Disgust

SUNY series, Intersections: Philosophy and Critical Theory

Rodolphe Gasché, editor

Disgust

The Theory and History of a Strong Sensation

Winfried Menninghaus

Translated by
Howard Eiland and Joel Golb

State University of New York Press

Die Herausgabe dieses Werkes wurde aus Mitteln von Inter Nationes, Bonn, gefördert.

The introduction and chapters 6, 7, and 9 were translated by Howard Eiland.
Chapters 1, 2, 3, 4, 5, and 8 were translated by Joel Golb.

Published by
State University of New York Press, Albany

© 2003 State University of New York

All rights reserved

Printed in the United States of America

No part of this book may be used or reproduced in any manner whatsoever without written permission. No part of this book may be stored in a retrieval system or transmitted in any form or by any means including electronic, electrostatic, magnetic tape, mechanical, photocopying, recording, or otherwise without the prior permission in writing of the publisher.

For information, contact State University of New York Press, Albany, NY
www.sunypress.edu

Production by Michael Haggett
Marketing by Fran Keneston

Library of Congress Cataloging-in-Publication Data

Menninghaus, Winfried.
 [Ekel. English]
 Disgust : the theory and history of a strong sensation / Winfried Menninghaus ; translated by Howard Eiland and Joel Golb.
   p. cm. — (Intersections)
 Includes bibliographical references (p.).
 ISBN 0-7914-5831-8 (alk. paper) — ISBN 0-7914-5832-6 (pbk. : alk. paper)
 1. Aversion. 2. Aesthetics, Modern. I. Title. II. Intersections (Albany, N.Y.)

BH301.E45M4613 2003
128'.37—dc22
                                                                                    2003057264

10 9 8 7 6 5 4 3 2 1

Contents

INTRODUCTION: BETWEEN VOMITING AND LAUGHING.
BASE LINES OF A PHILOSOPHY OF DISGUST   1

Exposition ... 1 / Subject Matter and Objectives of the Present Study ... 5 / Aurel Kolnai, "Der Ekel" (*Disgust*) ... 16 / Democracy as Source of Disgust: William Ian Miller's *The Anatomy of Disgust* ... 20

1   THE DISGUST TABOO, AND THE OMNIPRESENCE
    OF DISGUST IN AESTHETIC THEORY   25

The Beautiful as Vomitive ... 26 / Aesthetic Infinity as Antivomitive ... 31 / "Mixed Sensations" and the Exception of Disgust ... 33 / Pleasure and Displeasure ... 35 / The "Darkest of all the Senses" and the Collapse of Aesthetic Illusion in Disgust ... 38 / Semanticized and "Crude" Disgust ... 45

2   DISGUSTING ZONES AND DISGUSTING TIMES:
    THE CONSTRUCTION OF THE IDEALLY BEAUTIFUL BODY   51

The Ideal Skin and Disgust at Folds and Wrinkles, Layers of Cartilage and Fat ... 51 / Disgusting Depths and the Body's Openings ... 54 / Forever young ... 58 / The Gaping Mouth ... 60 / Nose-Disgust and the "Greek Profile" ... 64 / The "Flattened Ear" ... 66 / "Disgusting Breasts" and Ideal "Hills" ... 67 / Invisibility, Unseen Nakedness, and "Wetted Garments" ... 69 / A Body "Without a Belly" ... 71 / The "Spare Behind" ... 71 / Excision, Castration, Hermaphroditization: the Phallus in the Field of the Beautiful ... 72 / The "Hypergigantic" Sex of the "Colossal Woman" ... 75 / Wounds, Dismembered Limbs, Flayed Skin:

The Body as a "Disgusting Thing" . . . 78 / Beautiful Death and Disgusting Decay . . . 81 / The Ugly Old Lady . . . 84 / Repression or Differentiation? . . . 91 / Disgust, Purity, and Impurity in the Aesthetic . . . 96

3 "STRONG VITAL SENSATION" AND ORGANON OF PHILOSOPHY: THE JUDGMENT OF DISGUST IN KANT   103

Disgust and Pleasure . . . 103 / Disgust as a Goal of Education . . . 108 / Smell, Taste, and the "Vital Sensation" of Disgust . . . 109 / Disgust, Laughter, and "Dark Conceptions" . . . 112 / Disgust as an Organon of Intellectual Critique . . . 113 / Disgust as Organon of Practical Action . . . 115 / Disgust, Happiness and Unhappiness, Ennui . . . 118

4 POETRY OF PUTREFACTION: "BEAUTIFUL DISGUST" AND THE PATHOLOGY OF THE "ROMANTIC"   121

Classical Disgust and the Basic Alterations of the Aesthetic Field around 1800 . . . 121 / The Disgusting as Stimulus-Increase and Recipe of Modern "Shock"-Aesthetics . . . 123 / The License of "Disgusting Impotence" and the Decay of the Negative Principle . . . 125 / Disgusting Souls, Disgusting Times, and the Art of the Disgusting: The "Romantic" Ubiquity of the Once-Tabood . . . 128 / Rosenkranz on the Disgusting (1): Putrefaction as an "Inverse Becoming of the Already Dead" . . . 131 / Baudelaire's Poem *Une Charogne* . . . 134 / Rosenkranz on the Disgusting (2): The Return of Indigestibility in the System of Dialectic Appropriation . . . 139

5 THE "NO" OF DISGUST AND NIETZSCHE'S "TRAGEDY" OF KNOWLEDGE   147

Plato, Jesus, and Morals as World-Historical Agents of Disgust . . . 149 / "Ressentiment" and Weakness as Catalysts of Modern "Moralizing"—The Disgusting Mixture of Lies and Innocence . . . 151 / "Mollycoddling" as Disgust at one's own Cruelty . . . 154 / The Disgusting Body and Nietzsche's Physiology . . . 156 / "Great Disgust" and Contemporary Literature . . . 158 / Disgust and Cognition . . . 160 / Education for Disgust . . . 165 / Overcoming Disgust . . . 167 / Nietzsche *Vetula* . . . 178

6 THE PSYCHOANALYSIS OF STINKING:
   LIBIDO, DISGUST, AND CULTURAL DEVELOPMENT IN FREUD   183

   Interpretations of Disgust in Evolutionary Theory before
   Freud . . . 183 / Freud's Birth . . . 185 / Disgust, Aesthetic Culture,
   Antie-Aesthetic Libido . . . 186 / The Triumph of Libido: the
   "Perverse" Overcoming of Disgust . . . 193 / Perverse Father,
   Servant Girl, and Prostitute . . . 196 / *Habemus Vetulam* . . . 203 /
   Disgust and the Choice of Neurosis . . . 208 / Excretion as
   Prototype of Social Acts, and the Copro-Erotics of
   Language . . . 213 / "Disgusting Abuses," "Primeval Devil
   Worship," and the Equation of Analyst and Torturer . . . 218 / Art
   as Suspension of Disgust and Guiltless "Enjoyment" of the
   Rejected . . . 220 / Research on Disgust in Empirical Psychology
   after Freud . . . 222

7 THE ANGEL OF DISGUST:
   KAFKA'S POETICS OF "INNOCENT"
   ENJOYMENT OF "SULPHUROUS" PLEASURES   227

   7.1. Ugly Maidservants, Fat Old Whores, Sexual Disgust,
   and "Sulphurous" Obesssions . . . 228

   Felice and Other Women with Un-Greek Noses, Skin Defects,
   and Bad Teeth . . . 228 / "Old Maids" . . . 234 / "I Want Only
   the Stout Older Ones" . . . 236 / Disgust with Conjugal
   Sexuality versus Pleasure in Disgusting Sex Outside of
   Marriage . . . 241 / "Innocence" and "You Must Possess Every
   Girl!" . . . 248 / "Dirty Fellow," Dancing and Swinging Pigs,
   Stinking Bitches and Self-Knowledge . . . 249 / Kafka the
   "Flabby Worm:" The Method of Making "Abominable
   Peculiarities" Invisible through the Form of Their
   Disclosure . . . 254

   7.2. The Transformation of the Abject into
   "Guiltless Enjoyment:" Writing as
   Devlish-Angelic "Deceiving without Deception" . . . 256

   7.3. Disgusting Sexuality in Kafka's Novels . . . 261

   Amerika, or the Trajectory of Male Innocence in the Realm of
   "Repellent" Female Practices . . . 261 / Loathsome Power and
   K.'s "Sexual Etiquette" in *The Trial* and *The Castle* . . . 272

   7.4. A Poetics of Eating and Vomiting . . . 281

   Broken Engagements and Disgust with Meat, Spoiled Old
   Food, and Laxatives . . . 281 / On Hard Sausages and Filthy

Breakfasts: Nutrition and Narration in Kafka's *Amerika* . . . 286 / Breakfast, Old Woman, and Arrest: The Opening Chapter of *The Trial* . . . 291 / Orgies of Flesh-Eating and Intoxication with Blood in Kafka's (Hunger) Stories . . . 294

7.5. Incisions in Flesh and the Knife of Literature . . . 298
Torture, Truth, and Disembowelled Pigs . . . 307 / "Like a Dog:" K.'s Execution as the Summa of Kafka's Knife-Poetics . . . 310 / The "Stupidity" of Torture . . . 316

7.6. The Wound in the Text and the Text as Wound: The Story "A Country Doctor" . . . 318

7.7. Beer-Drinking Hearse-Drivers and Cheerful Gravediggers . . . 332

7.8 "Horrible Words" and Kafka's Physiology of Writing . . . 334

8 HOLY DISGUST (BATAILLE) AND THE
   STICKY JELLY OF EXISTENCE (SARTRE)   343

Anti-Aesthetic of the "Formless:" Materialism of the Debased, Pollution of the Beautiful, Self-Mutilation, and the "Bliss" of Anal-Sadistic Ravages . . . 343 / Disgust Prohibitions and their Transgression as Societal "Core" and Stimulating Medium of Erotic Violence . . . 348 / "La Nausée: c'est moi"—Sartre's Elevation of Disgust to the Sole Authentic Experience of Existence . . . 355

9 ABJECT MOTHER (KRISTEVA), ABJECT ART,
   AND THE CONVERGENCE OF DISGUST, TRUTH, AND THE REAL   365

Repression, Repudiation, Abjection . . . 366 / Abject Mother, Symbolic Order, Desire . . . 370 / Abjection, Disgust, and *Jouissance* . . . 372 / Literature as (Perverse) Reclamation of the Abandoned . . . 378 / Rhythm, Laughing Apocalypse, Happy Guilt . . . 381 / Abject Pleasure, Disgust, Truth and the Real . . . 385 / Grand Narratives of the Heterogeneous . . . 387 / AIDS, Disgust, and Affirmative Abjection: On the Political Appropriation of Kristeva . . . 389 / The Academic Career of the "Abject" . . . 393 / Abject Art . . . 395

NOTES   403

BIBLIOGRAPHY   453

Introduction

Between Vomiting and Laughing

Baselines of a Philosophy of Disgust

EXPOSITION

"Disgust" is accounted one of the most violent affections of the human perceptual system. Kant, one of the first theoreticians of disgust, called it a "strong vital sensation."[1] Such sensations "penetrate the body, so far as it is alive." Whether triggered primarily through smell or touch, eye or intellect, they always affect "the whole nervous system."[2] Everything seems at risk in the experience of disgust. It is a state of alarm and emergency, an acute crisis of self-preservation in the face of an unassimilable otherness, a convulsive struggle, in which what is in question is, quite literally, whether "to be or not to be." This accounts, even in apparently trivial cases, for the peculiar gravity of the distinction at issue in disgust, the distinction between digestible/wholesome/appetizing and unpalatable,[3] between acceptance and rejection (vomiting, removal from proximity). The decaying corpse is therefore not only one among many other foul smelling and disfigured objects of disgust. Rather, it is *the* emblem of the menace that, in the case of disgust, meets with such a decisive defense, as measured by its extremely potent register on the scale of unpleasureable affects. Every book about disgust is not least a book about the rotting corpse.

The fundamental schema of disgust is the experience of a nearness that is not wanted. An intrusive presence, a smell or taste is spontaneously assessed as contamination and forcibly distanced.[4] The theory of disgust, to that extent, is a counterpart—although not a symmetrical one—of the theory of love, desire, and appetite as forms of intercourse with a nearness that is wanted. Appetite and erotic desire aim at the overcoming of distance—the

1

establishment of a union. The ideal presence of this union that would dissolve unpleasureable tensions is disturbed only, if at all, by its fleeting character. For disgust, however, it is precisely this transitoriness that offers the desperately sought release from a "false embrace," an intolerable contact or union. Hollywood has long made use of the complementarity of disgust and love in generating as powerful an emotional impact as possible; it has developed different popular film genres which aim at agitating the feelings of either love or disgust, as well as narrative formulas designed to blend the opposite effects.

Stated very abstractly, the defense mechanism of disgust consists in a spontaneous and especially energetic act of saying "no" (Nietzsche). Yet disgust implies, not just an ability to say no, but even more a compulsion to say no, an inability *not* to say no. As this quasi-automatic ("instinctive") form of nay-saying, disgust stands on the boundary between conscious patterns of conduct and unconscious impulses. On the one hand, it comes to our attention in a particularly striking way and, accordingly, in no way escapes conscious perception. On the other hand, it attacks, it overcomes us, unannounced and uncontrollable, taking sudden possession of us. Viewed from this perspective, it does not stand under the sway of consciousness, but rather makes itself felt within consciousness as a voice arriving from somewhere else. In the volume of this voice from elsewhere, in this scandalous invasion of a heterogeneity, disgust brings eminent affective powers to bear: it processes elementary civilizing taboos and social distinctions between what is foreign and one's own. At the same time, it is a medium for the intercourse with strong libidinal impulses.

Eighteenth-century anthropology regarded the sensation of disgust as an unconditional given of human nature, as an elemental reaction type of very considerable importance for the physical, intellectual, moral, and social spheres of life. By the same token, evolutionary theory, empirical psychology, and finally neurology[5] have regularly, since Darwin, reckoned "disgust" as being one of the most elementary human feelings. For Freud, to be sure, disgust is the direct opposite of a simple natural given; that is, it is an effect of the passage into culture, a (neurotic) symptom of the repression of archaic libidinal drives. But *as* such, as sublimation effect and civilizing organ of inhibition, it nonetheless stands at the disposal of all human beings, allowing for a wide variety of individual determinations; Freud even speaks of a "hereditary fixture."[6] Walter Benjamin, too, has treated of disgust as an intrinsic and universal pattern of human subjectivity: "On the theory of disgust. There is no one who would be free of disgust. Only this is conceivable: that a man never in his life encounters the sort of sight, smell, or other sense impression that calls forth his disgust."[7] Although disgust, as compared with love, hate, or anxiety, belongs among the least documented sensations in human history, much speaks in favor of considering it to be a general and presumably distinctive pattern of human reaction.

The ambition to write a history of "actual" disgust—its far-reaching constant, as well as variable, forms, its fluctuations in intensity and its shifting objects, its de- and resensitizings, its natural and cultural models—meets with almost insurmountable difficulties. The relevant data have made only a negligible entrance into the cultural archive. As a rule, it has not seemed worthwhile to record such data; what is more, their recording would have been rejected as unworthy, indecent, and abominable. Even today, the few researchers in this area habitually make excuses for their interest in the subject. Accordingly, the present study also refrains from writing a history of the—widely undocumented—"reality" of disgust. Rather, it inquires into the most important theoretical approaches to disgust taken during the past 250 years. It is only through the medium of these theories of disgust that some fragments of the largely mute history of this strong sensation become accessible.

The historical starting point of the present study at the same time demarcates a major shift in the discourse about disgust. Ever since antiquity, literary texts have occasionally portrayed disgusting phenomena. Sophocles' *Philoctetes* goes particularly far in this direction; the dialogue keeps coming back to the stinking, suppurating, and always newly inflamed sore of the exposed hero. Among the mixed blessings in his miserable cave belong some drying "rags . . . full of the oozing matter from a sore."[8] The revolting appearance, foul smell *(dysosmía)*, and the vocal expression of suffering constitute Philoctetes as a multisensorial example of *dyschéreia*,[9] of disgust in the literal sense of what is extremely difficult to handle or manage, and hence repugnant. But the disgusting character of the "evil sore" is of interest to Sophocles and his audience nowhere for its own sake alone. What is stressed, first of all, is an argument of Odysseus to justify the shameful exposure of Philoctetes: with "his foot/diseased and eaten away with running ulcers," Odysseus argues, "we had no peace with him . . . / . . . and those terrible cries of his/brought ill luck on our celebrations."[10] Secondly, there are indications that the disgusting wound has been ordained by the gods and consequently entails a moral-religious hermeneutic. Thirdly, the exposure to what is disgusting has the aspect of a test: the nobility of a character is measured, as is later the case in many saints' lives, by the overcoming of physical disgust at this festering sore.[11] Analogously, the relatively infrequent evocation of physical disgust in medieval literature stands under the regime of other dominant passions. For the most part, these phenomena of disgust serve in the representation of actual or impending humiliation, and are thus "subsumed into the moral and social economy of shame and honor."[12] Beginning in the seventeenth century, however, and more fully in the eighteenth, disgust—as represented or reflected in texts—attains to "a life of its own,"[13] becoming worthy of consideration for the sake of its own (anti)aesthetic and moral qualities. Even the words *dégoût*, disgust, and *Ekel* first come into general usage in the sixteenth or seventeenth century and make a more than isolated entry into theoretical texts for the first time in the eighteenth century. The French term is particularly revealing in this context: the discursive career of *dégoût* constitutes the little noticed reverse side of that interest, so vehemently propagated since the later seventeenth century, in *goût*, in aesthetic, and to some extent, moral "taste."[14] The replacement of universal rules for poetry by a self-grounding logic of judging the particular (= taste) is a fundamental datum in the evolution of aesthetics as an independent discipline, and of art as an "autonomous," autopoetic system. When works of art are supposed to excel, above all, through their originality, their difference from their predecessors, then a faculty of judgment is likewise required that, without presupposing any fixed criteria, is capable of doing justice to the singular achievements of genius. Such a capacity for judgment is, by its nature, almost as delicate and imponderable as artistic creation itself. It breaks with the predominance of aristocratic etiquette and normative codifications and, to that extent, makes possible the bourgeois appropriation of aesthetics and art. According to Kant, this highly intricate faculty of aesthetic taste is actually the sole basis of the *sensus communis* and thus, in the end, of the informal coherence of society—a society, that is to say, whose subsystems henceforth must more and more ground and reproduce themselves (Luhmann), instead of merely obeying a hierarchical power.

Yet this taste is not something egalitarian. It presupposes refinement and higher education *(Bildung)* and in itself leads, while tending to overthrow the old aristocratic hierarchy of birth and of norms, to a new type of social differentiation, which not only divides the "barbarian" or "vulgar" taste of the lower classes from the "good" taste of the nobility and the upper middle classes.[15] Being an infinitely refined organ of discrimination of the particular, taste also allows many kinds of subtle and highly selective distinctions among the "cultivated." Especially the nobility, facing social degradation, tended to augment its powers of making refined distinctions and to direct these against the bourgeoisie, all the more so as the latter came to rival them in power and influence. The career of (aesthetic) pleasure and displeasure, of "pure" and "impure" judgments of taste, thus confirms Mary Douglas' theory according to which informal distinctions of pure and impure, as well as ideas of contamination and the respective practices of demarcation, are particularly relevant in social systems with weakened authorities and ambiguous hierarchies.[16] Analogously, in the perception of today's youth, nuances of aesthetic taste, often very subtle ones, make for decisive distinctions and determine the etiquette of "cool" or "disgusting." Advertising and fashion extract the yield of such distinctions; in an aestheticized consumer world, countless communicative "events" depend on attributions, which imply such judgments of taste. These judgments are not merely individual judgments—any more than the Kantian aesthetic judgement is merely individual; but even as the operator of group identities they allow, in an unprecedentedly flexible manner, for ever new demarcations of the boundaries of acceptability, group membership, and ever finer gradations of ever increasing and ever smaller "subcultures." The discourse of "disgust" is, not least of all, the reverse side of this enormous propagation and increasing significance of judgments of taste.

In today's colloquial French, German and, above all, American, the extremely negative predicate "disgusting" tends to be used exceedingly often—and in the rhetorical sense of an "exaggeration," of a hyperbole—for phenomena which literally do not seem to deserve so harsh a rejection. In eighteenth-century aesthetics, "disgusting" does *not* (yet) import the maximally negative predicate of an aesthetic judgment of taste, but rather a quality that wholly exceeds the conditions for the possibility of an aesthetic judgment. Aurel Kolnai, the author of the first comprehensive phenomenology of disgust, conforms to this view: for him even though disgust sensations partly depend on aesthetic judgment of taste, they essentially go beyond such judgment.[17] The transcendence which disgust implies *vis-à-vis* purely aesthetic judgment is primarily based on its normative and quasi-moral moment; for disgust apprehends qualities, not simply as givens, but always as something that *should* not be, at least not in proximity to the one judging. The current use of "disgusting" as an hyperbolical expression of dislike—even the weather can be "disgusting"—contains such elements of a "moral" negation too. In any case, even the apparently "weak," figurative usage represents no mere mannerism; in light of the modern success story of the judgment of taste, this usage is entirely consistent. For, in the world of taste, everything, even the smallest distinction, is literally decisive. And, in informal communication, no judgment is more decisive than that of disgust. *"Vive la différence"* is the watchword, not only of the modern system of art, of advertising, fashion, and recent French philosophy, but also of (modern) disgust. Since the eighteenth century, the German *eckel sein* not only signifies what is disgusting in the sense of being extremely offensive to the taste; it can likewise be ascribed to persons who are exceedingly delicate, oversensitive, hypertrophically addicted to making refined distinctions.[18] *Ekel* of this type is the essence of the judgment of taste itself. It stands, with almost equal prerogatives, side by side with that other sphere of the disgusting that is rude, obscene, and sexually "perverse," and hence an offense to "good taste"—which, however, it still presupposes in the very act of transgressing it.

Subject Matter and Objectives of the Present Study

From a historical perspective, the present study treats authoritative theoretical descriptions or appropriations of disgust since the specifically modern promotion of taste, *goût*, and *Geschmack*, to the rank of a self-legitimated organon of judgment. In other words: it treats disgust as the correlate *and* antagonist of a specifically modern "aesthetic culture" (Freud). The definition of the concept which serves as point of departure for the following inquiries confines itself thereby to the general pre-understanding of "disgust," with its three fundamental features: (1) the violent repulsion *vis-à-vis* (2) a physical presence or some other phenomenon in our proximity, (3) which at the same time, in various degrees, can also exert a subconscious attraction or even an open fascination. Any more exact preliminary definition would, in the end, amount to an obstacle when it comes to dealing with the often radical semantic calibrations of, say, a Nietzsche, who, without hesitation, and in sovereign disregard of the precise demarcations between loathing, aversion, and so forth, outruns and expands the boundaries of the concept. Taking all this into account, the present study pursues four desiderata and goals of presentation:

1. In order to meet the challenge of theorizing disgust, this study offers a multiple succession of approaches and theoretical idioms. The individual chapters below present disgust as a key desideratum of significant aestheticians, philosophers, cultural theorists and psychoanalysts: Mendelssohn, Winckelmann, Lessing, Herder, Kant, Rosenkranz, Nietzsche, Freud, Bataille, Sartre, Elias,[19] Douglas, and Kristeva. The arrangement of these authors is, to be sure, chronological, but it implies no linear development—neither progress nor obsolescence—of the theorems in question. What is remarkable is rather the relative durability of precisely the first explicit theories of disgust. Hardly any of the writers treated has before now been read systematically as theorists of disgust; the majority not at all. Bringing them together yields the possibility of new constellations, not so much in the history of concepts, as in the history of problems. This problem-oriented configuration at the same time places basic questions of theoretical and practical philosophy—questions of "truth" as much as of the springs of practical action—in a new perspective. The feeling of disgust makes a claim on (theoretical) cognition of its object; at the same time, it is at once an obligation, a categorical imperative of action—*that* is not to be, or to remain, in my body or in my proximity—*and* the realization of this imperative in vomiting or in turning away. Knowledge, aesthetic-moral-dietetic judgment, and its execution overlap in a syndrome that runs counter to the modern tendency toward division of powers, toward differentiation of claims and specialized subsystems (even when the new position of disgust is itself an effect of this tendency toward differentiation). In the interruptions of continuity and contiguity which disgust occasions, in its spontaneous act of rejection, a barely illuminated—and perhaps not too trustworthy—unity of our theoretical, practical and aesthetic faculties is brought into play. Academic philosophy has barely made a start in examining this problematic.

2. This study attempts throughout, along historical as well as systematic lines, to trace the position and function of disgust in aesthetics and in the sys-

tem of art since their respective "autonomization" some two hundred and fifty years ago. Eighteenth century's foundation of modern aesthetics can be described negatively as a foundation based on prohibition of what is disgusting. The "aesthetic" is the field of a particular "pleasure" whose absolute other is disgust: so runs its briefest, its only undisputed, yet almost wholly forgotten basic definition. Nevertheless, a careful reading of the "classic" aesthetic theories reveals unexpectedly complicated relations between "disgust" and aesthetic "pleasure." The most surprising discovery may be this one: like a sweet that is all too sweet, the beautiful is in danger—from the first and by its very nature—of turning out to be *in itself* something disgusting. This applies precisely to the extent that beauty's "purity" is *not* contaminated and supplemented by something that is not (only) beautiful. The absolute other of the aesthetic thus returns as the inmost tendency of the beautiful. Aesthetic theory, therefore, had to offer a kind of antivomitive, a remedy for the disgusting satiation brought on by the merely sweet or purely beautiful. The famous invention of aesthetic infinity can be read as this remedy for it opens up a reflective experience that never can close and thus never can fully sate. The motif of satiation avoided, a motif directly linked to the prohibition of the disgusting, and Lessing's "fruitful moment" or Kant's "aesthetic ideas" are, in this respect, two sides of the same coin.

The ideal of the beautiful—the classical statue and the human body in general—is subject, from head to toe, to a topography and chronography of "disgust." Disgusting zones, disgusting moments are the strategic entry points of the beautiful body's construction. Folds, wrinkles, warts, "excessive softness,"[20] visible or overly large bodily openings, discharge of bodily fluids (nasal mucous, pus, blood), and old age are registered, on the criminal index of aesthetics, as "disgusting." The positive requirements of the aesthetically pleasing body—elastic and slender contour without incursions of fat, flawless youthful firmness and unbroken skin without folds or openings, removal of bodily hair and plucked eyebrows forming a fine line, flat belly and "trim" behind, and so on—are at the same time prescriptions for the avoidance of disgust. The canonical sculptures of Apollo and Aphrodite function as veritable paradigms for avoiding all that might evoke disgust. They produce a visibility insofar as they make something invisible. For that which they make invisible, for that which they drive down obsessively into the Orcus of aesthetic impossibility, the "classical" authors make use, again and again, of a figure already sanctioned by a long-standing tradition: the figure of the disgusting old woman. She is the embodiment of everything tabooed: repugnant defects of skin and form, loathsome discharges and even repellent sexual practices—an obscene, decaying corpse in her own lifetime. With the single exception of Winckelmann, the disgusting has the attributes of female sex and old age with all the writers treated here. This book about disgust is thus, at the same time, a book entirely concerned with the (masculine) imagination of the *vetula*, of the disgusting old woman. Kant's *vetula*, Nietzsche's *vetula*, Freud's *vetula*, Bataille's *vetula*, Kristeva's abject mother—this series of abominable women opens perspectives into the depraved and abandoned underground of what Freud has called "the aesthetic culture."

In contrast to disgust, other "disagreeable sensations," such as the terror of tragedy, contribute positively to and, according to classical doctrine, even enhance the aesthetic stimulation of the affects. They prove the power of art to convert even depressing objects into objects of pleasure. With this pleasure taken in horror, the very aesthetics that constitutes itself in the taboo placed on everything disgusting provides a model for all later theories of aesthetic transformation of affect (Freud), or of transformation of repulsion into attraction (Bataille, Kristeva). According to this model, the pleasure taken in incest, or in the murder of spouses or mothers, as represented on the stage, essentially rests on the arousal of a vivid self-perception on the part of the viewer. Confronted with abominable actions, the "soul" of the spectator breaks through its anaesthetized state in the banal everyday, or in gloomy boredom, and feels itself to be "alive," because agitated by strong sensations of great emotional amplitude. To the extent that they are "passionate" and intense, disagreeable sensations may thus in themselves be "agreeable" and conducive to pleasure. Like Sartre's *La Nausée*, Bataille's theory of tragedy and the social extends this (sensationalistic) figure of the transformation of affect—which makes use of everything disagreeable for an enlivening of the observer's self-perception—to that one unique sensation which classical aesthetics had excluded from such a redemption: disgust.

The hunger for strong sensations seems to have changed but little in more than two hundred years. Already the eighteenth century occasionally bewailed a general cultural situation in which the growing burden of information and the chaotic flood of stimuli go together with the experience of an empty passage of time and with *ennui*. In this context, the sheer power of agitation which the feeling of disgust excites, in both the body in general and the affects in particular, could serve as an argument to lift the ban on the disgusting. Indeed, in early German Romanticism, it became an integral and positive category of poetics; Romanticism thus led the way in expressly seeking to license the disgusting for art. Schlegel sees the turn toward the disgusting as the natural tendency of an art whose unceasing and fully self-supporting striving for otherness—otherness being the mark of "genius"—exhausts the "old stimuli" and almost inevitably seizes on "ever more violent and penetrating ones": "Once the tendency . . . is toward aesthetic energy, then taste, which has become increasingly used to the old stimuli, will only desire ever more extreme and intense stimuli." The disgusting thus figures as an extreme subspecies of a modern aesthetics of the "shocking,"[21] and by 1798, it is recognized as the almost inescapable vanishing point, as the negative eschaton of the modern art system's accelerated *drain on stimuli*. Under these conditions, there remains almost no choice for the individual artist: the Romantic literature of "decomposition" *(Verwesung)*—including the interesting case of a special license for "disgusting impotence"—answers not least to this requirement inherent in artistic production itself.

Mendelssohn and Kant had defined disgust as a "dark" sensation that so categorically indicates something "real" that it strains the distinction between "real" and "imaginary"—and therewith the condition for aesthetic illusion: *I am disgusted—therefore I experience something as unconditionally real (not at all as art)*. Nietzsche's early book on tragedy gives a new meaning to "disgust," making it a hallmark of metaphysical insight. Whoever, in the grip of Dionysian rapture, has once seen through the veil of appearance will henceforth be disgusted by everyday reality: for he has recognized "the truth," "the eternal essence of things." The formula—*I am disgusted, therefore I have (had) access to a powerful insight* (in the sense of a cognition supported by "physiology")—has a manifold resonance throughout Nietzsche's work. As test cases for the power of distinction residing in disgust, Nietzsche recommends a whole series of objects: Jesus Christ, modern penpushers, German youth, and so forth. Only he who is genuinely revolted by these objects is not yet secretly infected by the "disgust with life." "Disgust" thus accedes to a double position. On the one hand, it is a symptom of modernity as "sickness"—as the epoch in which disgusting phenomena abound and proliferate. On the other hand, only the disgust of "distinguished men" can offer resistance to the universal "disgust with humanity." This homeopathic structure, however, is merely provisional, for Nietzsche at the same time regards the "great disgust" as the "great danger" to himself and to all freethinkers capable of distinction. Hence his motto: "We revaluate disgust" *("Wir lernen den Ekel um")*. In the "revaluation of all values," a decisive role falls to disgust: it is for this reason that Zarathustra is praised for being "the man without disgust, the conqueror of the great disgust." The trajectory of this overcoming terminates in the affirmation of repetition, of eternal return as an unending "rumination" without disgust. Nietzsche thus knows of a double disgust in the face of disgust: the first sort is the hallmark of cognition or critical insight, and the second is needed for overcoming this insight into what is disgusting in the interests of "life." All of Nietzsche's principal works contribute to this complex project of an ultimately self-surpassing revaluation of disgust.

Freud's theory of disgust is an integral part of the narrative he offers to explain the emergence of upright posture and the civilizing transformation of anal lust and olfactory pleasure with the genitals into something disgusting. The barriers of disgust define the massif of repressed libidinal drives. According to Freud, the libido must triumph again and again over the inhibitions codified in the feeling of disgust, and it must do so precisely in the form of "perverse" practices. Otherwise, the structural neuroticization that comes with organic and cultural repression threatens to pass over into an acute sickening of civilization itself, and finally a "fading away" of the will to live. All calls for liberating what has been made disgusting, for desublimating countermovements against civilization's tendency to sublimate libidinal drives, are rooted in Freud's nostalgically colored narrative of the sunken continent of anal and other pleasures which have fallen under the taboo of the disgusting. This narrative stands at the beginning of his psychoanalytic experience and informs the entire development of his theory.

Along with Freud's ground-laying "myth" of a paradise (a childhood) without disgust, of civilizing-neuroticizing "barriers of disgust," and the inextinguishable insistence of what has been made disgusting, Nietzsche's watchword about rethinking disgust has found a wide variety of echoes in twentieth-century thought. Bataille has discovered in *dégoût* an overtly sacred instruction. For him, the fundamentally inviolable prohibition entailed by dégoût in no sense operates to repress; on the contrary, it is considered to be the very means for setting free, through acts of sacred and erotic transgression, a maximum of pleasure—and thereby, at the same time, for grounding the *choses sociales:* "Society is grounded in disgust."[22] Kristeva has analyzed the "abjection" of the mother's body—and the symptom-like insistence of the "abject mother" in disgust for food, excrement, and bodily fluids—as a trajectory necessarily implied in every formation of the subject and in every integration into the symbolic order. She has also traced, throughout her work, the modes in which the rejected *corps maternel* and its *jouissance* is continued, adapted, and in part reconquered in affects, desires, religious and literary practices.

The "no" of disgust, therefore, leaves room for various dimensions—ranging from secret to overt—of affirmation. Not only does disgust, from Kant to Sartre, serve in numerous ways as a positive operator and signature of immediate cognition—cognition of the harmful (Kant), of the "eternal essence of things" (Nietzsche), of our existence in its pure facticity (Sartre). The disgusting in and of itself is also brought forward for a second-order acknowledgment in that it comes to represent the diverted "truth" of the human bestial nature and of the Dionysian (Nietzsche), or else of the polymorphous-perverse libido (Freud). Not a simple rejection, but the rejection of rejection, the overcoming of disgust and its integration into an economy of pleasure and knowledge form the core of thinking about disgust since Nietzsche. Without exception, there emerges, from Nietzsche to Kristeva—wherever this overcoming of a necessary experience of disgust, this immanent conversion of disgust, is at stake—the concept of "laughter." All theoreticians of disgust are, at the same time, theoreticians of laughter. The "vital sensation" of disgust might well be considered a property no less characteristic of humanity than the capacity to laugh—a property, in fact, that represents the negative complement of laughter. The sudden discharge of tension achieves in laughter, as in vomiting, an overcoming of disgust, a contact with the "abject" that does not lead to lasting contamination or defilement. On the other hand, laughing *at* something, as an act of expulsion, resembles in itself the act of rejecting, of vomiting in disgust. Disgust, which undergoes a countercathexis (or a sublimation), and laughter are complementary ways of admitting an alterity that otherwise would fall prey to repression; they enable us to deal with a scandal that otherwise would overpower our system of perception and consciousness. To be sure, the openly comical use of disgusting phenomena, as discussed already by Lessing, does not live up to the "tragic" implications of overcoming disgust in laughter, as theorized in Nietzsche, Bataille, and Kristeva; for this use suspends, from the outset, the seriousness of the conflict enacted in the feeling of disgust and turns it into something ridiculous. But even this particular type of the comical points to the close relation of disgust and laughter.

Precisely as that which transgresses civilized prohibitions, incites the (anal-sadistic) destruction of beautiful form, and laughingly transcends the symbolic order—precisely as this scandal, the disgusting advances into the abandoned positions of the inaccessible "real" and of quasi-metaphysical truth. The true is the disgusting, and the disgusting is the true, indeed, the "thing in itself." In this assumption, an important but widely overlooked movement of modern thought—stretching from Nietzsche through Freud, Kafka, Bataille, Sartre, and Kristeva—unexpectedly converges. With almost every author, this thesis entails another one: art is the praxis which, first of all, gives to this abject truth a place and a specific "reality"—one that explodes the symbolic order. By means of complex measures counteracting disgust, it reclaims as emphatic pleasure what has been rejected and abandoned. Art itself—and all the authors named above, provide their own particular models for theorizing this intriguing claim—is nothing less than the abject as "absolute" pleasure; it is disgust as a form of excremental-destructive and, at the same time, innocent enjoyment; it is the disgusting as intermittent being of the "true."

3. It was the original intention of this project to write a (counter)history of literature understood as just such a processing of the disgusting. Selected chapters were planned and the following studies prepared: on the disgusting and the fantastic (E. T. A. Hoffmann's *Sandman*, Mary Shelley's *Frankenstein, or The Modern Prometheus*, Alfred Kubin's *Die andere Seite*, H. P. Lovecraft's *Ctulhu* "myth"), and on Zola, Joyce, Kafka, Benn, and Thomas Bernhard. After lengthy work in this field, however, the utter arbitrariness of this selection became apparent. It turned out that, in the last analysis, every author—at least, since the Romantics—could be ranged under the figure of a transformed, appropriated, counter-cathexed disgust, and in a manner more than merely thematic. Which is just the point of Freud's, Bataille's, and Kristeva's reflections on disgust and art. On the other hand, the few indispensable theories of disgust, from Mendelssohn up through the present, already proved so unexpectedly rich that their treatment in a foreword spilled over into a sizeable book. As the sole relic of a literary history of disgust, there remained in

the end—alongside the readings of Baudelaire and of Sartre's *La Nausée*—only Kafka. What made this particular selection appealing was, not least, its improbability. Despite the "disgusting" beetle in "The Metamorphosis," or the execution machine in "In the Penal Colony," other authors lend themselves much more readily to an inquiry focused on the disgusting. In the vast secondary literature on Kafka, there appears to have been, up to now, no attempt to deal explicitly with this question. "Writers speak a stench"[23]—it is to this erratic utterance of Kafka's that a reading of his three novels, and of his short story, "A Country Doctor," will try to give due weight.

4. Over the past two hundred years or so, critics reflecting on the cultural situation of their day have regularly lamented the mounting prevalence of the disgusting. Today's contemporaries have every reason to make a similar finding. Children's tactile senses are willfully exposed to and readily engaged by disgustingly soft and sticky plastic masses. Their palates are delighted with such fascinating matter as "marshmellows," which satisfy the conditions for disgust in three areas simultaneously: that of excessive sweetness, of excessive softness, and of "kitschy" color. "Disgust-pops" *(Ekel-Lollis)*—with real insects enclosed within the colorful, transparent candy glob—pointedly test the boundaries between pleasure and disgust, insofar as they enlist customary objects of disgust for sweets-sucking consumption.[24] Slimy monsters seem to be the favorite heroes of children's movies. Contemporary artworks routinely work with parts of corpses and masses of excrement; photographic still lifes of vomit, mucus, bodily secretions, and genuine as well as plastic body parts of all kinds make for a focus of debate in aesthetics.[25] The editors of the German periodical *Kursbuch* thus rightly considered an issue on "Disgust and Allergy" as up-to-date.[26] Exhibitions of reconditioned corpses prove to be an irresistible draw for the public.[27] "Splatter videos" present, in serial form, various disgust-horror-porno-excesses and seem bent on establishing cannibalism as the quintessence of exciting visual entertainment. Meanwhile, the big cities of Western Europe are threatened, after the increase in the population of rats, with the reentry of cockroaches. But even the orderly reality of the German Federal Republic in the sixties could prompt the following tirade on a "new, universal brand of trash and disgust":

> These pedestrian walkways are what he means, these two-family dwellings, these lawn mowers, these streets named after asters, dahlias, and fuchsias, these Rudyard Kipling Ways, these ornamental firs are what he means, these yew shrubs, these collapsible lawn chairs, these inflatable swimming pools, these brass watering cans, . . . these liquid hair nets, these greeting cards, these postal area codes, these foot- and underarm-sprays, and sprays in general he means. These gratifications he means as well, these concessions, these local bonuses, these housing subsidies he means, these rates of

growth, these small credit unions, these easy installment plans, these flights to Majorca he means, these five-minute spaghettis, . . . these anti-knock gasolines, these structural improvements, these swing sets, . . . these miniskirts, these go-gos, these combos—quite generally, he means these things with all that appertains to them.[28]

Thirty years later, it was no longer the disgustingly "safe and sound" universe of the small town and its social network[29] that inspired a fulminating declaration of disgust. This role falls instead to the intense experience of bodily proximity and of "contacts with food"[30] to which we are exposed in public transportation vehicles in the big cities. The scandalous objects are no longer the same; but the model of disgust-operated social discrimination, as elucidated by Bourdieu and Mary Douglas, applies unchanged:

> The scandal of the domestic economy does not exactly stink. It produces a homogeneous emulsion in tremendous quantities, the scum of the food industry. Sweet stuff as a way of sliding through the day at the office. Bags of rubbish, the ornament of garden walls, contain, according to statistics, above all the slippery remains of best-quality grapefruit sold at reduced prices. Whoever would rather make immediate use of this runny slime, made from Unilever-Givaudan and Nestlé secretions, has it in public, say at tram stops. The quick-eater craves the wobbly undefinability of some chilled mass without any delay, and he downs it already in the supermarket or at the post office before the counter. That glaring yellow or unsteady brown substance that, vibrating, gives itself out to be mousse is devoured on the subway escalator by women seeking instant gratification. The connoisseur of post-pleasures is enticed by the dead spawn of fish, prepared in jelly, and by the dead stare of former egg yolks in the blood-clot of immature foetuses of uncertain animal origin, on cardboard, at the stand-up bar in Shopville. The result of this nests in and issues out of all the receptacles in the room. By the side of the tub, behind the waste paper basket, in the container and in the sink, appears a whole society of food inhalers, anorexic women, and diet fanatics: it is a society that spoons. It seeks the total pudding and, with it, the invulnerable consistency. One cannot give way before this society, and one cannot set anything over against it, because it offers no physical resistance. What goes in at the front comes out, so to speak, unchanged at the rear. The pap eaters are among us. And the horrible suspicion proves true: they are also within us. . . . Head-sealed plastic foil to be torn by teeth, and the eagerness with which one tears still sticks in the ruins of gaping plastic. Unchastity of the palate, with tin foil, styrofoam, cellophane, viscose, latex, polyethylene, and various chemical

additives and artificial colorings. Form and content are synthesized, and the remnants ground down to a putrid and pus-like slop. There is nothing left but to bend over and vomit, across the spilled and splattered yogurt, right into this disposable container; out with the fast food that clumps together with greasy cotton fibers, trash, crumbled cartons, and rotten leaves to stop up the drain pipe. Before long, I too will give up the contents of my microbe-infested, embittered stomach.[31]

The spread of humanity and the acceleration of its means of locomotion lead to an unprecedented density of traffic and communication and, along with this, to all sorts of experiences of proximity—experiences which, as disagreeable, can reach the level of disgust. On the other hand, the character of professional and private life in the contemporary world reduces precisely these experiences of bodily proximity to a statistical minimum. Those activities that carry the greatest threat of disgust—such as the care of the sick and elderly—have for a long time been delegated to anonymous institutions. The same people who shove against one another in buses and subways live in households with steadily shrinking numbers of heads; in many large cities, more than fifty percent of households are occupied by singles. Their professional life runs its course—at the other end of the disgust-ridden trajectory through the spaces of public life—more likely than not before computer terminals, which make possible worldwide communication without any direct bodily contact. This new situation in the private sphere and in professional life may, at the same time, account for that enormous need for positively consumable experiences of the body and of nearness, which is then filled, in some cases, by contemporary art and audiovisual media, partly in the form of (perverse) pleasure in the disgusting. Even the simulations of disgust in the media form a bridge of sorts to the dark, "dense" and "intense" continent of elemental, bodily (self-)perceptions.

The desperate bourgeois *dégoût* in the face of fast food fails to register the fundamental displacements in contemporary relations between eating and the feeling of disgust. It is more difficult than ever before for traveler's accounts to revel in detailed reports of the disgusting foods of other peoples. For not only the basic culinary distinction of foreign and familiar, but also its maximum degree (disgusting versus tasty and digestible), is threatening to disappear. In countries like Germany and the United States, restaurants offering German cooking or establishments like "American diners" are fast becoming folkloristic relics in the midst of ever more abundant offerings from all around the world. The talk of a "global village" applies to the stomach at least as much as to the currents of information and capital. The old dictum, "what the poor fool doesn't know . . ." has given way before a universal culture of pleasure and consumption, which slurs over earlier standards of disgust and welcomes the foreign as an adaptable attraction and gain in difference. What, in caste societies, can be said by only the poorest groups on the margin—"we have no religion; we eat everything"—appears to have become, with a delighted shuttling from one menu to another, the motto of highly industrialized countries.[32] To the extent that food taboos lose their force as "cultural charters" and as the "material basis of general decisions about alterity,"[33] the goal of all antidiscriminatory politics becomes at least culinary reality.

Along with this weaning of the stomach from disgust comes the "liberation" of table manners—according to Elias, one of the pillars of the civilization process—from discriminatory cultural regulations. Since sit-down meals in the family circle are becoming less common, eating habits are fast regressing in a direction squarely opposed to "good manners," "good taste," and "good breeding"—to values, that is to say, whose capacity for social distinctions readily goes back, in Pierre Bourdieu's analysis, to the aesthetic-affective code of *goût* versus *dégoût*.[34] Not only the snack on the run, but also the meal eaten before the television at home or the computer screen in the office dispenses with any mealtime company and often with even a knife and fork, to say nothing of a white tablecloth: "These days, we eat with our fingers once again; ... what a mess! And our contact with other bodies and other souls resembles this sort of contact with our food." The author of this finding, a representative of the Old Left, believes himself to be "old-fashioned and nostalgic" when he "stubbornly" persists in his "disgust" with these contacts and "in his loyalty to a level of civilization reached long ago and, lately, once again abandoned and betrayed."[35] The race, as it seems, to abrogate civilizing barriers of disgust is, in fact, not only grounds for rejoicing. In many respects, it secures for Marcuse's concept of repressive desublimation a new field of application.[36] The theory of civilization appears, so far, to have been little concerned with this "crack" in the wall of normative disgust—something to which the conscious dismissal, or at least considerable de-emphasizing, of "toilet training" for children may well belong.[37]

Unperturbed by such misgivings on the part of cultural critics, the vulgar, the low-minded, the perverse, the "abject"—which last is, according to its authoritative theorist, Julia Kristeva, closely akin to the disgusting—all these have enjoyed, in the 1990s, a downright epidemic and generally affirmative expansion in the realms of literature, art, and the humanities. Grossly simplified, the last three centuries provide the following panorama of a discursive appropriation of disgust: the eighteenth century affirms disgust as doing a thoroughly "right" and healthy job, propagates the cultivation of disgust as a spur to the progress of humanity and of civilization, and celebrates the codification of the aesthetic body as free from everything potentially disgusting;[38] the nineteenth and early twentieth centuries discover both the costs of this sort of cultivation and the (forbidden) attractions of the disgusting; since the end of the twentieth century, the cultivation of disgust itself becomes brittle, and at the same time—as though the (repressive) barriers of disgust have grown more decisive than before—the terrain of the abandoned becomes, in virtually programmatic fashion, the promised land of a fiercely asserted revaluation of the disgusting in artistic, political, and academic work. If philosophy, in Hegel's famous phrase, "is its own time apprehended in thoughts,"[39] then it seems crucial to understand why the outgoing twentieth century kept interpreting itself, with such unmistakable obsessiveness, in terms of the reclamation of what had been rejected as disgusting. This book is *also*, though not primarily, a book about such more recent phenomena of art, of political and (U.S.-)academic debate as it tends to draw on the "abject," and of the everyday "culture of disgust." Some of these phenomena the present study treats directly; for others, it offers more general keys to understanding, while leaving their specific application to the reader.

AUREL KOLNAI, *"DER EKEL" (DISGUST)*

The present study is the second monographic and, at the same time, the fourth extended study of disgust to date. After a phenomenological study by Aurel Kolnai, an empirical-psychological series of essays by Paul Rozin,[40] and a sociological-political monograph by William Ian Miller, it is the first work to focus primarily on the role of disgust in art, aesthetics, and philosophy. That makes for a straightforward bibliographic situation. The following survey of Kolnai's study, in particular, is not intended merely to fulfill academic obligations; it serves, above all, as a further introduction to the territory of disgust.

In 1929, Aurel Kolnai's *Der Ekel* presented what was a penetrating and, for a long time, the sole attempt comprehensively to map the "remarkably wide-ranging domain" of the extremely "acute" reaction of disgust (515).[41] Published in Husserl's *Jahrbuch für Philosophie und phänomenologische Forschung*, Kolnai's dense fifty pages, richer in distinctions than anything before attempted in this field, are still the basic prerequisite for any investigation of disgust. Since the study is not well-known today, a review of its principal findings may not be out of place. In general, Kolnai views disgust as distinguished from other "tonalities of rejection," like anxiety, hate, contempt, and displeasure, by its greater immediacy and sharper physiological coloring. Unlike anxiety and displeasure, disgust never relates to "inorganic, lifeless things" (516). Without directly "having to incorporate anxiety," disgust nevertheless always points "in some way to anxiety" (517). Appertaining to both "intentions" is "a force that, at least temporarily, fills the person" (517). But whereas "the intention of anxiety" is directed "chiefly toward an existential condition" of the subject, disgust is ignited preeminently by a "modality" of the object at issue (528):

> To the intention of anxiety there attaches something abstract, indifferent to essence: what is threatening is understood here, on the

whole, only as "danger," and the persona [of the one affected by anxiety, W.M.], on the whole, only as "existential unity." In contrast to hatred, anxiety does not "pursue" its object in any detail, does not seek to evaluate it.... The feeling bores into the subject's own self, its present conditions, its future lot.... Conversely, in the case of disgust, ... the point of the intention bores into the object, and, as it were, analyzes it.... Inherent to disgust is thus a cognitive function, such as is lacking in anxiety: anxiety can lead to recognition of the danger, but disgust is capable of immediately providing a partial knowledge—and, it may be, a quite graphic one—of its object (523–24). That is the paradox of disgust: like anxiety, it is a genuinely passive defensive reaction of the subject, ... and yet, once aroused, it seeks out its object, as hatred does, in its entire significance, instead of unfolding according to the persona's own condition. If anxiety intends to free itself from its object, and if hate, on the other hand, seeks to annihilate its object, ... then disgust occupies here something like a middle position.... What is felt to be disgusting is always something ... that one neither annihilates nor escapes, but rather clears away. (525–26)

The "macabre attraction," the "ambivalence" of disgust is explained by Kolnai simply in terms of this intimate relation to its object: although unwanted, the normative "proximity of its possible objects" enrolls what is disgusting among those phenomena "that, 'in other respects,' are properly determined for a positive use and contact" (527); as a result of this contiguity, "a shadow of the intention to unify" is always already "grafted" upon the reaction of disgust (530). This explanation is as insufficient as Kolnai's description of the ambivalence of disgust is apt:

Nevertheless, so much may be maintained: that the object of disgust has just as much a tendency toward the covert, the hidden, the many-layered, the impenetrable and uncanny, as it does, on the other side, toward shamelessness, obtrusiveness, and the lure of temptation.... Everything disgusting has something at once conspicuous and veiled, like a poisonous red berry or a gaudy cosmetic. (531)

In keeping with eighteenth-century anthropology, and variously elaborating on Karl Rosenkranz's *Ästhetik des Hässlichen (Aesthetics of the Ugly)* of 1853, Kolnai correlates disgust, in descending degrees, to the senses of smell, touch, and sight. His examples, likewise, offer no surprises: in addition to the olfactory "circle of associations—disgust-smell-corruption-decay-secretion-life-nourishment" (533)—Kolnai addresses the haptic sensations of disgust—sensations of "the flabby, slimy, viscous" (534), as well as of "the sticky, semi-fluid, and quasi-obtrusively clinging" (537),—and, finally, sensations (connected, by association, with smell and taste) of "visual disgust" at the sight of bodily disfigurations or of "crawling and swarming parts" full of a (repulsive) excess of life. All these sensations of disgust merge in the "phenomena of decomposition" which represent an optical-tactile-olfactory *Gesamtkunstwerk*, and hence are its "primal object" (536). Excrement and other forms of eliminated matter and filth have an immediate bearing on this paradigm, as do certain sores, illnesses, congenital "deformity" (544), and, of course, the corpse "in its oozing decomposition": "the death grimace, as intimated in the feeling of disgust, reminds us of our own affinity with death, our subjection to death, and our longing for death" (558–59).

This invocation of a *Todeslust* is one of the many vague references to Freud which Kolnai makes no attempt to elaborate upon. By contrast, the complex relationship of disgust to life and death receives more attention. The disgust reaction aims to protect us from contamination, defilement, and death, but is always already exposed to the immediate proximity of these things, a proximity that "is poised to crush us." Moreover, there is a disgust not only in the presence of the decaying corpse, but "in the presence of rampant life" itself. This is in keeping with the general distinction between two types of disgust: a prohibitive disgust, which excludes or interrupts the pleasure of eating or sexual activity, and a "satiation-induced disgust" (545), which follows upon too rich an indulgence in sweets, sex (548), or other things. Kolnai's characterizations of satiation-induced disgust, as occasioned by "luxuriant life-growth," have a starkly ideological cast. From the "manly" Otto Weininger the student of Husserl takes up the proposition, "All *fécondité* is simply disgusting," eloquently interpreting it with reference to "disgust at the sight of swelling breasts, swarming broods": "one need only think of the connection to vermin; or of what is disgusting to the spirit in the idea of effervescent vitality, of a qualitatively indifferent, reckless production of embryos and spawn" (544). There is no type of disgust that Kolnai has described more obsessively and more originally than disgust with "crude, unrefined, as it were 'sweating' and 'fuming,' thronging life," with the "*danse macabre* of animation that attends the cessation of properly 'personal' life" (554). Not only is disgust with insects and rats, for Kolnai, essentially disgust with "a teeming conglomerate ('vermin!')" (540–41), with excessive sexual fecundity and mobility in connection with dirt, refuse, rotting matter and fear of contact (in the case of insects, the slimy trail of their crawling adds to the picture). In addition, "disgust with incest" is expounded as a form of satiation disgust: "There is something uncommonly insipid, dreadfully mawkish and wearying in the thought that the original, child-oriented (pre-natal in the case of mother and child), intimate community of the family would also take up the sexual life into itself; this would amount to a prototypical thickening and buckling of the stream of life" (546). For Kolnai, even intellectual expressions and literary forms of representation, awaken such disgust with "'crudely organized' life," in its "unrestrained, undistinguished, indifferent luxuriance":

> The surplus life in disgusting artistic or theoretical works means: "highlighting," "exaggerated presentation," "overburdened expression," "swollen redundancy" of liveliness and organicity—as opposed to norm, a clear direction and a telos of life.... It is in this very excess of life that there dwells the nonliving, death. Admittedly, this deadening by means of an accumulation of life ... can also appear very "interesting." (554, 556)

Mendacity, guile, corruption, and hypocrisy are also elucidated, as the cardinal "types of the morally disgusting" (545), by analogy with disgusting haptic "softness" and with the "swampy flourishing of a, so to speak, 'carious' mass, grown formless and uniformly pulpy"—a "life-aping, corrosive mass which usurps the place and the vigorous diversity of healthy tissue" (551). Kolnai does see the dangers of disgust when conceived as a moral organon: as such "it must not ground any unrestrained destructive intention operating against the object in question"; rather, it constantly requires qualification and correction through other perspectives on the argument (567). This caution would not be necessary if the separation of disgust and hatred did not allow for transitions.[42] Nevertheless, Kolnai underlines emphatically "the powerful potential of disgust" in the "domain" of moral judgment (563).

Kolnai's own text attests to the problematic inherent in the judgments of rejection articulated by "disgust." He surveys the continent of the disgusting from the banks of a culturally conservative preference for the manly, firm, moderate, gestalt-endowed, and goal-oriented. In this preference Kolnai follows, often to the point of adopting specific formulations, Karl Rosenkranz's critique of the Romantic literature of disgust (which is examined more closely in chapter 4). The analysis of the disgusting is thus shored up with an ideology of the "healthy" and "correct" that itself goes unquestioned. On more than one occasion, this pattern of argument is stretched to the point where it results in statements that call upon the very impulse to reject which they are treating:

> A soldier's responding, at the first, to the order of a superior with an inquiry into its aptness, or other such cases of inappropriate critique and intellectual flabbiness, are often felt to be, not only impertinent, absurd, pernicious, but in some sense "disgusting." This is no less true of an aimlessly subtle, subjectivistic and self-indulgent ... over-refinement ... of one's mode of thought and representation. (548)

In political and social life, "dictatorship" appears to Kolnai as the quasi-natural reaction to "decaying disintegration" and "disorganization," and it is said to mark the "closing of the epoch of corruption, with its muck and morass" (556). In addition, the "healthy" response to homosexual advances is called simply "disgust" (543). In the field of literature, this same politics of disgust entails the following judgment:

> Many (including myself) feel disgust at the spectacle of that heavenly exaltation of the soul and the emotions which . . . typifies a segment of Russian literature. . . . In a deeper sense, of course, all this soulful bursting forth is also false and mendacious, since authentic vitality and greatness of soul, etc., always bespeak hardness, firmness, and the will to form. (553)

In the last resort—and thus Kolnai fully reveals the very specific coloration of his own sensory system of disgust—all these organic, moral, and artistic forms of disgusting "abundance" represent nothing less than "a desertion"—"a desertion of the total framework of life" (555). Kolnai's marked propensity for hardness and other virtues of a manly-soldierly stripe detracts from the merit of his groundbreaking survey of the field of disgust, although only slightly. *Every* study of disgust, in fact, runs the danger of disclosing as much about the author as about his subject. Walter Benjamin was of the opinion that an exact understanding of a person would prove itself in the divination of his cardinal object of disgust.[43] Conversely, an acquaintance with individual profiles in disgust—for which not so very much data is required—makes possible significant disclosures about a person.

DEMOCRACY AS A SOURCE OF DISGUST: WILLIAM IAN MILLER'S *THE ANATOMY OF DISGUST*

Miller's *The Anatomy of Disgust* (1997) is written in ignorance, not only of the entire German tradition of thought on the subject of disgust, from Mendelssohn to Nietzsche, but also of the work of his direct predecessor, namely, Kolnai's great study, *Der Ekel*. This conforms to the dramatic loss of familiarity with German-language scholarship within American universities since the Second World War. On the whole, this ignorance has done no great damage to *The Anatomy of Disgust:* Miller provides a highly differentiated account of the prototypical objects of disgust, of their sensuous and intellectual channels, and of the functions of the disgust sensations. In the first two-thirds of his book, however, this account repeats, practically point for point, Kolnai's phenomenology—in a different scientific idiom, to be sure, but with a degree of overlapping that often extends to identical coverage.

The few points at which Miller diverges from Kolnai are more likely to raise doubts about his own position than to make for convincing elaborations of the latter's analysis. Can different sorts of laughter and regional accents of language induce a feeling of disgust in the full sense of the term (83–84)?[44] Does a light touch on the arm (66), in the course of a conversation, actually pose "only one serious question: Do I disgust you?" Does "the mere thought of pubic hair" have a stronger "contaminating power" than excrement (55)? Is masturbation, "even by our present liberated standards," in every case at least "self-defiling" (51)? There are likewise grounds for puzzlement at the thesis that the nonpenetrability of the anus is "the footing on which [male] dignity depends. It must be secured or everything else built upon it crumbles" (101). Kolnai's concept of disgust with fertility is surpassed by Miller's thesis that semen—even for men themselves—is the most thoroughly polluting, and therefore the most disgusting, substance associated with the male body": "Whatever receives it is made woman. The feminizing power of semen can reduce men to women, even lower than women in some moral orderings.... Men can never quite believe that women aren't as revolted by semen as men feel they should be!" (103–4)

The real ambition of Miller's book, and also its difference from Kolnai's, comes to light only in the last three of his ten chapters: "My central mission in this book is to demonstrate that emotions, particularly ones like disgust and contempt, . . . structure various social, moral, and political orderings" (18). The theory of "sentiment," in the style of the seventeenth and eighteenth centuries, serves as model here, insofar as, in this type of theory, "the psychological was not yet divorced either from the moral or from the social" (xii). Aligning himself with Swift, Hume, Adam Smith and Samuel Johnson, Miller claims that disgust "has certain virtues for voicing moral assertions. It signals seriousness, commitment, indisputability, presentness and reality" (180). It is "the passion that fuels our disapproval" (185); it imports, in particular, a "warring against cruelty and hypocrisy" (197). What sources disgust might have for these desirable qualities is a question raised by neither Miller nor his predecessors. Miller is not unwilling to seize the bull by the horns and to credit disgust with a sort of self-supporting application of its basic structure to social phenomena (62): "Might it be that disgust itself has a structure which it imposes on cultural orderings?" "The capacity to be disgusted," without question a "feature of human psychic organization" (10), turns thus into a self-regulating agent. Hence, the reference to a "moral disgust" ultimately implies, as is often the case in the eighteenth century, an optimistic anthropology: we are provided, it is suggested, with a sort of sixth sense that spontaneously condemns moral vices.

In Miller's affect-oriented micropolitics of contemporary social relations, disgust fares rather badly at a first glance. For it "subvert[s] the minimal demands of tolerance" and, to that extent, appears as a "powerful anti-democratic force" (206). At a time when tolerance and nondiscrimination have become normative—and this development, in Miller's view, defines democracy today—there can even arise behavioral models of faked nondisgust; for the dissimulation of disgust seems to satisfy the demands of political correctness. Thus, for instance, the dissimulation of a supposedly given disgust with "the obese, the disabled, the deformed, the mentally ill, the grotesquely ugly" (199) can be narcissistically savored as a moral victory—not a victory *of* disgust, but a victory *over* disgust (200): "Wonderful of me, isn't it, that I am secure enough to be seen out for lunch with the obese X?" As Miller conceives the matter, democratic relations of tolerance require of us many such notable dissimulations of disgust.

On the other hand, contempt—so runs another of his provoking theses—is not only compatible with democracy, but "mutuality of contempt" is actually "much of what pluralistic democracy is all about" (234). Contempt is less immediate and bodily, is more intellectual and, above all, more ironic than disgust—this was already noticed by Kolnai. The upper classes, in earlier societies, could look down upon the lower classes with self-assured contempt. At the same time, they ran no danger of feeling any disgust; for such contempt essentially went along with indifference. According to Miller's diagnosis, two things about this situation have changed today. The "superiors" can look down upon "the low," if at all, only with various scruples and a bad conscience. But, above all, forms of "upward contempt" have evolved—forms which, ironically enough, are supposed to have inherited, from the classical aristocratic "downward contempt," the happy blend of self-assurance and general disregard of the disdained social strata (230). Miller conceives liberal democracy as an interaction between insecure, self-questioning, "effeminate," neurotic types of contempt "from above" and self-assured, "masculine" types of contempt "from below" (234).

The somewhat painful description of a relation—one marked by contempt and disgust—between law professor Miller and a mason (207–17) makes it more than clear that those who today still see themselves as belonging "above" have considerable emotional difficulties with the precarious balance of asymmetrical types of contempt. It is precisely here that the antidemocratic disgust comes into play once again. "The superior," who censure their own contempt, but are not requited by the "low" with equal self-restraint, see themselves unexpectedly overtaken by disgust—and therewith by a quasi-natural force which, on an emotional level, restores the weakened clarity of hierarchy. Those below stink—that is the core of Miller's discovery of a supposedly new micropolitics of the social. For this discovery, George Orwell's *The Road to Wigan Pier,* of 1937, is extolled as the foremost example of an authentic literature of disgust in the twentieth century: "The very matter-of-fact Orwell is the twentieth century's real poet of disgust, not the self-indulgent writers of sex and sexuality, sadism and masochism, pornography and criminality, not the likes of Genet or Bataille" (238). This assertion is all the more out of place as Miller nowhere reads Orwell's text as literature, but only as a political statement. According to this latter, members of the middle class can take it into their heads to adopt the concerns of socialism only so long as they do not come too close to the objects of their philanthropic aspirations. Should they happen to lose this safe distance, they experience, in Orwell's words, "the real secret of class distinctions in the West.... *The lower classes smell*.... You can have an affection for a murderer or a sodomite, but you cannot have an affection for a man whose breath stinks—habitually stinks, I mean" (240). Without attempting to actualize Orwell's account in any significant way, Miller juxtaposes, to the overly virile smell of sweat and bad breath, the excessive use of aftershave and cologne as distinguishing features he finds disgusting in lower-class men (247). To be sure, he readily admits that "the stench of the low seems to bear direct relation to the anxiety they generate in the high" (248): "Jews, blacks or workers smelled as a matter of principle. Whether they really smelled or not, a stench would be imputed to them, and presumably suggestion and wishful thinking made it so" (247; see also 155–57). The long excursus on Orwell, however, unequivocally asserts the reality of the stench correlated with disgust. Given these feelings of contempt and disgust, therefore, the micropolitics of the social comes down, in the end, to a state of affairs in which the presumed core of pluralistic democracy—a balance of asymmetrical types of contempt—tends to destroy itself insofar as it produces disgust in the upper classes:

> Disgust does not admit of equitable distribution, and it works against ideas of equality. It paints a picture of pure and impure.... Hierarchies maintained by disgust cannot be benign; because the low are polluting, they constitute a danger; a policy of live and let live is not adequate. Look at "live and let live." Is it not the fundamental principle of pluralistic democracy? Does it not embody a pure sentiment of contempt equitably distributed? The problem, however, is that democracy not only worked to ensure the equitable distribution of contempt across class boundaries but also produced the conditions that transformed the once benign complacent contempt or indifference of the upper classes into a more malign and deeply visceral disgust. (251–52)

Not without pathos, the book as a whole concludes with the finding that it is precisely democracy that pushes the upper classes out of the safely distanced contempt for the low into disgust with their stench (254). Does it then follow, as is explicitly the case in Kolnai, that the reaction to what is disgusting culminates in the specter of a restoration of the old, unequivocally hierarchical orders? Any further unraveling of this theory of disgust and democracy seems hardly worth the effort. Perhaps it is not by accident that both Kolnai's and Miller's study occasionally turn the intellectual stomach of the reader—and less through their disgusting subject matter than through many of their own perspectives on it, especially those that are, or claim to be, original.

1

The Disgust Taboo, and the Omnipresence of Disgust in Aesthetic Theory

In the short essays in footnote form that Johann Adolf Schlegel attached to his translation (1751; second edition, 1759) of *Les beaux arts réduits en un même principe* by Charles Batteux, "disgust"—*Ekel* (or *Eckel*)—is defined, for the first time in full, systematic sharpness, as the outer limit of the aesthetic: "Disgust alone is excluded from those unpleasant sensations whose nature can be altered through imitation. Art would here fruitlessly expend all its labor."[1] Indeed, the disgusting is so powerfully repellent that it even checks the reflexion on its abject nature: "We are scarcely inclined to consider why the disgusting always repulses, even in the form of artistic imitation."[2] Once defined as a concept, however, "disgust" proved highly useful, even indispensable, for articulating the difference between the aesthetic and the nonaesthetic. As a term, the concept thus evaded the very exclusion to which it was subjected: "I dare hope," Moses Mendelssohn writes on February 14, 1760, in his "82nd Letter Regarding Literature," "that you are not so delicate as to shy away from such an examination. Therefore I shall venture, indeed, on a closer consideration of the nature of *Eckel*."[3]

In a discrete manner, the insinuation here of delicacies to be avoided conveys one of the intricate linguistic peculiarities rendering *Ekel (Eckel)* "one of the most striking words in [the German] language."[4] In the eighteenth century: "to be *eckel*" denoted both that which repels and the (too) ticklish, (too) delicate sensibility, which (too) easily allows itself to be repelled by something. This double application of being "eckel" to both object and subject leads to a blockade of possible insight *vis-à-vis* disgust. Only those who are themselves not (too) *eckel* can attain insight into the "nature of *Eckel*." Lessing, Herder, and Kant followed Mendelssohn's "I shall indeed venture it." The 1760s thus saw the emergence of the first veritable theoretical debate over disgust, with numerous examples serving as canonized points of reference. For a foundational moment in the history of aesthetics, culminating in the reflections on disgust in paragraph 48 of Kant's *Critique of Judgment*, establishment of the aesthetic and of ideal beauty, on the one hand, and insight into the "nature of disgust," on the other, were two facets of the same endeavor. (There is no equivalent to this in French or English aesthetics. In a few passages, Addison and Diderot speak of "disgust"[5] and *dégoût*.[6] But these concepts neither possess the prominent systematic value nor share the specifically philosophical semantics that "disgust" comes to assume in the German aesthetic tradition.)

The Beautiful as Vomitive

Disgust's astonishing career already begins, in fact, at the center of the beautiful itself. In its virtually exclusive focus on the extreme countervalues to beauty, the explicit debate that originated in the 1750s conceals this cardinal locus of *Eckel*. A disgusting menace inherent in beauty itself fully emerges only outside the confines of the more narrowly defined debate. The "82nd Letter Regarding Literature" does at least hint at a form of disgust elicited by beauty; but it does so only under the rubric of a disgust at the merely pleasant and at "excessive sweetness." The mixed sensations, which transform unpleasant objects and sensations into sources of aesthetic pleasure, are superior to "purest enjoyment"[7] because they provide an enlivening sollicitation of our sensitivity to a heightened degree by means of changing sides—of performing a trajectory with a considerable amplitude of tension. This theorem can be reformulated inversely so that the role of disgust becomes apparent: the cumulation of unadulterated pleasantness passes over, through its own dynamic, into that quantitative sort of disgust connected to the feeling of (over)satisfaction: "What is merely pleasant soon produces satiation, and finally *Eckel*. . . . By contrast, the unpleasant that is mixed with the pleasant seizes our attention, preventing all too early satiation. Daily experience with those tastes that are sensual shows that pure sweetness soon leads to *Eckel*."[8] Other authors diagnose such an inherent reversal into displeasure and disgust for *all* "pleasing" feelings, explicitly including the sensation of the beautiful. In his *Essay on Human Knowledge*, Johann Karl Wezel writes as follows:

> Pain, particularly physical pain, tautens the nerves. Only when it reaches a very high pitch and lasts too long, does it cause the nerves to slacken. On the other hand, we cannot experience any sort of pleasant sensations for long without the organs being exhausted: surfeit and disgust *[Ueberdruß und Eckel]* are the constant companions of such sensations.[9]

All of us will have enjoyed, or experienced pleasure, at having our skin stroked by a tender hand or being gently tickled—at having our nerves soothed by a soft tone, a mild color, a moderately sweet smell. But as soon as the loveliest smell or color exceeds a certain level . . . it becomes oppressive and unenjoyable, thus producing displeasure.[10]

Breitinger's *Critische Dichtkunst* (1740) already applies the special structure of quantitative disgust from (over)satiation to poetic *elocutio:* "In the same way that immoderate lavishing of spices only spoils dishes and awakens *Eckel,* a glut of flowers and ornaments stifle the beauty of a work's material."[11] In his *Observations on the Feeling of the Beautiful and Sublime* (1766), Kant approaches social life and the relations between the sexes along the same lines: "In France, the woman sets the tone in all companies and all society. Now it can scarcely be denied that without the beautiful sex, social gatherings are rather savorless and boring; but if women supply them with a tone of beauty, it is up to men to supply a tone of nobility. Otherwise, social intercourse becomes equally boring, but for opposite reasons: because nothing evokes as much disgust as sheer sweetness."[12] Without beauty, savorlessness and boredom triumph; dominated by the beautiful sex alone, social intercourse is "equally boring," and even disgusting. Contemporary aesthetic theory provides, precisely, an exit between these poles of savorless absence and disgusting presence of the beautiful. The aporia's solution involves an imperative of *mandatory supplementation:* in order to be and remain beautiful, the beautiful has an innate need for completion through something other than it—through something non- or not-only-beautiful. This supplement comes under a variety of names: "grace," "calm grandeur" *(stille Größe),* "solemnity" *(Ernst)*—or simply "soul" *(Seele).* In Kant's "social" example, this law of mandatory supplementation reads thus: the feminine "beautiful tone" needs the counterweight of a tone that is masculinely "noble," in order not to be filled with boredom and disgust out of "pure sweetness."

Alongside the satietory values of sheer sweetness, wearying repetition, and all-too-exhaustive elaboration, one paradigm of *Eckel* above all assumes a leading role in the eighteenth century.[13] Its material is found, once again, outside the confines of the more narrowly defined aesthetic debate. It is the disgust from sexual fulfillment. The problematic, disgust-endangered moment of satiation is not the "enough" of joyful satisfaction, but the "too much" unfolding in just that satietory moment—namely, to the extent that the object of already fulfilled desire offers itself to further consumption. One piece of sugar too many, continued sexual suggestion converging with just-quenched longing—and satiety threatens to emerge from the joy of satiation. Satietory disgust is thus basically disgust from excess or overfulfillment. Spinoza formulated this point with great acuity: "One further point should be observed concerning love. It frequently happens, while we are enjoying what we were seeking, that from that very enjoyment the body changes to a new condition, as a result of which it is differently determined and different images are activated in it, and at the same time the mind begins to think of and desire other things." When, however, the "old" object presses us to further consumption, a conflict emerges between past and present desire; in the realm of sexuality just as in that of food, this can result in a state of "disgust" and "repugnance": "while we are enjoying food we were seeking, the stomach is being filled and the body is changing its condition. If therefore, with the body now in a different condition, the image of the said food is fostered by its being set before us, and consequently also the conatus or desire to eat the food, this conatus, or desire, will be opposed by the new condition of the body, and consequently the presence of the food which we used to want will be hateful, and this is what we call Satiety (fastidium) and Disgust (taedium)."[14]

Even when later authors cross the threshold of "enough" without plunging into disgust, excess thus being joyously affirmed, Spinoza's observation remains a model for both the avoidance of disgust at excess and the inversion of such disgust into pleasure. Barthes thus writes of a language of love allowing us to "leave every satisfaction" behind us and "transgress the bounds of satiation," without paying the price of *dégoût* and *nausée*.[15] And Benjamin offers an account of a form of voracity that only discovers its own terrain through victory over the disgust of satiety: "And then came the pass-heads of taste, upon which, once excess and disgust—the last curves—are conquered, the view opens up onto an unheard of gustatory landscape: a pale flood of desire without threshold . . . the full transformation of pleasure into custom, custom into vice."[16]

An elaborate "map" of love from 1777 very precisely marks the shift from satiation to disgust: on the one hand, the province of "satiation" still lies in "the land of happy love"; on the other, it neighbors directly on *"Eckel."*[17] According to Kant, disgust generally threatens the "vulgar acquaintance" with sexual fulfillment.[18] Among the many pre-Kantian articulations of sexual disgust, let us here simply note Shakespeare's famous misogynist variant.[19] For Shakespeare, *sex disgust* and *sex nausea* are the "natural" fate of male desire. The highest praise he can accord Cleopatra thus centers on her ability to avoid sexual satiety—and hence satietory disgust—through the art of endless variation. As one commentator puts it, "For the lover of Cleopatra there is no sexual disillusionment, no depression or depletion, and every time is as the first time: 'Age cannot wither her, nor custom stale/Her infinite variety: other women cloy/The appetites they feed, but she makes hungry/Where most she satisfies.'"[20] "Disgust satiates," it suppresses all appetite, Kant would say later;[21] but contrary to Shakespeare's portrayal of Cleopatra, he is in fact subscribing to the conventional motto for avoiding satiety: "abstain or infinitize foreplay."[22]

Endless variation and foreplay: in eighteenth-century aesthetics these antidotes to sexual disgust become constitutive elements of aesthetic experience. At the very moment when the beautiful is first and thoroughly subjectified, being defined as a special sort of pleasure *(Vergnügen, plaisir)*, rules for avoiding satiation, developed for the pleasures of eating as well as of social and sexual intercourse, are extended into the field of this new aesthetic pleasure. There they institute the genuinely modern law of an "aesthetic" *infinity* that thwarts any closure. Henceforth, even art is meant to offer only those pleasures capable of yet further elevation and/or an open-ended process of reflective consummation. In contrast, bringing the beautiful to the edge of "excessive sweetness" and "purest pleasure" would mean seeing it turn into disgust. Kant generalized this rule to a "chief maxim" of all behavior:

> Whatever the path may be upon which one seeks pleasure: it is ... a principal maxim to apportion it in such a way that one can always heighten its experience; for to be satiated by it produces that condition of disgust *[ekelnden Zustand]* which renders life itself a burden to spoiled people, and consumes women under the name of the vapors.[23]

Following a pair of long dashes, Kant comes out promptly with an ironclad recipe for success: "Young man (I repeat): enjoy your work! Do not place a check on *pleasures* in order to *renounce* them, but in order to reserve always as much of them as possible for future prospects." The recipe of "autonomous" aesthetics is no different: it propagates a "prospective" pleasure that can be infinitely elevated, a kind of everlasting *Vor-Lust*—or more exactly: an endless foreplay that turns into an endless afterplay without any excess or peak in between. Such a diet alone offers protection from satiation, and consequently from disgust at the "highest pleasure," "pure beauty" and "unadulterated sweetness." It alone prevents an immanent transformation of the beautiful into a vomitive. The aesthetic provides the unique kind of pleasure that by its own rules (which are not identical with the nature of the beautiful, but rather subject to a dietetic regime) conforms to the law prescribing exclusively non-finite forms of fulfillment. Aesthetic pleasure is aesthetic only to the extent that it inherently respects this law, whereas the other types of pleasure have no built-in features through which they can structurally avoid the self-destructive turn upon reaching the point of satiation.

With utmost precision, Lessing's famous rule of the "fruitful moment" *[fruchtbarer Augenblick]* renders the anthropological-aesthetic principle of avoiding satiation into an artistic imperative. It prescribes always avoiding the "climax" within "the full course of an affect." "The imagination" is only granted "free play" through such a ban on maximum satiation, which enables us to "add all the more" in imagination, or "thinking." Lessing promptly spells out the dangerous sensation his rule is meant to avoid: "that finally we feel disgusted with the entire object."[24] Aesthetic pleasure, then, does not allow an exhaustive, maximally fulfilling representation; it requires, instead, an economy of reserve: the retention of open possibilities for intensification, or of a "stairway" always offering another step to climb. The new discipline of aesthetics calls for virtuosos of infinite foreplay. This infinitely open process of fulfillment implies an equally infinite process of nonfulfillment. The aesthetic realm is thus grounded in an abysmal assumption: the beautiful tends in itself to become disgusting, hence to pass over into its extreme opposite; by virtue of its innate features, it is threatened with the danger of unexpectedly revealing itself as something *vomitive*. Laconically, the early Kant confirmed that "the very thing which is beautiful evokes disgust" *(die Sache selbst vereckelt die da schön ist)*—unless, Kant adds, it is mixed with something different.[25] And in another passage:

> [The beautiful] causes the soul as it were to melt in a soft sentiment, and by slackening the nerves sets all the feelings into a gentler emotion which, however, if carried too far, is transformed into lassitude, satiety, and disgust.[26]

Finally, Kant diagnosed an "admixture of disgust" in every strong "enjoyment of the senses"—with one remarkable exception and outer limit: "Under conditions of good health, the greatest enjoyment of the senses not accompanied by any admixture of disgust, is *rest after labor*."[27] The Protestant ethics of this sentence are deeply inscribed within the very foundations of aesthetics, namely in theories of the beautiful and of aesthetic pleasure. In Kant's "rest after labor," labor resounds ad infinitum; rather than comprising an autonomous, sensual self-presence, the sensual enjoyment of this "rest" is also, always, the enjoyment of "work" that has been accomplished. The unadulterated self-presence of "enjoyment of the senses" would involve its shift into the negative form of experiencing intimate presence: into disgust. As an antidote to the inherent danger of disgust, the theory of aesthetic pleasure similarly stipulates a potentially endless labor of the understanding—a labor that simultaneously figures as basis, motor, and content of aesthetic experience. Within this model, *Ekel* is both lower and upper limit, adversary and innate tendency of the beautiful. Though the aesthetic debate on *Ekel* emphasizes almost exclusively its role of being the extreme opposite of the aesthetic, disgust thus proves to be, even while placed under a ban, to be constitutive for the beautiful in a double manner. Between the contradictory sentences "the very thing which is beautiful evokes disgust" and "nothing is more opposed to the beautiful than disgust,"[28] the new discipline of aesthetics demarcates its space and its ideal. Referring to Goethe's "beautiful silhouette in complete form," Kafka once echoed this basic argument of classical aesthetics, ironically applying it to the classicist aesthetic itself: "Goethe's beautiful silhouette in complete form. Secondary impression of repugnance at the sight of this consummate human body, since surmounting this level [of perfection] is beyond the imaginable."[29] At the same time, disgust at beauty itself opens a perspective upon the category of *kitsch:* According to Adorno, *kitsch* is that type of the beautiful that "contradicts" itself precisely due to "the absence of its own opposite," or that turns into something "ugly," because it is not contaminated by something dissonant and other than itself.[30]

Aesthetic Infinity as Antivomitive

Art thus needs to master equally both the advantages and the deficits of the beautiful. Something in the beautiful itself demands supplementation through a not-beautiful: a contamination blocking the disgusting satiety that arises, precisely, from the purely and unadulterated beautiful. From their very inception, both the emerging "discipline" of aesthetics and the classical ideal of art respond to this danger of pure beauty. Baumgarten's notion of perfect sensual cognition postulates a form of perception that, while marked by clarity and exerting a striking effect on the senses, never achieves the distinctness of theoretical cognition because of its excessive endowment with sensual traits. This absence of distinctness grants aesthetic perception a capacity to draw ever more distinctions, ad in(de)finitum; it thus blocks arrival at any maximum value of full satiation. Winckelmann formulated an analogous rule:

> A beautiful face is pleasing, but will be more stirring when endowed, through a certain reflective bearing, with a quality of seriousness.... All stimuli achieve duration through enquiry and reflection, and that which is discretely pleasing invites deeper study. A beauty endowed with seriousness will never leave us completely sated and satisfied, but rather with the expectation of ever-new enticements; such is the particular distinction of Raphael's beauties, and those of the old masters.[31]

Whether the beautiful's supplement is named "truth" or "gravity," beauty requires a not (simply) beautiful moment, so that its "enticements" can take on duration—instead of leaving us "sated and satisfied." Already several years before similar reflections by Mendelssohn, Lessing, and Herder, Winckelmann had expressly named this satietory value *Ekel,* touching discretely on sexual disgust as its paradigm:

> All delights, including those robbing the greatest number of human beings of that unrecognized great treasure, time, gain their

endurance and protect us from *Ekel* and satiety, to the extent that they engage our understanding. Merely sensual feelings, however, are only skin deep, and have little effect on the understanding."[32]

For a painting whose charms exhaust themselves in "a short time," Winckelmann occasionally also uses the metaphor of that "lower sense" constituting the disgust-sense par excellence: such a painting "appears to have been made for the sense of smell."[33] Sensations of smell, taste, and touch are fleeting, they are bound to the here and now, and cannot be reflectively rendered infinite. Winckelmann's postulate that "a painting must permanently please" can thus only be satisfied by those senses capable of establishing inner connections with the "understanding." Along with transcending the sensory experience of disgust, this rule transcends the field of pure sensory experience in general. From now on, the aesthetic enters into narrow cooperation with the reflective understanding: senses and understanding are configured in such a manner that a virtual and nonterminable process of "information enrichment" unfolds. As a thoroughly finite defense reaction, as spontaneous as it is brief and as violent as it is decisive, disgust allows no room for reflection: all the less so for a type of reflection affirming its own nonterminability and undecidability. If the insertion of infinite reflection into aesthetic experience is one of the cardinal innovations from Baumgarten to Kant and Friedrich Schlegel, vomiting from disgust serves as that innovation's negative definitional model: an indigestible block of nonreflective finitude and decision.

To employ the understanding while resisting any finite, exhaustive determination by it: that is also Kant's formula for introducing the aesthetic idea, a paradoxical term serving as a means of successfully—and structurally—avoiding disgust. By an aesthetic idea, Kant means "a presentation by the imagination that prompts much thought, but to which no determinate thought whatsoever (i.e., no [determinate] *concept*), can be adequate, so that no language can express it completely and allow us to grasp it."[34] This idea is aesthetic precisely to the degree that it "opens a view upon a boundless realm of related impressions,"[35] thus maintaining its own unreachability for every finite interpretation. Put otherwise: aesthetic pleasure only remains pleasure if something remains to intensify or to discover—something postponing the maximal satietory value ad in(de)finitum through an unterminable employment of the understanding. Whenever, to the contrary, the aesthetic is "merely" centered on a self-exhausting "pleasure" *(Genuß)* and "leaves nothing behind in the idea," its "object gradually [becomes] disgusting."[36] From here emerges the tension which characterizes the foundational structure of the entire *Critique of Judgment*. On the one hand, the beautiful is meant to please free of all interest; on the other hand, only those taking an "intellectual interest in the beautiful" are immune to the dangers of the "vanity" and vapidity routinely affecting the purely aesthetic "virtuosi of taste."[37] Likewise, the beautiful is meant to please free of all concepts, while, on the other hand, it is linked to undetermined, and hence infinitely determinable, concepts. By his own account, Kant is here "impairing" the same "pureness" of the beautiful he lays out in such uncompromising fashion.[38] Ubiquitously, such impairment serves to increase the powers of aesthetic judgment through its contamination. Such contamination alone orients aesthetic experience toward infinite satisfaction; and it can do so only by generating an infinite deferment of a simultaneously complete and distinct comprehension that would "leave us completely sated and satisfied"—and hence on the verge of being disgusted. To a considerable extent, the often-conjured inexhaustibility and indeterminacy of aesthetic experience can thus be read as a remedy to the radical finiteness of disgust, since disgust not only defines and threatens the aesthetic realm from the outside, but, due to beauty's self-sickening tendency, has always already infiltrated its interior structure. This prominent feature of the new aesthetics inaugurated by Baumgarten furnishes an urgently needed *antivomitive:* an apotropaic response to the disgust of satiation that results from the unmixed and uncontaminated beautiful.

"Mixed Sensations" and the Exception of Disgust

Ancient 'theories' of the beautiful only occasionally touch on art, and do not form part of a specifically aesthetic discourse. In contrast, the modern elaboration of aesthetics into an independent 'discipline' is aimed at the isolation of phenomenal zones and subjective forms of experience that are first and foremost aesthetic—and nothing else. More than a hundred treatises on the beautiful accompany the phenomenon defined in the language of systems theory as the differentiation of art into an autopoetic subsystem. Although doubtless it is this system's highest programmatic value, its "ideal," the beautiful never figures as its exclusive principle player. Rather, the field of the aesthetic always covers more ground than just the beautiful. Indeed, precisely this incongruency prompts the aesthetic reflection to define the beautiful's *trans*-aesthetic and *inner*-aesthetic boundaries and supplements. Alongside the danger of disgust elicited by beauty itself, this becomes especially apparent in the marked importance accorded the problem of aesthetic pleasure at unpleasant objects. From the late seventeenth-century to Dubos and Batteux, and onward to Burke, Mendelssohn, and Lessing, aesthetic theory consistently addresses the paradoxical pleasure at the representation of all sorts of horror, including the pleasure taken in the representation of ugly, gruesome, and revolting objects or events.

Aristotle's intellectualizing explanation for the pleasure taken at horror[39]—a problem that has gained fresh topicality over recent decades—did not at all satisfy the eighteenth-century aestheticians. If this pleasure were in fact merely grounded in the "illusory," technically successful and hence beautiful imitation of horrible events, it would—when compared with the synergetic energy released by the beautiful imitation of the beautiful—be always merely a partial and hence partly deficient pleasure, or from Lessing's perspective, even a double displeasure.[40] Lucretius's topos of the shipwreck with spectators has comprised a second traditional explanation.[41] But it, as well, presents little more than pleasure at intellectual distance: we are pleased because as mere spectators we are ourselves safe, or because we can withdraw from aesthetic horror into our actual intactness. The "empathy" doctrine of the "moral sense" philosophers offers the inverse of this Lucretian model: we feel pleasure at horror because it sparks empathy with the victim, thus allowing us to sense our own humanity. To be sure, this doctrine also has palliative and apotropaic elements, it also evokes a dynamic of defensive pleasure; but the sort of positive affect resulting from horror itself conforms far more closely with the standards set for explaining the pleasure taken in horror by its most advanced eighteenth-century advocates. How is it conceivable that in art, unpleasant events *in themselves* spark pleasure—and not simply their distancing as something unreal? And further: why *must* art, in its own interest, not limit itself to beautiful "objects" when aspiring to furnish a pleasure as intense and enduring as possible?

The theory of the violently agitated passions in the tradition of Dubos and Burke ascribes the same salutary effect to tragedy's artificial horrors, and to the real ones at work in gladiator combat and gruesome public executions: both forms of horror agitate our mind to maximal degree; they thus generate a powerful self-apperception considered pleasant and beneficiary since it strengthens our will to self-preservation, guarding us from sluggishness, boredom, and—in extreme cases—suicidal predilections. The artful horrors provide such pleasing effects to a lesser degree than the real ones; but they do not pay for these effects with the sort of scruples coming into play, for instance, through the deadly results of the gladiator spectacle. This is, in effect, a hard theory of excitatory appetite: of an abstract hunger for stimuli that embraces, precisely, ugly and horrible phenomena as all the more durable sensations for the receptive sensual and spiritual apparatus. At that theory's side, we find the more complex theory of *mixed sensations,* developed exclusively to account for the horrors of art. No matter if the latter theory, in its fine and manifold ramifications, is based on a successive or a simultaneous mix of pleasant and unpleasant feelings: in either case, it leads to the paradoxical result that "a mix of pleasure and displeasure . . . is more stimulating than purest enjoyment."[42] To the extent, namely, that artistic "imitation" must prove its mettle by producing a sense of aesthetic pleasure at "unpleasant objects," it overcomes resistance and realizes a transformation whose shocks and dangers enhance the stimulatory effect. This theory does not only supply a license for unpleasant objects, but also diagnoses, with great critical acumen, their superiority *vis-à-*

vis "pure beauty." In the first place, horrible objects furnish us with particularly violent stimuli for our perceptive apparatus; in the second place, they furnish us with the joyful relief of these objects being "merely" artful illusion. In contrast, pleasant objects generate only moderate agitation of the passions; and furthermore, awareness of their nonreal nature rather produces disappointment. Correspondingly, Batteux states in his *Les beaux arts réduits en un même principe* (1746):

> These effects of imitation, so advantageous for disagreeable objects, turn entirely against agreeable objects for the same reason. The impressions are weakened. . . . Hence, all things otherwise being equal, the heart must be far less happy with agreeable objects in the arts than with those which are disagreeable. Subsequently we find that artists succeed much more easily with the latter than the former.[43]

Or as Mendelssohn put it:

> Our fear is seldom stripped of all hope; horror stirs all our capacities to evade the danger; rage is linked with the desire to take revenge, sadness with the pleasant representation of past happiness; and pity cannot be separated from the tender feelings of love and affection. The soul has the freedom of sometimes dallying with the enjoyable aspects of a passion, sometimes with the repugnant, thus according itself a mix of pleasure and displeasure that is more stimulating than purest enjoyment. Little self-attentiveness is required to observe this phenomenon everywhere; for what other reasons would those enraged prefer their rage and angry people prefer their anger to all the joyful images they are offered for the sake of comfort?[44]

The different theories centered on the aesthetic amenities of fear, horror, terror, and pity have been frequently discussed and are sufficiently well known.[45] They were here recapitulated as a pretext, from which *one* single "unpleasant passion" stands apart, as the scandal that *cannot* be incorporated into the field of aesthetic pleasure.[46] Or to repeat the words of J. A. Schlegel: it is *"disgust alone"* that "is excluded from those unpleasant sensations whose nature can be altered through imitation."

Pleasure and Displeasure

The domain of the aesthetic is hence not regulated by the distinction between beautiful (pleasant) and not-beautiful (unpleasant, ugly, horrible, sublime, ridiculous, etc.) alone. The beautiful itself is in fact defined as the unity of itself and a not (only) beautiful supplement that first shields it from the sickening satietory value of its own purity; in the framework of this self-contradiction, the beautiful can hardly be considered merely the positive value in a binary "informational" code (beautiful versus ugly). In fact, another aspirant here stakes a stronger claim to being the prime distinction of the aesthetic system: the distinction between (aesthetic) pleasure and displeasure, as traversing and overlaying *both* the phenomenology of the beautiful and the sliding scale of the not-beautiful.[47] This "code" as well, has its logical complications, since pleasure here also figures—indeed, preeminently so—as a mixture of pleasure *and* displeasure. Nevertheless, the lively and enlivening stimulation of an enduring contemplative pleasure is consistently considered as the positive distinctive feature of aesthetic "information"—regardless of the specific definitions, refractions, and mixtures the beautiful *and* the varieties of the unpleasant undergo. A negative proof of the aesthetically distinctive value of the pleasure-displeasure distinction is offered precisely by the fact that, at least in the case of its first theorists, *Eckel* represents both a transcendence of the aesthetic and the transcendence of possible feelings of pleasure:

> The soul's unpleasant passions have yet a third advantage over *Eckel* . . . in that they often flatter the soul even outside the realm of imitation, in nature itself. Their advantage is that they never prompt pure displeasure, rather always mixing their bitterness with delight. . . . The situation is very different, however, in the case of *Eckel* and related sensations. Here the soul does not recognize any perceptible admixture of pleasure.[48]

This binary exclusion from the group of mixed sensations—mixture versus nonmixture of pleasure—testifies less to any timeless insight into the "nature of disgust" as to the architectonic impulse steering Mendelssohn's differential specification. Long before Freud, later authors will emphasize, precisely, the ambivalence of attraction and repulsion at work in many disgust-eliciting phenomena; in disgust, they will diagnose a repressed or rejected ("foreclosed") pleasure, rather than the total absence of any relationship with pleasure. Mendelssohn discreetly leaves this possibility open by preferring the expression "no *perceptible* admixture of pleasure" to "no admixture of pleasure"—a choice certainly allowing for imperceptible or hidden admixtures. Beforehand, J. A. Schlegel had already defined the relation of pleasure to disgust by means of the dynamic model of an inverse balancing of two scalepans. The "unpleasant sensations" that are conducive to art are marked by a well-balanced alternating rhythm of pleasure and displeasure, with a light though decisive upperhand granted the feelings of pleasure; by contrast, in the case of disgust, the contribution of pleasure is overwhelmed by the accretion of displeasure:

> The most well-rendered depiction of an unclean old woman emphasizing more her repulsive than her ridiculous side will elicit a horror *[Schauder]*—whether or not in painting, I won't dare say, but certainly in poetry—that can be neither balanced off by pleasure at the discovery of similitude nor eradicated by the feeling that it is a fictive sensation. The more imitation succeeds in arriving at the truth—the more accurately and powerfully the disgusting features gain expression—the more violently do they revolt us.[49]

For the dietetics of the beautiful, the paradigm of satietory disgust is more important than all variants of disgust at touching or smelling an object at all; the ties it maintains with pleasure are far more than subcutaneous ones. For satietory disgust emerges at the locus of pleasure itself, where not too little or no pleasure is present, but in fact an excess: it is the trace, then, not of a lack, but of this excess of pleasure. Nevertheless, such a relation between disgust and excessive *Lust* should be distinguished strictly from the archaic-modernistic syndrome of a transgressive disgust-pleasure at excess itself (as in Bataille). This is because the pleasure preceding the experience of satietory disgust actually disappears within it, so that the pleasure is no longer felt *as* pleasure. In Condillac, we find a description of disgust's genesis at the locus of pleasure, in the context of revulsion at specific dishes.[50] For Condillac as for authors of the French Enlightenment in general, culinary judgments of taste are simply an arbitrary, culture-encoded expression of custom. For just this reason, with the onset of an attrition that can affect habit, he sees two paths leading from pleasure to disgust: either the accustomed and desired dainty ("certain fruits") turns directly into a source of *dégoût*, and is thus abandoned; or the road to pleasure's loss takes a detour through disgust from excess. The latter alternative results from the earlier pleasure's "shadowy image" spurring the desires "all the more violently" onward, "to rediscover the earlier relish" through repeated attempts at consumption. What follows an overeating whose "hopes" are repeatedly "disappointed" is a "punishment" which assumes the form of physiological "pain." For its part, this experience of digestive disagreement becomes part of the conception of the habitually desired object, culminating in this fashion likewise in distinct *dégoût*. In the moment of its experience, this disgust, as well, contains no pleasurable admixture; rather, it occupies, by virtue of its own genesis, the locus of a pleasure that has first been weakened by the corrosion of habit, then transformed into its opposite through stubborn and excessive efforts to preserve it or regain it.

The "Darkest of All the Senses" and the Collapse of Aesthetic Illusion in Disgust

For Mendelssohn, the defeat or exhaustion of aesthetic pleasure is merely one of three features distinguishing the trans-aesthetics of *Eckel*. The first feature is that "properly speaking" "no objects of disgust" exist or can exist in works of art. What is meant to be "excluded" is—always already and a priori— excluded. Why, then, the scandal? Mendelssohn answers with a theory of the dangerous metaphor. Something that "does not have the slightest role in the fine arts" can be "associatively" transferred to them. The stakes involved here are nothing less than an invasion of the "darkest of all the senses"—with a menace of collapse facing prominent features of the aesthetic:

> Let us consider how this feeling of disgust naturally emerges. Which senses are most of all subject to its experience? It seems to me these are taste, smell, and touch, the first two from excessive sweetness, the last from an all-too intense tenderness of bodies that do not sufficiently resist the touching fibers. These objects, then, can also become unbearable to the sense of sight through a simple association of concepts, in that we remember the displeasure they prompt for taste, smell, or touch. But, properly speaking, the sense of sight has no objects of disgust. In the end, when lively enough, the mere idea *[blosse Vorstellung]* of disgusting objects can, in itself and for itself, prompt revulsion—and indeed, notably, without the soul needing to imagine *[vorstellen]* the objects as real.
> Here, already, we have concrete reasons for *Eckel* being unconditionally excluded from the unpleasant sensations that please in imitation. In the first place, by its very nature, the sensation of *Eckel* can be experienced exclusively by the darkest of all the senses, such as taste, smell, and touch—and these senses do not have the slightest role in the fine arts. Artistic imitation labors solely for the more lucid senses, namely sight and hearing. Sight, however, has no disgusting objects of its own. And as for hearing, perhaps the only feeling of disgust linked to it results from a steady stream of perfect harmonies that would appear to have some similarity with excessive sweetness in regards to taste.[51]

The argument has been often repeated since antiquity: the experience of (artistic) beauty requires distance; paintings, poems, and musical compositions are neither tasted nor smelled nor touched. Even a number of languages acknowledge this distinction: rather than "tasting beautiful" or "smelling beautiful," they prescribe "tasting good" and "smelling good." Disgust figures primarily as an experience formed from the senses of contiguity or proximity: something tastes disgusting (the eighteenth century's standard example: excessive sweetness); something feels disgusting (favorite examples: excessively soft; flabby; pulpy-gluey); something smells disgusting (smell here possessing a wider radius for action than touch or taste, but demanding an as it were physical entrance of the "object" into the sense-organ). What excites disgust must be nearby—indeed this proximity is an essential part of the feeling of disgust. As Aurel Kolnai indicates, it is "not simply the source but also an accompanying object of the feeling of disgust," forming "the bridge between [its] catalyst and the subject-person affected by it"; for this reason, proximity assumes "a key position in the problematic of disgust."[52] Kant himself already put it quite succinctly: the disgusting "presses itself upon us."[53]

Mendelssohn's opposition between senses genuinely capable and incapable of disgust involves an intersection of the sensory feature *proximity versus distance* with that of *obscurity versus lucidity*. In turn, this opposition encapsulates a whole series of additional oppositions: directly material, substantial, and 'real' versus intellectually mediated, form-oriented, more proximate to language, and to this extent tending toward the 'ideal'; resistance to analysis (infinite) openness to analysis; concrete abstract. In view of such features, the distinction between senses capable of and senses removed from disgust sets in play distinctly ambivalent judgments. On the one hand, with the great exception of Herder, eighteenth-century aesthetics aligns the experience of the beautiful with the "distance"-associated senses, considered the superior senses. To be sure, when compared with the accomplishments of the pure intellect, sight and hearing lose in clarity what they gain in sensuality and their accessibility to pleasure. But compared with the "dark" proximity-related senses of "taste, smell, and touch," they indeed stand far closer to the "light" and "clarity" of reason. On the other hand, labeling the senses of proximity as the "dark senses" not only marks a deficit of intelligibility. From a materialist-sensualist perspective, and in the sense of the doctrine of the "dark conceptions" of the soul, that which is distant from reason provides an all the closer contact to the reflectively elusive basis of our physical and spiritual life: as a sensual, a-thetic proof of reality, evidence of an anchoring in the depths of the human soul.[54] Hence what Mendelssohn tends to exclude from the aesthetic can be inscribed soon after into Herder's linkage of beautiful form with the proximity-based sense of touch—this with direct recourse to Mendelssohn's reflections on *Eckel*. Herder thereby endows the relation of the beautiful to disgust with even more complications. Nevertheless, running through the various, disputed assessments of the dark and the more lucid senses is a consistent removal of art from the "actual" disgust-associated senses. Accordingly, Mendelssohn defines *Eckel* as a sensation that "by its very nature . . . can be experienced exclusively by . . . taste and smell . . . and these senses do not have the slightest role in the fine arts."

The consequence involved here is compelling: "properly speaking, the sense of sight has no objects of disgust"—and nor, subsequently, does art. Repeatedly, we find this insight accompanied by the authors noting that "genuine" examples of what needs to be excluded from art are indeed very hard to come by in the existing art works. According to Herder, "nature itself endowed no unpleasant sensation with so narrow a sphere as . . . *Ekel*"; the same sphere is said to be even far narrower within the realm of art. Laying as much stress as he can on the rarity—even the nonexistence—of that disgust destined for exclusion, Herder even coins the phantom-concept of "true *Ekel*."[55] Measured against its unheard-of rarity, the usual references to disgust are thus (dis)qualified as references to "untrue" simulacra: to inauthentic revenants of an original that can scarcely ever be experienced. Disgust can intrude into the field of art only as such a derivative, an inauthentic "association" or metaphoric transposition—as a figurative memory of itself. What quality predestines this inauthentic derivative, this "distant reminiscence" of "true" disgust,[56] to draw upon it all defensive powers of the aesthetic—indeed, to emerge as *the* tabooed sentiment, par excellence?

The answer lies in the configuration of disgust's first distinctive feature with its second—the feature Mendelssohn himself considered the most important. Put succinctly: the metaphors of disgust (or its figurative derivatives) are so dangerous because they are simultaneously *metonymies* of "the darkest senses." The figurative derivatives carry with them a "reminiscence" of the dark sensory substrate of the "true" sensation of disgust, thus providing this dark continent entrance into the bright field of art. And these lower senses—or their simulacra—cause the collapse of another key distinction of aesthetic experience: the distinction between nature and art (or "reality" and "artificiality"). It makes no difference to the unfolding of pleasures of taste and smell if that which tastes and smells good is, say, a superb dish or a smell of rose, an artificially prepared or natural material. *Cum grano salis*, the same can be said for the sense of touch. These senses are not accessible to aesthetic illusion because they neglect, and even cause to collapse, the constitutive distinction of aesthetic illusion: the distinction between "nature" and "art" (or "reality" and "artificiality" respectively the "imaginary"). Aesthetic illusion, from rationalist semiotics all the way down to Kant, processes these basic distinctions in a unique manner. Art deceives to the extent that it both suspends and maintains these distinctions. It conceals its own artificiality in favor of the illusory presence of what it represents, and thus appears to be "nature." Within the rationalistic model, it prompts us to forget the signs it employs, and seems to provide an immediate intuition of the represented object.[57] According to Lessing, even a poet must cause us to "believe" we directly see Helen or Achilles' shield, in the sense of a transformed rhetoric of producing the effects of real presence *(enargeia, hypotyposis)*.[58] And although Kant expressly breaks with the rationalistic model of representational transparency, he still offers his own variant of the time-honored topos *ars est celare artem:* "Nature, we say, was beautiful *[schön]* when it simultaneously looked like art; and art can be called fine art *[schöne Kunst]* only if we are conscious that it is art while it still looks to us like nature."[59] The lower senses rob all such exchange-grounded models of illusion, which define the formal structure of aesthetic experience, of their underlying premise. For they invest no differential value whatsoever in the poles which are to change sides (i.e., nature and art, or reality and fiction):

> Yet I believe there is a far more important difference between disgust and the unpleasant sensations that please in imitation. Representations of fear, sadness, horror, pity, and so forth can only prompt displeasure in so far as we take the evil for reality. Hence they can dissolve into pleasurable sensations with the recognition that they are an artful deception. Due to the law of imagination, the repellent sensation of disgust, however, emerges from an idea in the soul alone, whether or not the [causative] object be held for real. What help, then, could it be for the injured mind *[Gemüt]* when the art of imitation betrays itself, be it even in the most flagrant way? Its displeasure did not result from the assumption that the evil is real, but from the latter's mere idea, and this is really present. The sensations of disgust thus are always nature, never imitation.[60]

Aesthetic illusion, then, confuses the difference between art and reality, while disgust makes the poles completely collapse. Kant spells out the point with full clarity in his reworking of the triad Mendelssohn constructed out of the physical sensation of disgust, the "mere idea" of something disgusting, and an imagination prevailing without resistance: "For in that strange sensation, resting on nothing but imagination, the artful representation of the object is no longer distinguished in our sensation from the nature of this object itself, so that it cannot possibly be considered beautiful"[61]—namely, so long as "beautiful" signifies just that complex processing of the same distinction disgust undermines. To rest "on nothing but imagination" here in no way implies a positive assertion of disgust's irreality or nonexistence. In face of disgust's power to make collapse the distinction of nature and art, Mendelssohn's parallel definitions of the sensation as "always nature" and a "mere idea" of imagination rather confirm the *same* suspension of both the indication that something is real and the inverse indication that it is art; the suspension is simply emphasized from the two different poles of the collapsed distinction.

Johann Adolf Schlegel had already noted: "Disgust has the same effects in art as in nature. Against expectations, this is what we learn ... from experience."[62] Schlegel can only hold, in a very general manner, the "violent" nature of the disgust-experience responsible for this. Mendelssohn defines this violence more closely as the puncturing, indeed the eradication, of a difference;

in doing so he applies the concept of nature ("always nature") asymmetrically, as the unity of the *non*-distinction of nature and art, reality and illusion. This hyperreality of disgust suggests an analogy. For Freud, it is the unconscious that operates without an "indicator of reality *[Realitätszeichen]*,"[63] steadily preserving an impenetrable obscurity while still constituting the "real" libidinal basis for all behavior. In Freud's writing and elsewhere, disgust maintains narrow ties with unconscious drives, furnishing their suppression with an (anti)form; it thus marks the fate of the drives in civilization and upbringing. From the vantage of aesthetics, disgust participates in a reality that undoes the very distinction between "real," on the one hand, "artful deception," on the other. When it comes to the disgust-sensation, the Cartesian dictum "I think therefore I am" can be replaced by a new variant: "I am disgusted, hence something is real."

The conclusion "the sensations of disgust thus are always nature, never imitation" is only possible through an assumption on Mendelssohn's part—or the evocation, like Schlegel's after him, of an "experience"—that is anything but self-evident: "The repellent sensation of *Eckel* . . . emerges from a representation in the soul alone, whether or not the [causative] object be held for real."[64] It doubtless makes a difference for "representations of fear, sadness, horror, pity, and so forth" if we "take the evil for reality" or only for an "artful deception." Why should this not be the case for the sensation of disgust as well? Why should precisely this sensation, based in the dark, substance- and reality-bound senses of proximity, know no "indication of reality," rather being sparked by "mere ideas" of the imagination with the same violence as by a "natural" object, in full indifference to the distinction between imagination and the real? According to Mendelssohn, the relation between disgust and the imagination is clearly subject to a double logic of exclusion and incorporation. On the one hand, the extreme experiential model of disgust belongs to the "darkest of all senses" alone, and is thus strictly separated from imaginative realms mediated by distance and intellect. On the other hand, the imagination allows a re-entry of disgust into its other: in the mode of inauthentic "association" and "reminiscence," even a "mere idea" of something disgusting activates the structure of indifference to the art-nature difference, thereby imploding the distinction between "reality" and "imitation." The conditions making *beautiful representation* possible are thus bracketed, if not destroyed.[65] This is the reason why disgust, that dark, substantive, analysis-resistant feeling of reality, is simultaneously such a dangerous metaphor in the field of "higher" and "more lucid" senses. Both the aesthetic and the ideally beautiful classical body are constituted by the exclusion, not only and not so much of "true disgust," but of the imagined and conceptualized metaphors of disgust. Winckelmann's—and even Herder's—beautiful statues, and the tabooed "reminiscence" on disgusting bodies always already distant from art, are products of disassociation: two sides of the same thing, making contact along the boundaries of the aesthetic.[66]

The functional circle of disgust is short and quick. It allows no reflective shock-defense: there are no mediating links between a disgusting stench and the sensation of disgust, and hardly any possibility for conditioning and intervention. True, over large expanses of time, disgust reactions can be either learned or unlearned—they constitute no timeless natural occurrence. But the role of intellectual processing is far less important than with fear, horror, grief, or pity, and the relative distancing is thus far smaller: a further reason why these emotions are fit for "aesthetic" representation, while disgust is not. The absence of longer intellectually reflective sequences in disgust's regulatory circle is the source of this sensation's violence. The same absence allows the imagination completely unchecked sway, producing a short circuit between the "real evil" and a "mere idea." The unimpeded power of *association* has an effect identical to the source itself,[67] while those mixed sensations capable of illusion are subject to another law: the aesthetic-reflective weakening of truly disagreeable phenomena. Here as well, an irreconcilability with the temporality of reflection reveals itself as the decisive aesthetic defect of disgust. Being a violent response to an intrusion into our organs, the sensation simply leaves no room for reflection. It is a decisive and thoroughly finite reaction, while ever since 1750, aesthetic experience is meant to unveil reflective indeterminacy and infinity.

Pursuing its way from disgust's first distinctive feature to the second, Mendelssohn's theory thus traverses a field of considerable conceptual tensions. Regarding the first feature, he states that "properly speaking . . . no objects of disgust" exist for the aesthetic senses—only transpositions, memories, derivatives. Yet because of their non-intelligibility, their ties to the "dark" proximity-based senses, these distant simulacra are sufficiently powerful—according to the second feature—to make the reflective scaffold of aesthetic experience collapse (i.e., the configurative structure comprising suspension, exchange, and the maintenance of the "nature"-"art" distinction). In addition, the hyperfactual sense of reality, as experienced in disgust, provides another possibility for juxtaposing the mere opposition between the beautiful and the disgusting with a tendency toward convergence of these opposites. The beautiful is meant to deceive. Through its status as artificial sign, it is meant to engender the illusion of a real presence of something absent. The more deceptive, the more natural and real the effect of the beautiful representation. For its part, even as a "mere idea" of imagination, the disgusting "always" realizes this effect of nature. Hence the disgusting at the same time marks that value in which the beautiful's illusion-ideal is fulfilled with security and without strain, that is, "always." But precisely for this reason, it ceases to be a distinguishing accomplishment of artistic representation.

From this vantage, the "disgust"-cipher simply signifies the deception realized by the beautiful itself: a deception that operates irrespective of all differences, thus negating itself.[68] Like the unmixedly beautiful, when left entirely to its own devices, culminates in "pure sweetness," so, too, the successful aesthetic illusion of real presence undergoes an immanent shift into the disgusting: namely, when the illusion becomes absolute, and is no longer punctured by an accompanying awareness of its illusory character (i.e., by a residual noting of art's difference from "reality"). Mendelssohn diagnosed such an immanent shift of successful illusion into *Ekel* as occuring, in particular, when sculpture is painted: "I believe that when painted by the greatest artists, the most beautiful statues could not be contemplated without disgust." Ordinarily, the illusion of "nature" is evidence of beautiful representation; to the extent, however, that nothing recalls the artificiality of the representation, the law of art's success turns into a law of its disgusting failure: "painted statues are all the more unpleasant the closer they come to nature. . . . Life-size representations in wax, dressed in real clothes, evoke a highly repulsive impression."[69] Or as Hegel put it: "There are portraits that, as witty minds have rightly observed, are resemblant to the point of being disgusting."[70] This provides yet a further reason for the claim that the disgusting is not only beauty's maximal oppositional value, but rather is nondifferentiated beauty itself. It is pure sweetness, or the absolutely successful illusion of "nature" and real presence—an absolutely successful illusion that simultaneously ceases to be an illusion, since by causing oppositions to collapse, it erases every artistic difference as well as every distinctive "indication of reality."

Already in 1745, Johann Elias Schlegel—a brother of *Ekel*-theorist J. A. Schlegel—offered an advance variant on the thesis of a hyperreal reality even adhering to artificial *Ekel*:

> There are also sensations in which it actually cannot be taken for granted that an idea in imagination would be less powerful than a sensual perception of the very same thing. For at times, representation within the imagination feels as if a thing is being all the more accurately dissected, whereas one would turn one's eyes away if this thing were seen from the outside. It seems to me disgust belongs to this category. It is awakened far less by the view of a disgusting thing than by an accomplished narration. And I admit that I much prefer seeing a truly ugly old woman to reading a very detailed description of her.[71]

In contrast to the sequence of other unpleasant sensations, whose artful "representations . . . could never be as strong" as the "passion itself," in disgust, the difference in strength between real and artful source is here not only leveled, but even inverted. With disgust thus assigned the role of a pure "representation within the imagination," Schlegel's inversion disfigures a palliative against disgust, inscribed in disgust-theory itself, to the point of recognition. Through sleight of hand, disgust emerges as "an accomplished narration," a "view," a "very detailed description"—as everything that by definition, Herder's "true *Ekel*" is not. The theory of disgust's exclusion thus itself realizes what it propagates: disgust is, "properly speaking," excluded from the arts, from the very beginning (first exclusion); even the distant reminiscences on disgust must be excluded all the more tenaciously (second exclusion); at the same time, such derivatives and transpositions are transformed, entirely, into effects of what stands opposed, as theoretical and aesthetic modes, to physical-substantive disgust—into effects, that is, of imagination and representation (third exclusion). And nonetheless: the theory conveys more than it states. For Schlegel, "a truly ugly old woman" stands in once more for the unstated.

Semanticized and "Crude" Disgust

In the 83rd of his *Letters regarding Literature,* Mendelssohn returns to the previous letter's theory of disgust, now strengthening his rigorous rules of exclusion with an additional observation:

> Let us take note of the following difference between *Eckel* and the highest degree of the horrible. The former does not only cause displeasure on the stage, but also in descriptions and poetic portrayals, and can never serve as a source of the sublime. But however much the poet increases the horrible's intensity, he will continue to earn our praise, as the more violently he makes us shudder, the more sublime his work.[72]

If there is any theoretical-doctrinal "progress" from Mendelssohn to Lessing, it lies less in the technical refutation of this thesis as in its subversive application. For Mendelssohn, the horrible belongs to "the unpleasant sensations that please in imitation," since it can serve as a "source of the sublime." Disgust is blocked from this path of aesthetic ennoblement qua mixing. For Lessing, there is, however, a detour: namely, a *double* application of the mixing operation. The disgusting need only become an "ingredient"[73] of the horrible or monstrous in order to serve, with them and like them, as a "source of the sublime" or other aesthetic pleasure.[74] It can equally take on a functional role in the domain of the comic and ridiculous, being even coopted there to promote the joy of laughter:

> The drollest features of this sort are contained in the Hottentot tale "Tquassouw and Knonmquaiha," in the *Connoisseur,* an English weekly magazine, full of humor, which is ascribed to Lord Chesterfield. We know how dirty the Hottentots are and how many things

that awaken disgust and loathing in us are beautiful, comely, and sacred to them. A piece of flattened cartilage for a nose, flabby breasts hanging down to the navel, the whole body covered with a layer of goat's fat and soot and tanned by the sun, the hair dripping with grease, feet and arms entwined with fresh entrails—think of all this present in the object of a fiery, worshipping, tender love; hear this expressed in the noble language of sincerity and admiration, and try to keep from laughing.[75]

Is, then, the disgusting—the transcendence of the aesthetic, and of any mix with pleasure—indeed usable as part of, and medium for, aesthetic pleasure in representation? The answer is affirmative, to the extent that Lessing can in fact draw on an imposing sequence of disgusting details to be found in numerous literary masterpieces—among these, by Aristophanes, Ovid, and Dante. Johann Georg Sulzer thus begins his article on *Ekel* in his *General Theory of the Fine Arts* (1773–1775) with the following remark:

Some of our judges of art have made it a basic maxim of the fine arts that nothing disgusting should be represented in an artwork. But a closer consideration of the matter shows this prohibition to be not only ungrounded, but also trespassed by the greatest masters of art.[76]

In any event, Sulzer's argument falls short of properly restating the "basic maxim" he is dismissing with regard to aesthetic theory's foundational treatises. Disgust, for Sulzer, is not allowed for its own sake and as a moment of aesthetic pleasure, but only for didactic purpose: "to keep people away from evil through displeasure and repugnance." Lessing's model—disgust's entry into the field of "pleasing" representations through double subordination—is certainly incomparably more elegant; but it demands from disgust a similar self-annihilation through functionalization. Disgust now becomes a purveyor of meaning; it forms part of a symbolics of the ridiculous: as a signifying vehicle of mockery, whose substantive, physical weight—put emphatically, its being—is bracketed by the comical intention at work in it. As Lessing himself concedes, such a disgust, tamed by a signifying intention, is something altogether different from that nonsemanticized "bare" disgust,[77] which is subject to the taboo of exclusion. This distinction allows Lessing to license the disgusting in art while simultaneously maintaining the taboo placed on it—simply with somewhat less rigid borders. If art "does not favor the disgusting for its own sake," but to "thereby intensify the ridiculous and horrible," the imperative of its avoidance comes promptly into play as soon as anything disgusting "appears before us in its own crude form,"[78] free of this intensifying function. Lessing even conjures up the danger that with a second look, successfully blended disgust might once more become "entirely separate"—in other words, that from subdued and licensed, significatory disgust, "crude," unadulterated disgust might reappear.[79] His example is one of the standard references to be found in the contemporary tracts on *Ekel*.

> I come now to disgusting objects in painting. Even if it were an indisputable fact that there is actually no such thing as an object disgusting to the sight—an object which painting as a fine art would naturally renounce—disgusting objects would still have to be avoided, because the association of ideas renders them disgusting to the sight as well. In a painting of the burial of Christ, Pordenone pictures one of the bystanders holding his nose. Richardson objects to this on the ground that Christ has not been dead long enough for his body to have begun to putrefy. But in the case of the resurrection of Lazarus, he believes that the painter might be allowed to depict some of the bystanders in such an attitude, as the story expressly states that his body had already begun to smell. To my mind, such a representation would also be unthinkable, since it is not only actual stench that awakens a feeling of disgust, but even its very idea. We avoid places that stink, even when we have a cold. But painting, it may be objected, does not favor the disgusting for its own sake; just as is true of poetry, it needs it to intensify the ridiculous and the terrible. At its own peril! But what I have said about the ugly in this respect applies all the more to the disgusting. It loses incomparably less of its effect in an imitation meant for the eye than in one meant for the ear. Consequently, it will blend less closely with elements of the ridiculous and terrible in the former than in the latter case, for as soon as our surprise is over and our first eager look satisfied, the disgusting becomes a separate thing again, appearing before us in its own crude form.[80]

Mendelssohn's central theorem of disgust from a "mere idea" is here conveyed through an impressive example: even the "very idea" of stench awakens disgust. Lessing's incorporation of that "dark sense" into art thus culminates in a renewed exteriorization.[81] The same can be said for Herder's analogous effort to create a limited license for disgust by modifying Winckelmann's distinction between main and secondary work. As Winckelmann explains it, in an "accessory or *parergon*," "deficiencies in form and workmanship" must occasionally be tolerated, so long as in the main work "here the author, there the poet, have displayed their utmost skill."[82] Herder displaces this "lenient judgment" concerning "sloppiness"[83] in the direction of a supplementation of the beautiful by the not (only) beautiful: a supplementation not only tolerable to the beautiful, but that serves it and is even required by it. In light, Herder claims, of the many "repulsive figures" to be found in all mythologies and religions, even the Olympian, "much paper crammed with protests would have been spared by recognizing that in a composition comprised of various figures, a secondary figure cannot be subject to the rule of shaping that governs the main figure without the entire composition being ruined."[84] If the same mimetic rule aimed at beauty were applied everywhere, the result would be "a dull *one and the same* of long-limbed, straight-nosed, so-called Greek figures standing in line on parade."[85]

Herder's vision of uniformly beautiful runway-models evokes the disgust-value of oversatiation, hence the desire for variation—for ugly or repulsive antidotes. And yet, beyond such a contrastive, preserving and strengthening function for the beautiful, Herder himself leaves the decree of banishment aimed at disgust intact:

> Concerning Hesiod's depiction of sadness my feelings and those of Longinus are the same—be it for whatever reasons, I do not wish to see the running nose: I do not wish to see anything that awakens real disgust. Disgust as such simply cannot be mingled with other, pleasing, feelings.[86]

With this, the circle closes—albeit now expanded by an interior differentiation. "Disgust" is not only the direct antipole and, simultaneously, the inherent satietory value of the beautiful. Besides demarcating the extreme (counter)values of the aesthetic, it can be found at its very center: as a functional admixture of the other affects or as a necessary contrastive value *(parergon)* of the "principle rule." It thus tends to be found virtually everywhere and always: a multiple, ghostly quantity, a *shifter* taking on other values without a pause—and yet, or just for that reason, remaining oddly nonexistent. "Properly speaking," disgust is entirely absent from the aesthetic senses of sight and hearing, thus not having "the slightest role in the fine arts"—while nevertheless requiring exclusion with all apotropaic exertion. Where it is nonetheless admitted, it consistently turns out, despite deceptive phenomenal similitude, a harmless, domesticated doppelgänger of the "crude," "actual," and "true" original. As the aesthetic's entirely other, it remains basically unrepresentable, invisible, unidentifiable for the field that it limits: an empty cipher for that which the world of beautiful forms cannot appropriate or integrate. As soon as this absolute transcendence reifies itself into anything identifiably disgusting and, as such, appears *within* the aesthetic domain, it ceases to be what it (non)conceptually is, its monstrous alterity thus being reduced to the level of an inner-aesthetic phenomenon. Hence the difficulty of finding any fully convincing examples in works of art for transgression of the disgust-taboo: despite all authorial consensus to the contrary, even the runny nose that is nothing but a runny nose is not destined beyond all doubt to spark disgust. Inherently, every example is already, qua example or identifiable appearance in the domain of the aesthetic, a depotentiation of plainly heterogeneous *disgust* to a representable quantity of the *disgusting*.[87] And yet: regardless of all depotentiation and second order simulation, the phantom, the transcendental signifier "real disgust" remains intact. For still as a phantom, it serves to found that very identity of the aesthetic whose absolute transcendence it is supposed to be. Symbolically excluded, imaginarily plagued by the fury of vanishment, yet omnipresent, disgust marks the position of a tabooed reality: one that never stops returning to the field of the aesthetic, in order once again to be ejected. It is the beautiful's matter, matrix, *Marter* (the German word for plague or torment)—indeed even its disgusting old lady or banished *mater*. Everywhere, the articulation of the beautiful human body, the ideal of the "classical" authors, bears the traces of its emergence from this phantasmagoric body of disgust.

2

Disgusting Zones and Disgusting Times
The Construction of the Ideally Beautiful Body

With a quantitative culmination in the 1760s, the focus on "disgust" in aesthetic theory unfolds between 1750 and 1790—which is to say during the very emergence of both "aesthetics" as a philosophical discipline and the classical ideal of art. "Disgust" here assumes a key negative role in definitions of (aesthetic) pleasure and displeasure, mixed sensations, beauty, and the transformative power of "imitation." What has been surveyed in chapter 1 accounts for the general theoretical framework regulating the semantics, grammar, and function of the "disgust" cipher in individual treatises. The examples and concrete points of reference within the disgust debate cannot simply be derived from the general framework, nor are they merely a result of haphazard liberty of choice and accent on the part of the individual authors. Rather, the highly concrete matter and substance of the debate also has 'archaeological' dimensions, opening additional insights into the economy and iconology of disgust. Above all, it endows the concept with what it inherently requires: a body. This body turns out to be no natural body, but one constructed in unheard of fashion, and subject to a thorough cultural coding. And yet: it is very concretely a youthful, or old, or dead body; it has a highly specific skin and shape, and is quite unique with respect to its joints, nose, mouth, breast, and belly.

THE IDEAL SKIN AND DISGUST AT FOLDS AND WRINKLES, LAYERS OF CARTILAGE AND FAT

As Winckelmann formulates his old-new corporeal ideal, the "masterpieces" of Greek art show us a skin that is not taut, but smoothly drawn over healthy flesh. The latter thus fills out the skin without fatty bulges, and—in every bending of the fleshy parts—follows its movement in a harmonious manner. The skin never projects, as on our bodies, certain small wrinkles separately from the flesh. In the same manner, modern works distinguish themselves from the Greek through a multitude of small impressions, and through far too many and far too noticeable little furrows.... The probability always offers itself here that in the form of the beautiful Greek bodies, as well as in the works of their masters, there was more unity of the whole structure, a nobler union of the parts, a richer measure of fullness, without the skinny tensions and without the many caved-in hollows of our bodies.[1]

Noninterruption is thus the main feature of beautiful "lines"—both singular lines and those of the entire body: "The form of *true* beauty has *uninterrupted* portions. The *profile* of antique youthful heads is based on this thesis.... This rule implies, as well, that neither chin nor cheeks, interrupted by dimples or pockmarks, are adequate to the *form of true beauty*."[2] Herder came up with an incomparable expression for this continuum of the skin. He called it *das sanft verblasene Leibhafte,* the "softly blown corporeal": the corporeal as something softly blown like glass, or in other words a "beautiful line" that, in all its variations, is "never violently interrupted, never disagreeably forced out of its way" *(nie widrig vertrieben),* and never "knows anything of corners or angles."[3] Among the many meanings of *verblasen,* its use as a technical term is here specially revealing: "to cloak the objects with . . . as it were, a fog, French *effumer,* Italian *sfumare*."[4] In sculpture, a soft *sfumato* brings about a sort of comprehensive makeup for the skin, toning down all porosity, all surface variations. Or as Herder puts it, the skin becomes covered "with a palpable plaster."[5] Every fold, every dimple and hollow, every bodily corner (every *Ecke*), would be *eckel*. Such flaws would impair the smooth, harmonious surface as "disagreeably" "as does every pock-mark or fatal irregularity."[6] With a zeal that could easily match the sales-pitch of modern cosmetics representatives, the "classicists" extirpate every pit, pucker, wart, and fold. A few examples:

> in images whose beauties were of a lofty cast, the Greek artists never allowed a dimple to break the uniformity of the chin's surface.[7]
>
> Bad painters, who out of weakness cannot attain the beautiful, seek it in warts and wrinkles.[8]
>
> Wrinkles and folds are ruined regions, and each such swelling is more painful an illness than a bloated skin . . . might ever be.[9]
>
> Many of the wrinkles that are the necessary accompaniments of age are omitted.[10]

Again and again, Winckelmann praises the Greek "nature" for its resistance to "smallpox scars."[11] His sensitivity to "fatal irregularities" also includes body parts "that usually have gristle":

> It is common doctrine in our academies that the ancients really departed from the true contour of some parts of the body; and that at the collarbone, elbows, knees, and wherever much cartilage normally lies, the skin seems simply to be drawn over the bones, without revealing in a truly distinct manner the depths and hollows that the apophyses and cartilage form at the joints.[12]

For his part, Herder denounces the gristly deformation of smooth skin-surfaces as "unnatural excrescences" *(unnatürliche Auswüchse)* explicitly placing them in the disgust paradigm's horizon through the metaphor of "creeping worms": "these veins on the hand, this finger-cartilage, these bones in the knee must be handled delicately, dressed up so that they blend in with the whole— otherwise veins become creeping worms, and knuckles extruding excrescences."[13] That, Herder indicates, is "the basis of their disgusting nature. . . . It is as if they do not belong to the *one and integral whole of the body;* they are extra-essential accretions, or detached parts . . . like . . . an early death."[14] This is a fantastic anatomy, rich in bizarre details. The violence of its presumptions underscores that what is here at stake is a specific, classical-aesthetic encoding of the body, one rigorously applying—like any sort of binary encoding— the same distinctions to all parts of the body: the distinction between smoothness and roughness, and that between wholeness and "detachments." The desired result of this operation, the "softly blown corporeal," is not an inclusive but rather an exclusive whole: one whose "uninterrupted" completeness is based on detachments of presumed "detachments": on the body's exclusion from itself.

This radical formation of the body through deformation entails a politics and a morals. Everything disgusting solicits an ethical reaction: this thing here—the "crawling worms," anticipating our presence as stinking, rotting bodies—should *not be*, at least not for *us* and in *our* presence. It should *go away*. The theoretical equivalent of practically avoiding the disgusting is defining it "away" either as "unnatural excrescence," or simply as a disease. Both Winckelmann and Herder present their highly stylized ideal bodies as the quintessence of "health," born from a "happy engendering" and formed "through bodily exercise."[15] The "callipaedian" doctrine shows Winckelmann "how careful the Greeks were to engender beautiful children. . . . To further this intention, they also instituted beauty competitions. They were held in Elis: the prize consisted in weapons."[16] "Beautiful children," "beautiful lineage," "beautiful nature": whoever or whatever did not correspond to this eugenics of the beautiful—put euphorically: this "physical psychology of paradise"[17]—was promptly stamped with rubrics of weakness, incompletion, and illness.[18] It is striking how pitiless the Classicists marked physical defects, illnesses, and "misbirths" as disgusting.[19] At the same time, the selection of what is beautiful often has a gymnastic-ascetic rather than an erotic tenor. In this manner, the beautifully engendered and naked Greek can be smoothly imagined in the form of a naked American, the hunting Indian:

> Look at the swift Indian pursuing the deer on foot: how speedily his juices circulate, how pliant and quick are his nerves and muscles, how buoyant the whole frame of his body. This is the way Homer fashions his heroes for us, portraying Achilles mainly through speed of foot.
> From such exercises, bodies received the great and manly contours with which the Greek masters endowed their statues, without haziness and surplus fat. The young Spartans had to present themselves naked to the ephors every ten days; the latter imposed a stricter diet on those who had started to put on fat. Indeed, one of Pythagoras's precepts was to guard against surplus weight.[20]

The rule of contours "without haziness and surplus fat" completes the taboo on "fatal irregularities" of the skin and limbs through an avoidance-rule for the "healthy flesh," over which the skin is meant to be softly stretched: not one gram of fat too many, no waste or excess; but also: no plunge into gauntness, which would itself be punished with ugly "hollows." Located between these extremes is the "noblest contour" of the Greek, "set as if at the top of a hair."[21] If we take account, as well, of the "strict diet among those subject to Pythagoras' laws," meaning vegetarianism, then three pillars of a juncture between ideal of beauty and politics of health become present: a triad appearing to have more followers now than in the age of Winckelmann and Herder.

Disgusting Depths and the Body's Openings

Wrinkles, puckers, warts, and gristle are the least of the "revolting" threats to the uninterrupted skin-line of the softly-blown body. For obvious reasons, the physical interior, the inner organs, and all processes of resorption and excretion do not only remain invisible in a field focusing exclusively on the beautiful facade; more to the point, they are among the "extra-essential accretions" to be painstakingly avoided. For Winckelmann, ideally beautiful bodies are not only able to dispense with the disturbingly excrescent "nerves and sinews," they also have "no need of those parts destined for the nutrition of our bodies. And this explains Epicurus' view of the shape of the gods, to whom he gives a body, but *an apparent* body, and blood, but *apparent blood*—a remark

Cicero finds obscure and incomprehensible."[22] The aestheticians of the 1750s and 1760s, however, found the same remark to be as highly illuminating and to the point as their own "as-ifs." For they thought of a body's beauty precisely as a self-idealizing sensuality—a sensuality appearing at a maximum degree (as Plato put it, *ekphanéstaton*[23]), hence leading to the edge of the sensual, indeed opening a vista beyond the edge. It was for the sake of such immanent self-transcendence of the aesthetic that the integrity of uncovered skin had to be preserved most strictly. Otherwise, that maximal value of phenomenality alone allowing the beautiful body an "expression of aesthetic ideas" (Kant),[24] or an expression of "soul," would not be attainable. For this reason, the aesthetically pleasing body has no interior, hence allows no dissection or anatomy: "for thinking beings, art's highest subject is *man*, or [more precisely] his external surface alone."[25] Aesthetics and anatomy, which boom simultaneously in the second half of the eighteenth century, are thus opposing disciplines. According to one of Diderot's reflections, "peeking under the skin" is "highly dangerous," having "ruined more artists than it has perfected."[26] Goethe confirmed this rule *ex negativo*. In his "Outline of a Comparative Anatomy" he finds himself forced to expressly defend the sciences devoted to the inner body, "dissection as well as physiology," against the aesthetic reaction of disgust.[27] With regard to the skin's pure and uninterrupted surfaces, these sciences descend into a void: what appeared "as if" a body turns out to be an "ethereal" and hybrid "creature" of "supersensual sufficiency"—a creature that had simply been "cloaked on its outside . . . with a human form."[28]

In the realm of the ideally beautiful, when not only the body's excretions, but literally its inner organs become visible on the outside, what is at play can only be the disgusting in the service of the monstrous or ridiculous.[29] Thus Lessing's example from the "Hottentott Tales," when the protagonists have "wound fresh intestines around their feet and arms." In his *Analysis of Beauty* (1753), Hogarth correspondingly offered the following methodological suggestion: "In order to my being well understood, let every object under our consideration, be imagined to have its inward contents scoop'd out so nicely, as to have nothing of it left but a thin shell, exactly corresponding both in its inner and outer surface, to the shape of the object itself.[30] For Hogarth, this "shell-like manner" of "think[ing] about objects"[31] best allows an imagination of the soft lines composing the beautiful body's unity and completeness. Extending to the muscles located directly beneath the skin and responsible for its "fullness" and curvature, the Classical body sets this extreme conceptual model into practice. It is a body, "but an apparent body." Herder's troping of the softly-blown corporeal likewise implies a hollowing-out of the body. Among the meanings of German *verblasen*, in the sense of blowing fluid glass, one is here worth noting: "to consume through blowing: the entire glass-mass has already been blown into all sorts of bottles etc."[32] In this sense blowing devours its material, transforming it into beautiful hollow forms; the aesthetic body resulting from such blowing is a hollow bottle—or a glass puppet without an inner corporeal life. Carrying ad extremum Winckelmann's notion of ideally beautiful bodies "inflated as by a gentle breath,"[33] Herder ventures to speak of (marble) "sheaths" (or "veils"—his word is *Hüllen*), "tender as a soap-bubble."[34] Such imaginary orality and airiness of the statue—its beautiful stony form as an effect of "breathing" and "blowing"—realizes disgust's avoidance: through a consequent sublimation of all materiality and scripturality on and beneath the skin of the beautiful.

Considering that statues of gods represent the chief object of classical aesthetics, the theme of digestive organs may seem as abstruse as their absence qua "removal" seems redundant: one would not expect digestive organs in a statue, and even if present, they would more or less inherently be invisible. Nevertheless, for the classical ideal of beauty, these organs make a decisive difference. For in a variety of ways, the ideal is transversed and even shaped by *invisibility*. As the "expression"—or *Ausdruck*—of the beautiful figure, "soul" *(Seele)* and "spirit" *(Geist)* are meant to be visible in an invisible manner. On the other hand, the digestive and excretory organs are meant to be invisible in a visible manner. The figure must look *as if* it has no corporeal interior; put otherwise, it must appear in a manner necessarily suspending any thought of such interiority. This rendering visible of an inherent invisibility fuels the determination to focus on a phantasmatic inner corporeal life of statues. At stake in this apparently paradoxical logic is a different type of invisibility: one that accompanies and governs the sculpture's visibility like a shadow. Apparently, this second type of invisibility can be established only at the expense of the first type. To realize this effect, the statue sets in motion a game of changing sides and of mutual exclusion: the soul as the invisible "inside" can only become visible when—in a manner that is itself visible—the invisible corporeal inside has been eviscerated. One invisibility, then, makes way, through a paradoxical configuration of appearing and vanishing, for another invisibility; the latter weaves its becoming visible and ideal into the phantasm of a beautiful figure. The topos of "breathing" and "blowing" regulates the transition from one invisibility to the other: as a description of the beautiful fleshly line, it sublimates all "corners" and all the resistance of bodily material; and at the same time "breath" is itself a synonym, rich in tradition, for the soul—a metaphorical representation of its peculiar presence.

Still, even in the case of the beautiful hollow body, those zones leading *to* the body's inside *on* the body's outside remain ineffaceable: body apertures are the true *skandalon* of both "classical" aesthetics and politics of the body. They are *the* signified of disgust, thus requiring elaborate regulation. What the authors have to say concerning mouth, nose, ears, nipples reveals itself as up to this difficult task. When it comes to the lower body apertures, however, the theory itself becomes *eckel*, in the sense of German *heikel*, ticklish or thorny: this realm is touched upon with rather few comments.

In "The End of All Things," Kant speaks of four "disgusting similes" for the world as a whole. One of these is "the world as a *cloaca* to which all refuse from other worlds has been banished." Kant gives this simile a sympathetic reception as "in a certain sense original," reformulating the story of the Fall as a story of the discovery of excretion and its organs. According to this memorable account, paradise was

> transplanted to heaven. In this heavenly garden, many trees were present, amply provided with magnificent fruit. When these fruit were eaten, their digested residue vanished through an imperceptible evaporation; the exception was a single tree in the middle of the garden, which bore a fruit that was delicious but could not be sweated out in the same way. As our first parents were overcome by lust after this fruit—despite the prohibition against tasting it—, there was no other way to keep heaven from being polluted except to take the advice of one of the angels who pointed out to them the distant earth, with the words: "That is the toilet of the whole universe," carried them there in order to let them do what they had to do, and then flew back to heaven leaving them behind. That is how the human race is supposed to have arisen on earth.[35]

Paradise was the locus of pleasure without a "toilet," of excrement avoided. Bliss was the tracelessness of metabolism—an "imperceptible" and quasi-pneumatic "evaporation," or an ideal, invisible, and odorless transpiration. The relation of this "physiology of blissful nature"[36] to the earthly cloaca is analogous to that of the ideally beautiful statue-bodies—the "plastic art . . . of paradise"[37]—to the ugly depths and discharges of the "real" body. Under the title of "the grotesque body," Michail Bakhtin has described a construct governed by both positive and negative rules that are opposed, point by point, to those for the aesthetic body. The "extra-essential accretions" of the one mark the positive realm of the other:

> The grotesque body is not separated from the rest of the world. It is not a closed, completed unit; it is unfinished, outgrows itself, transgresses its own limits. The stress is laid on those parts of the body that are open to the outside world, that is, the parts through which the world enters the body or emerges from it, or through which the body itself goes out to meet the world. This means that the emphasis is on the apertures or the convexities, or on various ramifications and offshoots: the open mouth, the genital organs, the breasts, the phallus, the potbelly, the nose. The body discloses its essence as a principle of growth which exceeds its own limits only in copulation, pregnancy, childbirth, the throes of death, eating, drinking, or defecation. . . . The

age of the body is most frequently represented in immediate proximity to birth or death, to infancy or old age, to the womb or the grave, to the bosom that gives life or swallows it up.... The Renaissance saw the body in quite a different light than the Middle ages, in a different aspect of its life, and a different relation to the exterior nonbodily world. As conceived by these canons, the body was first of all a strictly completed, finished product. Furthermore, it was isolated, alone, fenced off from all other bodies. All signs of its unfinished character, of its growth and proliferation were eliminated; its protuberances and offshoots were removed, its convexities (signs of new sprouts and buds) smoothed out, its apertures closed. The ever unfinished nature of the body was hidden, kept secret; conception, pregnancy, childbirth, death throes, were almost never shown. The age represented was as far removed from the mother's womb as from the grave, the age most distant from either threshold of individual life.[38]

In the new bodily canon, the focus is on the individually characteristic and expressive parts of the body: the head, face, eyes, lips; on the muscular system; and on the body's position vis-á-vis the external world.[39]

With striking precision, the inversion of Bakhtin's description produces the ideally beautiful body in the sense of Winckelmann, Lessing, and Herder. To this extent, the Classical ideal appears to be only *one* aesthetic codification of the civilized and hygienic body, strictly regulated in its elementary functions, that Bakhtin sums up as *the* "new canon" emerging with the Renaissance aesthetic.

Forever Young

Upon closer examination, however, numerous grounds for differentiation emerge. It is the case that "ripened" youth, indeed even the "eternal youth"[40] of the gods, is the ideal age for the Classical body. Here as well, that body conforms with today's most up to date imperatives for beauty. "In the case of young children," Winckelmann explains, "the concept of a beautiful form does not actually come into play: we say that a child is beautiful and healthy; but the expression of form already comprises the maturity of a certain number of years."[41] Such ripe youth, however, is not only aesthetically "blissful"[42] by virtue of its roughly identical distance[43] between birth and death, or even because it "hides the ever unfinished nature of the body." Herder maintains just the opposite: *"eternal duration"* falls to the "mummy" alone, to the rigidity of the "grave" and "doing nothing."[44] The "perfection" inherent in youthful "blossoming" rests precisely in its positive incompletion—its nonidentity with itself. It is not simply a Being—or even merely a telos—out of and in itself: something that would seem to apply more aptly to our contemporary ideology of normatively enduring youth. Rather, it is always also a promise—a "view" onto something still outstanding. Herder refers to a "view of a laughing world" and to the "beautiful idea of hope" as a performative correlate of the beautiful body.[45] In this manner, the "forms of beautiful youth" leave room for charging the Apollonian perfection of the figure with a highly dynamic temporality, indeed to defigure all its apparent stability:

> The forms of beautiful youth resemble the unity of the surface of the sea, which at some distance appears smooth and still, like a mirror, although constantly in movement with its heaving swell. The soul, though a simple being, brings forth at once, and in an instant, many different ideas; so it is with the beautiful youthful outline, which appears simple, and yet at the same time has infinitely different variations.... The forms of a beautiful body are determined by lines the center of which is constantly changing, and ... has a stationary point in our sex still less than in the female.[46]

The aesthetic body's "eternal youth" is perfection qua imperfection, Being qua promise. Its forms correspond to the rule of the fruitful moment precisely in not yet being fully articulated, unfolding precisely in a withholding of their completion, "in an instant" of "infinitely different variations," and this within a realm without "a stationary point." This apparently small yet astonishingly dynamic difference between the almost-finished and—to speak with Lessing—the "climax" of articulation is what causes the beautiful to vibrate. Once again, the rule of avoiding satiation brings into play an exchange of "seeing" and "thinking" that cannot be finished. The image's configurative simplicity and stability gives way—as if an infinitely variable, wavering image—to an open sequence of deconfiguration and reconfiguration: "The more we see, the more we must be able to add in imagination."[47] Let us recall that just this supplementation comprises, simultaneously, the rule of avoiding disgust at merely beautiful figures "standing in line on parade." The classical aesthetics does not simply avoid birth and death, with the concomitant disgusting visions of a prefigurative becoming and a decomposition into stinking corruption. Instead, it attempts to inscribe both, as it were, "at once, and in an instant," upon the beautiful body. To be sure, this inscription takes a distinctly moderate form: for the defigurative infinitization of a particular fruitful moment shortly before maximal articulation is actually aimed at overcoming *every* disgustatory value—even disgust at the "merely beautiful" itself. Despite all vibration in the smallest detail, this eternity of beautiful youth is averse to decisive external alterations. It does not wish to endure birth and death as its other—but rather, through a process of infinitesimalization, to incorporate them into its own *confinium*. Apollo remains Apollo, Venus Venus. The extreme counterpole of their eternity is not represented by the gradual figurative transformation from birth to death, but by the *abrupt metamorphosis* in Ovid's sense. Contemporary film technique can offer dizzying visualizations of such monstrous, split-second transformations from human beings into animals. Even painted scenes capturing the moment of this event were sufficient proof for Goethe that "altogether Ovid's metamorphoses were of more harm to art than good": for "metamorphosis turns its object into a disgusting one."[48]

THE GAPING MOUTH

"The grotesque face," explains Bakhtin, "is actually reduced to the gaping mouth; the other features are only a frame encasing this wide-open bodily abyss."[49] The "wide entrance into the depths of the body" maintains close relations with the motifs of the open womb and bodily hell: "The bodily depths are fertile; the old dies in them, and the new is born in abundance.... The grotesque body has no façade, no impenetrable surface, neither has it any expressive features. It represents either the fertile depths or the convexities of procreation and conception."[50] The gaping mouth has left its stamp on mystery plays not only as something represented, but also as the law of scenic representation itself:

> In 1474 the author of a mystery play gave these stage directions, "Hell must be represented in the form of huge jaws which open and shut when needed." Thus the *gaping maw* was what all mystery-play viewers saw directly before them. This entrance to hell was located precisely in the middle of the stage foreground and at the eye-level of the viewer. The "hell maw" (*la guelle d'Enfer*, as it was usually called), seized the attention of the medieval public.... The public befriended the gaping maw in its cosmic aspect.[51]

In light of this now-forgotten prehistory, German classical aestheticians' attention to the gaping mouth attests to their highly developed sensorium for strategic approaches to debates. Bakhtin's general observation that "in the new canon, such parts of the body as the genital organs, the buttocks, belly, nose and mouth cease to play the leading role"[52] in no way applies to nose and mouth in the classical ideal. In fact, these body apertures are the objects of special attention. On the one hand, they are incorporated into the doctrine of the beautiful even as repudiated and disgusting entities. On the other hand, they are recoded into something thoroughly positive. Winckelmann's codification of the ancient Greek canon sets the tone for the subsequent circulation of the gaping mouth as a disgust-cipher in texts of Lessing and Herder:

> Next to the eyes, the mouth is the most beautiful facial feature. . . . The lips of figures in the most ancient style are usually closed; but in the later periods of art, they are not entirely closed in all figures of divinities, either male or female; and this is especially the case with Venus, in order to express the languishing quality of her desire and love. The same holds true of heroic figures. . . . Very few figures represented as laughing . . . reveal their teeth.[53]

According to Winckelmann, only one statue he knows of reveals the teeth of a god; such a degree of oral opening is normally reserved for "some *satyrs* and *fauns*," which is to say figures strewn along the edge of the Olympian canon. (In this regard, the now-habitual display of gleaming white teeth cannot appeal to ideal Olympian figures, but only to prototypes of a lower rank.) The rule of the most moderate possible lip-opening particularly proves its idealizing force in instances such as the expression of violent pain, where the represented object would be expected to have a wide-open mouth, as in a scream. This is the case of the *Laocoön*, which thus serves to epitomize the rule of the closed or slightly opened lips. Winckelmann's famous words on this theme are as follows:

> The pain which manifests itself in all the muscles and sinews of the body, and which neglecting the face and other parts we believe to feel from the belly alone, contracted in agony; this pain, I say, still does not express itself with fury, neither in the face nor in the entire posture. No awful cry is raised, as Vergil sings of his Laocoön: the opening of the mouth does not allow it.[54]

Lessing succinctly confirmed that a Laocoön with gaping mouth is irreconcilable with the "law of beauty." He also was the first to expressly define the oral danger to beauty as the danger of disgust:

> The master strove to attain the highest possible beauty under the given condition of physical pain. The demands of beauty could not be reconciled with the pain in all its disfiguring violence, so he had to reduce it. He had to soften the scream into a sigh, not because screaming betrays an ignoble soul, but because it distorts the face in a disgusting manner. Simply imagine Laocoön's mouth forced wide open, and then judge! Imagine him screaming, and then look! . . . In painting, the wide-open mouth—putting aside the fact that the rest of the face is thereby twisted and distorted in an unnatural and loathsome manner—becomes a mere spot, and in sculpture a mere cavity, with the most disagreeable effect in the world.[55]

Not the mouth, but the uninterrupted surface of the skin, is the dominant speech-organ of the sculptural body. As soon as the mouth speaks in excess, it disturbs—or indeed even destroys—the authentic discourse of plastic form, because it distorts this forms's beautiful curvature and generates an ugly crater. To this extent, a wide-open mouth is not "disagreeable" through offering a view into the body's depths, or to speak with Bakhtin, the "hell of the body's innards." From the perspective of Winckelmann and Lessing the mouth does not play such a role at all—or only to the extent of making visible the next external border, the rows of teeth. Rather, a gaping mouth is already *ekel* because in sculpture, it appears *in itself* as "a cavity," with the accompanying secondary effect that through the illegitimate opening, the adjacent surface is "distorted in a loathsome manner." The widely open mouth thus elicits disgust—in both a direct and a metonymical manner—simply by inscribing a "spot" onto the perfect skin of the aesthetic. Darwin's famous treatise on the expression of the emotions illuminates another source for the classicists' oral regulation: for Darwin, a "widely opened mouth" is the first physical sign of disgust[56]—its forbidding thus being directly identical with an exclusion of the disgusting from the realm of art.

The talk of "spots" and the distortion of the body's surface tends to attach the gaping mouth to the contaminative series folds, warts, wrinkles, and scars from smallpox—and not to the series within which it figures in the field of the grotesque: namely the gaping womb and gaping anus. It thus needs to be asked if the taboo on the gaping mouth is also, or above all, a masked proxy for the taboo on vagina and buttocks, birth and excretion;[57] or rather if the Classical body does not simply integrate the mouth in an entirely new series. The hypothesis of physical and sexual repression à la Bakhtin suggests itself so strongly only because Bakhtin identifies, in a relatively unmediated fashion, various discursive accounts of the body within different sign-systems directly with "real" attitudes to the body, food, and sexuality.

Lessing's politics of the gaping mouth is resistant to any direct alignment with Bakhtin's evocative oppositional schema already for the simple reason, that it argues, not for exclusion of the incriminated mouth from literature (i.e., from the field of Bakhtin's study), but for its ready *admission*. The "law of beauty" at work in representations of the body applies *sensu stricto* to the plastic arts alone, and not to literature—which "in modern times ... is ever ready to sacrifice beauty for the sake of higher aims." What is at stake here is another law, indeed possibly a "first law," its own ciphers being "truth and expression."[58] The nonidentity of beauty with either itself or with the realm of the aesthetic is already grounded in the deficiency of beauty in itself—in its necessary recourse to a supplement for avoiding disgust. Lessing makes use of this differentiation to offer an additional bifurcation: far from playing the solitary ruler in the realm of the aesthetic, the beautiful does not even need to enjoy *dominance* in all the arts—as long as the most general quality of the aesthetic is preserved, the pleasure experienced at vividly illusory representations. Winckelmann's assertion that "Laocoön suffers like Sophocles' Philoctetes" thus receives a decisive rebuff:

> But how does [Philoctetes] suffer? It is strange that his suffering has left us with such different impressions. The laments, the cries, the wild curses with which his anguish filled the camp and interrupted all the sacrifices and sacred rites resounded no less terribly through the desert island, and brought about his banishment there. . . . Screaming is the natural expression of physical pain. Homer's wounded warriors not infrequently fall to the ground screaming. Venus shrieks loudly at a mere scratch. . . . And Sophocles even lets [the dying Hercules] wail and moan, weep and scream.[59]

With the scream, the gaping mouth's disgust-value also receives its license in the realm of the aesthetic: that which has been excluded now returns as something included, through the introduction of a new distinction on the other side of the earlier distinction.

In any event Lessing's license of the gaping mouth cannot be seen as fully traversing Bakhtin's sharp oppositions. The licensing of the wide opening is not at all concerned with the biological site of exchange between inside and outside, the devouring and expelling entry into the corporeal cavity in the sense of the grotesque body. It applies to an entirely other mouth: the mouth which, even when opened to an extreme, is above all an individual speech-organ of the body's *surface*.[60] "Cavity"—*Vertiefung*—here does not signify depth, but rather an indented, injured surface: one that can even appropriate this lesion for its own expressivity. What is involved here is thus not identical elements in different corporeal systems, but—beneath the deceptive identity of name—a transformation of the elements themselves. As part of this transformation, the just-admitted gaping mouth immediately excuses itself anew, before choosing to withdraw into non-perceptibility. As the argument's first half would have it, no one should reproach Vergil's Laocoön for screaming—in contrast to the Laocoön of the unknown sculptor. The argument's second half again bows, however, before the incriminated taboo, in that it ranks the gaping mouth as a virtually invisible, merely secondary matter:

> When Vergil's Laocoön screams, does it occur to anyone that a wide-open mouth is necessary in order to scream, and that this wide-open mouth makes the face ugly? Enough that *clamores horrendos at sidera tollit* has a powerful appeal to the ear, no matter what its effect on the eye! He who demands a beautiful picture here has failed to understand the poet.[61]

Once more we see: in the system of Classical aesthetics, even incorporating the disgusting removes none of its distinctive value—even if this value sometimes comes down to a mere invisibilization of itself.

NOSE-DISGUST AND THE "GREEK PROFILE"

Something similar holds true for the nose, the second problem-zone of the Classical face. In the case of grotesque bodies, Bakhtin leaves no doubt concerning the "significance of the nose": it "always symbolizes the phallus."[62] The Classical nose is obviously no such analog or even indicator of the grotesque phallus's fruitfulness and monstrosity; at the same time, the simple counter-conclusion that "in the new canon, such parts of the body as the genital organs, the buttocks, belly nose and mouth cease to play the leading role"[63] is also off the mark. The nose's disturbing quality is not simply that, considered in itself, it *possesses* holes, but that it also, and for this very reason, *produces* holes with regard to the larger skin-line system. Like wrinkles, warts, and gaping mouths, these holes damage the law of least possible interruption and blemishlessness in surfaces of skin and speech. They also evoke an entirely other interior than that of a "soul's" "expression." The nose's material outflow is thus a cardinal paradigm of the disgust discourse within German Classicism. In this regard, one nose, above all, achieves notoriety: the nose of Achlys, a demonic personification of the "dark misty veil of death,"[64] read by Lessing and Herder more gently as the embodiment of "sadness." In a highly detailed description of Hercules' shield *(Aspis)* in the *Homeric Hymns* (now often ascribed to Hesiod), Achlys appears with a running nose:

> Clotho and Lachesis were over them and Atropos less tall than they. . . . By them stood Darkness of Death, mournful and frightening, pale, shriveled, shrunk with hunger, swollen-kneed. Long nails tipped her hands, and mucus was running out of her nostrils, and from her cheeks blood dripped down to the ground.[65]

With such features, Achlys has all right to claim the status of negative image to the "softly blown corporeal": hunger-hollows and withered skin-folds are as little reconcilable with that ideal as is flowing snot. (Pseudo-)Longinus, already, saw the latter feature as an example of the sublime's absence: "Hesiod . . . if indeed we are right in adding the *Shield* to the list of his works . . . has not made the image frightful, but revolting."[66] For Lessing, Achlys' dripping nostrils are first of all a means to demonstrate his distinction between a semanticized disgust, admittable as a furtherance of "the terrible," and a "crude disgust" that is to be avoided. The feature of the snot, Lessing argues, makes disgust become present "in its own crude form," and not as it were invisibilized through a functional relation to the terrible:

> The disgusting seems even capable of an ever greater degree of amalgamation with the terrible. That which we call gruesome is nothing more than the terrible which has been made disgusting. Longinus does not like that, in Hesiod's picture of Sadness "mucus was running from her nostrils;" not so much, it seems to me, because it is a disgusting trait, but because it is merely a disgusting trait that contributes in no way to the terrible. For he appears to have no objection to the long nails protruding beyond the fingers ... although long nails are scarcely less disgusting than a running nose. But long nails are also terrible, for they tear the flesh from the cheeks so that the blood streams to the ground.... A running nose, on the other hand, is nothing but a running nose, and I can only advise Sadness to keep her mouth shut.[67]

Despite being considered "scarcely less disgusting" than mucus, the "extra-essential accretions" represented by nails protruding far beyond epidermal confines are aesthetically licensed for one reason: they can serve to bloodily carve up the uninterrupted skin-line, and in this terrible capacity prompt a lively-sublime agitation of the spirit. For the running nose, however, which is "nothing but a running nose," the only thing left is harsh advice to "keep her mouth shut": a metonymic transposition of the mouth-taboo from the mouth-hole to the nose-holes and back. In this manner, the text of *Ekel* even interweaves the corporeal map's taediogenic zones on the level of linguistic articulation. With regard to Achlys's nose, Herder unhesitatingly aligns his stance with that of Longinus and Lessing: "I do not wish to see the running nose: I do not wish to see anything that awakens real disgust."[68] And again we can here add: this is so *within* art, within the realm of aesthetic *pleasure*. Nothing comes easier, yet is more problematic, than relating Lessing's and Herder's dicta to "reality" and to decide on neurotic-compulsive hygiene and corporeal repression. There is no record of either man being stricken with attacks of *Ekel* at his own snuffles, or that of his loved ones. Rather, their discourse of the flowing nose points, here again, to the eighteenth-century thrust to differentiate autopoetic functional systems: each has its own realm, laws, and taboos. The establishment of aesthetics as a new and distinct discipline has programmatically claimed just this for itself. For this reason, hasty conclusions passing outside the system's borders run the danger of leveling out the fine-grained logic of mutually irreducible *differences*. Still, the nonaesthetically oriented discourse over female noses has occasionally served an unmistakably misogynist purpose. As a remedy for erotic desire, Johannes Chrysostomos, for instance, recommends imaging the nasal contents of an attractive woman: henceforth the body's beauty will appear as a whitewashed crypt for nauseating matter.[69]

In art, running noses and hidden nasal content are both seldom and easily avoided. The classical nose is thus intent on other achievements than simply "shutting up" the snotnose. It also does not simply succumb to a form of antiphallic repression. Rather, in a highly subtle way, it is a nose invented anew: as an integral element of beauty itself. The nose precisely defines the "Greek profile":

> In the forming of the face, the *Greek profile,* as it is called, is the first and principal attribute of a high style of beauty. This profile consists of a nearly straight or slightly depressed line that the forehead and nose describe in youthful, particularly female, heads. . . . That such a profile represents a source of beauty is proved by its opposite; for the more the nose is depressed, the greater is the deviation of the face's line from the form of beauty.[70]

Again and again, Winckelmann and Herder return to this "nearly straight" line, this "unbroken form" descending from forehead to nose.[71] The Greek profile prevents three types of unsightly discontinuity in the skin-line: first, a concave curve between forehead and nose that Winckelmann called an *Einbug* (an indentation—or something like a "curved-in bow") and Herder a *Grabensprung* (rendered here as a "gaping ditch");[72] second a "flattened nose" *(gepletschete Nase)* that bends the forehead-line excessively inward; and third the "hawk-nose" *(Habichtsnase)* that projects outward in an extreme manner and evokes the phallic-grotesque nose.[73] At the same time, the Greek art-nose counters a defect sometimes mentioned together with the "collapsed, crushed nose,"[74] the "piece of crushed cartilage for a nose,"[75] this "greatest disfigurement of the face":[76] the projecting and/or excessively large nostrils. Lessing in fact wished to see "a flattened nose with prominent nostrils" established as an autonomous disgust-value for the sense of sight.[77] The straight-falling line from forehead to nose here works wonders. For the nose's altered starting angle in turn leads to an altered, less pointed closing angle above the upper lip—with the added, beneficent effect of less distended, in general smaller, nostrils.[78] Thus, like the gaping mouth, the gaping, disgustingly runny nose is not simply handed over to the grotesque body; it, as well, is recoded in a complex manner. The orientation toward the forehead-nose profile reveals—or better, produces—an artificial beauty that is beautiful not least because it removes and transfigures everything potentially disgusting to our sight. Even when it has become invisible in the transfiguration, the tabooed disgust value does not cease to regulate the realm of the beautiful.

THE "FLATTENED EAR"

In face of this highly elaborate politics of mouth and nose, it does not come as a surprise that a similar prescription is at play for the head's third opening.

"In ideal figures," Winckelmann explains in his detailed account of the ear in ancient art,[79] "one observes a highly special sort of ear." The ideal ear is indeed specially noteworthy, being "flattened out and swollen at the cartilaginous wings" *(platt geschlagen and an den knorpelichten Flügeln geschwollen)*. The flattening moderates the "fatal irregularities" of the cartilaginous excrescence; the swelling, in turn, furnishes the flattened-out ear with gentle roundness and fullness. Beyond this dynamic, the two opposing tendencies, flatness and swelling, join together to produce the desirable effect of diminishing the size of the ear-aperture: not only is the ear-hole rendered "narrower," but the entire "excrescence" of the monstrous ear, menaced by the "formless," appears "compacted and diminished in size."[80]

"Disgusting Breasts" and Ideal "Hills"

Between face and lower body, another body part is predestined to be subject to the classical-beautiful regime of avoiding openings: the female breast. The "aesthetic" breast is negatively defined by two features: it may not be "full to excess" *(gar zu voll)*[81]—not "large and fully developed"—and the nipples not "erect," "pointy," and "prominent."[82] Especially the 'haptician' Herder links the taboo on large breasts with the taboo on excessively soft breasts; he thus praises beautiful breasts for being "virginally hard."[83] An occasional, exceptional linkage of large to beautiful breasts is only admissible when large breasts are quasi-mandatory allegorical attributes, as with Ceres, goddess of earth and fruitfulness. In any case here as well this is only possible in the form of a conflict between the two predicates: "full breasts, but beautiful."[84] By contrast, the more than moderate breast-volume of Raphael's Venus, for which no similar allegorical investment can be claimed, is unhesitatingly admonished: "It is not necessary to admire everything: the sun also has its spots."[85] Herder provides a literary example for the disgust-value of sheer size: "Quantity matters as much as the sort of a phenomenon. In this respect, the story of Gulliver and the Brobdingnaks is highly instructive: how disgusting did Gulliver find the breasts of those women!"[86] Lessing's expression of "disgust and revulsion" *vis-à-vis* female breasts is related primarily to the quality of "the phenomenon"; it is focused on "flabby breasts hanging down to the navel."[87] Hovering behind all such breast-features to be avoided in aesthetic representation are taboos on nonaesthetic—that is, sexual and oral—pleasure: a large breast and erect, visible nipples "signify not virgins, but women,"[88] and evoke, as well, the function of nourishment.

The aesthetic taboo on the "woman who has suckled many children"[89] does not, in any event, exclude the act of suckling from the realm of the beautiful.[90] For what Winckelmann's formulation implicitly leaves open is rendered as an explicit chimera by Herder and Goethe: the very young woman, suckling her first baby—indeed, the suckling virgin. As typified in the famous case of Goethe's Ottilie, we find an evocation of images and positions of virgin and child, with no milk really flowing; rather, something emerges like an air-brushed impression of *virtual breast-feeding*. This hybrid suckling on the virginal breast is the only way to sate the thirst of the Classical ideal without paying the price of disgust-reactions to bodily apertures and secretions. Herder offers an especially inspired description of such ideal breast-feeding:

> Nature endowed the woman not with breasts, but with *a bosom* . . . washed with the milk of innocence and crowned with the rose of love. For the time that a little bud has emerged and the unripe hill is growing to harvest, the grace of virginity has wrapped her girdle around this rose, in which, according to the poet's description, love and longing reside. When the drink of innocence has been made ready and the helpless newborn hangs on the first fount of joy for mothers and children, and his little hand nestles and gropes and has 'nuff, and mother and child feel as one on the tree of sweet life—how inhuman would one have to be to not be moved at this sight and sense a lost paradise of innocence![91]

This passage evokes a closed cycle of "innocence" before the sexual "harvest." With finest nuancing, Herder avoids real sucking and drinking: the "immature" or "helpless" newborn, the *Un-mündige*, appears literally to lack a mouth—a *Mund*. Only "his little hand" finds satisfaction, nestling and groping and "having 'nuff" at the virginal breast. The grown Herderian "lover" of sculpture who is an expert in seeing as if he is touching,[92] here finds his nursery school in the inversion and displacement of the senses: already as an infant, he "gropes" *as if* he is drinking, and has entirely "'nuff'" from this phantasmagorical fulfillment.

What Herder wrote about the size and form of the aesthetic bosom is taken, down to its very metaphors, from Winckelmann. The *History of Ancient Art* establishes positive rules of beauty for those "unripe hills" that always leave open an expectation of something more and avoid any satiatory value of disgust precisely thanks to the infinitization of their prematurity. These rules thoroughly canonize the presexual woman:

> The breast or bosom of female figures is never endowed to excess. . . . The form of the breasts in the figures of divinities is all the more virginal in that their beauty was generally based in the moderateness of their size. A type of stone found in the island of Naxos was finely polished and placed upon them, in order to repress their swelling growth.[93]

When it comes to nipples, the taboo on "excessive endowment"—an echo of the rule of "noblest contour" beyond swelling and gauntness—is once more carried to the extreme of a self-invisibilizing form:

> Hence the breasts of the goddesses and *Amazons* are like those of young maidens whose girdle Lucina has not yet loosened, and who have not yet gathered the fruits of love; I mean to say that the nipple is not visible on the breasts.[94]

Winckelmann does not hesitate to apply this rule of invisible nipples for ideal figures quite practically. He draws from it the reverse conclusion that whenever a nipple is distinctly visible, the statue cannot represent a goddess: "Now, as the nipples are fully visible in the figure of the presumed life-size Venus in an old painting in the Barberini palace, I conclude that the figure cannot represent a goddess";[95]—hence that it "cannot be *Venus*."[96] A truly binary code (visible vs. invisible) is thus at work here, generating information and capable of producing surprising classifications.

Just as the ideal nose is shaped as the "almost straight" continuation of the forehead, the ideal nipple should look like an uninterrupted continuation of the breast-curve: "In the case of some less than life-size statues of Venus, the breasts are compact and resemble pointed hills, and this seems to have been considered their most beautiful form."[97] In this "most beautiful form" of the breast, then, there are no separate and prominent nipples, just as the ideal nose shows no prominent, visible nostrils. This parallel doubly inverts the traditional relation between sex and body-part: with regard to the phallic nose, the Classical canon places a taboo on its vaginal moment of opening and flowing efflux, while the female breasts are deprived of all potentially phallic features. Within the aesthetics of body parts, these crossovers suspend the moment of "mature" sexuality in both directions, replacing it with a kind of idealized sexuality: one in which visual pleasure taken in the body's beauty is offered only—and precisely—to the extent that the direct sexual function of the corporeal openings is made "invisible."

INVISIBILITY, UNSEEN NAKEDNESS, AND "WETTED GARMENTS"

The rules for the rendering invisible of digestive organs, mouth, ears, nostrils, nipples, and in general all openings and "excrescences" are not simply maxims for the material representation of potentially "disagreeable" phenomena. They point, as well, to *the* prominent formal device of aesthetic representation from Baumgarten until Kant: that of art's power to deceive through rendering itself invisible. Whatever variations we may find in different models of "illusion" extending from the rationalist self-erasure of the sign to the Kantian imperative regarding the self-concealment of art: what is constantly at stake in the theme of illusory *celare artem* is nothing less than the success and ideality of the aesthetic act—indeed, the capacity of art to be art. For this reason, the Classical rules for the beautiful body are likewise an allegorical presentation of what the (illusory) body of fine art itself is about. What blends the two together, the imperative of a beautiful—hence for its part visible—rendering invisible, faces its toughest challenge in relation to the gravitational center of the grotesque body, namely its lower half: belly and buttocks, penis and vagina.

From Winckelmann to Herder, the solution most immediately coming to mind, disguise through clothing, is decisively rejected. Such a solution would simply cloak the problem in a "Madras handkerchief,"[98] while not making the visible invisible—the only thing worthy of art. With Winckelmann, the pathos of the nakedness of ideally beautiful figures has, unmistakably, a gymnastic-athletic-calligenic tenor; in contrast, Herder's doctrine of sculpture's virtual feeling—the "eye becomes a hand," the "lover" sees *as if* he is touching[99]—tends toward the fetishistic. One assumption unites the two approaches: nakedness is above all a formal challenge to arts idealizing capacity. It belies all probability that Apollo strode away naked from his dispatch of Python, or that Laocoön was naked when the snakes attacked him. Why, then, this unreal nakedness, and what is so ideal about it? In Herder's words:

> The Greeks, . . . artists born for the beautiful, threw away raiments made of ore and drapery made of stone, instead sculpting what could be sculpted: beautiful *bodies*. Did Apollo emerge unclothed from his victory over Python? Did the artist struggle to remain true to the poor and ordinary form of customary appearance? By no means! He rather represented the god, the youth, the conqueror with his beautiful thighs, free breast, and young tree-like built. . . . Was *Laocoön*—the man, the priest, the royal son—indeed naked at a sacrifice before the assembled populace? Did he stand there unclothed as the snakes attacked him? Who in fact thinks about this when now gazing at the artist's Laocoön? Who ought to think about it?[100]

The rhetorical question contains its own answer: we give no thought to the question and "ought" not do so. For the art of sculptural representation rests precisely in making sure that the question does not even arise. It enjoys the elegance of a solution that hides the difficulty of the task: to display nakedness without displaying it; to "forgo" clothing in unusual and even inappropriate contexts, without this being at all startling. This nakedness is no less artful than the flattened ear or the skin-surface lacking cartilage. It is the effect of an ambitious technique of overcoming difficulties: "But the Greeks!

How they forwent clothes in the most beautiful images of their most beautiful periods! How many obstacles have they overcome, in order to show naked beauty itself."[101] To "show" in the mode of invisibilizing the obstacles that have been overcome—and even invisibilization of that which is actually seen: as such a paradoxical weave of the visible and invisible, nakedness obeys rules similar to those for the bodily surface's taediogenic zones.

For all those cases in which even a nakedness appearing not to be nakedness would be too inappropriate, Greek art invented a problem-solving kind of garments: the so-called "Coic dress," consisting of "fine and wetted garments"[102]—clothing that is no clothing for a nakedness that is no nakedness. "Apparently," observes Herder, the wet-clinging garment is "a device of the sculptor designed to evade obstructions and achieve goals attached to what is essential for his art."[103] In any case, whether invisibly naked or invisibly clothed, when it comes to the painstaking inspection of body parts for their values of disgust and beauty, the greatest difficulties are posed by the abdominal "excrescence"; in some cases, these difficulties are not tackled head-on through explicit theorems, but must be extrapolated from descriptions.

A Body "without a Belly"

While the belly is always a fat belly—a hyperbolic convexity of devourment and fecundity—,[104] the classical belly is its flat-out negation:

> Even in male figures, the abdomen is the same as in a person after a sweet sleep, and after healthy digestion—that is, *without belly*, and of the sort physiologists consider an indication of a long life.[105]

Winckelmann's rigid formula "without belly" again pushes the "excrescence" to be avoided to the point of becoming invisible. When Herder considers the "opposite" of this "soft" convexity, he spurns it as "a form and condition that repels even in description."[106] "Without belly" thus becomes readable as one more avoidance of a disgust-value.[107] Herder even endows the rejected belly-curve with a moral dimension (the faithlessness of the "lusty woman"; offense against "wise moderation").[108]

The "Spare Behind"

In its advocacy of what Winckelmann inimitably terms only "moderately full parts at that locus where *sedet aeternumque sedebit/Infelix Theseus* (Vergil)," in English: "that locus which unhappy Theseus sits on, and eternally will sit on,"[109] the Classical body conforms both to the rules of today's dietitians and our own ideal of slenderness. In Winckelmann's fictive-playful critique, in the *Circular Letter* ("Sendschreiben," 1756), of his own *Reflexions on the Imitation of Painting and Sculpture of the Greeks* (1755), the "spareness of nature" manifest in the "Greek behind" is admonished as a defect: one distorting the ideally beautiful body even more awfully than the *Blättergruben*—those disgusting pock-pits. A second disgust-value, monstrously "large ears," is hazarded as a negative parallel: "the spareness of nature in these [nether]parts had the same effect as nature's superabundance had with regard to other body parts in the case of the Enotocetes in India, who are said to have had such large ears that they used them instead of pillows."[110] But then, as a metacritique of this ironical self-critique, the "Explanation of the Reflexions on the Imitation of Painting and Sculpture of the Greeks" (1756) returns to the initial claim, providing both the key mythological reference and the authoritative "classical" reading of the curious discourse on the male butt:

> The *Circular Letter* uses a topos Aristophanes alludes to in order to prove a natural deficit among the Athenians. I take this topos as it must be taken. The poet's joke is based on a fable about Theseus. . . . It is said that Theseus was only freed by Hercules from his imprisonment at the hands of the Thesproti with a loss of those parts under discussion; and that he [i.e., Theseus] brought this loss to his descendants as a portion of their inheritance. Whoever looked like this, could boast of descending in a straight line from Theseus, just as a birthmark in the shape of a spear meant descent from the Spartans. We also see that Greek artists imitated the spareness of nature at this location among them.[111]

The rule of spare (male) buttocks avoids yet another "ugly" convexity. And it becomes clear once again that the putative "spareness of nature" is actually a dramatic result of art: the effect of a "liberation" that ancient comedy still evokes as a "loss" of bodily fullness, but that is elevated to the rank of "aesthetic beauty" by those formulating the Classical ideal.

EXCISION, CASTRATION, HERMAPHRODITIZATION: THE PHALLUS IN THE FIELD OF THE BEAUTIFUL

Without a doubt, the "repellent" convexities of belly and buttocks are immeasurably more easy to invisibilize on the level of the softly blown corporeal than is that "extra-essential accretion" par excellence, the male sexual organ. Paragraph 11 of chapter 6, book 5 of Winckelmann's *History of Ancient Art* takes up this problem—and in this one instance makes the problem itself, rather than the scandalon, invisible. Here is the passage in toto:

Even the private parts *[die Theile der Schaam]* have their special beauty. Among the testicles, the left is always larger, as is the case in nature, just as it has been observed that the left eye has sharper vision than the right. But in a few figures of *Apollo* and *Bacchus*, the genitals seem excised with diligence, leaving a hollow in their place. One should not take this for wanton mutilation. In the case of *Bacchus*, the secret meaning of this may be his occasional confusion with Atys, who was likewise deprived of his genitals. Since, on the other hand, Apollo was himself honored in the homage paid Bacchus, the mutilation of his own member had an identical significance.

I leave it to the reader and the seeker after beauty to look at the coin's flip-side, and study particularly the parts that the painter was unable to represent to the satisfaction of Anacreon, in the picture of his beloved.[112]

That differing testicular size has its "special beauty," seems to allude to an assumption widely held in eighteenth century aesthetics that pure symmetry is aesthetically less appealing than a sightly displaced symmetry, and that all unity and identity should be charged with as much difference and variety as possible. Yet even before the phallus itself is hinted at discretely—in order to then simply be dispatched from both the paragraph and entire book—Winckelmann has already taken the exit-path toward the beauty of those male figures whose "genitals seem excised with diligence." In their case, even the *vitium* of a "hollow" is accepted, as something that, in its commendable avoidance of phallic excrescence, should not be taken for "wanton mutilation" and possesses a "secret meaning." In this fashion, the paragraph seems to recognize only one way to unite the concepts of "male sexual organ" and "special beauty": amputation. Only the phallus's excision appears to allow a unified skin-surface, free of bulges, hollows, furrows, and spots. Literal dismemberment, however, is only one special instance of a general rule of virtual castration. Figures possessing an intact phallus—this can be extrapolated from the rules governing the other physical openings and protuberances—are to be represented *as if* it were absent, or more accurately, as if it were made in such a way as to be capable of being rendered invisible: of becoming "visibly invisible." Unfortunately, Winckelmann leaves it "to the reader and the seeker after beauty to look at the coin's flip-side"—to investigate the elegance of a visible penis's aesthetic *as-if* avoidance, and not only to appreciate the beauty of its 'real' excision. One is thus asked to search for a phallic analogon to the nose's "Greek profile" or the "flattened-out ear."

The solution to the difficult problem of how the penis can be represented as something beautiful is to be found in the idealization of hermaphrodites and castrati. Winckelmann and Herder were in fact by no means so *eckel*, so delicate, as to avoid naming and describing the male sex-organ. To the contrary, in the tables contained in his *Geschichte der Kunst des Altertums*, Winckelmann for the first time publicly presented an image of Jupiter pursuing Alcmene with a giant erect phallus. However, this grotesque Jupiter barely lays claim to beauty, thus transcending the very problem Classical aesthetics tries to cope with in other cases: how can the penis be represented as a *beautiful* penis? Even in the antique *Corpus Priapeorum*—the canon for all literary praise of the phallus—the claim to beauty is abandoned without contest in light of other, vastly superior capacities.[113] Winckelmann and Herder are here more exacting. As founders of an ideal of the beautiful human body, they also wish to discover a rule for the phallus that allows a purely aesthetic evaluation, with the predicate "beautiful" as its outcome. Pursuing this aim, they regularly link explicit descriptions of the phallus as an integral part of beautiful male statues to the striking stipulation that they be "unmanned" or hermaphroditic—or at least exhibit some female features. Repeatedly, Winckelmann identified "the type of the eunuch, for whom boys of handsome shape were chosen"[114] as the model of the exemplarily beautiful male figures Apollo and Bacchus. This "type" or "body-shape"—*Gewächs*—is "intermediate" between male and female: men with feminine backs, hips, and legs,[115] with a consistently "soft roundness" possessing the special advantage of "a little less harsh a suggestion of the muscles and cartilaginous portions."[116] Finally, with the hermaphrodite "art went still farther," extending the merger to the sexual features: "All figures of this kind have maiden breasts, together with the generative organs of our sex, and in other respects the body has female features."[117] Herder takes note—granted, in a travel diary not meant for publication—of "an unusually lascivious posture" on the part of such hermaphrodites, as well as "a male member" that is "rather long" and "elastic."[118] Such a member is rendered "ideal" and "capable of beauty" through two antigrotesque limitations: first, through a precisely-described moderation of the erection, meant to be merely "softly strained," with "the glans only somewhat unsheathed above"; second and above all, through its metonymic embedding in a body with hints of breasts, female hips, and so forth. Castrated or hermaphroditic bodies no longer possess predestined sexual partners, thus eradicating the thought of phallic-heterosexual consummation—however lascivious their forms and postures may be. At the same time, they can hardly serve any Graecophile revaluation of homosexuality.

A phallus capable of art and beauty is thus one that actually deletes and invisibilizes its phallicity: an as-if phallus, a phallus that is no phallus on a naked body that is not naked and is also "only an apparent body." Winckelmann, in any case, ends up choosing a more or less suprasexual reading of those rare and strange "creatures" who alone receive a relatively precise description of their sexual parts: "The ancients gave some gods the mystical significance of both sexes blended together."[119] Just as a purely aesthetic evaluation of the female breast leads to the invention of a woman who is not a woman, the phallus demands, for the sake of aesthetic beauty, the creation of men who are in fact not men. Indeed, Winckelmann speaks of the ease with which the ideally beautiful Bacchus, when represented in draped form, can be "taken for a disguised virgin."[120] The suckling virgin, the transvestite who seems a virgin, the castrated man, (herm-)Aphrodite with a penis: all these "creatures" are exotic "growths"—another meaning of *Gewächse*—resorted to by beauty in order to shield the purely aesthetic pleasure of form from any confusion with sexual pleasure.

The "Hypergigantic" Sex of the "Colossal Woman"

Aside from the "excessive endowment" of the bosom, Winckelmann spares the female sex the "equivocal beauties"[121] of excision, castration, and transplantation into a corporeal vehicle endowed with features of the other sex. The female "shame"[122] suffers another fate: it remains without a paragraph, and indeed without mention. The assumption comes readily enough: either the female sexual organ, as something displaced toward the interior and thus already invisibilized by nature, is in problem-free harmony with the ideal of the softly taut skin-surface, or it represents the maximum scandalon—its treatment thus subject to a total taboo.

In the grotesque body, the female womb consistently figures as gaping wide, or giving birth, or swallowing up the phallus; it thus directly corresponds to the gaping mouth. According to the rules of analogy, what succeeded in the case of the mouth (i.e., integration into "the beautiful" through reduction of the opening's "disgusting" expanse) should be even more easy with the female sexual organ. Sculptural representations actually need to invest little effort to hide an opening that is already quite invisible in itself. There seems to be no need for a delicate rule of invisibilization as with the openings of mouth and nose and ears—"nature" itself saved Winckelmann the trouble. Diderot thus did not hesitate to apostrophize the contours of the hairless female shame as an exemplary "serpentine line," hence as an embodiment of beauty in the sense of Lomazzo and Hogarth.[123]

Nevertheless, far more strongly for the German Classicists than for the author of the *Bijoux indiscrets,* the powerful phantasm of this bodily opening remains an obstacle for any glossing of its purely aesthetic "special beauty." The female sexual organ runs against the canon of the softly taut, uninterrupted, unblemished skin-line through another, much more visible anatomical feature: it has the form of a fold. Winckelmann disapproved of even "small skinfolds" as found in "most figures of the modern masters." By contrast, in ancient Greek art "the skin never projects . . . certain small wrinkles separately from the flesh."[124] The aesthetic defect marked by the fold was considered even more serious than that marked by the "fatal irregularities" of wrinkles, warts, and pockmarks. In the case of the fold, the skin is not damaged through "excrescences" and "accretions"; rather, as an intact surface, it is folded into itself. In this manner, it becomes an ambivalent "growth," traversing the guiding distinction of outside and inside, bodily surfaces and bodily depths. The fold arches the outer so thoroughly into the inner that the outer seems to loose itself into the inner. Where every little skin-crease is *already* a kind of invagination, violating the aesthetic rule of soft-stretched skin that articulates itself as pure surface, the skin-fold of the female sexual organ runs an even greater danger of falling into aesthetic disfavor. From the perspective of the Classical bodily canon, the double flaw of being both fold and opening thus poses obstacles for a purely aesthetic evaluation of that organ. Despite referring far more frequently to the female sexual organ as did Winckelmann, even Herder could not reconcile himself to an analogy with his formulas of praise for forehead, nose, bosom, belly, and so on. In any case the *omissum* within Winckelmann's system, the absence of both (phallic) phallus and vagina on the painstaking anatomical checklist of ancient Greek sculpture's ideal naked body, did not simply leave Herder perplexed and clueless until his trip to Rome; it spurred him toward a hypothesis and a project:

> I do not know if the ancients sculpted the shame—direct inspection must supply the answer. The feminine shame should always be *only half* revealed, and with the other sex I find even more reasons for caution. I must learn more about this.[125]

Even on the basis of absent knowledge and "inspection," Herder proffers a rule of semi-invisibilization (of "only half" revealing) that lays claim to universal validity ("always"). Within the dense constellation of texts here under discussion, the only direct indication that a threat through maximum disgust-value *also* accompanies the feminine sexual organ is reserved for Herder's critique of Lessing's *Laocoön* in the *First Critical Forest* ("Erstes Kritisches Wäldchen," 1769). Lessing had not only attested to the wonderful degree of "strength" and "speed" of the Homeric gods, but also to a "physical size . . . that far exceeds all natural measure."[126] Herder can only feel comfortable with Lessing's assumptions by emphasizing major qualifications. For, he explains, in those instances "where no superhuman degree of strength is being expressed," the rule of "hypergigantic stature" leads to an "insufferable contradiction"—indeed, directly to "disgust." Herder evokes the view of a colossal goddess as proof of his thesis:

> I believe my conclusions to be probably, and wish to make them certain. Let Homer be a witness: his Jupiter, his Neptune, his Minerva may be as large as they please; a Juno of royal beauty already rather less so. She may have as much greatness in her glance that he

names her cow-eyed; as much nobility in her limb-structure as befits the woman who rests in Jupiter's arms; she may shake great Olympus when she stirs in anger on her heavenly throne. All ideas of her highness and greatness! But, in their innermost essence, these ideas should not be presented to me first and foremost through physical stature—let my eyes not rest on the latter as if it were the main sight. If they do so, I lose sight of the queen of the gods, the most splendid of the goddesses: instead I see a colossal woman. In all the heavens, where would she then, the long-limbed one, have room? How large would her heavenly bridal chamber, built by Vulcan, need to be? How great the lock and key offering access to this chamber, to which no god has access but she? How many hundredweights ambrosia will she need to clean her body? How many tons of oil to anoint it? How large will her comb, her girdle, her adornments be? Where will she have room with Jupiter in her sweet embrace upon Mount Ida? How then, when he takes her in his arms and presses her on his royal breast—how will Ida and the earth both tremble?—I wish to say no more. 'Nuff! ... My sight fades when it is meant to peer into the monstrous *[ins Ungeheure]*; the admiration that I have been feeling turns into a kind of horrid self-sensation, and terror and disgust *[Schauder und Ekel]*.[127]

As if to simultaneously refute Lessing's critical words on the impossibility to generate an illusory aesthetic presence through successive literary description, Herder's ecphrasis of the hypergigantic Juno-colossus moves past the *augmentatio* to culminate in such a violent act of *sub oculos subiectio*, subjection before the eyes, that the threatening presence brings the observing subject to the point of fainting ("my sight fades"). Only the apotropaic break in the description ("'nuff!"), in the face of a vaginal maw and an orgasmic quaking that corresponds to the "tons of oil," prevents far worse. This "enough" of disgusting satiety—indeed of the arrival at a traumatic border—represents the precise counterpole to the softly satisfied "'nuff" of the "helpless" baby whose "little hand nestles and gropes and has 'nuff" upon the merely moderately endowed, virginal bosom. Just as Herder praises Ariosto's "satirical encomium to a beautiful but large-nosed maiden" for the device of fainting "at a depiction of the nose,"[128] Herder's powers vanish before another excessive—now hypergigantic—bodily opening. Herder thus ends up running through the entire gamut of displeasure, *Unlust*, until he arrives at its antiaesthetic maximal value: "disgust."

Among the Classical authors, no one was as inventive as Herder in imagining disgust-values that are primarily grounded in the "quantity of the phenomenon." In a manner similar to Gulliver's response to the breasts of the Brobdingnag women, he is *eckel* face to face with the sex of the "colossal woman." For the system of Classicist aesthetics, the result is not simply one more antigrotesque rule of moderate enlargement and diminution. Beyond that, Herder's fiction (as well as Swift's) reveals the phantasma of corporeal depths: of devouring fecund chasms of pleasure and channels of life, against which the aesthetic must establish a distinct type of pleasure and a distinct body, lest "the borders of beauty disappear."[129] This danger amounts to an undoing of the aesthetic altogether: facing the sex's monstrosity, not only does beauty vanish, or not only are its borders reached, but "the borders of beauty" also disappear. In other words, beauty's entire confinium is defigured; the transaesthetics of "disgust" takes over the field otherwise executing inner-aesthetic distinctions of beautiful and not-(so)-beautiful, yet still aesthetically pleasing, stimuli.

WOUNDS, DISMEMBERED LIMBS, FLAYED SKIN: THE BODY AS A "DISGUSTING THING"

The field of disgust-values within and against which the ideal of the aesthetic body is established is in no way exhausted by the taediogenic openings and cavities, excrescences and "accretions," folds and uneven regions that map out the topography of the body. Ciphers of disgust consistently serve as negative determinants, not only of the body's anatomy, but of its *history*, too: wounding, dismemberment, age, and death. As in the case of the disgust topography of the body, the phenomena of its disgust chronography can—with the help of semanticizing, diminishing, and invisibilizing devices—occasionally be made serviceable for aesthetic appeal.

Blood and pus are the "disgusting" effluxes of a "disgusting" wound; the scar is a flaw on the skin's closed surface—and a reminder of the chemical processes raging beneath it. And yet, even a chronic, stinkingly infected wound that will not heal can be eminently eligible for literature. In eighteenth century aesthetics, Philoctetes, in Sophocles' depiction, repeatedly vouches for this fact. At least according to his antagonist Odysseus, disgust at that defect relegates Philoctetes to the status of a scorned leper. As Herder objected in regard to Lessing, wounds and physical pain, comprising "merely disgusting" traits,[130] could "not constitute a tragedy's main idea."[131] But Lessing actually concurred entirely. He first stresses the "noteworthy" fact that in two of Sophocles' dramas, "physical pain is not the least part of the misfortune that befalls the suffering heroes";[132] he then himself qualifies the fact by indicating that such pain would "alone be insufficient to excite a marked degree of pity,"[133] in this way shifting over to the aesthetic pleasure of the mixed sensations. When linked with other "evils," blood, pus, and disgust can even provide dramatic representation with a final touch of perfection:

Let us read Sophocles' description of the wretched cave of the unfortunate Philoctetes. There is no trace of food or of life's comforts to be seen except for a trampled litter of dry leaves, a misshapen wooden bowl, a piece of flint. This is the entire wealth of the sick and deserted man! How does the poet complete this sad and fearful piece? By adding a measure of disgust: "Ha!" Neoptolemus gives a sudden start in shock "a heap of torn rags full of blood and pus is drying here!"[134]

A "measure of disgust" completes what a "merely disgusting trait" would condemn to aesthetic failure. Tied in with other affects, that which "in its own crude form"[135] "simply" cannot "constitute a tragedy's main idea" can indeed occupy the foreground of an entire play's dramatic action. In occupying the double position of an outer transcendence and immanent differentiation of the aesthetic, disgust once more demonstrates its inescapability. The power of art nowhere displays itself more forcefully than in the victorious metamorphosis of its enemy into the stuff it is made of; within the field of the soft-blown, continuously foldless and woundless epidermal-linguistic surface, there is no more severe test of this power than the skin's complete flaying, or indeed removal: a process resulting in the exposure of the bleeding, trembling, and dying corporeal innards. Ovid describes such a horrible case in Marsyas' flaying by Apollo. With his unique sure aim, Lessing supplied this episode from the *Metamorphoses* with its place in aesthetic debate. The dragging of Hector's corpse around Troy serves here as prototype and analogon:

> Homer's Hector too, once dragged over the ground, his face disfigured by blood and dust, his hair matted—*squalentem barbam et concretos sanguine crines,* as Vergil puts it—becomes a disgusting object. But he is for that very reason all the more terrible and moving.[136]

The fate of the Phrygian river god, Marsyas, is even worse. Skilled at the flute, he had challenged Apollo to a musical contest. Apollo won, but was not satisfied with the victory alone. Angered by the very challenge, he flayed the skin off his living opponent. Apollo, embodying Winckelmann's ideal of beautiful form, himself thus produces what should be at greatest possible distance from it: "disgusting" mutilation. *Quid me mihi detrahis?* screams Marsyas: "what are you tearing me off myself?" Lessing cites the event in toto, naturally only in Latin. An English version reads:

> And as he cried the skin cracked from his body
> In one wound, blood streaming over muscles,
> Veins stripped naked, pulse beating: entrails could be
> Counted as they moved, even the heart shone red
> Within his breast.[137]

Lessing's comment on the episode is remarkably placid: "But who does not feel, at the same time, that the disgusting is in its proper place here? It makes the horrible gruesome; and the gruesome is not altogether displeasing in nature, so long as our compassion is engaged. And how much less so in imitation! I do not wish to overburden the reader with examples."[138] The theory of mixed sensations makes aesthetic pleasure so elastic a phenomenon that in the case of an appropriate functionalization (making the "horrible" "gruesome") and presence of affective interest (pity), even the maximum catastrophe the aesthetic body can experience—even the worst possible example of "the disgusting"—"is in its proper place here" and "is not altogether displeasing." Just as, its skin torn away from itself, the beautiful, unblemished body is transformed into a "disgusting object," disgust at this object can, inversely, be "torn away" from itself in aesthetic representation, to be thus transformed into a source of something "moving." In this regard, Kleist's "Penthesilea" even manages to out-trump the Marsyas paradigm: Penthesilea does not only cut her beautiful antagonist Achilles into pieces, but proceeds to eat him. Here as well, a serious feeling of "bare" or "true" disgust never emerges—this not only because of the event's indirect representation through a second-hand account. More important is the cannibal consumption's intensifying function for the representation of love and hate, and thus a metaphoric suspension remaining in place even in the literalization of the "bite" of Penthesilea's passion.[139] The theory of mixed sensations, on the one hand, and the capacity of the complex mixing-operations to incorporate even the disgusting, on the other, incessantly and uncontrollably defers the border where "crude disgust" begins and everything aesthetic ends. Nevertheless, with great insistence, the phantom of this ever-deferred border haunts speculation about art, and even art itself.

In *Rabelais and His World*, Bakhtin analyzes beating-scenes in which the victims are made into "mincemeat" while laughing and jeering.[140] Already in any event comprising a non-individual, nonfigured conglomerate of openings and excrescences, the grotesque body is only experiencing its own principle of elimination, separation, and new connection when it is literally fragmented and "sown out" again.[141] As in the great metabolic cycles and the—in part grotesque—Ovidian metamorphoses, this body has no clear-cut end and, essentially, no death: the dynamic of organic life does not stop at a defiguration of transient "bundles" of body parts. Hector's dragging around Troy and Marsyas' flaying are as remote as possible from such corporeal dismemberment "in the popular-festive comic spirit."[142] Every injury to its individual demarcation destroys the ideal body's perfection; in turn, the rupture awakens a disgust that craves immediate subduing and overlayering by representational ends capable of pleasure. As a counter-image to the ideally beautiful state of *eternal youth* and the *springtime of life*, death thus represents the repellent vanishing point or last station of the disgust-series comprised by folds, wrinkles, openings, excrescences, and dismembered limbs. If not "handled delicately" and "dressed up," "these veins on the hand, this finger-cartilage, these bones in the knee" already remind Herder of "creeping worms, and knuckles extruding excrescences," and he even explicitly defines such "detached parts" as "an early death." The "detached parts" belonging to Ovid's Marsyas are only quantitatively different from the many lesser evils threatening the soft-blown corporeal. In the field of the aesthetic body, Marsyas is 'merely' the hyperbolic allegory of epidermal defect: of folds, wrinkles, warts, and cartilage. These "creeping worms" render the yet-living beautiful body into a rotting, stinking corpse. The wounded, dissected, dismembered body, as rendered artistically before, within, and after Winckelmann, Herder, and Lessing, is not as much the antidoton of a preceding ideal of beautiful form as the reverse: that ideal is itself in debt to a strenuous labor of invisibilizing all defects, separations, and inner deformities. The "forms of beautiful youth" are erected upon an omnipresent, only painfully hidden massif of disgust. Nietzsche—himself a disgust-theorist par excellence—was likely the first to polemically highlight (with in any case unequaled sharpness) the beautiful figure's birth from disgust:

> The *aesthetically* insulting at work in the inner human without skin,—bloody masses, muck-bowels, viscera, all those sucking, pumping monstrosities—formless or ugly or grotesque, painful for the smell to boot. Hence *away with it in thought!* What still does emerge excites shame. . . . This body, *concealed* by the skin as if in *shame* . . . hence: there is disgust-exciting matter; the more ignorant humans are about their organism, the lesser can they distinguish between raw meat, rot, stink, maggots. To the extent he is not a *Gestalt*, the human being is disgusting to himself—he does everything *to not think about it*—The *pleasure* manifestly linked to this inner human being passes as *baser:* after-effect of the aesthetic judgment.[143]

BEAUTIFUL DEATH AND DISGUSTING DECAY

With logical consistency, the law of "handling delicately" and "dressing up" also applies to that disgusting corporeal state whose imminence it battles, already, in every "little fold": to death itself. Lessing's essay "How the Ancients Represented Death" (1769) confronts a problem that in fact should not exist at all within the field of the ideally beautiful body's normative youthfulness. The only feasible way for death to enter into the aesthetic realm is to be rendered as invisible as folds and the gaping mouth. Lessing undertakes to demonstrate precisely this: the Greeks, according to him, represented death in the Apollonian mask of a beautiful youth. Lessing celebrates this "delicacy" *vis-à-vis* a "disgusting idea" as an admirable "euphemism of the ancients":

Finally I wish to remind my readers of the euphemism of the ancients; of their delicacy in exchanging words that might immediately awaken disgusting, sad, or gruesome ideas for less shocking ones. If as a consequence of this euphemism, they tended to avoid directly saying "he is dead" rather preferring "he has lived, he has been, he has moved over to the majority" and so forth; if one of the reasons for this delicacy was avoiding everything ominous as much as possible; then doubtless artists too would have toned down their language to this gentler pitch. They too would not have presented Death through an image unavoidably calling up all the disgusting notions of decay and corruption—the image of an ugly skeleton; for in their compositions as well, the unexpected sight of such an image could have been as ominous as the unexpected hearing of the actual word. They, as well, would have preferred an image leading us by an agreeable detour to what it is designed to indicate; and what image could be more useful here than that whose symbolic expression language itself likes to employ as the designation of death, the image of Sleep?[144]

This "image of Sleep" was of a winged youth with the torch turned upside down. As the "twin brother" and "perfectly similar duplication"[145] of the Sleep depicted under this image, Death was in fact hardly distinguishable from winged Amor: "Such an Amor is just on this account not yet an Amor," cautions Lessing,[146] thus setting at least certain limits on the euphemism. If, however, death is represented through a charming winged youth, what is the purpose of those actually quite terrifying skeletal and other creatures very much evoking "all the disgusting notions of decay and corruption?" Against Lessing, Klotz had pointed to the horrible Ker, imagining her as a skeleton. Lessing does not agree: "Fortunately Pausanias has preserved for us the image through which this Ker was depicted. It appeared as a woman with grisly teeth and crooked nails."[147] The affinity of this repellent figure with the disgust-paradigms of Achlys and the old lady is evident. Precisely for this reason, Lessing concludes against Klotz, what would seem likely cannot be the case: "Ker is not death." The introduction of a subtle distinction saves both Death and Lessing's argument from the disgusting hag: Ker is well read as *fatum mortale, mortiferum*, as the grisly-gruesome *agentess* of mortal fate; yet in this very capacity she falls short of being the personification of what she brings, namely death itself.[148] In an even more elegant fashion, Death is preserved from any confusion with skeletons:

Thus: since it is proved that the ancients did not represent Death as a skeleton; and since skeletons nonetheless appear on ancient monuments: what, then, are these skeletons? Stated bluntly . . . [they] are larvae: not because *larva* itself means nothing but a skeleton, but because *larvae* signified one sort of departed soul. . . . Departed souls of good . . . men . . . became peaceful, blissful household-gods for their progeny and were named *lares*. Those of the wicked, however, in punishment of their crimes, wandered restless and fleeting about the earth, an empty terror to the pious, a blighting terror to the malign, and were named *larvae*.[149]

A parallel is here manifest with Winckelmann's conclusion that Venus's visible nipples meant the statue, contrary to common belief, was in fact no Venus. With inimitable acuity, Lessing now demonstrates that everything appearing to be a noneuphemistic representation of death is, in truth, not at all a representation of death. It would be difficult for "the law of beauty" to discover a better exemplification of its complexity—its necessarily failed success and its successful failure. The excluded disgust is in no way simply disposed of; rather, it replicates itself with every new distinction, becomes increasingly differentiated, and thus completely surrounds the little island—the labile terrain—of the beautiful youthful body.

In his detailed critique of Lessing's text, Herder declined to give up the notion that "the Greeks' Thanatos (Death) was a fearsome being."[150] Quite to the contrary, he concluded that the beautiful youthful Genius had only been installed in the place of Death so as *not* to "represent" it, but to "banish" it—to successfully "evade" any "reminder" of it.[151] Precisely this seemingly moderate and critical position invests aesthetic idealization with an even more radical power, interpreting it in a manner that anticipates Nietzsche. For Lessing, the winged youth "really," albeit euphemistically, represents Death—this regardless of the fact that he is barely distinguishable from an Amor, and not at all distinguishable from his twin brother Sleep. For Herder in contrast, he in no way represents the "hated" Death, whom the Greeks termed "rather *phtonos* [Envy] than *thanatos*."[152] How, then, are we to ever even notice that the winged Genius assumes the "place" of Death, if he "is not to represent him," but rather to "avert" that we "think of him" at all? A substitute that does not represent what it replaces and even blocks any thought of the latter seems scarcely still identifiable as a substitute: all the more so when it is hardly distinguishable from the images of Sleep and Amor. And further: if a relation between representing and represented figures were indeed perceptible, the desired "averting" of any thought of the represented figure—the evasion of any "reminder" of his hovering presence—would have failed. Yet despite this radical nonrelationality—this relation consisting of an avoidance of relation—the beautiful winged creature is meant to engender the radical effect, not so much of a "euphemism" that would still evoke its "actual" relatum, as of a complete ban placed on "disgusting notions of [death's] decay and corruption."

In this regard, the performativity of aesthetic idealization consists once again in invisibilization—but now to the point of complete forgetting. Herder's particular device for avoiding disgust in death's representation gives rise to the suspicion that *all* Apollonian images are masking-images: images masking frightful, disgusting forces, processes, and phenomena that they not only assuage, but whose locus they *usurp*, in order to "avert." Read in this manner, beautiful idealization is in line with apotropaic rites. Nietzsche's reading of the Hellenic-Apollonian follows a similar pattern. It, too, explores all form-like beauty from the negative perspective of what it overcomes and transfigures; yet it replaces the position of frightful death with the Dionysian exuberance of life itself. As a reaction to the trans-aesthetic, disgust has its place in Nietzsche's model as well. But disgust now attains a new and positive function: as the signature and authenticity-marker of metaphysical insight—the glance into the abyss and groundlessness of "being."[153]

The Ugly Old Lady

Almost all of the defects addressed and rejected by the discourse on disgust are repeatedly compressed into one single phantasm: that of the ugly old woman. This phantasm conventionally brings together folds and wrinkles, warts, larger than usual openings of the body (i.e., mouth and anus), foul, black teeth, sunk-in hollows instead of beautiful swellings, drooping breasts, stinking breath, revolting habits, and a proximity to both death and putrefaction. Lessing's death-bringing Ker, with her grisly teeth and crooked fingernails, is as much at home here as the dark, much-cited Achlys with her running nose and her gruesome nails, or the ridiculous-disgusting beloved with her "squashed gristle nose" and "flabby breasts hanging down to the navel."[154] Herder presents us with an entire list of ugly crones, whom he would prefer to exempt from any physical description aiming at beauty: "Century-old Cybeles, and old mammies of the gods *[Altmütterchen der Götter]*, and matronal Junos and vestals."[155] In the *Plastik* of 1778, the differentiation of the—in the end honorable—gamut of ugly old types is widened to comprise a male specimen. Indeed, this specimen inaugurates the series: "philosophers, Cybeles, hundred-year matrons."[156] Since "a philosopher is always only portrayed through *head* or *bust*," he does not need to "stand before our eyes" as a beautiful, complete, and undressed statue "like a youth or warrior does." The philosopher as ugly old woman: many of Winckelmann's and Herder's reflections over the degenerative fate of the beautiful Greek body culminate in that image. The male Classicists thus themselves take on the position of what they aesthetically abjure. In a footnote to his early aesthetics, Kant offers a memorable anecdote: the account of a man who, in an inverted agon of beauty, lays fully explicit claim to the position of the ugliest old woman. In Kant's posthumous writings, we find numerous entries on matters such as "why an old lady . . . is disgusting,"[157] or "a kiss is bliss. Old lady evokes disgust *[Kuß ist Genuß. Alt Weib eckelt]*,"[158] or "the disgusting face of old ladies. Heidegger."[159] In the *Anthropology from a Pragmatic Point of View*, we find the following resolution to the enigmatic linkage of "Heidegger" with a disgusting old hag:

> Heidegger, a German musician in London, was fantastically deformed, but a clever and intelligent person with whom aristocrats liked to associate for the sake of conversation. Once it occurred to him at a drinking party to claim to a lord that he had the ugliest face in London. The lord reflected and then made a wager that he would present a face still more ugly. He then sent for a drunken woman, at whose appearance the whole party burst into laughter and shouted: "Heidegger, you have lost the wager!" "Not so fast," he replied, "let the woman wear my wig and let me wear her headdress; then we shall see." As this took place, everybody fell to laughing, to the point of suffocation, because the woman looked like a very presentable gentleman, and the fellow looked like a witch. This shows that in order to call anyone beautiful, or at least bearably pretty, one must not judge absolutely, but always only relatively. It also shows that no one ought to call a fellow ugly just because he is not handsome.[160]

Although it seems simply to be a humorous detour that makes the disgusting enjoyable in Lessing's sense, this anecdote teaches two things with dialectical rigor: first, a woman strikes us as uglier than an ugly man even when she is actually less ugly; second, a man can win the prize for ugliness only when he switches sexual signifiers and "look[s] like a witch." The adjectives "beautiful" and "ugly" are therefore in a very precise sense to be applied only relatively: relative, namely, to sexual difference. To be legitimate, "ugly" always and continuously requires this quasi-transcendental reference to the disgusting "old woman" regardless of whether we are dealing with a "real" woman or a disguised man: this, we may say, is the *lex Heidegger*. Kant's footnote both conceals and discloses an archeological rule of eighteenth century protoaesthetics. In disgust, we lose that freedom toward the object (Hegel) emphatically stamping our experience of the beautiful: the respectful, never distanceless involvement with something that, in an extraordinary manner, stands for itself and resides in itself. Disgust's intention toward the object only knows the "for us" of a strange "thing" with which no dialog takes place, but which simply deserves, because and to the extent it comes close to us, an immediate act of distancing. "What strikes us as disgusting is routinely something that we neither destroy or flee, but rather clear away."[161] Such a purely disagreeable "thing" does not so much threaten as disturb our sense of ease. It releases less a feeling of angst in face of a stronger person than a "feeling of superiority"[162] in face of one who is inferior, or dirty. For we can dispatch this "thing" from our proximity through a short but violent movement.

With negative obsession, the founding fathers of the new "discipline" of aesthetics incorporated aged femininity into their system as its maximum disgusting evil. This obsession by no means begins with Lessing's citation of Longinus's citation from Hesiod's *Aspis*. Barthold Heinrich Brockes merits recognition for offering a paradigm of decrepit old femininity in a new year's poem of 1722. In respect to both its drastic nature and impact on the emergence of the discourse on disgust, it far exceeds the figure of Achlys with her running nose.[163] Brockes had certainly not anticipated his long, didactic and edifying poem eventually gaining considerable critical prominence entirely through its depiction of a "poor old woman": a depiction that advanced to become the cardinal example of the disgusting to be avoided in aesthetic representation. It was a strictly functional depiction at that, occupying no more than one out of thirty pages. The critical career of Brockes' aged woman seems all the more surprising as the figure of the ugly old woman had been firmly established as a topos in various literary genres long before Brockes' depiction. The bitingly satirical castigation of the physical and moral evils of old women, in fact comprises an elaborate tradition in Greek and Latin literature. Ingeniously, Horace compressed nearly all its motifs into the eighth and twelfth of his *Epodes:*

VIII

You, with the stink of a long lifetime, dare to ask
   who's draining my manhood away,
when your teeth are blackened and old senility
   plows its wrinkles in your forehead,
and your filthy arsehole gapes between your shrunken
   buttocks, just like a leaky cow's!
It maddens me to see your breast and withered tits
   that look like a mare's udder,
and your flabby belly and your shriveled-up thighs
   and your swollen calves below them.
Enjoy your riches, as the ancestral statues
   lead the way for your funeral,
and may no matron be seen parading after
   freighted with rounder pearls than yours.
And what of your Stoic pamphlets that are apt to
   lie under little silk pillows?
Do the illiterate really stand less stiffly
   or their rods droop any sooner?
But if you should want to get a rise out of me,
   you'd better work at it by mouth.[164]

The twelfth epode completes the catalog of repellent features with "evil stink" *(malus odor)* and expressly introduces "disgust" *(fastidium)*. Alongside Old Attic comedy,[165] which in any case only evoked the disgusting for the sake of ridiculousness, it was above all Archilochos and Martial who had offered numerous variations on the *vetula*-topos beforehand.[166] Stretching from furrows and folds *(rugae)* to "yellowed teeth, the *femur exile*, the *aridae nates*, the *mollis venter*, the *mammae putres*, and grey hair," all the way to "evil bodily odor,"[167] the persistent disgust-related features of the old woman's bodily topography do not stand for themselves alone. Rather, they owe their cutting edge to the sexual insinuations emanating from the *vetula*. These insinuations comprise the following set of motifs: an unquenchable sexual desire, on the part of the old woman, for countless copulations; complaints over male slackness *(languidum membrum)* and impotence; references to both the hiring of male prostitutes (i.e., the inversion of accepted male sexual behavior, regularly accompanied by the role-exchange of female financial superiority) and the compensation for failing charms through a readiness for fellatio.[168] The epode of Horace providing this canonical articulation of male sexual disgust and disdain for the feminine is among the least-cited, least translated of his poems. Something similar holds for the more "hard-core" of Martial's dirty epigrams: in the *Loeb Classical Library* edition, they suffer the curious treatment of Italian translation.[169] Goethe here distinguishes himself—as he generally does in his politics of sexual disgust—from the large majority of his contemporaries. He expressly admonishes disgust at Martial:

> From too disgusted a taste, Nauger burnt Martial
> Do you toss silver away because it's not gold? Pedant![170]

Karl Rosenkranz declared the "wicked old woman," that Aristophanes, Horace, and other authors of antiquity depicted as "still tormented by impure desires despite her age" to be the canon of the witch: "This, one may well say infamous, personality forms the foundation for witches."[171] The Middle Ages and Renaissance were particularly inventive in imagining numerous variants of this traditional role of the repulsive woman.[172] Compared with the *vetulae* of the Augustinian-ideal poet Horace, Brockes' "old woman" may not be more beautiful but is certainly less sexually repulsive. And yet it was Brockes's "poor old woman" who emerged as the first news-peg in the discourse on disgust— as an exorbitant scandalon and object of strict aesthetic exclusion.[173] Brockes' poem has the form of a rhetorical disputation between *A* and *B*. *B* champions insight into the greatness and perfection of creation, which even human "nullity" can only serve to "glorify." In contrast, *A* first maintains the ubiquity of sad evanescence, decay, disgust; but he ends up converted, "ashamed of his crude error."[174] At the apogee of his antiperfection thesis—representing, within the poem's rhetorical texture, not what is meant to be rejected but only what is to be refuted—*A* turns to the "dirty" genesis of the human body and its dissolution into a "foul Maggot-sack." But subtle distinctions remain preserved in this panorama of deficiencies: the extreme value of disgust is ascribed to death, but not to our "dirty birth" from muck and slime:

> The Filthiness of Birth, the Grave's Decay and Dung,
> Thus a Lifetime full of Needs ends like it's begun.
> Tell me: what is a Man? In Seed he is but Slime,
> In Mother's Womb a Clot, a Curd in milky Whey
> An unperfected Flesh.[175]

> Once the Body, Noble Body, finally grows white
> And is shoved in a Coffin that's rather too tight,
> Putrefaction and Worms soon devour its fine Limbs:
> So gruesome an Image—Abomination grim!—
> That no Living Person ever might contemplate
> This foul Maggot-sack without Disgust, without Hate.
> No Mould looks so vile, no Slime or Phlegm so nasty,
> No Pus abominate, no Waste so disgusting,
> No Cesspool so ugly.[176]

The old age preceding death is at least as repulsive as death itself:

> Yet, ere he [=Man] finally dies, he ages more and more,
> The Spirit's Powers shrink, the Flesh's Shape distorts.
> Admit: how ugly does an aged Body grow?
> Observe just once, my Friend, a poor old Woman,
> Her scabby yellowed Skin a Field of Pocks and Folds,
> Her squinting Cock-eyes red and oozing from her Head,
> Her wobbling balded Skull, her toothless gaping Mouth
> That's filled with thickish Phlegm, the Lips all swoll'n and blue,
> Breasts that sag like Mats o'er skinny, brittle Ribs,
> Her Neck a crooked Bend, her Spine a jagged Curve,
> Her Jaw a fleshless Jut, her withered hollow Cheek—
> Shall this living Carcass reflect eternal Grace,
> Be deserving of Bliss, and worthy of Heaven?
> Say not this affects Body only. This old Soul's
> Strength, Knit and Quality are also not the Best:
> Forgetfulness and Strife, which always contradicts;
> Cunning, Sloth, and Stubbornness; Envy, Discontent;
> Fearful, stupid Grouchiness; Hatred, ever vexed;
> Forever telling Tales of long-forgotten Days,

While ceaselessly belittling present Woes and Ways;
Worry, Doubt, nagging Grief, and a relentless Urge,
A burning, thirsty Greed: these an aged Soul's Fruits.
Of Madness, Insanity, Disease, Anguish, Pain
That corrode and mutilate Skin, Sinew, and Vein—
I'd rather just not say.[177]

The evils of "old souls" are here entirely different from those Horace speaks of. This old woman is "poor" and in no way a sexual being; instead of living out her randyness through money, role-inversion, and fellatio, she only endures a gerontological diagnosis of progressive debility. The depicted social evils are certainly highly unpleasant, but represent no assault on the potency and status of the man. Bakhtin informs us of "curious figurines of *pregnant old women*, whose ugliness of old age and features marking pregnancy are grotesquely emphasized. Moreover," he notes, "these old hags are laughing."[178] Brockes' hag is even more removed from this laughing fertility of aging and transitoriness than from the unfulfilled sexual hunger of Horace's *vetula*. Still, the outer physical features are pretty much the same: the field of pocks and folds; the "hollows"; the "skinny brittleness" and "mat-like sagging" of contour; the "jagged" landscape of bones and cartilage; the "phlegm" and "oozing." What binds precisely this bitter gerontology so closely to the normative system of aesthetic idealization? And generally, wherein lies the *special* provocation of Brockes' description?

From the vantage of the beautiful skin's surface, Brockes does not only offer—like Horace, Winckelmann, and Herder—the uneven areas, the openings, the hollows. Rather, he furnishes the same phenomena with a resonant depth leading into the body's interior. The "living carcass" not only suffers from outer deficits, but in fact is entirely carrion: a "foul Maggot-sack." This baroque image offers a look "beneath the skin": onto that "anatomy" Diderot would later warn artists to shun. The skin thus figures as a mere cover, as a "sack" of medically relevant disgusting material, instead of as a hollowed out, autonomous shell speaking to itself and offering expression to exclusively spiritual signifieds. A further particularity produces highly ambivalent effects: the unusually detailed nature of the physiological *descriptio*, the elaborate unfolding of an inner dynamic through the descriptive metaphors. Within the framework of "descriptive poetry," this is considered one of the qualities enabling a vivid intuitive power of "poetic imitation," hence furnishing pleasure. In this fashion Johann Jacob Breitinger felt himself superbly entertained by the oozing maggots' sack. In his *Critische Dichtkunst* ("Critical Ars Poetica") of 1740, he cites Brockes' description as evidence of "vivid clarity of depiction" (of the rhetorical quality of *energeia* or *evidentia*). To him, "enjoying" the vivid clarity was self-evident: "And who is not pleased by the following portrait of an old woman in the new year's poem of 1722 in Brockes' Earthly Pleasure?"[179]

Brockes thus supplied a solid pleasure from *evidentia* for a poetics of the old style, grounded in rhetoric. The orientation changes strikingly in the field of the new aesthetics: only five years later (in 1745), J. E. Schlegel recommends, instead of the pleasure taken in similitude, a partial "prevention" and a "transformation" into the "dissimilar." Along with death,[180] the old woman again heads the list of examples: "one should not paint the disgusting quality of an old woman if one wishes to depict her ugliness."[181] In 1751, brother J. A. Schlegel concurs. Other than Breitinger, who still offers a bibliographic citation for Brockes' poem, the latter Schlegel simply refers to it as a generally known item: "the notorious Brockian portrait of an old woman." Only a "critique," he indicates, which "sets experience aside and simply draws conclusions from premises" can "discover" rhetorical "beauties" in the poem. To counter this type of "critique," Schlegel mobilizes "taste," the transcendental organ of the new aesthetics: taste, we are instructed, refuses being "prescribed"—even through the "rules" Breitinger draws on—"a pleasure conflicting with experience."[182]

In Christian Ludwig Hagedorns *Betrachtungen über die Mahlerey* ("Observations concerning Painting") of 1762, under the heading "Avoidance of the Ugly, and What Insults the Finer Feelings," we find alongside the Brockesian hag, and as if it were self-explanatory, Hesiod's not exactly well-known Achlys: an "object of disgust for the eyes."[183] A little later (1766), Lessing's *Laocoön* tacitly stages a contest of negative ideals between the two figures: which occupies top position in embodying *Ekel?* Brockes' old woman loses for noteworthy reasons. The contest is carried out on subcutaneous terrain, its only lasting trace being the sudden disappearance of Brockes' woman from the discourse on disgust. The paradigmatic ugly old woman does not cease to be "a disgusting thing";[184] but on purely poetic grounds, her portrayal is denied the power of illusory representation. As Lessing explains it, the more exact—hence more successive—the description, the more it fails to generate any deceptive simultaneous presence of what is being described: "Is not the effect of ugliness destroyed by the successive enumeration of its elements just as much as the effect of beauty is destroyed through a similar enumeration?"[185] Lessing does not hesitate in drawing the paradoxical conclusion of this doctrine: the more detailed and elaborate the portrait of ugliness, the "less offensive" its poetic "appearance"; indeed it "ceases, as it were, to be ugly in its effect." It is precisely on this account that the detailed description of ugly and disgusting traits "becomes usable" for the poet: namely, as (self-)invisibilization of these traits. In this manner, alongside the numerous devices for avoiding disgust through smoothing and softening, an opposite device comes to the fore, one operating precisely through the accumulation and painfully precise "enumeration" of the potentially disgusting features. With regard to this new aesthetic device, Brockes unintentionally emerges as a master of "dialectic" *Ekel*-transcendence. Inversely, within the field of the beautiful, a single attribute or adjective, a tiny "admixture of disgust,"[186] can be more effectively disgusting, hence more dangerous, than an entire catalog of *vetula* features. Hence Lessing's recourse to the Achlys of Hesiod and Longinus: for the most part, her features are "horrifying"; only *one* of them, the running nose, is disgusting—and precisely because this feature is no more than a single and tiny "admixture" of the disgusting, it is said to be all the more offensive to aesthetic taste.

In such a way, the distinction representation versus exclusion (invisibilization) of the disgusting defines even the most delicate troping and nuances at play within the field of aesthetic devices—this no matter if the mandatory exclusion takes the form of softening, smoothing, avoidance or paradoxical accumulation. It is remarkable that one feature remains constant—thus gaining a certain "archaeological" depth—throughout the various controversial models of illusion: the paradigmatic linkage of the scandalous disgust-pole to the body of an old woman. Kant's anecdote about the "fellow" Heidegger who has to change himself into a "witch" in order to look truly "ugly" points to a subsurface dimension of the aestheticians' old *Weib*. Along with the traumatic phantasma of the *magna mater*, whose cult was tied to the ugly-obscene Baubo,[187] the powerful and sexually potent witch is placed under a double spell: she is both disfigured into harmlessness as a withered, toothless, penniless, asexual old woman (an *"Altmütterchen"*); and dismissed—in a gesture bordering on derision *vis-à-vis* this diminished form of threatening femininity— as unaesthetic. To this extent, aesthetics is a continuation of the witches' trials by other means—at the very time when, in enlightened Europe, regular witch trials were just banned and about to become things of the past. (Henceforth even the witch's beautiful counterpole, classical Aphrodite, will itself offer only a distant memory, depotentiated and palliated, of the earlier predicates attached to this great goddess.)

Repression or Differentiation?

Bakhtin has furnished the grotesque body with a sentimental reading. He considers only this (anti-)body to be, in an emphatic sense, a body: the substrate of "life" and "history," of a fertility and developmental capacity persisting through all death and all dismemberment. Almost without any qualifications, Rabelais' "materialism"[188] is read 'realistically' as the index of an extra-aesthetic corporeal culture; at the same time, it is celebrated 'idealistically' as reflecting an authentically vital principle.[189] Inversely, Bakhtin's approach suggests a critique of the ideological implications of the body presented by the Classical canon and the new aesthetics: a critique postulating a degenerative-repressive move within that canon's presumed institution of the body as "official" hygienic facade, not stinking, not eating, not excreting, not copulating, not aging, but only existing as an expressive sign. In fact, the many exclusions constituting the ideally beautiful body make it quite difficult to speak of Winckelmann's, Herder's, and Lessing's corporeal ideal in terms of the body's "revalorization."[190] Rather, this body subsumed to aesthetic illusion, with its normative youthfulness, its smooth skin free of blemish, its slender-athletic elasticity and nonobscene nudity, anticipates a now-predominant regulation of the body, its sleekest forms emerging from the world of advertising, cosmetics, and—as analagon of the antique gymnasia so enthusiastically evoked by Winckelmann—the fitness center with its various machines.

From the antique *agon* of beauty to the modern "Miss" contests, the public fora chosen to celebrate and confirm the athletic body have maintained an—at least—external continuity. In contrast, the pertinent idols and icons have undergone an interesting history of substitution. In place of the gods and mythic heroes of antiquity, stage-actors and actresses emerge, already, within the eighteenth century's popular discourse; then come film stars, and finally supermodels. Although these substitutions partly point to changes in the body-related code itself, their negative values and anti-ideals have remained remarkably stable: folds, wrinkles, warts, fatty areas, deficient swellings or muscular elasticity, discolored or incomplete rows of teeth—in short everything together comprising the image of the ugly old woman. With the comprehensive cipher of disgust, the theoreticals aesthetics emerging as a separate discipline around 1750 has provided a particularly harsh articulation of the negative grounding (or: the avoidance values) of the beautiful, one taking on the semblance of a natural corporeal defense-reaction. This articulation evades not only the intellect, but any thought of tolerance and pity.[191] It knows only a vomitive judgment: *away* with it—from the belly, proximity, one's eyesight. Age thus emerges as a "problem" demanding eradication, or at least invisibilization through relegation to a separate sphere: responses only outdone through the soothing exclusion of the offenses death could impose on our delicate aesthetic taste.

All this suggests viewing the rules of disgust-avoidance constitutive for the ideally beautiful body as one of the many ideological reflexes pointing to a comprehensive suppression of the body in its basic being and functioning. Such a view would be in line with Nietzsche's and Freud's interpretation of disgust as something rooted in sexual repression; it would likewise conform to Norbert Elias' description of the "civilization" imposed on all the bodily functions in modern times,[192] as well as to Bakhtin's critique of the idealism of the bodily facade. Nevertheless, applying this hypothesis of suppression to Winckelmann's, Herder's, and Lessing's rules for the beautiful body is only conditionally justified.[193] That is, the hypothesis involves an equivocation running counter to everything that in fact motivates the emergence of aesthetics as an autonomous discipline. It *de*-differentiates what the Classicists carefully differentiate. To institute aesthetics as an independent, irreducible form of perception means creating and reflecting upon a realm that is *different* from all other realms. This implies a singling out of phenomena and reflective rules that are both possible and constitutive in this particular realm alone. Drawing boundaries was the cardinal operation not only in the Kantian critiques, but already of the hotly-disputed demarcation and ranking of the individual arts. A comparative theory of the *arts* accompanied the emergence of philosophical aesthetics, until *art* was invented as a collective singular and homogeneous referent. The Classical aesthetic discourse on the disgusting is one aspect of such a differential thrust, hence the effect of a process producing ever-more functionally refined differential systems. By its very nature, this process had to preserve the bodies destined for purely aesthetic pleasure from physical pleasures like eating and lovemaking, as well as from practical activities such as procreation and excretion—and also from the theoretical realm of reason. Rather than simply confirming, once again, the suppression of the body and its functions, disgust can thus also be read as the operative source of a distinction generating a new, irreducible phenomenal realm. Its novelty and singularity can perhaps best be grasped in the canonization of, precisely, a purely aesthetic hybrid body: a bodiless body without inner organs that that does not even lay a claim to being real. Many imperatives of the beautiful and of disgust-avoidance did not even apply to all the arts, let alone to everyday reality, but only to individual arts, mostly to sculpture.

To establish this point, two examples may be sufficient. The first is the prescription of a general "peeling" of all bodily hair and the reduction of the eyebrows to a fine stroke: again, a most concrete rule linking present-day models—and not only them—to antique statues. "Does hair also belong to the body's inessential features?" asks Herder, thus drawing an analogy with the "creeping worms" of cartilage, veins, and wrinkles. His answer is clear-cut: "the little dispersed hairs in any case; they would deform any statue."[194] As an "adornment for the body," head hair alone belongs in the "realm of art." But here as well, "the sculptor must come up with more than one trick" in order to prevent the individual hairs from emerging as "[all] too noticeable lumpy stone bodies." With single stony body hairs, the "tricks" used to make larger hair masses "more formable" prove useless. Hence the rule of general avoidance of these "disagreeable" and "extra-essential accretions." A compromise full of tricks accounts for the singular exception of the eyebrows. Winckelmann explains that "the beauty of the eye itself is enhanced, and, as it were, crowned, by the eyebrows; and the eyebrows are beautiful in proportion to the line that appears to be formed by thin little hairs."[195] Herder comments:

> It is known that the best statues do not have distinct little hairs, but simply a fine, sharp elevated thread extended over the eye. Winckelmann considers this as comprising the graces' eyebrows and the most beautiful nature; I do not doubt that it is the most beautiful

nature in art—but is it also such in living, Greek nature? At least, this must not be concluded from the statues alone . . . separate body hairs lay outside the essence and goals of art: they were not able to suggest anything of what a work of art was supposed to suggest, and even if they could have suggested a great deal, the artist still could not use them.[196]

The passage is clear enough: the rule of "peeling" and plucked eyebrows only applies for the material aesthetic of stone, and for "nature in art." To this extent, the rule's export to the field of daily corporeal cosmetics would constitute a transgression of borders—an unanticipated application. No canon, however, is immune to *misreading* and to illegitimate usage: the rule survived its artistic obsolescence thanks to a misplaced literalism—the transfer to a context against which it had been precisely invented as a differential "trick."

At least in part, the same holds for the entire aesthetic system's negative ideal: for the merciless exclusion of the "old woman." Occasionally, some of the authors expressly emphasize that they are, in fact, not disgusted by real old women—or at least not in first line. J. E. Schlegel, for instance, "confesses" to "much preferring the sight of a truly ugly old woman to reading a detailed description of the same"[197]—while Kant seems to have made no such distinction. Elsewhere as well, the debate is not about "real" old women but strictly about their "depiction" to a very special end: "beauty" and the achievement of aesthetic pleasure. Nevertheless, the aesthetic classification of the old woman as a "disgusting thing" remains an open wound within the system: the principle of aesthetic exclusion here both relies on a politics of age and sex and inversely paves the way for it. J. E. Schlegel's reference, for instance, to "the most precise depiction of an impure old woman, showing me more of her repellent than her ridiculous side"[198] draws entirely on a range of negative attributes; it allows nothing more than a selection between "impure," "repellent," and "ridiculous." And yet, classical aesthetics has itself issued the very same criticism. "He is completely correct," pronounced Hagedorn in regard to Schlegel, then commenting as follows:

> And yet, for the conceptualization of old age, the idea of impurity (which he links to it) is extraordinary, in that it would also be an insult to our taste in the representation of the most beautiful youth. One has thus rightly distinguished between a beautiful advanced age in both sexes and its pitiable form or ugly appearance, also in respect to the plastic arts. Where old age endows the skin with folds, but does not succeed in eradicating the features belonging to the morally developed soul, a beautiful old man by *van der Helst* and by *Denner*, and a worthy matron's face by these diligent masters, will in any event be more pleasing than a carefully sought out example of ugliness. In

his later years, a considerable time after writing his well-known poem, Herr Brockes judged and valued the half-length portrait of an older woman according to this principle—the portrait was painted beneath his eyes for my collection of *Denner*.

> Orderliness and purity prevail about her, and the appearance of age
> Thus becomes more mild and soft.
>
> Zachariä, "Four Seasons in a Woman's Age."[199]

With this, the claims of humanistic "correctness" appear to have been honored. Alongside the ugly old woman, we are offered the possibility of "a beautiful advanced age in both sexes." Yet even this strained rescue effort reveals the devaluation inflicted on old age through a purely aesthetic perspective. The strictest "order and purity" must "prevail" in order that the view of "folds" and the "pitiable form" become "more mild and soft"—instead of being an "insult." Hygienic, everyday "purity" is supposed to generate an analogon to the aesthetic rules regarding cartilage and folds: an invisibilization of the "ugly appearance." In face of actual old people, as well, the purely aesthetic perspective thus carries the day; in doing so, it renders itself impure by blending with another kind of purity. By virtue of the paradigmatic verdict concerning the "impure woman," this mixing or contamination is inscribed into the purity of the aesthetic at its very origin. It thereby *in itself* prefigures the "impure," extra-aesthetic career of the purely aesthetic ideals that had been conceived for the beautiful stony body of the plastic arts.

The cleansing of all direct sexual functions from this body has its own "archaeological" dimension. True, according to the theorem of differentiation, an aesthetic judgment can only be distinguished from "mere" sensual pleasure to the extent it does not shift into sexual or oral consumption. Here the self-grounding and self-maintenance of a particular aesthetic pleasure *necessarily* mark a border with the other pleasures: a border that cannot be instrumentalized unconditionally as evidence of sexual repression. And yet, more is at play than the 'autonomous' differentiation of mutually irreducible differences. Rather, the purely aesthetic body produces a double resonance in regard to the field and history of the sexual. On the one hand, aesthetics tends to use the establishment of its specialized code for (re-)hierarchizations in other fields. Accordingly, whatever does not produce a purely aesthetic pleasure is implicitly disqualified as *impure;* from Baumgarten to Kant, none of the founding figures of aesthetics fails to depreciate the "mere" pleasures of the "lower senses" when compared to the elevated level of purely aesthetic pleasure.

On the other hand, the purely aesthetic, ideally beautiful sculptural body itself generated a kind of sexual pleasure: the fetishistic worship of an idol removed from "regular" sexual contact. From Herder's scarcely-virtual handling of the Classical Greek statue, to Sacher-Masoch's abandonment to the statue become flesh, up through a wide range of early twentieth-century literature, we can trace out an interesting tradition of statue-erotics. Within this tradition, the devotee never assumes the double paternal role of Ovid's Pygmalion: creator of the statue and father of real children with her. Both sides of a sexual politics *internal* to the purely aesthetic body can still be studied through our own statues, the supermodels. Occasionally, a nude photo-take is accepted, albeit only as a sort of limit-value and exception; in contrast, a depiction in sexual action is quite strictly tabooed, being reserved for the baser profession of porno star. In both cases, as the most discrete form of a shift from purely aesthetic pleasure to sexual pleasure, the fetishistic gaze is paid steady and ample homage.

The ideally beautiful Classical body thus allows for various perspectives—cultural-historical, psychosexual, and even commercial—on its extra-artistic afterlife. The present study is concerned, above all, with identifying the rules producing this beautiful body. Beauty here figures as a problem-solving strategy—the precise reason for the ideal proving so rich in implications. The name, the multiple cipher, for the problem to be overcome and made "invisible" is—"disgust." Just as Nietzsche's Apollonian principle of form responds to the Dionysian frenzy of dance, rapture, and physical ecstasy, the Classicists' Greek-beautiful is erected against a background of deformity and disgust—this negative foundation taking on many individual variants and investments. The rules of the "beautiful" are the traces of disgust.

Disgust, Purity, and Impurity in the Aesthetic

In her book *Purity and Danger*, Mary Douglas has offered a general theory, set on a broad ethnological basis, of the application and functioning of the "pure"-"impure" distinction. According to this theory, we only have recourse to the idea of impurity, and to the sanctions connected with it, when a given social system cannot adequately process problems and ambivalences through the available social, juridical, and moral codes. For instance, "when a situation is morally ill-defined, a pollution belief can provide a rule for determining *post hoc* whether infraction has taken place or not."[200] Inversely, "when the sense of outrage is adequately equipped with practical sanctions in the social order, pollution is not likely to arise."[201] The many notions of pollution through sexual contact with women or through menstrual blood emerge as a similar processing of problems of social order. According to Douglas, such notions generally are not present in the framework of strictly hierarchical sexual relations. In an apparent paradox, notions of pollution through contact with women do not indicate, viewed sociologically, a discrimination against women, but precisely the inverse: a relative nondiscrimination which, however, men can only process as a threat to their power:

When male dominance is accepted as a central principle of social organization and applied without inhibition and with full rights of physical coercion, beliefs in sex pollution are not likely to be highly developed. On the other hand, when the principle of male dominance is applied to the ordering of social life but is contradicted by other principles such as that of female independence, or the inherent right of women as the weaker sex to be more protected from violence than men, then sex pollution is likely to flourish.[202]

According to this line of argument, ideas of feminine or other impurity, and the correlative rules for "separating, purifying, demarcating, and punishing," are no mythic archetypes or superstitious biologisms, but—again and again—'cybernetic' reactions to sometimes latent, sometimes open dangers threatening given social orders. The articulation of these ideas is regularly modeled on the human body, whose "orifices seem to represent points of entry or exit to social units." These dynamic zones are also the ones most threatened by disorder.[203] Inversely, "the idea of holiness was given an external, physical expression in the wholeness of the body seen as a perfect container."[204] Perfect self-containment, "physical . . . wholeness of the body," and a renunciation of sexual intercourse are also the Mosaic rules for the bodies of priests; they render the priest a spotless and thus "perfect man," and the representative of an ideally stable order. As a threat to this impermeable, "perfect container," which can also be represented by the Virgin Mary,[205] "bodily disintegration" represents "the final problem to which the perspective of pollution leads."[206]

It is tempting to view the aesthetics of the ideally beautiful body in light of such an order, which uses the distinction between purity and impurity to articulate and regulate the ambivalences and dangers along its edge. As a "discipline" that had just established its own autonomy, and thus needed to assert and ensure its boundaries, eighteenth-century aesthetics was doubtless in a situation of unstable order, laced with ambivalences and murky hierarchies. Many efforts were dedicated to newly defining and evaluating the relation of aesthetic experience to both theoretical and practical philosophy, as well as to sense perceptions. On the one hand, aesthetics was meant to be simply itself, autonomous and self-referential, different in code and function from the other disciplines; on the other hand, aesthetics either simply remained subordinate to theoretical philosophy or advanced to become the bridge between theory and practice. Far from constituting a harmonious unity, the triad of the beautiful, good, and true was ceaselessly engaged in a highly complex inner struggle over boundaries. Hence Kant's own, incomparably keen concern with avoiding anything that might pollute the aesthetic purity in the definition of the beautiful.

Order, however, was not only needed for the demarcation of aesthetic experience. Starting with antique cosmology, the concept of the beautiful is itself an ordering concept, corresponding to the double meaning of *kosmos* as "order" and ornament. Again and again, the female body figures here as a dangerous and deadly threat to the very harmonious order that, as something beautiful, it promises. From Helen to Atalanta we find a rich assortment of beautiful *femmes fatales*, including goddesses such as Dido and intermediary beings such as the sirens. Clever male heroes like Odysseus knew how to enjoy the beautiful without succumbing to its dangers. Eighteenth-century aesthetics took on the role of another Odysseus: along the map of aesthetic pleasure, it tried to find a path purified of all dangerous contaminations by sexuality and death. The effort of distancing the aesthetic from normative doctrines of harmony and proportion did not imply a break with its status as an eminent ordering phenomenon. Quite to the contrary: the aesthetic was promoted to the very condition of possibility, indeed the only medium of the intricate unity of our capacities—and of our experience (compare Kant). With this, we are furnished with precisely the criteria Mary Douglas speaks of: an order imperiled by numerous ambivalences and unsafe boundaries, thus making an invocation of the pure-impure distinction probable.

By its very nature, the highest programmatic value of aesthetics, the ideal of the beautiful, required a specially painstaking labor of separation and purification. For Kant, even the *concept* of the ideal was infected by transaesthetic impurity—this in its very presumption of a theoretical concept of perfection.[207] From Baumgarten to Herder, aestheticians remained insensitive to this point, namely the aesthetic impurity of perfection itself; rather, they turned all their purificatory attention to the *body* of the ideal. One of classical aesthetic's basic assumptions was that the embodying body could only be the human body. In more than one sense, therefore, this aesthetics was anthropologically grounded—and it would remain for Herder to furnish this anthropocentricism with a strictly relativistic formulation:

> A lizard is in itself as beautiful as divine Venus. Not, to be sure, for every feeling being in every place in the world. For here the scope of everyone is limited; none can grasp the perfection of all the others—less so recognize it at first sight or on first sensing its forms and portions, in other words feel its beauty straightway. For such perception, an intimate familiarity with the nature of the being is called for, and [we have this familiarity] most properly only with ourselves alone.[208]

The very human body, which alone we are "able to judge" in an "unmediated way,"[209] is subject to a work of aesthetic idealization that structurally executes the same distinctions Mary Douglas found at work in the processing of social problems through concepts of pollution. The impermeable, closed body as "perfect container" takes on a position of pure and ideal order, while all openings, "border-regions," and surface defects mark the danger of pollution. By means of Douglas' relatively uncomplicated cybernetic classificatory model, the femininity (either overt or latent) of all these defects, ranging from the fold to the bodily secretions, can be accounted for by one basic interpretation: in the new and ambitious discipline of aesthetics, the principle of male supremacy runs into danger. More physical strength, more (theoretical) reason, and likewise stronger moral principles: for the anthropology of the period, all these putative male advantages meant an unquestionable legitimation of clear-cut hierarchical relations between the sexes. With beauty, however, male aestheticians gave up the priority of their own sex, and thus found themselves facing a dangerous complication of the otherwise unequivocal sexual order. For beauty was by no means merely a nice accessory or pleasing decoration. Rather, it represented the eminent locus of unity for all our capacities—even, in fact, the locus of the Absolute, or, one might say, a kind of secular replacement for God.

The ceding of beauty is thus not only a gallant gesture to the "lovely lady"—the *Frauenzimmer*—but a serious problem. This becomes clear precisely in the case of Winckelmann, defining as no other the Classical ideal, while nevertheless turning out incapable of preventing its prompt subjection to a sex-change. Winckelmann himself evoked "the young Spartan girls . . . clad so lightly and so short, that one called them on this account 'displayers of hips'"[210] as readily as the naked young Spartan boys in their gymnastic contests. Still, his comprehensive inventory of male and female beauties, with idolized Apollo and Venus at its head, reveals a distinct tendency to grant the male sex superiority in beauty's realm as in all the others: no female statue, for instance, brings Winckelmann to "tears" as promptly as that torso of Bacchus, which—despite the lack of head, breast, and arms—provides an incomparably "high idea of what Anacreon terms a belly of Bacchus."[211] By contrast to his own sensitivity for male beauty, those "who are little or not at all stirred by the beauties in our sex" are said to lack an easy and genuine access to "the perception of the beautiful in art," "since the greatest beauties in Greek art are more from our own than from the other sex."[212] The figures of the various female deities, Winckelmann explains, "differ only according to their age," otherwise "the limbs are equally rounded and full [in all cases]." This discovery of a lack of corporeal individuation shifts seamlessly into a far-reaching speculation:

> For the same reason that I find less to notice in the beauty of the female sex, the study of the artist in this department is much more limited and easy; even nature appears to act with more facility in the formation of the female than of the male sex, since there are fewer male than female children born. Hence Aristotle says, that the operations of nature tend to perfection in the formation of human beings, too, the male sex being this final goal of nature; yet if this goal could not be arrived at, due to the resistance of matter, then a female is the result.[213]

Precisely because Winckelmann was the only Classicist to grant the male sex precedence in the contest for beauty as elsewhere, he does not have to respond as drastically as his colleagues to a threat of the sexual order. And for just this reason, it is only in Winckelmann's case that at least the emblematic maximal value of the threat posed to beauty—the wrinkled hag with gaping body-openings and visible secretions, nearly ubiquitous among the other important authors—is *absent*. On the other hand, even for Winckelmann male dominance is not unquestionable. In their very zealousness, his programmatic-pedagogic remarks reveal the losing nature of his battle against "those who are attentive solely to the beauties of the female sex."[214] In Winckelmann's writings as well, we find an exclusion of all signs of mature feminine sexuality, and a correlative idealization of virgins and amazons. But the problem-solving mechanism of applying notions of (sexual) pollution does not reach its full articulation until the feminine body has become the prevailing icon of beauty.

Lessing's, Herder's, and Kant's corporeal descriptions from the 1760s are less complete and systematic than Winckelmann's great normative œuvre. At the same time, in a partly discrete, partly programmatic way, they abandon the male claim to aesthetic superiority. Certainly, for both Lessing and Herder, Laocoön and Apollo maintain their preeminence in the aesthetic debate, but the number of female beauty-paradigms is ahead of their male counterparts by a wide margin. Herder colors the relation between viewer and statue as that of an enthused, "visually feeling" male "lover" to beautiful feminine "flesh" *(Fleisch):* "Let us touch a Venus emerging from her bath, with the beautiful behind etc., a Juno, Diana—what else?"[215] The promotion of femininity to the rank of an ideal with considerable philosophical power has its price: a complimentary move defining the same femininity as embodying a permanent danger of disgusting impurity. Edmund Burke probably formulated the simplest solution: female beauty is in fact only beauty *for the male*, a stimulant purposively invented by nature for the sake of perpetuating the species.[216] Kant countered the superior beauty of the female sex, while not challenging it directly, through a major redistribution of the aesthetic realm. He reserved the register of the sublime exclusively for the male sex, reevaluating this register markedly upward, thus ensuring that the feminine was surpassed in the aesthetic realm as well as all the others.

This, however, seems to have not sufficed. In a relatively crude manner, Kant also makes use of the same degradative strategy that Lessing and Herder lodged, masterly and discretely, within their learned discourse over aesthetic models. All three, Lessing, Herder and Kant—like many other authors—wrap the female body in an ambivalence neutralizing every virtue through a *vitium* located at another point in the system. Here Mary Douglas's model of impurity-attribution as a problem-solving strategy takes on resonance. To be sure, the female body (naturally with a virginal form) may well constitute the ideal of beauty—but this beauty would have no need to be quite so beautiful, quite so ideal, quite so illusory, if it were not simultaneously covering up a female abyss of disgusting ugliness. In this manner, the "impure old woman"—as Douglas puts it, "the idea of woman as the Old Eve"[217]—becomes a wild card in the field of theoretical aesthetics. The wild card allows all the gestures of expulsion and exclusion that, on the other side, make it possible for male aestheticians to subordinate their sex aesthetically under the image of the young Eve. Kant got at the heart of the matter: "Nothing is so much set against the beautiful as disgust. . . . On this account no insult can be more painful . . . to a woman, than being called *disgusting.*"[218] And it is precisely for this reason that this insult is produced with so much obstinacy in the system of the beautiful, even being extended, in its capacity as a generalized ascription of impurity, to young women. The female body, the ideal of beauty, needs a ceaseless effort of self-idealization in order not to succumb to its inner propensity for the impure and the disgusting. As Kant puts its: "To distance oneself as much as possible from what might evoke disgust, *cleanliness,* while becoming for everyone, counts among the most high-ranking virtues for the beautiful sex, which can scarcely carry it too far."[219]

At the ideal locus of the beautiful Venus, a drama of the *disgusting* female body is thus raging. A threat to male supremacy is redefined as a threat to female aesthetic superiority from within the female sex. Once again, impurity and disgust function as a paradoxical instrument of order, as the processing of a threat to a specific hierarchy. Within the field of the aesthetic, the emergence and function of representations of female impurity thus appear to obey the same temptingly simple—perhaps too simple—model Mary Douglas discovers at work in social organizations. Still, the model's explanatory value has rather narrow limits. It may indeed offer an elegant solution for a "disturbance of order" inscribed within the system of aesthetics. It does not, however, address the particular forms taken on by the ciphers for problem-marking and problem-solving—Old Eve, disgusting lady, witch—in the writings of individual aestheticians. And it does not account for their centrality, in very different contexts, for practically all theories of disgust. Answers to these problems cannot emerge by approaching both the body and concepts of sexual pollution strictly in terms of functional metaphors of (dis)order, as in fact does Mary Douglas. Rather, it seems just as crucial to take the body's imagination literally—in its materiality and originary relation with desire, with consciousness, and with unconscious contents. As examples of the latter approach, the present discussion will focus principally on three models: Freud's; Bataille's; and Kristeva's reflections on the "abject," anti-aphrodisian woman, smelling of blood and linked "perverse" behavior. (An interpretation of specific variations on the *vetula*-cipher by different authors—the sort of psychological interpretation that will *not* here be offered—would need to go beyond such models, in order to consider classical patterns of misogyny and the entire imaginative field of witches and Baubos.)

3

"Strong Vital Sensation" and Organon of Philosophy

The Judgment of Disgust in Kant

Among the early theorists, disgust appears mainly in marginal textual positions, its literally *deciding* role as border and taboo notwithstanding. J. A. Schlegel assigned his reflections on disgust to a footnote of his Batteux-translation. Mendelssohn's prominent disgust-theory is not located in his more substantial treatises on the beautiful and the sublime, the arts and the sciences, but in a very short "letter." In contrast, with Lessing's *Laokoon* und Herder's *Plastik*, disgust has gained an unmistakable presence within the main literature on aesthetics. But Kant's *Critique of Judgment* already remarginalizes the category on a compositional level: the analyses of the beautiful and the sublime manage very well without it. The only paragraph touching on disgust—merely in order, however, to reinforce its exclusion—is stuck at the end of the "Deduction of the Aesthetic," in a paragraph whose title in no way indicates the appearance of disgust: "§ 48. On the relation of genius to taste." Kant scholars have entirely neglected the *Ekel*-passages in this paragraph.[1] It took Pierre Bourdieu's sociological insight and Jacques Derrida's "marginal" acumen to sense more than a marginal problem in Kant's postponed and isolated paragraph on disgust. Neither author, however, has realized that the paragraph is almost entirely a citation, less a continuation than a burial of the elaborate disgust-debate of the 1750s and 1760s.[2] The more interesting and entirely new facets of the Kantian philosophy of disgust are to be found in the early texts and the anthropology, rather than in Kant's main aesthetic œuvre.[3]

DISGUST AND PLEASURE

The reprise of Mendelssohn—and Lessing—in the *Critique of Judgment* runs as follows:

Fine art shows its superiority precisely in describing things as beautiful that in nature would be ugly or displeasing. The Furies, diseases, devastations of war, etc. are all harmful; and yet they can be described, or seen presented in a painting, very beautifully. There is only one kind of ugliness that cannot be presented in conformity with nature without obliterating all aesthetic pleasure, hence artistic beauty: namely, the ugliness arousing disgust. For in that strange sensation, resting on nothing but imagination, the object is presented as if it were pressing us to consume it [zum Genusse aufdrängen],[4] although this is just what we are violently resisting; and hence the artistic presentation of the object is no longer distinguished in our sensation from the nature of this object itself, so that it cannot possibly be considered beautiful. Being nearly confused with nature in its products, the art of sculpture, too, has excluded from its creations any direct presentation of ugly objects. Instead, it has permitted, for instance, death (as a beautiful genius), or a warlike spirit (as Mars) to be presented through an allegory or an attribute that stands out as pleasing. It has hence only permitted them to be presented indirectly and by means of an interpretation of reason, rather than for the merely aesthetic faculty of judgment.[5]

The Aristotelian paradigm of the "beautiful description" of ugly or "displeasing" objects; the exception of disgust; the basis of this sensation's strength in "nothing but imagination," resulting in the eradication of the nature-art difference; the especially rigid taboo on ugliness in the plastic arts; death's mitigation in a "beautiful genius": these are all old themes from the pertinent texts of Mendelssohn and Lessing. Kant dispenses with many finer distinctions, such as the distinction between a technically beautiful imitation of "ugly things" and the special effect of mixed sensations. At the same time, in a short clause he adds a trait absent from his predecessors' aesthetic writings. Before Kant as well, the aesthetic unpalatability of the disgusting—whether it took the form of pockmarks or nose-snot, foul smells, maimed bodies, or the "impure old woman"—was undisputed. But it was *not* assumed that such disgusting entities in themselves "press us to consume" them. Kant maintains precisely that: the defense-reaction of disgust does not only involve the proximity and presence of something repellent; rather, it is also the correlative of an intruding act of consumption. This figure appears to move beyond Condillac's anthropological linkage of gustatory disgust to a pleasure exhausted through habit or excessive consumption. Condillac's *dégoût* comes into play only when a formerly habitual pleasure is fruitlessly and despairingly *searched* for in specific objects.[6] In contrast, Kant attributes the disgust-object with the power to itself "press consumption" on us. Further, only to the extent that there is consumption—sexual, gustatory, olfactory—there can also be disgust: "What is felt in us as present is consumed *[genossen]:* tasting and smelling. *Ekel.*"[7] *Genuss* does not necessarily here imply the meaning of pleasure or enjoyment, but simply signifies consumption, inner "intake"[8] in general, as the modus operandi of all tasting and smelling. The sensation of disgust rests precisely on this distinction: in order to experience something as disgusting, it must first have entered—however partially—our sense of smell or taste; it has to be "taken in" or "consumed" before being judged as totally unenjoyable (at least as long as disgust does not wholly depend on a transfer by means of association).

Bourdieu reads the disgust-taboo reinforced by Kant generally as "a disgust for objects which impose enjoyment"—the more proper translation of Kant's formula being: "which press consumption on us."[9] In doing so, he ends up eradicating the distinction from the "merely agreeable" of purely sensuous taste: the "pressing" nature of the disgusting is the same, for him, as the "enslaving force of the 'agreeable.'"[10] Sensual enjoyment itself is what here is classified as disgusting and barbaric—the purely aesthetic judgment thus establishing itself as a distinguishing trait of the higher, "educated" classes. This may have some justification as a general critical reading of the ideology of aesthetic autonomy; but it does scant justice to Kant's reinforcement of the disgust-taboo, Bourdieu apparently being as unfamiliar with its pre-Kantian variants as Derrida is after him. It is not simply that in the cited passage *"Genuss"* signifies inner intake alone and precisely not enjoyment; at the same time, Kant extends the sphere of the disgusting well beyond the spheres of smell and taste. His concept of disgust refers just as strongly to the *morally* disgusting, hence to phenomena subject, in any event, to an intellectualized judgment. Furthermore, the paradoxical equation of the disgusting and the pleasant is indeed correct to the extent that both annul the reflecting distance and disinterest of the imagination. But the scandalous, revolting presence, the incompatibility with pleasure, and the hyperreality of the disgusting—hence its three distinctive characteristics—are here left fully unconsidered. The same is true for the special position of the disgusting in the contemporary anthropology of "agreeable" and "disagreeable" sensations. Kant's sentences on the aesthetic nonrepresentability of the disgusting in no way articulate a "a disgust for the crude, vulgar taste which revels in this imposed enjoyment."[11] Such pleasure at the disgusting is all the more absent in Kant as he declares it to be impossible—at least in the case of aesthetic pleasure. The paradigm of disgust at pleasure at the disgusting will only emerge in the conservative critique of romantic literature. Hence, as plausible as Bourdieu's overall reading of aesthetics as a class-specific mechanism for distinction may be, his interpretation of Kant's disgust-paragraphs represents a drastic distortion, one offered in the service of a decidedly non-aesthetic approach to the text.[12]

For Kant, the field of disgust is that area *within* the field of possible enjoyment where the reality of consumption ("intake") turns into the convulsive rejection of itself. Kant takes the model of vomiting that always presupposes a previous "consumption" more literally than his predecessors: even in its metaphoric variants, disgust is for him "a stimulus to discharge what has been consumed through the shortest path of the gullet (to vomit)."[13] It is an "attempt . . . to expel an idea that has been offered for consumption."[14] Only two of the many disgust-paradigms in the pre-Kantian debate correspond with Kant's vomitive model: satiatory disgust and the representation of hunger. "In dishes," the disgusting is "excess. very sweet or fat."[15] Disgust at sweetness and its transposed variant, disgust at the "merely" beautiful, presumes a "gorging with consumption *[Überfüllen mit Genuß]*."[16] The representation of hunger is another example where Kant's juxtaposition of "appetite" and "disgust"—in terms of both being "related to consumption"[17]—proves to be useful. As Lessing indicates, other forms of the terrible *can* be intensified by an addition of the disgusting; by contrast the poet has access to hunger's horrors "virtually only and alone" through the disgusting: "Even in ordinary life we can express an extreme degree of hunger only by recounting all the unnutritious, unwholesome, and especially disgusting things through which the stomach must be satisfied."[18] The poetic "portraits of *Fames* [hunger's impersonation]" were most inventive, Lessing observes, in furnishing disgusting objects for the "satisfaction" of raging hunger; he presents a rich literary panorama, from falling upon cats and "filthy leftovers" to the devouring of one's own limbs, longing for wound dressings, enema tubes, and the "princely banquet" of a surgically removed fatty tumor.[19] But the relation here between the disgusting and both consumption and satisfaction simply constitutes something perfidious that wholly depends on the special emergency situation defined by hunger.[20]

If Kant, in contrast, sees disgust generally "related to consumption," this necessarily has consequences for his reading of the established stock of examples. Snot, for instance, rejected by Herder and Lessing in Hesiod's Achlys on grounds of disgusting sight alone, returns literally as an object of "swallowing" and hence "innermost intake"[21]: "The view of other people consuming disgusting things (e.g., when the Tunguses speedily suck out and gulp down the mucus from their children's noses) causes the witness to vomit, as if he were being forced to indulge in such consumption himself."[22] The ugly old woman similarly figures as a being who presses toward sexual "consumption." She thus regains the provocative randiness of the antique *vetulae*, eliminated from the field of the "impure old woman" by Brockes, as well as by Schlegel, Lessing, and Herder. For these authors, purely physical-aesthetic flaws already served as grounds for rejection. The proximity of old women to—itself disgusting—death was here more at play than any sexual insinuation. Or at least the authors' explicit remarks fail to hint at a temptation or prompting to sexual enjoyment. In this context, only a psychoanalytic diagnosis of *suppressed* sexual anxiety could manufacture the connection that Kant's *vetula*-reflections openly articulate. The most laconic form of this connection is the juxtaposition of two short phrases: "A kiss is bliss. Old lady evokes disgust."[23] Or at greater length:

> Indeed the platonic love might well be somewhat too mystical, which an ancient philosopher asserted when he said of the object of his inclination, "The Graces reside in her wrinkles, and my soul seems to hover upon my lips when I kiss her withered mouth"; but such claims must then be abandoned. An old man who acts infatuated is a fool, and similar presumptions by the other sex are disgusting.[24]

For such reasons, in order not to inevitably decline into something disgusting, Kant's "old woman" must not only follow a purity-regime that "can hardly be pushed too high."[25] She must in fact satisfy a *double* requirement: "an old woman is an object of disgust for both sexes except when she is very clean & not coquette."[26]

The disgusting in Kant's sense thus in fact takes on the character of the "shameless and as it were dissolute self-offering" that Kolnai attributes to the phenomenology of disgust in general.[27] In (re)sexualizing the cardinal *Ekel*-cipher of the old woman, and treating it equally as something both aesthetic (bearing only on the question of representation for the sake of formal beauty) and extra-aesthetic ('real' old women), Kant is denying the claim of aesthetics to the differentiation of an ideal special sphere. Through such a denial, Kant legitimates a 'realistic' reading of aesthetic "disgust." With the leveling of the systemic references, the aesthetic insistence on a distinction from sexual enjoyment shifts into 'ethical' disgust at sex.[28] Its highest value is "lecherous self-pollution" that "renders a man into not only an object of enjoyment but through this simultaneously into an unnatural thing, *i.e.*, a *loathsome* object." "Through its form (its attitude)," such an "unnatural vice" even seems "to surpass that of self-murder." For "we consider it indecent even to call this vice by its proper name. This does not happen in the case of self-murder." Indeed, "the defiant casting away of oneself ... as a life-burden" is closer to ethical action, since it is "at least not making a feeble surrender to animal impulses, but requires courage."[29] Other than with self-murder—and other, as well, than with the terrible or piteous—in being robbed of any courage, disgusting self-enjoyment is also robbed of any higher pathos. It thus marks the anti-ideal identity of "lower" (i.e., sexual) enjoyment and moral abomination. The onanist vomits himself out of himself, thus making himself into a "disgusting thing." In his position, the disgust-subject and disgust-object intersect.

Disgust as a Goal of Education

In the field of a generalized implication of "consumption" for all disgust, evoking the consumption of disgusting dishes is no longer contingent on starvation. Kant describes the eating habits of Asian peoples at some length, and in eyewitness mode: a "taste for spoiled, stinking fish," "half-rotten crabs," "entrails," and "warm brandy made from horse-milk" that is "distilled over mutton."[30] The condition of hunger is here replaced by an ethnological vantage, oriented around the distinction between what is alien and what is familiar. This does relativize the figures of both disgust and enjoyment; but precisely such relativism allows insight into disgust's cultural content: it connects it to history and the civilizational process. The seemingly natural and uncontrollable reaction of the dark senses advances to the position of a supreme cultural sign:

> Filth is an object of vision; but it cannot directly excite visual aversion, rather drawing our imagination to smell and taste. Filth produces disgust, but not through our fantasy. We also find that disgust at filth is only present in cultivated nations; the uncultivated nation has no qualms about filth. Cleanliness demonstrates the greatest human cultivation *[Bildung]*, since it is the least natural human quality, causing much exertion and hardship.[31]

In Kant's *Pädagogik*, cultivating disgust thus figures among the highest educational goals: "Everything in education rests upon establishing correct principles, and leading children to understand and accept them. They must learn to substitute abhorrence grounded in the feeling of disgust or of absurdity for the type of abhorrence that is hatred; aversion out of inner beliefs for that induced by other people or by the idea of divine punishment; self-respect and inward dignity, for a dependence on others' opinions."[32] The common feature at play here involves an inclination toward interiorization and an avoidance of outer force. Abhorrence on the basis of hatred would lead to violent acts, in the end to murder; abhorrence on the basis of disgust to an avoidance of the object—or its removal from our proximity.[33] Condillac's *Traité des sensations* (1754) defines the relation between hatred and disgust as one of simple gradation, disgust involving a "weaker degree" of rejection. But Condillac immediately relativizes his own definition, indicating that even if one disregards this gradative distinction, the words "hatred" and "disgust" are not interchangeable.[34] Given his stress on the particular "vital" strength of the *Ekel*-sensation, Kant would have found defining it through its weakness preposterous. He distinguishes disgust from the sensation of hate a priori according to type, not degree, the two sensations being mutually irreducible and having differing orientations. As violent as disgust's rejective verdict may be: it hardly encourages, ipso facto, the aggressive and annihilatory intention toward its source that is typical of hate. We turn away from the many catalysts of disgust—excrement, the scent of rot, slimy-slippery matter, repellent filth, excessively sweet dishes, and so forth—without wishing to destroy them. Inversely, we can hate all sorts of things without being at all disgusted by them. This categorial demarcation does not exclude the possibility of the two "passions" working on and strengthening each other. In venting itself on its object, hate can take on disgust as a supplement; and disgust can lower the threshold for hate-grounded annihilatory impulses.[35] But such hybridizations do not define Kant's perspective. Disgust allows him, above all, to establish through education, and to maintain, decisive moral border-demarcations, while sublimating directly annihilatory impulses that are aimed at what is rejected. The "nature of disgust" is consequently to civilize. Kant perceived this long before Freud and Elias, and erected a politics and morals of disgust upon the insight. The underlying schema here involves making precisely the dark, sensory basis of *Ekel* serviceable for "higher" goals.

SMELL, TASTE, AND THE "VITAL SENSATION" OF DISGUST

For Kant, the three "higher" senses—comprising touch along with sight and hearing—"lead the subject through reflection to cognition of the object as something outside ourselves."[36] They are senses "of perception (of the surface)," working via various forms "of mechanical operation." In contrast, the "lower senses" of taste and smell work through a chemical "intake" of their objects into the body's interiority. This "innermost intake" certainly reduces the possibility of distanced perception, rendering these senses "more subjective than objective."[37] But the formulation "more than" has been chosen deliberately over mere opposition. For "intake" does not only solicit practical action, but also implies cognition:

> Smell serves to distinguish what is meant to enter the lungs. Taste: what enters the stomach, but with the most sensitive tool. Smell is sensitive because the lungs are insensitive; what enters the lung is sent directly into the blood and is deadly.[38]
>
> Affinity between smell and taste: both tests of wholesomeness.[39]

The difference defined by smell and taste through inner "intake" of their objects is that between *wholesome* and *unwholesome*, health-promoting versus health-damaging—leading up to deadly. Theoretical cognition "with the most sensitive tool" thus precedes practical "discharge" through vomiting or exclusion. In this manner, Kant participates in the sensitivity regarding smells that had been rapidly intensifying since the mid-eighteenth century: presumably harmful smells in particular, thought to enter the blood directly as so-called *miasmas*. Along with "vapor from a stove, or the stench from a swamp or from dead animals," Kant here mentions many objects of olfactory disgust found "especially in densely-populated places."[40] According to contemporary opinion, no more suitable instrument was available for classifying these smells than the nose. Alain Corbin has impressively described the theory and praxis of "sniffing" applied by state officials and scholars to confront the dangers of all sorts of disgusting smells resulting from rot, decay, mold, dung-ditches, knacker's yards, and the "sick city" in general.[41] The lower senses thus become measuring-instruments that directly cognize their objects by virtue of "innermost" contact with them. They offer, in other words, what Kant otherwise only accords the divine spirit: direct cognition, not grounded in intuition. Through their cognitive capacity, these agents of hygiene both warn of and guard from uncleanliness and death. The psychology of disgust has always stressed disgust's "cognitive sophistication"; for long before modern knowledge of infection, the idea of contamination already implied the presence of invisible and dangerous materials.[42] Kant, therefore, does not subscribe to the strict focus on cultural factors and habit informing the interpretation of (nutritive) disgust found in d'Holbach and other French Enlightenment authors.[43] Rather, he stresses disgust's cognitive role and—despite all insight into the sensation's cultural production and function—describes its inedibility-judgment from the perspective of the ideas of contamination inscribed within it.

Alongside the cognitively oriented "test," olfactory "consumption" always had a darker, libidinous aspect in the eighteenth century. As an uncivilizable, phallic organ, the nose was here directly connected to sexual pleasure. Kant's notion of "innermost intake" entwines these semantic fields: the decision over life and death with that over *union versus corporeal expulsion*. Whereas "the beautiful contains in itself the concept of the invitation to the innermost union with the object, that is, to immediate [pleasurable] consumption," the disgusting sparks "an effort to expel an idea that has been offered for consumption."[44] In his *Anthropology from a Pragmatic Point of View*, Kant terms this fusing of "consumption" and expulsion into the feeling of disgust a "vital sensation":

> For this reason disgust, a stimulus to discharge something that has been consumed through the shortest path of the gullet (to vomit), is given to the human being as such a strong vital sensation, since such an inner intake . . . can be dangerous.[45]

The strong emphasis on the paradigm of vomiting is, however, only one aspect of Kant's semantics of *Ekel*. The other side involves his definition of olfactory disgust as the true basis and "innermost" form of impurity-linked disgust:

"Filth seems to awaken disgust less through what is repulsive to eye and tongue than through the stench that presumably comes with it. For intake (into the lungs) through smell is an even deeper inner intake than through the ingestive vessels of mouth or gullet."[46] Kant's posthumous notebooks indicate that smell might not be serviceable as a model for disgust's theoretical definition, despite its status as the preeminent disgust-sensation. The sense of smell, Kant notes, is so dark that precious little—"properly" nothing at all— could be revealed by the light of language. For the sensation lacks "appellations," *Benennungen:*

> All sensations have appellations of their own, e.g. for sight red, green, yellow, for taste sweet, sour, etc., but smell cannot have proper appellations; rather, we borrow the appellations from other sensations, e.g. it smells sour, or has a smell of roses or carnations, it smells like moschus. These are all appellations from other sensations. Hence we cannot describe smell.[47]

In any case, even more than through the role of smell, the orientation toward the mouth, hence toward taste-grounded disgust, is relativized through the general definition of disgust as a "vital sensation." Just as free beauty *(pulchritudo vaga)* sets all our "higher" capacities into interplay, the vital sensation, as a *sensus vagus,* affects the *entire* system of bodily feelings; it cannot be localized in any single organ:

> To begin with, we can divide the senses of corporeal feeling into those of the *vital sensation (sensus vagus)* and those of *organic sensation (sensus fixus);* and, since they are met with only where there are nerves, into those affecting the whole system of nerves, and those which affect only those nerves belonging to a certain member of the body. The sensations of warmth and cold, even those aroused by the mind (for example, through quickly rising hope or fear), belong to the *vital sensation.* The *shudder* seizing people even at the idea of something sublime, and the terror with which nurses' tales drive children to bed late at night, belong to the latter type. They penetrate the body, so far as it is alive.[48]

If disgust is thus "given to the human being as such a strong vital sensation," then smell and taste, the senses of both consumption and disgust, are simply synecdoches and transmitters of a *sensus vagus,* a freely wandering sensation, place uncertain, that "penetrates the body, so far as it is alive." For Kant, the beautiful "directly conveys a feeling of life's being furthered,"[49] and the aesthetic pleasure of laughter "seems always to consist of a feeling that a person's life, including bodily well-being, i.e., his health, is generally being furthered."[50]

Similarly, as a "serious and unpleasant sensation,"[51] Ekel uses the same wide radius of action to warn of "unwholesome" and unhealthy affections menacing the very life that beauty and laughter positively "further." Beauty and laughter are life's elixirs; disgust an apotropaic response to death. (The feeling of the sublime offers a third possibility, taking on the defeat, the virtual death of our sensory capacities, and compensating for it by "stirring" the powers of our "supersensuous character.")

Disgust, Laughter, and "Dark Conceptions"

Disgust is thus "a negative condition of well-being";[52] as a "test of wholesomeness," it operates on the negative pole of the vital sensations to make safe the field and possibility of the positive. It is a negative form of laughter, similarly catalyzing convulsive movement and shaking the entire body. Both start suddenly and are usually of short duration. Laughter, according to Kant, brings about a rapid collapse of a previously built-up tension: it is "the sudden transformation into nothing of a tense expectation."[53] Disgust just as suddenly generates a maximal defensive tension in face of disappointed expectation—that of the "wholesomeness" of what was (about to be) taken in—in order to then immediately "discharge" the tension. In both laughter and disgust, the rapid discharge of a high tension leads to a state of pleasant relaxation, or a soothing sense of "all clear." Since Kant is among those seeing laughter as a distinctly human trait, along with language and reason alone, disgust accrues considerable anthropological meaning from this side as well as laughter's negative *Doppelgänger*.

One important aspect of any definition of disgust is the absence of a strictly symmetrical counterconcept. *Ekel* twists and asymmetricizes all oppositions, thus removing itself from any binary semantics. In Kant, though belonging to the dark senses, it is also a pedagogic goal and certificate of a high cultural level. It is a negative laughter, and yet not the weeping opposite of laughter. It represents the contrasting vital sensation to that of the beautiful, but also knows the disgust-value attached to the beautiful itself—just as, inversely, the "ugly" qualifies more than the "disgusting" as a symmetrical countervalue to the beautiful. Occasionally, disgust figures in Kant as the opposite of "appetite"[54]—to the extent, that is, that "disgust satiates."[55] On the other hand, Kant stipulates that both equally imply an "intake"; "appetite," however, operates rather through the oppositions well-tasting versus bad-tasting and satiating versus nonsatiating than through the medical-dietetic oppositions wholesome versus unwholesome (life-sustaining vs. deadly). The scale of negative parallel concepts stretching from the disagreeable to the repellent also requires highly complex demarcations. Early Kant had thus not hesitated to include *Ekel* among those complex "elementary concepts" of "world wisdom" that "are only incompletely, or almost not at all, capable of analysis." Aside from the categories of space and time this applies to "many *feelings* of the human *soul*, the feeling of the *sublime*, the *beautiful*, the *disgusting*, etc.: without their precise knowledge and analysis, the mainsprings of our nature are insufficiently known; and yet a careful observer will note that the analysis falls far short of what is needed."[56] Kant indicates that the role of critical philosophy is not to lament this situation, but to acknowledge it as "unavoidable"—as a resistance to analysis affecting every "discipline," to be sure mathematics far less than "especially metaphysics." Regarding the capabilities of the human power of "imagination"—which is a central category of the entire Kantian system—the *Critique of Pure Reason* speaks of "an art hidden in the depths of the human soul, whose true operations we are hardly likely to ever divine from nature and lay down unveiled before our eyes."[57] According to the doctrine of the soul's "dark conceptions," resistance to full analytic transparency and proximity to our "true mainsprings" are reciprocal notions. Kant incorporates disgust into this register of the dark conceptions—their insolubility being both sign and promise, albeit in no way proof of proximity to the unintelligible ground of our existence:

> Dark conceptions. . . . Our soul does most of its work in the dark, and has its greatest treasure in the dark as well. A great charter, illuminated in few places. . . . We are partly a play of dark conceptions (sympathy, disgust, fear, hate, none of which we can offer a reason for), and we partly play with dark conceptions, in order to stimulate someone through something without him knowing how it happens. (Non-awareness as the true mainspring of our virtue.)[58]

To be sure, so much great critical modesty does not alter the goal of *illuminating the illuminable* with the greatest possible clarity and analytic acumen. At the same time, it burdens every metaphorization, every transfer of the dark conception of disgust into the field of the intellect, with a double danger: the danger posed by a temptation to give up on argumentation, indeed a license to supplement a lack of theoretical analysis with "dark" sensations, irresolvable to the understanding; and the danger posed by a tendency to assert relevance and original meaning precisely for what escapes theoretical elucidation. As an organon of philosophy, disgust was attractive for Kant precisely on account of the chances and possibilities inextricably entangled with these dangers.

Disgust as an Organon of Intellectual Critique

Consumption, testing of wholesomeness, and expulsion remain the model for the disgust-sensation in face of "food for the intellect," too:

There is also, however, an *intellectual consumption* consisting in the communication of thought. But when such consumption is pressed upon us, even though it is not wholesome as nourishment for the intellect, the mind finds it repugnant. (A good example of this is the constant repetition of amusing or witty quips, which can become indigestible through sameness.) Thus the natural instinct to get rid of such nourishment is by analogy called disgust, although it belongs to the inner sense.[59]

In this way, the "communication of thoughts," even philosophical thoughts, is itself subject to the wholesomeness-test performed by that "most sensitive tool," disgust, the schema for the physical disgust-sensation remaining uncurtailed. The sensation applies the code wholesome versus unwholesome in both realms; here as there its function is to defend against damages to "health"—in the end to avoid physical or intellectual death. In the interest of healthy "nourishment," an "instinct from nature," a corporeal-affective judgment, is also allowed to regulate the intellectual diet. Its scent is sharper, more distinctive, than that of merely rational judgment. Dogmatic philosophy? Disgusting! When such "intellectual consumption . . . is pressed" upon us, it experiences the same repellence by the "inner sensation" of disgust as does the ugly old woman from the outer sensation: "This much is certain: whosoever has once tasted of critique forever loathes all the dogmatic chatter with which he previously had to be satisfied out of necessity, since his reason was in need of something and could not find anything better for its sustenance."[60] Disgust can thus also be calibrated on the taste for (transcendental) critique. Through employing its differentiating capacity in the service of an intellectual diet, it emerges as an aesthetic organon of philosophy—one to whom the "descending to popular concepts," with their "disgusting mishmash of compiled observations and half-reasoned principles,"[61] tastes no better than dogmatic schoolphilosophy. And facing the natural instinct of he who "once has tasted critique," a third, concurring type of philosophy, the "witty" type, also enjoys no mercy:

> Wit snatches at *sudden ideas;* judgment strives toward insight. . . . Wit usually prefers the *broth,* whereas judgment usually prefers the *repast.* The hunt for witty words (bons mots) . . . makes for shallow minds or turns a conscientious man away in disgust. Wit is inventive when it comes to *fashions,* that is, assumed rules of behavior, which are pleasing only because of their novelty.[62]

The sensation of disgust judges, as it were, on physical, aesthetic, and moral levels, thus occupying—very much like the sensation of beauty—within the Kantian system a strategic point that unites all faculties. It supplements the purely theoretical critique with a test of taste—with a dietetic organon judging all sorts of "food for the intellect." For Sulzer, theoretical aesthetics far from all artistic praxis is to be rejected as sparking disgust,[63] and for color-theorist Goethe, there is another preordained disgust-object: "Newtonian optics, this confused mishmash, will finally appear just as disgusting to a more cultivated world as it does to me now."[64] Here once again, the analogy to the lower senses' "natural" judgment is at the same time a demonstration of superior cultivation.

Disgust as Organon of Practical Action

At least in Kant's case, rejection based on disgust is by no means merely the aesthetic abbreviation, or the hyperbole, of a critique based on purely theoretical grounds. Rather, disgust fills in and substitutes for a lack—a theoretical deficit in philosophy; it is in actuality, and entirely unmetaphorically, an originary philosophical organon. Kant's philosophy suffers from numerous foundational weaknesses. Not only does it abandon any possibility of objectively grasping God, the thing in itself, or the ego as the point of unity of experience. At the same time, it can regularly only *postulate* its own subjective laws as possible or necessary in thought, not, however *deduce* them from higher principles or preceding insights. Aesthetic judgment, for instance, simply presumes a priori, as a transcendental principle of itself, the concept of an objectively unknown and even unknowable "purposiveness of nature," and with it a "harmony of nature with our cognitive power." Only in this manner can it salvage "the possibility of the unity of experience" and of a "continual coherence of empirical cognitions" in face of "the possibility of an endless diversity of empirical laws."[65] According to Kant the beautiful represents precisely this principle *for feeling,* to the extent that the pleasure from beauty is essentially a pleasure at the harmonious interplay of understanding and sensuousness—at the (apparent) commensurateness of "our powers of comprehension" with the "order of nature." The feeling of aesthetic pleasure is the sole, highly problematical "proof" or indicator that any kind of 'reality' is attached to the postulated principle.

Even more virulent gaps emerge within Kant's practical philosophy. As the supreme imperative for action, the moral law is not derivable from higher laws; it can only be stipulated as an underivable "fact of pure reason."[66] Furthermore, the practical implementation of this precarious *factum* as a universal law lacks a compelling mechanism. Even if, as Kant holds, an awareness of the moral law ipso facto implies a *"necessitation* to act" accordingly,[67] and hence is strictly imperative, a prior question remains open: what brings us to the point of ever conceiving this simply stipulated "fact"—of becoming aware of it in the first place? Relying on its own powers, practical philosophy is capable of producing neither a secondary proof of its underivable law nor a supplemental impulse to conceive it at all. Here as well, an aesthetic feeling has to help out: the feeling of the *sublime*. That is, the sublime "compels us to subjectively *think* nature itself in its totality as the exhibition of something supersensible."[68] Exposing us to a might and grandeur incommensurate with our sensuousness, it provokes the resistance of our "supersensuous character," and thus stirs up noumenal ideas that are positively neither provable nor representable.[69] Practical philosophy can only *suggest [ansinnen]* its ideas; it therefore leaves open possibilities of not living up to this suggestion. In contrast, the aesthetic feeling of the sublime tends to dispose of an *irresistible* sensuous-affective power urging us to think these ideas. Aesthetic feeling alone can *compel* us "to think" freedom or the morally-good in the first place. In this way, the "vital sensations" of the beautiful and sublime are also organs of theoretical and practical philosophy—this corresponding to the Kantian inclination to burden the aesthetic with the 'solution' to problems not to be solved on the grounds of theory and praxis alone.

While virtually all pertinent scholarly work on Kant focuses on the duality of the sublime and the beautiful, the Kantian system is in fact distinguished by a triad—that of "the feelings of the *sublime*, the *beautiful*, and the *disgusting*."[70] This triad proves to be highly functional with regard to the paradigm of philosophical organa. The vital sensation of disgust offers negative counterparts to the ways in which both the beautiful and the sublime supplement philosophy's shortcomings. The latter furnish the purposiveness of nature and the noumenal ideas of freedom and morality with a reality in the "feelings," either disposing us or compelling us to conceive these unprovable ideas. Disgust, on the other hand, disposes us and compels us to decisively repel that which runs counter to morality, is unfree, and appears in disharmony with the "wholesome" and "beautiful" coherence of nature. In doing so, it likewise furnishes—albeit now in the mode of critique and avoidance of the opposite—the noumenal ideas of morality and freedom with a reality in the feelings. The beautiful and sublime positively compensate for theoretical deficits of foundation and practical deficits of motivation; the feeling of disgust warns us away, and shelters us in negative-apotropaic fashion, from giving in to what would be opposite to the (groundless) good or the (unknowable) purposiveness of nature. As an effect of cultivation, such desirable achievements do not constitute a miraculous natural phenomenon, proving that the human being is naturally good in essence. Rather, to speak with Freud, in the end these positive functions of disgust are instituted by the superego.

What Kant rejected under the rubric of "moral feeling," as "one more sense with which to enjoy oneself," is countenanced as the aesthetic feeling of the sublime—and of the disgusting: "There is something in morality for taste to judge." An aesthetic feeling that incorporates and works in favor of the moral law "always raises the worry of becoming a rightful object of *Ekel*."[71] The metaphysics of virtue thus needs the support of an "aesthetics of morals"—an aesthetics "in which the feelings that accompany the necessitating power of the moral law . . . make the efficacy of that law felt."[72] Disgust and horror thus "sensualize" the "moral antipathy," and are part of "an aesthetic machinery that does, however, point the way to a moral sense." Disgust is consequently a negative form of the sublime: an organon for the "worried" avoidance of vices, standing at the negative pole of our possibilities, alongside the sublime sense of our moral vocation's superiority to all natural obstacles. It is a "most sensitive tool" *not only* for the health-preserving test-taste of smells and food, and aesthetic taste's judgment of "food for the intellect," including philosophy. At the same time, it aids in the aesthetic-physiological repulsion of "vices" that "press consumption on us," and through this in a negative safeguarding of the morally-good.[73]

In its affective organa-function, the triad comprised of "the feeling of the *sublime*, the *beautiful*, and the *disgusting*" correlates with the triad of the three "higher" faculties: the beautiful is linked above all with the understanding, the sublime with reason, the disgusting with imagination. The surprising affinity of disgust with pure imagination—"imagination alone"[74]— loses its counterintuitive quality in view of two factors. First, as a faculty of intuition, the imagination is essentially less mediated than the two other faculties, standing essentially closer to our "dark" physical being. Second, precisely the moral organon-function requires considerable associative achievement by the imagination: otherwise, practical actions could not be judged in analogy with smell and taste. Later, Darwin as well would stress the special ease with which disgust can be sparked by a "mere idea."[75] To this extent, Kant's modeling of "the feeling of the *sublime*, the *beautiful*, and the *disgusting*" on the faculties understanding, reason, and imagination is only consequent. At the same time, the manifestation here of the triadic architectonies of Kant's thought pointedly underscores his interest in the "strong vital sensation"[76] of *Ekel*.

In the aftermath of the linkage with consumption and the open sexualization of the disgusting, Kant offered an analogon to disgust as vice-avoidance that Freud will later regularly mention in the same breath as disgust: the feeling of shame. For Kant, shame precedes the feeling of disgust. This additional "secret of nature" prevents any "all too common acquaintance" with sexuality, thus avoiding such acquaintance taking on the otherwise threatening value of disgust. Disgust furnishes us with a dramatic impulse for avoiding contamination; shame checks the last, vomitive safety-brake ever having to be activated, in order to negatively preserve our behavior's conformity with the demands of virtue. What Kant says about the moral function of shame applies at least as much for disgust: "it is most needed, as a supplement to the [moral] principles."[77]

Disgust, Happiness and Unhappiness, Ennui

Despite so many estimable virtues, for Kant, the feeling of disgust is itself not free of dangers. The "most sensitive tool," which is capable of comprehensively regulating the dietetics of the physical, moral, and aesthetic life, itself needs dietetic guidance, in order not to become too sensitive, too delicate, too touchy—in short, too *ekel*. Otherwise a pair of dangers threaten: a "hypertenderness"—*Verzärtelung*—of taste[78] and *ennui*. In general, Kant advanced a dynamic law for the vital sensations: "The more receptive to impressions the vital sensation is (that is, the more delicate and sensitive), the more unhappy is the human being; the more receptive to the organic sensation . . . and, on the other hand, the more hardened he is toward the vital sensation, the more happy he is; I say happier, certainly not morally better, for he has the feeling of his own well-being more under control."[79] Those especially receptive to the vital sensations of beauty and disgust are thus specially menaced by unhappiness. This results in the rule of the most robust possible basic disposition of the inner sense of *Ekel*: aesthetic rejection of the "unwholesome," to be sure; but no "all-too disgusting taste."[80] Otherwise, the sensitive *Ekel*-sensorium might, in the end, even turn against metaphysics Kantian style,[81] or against virtue itself.[82]

Once again, the "lady"—*Frauenzimmer*—has it particularly difficult in searching for an appropriate meta-dietetic within the *Ekel*-dietetic. On the one hand, "women have a stronger inborn feeling for all that is beautiful, elegant, and ornamented. Even in childhood, they like to be dressed up, and take pleasure when they are adorned. They are clean and very delicate in respect to all that provokes disgust."[83] This tenderness of the disgust-sensation "can hardly be pushed too high by the fair sex," since, as Kant holds, that sex is particularly threatened by uncleanliness, hence by the danger of itself becoming an "object of *Ekel*."[84] And yet, in face of men, women are meant to give up this great "tenderness" of taste and abandon "delicate" distinctions by means of the disgust-sensation:

> Nature wants the woman to be sought after; therefore she does not have to be as delicate in her choice (in matters of taste) as the man, whom nature has built more coarsely, and who already pleases the woman if his physique shows that he has the strength and skill to protect her. If she were delicate *(ekel)* with respect to the beauty of his body, and fastidious in her choice, then she would have to do the courting in order to fall in love, while he would have to show himself unwilling. This would entirely degrade the dignity of her sex, even in the eyes of the man.[85]

The outcome here is a delicately problematic situation for the *Frauenzimmer*: if she is not "very tender" and *ekel vis-à-vis* herself, she becomes easily disgusting for the man; if, to the contrary, she is "*ekel* and fine in choice" *vis-à-vis* men, this "would entirely degrade the dignity of her sex," and she would likewise become an "object of *Ekel*." Thus ubiquitously encompassed by positions of disgust, the female sex has all prospects of confirming Kant's law of a proportional relation between vital sensation-sensitivity and the state of being unhappy. This correlation does not only lead to excessively tender taste, but also to a second *vitium* of the disgust-sensation: that general "disgust at one's own existence"—the *ennui* cited so often in the eighteenth century. In the work of the Schlegels, Winckelmann, Lessing, and Herder, such a bridge from *Ekel* to *ennui* is not yet apparent. Both Kant and Goethe establish it as one of the many filiations that do not at all, however, manage to bring disgust's highly diverse field into confluence with the field of *ennui*.

On the side of disgust, the bridge to *ennui* emerges through a special application of the inner disgust-sensation: not so much to the physical or aesthetic body or the morality of actions as to the entirety of one's own social "existence." *Ennui* here appears as a special sort of satiatory disgust: a sort in which the "satiety" does not involve a "gorging with consumption," but with emptiness, or meaningless repetition[86]—a tormenting, pressing absence of invigorating movement of the feelings: "A *disgust* at one's own existence emerges from the mind's emptiness of any sensations toward which it continually strives, and hence from *boredom*. This type of disgust simultaneously involves a powerful tendency towards inertia, i.e., a satiety with any occupation that could be called work, and that could drive away such disgust because it is associated with hardship. Disgust at one's own existence is a highly unpleasant feeling."[87] With particular forcefulness, Goethe describes this "so often elaborated matter"[88] as a kind of satiatory disgust:

> The more open we are for these enjoyments, the happier we feel; but if the variability of these phenomena ebbs and flows before us without our participation, if we are unreceptive to such pleasing offerings: than the greatest evil sets in, the worst sort of sickness, we think of life as a disgusting burden. We are told of an Englishman that he hanged himself in order to avoid having to clothe and unclothe daily. I knew a hearty gardener, responsible for spacious park-grounds, who once cried out unhappily: am I to then always see these rain-clouds pass from the west to the east? Concerning one of our most excellent men, we are told that he unhappily observed spring's reemerging greenery and wished that it would once appear in red for the sake of change. These are actually the symptoms of a satiety at life that not rarely culminates with suicide, and that has been more frequent among thoughtful, introverted men than we might think.[89]

The inverted proportionality of openness for "enjoyments"—as the "actual mainspring of earthly life"—and the proneness to *ennui* corresponds to the Kantian law of the inverse effect of organic sensation- and vital sensation-sensitivity on the feeling of happiness and unhappiness. Goethe also recommends the same antidote for ennui as Kant: work. "Nothing is more miserable than the comfortable man without work, the most beautiful of gifts becomes *eckel* to him. The difficulty of setting earthly machines in motion, and keeping them so."[90]

The recipe of work and enjoyment as antidotes to a disgust-prone taste of one's own existence does not turn the reformulation of ennui as a kind of disgust into an original contribution to the "so often elaborated matter" of "emptiness" and "boredom." It does, however, once more reveal disgust as an unheard-of multiple talent—a conceptual chameleon or ideal shifter. There is hardly one set of problems to which it does not offer *both* possible solutions and intensifications of the evil; and this often enough in an amalgamation whose elements are hard to isolate. *Ekel* ties false humor with fatty dishes, often-repeated whims with excrement, disgusting diseases with sweets, hazel hen with Heidegger, the "face of old women" with self-praise:

> False humor is disgusting, along with often-repeated quips, boring narration, self-praise. In dishes excess. very sweet or fat. repeatedly one kind of hazel hen. The disgusting face of old women. Heidegger. Particularly the rotten and excremental of animal bodies in general. Disgusting diseases.[91]

This panorama is by no means complete. The things to be avoided or vomited return as an organon of avoidance: nothing protects better than *Ekel* against *Ekel,* nothing better than the subject's vital disgust-sensation against the disgusting object. Through disgust, all kinds of nourishment and possibilities for action undergo an aesthetic test of wholesomeness. Its judgment is at once a first and last instance; it knows of no appeal, is executed ipso facto, and does not rest on principles simply adoptable from other fields of "world wisdom." Rather, disgust judges according to its own binary code, thus supplementing foundational and motivational deficits of theoretical and practical philosophy. While Kant reduces the inner-aesthetic differentiation of *Ekel* to several basic lines, he multiplies *Ekel's* functions beyond the narrow confines of philosophical aesthetics, disgust thus circulating as a magic token—a powerful operator of differentiation, decisive action, and aesthetic-dietetic grounding—through all philosophical disciplines. Just as, body part by body part, the beautiful luminous figure of the classical statue rests on the most sensitive registering and avoidance of possible disgust-values, disgust remains inscribed in the enlightening labor of critical philosophy, in the double role of taboo and organon.

4

Poetry of Putrefaction

"Beautiful Disgust" and the Pathology of the "Romantic"

The birth of aesthetics and the ideal of the beautiful body generates a network of intersections and common features whose field is negatively demarcated through the rules of disgust-avoidance. The mutual interference of these elements can be dated, at the most, to the period between 1740 and 1790, with the greatest density lying in the 1760s and 1770s. From its onset, this configuration—the opening of an aesthetic experience without closure, on the basis of the closing of corporeal openings—was riddled with instabilities and incongruences. The starting point for Baumgarten's inauguration of the new discipline of aesthetics is not sculpture or painting but literature. And it is precisely literature that, for Lessing and Herder, is granted the widest space for maneuver *vis-à-vis* the sculptural "law of beauty" and with it the rules of disgust-avoidance. Kant's *Critique of Judgment*, too, displays tensions between the structure defining "purely" aesthetic experience and the classical ideal of the beautiful body. On the one hand, for Kant the human body remains the "ideal of the beautiful"; on the other hand, he enthrones literature as the highest form of all the "beautiful arts." The fact that Kant, once again, underscores the demarcating validity of the disgust-taboo for *all* the arts cannot check the subsequent dissociation undergone by this cornerstone of aesthetic theory.

CLASSICAL DISGUST AND THE BASIC ALTERATIONS OF THE AESTHETIC FIELD AROUND 1800

In Romantic aesthetics, the classically beautiful body of sculpture not only surrenders its leading role to the other arts; at the same time, it can no longer maintain its power via the bridge of *ut pictura poesis*. Music becomes the new ideal of the "poetic," thus also serving as a fantasma of literature itself. The triumph of music shatters the framework of the "classical" *Ekel*-debate, since until then it had not been decided whether music could produce any sensation of disgust at all. Mendelssohn had in any event suggested that in the auditory realm "an uninterrupted sequence of perfect consonances" could produce an analogy to taste's disgust at excessive sweetness.[1] But in view of the "all-too little clarified rules of tonal art," he had immediately abandoned any additional arguments. Lessing, Herder, Winckelmann, Kant, and Goethe do not even consider auditory disgust as a vague possibility. Kolnai states categorically: "the idea of a disgust from hearing is completely unrealizable, if we disregard more or less subtle exceptions. . . . In the realm of hearing, we would search in vain for half-way equivalent parallels to a foul odor, a body flabby to the touch, a corpse slit open."[2] Consequently, with just that art possessing the weakest link to the disgust-sensation coming to dominate the post-1800 stage of aesthetic reflection, the older disgust-taboo loses a considerable amount of its powers of distinction.

In its temporary (pseudo)stability, the aggregate of aesthetic experience and unblemished body was not menaced by upheavals in the hierarchy of the arts alone. A fundamental demand placed on aesthetic production itself served as a powerful source for reconsidering the disgusting: the demand to be ever new and different. It derived from the two concomitant requirements that aesthetic pleasure be exclusively self-referential and solely aesthetic; and that its appeal no longer be based in any conformity to preexistent poetic rules. Given these basic assumptions of aesthetic theory, the thrill of the artwork could only spring from an incessant striving for otherness—from the incommensurable novelty distinguishing the creation of "genius." For obvious reasons, all determinate rules for an ideal of the beautiful are ultimately at odds with the internal dynamic of a system of art favoring a relentless promotion of difference. Following 1780, this soon led to a devaluation of the classically beautiful. Cast in the light of the need for novelty, the two disgust-avoidance massifs—the inner structure of aesthetic experience and the beauty-ideal of the unblemished body—split asunder. For the inner dynamic of aesthetic innovation, nothing would thus suggest itself more strongly, and prove more productive, than an increasingly radical distancing from the "softly blown corporeal." Stamped with the seal of the "interesting," a poetics of defiguration, the grotesque, and ironic disruption banished the ideally beautiful body of disgust's avoidance to the prehistory of modern taste. In line with this development, the disgusting was expressly licensed and incorporated into art. Inversely, classical sculpture could take on the role of just those disgusting entities it had been meant to exclude: "Our museums are filling up," complained Nietzsche; "I always feel *Ekel* when I see pure naked figures in the Greek style."[3]

After 1790, as the early Romantics as well as Schelling and Hegel transform aesthetics into an "objective" philosophy of art, the subjective sensations of pleasure and displeasure largely lose their distinctive value for reflecting about the beautiful and its antipodes. Within the field of an absolutized aesthetic reflection, there are no longer any references to the metaphors of the disgust-sensations smell and taste—or in fact to any anthropology of the (lower) senses. Where beauty no longer figures primarily as a correlate to the feeling of pleasure—rather serving as an objective manifestation of the Idea, as the "absolute," and so forth—disgust, that maximal feeling of displeasure, loses its transcendental value as the very exorbitance of the aesthetic. Hermeneutics and dialectics contribute their share to an immanent embrace of the disgusting. Hermeneutic understanding is sparked precisely by what is strange and other, being aimed in general at a totalizing integration instead of an evaluative purification and exclusion. Dialectical aesthetics is akin to hermeneutic understanding in that it does not want to leave the negative simply as negative, but strives to integrate the negative into the positive's own movement. For this reason, the elementary biological phenomenon of excretion, seen as an "abstract rejection of oneself from oneself" *["abstraktes Abstoßen seiner von sich selbst"]*, poses a philosophical challenge for Hegel. From the perspective of an integral economy, he defines an organism's "being disgusted with itself" in "separating itself from itself" as a lack of "confidence." The common view of excretion—"as if only the useless and unusable were to be eliminated"—does not at all convince Hegel: "The animal does not need to take in anything useless or unusable."[4] For Hegel, that which has been "eliminated" essentially consists of one's own digestive substance, instead of strictly unassimilable material; and beyond this: "It is the same particles from which animal organs are constituted." In the end, excretion no longer appears as a lack of confidence in complete assimilation—the definition of disgust from the perspective of optimistic dialectics—but as a special self-relation, "as the organism's own process." Karl Rosenkranz drew his lessons from this, seeking to avoid the production of pure waste within aesthetics. His work expressly aims at "integration."[5] The ugly and, to a certain degree, the disgusting are to be salvaged for the immanent economy of beauty's self-realization.

The Disgusting as Stimulus-Increase and Recipe of Modern "Shock"-Aesthetics

In a complex manner, the boundaries of both the aesthetic and the disgusting are thus being redefined and rendered porous. The differentiating power of *Ekel* is transferred into the internal aesthetic system: it no longer designates the unique and transcendental border phenomenon founding and disrupting the aesthetic, but comes to articulate a variety of diverse, local phenomena and effects within the confines of "romantic" literature and "idealist" aesthetics. At the end of the eighteenth century, *Ekel* comes to function above all as a key category in diagnosing the contemporary historical situation. Oscillating in a variety of ways between description and judgment, insight and polemics, *Ekel* delineates the condition of modern "taste" and the modern soul. Apparently, Friedrich Schlegel was the first to designate the disgusting as a signature of contemporary taste. To a certain extent, his early text "On the Study of Greek Poetry" (1795) still defines the disgusting from a classically negative perspective. Compared to the Greeks' "natural history of taste," modern disorientation and the increasing subjectivity of the arts generally appear as a "crisis," and the disgusting as "dying taste's last convulsion." Schlegel views the trend toward the disgusting as the inevitable "catastrophe" of the very modern system of art whose unremittingly self-referential striving for the otherness of "genius" consumes all the "old stimuli," thus moving compulsively forward to "ever more extreme and intense stimuli." "If the tendency . . . is toward aesthetic energy," Schlegel explains, "then taste, which has become increasingly used to the old stimuli, will only desire ever more extreme and intense stimuli." The trajectory of a taste unrestrained by normative rules leads "quickly enough" from the "piquant" and the "astounding" to the "shocking":

> The *piquant* is that which frantically stimulates a sensibility grown dull; the *astounding* is a similar goad for the imagination. They are the harbingers of impending death. The *insipid* is the thin nourishment of the fainting taste and the *shocking*, whether adventurous, disgusting, or horrible, the last convulsion of the taste that is dying.[6]

Probably for the first time, the disgusting here is explicitly labeled as part of a modern aesthetics of shock, and as the nearly unavoidable vanishing point—the negative eschaton—of an accelerated stimulus-drain within the modern system of art. Sixty years later, Karl Rosenkranz will confirm Schlegel's insight: the "most extreme" stimuli are "not infrequently also the most disgusting."[7] Schlegel himself only diagnoses this taediotropic "tendency" of a self-corroding art in order to hope for another "catastrophe" from the moderns: namely, "to forcefully gather their strength," and turn to a new "objectivity" of beauty, rather than "exhausting" themselves through embracing "the most extreme affects"—in the end "succumbing" to a perilous trend to self-corrosion. In this manner, while the disgusting remains the extreme countervalue to the objectively beautiful, it is no longer excluded from the realm of art due to a timeless anthropology of the lower senses. Rather, it now designates the most inherent inclination of modern taste, and the inner temporalization of the modern art-system. The sharp distinction, characteristic of classical aesthetics, between the disgusting and all other "unpleasant sensations" thus falls by the wayside. Instead, the disgusting emerges as one, albeit maximal evil among the many evils of modern taste. Once the positions within the aesthetic field have been redistributed in this way, it is only a short step to an egalitarian admittance of the disgusting. As soon as the power and relevance of the Classical ideal of beauty fades—as soon as the critical recognition of art's inherent tendency to *Ekel* becomes an acknowledgment of this tendency—an indisputable conclusion emerges for the Friedrich Schlegel of the "Athenäum-Fragments" (1798):

> If one writes or reads novels out of psychological interest, then it is very inconsistent and petty to want to shy away from even the slowest and most detailed dissection of unnatural pleasures, horrendous tortures, outrageous infamy, disgusting sensual or intellectual impotence.[8]

Even here, Schlegel maintains a final reservation: the prohibitions only become invalid when novels are not written out of pure artistic but "out of psychological interest." With the emergence of the modern novel, however, precisely this boundary has begun to fluctuate. Schlegel's stress would thus seem to lie not so much on a normative delimitation of various attitudes towards art as on a historical diagnosis: the modern incorporation of the disgusting into the realm of art is *also* the effect of coupling the aesthetic, and primarily literature, with the modern science of psychology (and later psychoanalysis).

THE LICENSE OF "DISGUSTING IMPOTENCE" AND THE DECAY OF THE NEGATIVE PRINCIPLE

Schlegel's 124th "Athenäum"-Fragment more or less defines the field of what later would be called "dark romanticism":[9] "the slowest and most detailed dissection of unnatural pleasures, horrendous tortures, outrageous infamy, disgusting sensual or intellectual impotence." The arrangement of the predicates leaves no room for doubt: the disgusting in no way encompasses this entire list, but rather a highly specific group of phenomena. Why, then, "disgusting sensual or intellectual impotence?" Why does the predicate "disgusting" not extend, as well, to the "unnatural pleasures," "horrendous tortures," and "outrageous infamy?" From a literary-historical vantage, this question can also be put in the following manner: why do the works written by the Marquis de Sade in the 1790s not figure as cardinal ciphers of disgust (regardless of the fact that Friedrich Schlegel did not know them)? After all, Sade's œuvre can hardly be overtrumped in its dissection of "unnatural pleasures," "horrendous tortures," "outrageous infamy"; Sade might have invented the categories of the "shocking" and "ever more extreme and intense stimuli," and his œuvre leaves little to desire when it comes to flaying the "softly blown corporeal." Why is the disgust-sensation nevertheless not the preeminent aspirant for an aesthetic classification of "sadistic" deeds? And what does "impotence" signify in connection with the romantic category of the disgusting?

The answer to these questions shows, above all, how inadequate—indeed impossible—a motif-centered history of the disgusting-corporeal is. The founding theorists of the disgusting, in the forefront Lessing, observed just that. In themselves, bloody entrails may be disgusting; but when the context is the flaying of Marsyas by Apollo, they serve an aesthetic of the "monstrous" rather than the disgusting. Disgust at stench, excessive sweetness, all-too soft and sticky, disfigurement, and rot may indeed be allied with angst; but it implies only a diffuse quality of violence, rather than an active, directed violence on the part of the object of disgust. To this extent, intentional acts of violence like murder, violation, and torture slip outside the register of the disgusting and are generally linked with other repudiating predications: horrible, detestable, monstrous, and so forth. Hence Schlegel's talk of "horrendous" rather than disgusting tortures.[10] Analogously, when considered in relation to the spectrum of Schlegel's predicates, the torments, flayings, and repeated murders in Sade's work are more prone to classification as horrible, detestable, or opprobrious than as disgusting.

De Sade's characters are excellent ideologues, competent directors, and potent executors of their dreadful deeds; they thus need not fear the reproach of "disgusting sensual and intellectual impotence." For Freud, as well, "perverse" sexual practices are not so much disgusting in themselves as manifestations of an all-too successful conquest of the disgusting.[11] From this perspective, De Sade's novels are narrations, not of the disgusting, but of the end of disgust: the complete—Bataille would say: "sovereign"—annulment of cultural disgust-barriers. To be sure, upon second reflection this overcoming of disgust can itself be experienced as disgusting. But such a disgust-judgment does not regard the pleasure-murder, coprophagy, sodomy, or any other physical act *as such*. Rather, it regards the annulment—more precisely: the intentional annulment, reflectively celebrated by protagonist and narrating voice—of all "morally" and intellectually grounded inhibitions on performing (forbidden) violent and disgusting deeds. Sade's characters can only be related to Schlegel's license of a "disgusting sensual and intellectual impotence" in this special sense (i.e., a complete, explicit, and affirmative invalidation of distinctions normally made by both the ego and the superego). Although they certainly violate all the rules for the unblemished body, their acts rather correspond to the licenses, distinguished from these rules, of "unnatural pleasures," "horrendous tortures," and "outrageous infamy." In addition, they are not orchestrated with great eruptions on the scale of the soul's sensations, or aesthetically embellished, but depicted soberly, indeed mechanically, as skilled orgasm-production.

In Karl Rosenkranz's *Aesthetics of the Ugly*, the terms "impotent," "diabolic," and "beautiful disgust" merge into an eloquent critique of decadence.

This critique addresses precisely the phenomenal realm made accessible to art by Schlegel "out of psychological interest." In full agreement with Schiller's legitimation of the grand criminals, Rosenkranz acknowledges "a certain naive healthiness of the negative principle" among active villains in the mold of Judas, Richard III, Vautrin, and Franz Moor. In contrast, he denounces another type of romantic diabolicism as a disgusting "weakness" on the part of a civilization greeting its own "decay"—or, more precisely, embracing "putrefaction":

> A certain naive healthiness of the negative principle is still to be found in those active villains, but in these contemplative devils [such as Roquairol and Manfred] the sophistic play of a rotten, hollow irony transforms evil into a hideous putrefaction. Out of the man of today—restlessly exhausted, pleasure-craving yet impotent, bored out of satiation, genteelly cynical, futilely educated, ready to submit to every weakness, thoughtlessly depraved, flirting with pain—an ideal of satanic pretense has now developed. In the novels of the English, French, and German authors, this ideal appears on the scene with a pretense to nobility, these heroes customarily traveling a great deal, eating and drinking well, having the finest grooming, smelling of patchouli, and possessing elegant, sophisticated manners. But this noblesse is nothing more than the anthropological appearance of the satanic principle in its latest form.[12]

According to Rosenkranz, then, specifically Romantic villains are disgusting revenants of the great criminals, their impotence being both reflective and provocatively intentional. The "healthy" satanism of formal freedom and deliberate atrocity is here compromised by a "satanic indulgence in (decadent) beauty." "Submitting to every weakness," such satanism renders an object of refined pleasure out of its own inability to realize a "classical" form in character and deed. The description of this "satanic pretense" evokes both the quantitative *Ekel*-paradigm of satiation (boredom from surfeit, disgustingly refined manners in dress, food, and the application of fragrance) as well as the qualitatively disgusting paradigm of deformation ("hideous decay" of the principle of evil itself). "Beautiful disgust" is the paradoxical formula for an epidemic illness inflicted on the good old devil: for the particular "indulgence" in one's own depravity that, as "aesthetic satanism," lays claim to the locus of the Romantically beautiful, since it offers the stimulation most suited to the age.[13] The disgusting that appears as a "decadent," yet all the more contemporary beauty, the decaying yet perfumed and sophisticatedly elegant corpse of the devil: these are the figures transforming the transcendental incompatibility of the beautiful and the disgusting into a "perverse" identity.

Disgusting Souls, Disgusting Times, and the Art of the Disgusting: The "Romantic" Ubiquity of the Once-Tabood

Whether the "slowest and most detailed analysis . . . of disgusting intellectual or sensual impotence" is admitted, with Schlegel, as an integral moment in modern "universal poetry,"[14] or rejected, with Rosenkranz, as the "pleasure-craving yet impotent" abandonment of the disgusting to its own 'sick' beauty:—under the banner of the "Romantic," *Ekel* has clearly and irrefutably stepped onto the aesthetic stage. Instead of making the aesthetic possible through being categorical excluded from it, the disgusting is always already there. Art has now undeniably and provocatively come to incorporate that upon which it presumably would "fruitlessly expend all its labor": it has grasped the disgusting as one of those "ever more extreme and intense stimuli" needed as a result of art's own logic. Even Rosenkranz acknowledges that the disgusting is *up-to-date*, when he links its Romantic literary form to the "man of today," "futilely educated, ready to submit to every weakness, thoughtlessly depraved, flirting with pain." A double transformation of the disgusting forms an integral part of what is called "Romantic": the extra-aesthetic category becomes a disputed locus in the field of the aesthetic itself; and it gains, in addition, a dimension of psychohistorical diagnosis entirely alien to the earlier system. Even when the disgusting is condemned as a decadent phenomenon, it still is presented as an adequate cipher for the actual status of human passions and human history—a history "that is afraid of the possibility of an authentic history."

Three years after Rosenkranz,[15] Baudelaire presents a similar diagnosis to himself and his "likeness" *(mon semblable)*, the reader of the "Flowers of Evil."[16] In the introductory poem "To the Reader," "our soul" appears as the playground for disgusting vices and pleasures. After feeble attacks of regret and "fatly"— *grassement*—paid confessions, "we return cheerfully to the muddy path." Indeed, we even "feed our dear pangs of remorse/like beggars nourish their vermin," thereby instituting a new parasitism of the disgusting in and on itself, a closed circle of self-perpetuating *Ekel*. In diagnosing the "lure" *(appas)* of the repulsive as common denominator for both author and reader, Baudelaire simultaneously designates it as the staging ground for his literary work. Neither "a million helminths," nor the lascivious impotence that "kisses and eats the martyrized breast of an ancient whore" are absent from Baudelaire's clinical diagnosis of his age. The contemporary observer not only exposes himself "without horror" to the most "repugnant objects," but also manages the feat of their direct libidinal (counter)cathexis: the creation of an affirmative aesthetics of the disgusting whose appetite can only be spoiled through boredom *(ennui)*.

Long before Baudelaire and Rosenkranz, the proto-Romanticist Ludwig Tieck had equated the terms "romantic," "disgusting," and "putrefaction." Tieck's early novel *William Lovell* (begun in 1792; published 1795–96) certainly earns a place of honor in Rosenkranz's paradigm of an aesthetic-satanic "sickening" of the negative principle. In contrast, late Tieck criticizes the "romantic" transformation of the satanic as a self-destructive propensity of freedom. His verdict concerning the "desire to destroy oneself," and to simultaneously enjoy this destruction as an enthused "transport," nevertheless acknowledges the death-drive as something "necessary to the existence of us all"—as an "eternal riddle" and a "mystery." In the very moment of their rejection, the "abominable beings" who have "voluntarily" embarked on the road of aesthetic satanism thus experience a certain ennoblement, inherent in a "mysterious" longing of the soul itself:

> Since time immemorial, it has been the case that in the highest and most tender creatures, a germ often develops that is necessary to the existence of us all, the germ of a desire to destroy oneself, to step outside the holy, voluptuous, blissful bounds within which alone our freedom is possible, and to exchange this genuinely beatifying freedom, in which all our powers spread their wings, for senseless caprice, hollow absoluteness, slavish boundlessness. Even in men who are blessed, a transport of rapture flashes within the joy of cognition itself; how it happens that the soul so often then voluntarily plunges from enthusiasm to passion, is an eternal riddle and eternal mystery. Now the intellect speeds forward, as if in spite of itself, along the fiery path, scorns the light as ineffectual, and sinks and deepens into what is most offensive to its nature, now believing it has found its most characteristic quality in the wild, rough, and injudicious. Now it lives in lies and untruth, sinning against beauty and holiness as if these were the lies. From excessive transport of freedom, the intellect must now become a slave of ugliness, and the tighter the chains that bind it, the more it boasts, scornfully laughing, about its boundlessness.[17]

In the very same *Old Book* of 1835, Tieck uses the predestined cipher of *Ekel* to denote this "sinking and deepening" into "what is most offensive," furnishing the "eternal" tendency toward an exchange of "false" for "true" freedom a contemporary signature. In an extended literary and political reflection, the late Tieck here attempts to shift the Romantic explosion of the disgusting above all to France, and to limit German "complicity" to a misunderstanding of E. T. A. Hoffmann. Tieck thus arrives at a canonical equation of "romantic," "disgusting," and "putrefaction":

> Romantic school! That is a word, ambiguous, incomprehensible, and on occasion stupid. In Brandenburg, my homeland, *manschen* or *mantschen* means to throw together and mix something unpleasant and disgusting, as for instance when handling the blood of a slaughtered animal, thus making common cause with what belongs to putrefaction. . . . Oh, you gentle spirits and delicate poems of Gottfried of Strassburg, you holy Parcifal, you mystic Titurel, you noble, spiritual, witty Ariosto, you gloriously temperate Tasso, you shining Camoens, you Cervantes, roguishly smiling in the company of all the muses, you Calderon, grasping a bouquet of dark, purple flowers, singular W. Shakespeare before whom the muses and Apollo himself bow, you German Goethe, who as a shining heavenly body guides the sun's path to eternal spring—you Romantics, you genuine Romantics are thus the models and inspiring examples for the shameless who sing of vice, putrefaction, monstrosity, and the works of darkness, and who stamp like Victor Hugo on everything noble, revel in the decay of vice, and [are] drunk on the disgusting. Is it possible, then, that you, the better ones, Balzac, Nodier, and few others, follow this sick desire?[18]

Hence it is no longer the classical distinctions of aesthetic and transaesthetic, art and the impossibility of artistic illusion that is at stake in the disgusting; rather, the focus is now on two different sorts of "romantic" literature. One aspect of the category's new literary-political immanence is the fact that "healthy" Romanticism in no way simply locates its field outside the disgusting. Instead, it acknowledges the contemporary nature of the disgusting, and even the metapsychological universality of a pleasure at one's own putrefaction. But at the same time, it lays claim to a resistance against an unbroken "satanic indulgence in (decadent) beauty" in complicity with such a power. Consistently, this resistance to disgust *within* the field of disgust presents itself as a conservative allegiance to a "true" Romanticism, itself bound to the classical laws of beauty. The classical rule of exclusion thus returns as an internal differentiation within Romanticism; and the rule maintains intimate contact with art's historical development precisely through this metamorphosis. After 1800, direct repeats of the old disgust-taboo are only possible with complete absence of such historical contact—as for instance in paragraph 40 of Schopenhauer's *World as Will and Idea* (1818). More rigorously than anyone since Kant, Schopenhauer banishes everything "stimulating" from the "realm of art," as it "excites the will." Even more than the "stimulating quality in naked figures," sparking "lustfulness," the disgusting "instantly annuls purely aesthetic contemplation":

> There is also something negatively stimulating that is even more objectionable than the . . . positively stimulating: and this is the dis-

gusting. Just like the stimulating in the proper sense, it awakens the beholder's will, thus destroying the purely aesthetic contemplation. But what is sparked through it is a violent unwillingness, an aversion: it awakens the will in presenting it with objects of its abomination. For this reason, it has always been recognized that it has no place whatsoever in art, while even the ugly, as long as it is not disgusting, can be accepted in the right place.[19]

In the context of their time, Schopenhauer's observations fall short of offering a rule for the transcendental constitution of the aesthetic; instead, they secretly become an allegorical application of the formulas they repeat as citations: a vehicle for empirical and literary-critical resistance to the Romantically "stimulating." With the major exception of the 124th "Athenäums-fragment," where the "disgusting" figures as a purely descriptive category without being promptly evaluated through the same rejection it defines, between 1795 to approximately 1860, the explicit thematic treatment of the disgusting suffers from a normative distaste for its subject: a distaste stamped by fidelity to the classical-aesthetic. A redistribution of the classical positions of disgust and beauty within the field of the "Romantic" is merely diagnosed, in order to be placed straightaway on the aesthetic criminal index: as an artistic sickness, and a sign of inadequate resistance to both the disgusting frailties of the human soul and the historical syndrome of decadence. An aggressive and affirmative aesthetics of the disgusting—one relating positively to its object—can hardly be found. For the most part, the new aesthetics of the disgusting remains trapped within a disgust at disgust; it only unwillingly acknowledges the powerful appeal of what, at the same time, evokes the strongest rejection.

Rosenkranz on the Disgusting (1): Putrefaction as an "Inverse Becoming of the Already Dead"

Albeit intent on "integrating" all forms of aesthetic negativity, Karl Rosenkranz's *Ästhetik des Häßlichen* itself remains thoroughly caught up in such an ambivalence. From the very beginning, the work makes manifest an idealistic presupposition to conceive of the desired integration exclusively as an integration into the beautiful—which is to say: into the only positive element in the aesthetic system. Rosenkranz's broad knowledge of his subject and obvious enthusiasm for it nonetheless offered him space for numerous observations not altogether fitting into beauty's dialectic success-story. His chapter on "The Disgusting" merits closer attention if only for the simple reason that it is the first cohesive (if only eleven-page) treatment of the topic since J. A. Schlegel's mini-essays in footnote form and Mendelssohn's four-page letter (i.e., in around a hundred years). In the pertinent chapter of Rosenkranz's study, the concepts and theses marking the earlier debate have almost completely vanished from the scene. No trace is to be found of the distinction between pleasure and displeasure and their mixing; the theory of a disgust from a "mere idea"; the indifference toward the nature-art distinction and the model of illusion connected to it; the hyperreality of the disgusting. It is true that the examples of Philoctetes' wound and Lazarus's putrefying stench point back to Lessing's famous *Laocoön*. Yet beyond this, there are no indications of Rosenkranz even being aware of the other contributions to the debate on *Ekel*, from J. A. Schlegel down to Kant. His commentary on the disgusting is not steered by excessive sweetness and satiation, or excessive softness, or vomit, but simply—putrefaction. Mendelssohn's and Kant's reflections on disgust did not address putrefaction at all. In Rosenkranz, however, it gains far-reaching significance as a key symptom of modern life and Romantic art. It becomes both the literal and metaphorical determinant of the disgusting:

> The disgusting is the outer aspect of [the hideous], the negation of the appearance's beautiful form through a non-form arising from physical or moral decay. According to the old rule *a potiori fit denominatio*, we call all the lower reaches of the unpleasant and base disgusting because everything that offends our aesthetic feelings through the dissolution of form fills us with disgust. But for the notion of the disgusting in the narrower sense we have to add the criterion of putrefaction, because it contains the process of death *[Werden des Todes]* that is not merely a withering and dying, but rather an inverse becoming, an emergence of life out of what is already dead *[Entwerden des schon Todten]*. The appearance of life in what is in itself dead is the infinitely revolting within the disgusting.[20]

Remarkably enough, this Hegelian definition of the disgusting apes, in a new way, that of the beautiful itself. Drawing on the model of Pygmalion's statue, Lessing and others characterized aesthetic illusion by a deceptive aliveness; on the other hand, "the appearance of life" is now meant to constitute "the infinitely revolting within the disgusting." The disgusting thus appears as a particular, self-destroying instance of aesthetic illusion: where "the semblance of life" is not derived from the stone, the image, or the linguistic sign, rather making itself manifest in something "in itself dead," then, as Kolnai analogously indicates, we are dealing with a repulsive sort of life "in the wrong place."[21] Yet even this distinction does not manage to establish any firm borders. For the medium of aesthetic illusion is itself often enough described as "in itself dead," as dead stone or letters. Rosenkranz only avoids unwillingly conflating the "infinitely revolting" with the classical model of beautiful illusion through an additional determination of putrefaction. In order to be disgusting, the medium of illusory life must itself be an organic material, or at least an "analogy" of the organic:

The disgusting as a product of nature—sweat, slime, filth, sores, etc.—is something dead that the organism expels from itself, thus delivering it to putrefaction. Non-organic nature can itself be relatively disgusting, but only relatively, namely in analogy or linkage with the organic. But in itself the concept of putrefaction cannot be applied to it, and for this reason it is thoroughly impossible to designate stones, metals, soils, salts, water, clouds, gases, colors as disgusting.[22]

It needs not be decided here whether bodily excretions are in general "something dead" and categorically merit the predicate "disgusting," and whether, inversely, gases or colors are in fact incapable of "thoroughly" generating disgust. One thing is clear: Rosenkranz needs the opposition organic versus nonorganic. It is not at all clear, however, what his nature-philosophical opposition is meant to achieve in the context of a theory of art in which sweat and slime seem as marginal as metals and salts. Even the differential gain *vis-à-vis* the model of a *beautiful* "semblance of life" remains in need of explanation. For to the extent that the beautiful appears as living, while life is understood as a counter-concept to the mechanical, organism-metaphors occasionally intrude into the description of the aesthetic phenomenon; Herder even referred to the "flesh" of statues.[23] As only Rosenkranz' examples make clear, one important purpose of the organic versus nonorganic distinction is to tie the field of excrement and putrefaction to the dialectical process inherent in the unfolding of his concept of freedom. For starting no later than the Romantic debate over mechanism and organism, organic life was viewed as a form that bypassed the strict determinism of cause and effect, allowing space for nonderivable and unpredictable developments, or philosophically speaking: for freedom. As will become clear below, a "false" life or disgusting "sickness" of freedom is not least of what is at stake in nature's putrefaction. Mary Shelley's *Frankenstein* transformed this linkage into a canonical plot: the novel's titular Promethean scientist studies putrefaction and worm-devoured bodies in order to gain new life and "beauty" from them. He spends "days and nights in vaults and charnel-houses," acquiring the "materials" for his "creation" in "the dissecting rooms and the slaughter-house." At the very instance of his animation, the resulting hybrid creature instills "disgust" in his creator: this despite the creature's "limbs in proportion" and "beautiful features." Here as well, "disgust" marks a moment of "false life"—and this life is itself tied to a "sick" freedom.[24]

In the negative sense of avoiding violations of the skin's beautiful surface, classical aesthetics directs its attention primarily toward the orifices, only occasionally toward their excretions. In the latter regard, Achlys' snot is the only pertinent example. In contrast, Rosenkranz glosses—without any rules for the excretory organs—the excretory material itself. He feels no aesthetic pain at the "dying and withering" of the living—for the German Classicists, a threat to the normative "eternal youth." Rather, he invokes the *inverse withering*—the repellent reblooming, as putrefaction, of what is already dead—as the great danger represented by the disgusting, ascribing it not so much to the corpse as to excrement. In this manner, for Rosenkranz excrement becomes the master trope not only of decadent Romantic literature, but also of contemporary culture in general. For its part, as "an inverse becoming of what is already dead," putrefaction emerges as something other than the continuance of dying and passing away. Instead, it is a perverse reversal, a rendering inside out, a turn of and toward vomit within the temporality of life and death, a ghostly post-mortal life. With its various "scraps of cultural decay," the city—space of culture—provides the natural excretions with a "dreadful" intensification:

> If one could turn a big city like Paris upside down so that the lowest would rise to the surface and not only the sewer-filth, but also those animals that shy away from the light, the mice, rats, toads, and worms living from putrefaction, would emerge, this would be a dreadfully disgusting picture.[25]

This image had already figured as a cardinal disgust-paradigm in the eighteenth century's discourse on public hygiene. It not only locates putrefaction in the cultural cipher par excellence, in Paris as capital of the nineteenth century. It acquires an even more striking power for both aesthetics and the critique of contemporary culture when read in terms of yet another reversal: not only as an image of the underbelly of culture, but also as an image of the above-ground state of civilization itself. The "ideal of satanic pretense" in contemporary art and reality, the deliberate reveling in "depravity" and "beautiful disgust," present the same image of "abominable putrefaction" on the street and in the drawing room: a radical decay striking "people of the present age" already in their living bodies. The ingredients of this "putrefaction" are not sewage, rats, and worms, but rather: pleasure-craving impotence, satiated boredom, refined cynicism, a brilliant impudence of the immoral, an abandonment to evil in the affirmation of aestheticized satanism. To repeat an observation of Rosenkranz: in the Romantic age, "putrefaction" has seized the "negative principle," robbing good, old evil of a "certain naive healthiness." Analogously, Tieck repeatedly employs "putrefaction" as a key signifier of a disgusting sickening of the "Romantic,"[26] and he, as well, describes the deliberate indulgence in "what is most offensive" as an unfettered disdain for "genuinely happy freedom," for the sake of "senseless caprice" and "nullifying absoluteness."[27]

BAUDELAIRE'S POEM *"UNE CHAROGNE"*

Just as in Rosenkranz's image of the big city, below-ground putrefaction is mirrored in above-ground putrefaction, in his famous *"Une Charogne"* ("A

Carcass")[28] Baudelaire splits an allegorical depiction of organic putrefaction into two analogous and complementary images. Yet instead of the double opposition of above-below and physical-moral, the analogies are here articulated by way of the double opposition anonymous animal-beloved human being and present-future. In the mode of memory, the first image unfolds, not below the city, but apparently before its gates:

> Rappelez-vous l'objet que nous vîmes, mon âme,
> Ce beau matin d'été si doux:
> Au détour d'un sentier une charogne infâme
> Sur un lit semé de cailloux,
>
> Les jambes en l'air, comme une femme lubrique,
> Brûlante et suant les poisons,
> Ouvrait d'une façon nonchalante et cynique
> Son ventre plein d'exhalaisons.

[Recall, my beloved, the object we saw on that summer morning, so sweet and beautiful: at the bend of a path, a vile carcass on a stone-strewn bed,

legs in the air like a lustful woman, scorching and sweating its poisons, offering, in nonchalant, cynical fashion, its belly full of exhalations.]

Perhaps Baudelaire's "so sweet and beautiful" summer morning not only offers a contrast to the disgusting scene, but also alludes to the disgust-paradigm of the *excessively sweet*. Be that as it may, on such a morning a couple out for a walk chances on an animal's rotting carcass, "at the bend of a path." The poem's locus of the disgusting is thus a locus of discontinuation, its time that of sudden confrontation. From the start, the putrefying body is depicted as a figure of sexual desire. It can only be called *infâme* (vile) because it still, in a way, lives and acts—because it submits and gives birth shamelessly and ardently (cf. *brûlante*—"scorching" or "burning"). Resembling a "lustful woman" with its spread-out legs and exposed belly, the carcass lies on a bed *semé de cailloux:* disseminated with pebbles as with male semen. Indeed, the entire organic mass is in a state of orgasmic movement, "sinking and rising," it reads in the next strophe, "like a wave." The maggots that gather in the carcass's swollen belly are depicted as a result of this sexual union—as the analagon of a pregnancy, or repellent life in something dead.[29] At the same time, moving beyond mere disgust at a hyperanimated mass of insects,[30] "black battalions of maggots" vary and intensify a disgust-paradigm prevailing throughout the poem: the paradigm of the *excessively fatty*. The maggots pour forth from a woman's exposed belly like an unctuously "thick liquid"; her "lubricious"—*lubrique*—lustfulness even opens up the series of the fatty. In the end, a third form of the disgustingly fatty, "fat flowers," will cover the grave of the beloved as she turns, in the imagination of the speaking "I," into food for worms.

The carrion's view is thus not merely voyeuristically depicted, but is also *staged* as a hybrid mix of sexual act and birth. As a "superb carcass," the putrefying body, far from marking the death of (male) desire, is itself that desire's object and trophy. The disfigured image of the female carrion also represents the "superb" beloved—if not, entirely, her convulsive sex—through an inversion of two stereotypical evocations of attractive femininity: the corporeality of the woman as flower is rendered into a flower of decay, and the irresistibility of this flower's scent becomes an intolerable stench. The blending together of carrion, flower, and lustful woman reveals Baudelaire's carrion as a figure, if not as *the* figure of the *fleurs maladives* furnishing the title *Les Fleurs du Mal*. The sun cooks the rot of this abject femininity "till done"—*à point*. In doing so, it intensifies both the stink and magnificent blossoms of rot and putrefaction to the peak of their unfolding. At the same time, the culinary metaphor points once more to the status of the flowery flesh as object of consumption and pleasure. The vapors of cooking and putrefaction emanating from this flowery flesh replace—indeed are themselves—the scent of blossoming. If there is one poet who knows how to evoke smells—hence the strongest disgust-sensations—with words, it is Baudelaire. Many of his poems in fact appear to have been "produced for smelling," thus undermining the formula through which Winckelmann designates the absence of the aesthetic.[31] Emerging now in *"Une charogne"* to accompany stench is the idea of an avid devouring of the cadaver: a carrion-loving bitch—specifically no male *chien*, but a female *chienne*—impatiently awaits its chance, with malevolent mien. At this point, the apostrophe intervenes, introducing the second putrefactive image. It is not just that only memory of the carrion remains from the sweet summer walk, but the lyric voice's accompanying beloved is also imagined prospectively as moldy food for worms:

> Et pourtant vous serez semblable à cette ordure,
>   A cette horrible infection,
> Étoile de mes yeux, soleil de ma nature,
>   Vous, mon ange et ma passion!

[And nevertheless, you will resemble this ordure, this horrible infection, star of my eyes, sun of my nature, you, my angel and my passion!]

The adversative "and nevertheless" here hangs oddly in the air. It evokes the supplementation of a thesis whose qualification or antithesis is articulated in what comes after. Something like the following might be extrapolated: "nothing, dear beloved, could resemble you less than this carrion in the most extreme state of lewd putrefaction." Just as the dedicatory poem in Baudelaire's collection, *Au Lecteur* ("To the Reader"), has embraced the reader as "my likeness"—*mon semblable*—on the basis of shared repellent vices, *"Une charogne"* performs a disgust-equation via the word *semblable*. This time, the beloved woman is apostrophized as lewd, putrefying old woman—beauty as the material for disgust. Even the sun, initially appearing present in the poem's first putrefactive image as part of the positive, scenic contrast to the unanticipated sight of the cadaver, falls victim to putrefaction. Proceeding, already in the first image, from merely illuminating the scene to serving as putrefactive agent and accomplice, the sun now becomes directly, by way of equation with the beloved, the body of putrefaction itself. Hence even light putrefies in this scenario of all-devouring, cannibalistic decomposition.[32] Above ground is thus revealed as no brighter than "beneath the grass and the fat flowers"—the second flowery disgust-figure, marking the grave where the "queen of graces" putrefies among her bones. The disgust-predicate "(too) fat" here also represents one more link to the soul's "fat"—*grasse*—payment for confession cited in *Au lecteur*. The semantic opposition as well as phonetic indiscernibility between *"grasses"* (fat) and *"graces"* even condenses the movement of the entire poem into a single pun.[33]

The address to the beloved closes with a request that she proffer her own words to the worms:

> Alors, ô ma beauté! dites à la vermine
> Qui vous mangera de baisers,
> Que j'ai gardé la forme et l'essence divine
> de mes amours décomposés!

[Then, oh my beauty! tell the worms devouring you with kisses that I preserved the form and divine essence of my decomposed stirs of love!]

Similar swings from drastic evocations of transiency to invocations of *constantia* are present in many Renaissance and Baroque poems of love and *tombeau*. But Baudelaire only cites this structure in order to dissimulate it in a sustained fashion. We find no trace of Baroque mourning at the loss of a blissful state of human grace. The carrion's depiction unmistakably emanates a libidinous obsession with the carrion; Baudelaire is here—and not only here—enthusiastically imagining coition as the metonomy of one cadaver and another cadaver ("as a cadaver stretched out along a cadaver").[34] Both from a metonymic and metaphoric vantage, the "sinuous folds of old capitals" and old women possessing virtually all of Horace's *vetula*-defects are reciprocal figurations; through one and the same credo, Baudelaire is irresistibly drawn to the charms of both "flabby monsters."[35]

Read precisely, the apparently edifying final lines of *"Une charogne"* likewise reveal neither the need nor the intent of offering a *consolatio*. The lyric voice's affection *vis-à-vis* the beautiful living beloved does not at all survive putrefaction; rather, it putrefies in its turn—in the plural *(mes amours décomposés)*, as it were piece by piece with each of the worm-devoured body parts. Hence the putrefaction of *amours* has arrived to accompany that of the sun and the beloved: a closed circle of putrefactive material. Elsewhere in Baudelaire's poems as well, "the image of multiplication through demonic vermin and decomposition" serves as a "central metaphor."[36] And yet, or precisely on that account, the poem ends with an affirmative gesture. What is preserved as the transcendental form and divine essence of the putrefied *amours* can hardly be considered a simple Platonism[37] or a transfiguration of the transient beauty of the body into the enduring beauty of poetry.[38] For in Baudelaire's poem, desire in no way experiences the putrefaction of the desired body and one's own putrefaction as simply a border and the other to itself, in order to then offer the "classical" metaphysical remedy of a time- and rot-resistant life beyond the grave or in the poem. Rather, from *itself* and *the very beginning*, desire aims, in scarcely hidden form, at precisely the imagination of the putrefying body as something excessively alive—if not as the cipher of sexuality itself.[39] Such a desire that obsessively plunges into putrefaction clearly does not need conventional reassurance of putrefaction's powerlessness, or of indifference *against* the evils of putrefaction. It is also by no means the lover who assures an enduring form beyond death for his putrefied *amours*. For as just one more of this taediophilic-moribund obsession, this lover simply imagines an erotic relation between his beloved and the worms that kiss her and devour her.[40] In its course, even in face of her new partners, the corpse itself is meant to assert—as prompted discourse—the fidelity of the former lover: to be sure, not a fidelity to the beloved herself, but only to the *form* of his decomposing *amours*. Baudelaire thus imagines a truly unusual funeral-oration: not held for and upon the putrefying corpse, but from her, addressed to her kissing-devouring worms and offering the sole consolation of the former lover's *constantia* sending his *amours* themselves ahead on the putrefactive path. The *amours*—and not simply their objects—thus become food for the worms; paradoxically enough, precisely in their own putrefaction, the same *amours* preserve the law of their being. The Baroque turn in the representation of transiency would promise an allegorical salvage of the repulsive proceedings; by contrast, Baudelaire's text, in the deferring repetition of the *constantia*-gesture, separates the more-than-subterranean pleasure taken in the disgusting itself from any hope—and, apparently, any need—for a transcendental redemption.

Nevertheless, Baudelaire does not here offer a depiction of the disgusting for its own sake, "true disgust" in the sense of eighteenth-century aesthetics. Just as his dedicatory *"Au Lecteur"* presents its flowers of evil and the disgusting as a contemporary syndrome of vices, many perspectives suggest a functional or allegorical reading of *"Une Charogne"*: as a powerful resource, typical of the times, for qualitative and quantitative stimulus intensification;[41] as a stylistic device for aesthetic satanism; as a *mise-en-abîme* of the juncture between *décomposition* and (poetic) *création*;[42] as an (ironic) self-exhibition of misogyny and sexual disgust; as an exposure of abysses of sexuality or dark areas of the human soul; as the negative medium of a metamorphosis, a "self-overcoming of the ugly"[43] demonstrating, precisely, the triumph of poetry—of representational beauty—over the vileness of what is represented. Obviously, Rosenkranz's theorem of a "putrefaction" of the "negative principle" does scant justice to the poem, which rather presents a putrefaction of the "positive principle" per se, namely love and sexual desire. Be this as it may: in the present context, a superficial reading suffices—one not delving closely into the functional and allegorical load of the disgusting. It is sufficient to establish a—manifestly doubled—relevance of putrefaction for a nineteenth-century disgust termed "romantic" in the widest sense: as an organic process, "putrefaction" is a(n) (ironic) figure of defiguration that, starting with the advent of Romanticism, is repeatedly used in the description of libidinous desire, vice, and the historical signature of the passions in general. This figure—and with it an explicit license to represent the disgusting—corresponds to the Romantic discovery of a formal self-irony in art: precisely by subjecting its own laws and taboos to continual de-figuration and decomposition, art paradigmatically achieves an ironic "self-creation" through "self-destruction."[44] If the skin-surface's uninterrupted line is the law of the beautiful body, then the anti-illusional disruption of the textual body of art is the schema of romantic irony; it here readily invokes the parekbasis of Aristophanian comedy.[45] Disrupting the very form of aesthetic illusion, the disgusting is a powerful intermitting agent. To this extent, it promotes the Romantic art work's formal tendency toward self-irony, although (or precisely because) the disgust-reaction proper leaves no room for ironic reflection, but rather disrupts any reflective maneuvering-room through a decisive and finite act of expulsion.

ROSENKRANZ ON THE DISGUSTING (2): THE RETURN OF INDIGESTIBILITY IN THE SYSTEM OF DIALECTIC APPROPRIATION

Seen from the above perspective, the revalorizing of putrefaction in contemporary theories of the disgusting responds to a development within art itself. At the same time, the inadequacies of Tieck's and Rosenkranz's aesthetic reflections become evident precisely in their discussion of putrefaction. Rosenkranz's treatise begins on a heroic note:

Hell is not simply religious-ethical but also aesthetic in nature. We are situated in the middle of the malevolent and evil, but also in the middle of the ugly. The horrors of malformity and deformity, of coarseness and repulsiveness, surround us in countless forms, extending from the pygmy-like to those monstrous distortions from which infernal wickedness grins at us, baring its teeth. It is into this hell of the beautiful that we intend to descend here.[46]

For the sake of caution, Rosenkranz immediately announces the worst: "The aesthetics of the ugly makes it incumbent to treat those concepts whose discussion or even mention can ordinarily be considered a violation of proper tone. Whoever embarks on a pathology and therapy of illnesses must prepare himself for the most disgusting. And so here as well."[47] Following Hegel's critique of Romantic-ironic art, the perspective of "pathology" colors all subsequent observations and language according to a predetermined difference between healthy and sick; the perspective of "therapy" compromises the claim to a comprehensive "integration" of the not-beautiful through a judgmental gesture of normative poetics. In the end, Rosenkranz knows only *one* aesthetic theodicy of the ugly: its reflected self-overcoming in satire and caricature as two highly distinctive forms of the comic:

The ugly analogon of the absolutely beautiful is that aesthetic formation *[Gestaltung]* depicting the finitude of unfreedom in the condition of the unfreedom of the finite, but in such a manner that unfreedom takes on the *appearance* of freedom and finitude the appearance of infinitude. Such a form *[Gestalt]* is ugly, for the truly ugly is the free that contradicts itself through its unfreedom; within the finite, it sets a limit on itself that should not have been. But through the appearance of freedom, ugliness becomes milder; we compare it with that form representing its ideal counter-image; a comparison pushing the ugly appearance toward a verging on the comic. The self-destruction of the ugly through the appearance of freedom and infinitude, emerging precisely in the distortion of the ideal, is comic. We call this peculiar form of the ugly caricature.[48]

This argumentation brings two complementary premises into play, setting them in dialectic motion. The first premise is *kalokagathia*, aesthetico-ethical parallelism: "Ugliness does not lie in the concept of the human being. His concept, as that of reason and freedom, requires that he also realize himself in regularity of form, in the distinction of hands and feet and upright posture as external appearance."[49] This law applies to physically "ugly" people only under the stipulation that the "expression" of their free spirit "not only can induce a forgetting" of even deformities and pockmarks, "but even more, that they are capable of animating these unhappy forms from within with an expression whose magic irresistibly transports us."[50] Consequently, beauty of appearance is nothing other than the aesthetic side of the free spirit:

> The final ground of beauty is *freedom;* this word here not merely in the exclusively ethical sense, but also in the general sense of the spontaneity finding its absolute consummation, to be sure, in ethical self-determination, but that also becomes an aesthetic object in the play of life, in dynamic and organic processes. Unity, regularity, symmetry, order, truth to nature, psychological and historical correctness alone do not account sufficiently for the concept of the beautiful. This requires, in addition, an animation *[Beseelung]* through self-induced activity, through a life streaming out of the beautiful.[51]

The second, complementary premise of Rosenkranz's aesthetic theodicy emerges from the assumption that ugliness is not simply based on the inversion of the harmony of beauty and freedom. On the one hand, Rosenkranz's diagnosis points to the actual presence of a moment of "unfreedom" in everything ugly; it even assigns a "specific physiological expression" of ugly unfreedom to different "individual forms of folly and vices." On the other hand, he recognizes a "paradoxical" transformation into a harmony and beauty of its own sort, taking place as soon as the wicked and diabolical is consequently and freely desired as the "spiritually ugly":

> The ugliness must naturally be even greater when wickedness is desired in and for itself. But as paradoxical as it sounds, through the fact that in this case wickedness fixes itself as a systematic totality, a certain harmony of the will and hence of the appearance is produced once again; this aesthetically tempers the forms. Often, the folly of individual vices can have a much more harsh and unpleasant expression than straightforward wickedness, which in its negativity is again a whole.[52]
>
> This context also forms the basis for the demand, so often repeated since Schiller, that in order to be aesthetically possible the crime has to be great, since it then requires courage, cunning, cleverness, strength, endurance to an unusual degree, thus containing at least the formal side of freedom.[53]

According to Rosenkranz, then, within the ugly and wicked there are points of aesthetic reversal into the opposite: a degree of ugliness and wickedness indicates unfreedom; intensified ugliness and consequent wickedness win back "the formal side of freedom," and with it access to "the final ground of beauty." What the great criminal realizes for the aesthetic salvaging of wickedness, the art-form of caricature realizes for that of ugliness. The capacity of both wickedness and ugliness for beauty has the same grounding as beauty itself—the principle of freedom and self-determination. In this manner, a renewed convergence opens between the beautiful and its opposite. A collapse of the distinctions is only avoided through the introduction, in line with Kant and Hegel, of an idealistic concept of "true" freedom: a freedom that only desires the good and hence freedom itself. The "formal freedom" of affirmative ugliness and wickedness is then merely the "null" or "hollow" *(nichtig)*, substanceless counterpart to this "genuinely beatifying freedom."[54] To be sure, this moral difference is aesthetically un-differentiated, as soon as "untrue" freedom, equal to unfreedom, nullifies itself through reflective intensification, thus taking on the appearance of "true freedom."

At first sight, Tieck's and Rosenkranz's descriptions of the romantic-disgusting seem to imply analogous possibilities for rescue into the realm of aesthetic freedom. For the putrefaction of the negative principle in aesthetic satanism's beautiful disgust is not so much meant to consist in the description of the vices as in the attitude of free, intentional abandonment to the repellent: "From excessive transport of freedom, the intellect must now become a slave of ugliness."[55] However, the abandonment to vileness, diagnosed as typical of the period, does not seem to know a turning point where the intensification of the formal degree of freedom provides a dialectical aesthetic "therapy." The decomposition of the negative principle leads to a decomposition of dialectic itself. Instead of a movement of comprehensive integration, the older paradigm of indigestibility and "healthy" rejection of the unassimilable maintains the upper hand. The exorbitance of the disgusting is reconfirmed on a new level in that it even inverts the "confidence" of the dialectic appetite for appropriation into decisive repulsion. The "brilliant audacity that leaves morals to the philistines," the "'beautiful disgust' in this diabolics, that intentionally plunges into sin in order to then enjoy the sweet shudder of repentance," and all other vices of the "man of today," "restlessly exhausted, pleasure-craving yet impotent, bored out of satiation . . . ready to submit to every weakness," face the same judgment as that implied in the presentation of venereal diseases that might have been avoided out of "free morality": "Art must exclude disgusting diseases resting on immoral ground. Poetry prostitutes itself when it depicts such things. . . . They represent aberrations of a period that, as a result of its morbidly pathological interest in corruption, considers the misery of demoralization to be poetic."[56] Putrefaction and corruption, both read as moral ciphers, are joined in the (non)concept of the disgusting, thus forming one chief category in a pathology of the modern age—more generally, in a pathology of decadence. The prostitution of art at the hands of all these evils revolts the dialectical system, leading it to take recourse to the classical devices of border-demarcation and exclusion. Time and time again, it is urban life that provides Rosenkranz with striking examples of aesthetic impossibility:

The disgusting is also rendered aesthetically impossible when it mixes itself with the *unnatural*. Decadent epochs of nations like those of individuals, tease the slack nerves with the most intense and thus not infrequently the most disgusting stimuli. How hideous the newest fashionable entertainment of London idlers, the rat fight! Can anything more disgusting be imagined than a mass of rats in mortal agony defending themselves against a bestial dog? Some would say: but yes, those gamblers standing around the brick pit with their watches in hand. However, in his first, immortal letters of a deceased person, Pückler Muskau relates something yet more disgusting. Namely, that on the Boulevard Mont Parnasse in Paris he saw how the petit bourgeois shot at a rat they had bound to a crooked board so that it desperately ran back and forth in this narrow space. To shoot at a rat for pleasure! Infernally disgusting.[57]

The "fashionable pleasures" Rosenkranz describes here are indisputably disgusting. But the metaphorical and metonymical effect of this portrait of manners is problematic. For the factual analogy and spatial proximity to the diagnosis of moral putrefaction in "romantic" art suggests that such art and its "pleasure-craving yet impotent" heroes in fact do the same thing as "shooting at a rat for pleasure." By virtue of a specific doubling of the disgusting—disgusting pleasure being directed at a prototypically disgusting object ("a mass of rats")—the selected street-scenes ape an analogous doubling of disgust in the field of aesthetic satanism. Within that field as well, disgusting desire *and* disgusting objects of desire configure themselves to a syndrome of self-intensifying "reveling in depravity." The "pleasure-craving yet impotent man of today" seems so advanced in the expression of his "morbid desires" that even the big city's rat-heaps have to be protected from an affirmative aesthetics of the disgusting. Against this backdrop, Rosenkranz's exclusionary gesture no longer confirms—in Classical manner—the fundamental limits and rules of aesthetic illusion. Rather, it is engaged in a despairing, doomed defensive battle against an already executed and acknowledged self-dissolution—indeed overturning—of the classical-aesthetic system.

Blending the dialectic project with a recourse to the old demarcations and an almost unwilling diagnosis of new historical coordinates, Rosenkranz's view on the disgusting is paradoxical. On the one hand, in the mode of pathology, Rosenkranz offers a phenomenology of the disgusting comprising its "modern" form. On the other hand, his own disgust-licenses are anything but an extension of, say, Lessing's. From Lessing's panorama of admissible intensifying functions of the disgusting—the monstrous, frightful, sublime, and ridiculous—only the comic and an edifying sublimity remain. In his aesthetic legitimation of the flaying of Marsyas, Lessing goes further than Rosenkranz in any of his positive examples. It comes as no surprise that

Rosenkranz allows sweat, "filth and excrement . . . for the grotesquely comic," only.[58] And from the category of putrefaction governing the entire chapter, and in fact the definition of the disgusting itself, only its religious overcoming "through the divine life emanating from Christ" is aesthetically licensed. Rosenkranz's example in this respect, the "Resurrection of Lazarus," had already been discussed by Lessing. It is perhaps the only matter in which the approach of the *Laocoön* is less liberal than that of the *Aesthetics of the Ugly*. In distinction to Jesus's corpse, the Bible speaks expressly of a putrefactive stench in the case of Lazarus. Nevertheless, Lessing explains, the pictorial representation of the stench through the nose-holding of bystanders is "unbearable here as well, for not only actual stench, but even the very idea of it, awakens a feeling of disgust."[59] Rosenkranz has no use for a disgust out of "a mere idea" and the complimentary aesthetic model of illusion. Instead, he recalls the anti-illusionistic "truth"—"it should above all not be forgotten that painting does not represent this smell"—in order to then celebrate, in a second step, the death-conquering "freedom of the spirit," and with it the aesthetic ennoblement of putrefaction. According to this model, even mass epidemic infection can "take on a sublime character" through a "ray of life":

> Considered aesthetically, the Resurrection of Lazarus will serve as the canonical model for all such scenes, and life, as the eternal power of death, will need to step forward victoriously against the process of dying.[60]

Although Rosenkranz here oddly defines life itself as the power of death, one does not need to call any of his examples into question in order to see the anachronism of their selection. An unbridgeable gap opens between the contemporary form of a "decomposition" of the negative principle in "beautiful disgust"—the aesthetic Satanism of dark Romanticism—and the examples of aesthetically permissible putrefaction—religious history and large historical paintings. For Rosenkranz, the dialectical movement of the ugly is meant to pass through its maximal intensification to a point of self-destruction: the free denouncing of the unfreedom inherent in ugliness is supposed to lead in the end to an integration of the ugly into the beautiful. But Rosenkranz's chapter on the disgusting leaves behind a fissure in his project. The parallel pathology of modern life and Romantic art is precisely this fissure. The scandalous, unassimilable character of the disgusting is confirmed once again, this time not in the realm of anthropology or transcendental philosophy, but above all in the realm of history. The disgusting spoils the appetite of the dialectical system and disrupts its all-absorbing "confidence." Despite its contemporary omnipresence, the disgusting does not cease to be *choquant*. Aesthetic reflection registers the traces of this shock through interrupting its intended course and damaging its own system. But it does register the traces.

Corresponding to his philosophy's general design, Kant had conceived the "vital sensation" of disgust in terms of a subjective reaction, hence focusing on the act of vomiting. In contrast, reflecting his debt to Hegelian dialectics, Rosenkranz places an objective structure of the disgusting—putrefaction—at the center of his discussion. Vomiting nonetheless returns at the discussion's end; for like excretion, it is the expulsion of organic material, destined for putrefaction. In their basic features, Rosenkranz's comments on vomiting are entirely in line with his general formulas for disgust: the imperative of a turn to the comic and his verdict when this rule is not followed. But the examples he offers in illustrating these formulas for the realm of vomit point beyond their intended role:

> Vomiting, as well, has been mentioned earlier. Whether it is an innocent pathological affection or the results of gluttony, it is always most disgusting. Nevertheless both poetry and painting have depicted it. Painting can suggest it through pose alone, although in his "Dance of Death," *Holbein* was not embarrassed by having the glutton in the full foreground regurgitate the victuals he has just enjoyed. The Dutch were themselves not shy about the theme in their market and tavern scenes. The admissibility of such repellent features will greatly depend on the remaining aspects of the composition and on its style, for even a comic turn is possible, as in *Hogarth's* punch-parties or in that picture on a Greek vase showing *Homer*, stretched out on a cushioned bed, vomiting into a vessel standing on the ground. A female figure, poetry, holds his divine head. A number of figures of dwarfs stand around the vessel, assiduously inserting the regurgitated matter back in their own mouths. These are the later Greek poets, nourishing themselves on the cynically thrown-out leftovers of the great poet. Another apotheosis of Homer! But if poetry goes so far as to not simply tell of vomiting but bring it on the stage, this is a transgression of aesthetic measure whose effect cannot be comic. In this respect *Hebbel* misjudged things in his "Diamond." The Jew who has swallowed it vomits it out on the stage, and he not only vomits it out but even sticks his finger in his mouth to do so. That is too repellent! As a necessary natural act, birth does not have this repulsive quality, even when it does not take a comic turn . . .[61]

It is remarkable enough that birth is treated in a passage treating vomit—even if Rosenkranz immediately limits the parallel and, exceptionally, does not prescribe the comic turn as obligatory for this singular form of vomiting. This example can be related to a series of others pertaining to female genital and excretory organs; Rosenkranz tends to depict these examples in great detail, in order then to denounce them, all the more severely, as "boundlessly disgusting, common, shameless."[62] In this manner, perspectives open up not only on the survival of the *vetula*-topos, but also on the psychosexual fixations that may have accompanied Rosenkranz's erudition. Another topos, as well, comes into view, perhaps for the first time in a philosophical treatise on aesthetics: a topos with a considerable history before Rosenkranz, and with a straightforwardly monstrous twentieth-century career. This is the topos of the *disgusting Jew* (here, to be sure, only subcutaneously present beneath the evocation of a Jew who does something disgusting). Both topoi can here only be suggested, not elaborated on in detail. In contrast, the image of vomiting Homer is of direct poetological relevance for the *écriture* of disgust in Nietzsche and in the twentieth century. Words as a material of disgust and hence as something that can be vomited, reading as a process bringing this vomited substance back to one's mouth, writing as the renewed vomiting of the redigested vomited matter of earlier writing: having no precedents in the earlier tracts on disgust, these themes address disgust-desiderata far exceeding the goals of caricature and the comic. Within the field of the disgusting, Rosenkranz's *Aesthetics of the Ugly* thus exceeds itself in two respects: in the mode of pathology, it describes what it cannot incorporate; and it incorporates much that it would have to promptly regurgitate, were it to take the material more seriously than as a vehicle for comic-satirical freedom.

5

The "No" of Disgust and Nietzsche's "Tragedy" of Knowledge

Among the yelping and howling, carrion-eating and poisonous monsters in the realm of our vices, one in particular is stressed by Baudelaire at the end of his poem "To the Reader." This vice is both nastier and more gentle than the others: *C'est l'Ennui!* Kant had named this evil "disgust at one's own existence," caused by boredom and weariness of life.[1] In ennui, disgust becomes self-referential: what is rejected is not an alien indigestible entity, but one's own life—which itself thus assumes a position of indigestible alterity. Facing this satiety at one's own, desolate existence, Baudelaire fabricates an arsenal of charms and passions that are certainly not one thing: boring. To this extent, disgust appears in the role of evil and therapy at once; the lethargic disgust-type of *ennui* is challenged by other types of the disgusting, which are both actively desired and provocatively affirmed. At the same time, however, ennui threatens to swallow up *(avaler)* even the very appetite for the powerful stimuli of the disgusting, thus emerging as more dangerous than the disgusting's other forms. For to the extent that the strongest stimuli tend to exhaust themselves faster than all others, the positive cathexis of disgusting desires and objects is threatened, ubiquitously, with the fate of *anaesthetization*—and hence to turn, itself, into a source of ennui. In this manner, ennui serves as both counterpole and most innate tendency of the diabolical affirmation of disgusting lusts. The treatment of disgust with its own means is thus a dangerous enterprise; it can never count on gaining a stable position beyond satiation.

Friedrich Nietzsche's consideration of disgust faces similar challenges of processing the disgusting in a nonpessimistic manner. The disgusting evils that Nietzsche diagnoses in the contemporary forms of "satiety with life, fatigue, the wish for an 'end'"[2] are all in all less conspicuous, less diabolic-extroverted and unabashedly sinful as is the case with Baudelaire. And Nietzsche does not so much take the path of a provocative-affirmative countercathexis as that of a critical "self-overcoming" of disgust.[3] But with this overcoming itself operating via the means of what has to be overcome, Zarathustra—the ideal (super-)man without disgust"[4]—himself in the end remains trapped in the snares of disgust. The ennui of Baudelaire's "To the Reader" consigns life to the "scaffold," this image blending two elements that were mutually opposed in the eighteenth century. The danger of suicide was part of ennui's boredom, while the spectacle of public execution on the scaffold figured as, precisely, a maximal *antidote* to the melancholic tendency to suicide. The hybrid mixing of suicide and execution suggests that for Baudelaire, already, the substrate of experience and the structure of weariness with life had radically changed. Ennui's social substratum was no longer the disempowered early-eighteenth-century noble upper caste, condemned to inactivity and searching for distraction; rather, ennui had found a new circle of victims. Benjamin describes it through the flaneur, the gambler, and other "heroes" including the poet; all such figures undergo the calvary of socially determined "impotence," and all must struggle in different ways with *spleen*.[5] Nietzsche's diagnosis of life-weariness goes far beyond this phenomenal complex. His protagonists, victims, and conquerors of "disgust," open an entirely new field in the history of this sensation: "we're learning disgust anew!" *[Wir lernen den Ekel um!*[6]*]*.

Through a distinction between the wholesome and unwholesome, Kant had assigned a preservative function for health and life to the "vital sensation" of disgust. On an increased level of abstraction, Nietzsche defines the "binary code" of disgust as "yes"-saying versus "no"-saying. The cardinal object of this judgment is no longer, as with Kant, one or another sort of physical or spiritual "nourishment," but "life" itself—life considered not as a source of boredom, but precisely in all its energy, its injustice, suffering, desire, and amoral "will to power." To the extent that disgust says "no" to life itself, it inverts the Kantian function of life-preservation into its opposite and becomes the agent of a "will to decline, at the very least a sign of the most profound affliction, fatigue, sullenness, exhaustion, impoverishment of life."[7] In this function, disgust acquires a prominent place in the "history of European nihilism." It in fact denotes the "culmination-point" of "complete nihilism." Nietzsche cites "the great *contempt*," "the great *pity*," and "the great *destruction*" as its "symptoms" and "three great affects": "its culmination-point: *a doctrine* declaring precisely that life which stirs up disgust, pity, and the desire of destruction as *absolute* and *eternal*."[8] Again and again, Nietzsche returns in his writings to this configuration of disgust, pity, and nihilism. Disgust thus occupies a central juncture—if not *the* central one—in Nietzsche's thought: under nihilist conditions—the death of God, the end of the great narratives—how can a disgust at life that lurks everywhere be reconfigured into a "yes"-saying of a new type?

Plato, Jesus, and Morals as World-Historical Agents of Disgust

Nietzsche's genealogy of nihilism uncovers a radically new circle of—mostly hidden—catalysts and agents of disgust. The archetype of disgust-imbued life is not represented by those suffering from eighteenth- and nineteenth-century ennui—not by nobles needing distraction or Baudelaire's contemporaries and poetic personae—but by no lesser figures than Plato and Jesus. Both invent "a transcendental world in order to all the better slander this one." Metaphysics, philosophy of virtue, and Christian salvational religion are merely disguised and ornamented forms of a "hatred of the 'world,'" a "curse cast on affect," a "fear of beauty and sensuality . . . basically a longing for nothingness."[9] In "more noble" observers, this disgust at the worldly life evokes a second-degree disgust—a disgust at the disgust at life: "All deeper natures in antiquity have felt disgust at the *philosophers of virtue:* squabblers and actors were seen within them. Judgment over Plato: on the part of *Epicurus* and on the part of *Pyrrho.*"[10] In the "Attempt at a Self-Criticism" that Nietzsche prefaced to a new edition of *The Birth of Tragedy* (1866), Christian "disgust and weariness by life for life" is portrayed as the sharpest contrast to the Nietzschean project:

> In truth, nothing could be more opposed to the purely aesthetic interpretation and justification of the world as taught in this book than Christian doctrine, which is *only* moral, and seeks only to be moral, with its absolute standards: the truth of God, for example, which relegates art, *all* art, to the realm of *falsehood*—which is to say it denies, condemns and damns it. Behind such a system of ideas and values, which by necessity is hostile to art as long as it is authentic at all, I had always sensed *hostility to life,* the furious, vindictive distaste for life itself: for all life is based on appearance, art, deception, optics, the necessity of perspective and error. From the start Christianity was, essentially and fundamentally, disgust and weariness by life for life, which only disguised itself, concealed itself, ornamented itself beneath a belief in an "other" or "better" life. Hatred of the "world," a curse cast on affect, a fear of beauty and sensuality, a transcendental world invented in order to all the better slander this one, basically a longing for nothingness, for repose until the "Sabbath of Sabbaths"—all this, along with Christianity's unconditional will to acknowledge *only* moral values, struck me as the most dangerous and sinister of all possible forms of a will to decline, at the very least a sign of the most profound affliction, fatigue, sullenness, exhaustion, impoverishment of life—for in the face of morals (particularly Christian, meaning unconditional morals), life *must* be experienced as unworthy of being desired, as valueless in itself, crushed beneath the

weight of contempt and the eternal "no." As to morals themselves, might they not be a "will to the denial to life," a secret instinct for annihilation, a principle of decay, trivialization, slander, the beginning of the end? And, hence, the ultimate danger? . . . So then, with this questionable book, my instinct, an affirmative instinct for life, turned *against* morals and invented a fundamentally opposite doctrine and valuation of life, purely artistic and *anti-Christian*. What should I call it? As a philologist and man of letters, I baptized it, not without a degree of license—for who knows the true name of the Antichrist?— with the name of a Greek god: I called it the *Dionysian*.[11]

On the basis of "morals themselves," Nietzsche's depth-psychological scrutiny uncovers a systematic denial disguised as a positive doctrine of "true" life. As "the most extravagant elaboration of the moral theme,"[12] Christianity thus assumes the position of a master trope of disgust; at the same time, Dionysos represents a prosopopoeia of the counterpole—nondisgust or the overcoming of disgust. The "disgust and weariness by life for life" inherent in Christianity not only provokes Nietzsche's penetrating-skeptical deconstruction of morals. Rather, it itself becomes the object of a disgust-based "no"—an instinct-guided rejection:

A test of whether someone has some *classical taste* in his body is his stance regarding the New Testament (cf. Tacitus): whoever is not revolted by it—whoever does not honestly and thoroughly feel some *foeda superstitio*, something from which the hand withdraws in order to not be dirtied—does not know what is classical. One needs to feel the cross like Goethe. . . . —If one admits one's first impression of the New Testament: something disgusting and repellent from bad taste, a sanctimonious sentimentality, nothing but repellent symbols in the foreground; and the spoiled air of the cranny and conventicle:—one does *not* sympathize . . .

Even if one is so very modest in the demand for intellectual cleanness, in contact with the New Testament one cannot prevent feeling something like an unspeakable disgust: for the dirty and dissolute insolence of thoroughly incompetent persons in having their say about the great problems—indeed their claim to judges' status in such matters—exceeds all measure. The unashamed recklessness with which the most inaccessible problems are here discussed, as if they were no problems—life, world, God, purpose of life—but simple things which these little bigots *know*.[13]

In this context, Nietzsche is only pleased by a single role. Pilate advances to the prototype of that noble disgust of the second degree guiding Nietzsche's diagnosis of the age:

Pilate—the only honest person, his disdain for this Jews' blather about "truth," as if such people could have a say when it comes to truth, his *ha gégrapha*, his well-meaning effort to release this absurd criminal, in whom he had difficulty seeing anything else but a fool . . . his disgust regarding that never sufficiently condemned phrase "I am the truth."[14]

Under the guiding category of—hidden or open—life-denial, Nietzsche discovers a prototype of modern life exhaustion in Platonic doctrine of virtue and Christian morals. Late Tieck and Rosenkranz still used normative moral concepts to criticize aesthetic-satanic abandonment to depravity as disgusting. In inverting this conceptual pattern into its opposite—here revealing greater affinity with "dark Romanticism"—Nietzsche defines morality itself as the chief evil in a pathology of the modern.

"Ressentiment" and Weakness as Catalysts of Modern "Moralizing"— The Disgusting Mixture of Lies and Innocence

Nietzsche's essay *On the Genealogy of Morals* (1887) is the central document of the philosopher's disgust at all those forms of disgust for life, whose presence among his contemporaries he revealed with passionate acuity. The analysis of a general life-denial qua morals here recedes in favor of two other questions, both oriented toward historical differentiation: *Who* makes use of the medium "morals?" And *how* or *to what (hidden) ends* does he use this medium? In these question's horizon, contemporary "culture" appears as a panorama of disgusting pathologies, in its refinement of the negative and ignorance of itself far surpassing early Christian "sanctimony," characterized as it is by "bad manners," "bad air," and "resentment." In view of such phenomena, "disgust" is simply articulated as a self-evident judgment needing no additional justification: "There are many things against which I have not found it necessary to speak: it is a matter of course that I find the 'literary man' repellent, that all contemporary political parties are repellent to me. . . . My patient and mild disgust at the self-satisfaction of our scholary and large city-inhabitants fondly displaying their *Bildung* as ornament of their own persona."[15] Nietzsche expends more energy regarding other objects of his disgust-judgment, particularly in his depth psychology of moralist discourse. Latent self-contempt is revealed to be the agent of modern moralizing, as well:

> Those who are from the start casualties, defeated, broken—they are the ones . . . who most dangerously poison . . . our trust in life, in human beings, in ourselves. . . . Such an individual speaks to himself . . .

"I wish I were anyone else! . . . but there's no hope of that. I am who I am: how could I escape from myself? And yet—*I've had enough of myself!*" . . . On such soil of self-contempt, a real quagmire, every weed will grow, every poisonous plant, and all so tiny, so hidden, so dishonest, so sweet. Here the worms of vindictive feeling and reaction squirm; here the air stinks of things kept secret and unacknowledged; here the net of wickedest conspiracy is continually spun—the conspiracy of the suffering against the fortunate and the victorious, here the victor's sight is *hated*. And the mendacity needed in order not to acknowledge this hate as hate! What a display of grand words and poses, what an art of "honest" defamation! These failures: what noble eloquence streams from their lips! How much sugary, slimy, humble devotion is swimming in their eyes! What are they really after? To *represent*, at least, justice, love, wisdom, superiority—such is the ambition of these "lowest of the low," these sick souls! And how skillful such an ambition makes them! Admire, in particular, the forger's skill with which the stamp of virtue, even its cling-clang and golden sound, is faked here. . . . There is, among them, an abundance of vindictive men disguised as judges, their mouths continually secreting the word "justice" like a poisonous saliva, their lips always pursed, ready to spit at everything that does not look unsatisfied and goes its way in good spirits. Among them, there is also no shortage of that most disgusting species of vain men, the mendacious deformities out to play the part of "beautiful souls," and for instance, dressed up in poetry and other nappies, to market their ruined sensuality as "purity of heart": the species of moral onanists and indulgers in "self-satisfaction."[16]

Quagmires, worms, stench, sugary sweets, saliva and slime: Nietzsche here serves up the entire arsenal of disgust-topoi in order to drag into view the self-sickness and satiatory disgust, the "no" to oneself and to life, that secretly characterize the agents of morals. He sees "whole epidemics of such satiety" at play in history.[17] Schlegel's "disgusting sensual and intellectual impotence" returns in a "weakness" that is both the agent of disgust, first degree, and object of disgust, second degree. Those historians, for instance, who are "sweetly witty" and have "wholly and entirely rented out the praise of contemplation for themselves" serve for Nietzsche as models of such "impotence":

I could think of nothing so disgusting as such an "objective" armchair scholar, such a scented little historical hedonist, half-Pope, half-satyr, perfume Renan, his high falsetto applause immediately revealing what he is lacking and where, *where* the Fates have in this case applied their cruel shears in an oh! all too surgical manner! This offends my taste, and also tries my patience. . . . Nature, which gave the bull its horns and the lion its chasm' hodónton—why did this Nature give me feet? . . . For treading . . . and not just for running away: for trampling these decayed armchairs, this cowardly contemplation, this prurient eunuchdom in the face of history, this flirtation with ascetic ideals, this justice-Tartuffery of the impotent! All my honor to the ascetic ideal, *so long as it is honest,* so long as it believes in itself and avoids playing the fool for us! But I dislike all these coquettish bedbugs whose insatiable ambition is to smell of the infinite, until in the end the infinite smells of bugs; I dislike the whitewashed graves that play the part of life.[18]

Nietzsche here imagines nothing less than a recastration of someone already castrated. Shears, tread, bull-horns, and lion's maw are aimed at an "impotence" which, in fact, is potent to an unheard-of degree: its "moral posing" successfully renders invisible its own foundation (i.e., its own failings), and indeed manages to endow itself with the aura of a "beautiful soul." Regularly, Nietzsche presents anti-Semitism as an especially repellent figure of this "vicious mendacity" from weakness, a mendacity that masks its own resentment-born vindictiveness with a good conscience:

It would like to make itself heard even on the consecrated ground of science, this hoarse indignant bark of the sickly dog, the vicious mendacity and rage of such "noble" Pharisees (—once again, I remind readers who have ears to hear of that apostle of revenge from Berlin, Eugen Dühring, who is making the most indecent and repellent use of moral mumbo-jumbo in Germany today: Dühring, the foremost moral bigmouth around at the moment, even among his kind, the anti-Semites). They are all men of *resentment* . . . inexhaustible . . . in pretexts for revenge.[19]

Recently, I received a letter from Herr Theodor Fritsch of Leipzig. There is no more shameless and stupid gang in Germany than these anti-Semites. As thanks, I gave him a regular epistolary kick. This rabble dares use the name Z[arathustra]! *Ekel! Ekel! Ekel!*[20]

It is Nietzsche's conviction that "*not* the evil, *not* the 'predators'" pose "the greatest danger to man," but those *"sickly"* individuals who, out of weakness and for the sake of masking their own failings, collapse the difference between honesty and dishonesty, lies and innocence.[21] Nietzsche's entire "pathos of distance" and difference—the pathos of his *own* disgust—is directed against "the shamefully *moralized* form of speech smeared over practically all modern judgments of men and things. For make no mistake here: the most distinctive characteristic of modern souls, and modern books is not lying, but an inveterate *innocence* in moralistic mendacity. To be obliged time and again to uncover this 'innocence' everywhere—that constitutes perhaps the most repulsive aspect of our work, of all the in itself not-undangerous work a psychologist has to undertake today; it represents a great danger *for us*—a path perhaps leading precisely *us* to the great disgust. . . ."[22] Such work is repulsive "for us psychologists" because it leads to a slimy-swampy terrain of soggy differences and "worm-ridden" defigurations of moral concepts: a moral analogon to "physical disgust at something fungous, mollified, bloated, suppurating."[23]

"Mollycoddling" as Disgust at One's Own Cruelty

Mendelssohn's disgust at the "all-too great softness of the body"[24] returns in another form as well. As a follow-up to mendacious-moral innocence, its second referent is "shame" at one's own "instincts, "sickly mollycoddling and moralization." The hard "human-all-to-human proposition" that Nietzsche opposes to this self-denial from shame is provocative enough: "To see suffering is delightful; to inflict it is even more so."[25] The affirmation of a pleasure from cruelty counts among the most problematic basic features in Nietzsche's *Herrenmoral*. It would, however, be mistaken to read the pertinent paragraphs of his *Genealogy*, in undiscriminating fashion, as a legitimation of all past barbarity and a forerunner of that to come. Not only the text's rhetorical-polemical thrust here needs considering: its contemporary addressee is clear ("false" morals), as is the goal of provoking this addressee. At the same time, Nietzsche's "proposition" regarding cruelty seems firmly limited in its applicability. Expressly *not* covered by it is murderous activity from resentment—the "vindictive feeling and reaction" resulting from one's own weakness; the entire complex of "Christian-Aryan-philistine violence" cloaked in "the cheapest means of agitation and moral posing."[26] For such activity veils its cruelty ideologically, striving for secrecy instead of openly acknowledging its nature. Nietzsche's examples possess, to the contrary, a thoroughly premodern festive-spectacular quality, often resembling Bakhtin's description of the carnival. They extend from the Trojan War and archaic sacrificial practice—as a theater of cruelty for divine spectators—to royal marriages, and the world of Don Quixote:

> It seems to me that such false delicacy, indeed the Tartuffery of tame housepets (meaning modern man, meaning us) likewise fails to acknowledge the extent of naiveté and innocence with which prior generations' need for cruelty presents itself, and how fundamentally they regard precisely "disinterested malice" (or, to speak with Spinoza, *sympathia malevolens*) as a *normal* human characteristic—hence as something to which the conscience heartily says *yes!* Perhaps even today a more profound eye would discern enough of this earliest and

most basic human festive joy; in *Beyond Good and Evil* ... I pointed a careful finger at the transformation of cruelty into something ever more spiritual and "divine," a process running through the whole history of higher culture (and, in a significant sense, even constituting it). In any case, it is not so long ago that royal weddings and popular festivities in the grandest style were inconceivable without executions, torture, or for instance an auto-da-fé, or similarly a noble household without a creature upon whom one could unhesitatingly vent one's malice and cruel teasing (—remember, for example, Don Quixote at the court of the Duchess: today we read the whole *Don Quixote* with a bitter taste on the tongue, almost in torture, and we would thus seem very alien, very obscure to its author and his contemporaries—they read it with the best of all consciences as the most cheerful of books, they almost laughed themselves to death over it).[27]

In the eighteenth century, aesthetics already had acknowledged the avid interest in public executions as a fact of the human soul, and had offered explanatory models not wholly consistent with moral correctness. The widespread, and in the end, dominant theory of powerful emotions postulates an abstract hunger for the strongest possible stimuli; affected by powerful passions, the soul experiences the pleasure to sense itself as something active and alive. Cruel scenes extending from gladiator combat to the corpse-strewn baroque stage regularly served as specially suitable catalysts of this pleasurable *se sentir s'émouvoir* (Descartes)[28] of the soul. Nietzsche frames his own aesthetic-anthropological explication of the pleasure at cruelty in terms of civilizational history: as would be the case with Freud and Elias, he sees modern civilization as bound to an internalizing of violence—and "shame" as an instance of this self-censorship. In psychic cruelty, he surmises an everyday, modern substitute of the premodern, shameless liaison between cruelty and festive pleasure:

> Perhaps the possibility might even be entertained that pleasure in cruelty need not actually have died out: . . . all that it had to do was sublimate and refine itself—that is, it had to appear translated into the imagination and the psyche.[29]

Freud's insight into the ambivalence of civilizing drive-sublimation is anticipated by Nietzsche through stressing the psychohistorical costs that need to be expended for the development of "man's shame *before man*." These costs amount to self-disgust—a "standing before oneself with pinched nose," a "tired pessimistic gaze" and a "ruined stomach" in face of that "taste" for cruelty[30] that Freud, too, counted among the features of "normal" psychic life (at least within the boundaries of a sadistic drive-*component*). Nietzsche's disgust at self-denying "delicacy" and the excessively sensitive shame of "tame housepets (meaning modern man)," is aimed at an undiscriminating complicity with the cultural repression at work in shame.

The Disgusting Body and Nietzsche's Physiology

In Nietzsche's diagnosis of disgust, modern rejection of one's own body stands directly alongside "mollycoddling" and mendacious moralizing in thought and action. Not the body's aesthetic contemplation but rather its moralizing appropriation leads to the "utterly ghastly fact . . . that contempt has been taught for the primary instincts of life; that a 'soul,' a 'spirit,' has been *mendaciously invented* in order to destroy the body; that one is taught to sense something unclean in sexuality, life's precondition."[31] Aesthetic judgment—this at least Nietzsche's opinion in the *Gay Science*—makes no demands; rather, it promises something—and indeed bestows it. In contrast, moral judgment subsumes aesthetic distinctions to the demands issuing from the position of "truth": "The beautiful, the disgusting, etc. is the older judgment. As soon as it is appropriated by *absolute truth*, the aesthetic judgment is inverted into moralistic *demand*."[32] Then "the *aesthetically* offensive quality of the inner man without his skin—bloody pulp, fecal bowels, entrails"—leads to the imperative of exclusion: "Hence *away with in thought*."[33] In this case, the aesthetic judgment of the body shifts into a "prejudgment" of it: "All excretions disgusting . . . disgust increasing with refinement. The functions linked to this also disgusting."[34] Placing moral demands on the body thus institutes shame and disgust at one's own physical nature:

> What emerges from this in fact sparks shame (stool, urine, spittle, semen). Women would prefer not hearing of digestion. Byron not seeing a woman eat. The less knowledgeable a person is about his organism, the more often raw meat, corruption, stench, maggots together enter his head. The individual, so long as he is something else than form, sees himself as disgusting—he does everything *not to think about it.* The *pleasure* that is manifestly connected to this inner person is considered *inferior.*—After-effect of the aesthetic judgment. The idealists of love are enthusiasts for beautiful *forms;* they want to delude themselves and are often indignant at the presentation of coitus and semen.—The individual has ascribed everything painfully awkward, tormenting, overheated to this inner body: he has elevated seeing, hearing, form, thinking all the higher. The *disgusting* was meant to be the source of *unhappiness! We're learning disgust anew!*[35]

Nietzsche was perhaps the first to inquire rigorously into what is being denied with every "ideal": "Have you ever adequately asked yourselves how much the establishment of *every* ideal on earth has cost? How much reality had to be defamed and denied here, how many lies sanctified?"[36] From this perspective, idealism of beautiful "form," "soul," and an uninterrupted continuum of the skin emerges as a consequent moral denial of the body (i.e., the entire organism and its pleasure). Still, as an artful "concealment of naturalness" and proof of the "strength of dream," the body without an interior is also legitimated by Nietzsche. He views idealization in love as a sign of the strength of illusion, necessary for life: "When we love a woman, we easily harbor a hatred for nature, thinking of all the repulsive natural functions to which every woman is subject. . . . Then one shuts his ears to all physiology, secretly decreeing 'I want to hear nothing about humans being something other than *soul and form*.' For all lovers, 'the human being beneath the skin' is a horror, something unthinkable, a blasphemy against God and love."[37]

Despite all critique of body-denial, Nietzsche thus distinguishes very sharply between its forms in aesthetic and amorous illusion, on the one hand, and, on the other, the moral insistence on such denial from an alleged interest in "the truth." The highest success enjoyed by the moral denial of the digesting, excreting body is the habitualized taboo on speech and thought: "You've extended the pudenda's realm to the point where a conversation over digestion, indeed over toothbrushes, is already thought rude. And as a consequence finer souls do not even *think* about such things."[38] The "conversation over digestion" thus occupies more than a little space within Nietzsche's "revaluation of values." Disgust at the "inner man" is literally "learned anew," transformed from a putative "source of unhappiness" to one of happiness, health, and new thinking. *Physiology* is the conjuring word for such fresh knowledge of the body, in the end replacing all precritical play of truth. The autobiographical *Ecce Homo* ascribes the quality of a reawakening to the discovery of "a question upon which the 'salvation of mankind' depends far more than upon any quaint theologians' curiosity: the question of *nutrition*." Nietzsche admits that "on precisely this point I was backward to the point of holiness," from this deriving "the perfect worthlessness of our German education."[39] It would appear that no other nineteenth century philosopher lingers so readily and seriously with questions of diet and digestion. The history of the stomach here advances to a subtext in the history of thinking; dietetics returns as cognitive and moral critique. Hence German cuisine must count among the reasons for Nietzsche's disgust at Germany:

> In fact, until my maturest years I ate only *badly*—in the language of morals "impersonally," "selflessly," "altruistically," for the salvation of cooks and other fellow Christians. For example, I very earnestly denied my "will to live" with the aid of Leipzig cookery,

accompanying my earliest study of Schopenhauer (1865). To ruin one's stomach for the sake of receiving inadequate nutrition—the aforesaid cookery seemed to me to solve this problem wonderfully well. (It is said that 1866 produced a change here.—) But German cookery in general—what does it not have on its conscience! Soup *before* the meal (in Venetian cookbooks of the sixteenth century still called *alla tedesca*); meat cooked to shreds, greasy and floury vegetables; the degeneration of puddings to paperweights! If one adds to this the downright bestial dinner-drinking habits of the old, by no means only *old* Germans, one will also understand the origin of the *German spirit*—distressed intestines. . . . The German spirit is an indigestion, it can have done with nothing.[40]

In Winckelmann's opinion, ideally beautiful bodies have "no need of those parts destined for our body's nutrition."[41] Nietzsche's discourse on digestion breaks, above all, with this rule of disgust avoidance. At the center of his "learning anew" of body-disgust we find, not physical excretions and sexuality, nor vomit, nor decay, but the "entrails"—*Eingeweide*—in their function as digestive organs. In fact, a special type of digestion, rumination, advances—for reasons that will be explained—to a model for every overcoming of life-denying disgust. In this "physiological" turn, body-disgust of the first order itself becomes the target of a disgust of the second order. "Stern spirits," Nietzsche observes in a direct inversion of Winckelmann's ideal of beauty, distinguish themselves through "a genuine disgust for all such fawning enthusiasm, idealism, feminism, hermaphroditism."[42] Consistently, they prefer the satyr—with his stress on belly, phallus, bodily swellings, eccentric movements—to the softly marked hermaphrodite. Long before his explicit insight into "idealist" body-disgust, Nietzsche's emphasis on the importance of the chorus of satyrs for the "yes"-saying moment within Greek tragedy[43] prefigures the late philosophy of entrails and the pleasure of digestion. The satyr is *the* trope for the overcoming of disgust in the field of the body.

"Great Disgust" and Contemporary Literature

On the Genealogy of Morals progresses in a self-reinforcing loop of disgust. Nietzsche reacts to every diagnosis of first-order disgust—the "no" of morals to life; the latent self-satiety typical for the agents of "morals"; the mendacious-innocent and "mollycoddling" use of morals—with the manifestation of a second order disgust at all this "disgust and weariness by life for life." Hence the threat, unwillingly, of a closed cycle of disgust. In rhetorical self-apostrophe, Nietzsche repeatedly recalls this danger of infection:

And hence, let us have good air! good air! and away, in any case, from the vicinity of all asylums and hospitals of culture! And hence, let us have good company, *our* company! Or loneliness, if need be! But away, in any case, from the evil vapors of inner corruption and the secret worm-fodder of the diseased! . . . So that we, my friends, can defend ourselves at least a little while longer against the two worst plagues that could have been reserved precisely for us— against *great disgust at the human being!* against *great compassion for the human being!* . . .[44]

Great disgust at the human being would be the closure of the individual facets of Nietzsche's panorama of disgust into a system without egress. In the figure of great disgust, the diagnosed evils of modernity and Nietzsche's affective response to them would be so intertwined that his own project of a "tragic" saying "yes" to life would risk drowning in the "no" of disgust:

What is to be feared, as having an incomparably disastrous effect, would not be a great fear, but great *disgust* of the human being; the same with great *compassion*. If these two ever mated, something most uncanny would unavoidably and immediately come into the world, the human being's "last will," his will to nothingness, nihilism.[45]

Nietzsche classifies contemporary literature with, precisely, this grid of double danger from "great disgust" and "great compassion":

To *"great disgust," sometimes* suffering from it, *sometimes* producing it
nervous-Catholic—erotic literature
France's literature-pessimism/Flaubert. Zola.
Goncourt. Baudelaire.
the *diners chez* Magny
To *"great compassion"*
Tolstoy, Dostoyevsky
Parsifal[46]

Counting them agents of "great compassion," Nietzsche has little mercy to spare for Tolstoy and Dostoevsky. On the other hand, some of the authors consigned to "great disgust" are granted a double relation to disgust: "*sometimes* suffering from it, *sometimes* producing it." This doubling allows literature to move past a simple example of the contemporary-disgusting, aligning it with Nietzsche's own politics of disgust. In particular, Nietzsche perceives affinities with Baudelaire, the "very first *intelligent* disciple of Wagner"— although he directly singles out Baudelaire's "pessimism" for rejection.[47] In contrast, "Paris naturalism" is censured as a movement "drawing forth and exposing only the part of nature that prompts nausea and simultaneous amazement—today people like to call this part *la verité vraie*."[48] In his register of "my impossible ones," Nietzsche reserves a separate entry for this "disease of will": "*Zola:* or 'delight in stinking.'"[49]

The "great disgust" threatening, according to *On the Genealogy of Morals*, the man of cognition expressly reappears as a basic feature of Zarathustra's life-trajectory. Before his ascent into the mountains, Zarathustra has almost "stifled" on "disgust";[50] he also sends forth his followers on the path of a self-overcoming of "great disgust."[51] This "great disgust, the great sea-sickness" only seizes the individual when he shatters "false shores and false securities," the mendacious "tablets of the good."[52] The dictum then applying is "Not my hate but my disgust hungrily devoured my life!" And Zarathustra continues with a question motivating Nietzsche's entire work: "Yet what happened to me? How did I free myself from disgust?"[53] Nietzsche's answers to this question not only pass beyond disgust, but, above all, enter it more deeply. This becomes clear through a related, intermediary question: why is *On the Genealogy of Morals* not satisfied with a depth-psychological analysis of the disgust at life concealed within the origin of morals? Why does Nietzsche consider it necessary, in the first place, to intensify this diagnosis through the affect of a disgust—in this case open and explicit—at disgust? Beyond mere polemic, what is the cognitive and practical-performative function of Nietzschean negation out of disgust?

Disgust and Cognition

As is well known, Nietzsche's physiological aesthetics and his physiology of cognition are aimed, in their entirety, at a reconnection of even the most abstract thought processes to affects and corporeally grounded needs: "Most of a philosopher's conscious thinking is both secretly directed and forced into fixed channels by his instincts. Behind all logic too, and its apparent autonomy, stand evaluations, stated more clearly, physiological demands for the preservation of a certain species of life."[54] If all (philosophical) cognition thus stands in an inner relation to the body and to an affective economy, deriving not only its weaknesses but also the strength of its "will" from this relation, then the traditional absolutizing of cognition *against* the body and affects needs to be inverted. Then unconscious drives not only need to be made conscious, but cognitive achievements need to be transformed (back) into instincts, hence incorporated into the body:

> *Incorporating knowledge* and making it instinctive remains an entirely new *task*, hardly clearly perceptible and only now dawning to

the human eye—a task only seen by those who have understood that so far, we have incorporated only our errors, and that our entire consciousness is connected with errors.[55]

Chapter 26 of *Beyond Good and Evil* expounds on this basic idea in terms of the relation between philosophical knowledge and the strong "instinct" of disgust. Disgust, it turns out, is a necessary condition and catalyzer of cognition; and for the "favored child of cognition," it even returns, mixed with "enchantment," in the form of knowledge itself:

> Every elect human being instinctively aspires for his castle and secret spot where he is *delivered* from the crowd, the many, the almost everyone, where he may forget the rule "man" himself being its exception—that one case excepted where, as a man of cognition in the great and exceptional sense, he is impelled directly toward this rule by an even stronger instinct. He who, when dealing with human beings, does not occasionally scintillate with all colors of distress, green and gray with disgust, satiety, sympathy, gloom, and loneliness, is certainly not a man of elevated taste; but if he does not voluntarily assume this burden and displeasure, if he continually avoids it and, as said, hides himself away quietly and proudly in his castle, then one thing is certain: he is not made, not predestined for cognition. . . . The study of the average human being, protracted, serious, and to this end much dissembling, self-overcoming, intimacy, bad company . . . this comprises a necessary part of the life-history of the philosopher, perhaps the part that is most unpleasant, bad-smelling, and disappointing. If he is lucky, however, as fitting a favored child of cognition, he will encounter people shortening and easing his task—I mean so-called cynics, hence those simply recognizing the animal, the baseness, the "rule" in themselves, and yet still possessing a degree of spirituality and appetite that constrains them to speak of themselves and their kind *before witnesses*—sometimes they even wallow in books as in their own dung. Cynicism is the only form in which common souls come close to honesty; and the higher man must prick up his ears at every cynicism, coarse or refined, and congratulate himself whenever a shameless buffoon or scholarly satyr speaks out in his presence. There are even cases in which enchantment mingles with disgust: namely where, by a caprice of nature, such an indiscreet goat and monkey is touched with genius, as in the case of the Abbé Galiani, the profoundest, most sharp-sighted, and perhaps also dirtiest man of his century—he was far more profound than Voltaire and consequently also a good deal more silent. . . . And whenever anyone speaks without bitterness, rather innocuously, of

man as a belly with two needs and a head with one; wherever anyone sees, seeks, and *wants* to see nothing but hunger, sexual desire, and vanity, as if they were the actual and only motives of human actions; in brief, whenever anyone speaks "badly"—and not even nastily—of the human being, the lover of cognition should listen carefully and diligently, and in general he should lend an ear whenever anyone speaks without indignation. For the indignant man, and whoever is continuously tearing and lacerating himself to shreds with his teeth (or, instead of himself, the world, or God, or society) may indeed, morally speaking, stand higher than the laughing and self-satisfied satyr, but in every other sense, he is the more commonplace, less interesting, less instructive case. And no one *lies* so much as the indignant man.[56]

The opposition between "indignant man" and "laughing and self-satisfied satyr" is a variant of the opposition between moralistic-mendacious denial and amoral life-affirmation. Sigmund Freud would have had good chances of figuring among such laughing satyrs, who, with absolutely no indignation, see "nothing but sexual desire, and vanity . . . as if they were the actual and only motives of human actions." According to this memorable narrative of the "life-history of the philosopher," disgust—above all in its function as pathos of distance and the experience of difference—is located at the origin of the movement of cognition. But it only *transforms* itself into cognition when it overcomes its own fear of contact, opening itself to the unpleasant, stinking, and disappointing object. Upon the path of such "self-overcoming," that which disgust would have initially simply rejected (a wallowing in one's own dung; the dirtiest of men) can then indeed return, but now in a new mixture and on the side of knowledge. A posthumous fragment directly defines the necessary exposure of cognition to disgust as the "fate" that "henceforth rests upon Europe"—a fate stamped by the fact

> that precisely its strongest sons rarely and belatedly arrive at their springtime,—that for the most part they perish young and full of disgust, winter, gloom, precisely because they drank, drained, the cup of disappointment—and that is presently the cup of *cognition*—with all their strength's passion—and they would not be the strongest if they were not also the most disappointed of men![57]

Without this interplay of disgust, "cup of disappointment" and "cup of cognition," cognition would be cut off from its strongest source of power. It needs a disgust-engendering experience passing with "all [its] strength's passion" through "all the age's illness": a dialectic model defining negativity in the form of a heroically desired suffering from the disgusting as the signature of cognition. "The elect man of cognition" is an individual who has "almost" been "sacrificed" to disgust[58]—what this terminology reveals has already been depicted in The *Birth of Tragedy* in the medium of art, indeed as *the* accomplishment of art: as the "saying 'yes' to life even in its strangest and hardest problems; the will to life rejoicing in its own inexhaustibility through the *sacrifice* of its highest types—*that* is what I named Dionysian, that is what I recognized as the bridge to the psychology of the *tragic* poet. . . . In this sense I have the right to understand myself as the first *tragic philosopher*."[59] The "tragedy" of the man of cognition[60] only finds its "new way to 'yes'" in self-exposure to disgust's "no":

> As I have understood it and lived it until now, philosophy is the voluntary search for even the execrated and vile aspects of existence. From the extensive experience offered by such wandering through ice and desert, I learned to see everything that has been philosophized until now in a different manner. . . . The sort of experimental philosophy that I live tentatively anticipates even the possibilities of a fundamental nihilism: without this meaning that any move beyond negation, "no," a will to the negative is precluded. Rather, such a philosophy desires to break through to the inverse—to a *Dionysian affirmation* of the world as it is, without subtraction, exception, and selection.[61]

In *Thus Spoke Zarathustra*, Nietzsche stages the almost-sacrifice of those who are both knowledgeable and filled with disgust as a literal almost-death: as the protagonist's seven-day coma and near-death-experience. The crisis of symbolic death arrives on the scene when Zarathustra "summons [his] most abysmal thoughts" aloud and "turns [his] ultimate depth out into the light" by an act of vomiting. With a threefold *Ekel, Ekel, Ekel*, seemingly applying to both his own "abyss" and the process of "turning it out into the light," Zarathustra collapses, before emerging from just this crisis as "the convalescent."[62] The path of such cognition, its emphasis on "the execrated and vile aspects of existence" and the almost-sacrifice of the perceiving subject, confronts the Enlightenment model of cognitive light with a disgust-bathed "gloom" and "winter" to cognition. *I feel disgust, therefore I am predestined for cognition:* this the later doctrine of *Beyond Good and Evil* and *On the Genealogy of Morals*. According to *The Birth of Tragedy*, this "main thesis" comprises another thesis, aimed at the knowledge already achieved within disgust: *I feel disgust, therefore I have recognized something*. Disgust is what arrives with a return from the "transport of the Dionysian state," as a "true look into the essence of things":

> For its duration the transport of the Dionysian state, abolishing the usual barriers and boundaries of existence, contains a lethargic

element into which all past personal experience is plunged. Through this gulf of forgetting, the worlds of everyday and Dionysian reality become separated. But as soon as the everyday reality again emerges into consciousness, it is experienced as such with disgust; an ascetic, will-denying mood is the fruit of this state of affairs. In this sense, Dionysian man is similar to Hamlet: both have once cast a true glance into the essence of things, they have *understood,* and action disgusts them; for their action can change nothing in the eternal essence of things—they consider it ludicrous or shameful that they are expected to restore order to a world out of joint. Understanding kills action; action involves being cast in a veil of illusion—this is what Hamlet teaches us, not that cheap wisdom of Hans the Dreamer who, from too much reflection, as it were from an excess of possibilities, never gets around to action; not reflection! no!—true understanding, insight into the terrible truth, outweighs every motive for action, for Hamlet and Dionysian man alike. No consolidation avails any longer; longing passes beyond a world after death, beyond the gods themselves; existence, including its glistening reflection in the gods or in an immortal beyond, is negated. In awareness of the once-seen truth, the human being now sees only the horrible or absurd within existence; he now grasps the symbolic quality of Ophelia's fate; he now understands the wisdom of wood-god Silenus: it disgusts him.[63]

Nietzsche's early and later doctrines of disgust and cognition converge in presuming disgust as correlate to an extraordinary condition or sign of "election." Consequently, cognition as the effect or implicit accomplishment of such disgust is here bound up with an anti-modern and anti-egalitarian model of tragic-heroic distinction. Hence despite the epidemic increase of disgusting phenomena in modernity, in Nietzsche's specific definition both the sense of disgust and cognition are radically untimely: "In heroism, *disgust* is very strong.... The *weakness* of disgust defines industrial and utilitarian culture."[64] In view of its universal utilization interest, such culture cannot favor the disgust linked to "elect" human beings of refinement and distinction. That culture truly marks, for Nietzsche, the victory of optimistic dialectics, whose "confidence" (Hegel) shoves nothing aside. It thoroughly betrays the "lack of shame" Nietzsche attributes to an all-pervasive journalism:

> Much has been gained when the feeling has at last been instilled into the great multitude (into the shallow-pates and greedy-guts of every sort) that there are things they must not touch; that there are holy experiences before which they have to take off their shoes and keep their unclean hands away,—it is almost their highest advance

towards humanity. Conversely, there is perhaps nothing about the so-called cultured, the believers in "modern ideas," that arouses so much disgust as their lack of shame, the self-satisfied insolence of eye and hand with which they touch, lick, and fumble with everything; and it is possible that more *relative* nobility of taste and reverential tact is to be discovered today among the people, among the lower orders and especially among peasants, than among the newspaper-reading *demi-monde* of the spirit, the cultured.[65]

Like the peasants, the other agents of Nietzschean disgust-knowledge are historically marginalized. Nietzsche favors a polemically generalized concept of the "Germans" to denote the contemporary norm contrasting with the "elect" of disgust-led insight. "German" here signifies "*my* bad air," an "uncleanliness *in psychologicis* become instinct" ("one does not *want* to be clear about oneself"), absent "feeling for distance," no "finger for *nuances*," no "délicatesse," and "no esprit in his *feet*." Where all such disgust-sensoria are lacking, Nietzsche sees no chance for himself and his project: "woe is me! I am a *nuance*."[66]

EDUCATION FOR DISGUST

Already for Kant, the feeling of disgust is culturally coded and an effect of upbringing. Nietzsche shares this insight, referring—as Freud will later—to the absence of both disgust and shame in the child, who "reveals all qualities shamelessly, like the plant its sexual organs . . . upbringing is learning to rename or feel otherwise."[67] For Nietzsche, even the cognition-promoting disgust-type he favors needs to learn to feel otherwise. It needs, Nietzsche stresses, an upbringing—a "proper and strict education." But as the pessimistic diagnosis in his talk "On the Future of our Educational Institutions" will have it, "the present-day gymnasium" cannot "inculcate" such education. Indeed, it no longer even has the will to do so: "in the best of cases," it limits itself to "stimulating and fructifying the scientific impulse as such"—then leaving this to its own devices, instead of providing "serious and strict habituation," a training also implying "obedience." For the early Nietzsche, the goal of such "discipline and habit," increasingly absent from modern hermeneutic culture and its emphasis on early, unfettered spontaneity, is nothing other than language itself: learning to walk, linguistically, in the path of the best authors. And crucially, the "physical disgust" needed as a supplement to "noble" insight can only be developed "through such discipline . . . on the thorny path of language":

> In sum: up to now the gymnasium has neglected the foremost, most proximate object for the onset of authentic education, the

mother-tongue: as a result the natural, fruitful ground for all further educational efforts is lacking. For a proper sense of the greatness of our classical authors can only be strengthened by a strict, artistically careful linguistic discipline and habit; up to now, the gymnasium's recognition of these authors has only rested on a doubtful, aestheticizing dilettantism by individual teachers, or on the purely content-based effect of certain tragedies and novels: but one should himself know from experience how difficult language is; one should arrive at the path taken by our great poets in order to reexperience the ease and beauty with which they took it, and how awkwardly or swaggeringly others have followed.

Only through such discipline, the adolescent can gain physical disgust at the so loved, so praised "elegance" of our newspaper-factory workers and novelists, at the "select diction" of our literati; at one stroke and with finality, he is elevated above a row of downright comic questions and scruples, e.g. if Auerbach or Gutzkow are really poets: out of disgust, one can simply no longer read them, and this resolves the question. No one should think that it is easy to develop his feelings to the point of that physical disgust: but also, no one should hope he can arrive at aesthetic judgments in another way than along the thorny path of language, and indeed not linguistic research, but rather linguistic self-discipline . . .

Education begins with a proper linguistic gait: once adequately started, it generates a physical feeling in face of those "elegant" writers—a feeling termed "disgust."[68]

Physical disgust as the effect of linguistic discipline in the medium of literature: with this plea for a "classical" linguistic education—one meant to resemble an education in military movement more than the contemporary humanistic gymnasium—Nietzsche radically stresses the interference present between physical disgust and symbolic order. Hence the valorization of "instinct" over "knowledge" does not allow a naturalistic reading: the "instinct" of such language-trained disgust is "a new habit and a second nature,"[69] not an archaic inheritance and first nature. Its "nobility" does not derive from birth, but from learning to speak and move in the right manner. That it nevertheless is the property of "elect" human beings alone is grounded by Nietzsche in, not least of all, a failure of the "educational institutions." Cognition-guiding disgust only falls into a position of historical improbability in face of structural illiteracy—an epidemic incapacity for distinguished reading, writing, and speaking.[70] Three cognitive functions can be distinguished within this "disgust": it makes cognition *possible;* it is the *path* of cognition; and/or it is a *substitute* for cognition itself. In the last case, it is removed from all argumentation, simply affirming itself as a "physiological" affect of decisive negation. This is the case with bad poets: "one can simply no longer read them, and this resolves the question." It is the case, as well, facing the protoagents of morals: "Whoever not only understands the word 'Dionysian' but understands *himself* in the word 'Dionysian' does not have to refute Plato or Christianity . . . *he smells decomposition* . . ."[71]

Alongside industrial-utilitarian culture, the "democratic mingling of classes and races"[72] and a modern educational system using classical literature more for the hermeneutics of its content values than as the grounds for linguistic "self-discipline," Nietzsche identifies an additional reason why the disgust-based capacity for making distinctions has become anachronistic: the modern "historical sense." As is well known, Nietzsche is not frugal in his critique of nearly all contemporary varieties of historical thinking, from the positivist to the historical-optimistic; occasionally, he even condemns them as disgusting.[73] Still, in more than one respect he counts himself among "men of the 'historical sense.'"[74] The historical sense, however, stands in a goal-conflict with the "classical" or "good" taste—with that "noble" yes and no—upon which Nietzsche otherwise prefers to base his theory of disgust. For the modern historical sense has "virtually the sense and instinct for everything," developing "secret access everywhere, such as a noble age never had." It extends the borders of the palatable far afield, even including works of art that confront us with "repellent fumes" and "sewers of the plebeian quarters." In doing so, "the very definite yes and no" of the refined palate forfeits much of its rigid essence; "easily aroused disgust" is replaced with a disgust of far greater tolerance and more difficult rules of application. In Nietzsche's diagnosis, the reason for the invention of disgust in the 1750s and 1760s—fixing the borders of a purely aesthetic pleasure and an ideally beautiful body—can no longer be "retasted, reloved" in the late nineteenth century. In this respect as well, Nietzsche's disgust "instinct" represents a capacity for distinctions that, despite its untimely nature, is subsumed to historical evolution.

Overcoming Disgust

As the effect of a "strict discipline" in the field of language, the condition, path, and signature of cognition, the *affect* of disgust is always already in contact with that disgusting object which the philosopher engages—in voluntary heroism and up to the borders of almost sacrificing himself—in his descent into the hell of insight. Representing the other side of the (post)modern tendency toward an annulling of all disgust-limits: through what can this disgust-steered insight itself be saved from the danger of "great disgust?" In the voluntary contact between disgust-sensation and disgust-object, what checks disgust from becoming absolute?

The penetrating insight into what elicits disgust already implies a first "self-overcoming" of disgust within "the elect man of cognition": he has, after all, to open himself to the repellent in order to diagnose it. But this first overcoming leads precisely to the danger of "great disgust"—the danger of a circular reinforcement of disgust-sense and disgust-object into a closed system. A second overcoming of disgust is thus necessary at the end of its processing in the field of cognition. Nietzsche specifies only this second stage as an affirmation of life, or aesthetic legitimation of existence. According to *The Birth of Tragedy*, "metaphysical consolation" emerges from art's self-doubling into a Dionysian and opposing Apollonian tendency. With the return from the "transport of the Dionysian state, everyday reality . . . is experienced as such with disgust"; but in the course of just this danger, art shows itself to be a "healing enchantress":

> In awareness of the once-seen truth, the human being now sees only the horrible or absurd within existence; he now grasps the symbolic quality of Ophelia's fate; he now understands the wisdom of wood-god Silenus: it disgusts him.
>
> Here, in this supreme danger to the will, *art* approaches as a redeeming, healing enchantress. She alone can turn those thoughts of disgust at the horrible or absurd element in existence back into ideas that can be lived with: these are the *sublime*, as the artistic taming of the horrible, and the *comic*, as the artistic release from the disgust at the absurd. The satyr-chorus of the dithyramb is Greek art's agent of salvation; the nihilistic mood described earlier exhausts itself facing the intermediate world of this Dionysian escort.[75]
>
> The metaphysical consolation,—with which . . . every true tragedy leaves us—that despite all changes of outward appearance, life is in essence indestructibly powerful and joyful: this consolation appears in bodily distinctness as a satyr-chorus, a chorus of natural creatures, living, as it were, ineradicably behind all civilization, remaining the same for ever despite all change of generations and the history of peoples.[76]

The "turning" of disgust into the sublime and comical corresponds to the devices of disgust's "classical" domesticizing from Lessing to Rosenkranz. Nevertheless, a basically different model is at work here. Lessing and Rosenkranz wish to admit disgust into the field of art solely as something functionalized from the very beginning—as an intensifier of other aesthetic goals. In contrast, "Dionysian Tragedy" creates nothing short of *genuine* disgust at action and existence—a disgust located on the flip-side of ecstasis. It offers negation *as such* an intermediate space within which the "turning" can then take place. Nietzsche thus shifts the process of disgust and against disgust into the artwork itself; he abandons a demand for a functional use of the disgusting as a prerequisite for entry into the aesthetic. Put otherwise, art stages what amounts to a drama of disgust; within its doubled interior, it prompts a transgression and new establishment of those boundaries the classical model defines as representing its absolute outside. Around ten years later, Nietzsche presents a variation of this model for overcoming disgust as the "blissful art" and "fool's cap" of the intellectual "fool":

> *Our ultimate gratitude to art.*—If we had not welcomed the arts and invented this kind of cult of the untrue: then the insight into the general untruth and mendaciousness that now comes to us through science would be completely unbearable—the insight into delusion and error as a condition for our intellectual and sensual existence. *Honesty* would be followed by disgust and suicide. But now our honesty has a counterforce that helps us to avoid such consequences: art as the *good* will to illusion. . . . As an aesthetic phenomenon existence is still *bearable* for us, and through art we are furnished with eyes and hands and above all the good conscience to be *able* to turn ourselves into such a phenomenon. At times, we need a rest from ourselves by looking up and down ourselves and, from an artistic distance, laughing *over* ourselves or crying *over* ourselves. We must discover both the *hero* and *fool* hiding within our passion for cognition; we must now and then enjoy our folly, in order to keep on enjoying our wisdom! And precisely because deep down we are ponderous and serious human beings—really, more weights than human beings—nothing does us as much good as a *fool's cap:* we need it waving before us—we need all exuberant, floating, dancing, mocking, childish, and blissful art, in order not to lose that *freedom above things* that our ideal demands from us.[77]

The "free spirit" of cognition has here emerged in place of tragedy's spectator. Correspondingly, the transfiguration of disgust is no longer present before the contemplator of art in the form of a satyr-chorus; rather, "from an artistic distance," he discovers both hero and fool *in himself.* In the medium of the experience of art, the agent of cognition himself becomes a satyr, henceforth a scholarly satyr, preserving the "honest" disgust of his insight from the full denial of life ("suicide") through floating, dance, and exuberance. The tense field of disgust and its overcoming is maintained, but all the positions in this field are newly occupied. *The Birth of Tragedy* still could proudly announce that "as an *aesthetic phenomenon* existence and the world is eternally *justified.*"[78] Now, far more cautiously: "As an aesthetic phenomenon existence is still *bearable* for us." The prologue to the second edition of *The Gay Science* stresses the abyss of "exhaustion, disbelief, icing up" from which this "element of pleasure," both foolish and wise, is wrested as "consolation":"this radical self-isolation as a defense against a pathologically clairvoyant contempt for human beings, this fundamental self-limitation to the bitter, harsh, and hurtful contents of knowledge, prescribed by the *disgust* that had gradually emerged from an incautious intellectual diet and pampering called romanticism—oh, who could reexperience all of this?"[79] From the perspective of its overcoming, the fixation on the disgust-diet is given a familiar, historicizing name. This is "romanticism," criticized discretely as "incautious intellectual . . . pampering *[Verwöhnung]*": an habituation—*Gewöhnung*—in the false direction (a meaning implied by the prefix *ver-*) that at the same time represents a *self-indulgence*—*Sich-Verwöhnen*—or excessive enjoyment without censure. At play here is a mild echo of the moralizing and entirely non-Nietzschean polemic that classifies the "romantic" as an unqualified abandonment to the disgusting.

Nietzsche's subsequent work itself remains faithful to this peculiar "diet and pampering," while varying the proportions of abandonment to disgust and resistance to it. In *Thus Spoke Zarathustra*, he tries to go far beyond the fool's cap donned for compensatory reasons and the occasional satyr's leaps of the free spirit of cognition. The Übermensch ("Zarathustra himself") is no less than "the man without disgust . . . the overcomer of the great disgust."[80] The provocative guiding principle *"I'm teaching you the Übermensch*. Man is something that should be overcome"[81] can, not least of all, be translated as follows: "I'm teaching you an existence beyond disgust. Disgust is something that should be overcome." When Zarathustra, now recovered, descends from the mountain, he is recognized despite his transformation: "Yes, I recognize Zarathustra. His eyes are clear, and no disgust lies concealed on his mouth. Doesn't he move along like a dancer?/Zarathustra has been transformed, Zarathustra has become a child, Zarathustra has awakened: what do you now want with the sleepers?"[82] A dancing gait, laughing, and being cleansed of disgust are the signs of the transformation Zarathustra has painfully experienced:

> I favor everything clean; but I do not like to see the grinning mugs and thirst of the unclean. . . .
> Are poisoned wells necessary, and stinking fires, and dirtied dreams, and maggots in the bread of life?
> Not my hate but my disgust hungrily devoured my life! Alas, I often grew weary of the spirit *[Geist]* when I found the rabble, too, full of wit *[geistreich]*
> And I turned my back on the rulers when I saw what they now call ruling: bartering and haggling for power—with the rabble!
> I lived with stopped ears among peoples with a strange tongue: that the tongue of their bartering and their haggling for power might remain strange to me.
> And holding my nose, I went ill-humoredly through all yesterdays and todays: truly, all yesterdays and todays smell badly of the scribbling rabble!

Like a cripple gone blind, deaf, and dumb: thus I lived for a long time, that I might not live with the power-rabble, the scribbling-rabble, the pleasure-rabble.
My spirit mounted steps wearily and warily; alms of delight were its refreshment; the blind man's life crept along on a staff.
And yet what happened to me? How did I free myself from disgust? Who rejuvenated my eyes? How did I fly to the height where the rabble no longer sits at the well?
Did my disgust itself create wings and water-divining powers for me? Truly, I had to fly to the extremest height to find, once more, the fountain of pleasure![83]

Zarathustra describes the crisis and joy of such rediscovery of life as a "fountain of pleasure" in the vision of a "heavy black snake" that has "crawled into the throat" of a twisting, choking, twitching shepherd; while its body hangs "out of his mouth," it has nonetheless first succeeded in biting into his innards:

Had I ever seen so much disgust and pale horror on a face? . . . My hands pulled and pulled at the snake—in vain! they could not pull the snake from the throat. Then it screamed out of me: "Bite away! Bite away!
Its head off! Bite away!"—thus it screamed out of me, my horror, my hate, my disgust, my pity, all my good and bad screamed out of me with one scream . . .
—The shepherd, however, bit as my scream had advised him; he bit with a good bite! He spat the snake's head far away—: and sprang up.—
No longer a shepherd, no longer a man,—a transformed being, surrounded with light, *laughing!* Never on earth had any man laughed as *he* laughed!
O my brothers, I heard a laughter that was no human laughter.[84]

The attack by "great disgust" is here once again represented as an oral attack. But simple vomiting no longer helps—what is now necessary is a determined bite into the "heavy, black snake" of life-satiation, in order to transform choking disgust into the light dance-step and superhuman laughter. This primal scene prefigures a repetition by Zarathustra himself, and a repetition of this repetition by all "convalescents." In the process, it points to the limits of outside help in the cathartic crisis: no helping hand can replace the liberating analogon of involuntary vomiting—the intentional combination of biting and spitting. As Zarathustra indicates, the attack by disgust can itself "create wings."[85] For just this reason, he prescribes his "brothers" with "the great lookout, the great sickness, the great disgust"[86]—in order, that is, to reach the point where the self-overcoming of disgust leads to a new affirmation. Those who betray "great longing, great disgust, great satiation," are called "higher men"; nevertheless, they only satisfy Zarathustra's taediophobic claims as an "omen" of other beings they still need to become or whose arrival they announce: "more victorious, joyful men, those square-built in body and soul: *laughing lions*."[87] In any event, with the intermediate "higher men," Zarathustra does see himself as already rewarded for his verbal "man's fare" and "conquerors' fare" (remaining tied to the "incautious diet" of disgust as its antidote) with omens of recovery:

> They are biting, my bait is effective, before them their enemy, the spirit of gravity, is also wavering. They are already learning to laugh at themselves: do I hear correctly? . . .
> The *disgust* of these higher men is wavering: very well! that is my victory. They are growing assured in my kingdom, all stupid shame is leaving them, they are unburdening themselves.
> They are unburdening their hearts, good hours are coming back to them, they celebrate and ruminate once again . . .
> They are *recovering!*[88]

In the generally unsettling linguistic world of *Zarathustra*, praise of rumination as a sign of disgust's overcoming counts as one of the most singular amalgamations of high tone, Biblical allusion, course realism, and physiological philosophizing. In the encounter with the "voluntary beggar," it is cows that Zarathustra already senses from afar as "unknown companions": "Already I am less alone . . . their warm breath touches my soul."[89] "Apparently" listening, the cows surround "a peaceable man and mountain sermonizer," who immediately recognizes Zarathustra as the "man without disgust." The preacher knows how to offer a memorable response to a query concerning his address to the cows:

> What do I seek here? . . . the same as what you seek, you troublemaker! Namely, happiness on earth.
> To that end, however, I should like to learn from these cows. For, let me tell you, I've already been talking to them for half a morning, and they were just about to answer me. Why do you disturb them?
> If we do not alter and become like cows, we shall not enter the kingdom of heaven. For there is one thing we should learn from them: rumination.
> And truly, if a man should gain the whole world and not learn this one thing, rumination: what would it profit him! He would not be free from his affliction—his great affliction: that, however, is now called *disgust*. Whose heart, mouth, and eyes are not presently filled with disgust? You too! You too! But look at these cows![90]

This sermon on good rumination has frequent echoes throughout Nietzsche's writing. It is not only that in the end Zarathustra expressly defines rumination as a signature of "salvation." In the prologue to *On the Genealogy of Morals*, the author Nietzsche himself claims the repeated rumination of an aphorism in a chapter it opens as his own "model" of an 'art of interpretation,' and of an art of reading that has been forgotten:

> In the third treatise of this book I have offered a model for what in such a case I call "interpretation"—the treatise opens with an aphorism and is itself a commentary on it. To be sure, one thing above all is required to practice reading as an *art* in this way, and it is something thoroughly unlearnt at present—a fact explaining why it will be some time before my writings are "readable"—something for which one must be almost a cow and certainly *not* a "modern man": *rumination*.[91]

Rumination is suited for being the extreme countermodel to "disgust" for one simple reason: it is an enjoyment of the (almost) regurgitated. Rumination fills the mouth with the stomach's repumped contents. But rumination dallies, peacefully and agreeably, with one's own half-digested matter, instead of seeing to its convulsive expulsion. It is thus at once vomiting and not-vomiting—in its repetition, a virtually endless vomiting and equally endless pleasure taken at what has been vomited. This figure of an immanent transformation of disgust into a "fountain of pleasure" is likewise *the* physiological cipher of eternal return. For in both cases, pleasure in return is the prominent sign—rather: the only one—of affirmation. In the last chapter of *Zarathustra*, the "convalescents" arrive at the "child-like" insight that what is good is meant to be repeated and again repeated. "The ugly man" rises to the level of Zarathustra's doctrine:

> *I* am content for the first time at having lived my whole life. And it is not enough for me to attest only this much. It is worthwhile to live on earth: one day, one festival with Zarathustra has taught me to love the earth.
> "Was *that*—life?" I will say to death. "Very well! Once again!"
> My friends, what do you think? Will you not, like me, say to death: "Was *that*—life? For Zarathustra's sake, very well! Once again!"[92]

Saying "yes" means saying "once again"; becoming aware of one's own life without shame means wanting it "once again." For this reason, the "man without disgust," the "child-like" Zarathustra, is simultaneously the philosopher of eternal return. And for this reason, the laughter of the transformed shepherd, who has bitten off and spat out the heavy, black disgust-snake's head, figures as a metonomy and interpretation of the eternal return, captured immediately before in another image.[93] Much puzzled over, this doctrine may be less a positive assertion of both a cyclical philosophy of history and reincarnation, more a means of formulating one, particular thing in other than negative terms: an overcoming of disgust as the prototypical "affliction of the age." The ruminative image captures this doctrine more precisely than would any abstract conceptualization—which according to Nietzsche generally amounts to a rhetorical trick. Ruminating, we say "yes" to what our "stomach" has pumped into our mouths, hence to the threshold of regurgitation. Nietzsche demands this diet, and this demanding practice, from a process of disgust-supported cognition that must not end as "great disgust"—as the definitive rejection of the world in a convergence of disgust-sensation and disgust-object.[94] And just as physical disgust is not least of all the effect of linguistic discipline and "self-discipline," contact with language through reading, and interpreting represents a cardinal "model" for the art of rumination. Where in Nietzsche's diagnosis, the metaphysician is above all a "no"-sayer—someone tossing disgust at this-worldly, sensual life—he discovers an analogous disgust in the modern hermeneutic reader: a "no" to language and its paths of sensuality, its gait and dance. *Geist*, intellect or spirit, is his cipher for this disgust at the text. Hence his biting prophecy: "Another century of readers—and *Geist* itself will stink"[95]—namely, to the extent that it owes its transcendental existence to disgust at the letter at work in (reductive) reading. In contrast, a ruminative reading dwells repeatedly and in ever new variations on the material figurations of language and writing. It never digests completely, rather describing the paradoxical paths of a digestion of the indigestible in the mode of its repetition.[96] If Kant and Goethe saw persistent repetition as a catalyst of intellectual disgust or *ennui*,[97] an overcoming of disgust now proves itself in the praise of eternal return. Since Baumgarten and Kant, the aesthetic has served as the paragon of an experience infinitely resistant to definitive "digestion" in the concept, its pleasurable digestive repetition thus also being maximally disgust-resistant. Nietzsche's project of a disgust-free repetition of life is expressly stamped by this will to repetitive experience *vis-à-vis* the artwork: "We want to repeatedly experience the artwork! One should form one's life so that one has the same wish regarding its individual parts! That's the main thought!"[98]

Nowhere else does Nietzsche present the project of an affirmative overcoming of disgust as pathetically—indeed, serve it up as thickly—as in *Zarathustra*. Hence nowhere else does Nietzsche's tragedy of knowledge shift as easily into paratragedy—into parody. A significant part of what makes *Zarathustra* so disturbing results from the reader being at a loss concerning whether and when the parody begins, whether and when it is desired or involuntary self-parody. The prologue to the second (1887) edition of the *Gay Science*, written soon after *Zarathustra*, points to the shift from tragedy to parody in enigmatic-warning fashion: "Incipit *tragoedia*," we read at the end of this book, which is both disquieting and innocuous. Let people beware! Something downright wicked and malicious is announced here: incipit *parodia*, no doubt."[99] The sublime *sermo humilis* of Zarathustra—the "dumb cow" as protophilosopher and model of the "man without disgust," rumination as an ideal of life and reading—sparks at least a suspicion that the guiding figure of the satyr, after running through the explicit disgust-overcoming roles of tragic chorus and scholarly satyr, has now slipped inexplicitly into textuality itself. In this capacity, it occasionally smuggles verbal fools' caps into the sermons of all-too serious anchorites and gurus. These are, to be sure, fools' caps that only display foolishness indirectly—through the detour of an increase in gravity: those discretely wearing them display such an earnestly philistine gaze, one so humorlessly existential, that the border of (self-)parody appears to have been reached. Shortly before ending, Nietzsche even stages—in an open reference to the like-named medieval institution—a "donkey festival": a festival of donkeys surrounding a donkey, and an appearance on the scene of foolish folly. The chapter "Awakening" above all celebrates the recovery of Zarathustra's followers as Zarathustra's "victory"; but the receding of disgust then shifts to a "mad" scene of donkey worship. A "strange, pious litany" is sung, containing sequences such as the following:

> He does not speak, except always to say "yes" to the world he created: thus he praises his world. It is his cunning that refrains from speaking: thus he is seldom thought wrong.—The donkey, however, brayed "yee-a."[100]

After the eighth refrain of "the donkey, however, brayed 'yee-a,'" Zarathustra intervenes: he "could no longer master himself; he cried out 'yee-a' even louder than the donkey"; he scolds the recovered ones as "the worst blasphemers."[101] These, however, prove themselves bright pupils, striking at Zarathustra with his own devices—with an appeal to an overcoming of gravity that is crowned in laughter: "And whoever has too much spirit might well become infatuated with stupidity and folly itself. Consider yourself, O Zarathustra!/You yourself—truly! You, too, could become a donkey through abundance and wisdom."[102] Zarathustra succumbs after some resistance, acknowledging "a little brave nonsense" as a "good omen" of regained joyfulness and as a suitable celebration for the "joyful old Zarathustra-fool."[103] With his yee-a bray, the parody of his own "yes" saying, he had already spontaneously enacted, beforehand, the identity that nevertheless escaped him: the worshipped donkey is in actuality a cipher for Zarathustra himself. Behind his back, the *Übermensch* is promoted from dumb cow to dumb donkey. The two animals represent a single quality: a ruminative overcoming of disgust becomes yee-a; the "once again" of happy digestion becomes an eternal return of one and the same bray.

The philosopher of disgust as worshipped donkey; the pathos of life-affirmation as yee-a: this surprising turn is open to a double reading. Most obviously and importantly, within the "tragedy" of knowledge—as the "affirmation of life even in its strangest and hardest problems"[104]—it repeats the role of the satyrs' chorus. As the analogon to a satyrs' performance,[105] the donkey festival of *Zarathustra* inherits the overcoming of "great seriousness" through disgust-free laughter that Nietzsche ascribed to the Aeschylean satyr in *The Birth of Tragedy*, and to the scholarly satyr's gambols in *The Gay Science*. It is precisely *as* a tragedy of knowledge that *Zarathustra* must embody "an excess of the highest and most mischievous parody of the tragic itself, of the whole horror of earthly seriousness and earthly misery":[106] this the requirement of Nietzsche's antipessimist reading of tragedy. To this extent, the foolishness of the donkey festival in no way denies the psychology of tragic knowledge; rather, it completes it. In *Twilight of the Idols*, Nietzsche even asks if, as a yee-a sayer, the donkey might not be as tragic as the philosopher of tragic affirmation: "Can a *donkey* be tragic?—To be crushed by a burden one can neither bear nor throw off? . . . The case of the philosopher."[107] The case of Zarathustra?

Nonetheless, the parody does not simply dissolve, upon second reflection, into a confirmation of "tragic" affirmation. Rather, it remains the agent of a critical (indeed satirical) moment—if not regarding the tragedy of knowledge, than at least regarding its protagonists. For Zarathustra is regularly *not* on the same height as the text itself. Instead of laughing over himself, the donkey, he has to be laboriously convinced at least not to be annoyed. When in the mountains, instead of overcoming his "great disgust" at the human, he merely replaces it with another disgust: "I am weary of my wisdom."[108] Even at the end of his journey, Nietzsche's hero is exposed as falling into the trap and "sin" of compassion.[109] This, as well, can pass as the tragic hero's form-determined flaw, since otherwise he could not be destined for failure. But in rendering Zarathustra into a literal example of what it teaches, the text denies an integral moment of the same doctrine. To the extent that Zarathustra is a return, a reincarnation, not only of the shepherd with the snake hanging out of his mouth, but also of the ruminative cow and the braying donkey, the parodic effect is not limited to the excessive concreteness of the doctrine meant to be confirmed. For cow and donkey also very directly deny an integral moment of this doctrine: as house pets, they are both too good and too tame for either Nietzsche's affirmation of the amoral "beast of prey" or for his ideal of the "laughing lion."[110] They cannot pass fully as embodiments of "noble taste." The house pets' turn into the satirical is more than a latent semantic energy; occasionally, Nietzsche classified as "cow-warm milksops" all those "who have nothing from life but its most precarious distinction, *not to know us*": "the blind, the trusting, the simple, the peaceful . . . 'German youths' and other rapturous horned animals."[111]

Nietzsche's pronouncement "I am the *anti-donkey* par excellence"[112] can hardly apply to the Zarathustra of the donkey festival. Rather, what applies here is the law of self-disclosure that Nietzsche formulated in *Beyond Good and Evil* as the law of the unavoidable arrival of the donkey:

> In every philosophy, there is a point where the philosopher's "conviction" appears on the scene: or, to put it in the words of an ancient Mystery:
>
> *adventavit asinus*
> *pulcher et fortissimus*[113]

The donkey festival can be read as Nietzsche's effort to have this critical "point"—this donkey "in every philosophy" and indeed every text—emerge in a conscious and controlled manner: a parodic trick of the philosopher-author, at the expense of the philosopher-protagonist (i.e., Zarathustra) presented, nevertheless, as the wise man par excellence. Hardly has the overcoming of great disgust—*Ekel*—apparently succeeded than the great donkey—*Esel*—comes on the scene. Through his parodic excess, he attests to Zarathustra's distance from his own philosophy of laughing "yes-saying and amen-saying." Within the project of "tragic" affirmation, the distancing from disgust's "no" is neither stable nor a matter of any binary opposition between yes and no:

> The psychological problem in the type of Zarathustra is how he, who to an unheard-of degree says "no," *does* "no," to everything to which one has up to now said "yes," can nonetheless be the opposite of a "no"-saying spirit; how he, a spirit bearing the heaviest of destinies, a fatality of a task, can nonetheless be the lightest and most other-worldly—Zarathustra is a dancer.[114]

While Zarathustra may carry little conviction as a *dancer*, Nietzsche's thinking remains very much attached to a working through of disgust's "no," on whose horizon the laughing "yes" is meant to hover. Occasionally, the programmatic effort to reach the point of laughing "yes"-saying seems to represent a burden on Nietzsche's thought. It sounds like a relief from such a strain when his autobiography asserts: "After the 'yes'-saying part of my task [i.e., *Thus Spake Zarathustra*] was done, it was the turn of the half that was 'no'-saying and *no-doing*."[115] This no-doing side, the "critique of modernity, the modern sciences, the modern arts, even modern politics," does not omit any opportunity to make a finding of disgust. In doing so, it contradicts the dietetic imperative of avoiding "defensive expenditures" through a detour around the disgusting:

> Not to see many things, not to hear them, not to let them approach one—first piece of ingenuity, first proof that one is no accident but a necessity. The customary word for this self-defensive instinct is *taste*. Its imperative commands, not only to say "no" . . . but also to say *"no" as little as possible*. To separate oneself, to depart from that to which "no" would be required again and again. The rational element here is that defensive expenditures, be they ever so small . . . lead to a completely superfluous impoverishment. . . . In face of this, would I not have to become a *hedgehog*? But to have spikes is a waste, even a double luxury, if it remains free to have no spikes, but rather hands that are *open*.[116]

For Nietzsche, "it" apparently did not remain free: the *Genealogy of Morals* is anything but a text with open hands. It moves more decisively than ever to that disgust-steered "no"-saying on whose dangerous "diet" Nietzsche had already long since "pampered" himself. The spike of disgust survives rumination along with all repetitions of "yes"- ("yee-a"-) saying. But this survival implies a shift from a "defensive expenditure"—a negative reaction to the dangers of contamination—to an "*aggressive* pathos," to a weapon in that "war"[117] Nietzsche had named the "revaluation of values": "we're learning disgust anew!"[118]

NIETZSCHE *VETULA*

Lion and cow, donkey and hedgehog—among Nietzsche's multiple identities beyond the human, one still remains. It is the least predictable: "that I am in actuality a female elephant."[119] As a direct motive for this "thought," Nietzsche mentions the eighteen-month "pregnancy" preceding *Zarathustra*'s "delivery." But the figure of both great woman and great mother also belong to the ranks of a (male) disgust at the female: a disgust sparked—in Herder's words—by the "quantity of the phenomenon." The breasts of the giant women of Brobdingnag here served as an example to the same extent as the sexual organ of a "hypergigantically" imagined Juno.[120] Baudelaire's libidinous cathexis of nearly all topoi of disgusting femininity had itself not halted before sheer size. In three sequential poems, *La Beauté, L'Idéal, La Géante*,[121] he portrays himself as an admirer of oversized women, their charms being "fashioned for the mouths of Titans"; he wishes "to explore her magnificent forms at leisure" like a lascivious cat, and to sleep "nonchalantly" in the shadow of her breasts as at the foot of a mountain. When Nietzsche imagines himself the largest land-based mammal on earth, he shows himself to be a good reader of Baudelaire once again.

But Nietzsche's work not only contains numerous, extremely unconventional variations on Baudelaire's gigantic women; the poet's old, ugly, and offensive women are also present—hence the entire spectrum of the *vetula-topos*.[122] Nietzsche uses the "repellent old woman" above all as the prosopopoeia of truth itself: she simultaneously embodies and denounces philosophy's classical goal. To "burned" spirits, savvy when it comes to the psychological tricks and linguistic traps of thought, the striving toward "naked" truth appears "youthful madness":

> No, this bad taste, this will to truth, to "truth at any price," this youthful madness in the love of truth, have lost their charm for us: for that we are too experienced, too serious, too merry, too burned, too deep.... We no longer believe that truth remains truth when the veils are withdrawn; we have lived too much to believe this. Today we consider it a matter of decency not to wish to see everything naked, or to be present at everything, or to understand and "know" everything. "Is it true that God is present everywhere?" a little girl asked her mother; "I think that's indecent"—a hint for philosophers! One should have more respect for the *shame* with which nature has hidden behind riddles and bright-colored uncertainties. Perhaps truth is a woman with grounds for not letting us see her grounds? Perhaps her name is, to speak Greek, *Baubo?* ... Oh, these Greeks! They knew how to *live*. This requires stopping courageously at the surface, the fold, the skin, to adore appearance, to believe in forms, tones, words, in the whole Olympus of appearance! Those Greeks were superficial—*out of depth!*[123]

As part of Demeter's retinue, Baubo is said to have raised her gown at certain occasions and to have made sexually provocative pronouncements.[124] For this reason, she is considered both "personified vulva"[125] and "embodied obscenity."[126] Representations of naked women with spread-out thighs, occasionally riding on a pig's back, were readily linked to her name.[127] *Vis-à-vis* Demeter or among other women performing the same acts, Baubo's obscenities served functions of female self-affirmation and diversion from bitter experience. Men, on the other hand, have regularly classified this type of feminine self-exposure as offensive or even disgusting, thus reacting to the latent threat of castration emerging from an aggressive presentation of female sexuality. In Goethe's *Faust*, Baubo appears on the scene as the leader of Walpurgisnacht:

> VOICE
> The old Baubo's come alone;
> she's riding on a mother-swine.
>
> CHORUS
> Give honor then to whom it's due!
> Frau Baubo forward! Lead the crew!

> A proper pig and mother too,
> The witches' train will follow you.[128]

For Nietzsche, the name Baubo correspondingly stands for the "indecent" self-exposure of "naked" truth. Nietzsche insinuates that the sight is ugly and witch-like, if not disgusting: he views the self-revealing Baubo as "a woman with grounds for not letting us see her grounds." Sight of this naked "ground" puts in jeopardy—even more than Baubo herself—her admirer, the seeker after truth, indeed the project of philosophy itself. "When the veils are withdrawn," truth does not remain truth, but becomes inverted into disgusting nakedness. Paradoxically enough, it remains truth only when veiled and in itself possessing the form of nontruth: veil, surface, appearance, forms, tones, words. Nietzsche approaches another concept beloved by the philosophers, humanity, in the same manner, as an equally ranked sister of the truth-Baubo:

> We are no humanitarians; we would never dare allow ourselves to speak of our "love of humanity"—our kind is not actor enough for that! . . . Humanity! Has there ever been a more hideous old woman among all old women? (—unless it were "truth": a question for philosophers).[129]

Nietzsche's imaginative new variations on the old woman by no means exhaust themselves on the register of misogynist figurations. The old woman does not only assume the place of a naked "truth," its revelation compromising the search itself. At the same time, she is presented as the ideal subject of a skeptical form of knowledge, adhering to the surface of existence and—in a direct inversion of "classical" logic—viewing "truth" as an ideological self-veiling effect of just this surface:

> *Skeptics.*—I am afraid that old women are more skeptical in their most secret heart of hearts than any man: they believe in the superficiality of our existence as in its essence, and all virtue and depth is to them merely a veil over this "truth," the very welcome veil over a pudendum—a matter of decency and shame, and nothing more![130]

All positions have been exchanged here: the old woman is no longer object of knowledge, but now rather its subject. And the surface no longer appears as a shameful veil placed over an indecent-offensive truth, or Baubo; rather, the "depth" itself is merely a surface-effect: a shameful veil placed on that identification of "essence" and "surface" whose "truth" amounts to life having no depth and being only surface. Nietzsche apostrophizes even the result of this skeptical perception—"wisdom" as the knowledge of "truth's" nonexistence, as the burned-brave adherence to the surface and its deceptive truth-*effects*—as a female position. Philosophy is desiring this female position, this woman; and even more so, it means being desired by her: "Courageous, carefree, mocking, violent—that's how wisdom wants us to be: she is a woman."[131]

Nietzsche's philosophizing circulates between these multiple positions of the (old) woman, and it is thus only consequent that he describes himself in a notably prominent passage—the first sentence of his autobiography—as an aging woman: "The good fortune of my existence, its uniqueness perhaps, lies in its fatality: I have, to express it in the form of a riddle, already died as my father, I live on as my mother and grow old."[132] The affirmation of this "good fortune" contains all features of "tragic" existence. For Nietzsche does not hesitate to shed a drastic light on the "fatality" of his aging in the role of his own mother. His portrait of his own family begins with the assertion that "I consider having had such a father a great privilege," then continuing:

> When I look for my profoundest opposite, the incalculable baseness of the instincts, I always find my mother and my sister,—believing myself related to such *canaille* would be a blasphemy against my divinity. The treatment I have received from my mother and my sister, up to this moment, fills me with unspeakable horror: an absolutely hellish machine is at work here operating with infallible certainty precisely at the moment when I can be bloodily wounded.... I confess that the deepest objection to the "eternal return," my genuinely *abysmal* idea, is always mother and sister.[133]

For Nietzsche, continued existence as his own mother thus lacks any idealizing filial love. To the contrary, it is the hardest test of the "once again" to his own life. And just for this reason, by virtue of a suffering extending to "unspeakable horror," the very possibility of Nietzsche's philosophy is at stake here. The old women's deep skepticism is ascribed to an analogous suffering, which Nietzsche similarly endows with the predicates "monstrous," "gruesome," and "dreadful": the paradoxical and sudden submission to a sexual role in marriage under the widely agreed-upon precondition that young women "are to be brought up as ignorant as possible in eroticis."[134] Living on as his own widowed mother, Nietzsche sets out more on this psychosexual track of the "skepticism of the old woman" than in the role of the mother's son. Just as "all the world" demands from women that they discover their good fortune in their "dreadful" role, Nietzsche demands from himself the philosophical feat of affirming his own "fatality"—including the familial fatality—as the "good fortune of existence." This, to be sure, with a significant difference: *his* fatality is no general fatality of sexual role; rather, it is claimed to determine his "uniqueness." In this manner, a gallery is presented that extends from Nietzsche, the child-bearing elephant-cow to Nietzsche, the aging, knowing woman whose skepticism reveals "truth" and "humanity" to be nothing but offensive figurations of herself; and who, as a philosopher, is desired by "wisdom" as by the very power of female experience. As is the case with Baudelaire, these variants of the old woman amount, in part, to a positive countercathexis: one centered on those figures of disgusting femininity whose exclusion constitutes the system of aesthetics. Nietzsche's efforts at an aesthetic legitimation of existence thus attest, precisely, to a shaking of classical aesthetics' very foundations.

6

The Psychoanalysis of Stinking

Libido, Disgust, and Cultural Development in Freud

INTERPRETATIONS OF DISGUST IN
EVOLUTIONARY THEORY BEFORE FREUD

Darwin's study of the expression of feelings in tones, facial expressions, and gestures (1872) is generally seen as the first significant work of empirical research on disgust. Drawing on reports of various informants from across the world, Darwin comes to the conclusion that a wide open mouth—accompanied by other facial expressions that signify spitting, retching, and vomiting—is a universal indicator of the feeling of disgust. As to this feeling itself, Darwin's definition is not very specific: "The term 'disgust'... means something offensive to the taste."[1] Whereas vomiting brought on by the indigestibility of too much food, or of spoiled food, usually occurs a few hours after consumption, disgust can bring about retching and vomiting immediately and even by means of the "mere idea" of eating certain foods. The latter need not contain anything physically harmful; instead, Darwin defines the binary code of disgust simply in terms of the distinction between *unfamiliar* and *familiar*. The curious human capacity of "vomiting so quickly and so easily" at the "mere idea [of some unusual food]" leads Darwin to a bold speculation in the field of evolutionary theory. For this, he relies on an observation made by a Mr. Sutton, who reports "that the monkeys in the Zoological Gardens often vomit whilst in perfect health, which looks as if the act were voluntary." Like these monkeys, Darwin holds, our ancestors had the ability to vomit at will, according to a basic distinction they made among the various types of food they had ingested. The development of language eventually made this ability superfluous: for now man could "communicate by language, to his children and others, the knowledge of food to be avoided." In place of this capacity for voluntary vomiting—which, after becoming superfluous, was then lost—there remained a feeling that acted involuntarily: "now, though this power has been lost, as far as the will is concerned, it is called into involuntary action through the force of a formerly well established habit." Thus, the feeling of disgust is the erratically operating relic of a capacity for voluntarily vomiting up unfamiliar foods—a capacity since usurped by language. Darwin does not take up the question of whether or not animals too could pass on their aversions to food in some way other than through voluntary vomiting. At any rate, it is only by virtue of the disempowerment and displacement of an animal capacity, as carried out in the area of language, that disgust is specifically human. Darwin recognizes no present-day function for this "curious" vestige; he is prevented from doing so not least because our ancestors' capacity for distinguishing types of food involved the rejection, not only of 'genuinely' harmful stuffs, but of everything "which *they thought* would disagree with them." How such classifications of certain foods as "disagreeable" might have emerged, and what function they might have served, Darwin has left entirely unanswered. Not surprisingly, therefore, his narrative of disgust's evolution has not found any followers to date; indeed, in psychology, it has been deemed hardly worth the effort of a commentary.

In 1884, Charles Richet published a different interpretation of the evolution, symptomatic range, and purposefulness of the sensation of disgust from a more orthodox physiological perspective. In this account, disgust appears as an involuntary affective response of self-preservation and of defense against harmful substances; formed through the long experience of our ancestors, and transmitted hereditarily, it has become an "instinct" in the full sense of the term.[2] Accordingly, reptiles, frogs, snakes—which, for Richet, trigger our strongest and most unconquerable feelings of disgust—but also spiders and insects awaken disgust because, with their various poisons, they are genuinely dangerous.[3] It is literally the principal achievement of disgust, in Richet's view, that it identifies and defends against poisonous substances.[4] Richet does not fail to recognize the individual differences among triggers of disgust and the role of association in evaluating everything connected with death and decomposition, as representing the quintessence of all (ideas of) danger and harmfulness. Also, he acknowledges that the sense of disgust would not be able to distinguish between the usefulness of certain toxic substances in small dosages and their harmfulness in higher concentrations, or between highly poisonous and non-poisonous reptiles. Disgust, for Richet, embraces a few "wholesale" distinctions[5] on the basis of one or another *"forme total,"*[6] and, performing its function as an evolutionary organ of self-preservation, disgust cannot but subsume certain harmless animals or foods as well under the elementary categories of harmfulness, if striking resemblances work in favor of this non-distinction. Nevertheless, Richet claims that, in general, "only harmful and useless animals arouse our disgust"; by contrast, those animals which we eat cannot be disgusting to us.[7]

Richet's reflections cannot account for the possibility of profound disgust at the consumption of thoroughly "unthreatening" forms of life that may moreover be highly "useful" to us—cats, dogs, horses, other human beings. Where the "laws" of physiological "uselessness" and "noxiousness"[8] exclusively determine the criteria for what is sensed as disgusting, pus, bodily secretions, and all matter of decay are also disgusting simply because they are, first, "useless" and, second, "toxic" for the living human organism.[9] Richet freely admits that his hypotheses cannot account for such things as a dog's wanting to sniff at an infectious cadaver;[10] by the same token, he could not yet have known of contemporary investigations into the nutritional value of excrement.[11] His physiological interpretation not only pales before Darwin's well-founded caution as regards the purely biological value of the distinction entailed by disgust; by focusing exclusively on the function of defensive self-preservation, it also completely fails to account for the relevance of disgust to that other great "purpose" of every living being—active self-preservation through propagation. Furthermore, Richet makes no distinction at all between danger and bad taste, or between antipathy, anxiety, and disgust. The limited value of the resulting theory becomes still clearer with the following consideration: if it is true that disgust, as an organ of defense against harmful, dangerous, or at least useless things, arose solely from long experience with foodstuffs, then it should be far more at the disposal of animals than of human beings, since instinct-guided or instinct-like distinctions play a more important role with animals. According to almost unanimous opinion, however, this is not the case. Animals obviously distinguish between foodstuffs they eat and those they do not eat; but no reaction comparable to disgust seems to be involved in such distinction. The specifically human character of disgust is therefore better grasped by psychology than by physiology. It was only twenty-five years after Darwin, and thirteen years after Richet's treatise, that Freud's theory of disgust and sexuality was "born" to the world—and in a form requiring little future elaboration. Its difference from its immediate predecessors is immense.

FREUD'S BIRTH

"Another presentiment told me," writes Sigmund Freud, on May 31, 1897, to Wilhelm Fliess, "that I shall very soon uncover the source of morality."[12] A good five months later, on November 14, comes a formal "birth announcement," with detailed description of the newborn "piece of knowledge," which is not least a theory of disgust.[13] The "source of morality"—and at the same time "the essential factor in the development of repression" as well as in the development of civilization—is upright posture. For, in the evolution of human beings, it brings about decisive changes in the relations of sight and smell to the organs of excretion, reproduction and birth. Walking upright represents a break with the interrelation of smell, excretion, and sexuality that is characteristic of animals, and it transforms even the memory of the formerly libidinous fusion of nose, eye, sex, and anus into an "internal sensation" that is "analogous to disgust." The birth of olfactory disgust—"[The] feelings [of disgust] seem originally to be a reaction to the smell (and afterwards also to the sight) of excrement"[14]—is at the same time the birth of sexual repression and of the aesthetic and ethical ideals of cultural development. "The principal sense in animals (for sexuality as well) is that of smell, which has been reduced in human beings. As long as smell . . . is dominant, urine, feces, and the whole surface of the body, also blood, have a sexually exciting effect."[15] At the origin of the affect of disgust stands the phylogenetic "abandonment of former sexual zones." The withdrawal of sexual energies from those zones in turn engenders the dark continent of "sexuality gone under (and become virtual)." At the same time, it is the condition for the possibility of all repression, all perversion, and all neurosis:

> I have often had a suspicion that something organic plays a part in repression; I was able once before to tell you that it was a question of the abandonment of former sexual zones . . . ; in my case, the notion was linked to the changed part played by sensations of smell: upright walking, nose raised from the ground, at the same time a number of formerly interesting sensations, attached to the earth, becoming repulsive—by a process still unknown to me. (He turns up his nose = he regards himself as something particularly noble.) Now, the zones which no longer produce a release of sexuality in normal and mature human beings must be the regions of the anus and of both the mouth and throat. This is to be understood in two ways; first, that seeing and imagining these zones no longer produce an exciting effect, and second, that the internal sensations arising from them make no contribution to the libido, the way the sexual organs proper do. In animals these initial sexual zones continue in force in both respects; if this persists in human beings too, perversion results. We must assume that in infancy the release of sexuality is not yet so much localized as it is later, so that the zones from which sexual cathexis withdraws later (and perhaps the whole surface of the body as well) also instigate something that is analogous to the later release of sexuality.[16]

Disgust, Aesthetic Culture, Antiaesthetic Libido

The story of how nose, mouth, and anus, as "sexual zones," are rendered disgusting remains a *basso continuo* of the Freudian theory of libido, repression, and civilization, all the way up through the late work. In various ways, this narrative involves the same basic distinction that makes possible the emergence of aesthetics as an autonomous discipline: that of "disgusting" versus "aesthetic." Unlike the optical attractions of the skin at the body's surface, the odors, growths, and secretions of the body remain "incompatible with our aesthetic culture." Along with Winckelmann and Lessing, Freud regards "the genitals" themselves as incompatible with the law of "beauty":

> It is above all the coprophilic instinctual components that have proved incompatible with our aesthetic standards of culture, probably since, as a result of our adopting an erect gait, we raised our organ of smell from the ground. The same is true of a substantial part of the sadistic urges which are part of erotic life. But all such developmental processes affect only the upper layers of the complex structure. The fundamental processes which produce erotic excitation remain unaltered. The excremental is all too intimately and inseparably bound up with the sexual; the position of the genitals—*inter urinas et faeces*—remains the decisive and unchangeable factor. One might say here, varying a well-known dictum of the great Napoleon: "Anatomy is destiny." The genitals themselves have not taken part in the development of the human body toward beauty: they have remained animal, and thus love, too, has remained in essence just as animal as it ever was.[17]

As is already the case in Nietzsche, the evolution of disgust, of aesthetic culture, and of ethical ideals are closely intertwined and grounded in one another. The human anatomy itself contributes to the "cultural repression" which prescribes the "transformation of affect":[18] where there was oral and anal libido, there disgust shall be. The partial failure of this law has two results: (1) perversions and (2) neuroses as "the negative of perversions."[19] The possibility of failure follows from the fact that walking upright—and, with it, the cultural code of disgust—must be learned anew by every child. To be sure, given the genetic programming, the acquisition of the erect gait is something conditioned by heredity; to that extent, even the trajectory that leads from the absence of disgust in childhood to the construction of instinct-sublimating barriers of disgust is "organically determined and fixed by heredity, and it can occasionally occur without any help at all from education."[20] But "education has much to do with it," even if it merely "limits itself to highlighting the lines which have already been laid down organically and to impressing them somewhat more clearly and deeply." On an individual level, of course, the barriers of disgust are "purely conventional,"[21] and the success or failure of their operation can vary considerably in individuals depending on their childhood sexual experiences.

Above and beyond the ontogenetic return of the prehistoric absence of disgust, Freud also appears to posit, within the course of human evolution, a direct insistence of that libidinal organization that gets "repressed" with the emergence of upright posture. The memory of extinct pleasures cannot be entirely obliterated: we never quite cease being four-footed sniffers. Repression is by definition always "incomplete"; persisting in our defense mechanisms is precisely what we defend ourselves against. It is therefore not without pathos that Freud diagnoses "the survival of primitive, truly ineradicable coprophilic interests."[22] Upright posture may indeed have led to the devaluing of olfactory stimuli and of excrement, but it has not affected the contiguity or—in the case of masculine anatomy—the functional overlap of the sexual organs and the organs of excretion. Furthermore, it is through standing upright that the sexual organs first become properly visible and hence "indecent." And, with the uncoupling of the woman's olfactory appeal from her menstrual periods, there came a moment "when the need for genital satisfaction [in males] no longer made its appearance like a guest who drops in suddenly and, after his departure, is heard of no more for a long time, but instead took up its quarters as a permanent lodger."[23] Thanks to upright posture, then, "the male acquired a motive for keeping the female, or, speaking more generally, his sexual objects, near him"; upright posture thus provides the incentive for "founding families." Even the progress of civilization, however, is not capable of reliably domesticating the archaic and anarchic inheritance of sexuality. Those impulses that are "hard to educate"[24] survive their cultural subjugation as "demons" and, like demons, are placed under "taboo." The "dread of contact with it" is something that the demonic and the tabooed share with the "sacred"—this being, for Freud, "evidence that the ground covered by the two was originally one."[25] Not only for "mythology" but for cultural development in general, it is a law "that a stage which has been passed, for the very reason that it has been overcome and driven under by a superior stage, persists in an inferior form alongside the later one, so that the objects of its veneration turn into objects of horror."[26] Civilization is the permanent production of abject antiworlds, counterworlds, and underworlds, which are labeled "disgusting, abhorrent and abominable."[27] Disgust is the name for this transformation of affect. The ambivalence and the costs of this transformation constitute the discontents of civilization. In a long footnote to his 1930 *Civilization and Its Discontents,* Freud reformulates the speculations which the 1897 letter to Fliess had dedicated to the subject of man's rendering his own four-footed animal nature disgusting:

> The organic periodicity of the sexual process has persisted, it is true, but its effect on psychical sexual excitation has rather been reversed. This change seems most likely to be connected with the diminution of the olfactory stimuli by means of which the menstrual

process produced an effect on the male psyche. Their role was taken over by visual excitations, which, in contrast to the intermittent olfactory stimuli, were able to maintain a permanent effect. The taboo on menstruation is derived from this "organic repression," as a defense against a phase of development that has been surmounted. All other motives are probably of a secondary nature.... This process is repeated on another level when the gods of a superseded period of civilization turn into demons. The diminution of the olfactory stimuli seems itself to be a consequence of man's raising himself from the ground, of his assumption of an upright gait; this made his genitals, which were previously concealed, visible and in need of protection, and so provoked feelings of shame for him. The fateful process of civilization would thus have started with man's adoption of an erect posture. From that point, the chain of events would have proceeded through the devaluation of olfactory stimuli and the isolation of the menstrual period to the time when visual stimuli were paramount and the genitals became visible, and thence to the continuity of sexual excitation, the founding of the family and so to the threshold of human civilization ...

A social factor is also unmistakably present in the cultural trend towards cleanliness, which has received ex post facto justification in hygienic considerations but which manifested itself before their discovery. The incitement to cleanliness originates in an urge to get rid of the excreta, which have become disagreeable to the sense perceptions. We know that in the nursery things are different. The excreta arouse no disgust in children. They seem valuable to them as being a part of their own body which has come away from it. Here upbringing insists with special energy on hastening the course of development which lies ahead, and which should make the excreta worthless, disgusting, abhorrent and abominable. Such a reversal of values would scarcely be possible if the substances that are expelled from the body were not doomed by their strong smells to share the fate which overtook olfactory stimuli after man adopted the erect posture. Anal eroticism, therefore, succumbs in the first instance to the "organic repression" which paved the way to civilization. The existence of the social factor which is responsible for the further transformation of anal eroticism is attested by the circumstance that, in spite of all man's developmental advances, he scarcely finds the smell of *his own* excreta repulsive, but only that of other people's.[28]

Like several eighteenth-century authors—and in contrast to his immediate predecessors Darwin and Richet—Freud associates disgust, first of all, with the sense of smell; he sees in its evolution, however, an achieved break with the archaic economy of scenting and with the libidinal impulses rooted in the olfactory. Disgust originates in the interstices—in fact, *as* the fracture—of nature and civilization. It is a "defensive symptom" *vis-à-vis* the very nature to which, owing to its connection with the "lower" and "more obscure senses," it has often been ascribed. Like all other such symptoms, "the defensive symptom of disgust"[29] is a compromise formation: it not only testifies to the power of repression but, in the mode of "conversion," it also brings the repressed impulses to a negative "presentation"[30] in conformity with censorship. Instead of being, as in Mendelssohn, the only one of the "unpleasant sensations" incapable of assimilation to (aesthetic) pleasure, disgust is in itself pleasure—pleasure both abandoned and surviving in the form of conversion: "libido and disgust," so runs the early letter, "would seem to be associatively linked."[31] If, according to eighteenth-century aesthetics, the effects of disgust escape the (illusory) processing of the nature-art distinction, with Freud this nonapplicability of the nature-art distinction to disgust can be stated differently: disgust cannot be grasped in terms of the distinction between nature and art, because it first of all grounds this distinction. Up through Kant, it is not only the "life" of aesthetic illusion and aesthetic ideals, but also the life of the body itself that depends on the rejection of the disgusting. If the "vital sense" of disgust stops working, then one is threatened with the danger of incorporating the unwholesome and, finally, with death. Freud has set down the reverse side of this success story. With its power of rejection, the affect of disgust in the end threatens the foundations of life itself and also of the very civilization which is furthered by the evolution of disgust. Disgust is the catalyst for order and cleanliness and yet, precisely as such, it also powers a disruptive trend that Freud evokes as nothing less than a secular apocalypse, as "the danger of the extinction of the human race."[32] Given the rejection of all "instinctual components which have proved incompatible with our aesthetic standards of culture," the affect of disgust serves to further a structural "non-satisfaction" of the sexual instinct:

> What civilization aims to make out of [the instincts of love] seems unattainable except at the price of a sensible loss of pleasure; the persistence of unrealized impulses makes itself present in sexual activity as the feeling of non-satisfaction. Thus, we may perhaps be forced to reconcile ourselves to the idea that it is quite impossible to adjust the claims of sexual instinct to the demands of civilization; and that—in consequence of our cultural development—renunciation and suffering, as well as the danger of the extinction of the human race in the remotest future, cannot be avoided.[33]

Freud's narrative of the suppression of instinct is the basis of all sexual-political rehabilitation of abandoned practices in the field of culture itself. As a matter of fact, nearly all of Freud's thinking is in some degree oriented, with a considerable touch of nostalgia, toward the continent of "sexuality gone under (and become virtual)" of which the letter to Fliess speaks in connection with disgust and repression.[34] The theory of a childhood sexuality originally free of disgust retraces, on an ontogenetic level, the incessantly repeated process by which oral, anal, and excremental pleasure is made disgusting. The theory of perversions considers the insistence of culturally "overcome" practices in the field of fully developed barriers of disgust. The theory of neuroses shows what can happen to suppressed libidinous impulses when the way to open perversion is not followed. And, finally, Freud's studies of religion, language, superstition, literature, and art address above all the traces of censured desires and pleasures formerly rendered disgusting. All these expeditions into the underside of disgust breathe an unmistakable sympathy with their object—an affect for the uncivilized, which habitually infuses even the most striking "perversions" as proof of the power of the abandoned positions of libido.

In terms of its metapsychological and epistemological implications, such an archaeology of the "disgust sensation" presupposes the indestructibility of unconscious desires and libidinous impulses: "It is a prominent feature of unconscious processes that they are indestructible. In the unconscious, nothing can be brought to an end, nothing is past or forgotten."[35] "Every earlier stage of development persists alongside the later stage which has arisen from it," but "the primitive stages can always be reestablished; the state of the soul is, in the fullest sense of the term, imperishable."[36] For the life of individuals and for the work of therapy, this "indelibility that is characteristic of all mental traces"[37] can often make for a heavy burden. For the "fateful development of civilization," however, these "wishful impulses . . . which can neither be destroyed nor inhibited"[38] signify a hope: namely, that the forfeitures of pleasure through the cultural process—instead of terminating in the "extinction of the human race"—will be countered by the stubborn obtrusion of archaic libido-positions. The child, the "uncultivated lower strata of society," the perverts, and the neurotics are, each in their own way, tropes for the persistence of certain pleasures in the civilized field of disgust—pleasures which, in primordial times, held no suggestion of disgust:

> To understand the mental life of children we require analogies from primitive times. Through a long series of generations, the genitals have been for us the *"pudenda,"* objects of shame, and even (as a result of further successful sexual repression) of disgust. . . . What is to be found among us in the way of another view of sexual life is confined to the uncultivated lower strata of society; among the higher and more refined classes it is concealed, since it is considered culturally inferior, and it ventures to put itself into practice only in the face

of a bad conscience. In the primeval days of the human race, it was a different story. The laborious compilations of the student of civilization provide convincing evidence that originally the genitals were the pride and hope of living beings; they were worshipped as gods and they transmitted the divine nature of their functions to all newly learned human activities. As a result of the sublimation of their basic nature, there arose innumerable divinities; and at the time when the connection between official religious and sexual activity was already hidden from the general consciousness, secret cults devoted themselves to keeping it alive among a number of initiates. In the course of cultural development, so much of the divine and sacred was ultimately extracted from sexuality that the exhausted remnant fell into contempt. But in view of the indelibility that is characteristic of all mental traces, it is surely not surprising that even the most primitive forms of genital-worship can be shown to have existed in very recent times and that the language, customs and superstitions of mankind today contain survivals from every phase of this process of development.[39]

Julian Hirsch has extended the Freudian conception of disgust with sexual organs and sexual functions to disgust with bodily secretions of all kinds, with the corpse, and with cannibalism. Hygienic considerations are not sufficient to explain the range and strength of this disgust. Instead, Hirsch sees in such phenomena the misunderstood relics of archaic taboos that have their source in magical thought. "Everything that once belonged to the body of the primitive man and then was separated from him—that is to say, his hair, his nails, his feces, his urine, his sweat, his saliva"—was considered a valuable "component of his person." Such "refuse" had to be hidden away, because any damage it suffered at the hands of an enemy would be felt by the one to whom such parts used to belong. On the other hand, there could be "good" as well as "bad" influences emanating from such excreta, or from the corpse and flesh of a slain enemy. Bodily excreta and (parts of) corpses were therefore regarded as "curative objects to be venerated, on the one side, and cursed objects to be avoided, on the other."[40] To the question of "why only the second of these two attitudes toward human waste and refuse was retained in our civilization," Hirsch responds with an observation already made by Freud: "In the course of cultural development, what is found over and over again is a survival of a loathing and a disappearance of veneration. For what is tabooed belongs always to a cultural form that is repressed and that, as a consequence of its repression, appears as inferior, despised, abominable."[41] Disgust with the smell of decomposition, with worms and excrement, would not then constitute a primary, unmediated expression of the human sensorium, but rather a "vestige" of magical-religious taboos, whose affective value has outlived its long forgotten ritual significance and subsequently come to be rationalized on all sorts of seemingly plausible grounds. While Freud's theory provides an account of the origins of disgust (in upright posture, devaluation of the nose and of excrement), as well as an account of its function (in civilizing, sublimating instinct), Hirsch's modification of this theory presents merely a "causal" model for the emergence of the affect in magical contexts, not a "means-ends" model[42] for the present-day function of its one-sided and misunderstood survival. Freud himself would presumably never have ascribed any self-sufficient explanatory value to an ethnological account of "primitive thinking," but would have used it, if at all, only as a middle term or example for psychoanalytic argumentation.

THE TRIUMPH OF LIBIDO:
THE "PERVERSE" OVERCOMING OF DISGUST

In the *Introductory Lectures on Psycho-Analysis*, Freud briefly summarized his canonic theory of infantile sexuality and its phenomenal similarity with a variety of perversions:

> What in adult life is described as "perverse" differs from the normal in these respects: first, by disregarding the barrier of species (the gulf between men and animals); secondly, by overstepping the barrier of disgust; thirdly, by overstepping the barrier of incest (the prohibition against seeking sexual satisfaction from near blood-relations); fourthly, by disregarding the prohibition against sexual intercourse with members of one's own sex; and, fifthly, by transferring the part played by the genitals to other organs and areas of the body. None of these barriers exist from the beginning; they were only gradually erected in the course of development and education. Small children are free of them. They recognize no frightful gulf between human beings and animals; the arrogance with which men separate themselves from animals does not emerge until later. At the first, children exhibit no disgust at excreta but acquire this slowly under the pressure of education; they attach no special importance to the distinction between the sexes, but attribute the same conformation of the genitals to both; they direct their first sexual lusts and their curiosity to those who are nearest and for other reasons dearest to them—parents, brothers and sisters, or nurses; and, finally, they show (what later on breaks through once again at the climax of a love-relation) that they expect to derive pleasure not only from their sexual organs, but that many other parts of the body lay claim to the same sensitivity, afford them analogous feelings of pleasure, and can accordingly play the part of genitals. Children may thus be described as "polymorphously perverse."[43]

"Perversion" is therefore, first of all, an anachronism, a false coincidence of infantile practices and post-infantile behavior, a desynchronization of sexual and cultural development: "When, therefore, anyone has become a gross and manifest pervert, it would be more correct to say that he has *remained* one, for he exhibits a certain stage of *inhibited development*."[44] The barrier of disgust figures as one of the five "barriers" whose transgression serves to measure the deviation from the "normal." It remains peculiarly vague because, in contrast to the other four barriers, it is not elucidated by any set of specific phenomena. Other texts—above all, the *Three Essays on the Theory of Sexuality*—present the overcoming of disgust as an intrinsic factor in the overcoming of the other four barriers. Thus, perversion and the violation of postinfantile barriers of disgust appear as coextensive. "Perverse" is then the absence of disgust in a context where reactions of disgust and repression are normally expected; it is the untimely persistence of infantile libido, the breakdown of the civilized devaluation of smells, excrement, mouth and anus (a devaluation serving to promote purely genital sexuality). Wherever Freud observes "perverse" violations of the barriers of disgust, a memory of the archaic nobility of these practices is not far away—be it only in the form of a wary proviso:

> The use of the mouth as a sexual organ is regarded as a perversion if the lips (or tongue) of one person are brought into contact with the genitals of another, but not if the mucous membranes of the lips of both of them come together. This exception is the point of contact with what is normal. Those who condemn other practices (which have no doubt been common among mankind from primeval times) as being perversions, are giving way to an unmistakable feeling of *disgust,* which protects them from adopting sexual aims of this kind. . . . Here, then, our attention is drawn to the factor of disgust, which interferes with the libidinal overvaluation of the sexual object but can in turn be overridden by libido. Disgust seems to be one of the forces which have led to a restriction of the sexual aim. These forces do not as a rule extend to the genitals themselves. But there is no doubt that the genitals of the opposite sex can in themselves be an object of disgust and that such an attitude is one of the characteristics of all hysterics, and especially of hysterical women. The sexual instinct in its strength enjoys overriding this disgust. Where the anus is concerned, it becomes still clearer that it is disgust which stamps the sexual aim as a perversion. I hope, however, I shall not be accused of partisanship when I assert that people who try to account for this disgust by saying that the organ in question serves the function of excretion and comes in contact with excrement—a thing which is disgusting in itself—are not much more to the point than hysterical girls who account for their disgust at the male genital by saying that it serves to void urine.[45]

Like "libido" or "morality," "disgust" figures here as a quasi independent agent, a prosopopeia of an affect. Its psychohistorical achievement in transforming childhood sexuality is twofold. It is "one of the forces which have led to a restriction of the sexual aim," and as such contributes to "cultural repression." At the same time, and precisely in this capacity, it has a cognitive function: it "counteracts the libidinal overvaluation of the sexual object." In this way it constitutes the "realistic" antidote to the disposition of infatuation which, in the grip of blind libido, transfigures its "object" with all possible desirable attributes and hence "cannot be easily reconciled with a restriction on the sexual aim to union of the actual genitals."[46] Despite the irony infusing Freud's treatment of infatuation in his theory of sexual overvaluation, he does not even here give the last word to the disillusioning corrective that is disgust. On the contrary: Freud cautions against "using the word perversion as a term of reproach"—and precisely in cases where "the sexual instinct, overcoming various resistances (shame, disgust, horror, pain) makes for astonishing achievements (licking of feces, abuse of corpses)."[47] Only when the highly unlikely condition is met that such sexual practices—which also include "looking on at excretory functions"[48] as well as "cannibalistic desires,"[49]—comprise the only and "exclusive" form of sexuality, does Freud accept the term "pathological" as legitimate. Indeed, he "acknowledges" precisely in those sexual practices that "are so far removed from the normal" a supreme triumph of love:

> It is perhaps in connection precisely with the most repulsive perversions that the psychic factor must be acknowledged as playing an extremely important role in the transformation of the sexual instinct. It is impossible to deny that in their case a piece of mental work has been performed which, in spite of its horrifying result, is the equivalent of an idealization of the instinct. The omnipotence of love is perhaps nowhere more strikingly proved than in these aberrations. The highest and the lowest are always closest to each other in the sphere of sexuality: "from heaven through the world to hell."[50]

In view of Freud's theory of civilization, the acknowledgment of what "perverse" libido is able to achieve is more than simply reluctant. It is by the repression of precisely these "achievements" that Freud measures the "fateful development of civilization": "something is considered 'holy' because human beings, for the benefit of the larger community, have sacrificed a portion of their sexual liberty and their freedom to enact perversions. . . . Civilization consists in this progressive renunciation. It is otherwise with the 'superman.'"[51] The laconic reference to the *Übermensch* as an antidote to cultural repression may well indicate a direct acquaintance with Nietzsche's doctrine, which deplores, in the working of disgust, the cultural repression of all animal instincts and presents the superman (the "man without disgust") as the project destined to counter this repression. Without doubt, Freud's interpretive skills were more than sufficient to appropriate Zarathustra for his gallery of "perverse" overcomers of disgust. The typical representative of unrelinquished sexual liberty and "freedom to enact perversions," however, was the perverse father and—on a somewhat different level—the servant-girl, or the prostitute.

PERVERSE FATHER, SERVANT GIRL, AND PROSTITUTE

Two months before the great letter on "the essential factor in the development of repression," Freud had written Fliess about decisive lessons and disappointments arising from his analyses. Among them was "the surprise that in all cases the *father,* not excluding my own, had to be accused of being perverse."[52] An earlier letter was already unambiguous on the subject: "Unfortunately, my own father was one of these perverts and is responsible for the hysteria of my brother (all of whose symptoms are identifications) and that of several younger sisters. The frequency of this circumstance often makes me wonder."[53] The character of Jakob Freud's perversion has not been elucidated to date. Marianne Krüll proposes[54] that, in view of the very small apartment he and his parents lived in, Freud may have occasionally observed his father masturbating and later come to consider this as a perversion which would have "tempted" the son himself to behave analogously and would have thereby occasioned his "tendency toward neurasthenia."[55] In view of the practices which Freud elsewhere presented as perversions on the part of "all" the fathers of his patients, it is hard to credit this onanism thesis.[56] By the same token, Freud's own incest fantasy of "overaffectionate feelings" for his daughter Mathilde presents a far more aggressive variant of fatherly perversion. On the other hand, Freud immediately defuses the reported dream, reducing it to a second-order wish-fulfillment dream—to a dream, that is, representing not a sexual desire for his daughter but rather only an event within the context of his theory of neurosis: "the fulfillment of my wish to catch a Pater as the originator of neurosis."[57]

In 1886, not long before this wish-protocol of May 31, 1887, Freud had provoked his contemporaries by maintaining that the sexual abuse of children by parents and servants was a widespread and notorious fact, constitutive for the sexual trauma of hysteria. Furthermore, given the impossibility of "normal" sexual relations with children, these "assaults"[58] inevitably "include all the abuses known to debauched and impotent persons, among whom the buccal cavity and the rectum are misused for sexual purposes. For physicians," Freud adds, with notable sang-froid, "astonishment at this soon gives way to a complete understanding."[59] Freud's subsequent doubts regarding the alleged frequency of this double perversion committed against children—violation of the incest taboo and substitution for the sexual organs—were not something he arrived at after reading published critiques of his article; rather, what made him suspicious was precisely the fact that in his psychoanalytic practice the frequency with which he encountered cases of child abuse amounted to practically one hundred percent ("that in all cases the *father*, not excluding my own, had to be accused of being perverse"). To be sure, Freud by no means (entirely) dismissed his seduction theory; what he learned in analysis, however, caused him to modify the theory by assuming corresponding sexual fantasies on the part of the children.[60] This experience also led Freud (as recorded in the same letter to Fliess) to the famous "insight that there is no indicator of reality in the unconscious, so that one cannot distinguish there between a truth and an affectively charged fiction."[61] Both before and after this insight into the role of sexual fantasies, Freud acknowledged an enormously widespread occurrence of child abuse; his readiness to do so may have been strengthened, not only through remembrance of his own father's "perversion," but also by his general hypothesis concerning the ineradicable insistence of precivilized sexual impulses. It is not just a matter of pride in discovery, or of therapeutic thoroughness, if the letter to Fliess, for all its stylistic concision, openly relishes the account of a sexual "hell" while portraying a series of devlish fathers:

> I can also give you some news about G. de B. Your diagnosis was absolutely correct. Herewith the circumstantial evidence:/As a child she suffered greatly from anxiety. At age 8–10, fluor albus (white discharge)./As a child she had painful sensations in the vagina when she beat her little sister. She has the same sensations today when she reads and hears about horrors, cruelties. This youngest sister is the only one who, like herself, loves the father and suffers from the same illness./A conspicuous tic; she forms [her lips into] a snout (from sucking)./She is suffering from several eczema around her mouth and from lesions that do not heal in the corners of her mouth. During the night, her saliva periodically accumulates, after which the lesions appear. (Once I traced back entirely analogous observations to sucking on the penis.)/In childhood (12 years) her speech inhibition appeared for the first time when, with a *full* mouth, she was fleeing from a woman teacher./Her father has a similarly explosive speech, as though his mouth were full.
> *Habemus papam!*[62]

> Dear Wilhelm,
> Would you please try to search for a case of childhood convulsions that you can trace back (in the future or in your memory) to sexual abuse, specifically to *lictus* [licking] (or finger) in the anus.

There must, after all, be some indications or reasons to suspect this where it has occurred. This would then cover the [well-]known functional category in the literature: worm irritation, dyspepsia, and the like. For my newest finding is that I am able to trace back with certainty a patient's attack that merely resembled epilepsy to such treatment by the tongue on the part of his nurse. Age 2 years.—If you transfer [such treatment] to early infancy, you get the semblance of epileptic psychosis in the reproduction [of the scene]. I have firm confidence in this novelty, as well as in yesterday's about the precondition of age in psychosis.—In the case of R. L. who was the subject of the dispute between B. and me, convulsions occurred once a year ago; two younger sisters are completely healthy, as though the father (whom I know to be a disgusting character) had convinced himself of the damaging effects of his caresses.

Cordially, Your Sigm.[63]

The intrinsic authenticity of infantile trauma is borne out by the following little incident which the patient claims to have observed as a three-year-old child. She goes into the dark room where her mother is coping with her [assaulted] state and eavesdrops. She has good reasons for identifying with her mother. The father belongs to the category of *men who stab women,* men for whom bloody injuries are an erotic need. When she was two years old, he brutally deflowered her and infected her with his gonorrhea, as a consequence of which she became ill and her life was endangered by the loss of blood and vaginitis. Her mother now stands in the room and shouts: "Rotten criminal, what do you want from me? I will not give in to that. Just whom do you think you have in front of you?" Then she tears the clothes from her body with one hand, while with the other hand she presses them against it, which creates a very peculiar impression. Then she stares at a certain spot in the room, her face contorted by rage, covers her genitals with one hand and pushes something away with the other. Then she raises both hands, claws at the air and bites it. Shouting and cursing, she bends over far backward, again covers her genitals with her hand, whereupon she falls over forward, so that her head almost touches the floor; finally, she quietly falls over backward on the floor. Afterward she wrings her hands, sits down in a corner, and with her features distorted with pain she weeps./For the child, the most conspicuous phase is when the mother, standing up, is bent over forward. She sees that the mother keeps her toes strongly turned *inward!*/When the girl was six to seven months (!!) old, her mother was lying in bed, bleeding nearly to death from an injury inflicted by the father. At the age of sixteen years, she again saw her

mother bleeding from the uterus (carcinoma), which brought on the beginning of her neurosis. The latter breaks out a year later when she hears about a hemorrhoid operation. Can one doubt that the father forces the mother to submit to anal intercourse? Can one not recognize in the mother's attack the separate phases of this assault: first the attempt to get her from the front; then pressing her down from the back and penetrating between her legs, which forced her to turn her feet inward.
    Enough of my smut. See you soon. Your Sigm.[64]

Just as, at the close of this letter of December 22, 1897, the ironic self-interruption ("Enough of my smut") is immediately followed by the gleeful wish to resume before long the intimate communication, so the next letter starts on a downright humorous note while promising more "smut": "Otherwise, I am resolutely tramping along in the *Dreckology*."[65] And a few days later: "Today I am sending you Number 2 of the *Dreckological Reports*, a very interesting journal published by me for one single reader."[66] The letter concerning the "men who stab women" furnishes the motto for these serialized reports on men perversely overcoming the barriers of disgust, and on their "freedom to enjoy perversion" without disgust inhibiting them: "I can scarcely detail for you all the things that resolve themselves into—excrement for me (a new Midas!). It fits in completely with the theory of internal stinking."[67] Turning up occasionally in the "perversions of the seducers," although transformed by the clinical context, is Nietzsche's master trope for the overcoming of disgust—the dancing and leaping satyr: "The explanation for the phase of 'clownism' in the Charcot seizure model lies in the perversions of the seducers who, due to repetition compulsion, obviously even after their years of youth, seek satisfaction while performing the wildest capers, somersaults, and grimaces."[68] In his facetious dreckology, Freud himself plays the role of a scientific satyr who, void of disgust, faces man's animal nature: "Perversions regularly lead to zoophilia and have an animal character."[69] This is not necessarily to be understood as a pathological finding. To be sure, Freud's perverse fathers certainly produce hysterical or compulsive-neurotic patients, but they themselves can well be psychically "healthy." It is in full accord with his earlier libido theory, and his "theory of internal stinking," when Freud at one point writes: "Until the father fell ill himself, he had been a pervert and hence healthy."[70] The same theme informs a case history:

> A fragment from my daily experience. One of my patients, in whose history her highly perverse father plays the principal role, has a younger brother who is looked upon as a common scoundrel. One day, the latter appears in my office to declare, with tears in his eyes, that he is not a scoundrel but is ill, with abnormal impulses and

inhibition of will. He also complains, entirely as an aside, about what surely are nasal headaches. I direct him to his sister and brother-in-law, whom he indeed visits. That evening, the sister calls me because she is in an agitated stage. Next day, I learn that after her brother had left, she had an attack of the most dreadful headaches—which she otherwise never suffers from. Reason: the brother told her that when he was 12 years old, his sexual activity consisted in kissing [licking] the feet of his sisters when they were undressing at night. In association, she recovered from her unconscious the memory of a scene in which (at the age of 4) she watched her papa, in the throes of sexual excitement, licking the feet of a wet nurse. In this way she surmised that the son's sexual preferences stemmed from the father, and that the latter also was the seducer of the former. Now she allowed herself to identify with him and assume his headaches. She could do this, by the way, because during the same scene the raving father hit the child (hidden under the bed) on the head with his boot./The brother abhors all perversity, whereas he suffers from compulsive impulses. That is to say, he has repressed certain impulses which are replaced by others with compulsions. This is, in general, the secret of compulsive impulses. If he could be perverse, he would be healthy, like the father.[71]

The acknowledgment of one's own "perversity"—which involves overcoming the barrier of incest and the pleasure-sapping "respect for women"—is precisely what enables sexual "happiness" amidst cultural repression: "It sounds not only disagreeable but also paradoxical, yet it must nevertheless be said that anyone who is really to be free and therefore also happy, in the sphere of love, must have overcome his respect for women and made peace with the idea of incest with his mother or sister."[72] Moreover, being free—"really . . . free and therefore also happy"—means being free from the inhibition of disgust and hence free for perversion—like Freud's own father, and like all the fathers of all the hysterics and compulsive neurotics analyzed by Freud. "In our present cultural situation," however, this positive "freedom to enact perversions" can be had only at the price of an ironical "psychic impotence" and a "debasement of the sexual object." Conforming to the cultural rules of respect, the "educated" man suppresses his perverse tendencies toward his own wife and thus experiences with her only a sharply reduced sexual pleasure. By the same token, he can develop "his full potency" only in the company of "inferior" women, to whom he "need not attribute aesthetic scruples":

> There are only a very few educated people in whom the two currents of affection and sensuality are properly fused; the man almost always feels his respect for the woman acting as a restriction on his

sexual activity, and only develops full potency when he is with a debased sexual object; and this in turn is partly caused by the fact that among his sexual aims there are perverse components, which he does not venture to satisfy with a woman he respects. He is assured of complete sexual pleasure only when he can devote himself unreservedly to obtaining satisfaction, which with his well-brought-up wife, for instance, he does not dare do. This is the source of his need for a debased sexual object, a woman who is sexually inferior, to whom he need not attribute aesthetic scruples, who does not know him in his other sexual relations and cannot judge him in them. It is to such a woman that he prefers to devote his sexual potency, even when the whole of his affection belongs to a woman of a higher kind.[73]

The "average uncultivated woman," the servant girl, and the prostitute thus come to be seen as virtually unavoidable correlates of the "educated man's" desired—because healthy—freedom from disgust and freedom for perversion. In Freud's eyes, the wholesale "aptitude" for prostitution on the part of countless women, their aptitude for all the "perversions" practiced in this "profession," puts the "definitive" seal to his theory that perversions are "a general and fundamental human characteristic":

> According to the age of the child, the mental dams against sexual excesses—shame, disgust and morality—have either not yet been constructed at all or are only in the process of being constructed. In this respect, children behave no differently than an average uncultivated woman in whom the same polymorphously perverse disposition persists. Under ordinary conditions she may remain normal sexually, but, if she is led on by a clever seducer, she will find every sort of perversion to her taste, and will retain them as part of her own sexual activities. Prostitutes exploit the same polymorphous, that is, infantile, disposition for the purposes of their profession; and, considering the immense number of women who are prostitutes or who must be supposed to have an aptitude for prostitution without being engaged in it, it becomes impossible not to recognize that this same disposition to perversions of every kind is a general and fundamental human characteristic.[74]

For their part, the women "of a higher kind" also seem bent on confirming Freud's theory. They develop phobias which reveal that they are barely able to suppress their own talent for prostitution and for "perversions of every kind":

> I have found all sorts of nice explanations in my field. I actually confirmed a conjecture I had entertained for some time concerning

the mechanism of agoraphobia in women. No doubt you will guess it if you think of "public" women. It is the repression of the intention to take the first man one meets in the street: envy of prostitution and identification with prostitutes.[75]

Once aroused, the woman's dormant perverse "dispositions" can develop on their own. Having been seduced at some point, women now become seducers themselves and, like the fathers, ply their injurious trade with children; this makes up the second part of Freud's insight into the *"role of servant girls"* in the typical bourgeois family. Whether careless or deliberate, their occasional stimulation of the children's genitals during bathing and dressing can subsequently engender all sorts of neuroses; their tonguing of the anus (see above) can cause "quasi-epileptic seizures" later on. The following report on another servant-girl-perversion blends seamlessly with the aforementioned account of hysterical agoraphobia: "Will you believe that the reluctance to drink beer and to shave was elucidated by a scene in which a nurse sits down *podice nudo* [with bare buttocks] in a shallow shaving bowl filled with beer, in order to let herself be licked, and so on?"[76] The formula "and so on" invites excessive interpretation. The presence of such sexually available servant girls regularly represents a burden for the numerous hysterical daughters in Freud's case histories:

> An immense load of guilt, with self-reproaches (for theft, abortion), is made possible by identification with these people of low morals, who are so often remembered, in a sexual connection with father or brother, as worthless feminine material. And, as a result of the sublimation of these girls in fantasies, highly improbable charges against other people are contained in the fantasies. Fear of prostitution (fear of being in the streets alone), fear of a man hidden under the bed, and so on, also point in the direction of the servant girl. There is tragic justice in the circumstance that the master's stooping to a maidservant is atoned for by his daughter's self-abasement.[77]

The "universal tendency to debasement" in the erotic life of civilized man thus dramatically affects the "family romance." This debasement can be understood in terms of the position and the value it assigns to sexuality and its agents within the highly charged field of three overlapping oppositions: disgust versus overcoming the disgust barrier; "normal" sexuality versus "indestructible" perverse impulses; morality/respect/civilization versus archaic-anarchic-unrespectful-antisocial "pleasure."[78] The "healthy" acting-out of "perverse sexual aims" forms a trajectory leading over the disintegration of "heavenly and earthly," social and sexual love to a "tragic" debasement of all positions within the sexual field. So "fateful" is the "development of civilization" that the underlying fund of "animal" sexuality—wherever it has not already succumbed to repression—finds itself, in the very midst of its triumph, converted to impotence and debasement. The "educated man of culture" who, in the face of his own perverse impulses, "subjects himself to a serious self-examination, will be sure to find that he regards the sexual act as basically something degrading, which defiles and pollutes not only the body."[79] This latent feeling of self-debasement is in line with the overt "condition of debasement" required in the sphere of those sexual objects (maidservant, prostitute) who alone make it possible for the civilized man "freely to express his sensuality, while developing considerable sexual capacities and enjoying a high degree of pleasure."[80] At the same time, this man's wife is herself debased out of "respect"; that is to say, with the abatement of the man's potency and libido in her presence, she is deprived of her own sexuality: "it is naturally just as unfavorable for a woman if a man approaches her without his full potency as it is if his initial overvaluation of her when he is in love gives place to undervaluation after he has possessed her."[81] In her fantasies and phobias, this same woman can then experience "envy of prostitution" and go on to identify with prostitutes. The daughter, finally, is incorporated into this cycle of debasement either directly through acts of perversion and abuse or by detour through hysterical fantasies, with which she inwardly digests the "master's stooping to a maidservant" and the diffused sexual relations of brother and servant girl.

Faced with this apocalyptic picture, Freud at first emphatically demanded far-reaching reforms in the area of sexual relations as the only chance for civilization's survival.[82] Later, his belief in the necessity of reform coexisted with doubt as to its possibility. Where the "development of civilization" is itself what is "injurious," the danger arises that every new attempt to regulate the barriers of disgust and of perversion would necessarily entail—given the presence of "indestructible desires"—only new calamity and perhaps even "graver sacrifices."[83] Despite the "universal tendency to debasement in the sphere of love," which follows from the persistence of "perverse" impulses, Freud has left no doubt about one tenet in particular: worse than the normal "hell" of realized perverse practices is the repression of the polymorphous-perverse inheritance in the various pathological forms of neurosis. The greater and more invariable the successes of the culturally sanctioned barriers of disgust, the more certain is the individual's miserable subjection to henceforth fully unconscious powers severed from the ego.

Habemus Vetulam

Freud has confirmed in rather spectacular fashion the considerable "role played by the maidservant" and her perverse "talents" in his own sexual and intellectual development. It is not only among the data preparatory to the formulation of the Oedipus complex that the dream of a maidservant (having reference to Freud and his wife) shows up: "Hostile impulses against parents (a wish that they should die) are also an integrating constituent of neuroses. It seems as though this death wish is directed in sons against their fathers and in daughters against their mothers. A maidservant makes a transference from this by wishing her mistress to die so that her master can marry her. (Observation: Lisel's dream [relating] to Martha and me)."[84] In his self-analysis, Freud sought to unearth the role of the "nurse in whose charge I had been from some date during my earliest infancy till I was two and a half." In *The Interpretation of Dreams*, this "female servant" was remembered as a "prehistoric old nursemaid," as "old and ugly," but also "sharp and efficient"; "her treatment of me was not always lavish in its amiability, and her words could be harsh." Nevertheless, Freud identified this "prehistoric old nursemaid" as the true addressee of the exhibition wish which he uncovered within one of his own dreams of being naked. The analysis of the dream concludes on a cautious note: "It is reasonable to suppose that the child loved the old woman . . . in spite of her rough treatment of him."[85]

The letters to Fliess go much farther than this modest indication. Enigmatically enough, one of the early dream anamneses not only notes the return of the "old liking" for the "old woman," but explains "that my 'authoress' was an ugly, elderly, though clever woman." Biographies of Freud have had great difficulty in discovering even the name of this woman. At present, nothing more is known than that the "old woman" apparently was named Resi Wittek, although initially she had been identified as Monica Zajíc.[86] This Resi Wittek appears to overshadow even the "old man"—Freud's father—and the Oedipal love for his mother:

> For the last four days my self-analysis, which I consider indispensable for the clarification of the whole problem, has continued in dreams and has presented me with the most valuable elucidations and clues. At certain points I have the feeling of being at the end, and so far I have always known where the next dream-night would continue. To put it in writing is more difficult than anything else for me; it would take me too far afield. I can only indicate that the old man plays no active part in my case, but that no doubt I drew an inference by analogy from myself to him; that my 'authoress' was an ugly, elderly, though clever woman, who told me a great deal about God Almighty and hell, and who instilled in me a high opinion of my own capacities . . . I have not yet grasped anything at all of the scenes themselves which lie at the bottom of the story. If they come [to light] and I succeed in resolving my own hysteria, then I shall be grateful to the memory of the old woman who provided me at such an early age with the means for living and going on living. As you see, the old liking is breaking through again today. I cannot convey to you any idea of the intellectual beauty of this work.[87]

The letter itself provides no clue as to why and how the ugly old servant woman was Freud's "authoress"; it leaves the whole matter in a dreamy obscurity. There is no reason given for the degree of affect that is evidently bound up with the "memory of the old woman." The biographies of Freud have yet to provide any details about "whatever it was that Resi Wittek actually did with or to him."[88] Neither mother nor midwife *(Hebamme)*, this nursemaid nonetheless played the role of a prime mover *(Ur-Heberin)*, an authoress *(Urheberin)* of Freud's "own capacities"—indeed, his "means for living and going on living." The letter's sole concrete explanation for this distinctive authorship gives the impression of a fruitful intellectual curriculum: "[she] told me a great deal about God Almighty and hell and . . . instilled in me a high opinion of my own capacities." Yet, on the following day, a new dream is reported in which the old woman now appears as an instructor and initiator in sexual matters. In this particular area, she by no means promoted little Sigmund's "high opinion of [his] own capacities" with encouraging words, but rather scolded him violently for his incapacity:

> October 4. The children arrived. The fine weather is gone. Today's dream has, under the strangest disguises, revealed the following: she was my teacher in sexual matters and complained because I was clumsy and unable to do anything. (Neurotic impotence always comes about this way. The fear of not being able to do anything at all in school thus obtains its sexual substratum.) At the same time, I saw the skull of a small animal and in the dream I thought "pig," but in the analysis I associated it with your wish two years ago that I might find, as Goethe once did, a skull on the Lido to enlighten me. But I did not find it. So [I was] a "little block-head" [literally, a sheep's head]. The whole dream was full of the most mortifying allusions to my present impotence as a therapist. Perhaps this is where the inclination to believe in the incurability of hysteria begins. Moreover, she washed me in reddish water in which she had previously washed herself. (The interpretation is not difficult; I find nothing like this in the chain of my memories, so I regard it as a genuine ancient discovery.) . . . A harsh critic might say of all this that it was retrogressively fantasized instead of progressively determined. The *experimenta crucis* must decide against him. The reddish water would indeed seem to be of that kind. Where do all patients get the horrible perverse details which often are as remote from their experience as from their knowledge?[89]

According to Freud's own theory of the dream as wish fulfillment, the "mortifying" sequence of sexual impotence-pig-sheep's head-therapeutic incapacity would function less as the "dream-thought" of this dream than as a diversionary tactic designed to circumvent the courts of censorship, while in other respects conforming to the demands of the (super)ego. In itself, the trajectory from the sexual impotence of the child to the professional impotence of the therapist would hardly correspond to the emphatically declared libidinal bond and intellectual gratitude toward the ugly old woman. In view of the closing remark, "where do patients get the horrible perverse details?" and in view of Freud's special interest in the fate of perverse impulses, the memory introduced by "moreover" may be what is decisive: "Moreover, she washed me in reddish water in which she had previously washed herself." The interpretation, as he says, does not appear very difficult: the boy was washed in menstrual blood. In his *Poetics*, Aristotle offers a paradoxical proof of reality that proceeds precisely from emphasizing the striking improbability of an event or an action: something that is extremely improbable can only be real—because it is too unlikely to have been invented—and thus deserves more credence than any average probability.[90] By the same token, Freud also infers the presence of a "genuine ancient discovery"—namely, of something repressed—on the basis of its absence from his conscious "chain of memories." The "taboo on menstruation" was for Freud the quintessence of all "organic repression," such as developed in consequence of upright posture. Menstrual blood is *the* abject phenomenon in the development of civilization; its libidinal cathexis is therefore the surest sign of "animal" sexuality, whose forms henceforth are reckoned as "disgusting, abhorrent, and abominable."[91] The "prehistoric old nursemaid" would have thus introduced little Sigmund into prehistoric, now "perverse" practices in which "blood, too, [has] a sexually exciting effect":[92] a classic case of Freudian seduction theory. As Siegfried bathed in dragon blood, so Sigmund in menstrual blood, and by this means he was rendered (almost) totally resistant to disgust; and hence to the urge to adapt to the cultural repression which is sedimented in the barriers of disgust. This perhaps explains his gratitude to the "memory of the old woman": Siegfried was made (almost) invulnerable by the bath in blood, while Sigmund sees himself thereby "provided . . . at such an early age with the means for living and going on living." For overcoming the taboo on menstruation paves the way—at least in the wishful thinking of the dream—to further intellectual overcoming of the barriers of disgust and unpleasant contact; it prepares the liberation of Freud's particular "capacities" through acknowledgement of a "perverse," and therefore tabooed instinctive component and through the theory and practice of psychoanalysis that rests on such acknowledgment.

Freud liked to dream self-referential dreams not only *to the benefit* of his self-analysis and its elaboration for theoretical purposes but also *on the subject* of these things: "I can have dreams like that on order."[93] If subsequently it turned out that the dream did not conform to the use it was intended for and hence did not please Freud, he could allegedly order a "replacement dream," which was supposed to "improve on" particular elements. In the case of the "prehistoric old nursemaid" who was his "authoress," Freud apparently found no occasion for improvement. The bath in her blood was upheld as a "genuine ancient discovery" in the field of his own prehistory, and preventively shielded against any suggestion that it might have been fantasized: the *"experimenta crucis* must decide against [such criticism]." This claim to truth holds not only insofar as the dream-thought underlying the manifest content of the bath in Freud's dream transforms—through his feeling of gratitude—the old woman's rough handling of him into a source of pleasure; it holds all the more since the dream has a directly sexual wish dimension: Freud regards the "memory of the old woman," and the "story" to which she is linked, as decisive for "resolving [his] own hysteria." To the extent that hysteria essentially "is not repudiated sexuality but rather *repudiated perversion*,"[94] the aetiology of his own hysteria too can disclose the possibility of a resolution only through anamnesis of "perverse details." The "perverse" bath in menstrual blood would then be "genuine" precisely because it was discovered only, conforming to Freud's concept of original "deferral," belatedly. It provided a "resolution" not of any factual circumstance but rather of the *wish* to be free of the hysteria occasioned by his father's perversion, as well as that occasioned by his own perverse impulses, and thus also to be free of the regulations imposed by the "normal" barriers of disgust; beyond this, it answered to the wish to have a prehistoric-mythological *authorization* for such freedom. *"Habemus papam!"*[95] Freud exclaimed on uncovering another "perverse" story of seduction. There, the "genuine ancient discovery" in the prehistory of a woman patient with eczema around her mouth and fluor albus—"sucking the penis" of the father—serves analogously the "resolution" of a hysteria. For Freud himself, despite the explicit reference to a similarly perverse father, the case is otherwise: *Habemus vetulam!* The ugly and lascivious old woman of ancient literature and of eighteenth-century aesthetics returns anew; but instead of being demonized as witch and hag, she is venerated now, in grateful remembrance, as "authoress" and relic of an older religion of pleasure.

It is in keeping with this conversion of affect that the figure of the ugly old woman with her "perverted" practices—practices that transgress the demands of "aesthetic culture"—is nowhere qualified with the predicate "disgusting." This is the case with perversions in general: even where "the sexual instinct goes to astonishing lengths in successfully overriding the resistances of . . . disgust,"[96] these perverse "achievements" are at no point labeled disgusting in themselves.[97] To be sure, Freud speaks throughout of "aesthetically repulsive,"[98] indeed of "the most repulsive"[99] perversions. He even sees the project of psychoanalysis itself as caught in this "hellish" undertow—"I know that what I am doing is odious to the majority of people"[100]—and, therefore, he regularly feels himself obliged to justify, as an object of scientific study, "all the abominations which we are supposed to have discovered on the basis of our premises."[101] But he consistently maintains a certain distinction: the transgressions against the cultural barriers of disgust are disgusting only for this culture itself, not for the psychoanalyst. Furthermore, the affect of disgust is an aspect of the "illness" from which it promises escape. In the context of evolutionary and cultural history, this affect belongs to the "fateful" syndrome of "organic repression" and "cultural repression." In terms of individual pathology, it belongs—as a sensation affecting the individual on an (apparently) false, or inadequate occasion—to the neurotic symptoms.

Disgust and the Choice of Neurosis

"The instincts of love are hard to educate; education of them achieves now too much, now too little."[102] In the case of "too little" cultural restraint, an overt— and "healthy"—acting-out of the variety of "perverse" impulses results. In the case of "too much" repression, "a constant danger" develops, one "to which, in the form of neurosis, the weaker are succumbing today."[103] Neuroses, as Freud never tired of repeating, are "the *negative* of perversions."[104] Between the poles of "now too much" and "now too little," there is little room left for the phantom of "normal" sexuality. This latter has to comply—at one and the same time, and in equal measure—with two opposed imperatives: that of the cultural barrier of disgust and that of the libidinal overcoming of genital-focused disgust in the interests of sexual fulfillment. Burdened with this delicate, if not impossible balancing act between two opposed claims, "normal" sexuality routinely ends up passing over into the two forms of failed balance and thus turns into either the positive or "the negative of perversions." Neurotic symptoms "give expression (by conversion) to instincts which would be described as *perverse* in the widest sense of the word, if they could be expressed directly in fantasy and action without being diverted from consciousness."[105] A hysterical cough, for example (this is Freud's famous example of Dora), can then be read as a symptom of defense against the wish to have oral intercourse with one's father, while disgust at the sexual advances of a beloved man can be read as deferred disgust at one's own habit of masturbation and its (alleged) organic consequence, fluor albus.[106] In hysterical vomiting Freud regularly discovers the wish "to be . . . continuously pregnant and have innumerable children," and, to be sure, "by as many men as possible."[107] In order more fully to convince the skeptical reader of the quasi-natural propagation of such fantasies among young people, Freud occasionally has recourse, once again, to that "anatomy" which is our "destiny": "So we see that this exceedingly repulsive and perverted fantasy of sucking a penis has the most innocent origin. It is a recasting of what may be described as a prehistoric impression of sucking at the mother's or nurse's breast—an impression that has usually been revived through contact with children who are nursing. In most instances, a cow's udder has aptly played the part of an image intermediate between a nipple and a penis."[108] Freud's own "prehistoric old woman" and nursemaid may also have been helpful in this regard. (Empirical psychology, in several statistical studies, has confirmed Freud's positive correlation of neuroticism and susceptibility to disgust.[109])

In order to distinguish between types of neuroses, and, above all, between hysteria and obsessional neurosis, Freud made use of a range of dichotomies and trichotomies. The "birth announcement letter" to Fliess makes the "choice of neurosis" dependent, first of all, on the moment of pleasure's conversion into disgust:

> It is probable, then, that the choice of neurosis—the decision whether hysteria or obsessional neurosis or paranoia emerges—depends on the nature of the thrust (that is to say, its temporal determination [i.e., occurrence on the axis of age or phase of psychic development]) which enables repression to occur; that is, which transforms a source of internal pleasure into one of internal disgust.[110]

The types of neurosis not only differ in terms of the age at which their onset *as* neurosis typically occurs;[111] the nature of the traumatizing event itself (as it occurred years earlier) allows for another distinction: "Hysteria is the consequence of a presexual *sexual shock*. Obsessional neurosis is the consequence of a presexual *sexual pleasure*, which is later transformed into [self-]*reproach*."[112] Presexual here means "actually before puberty, before the release of sexual substances; the relevant events become effective only as *memories*." The concept of an originally deferred or belated effect is integral to Freud's proud announcement in the letter of November 14, 1897:

> A release of sexuality . . . comes about, then, not only (1) through a peripheral stimulus upon the sexual organs, or (2) through the internal excitations arising from those organs, but also (3) from ideas—that is, from memory traces—and therefore by the path of deferred action. (You are already familiar with this line of thought. If a child's genitals have been irritated by someone, years afterward the memory of this will produce by means of deferred action a release of sexuality far stronger than at the time [of the traumatizing occurrence], because the decisive apparatus and the quota of secretion have meanwhile increased.) . . . Deferred action of this kind occurs also in connection with a memory of excitations of abandoned sexual zones. The outcome, however, is not a release of libido but of an unpleasure, an internal sensation analogous to disgust in the case of an object./To put it crudely, the memory stinks in the present, just as in the present the object stinks; and just as we turn away our sense organ (the head and nose) in disgust, the preconscious and the sense of consciousness turn away from the memory. This is *repression*.[113]

With regard to this year-long delay in the emergence of disgust as a neurotic symptom, Freud's theory of disgust diverges from widely-held anthropological assumptions at two key points. For eighteenth-century anthropology, as for Aurel Kolnai's phenomenology of disgust, obtrusive physical presence or proximity—and hence a particularly striking case of "object" experience—was *the* indicator of an excitation of the prototypical senses of disgust, smell, and taste. With Freud, on the other hand, disgust originates in a virtual space, as a memory-bridge between two data which, in themselves, each lack what is disgusting. The traumatic event, the presexual sexual shock is not experienced as disgusting at the time of its occurrence, despite its having the character of an assault, because the physical (and moral) "apparatus" necessary for the experience of sexual disgust is not yet developed. And the later, factical trigger of "disgust," in its presence to the senses, can lack every ostensible mark of the disgusting. It is the short-circuiting of the two experiences in the memory that first engenders, in the mode of deferral, the feeling of disgust in regard to some nondisgusting later experience, while at the same time, obliquely and belatedly, rejecting the earlier experience. To be a "defensive symptom" has a radical consequence for disgust: it means that disgust "can arise only from memories," that only in memory can it "stink in the present." "Real" experiences, on the other hand, have no such effect: "None of the later scenes, in which the symptoms arise, are the effective ones; and the experiences which *are* effective have at first no result."[114] The affect of disgust thus arises as a deferred "effect" in a virtual space between two noneffects. It attains its present actuality as a stink-reaction only after years of deferral through a "false" object: in this respect also, Freud's theory of sexual "hell" is a "theory of *internal* stinking." Eighteenth-century aesthetics took its point of departure from the overwhelming presence and reality of the disgusting object for smell and taste; it therefore had some difficulty explaining how anything defined in this way as disgusting could appear at all in the illusory field of the aesthetic and disrupt it. For Mendelssohn, the solution lay in the concepts of "association" and "remembering"; by calling up the memory of disgusting olfactory or gustatory sensations, those "objects" that are merely seen or read about could also excite a corresponding "aversion." This model already uncouples the reality of disgust—"The sensations of disgust are always nature"—from the reality of its "actual" trigger. But it maintains the reference to a previous experience of disgust through an "inferior sense." By contrast, Freud's symptom of (neurotic) "disgust" not only arises exclusively in memory; it is also, from its very first appearance, belated, deferred and supplementary—originally nonoriginary.

"In hysteria it is the memories; in obsessional neurosis, the perverse impulses . . . which penetrate into normal life amid distortions due to compromise."[115] According to Freud, those who develop into obsessional neurotics were introduced into a presexual sexuality, with "perverse" aims and practices, either through a perverted seducer or through oedipal-incestuous fantasies.

Their efforts to repeat a pleasure experienced in the past, to be sure, subsequently run into the cultural barriers of disgust, but they do not therefore slacken. This obstinate fixation implies that "the genital organization (of the phallic phase), in whole or in part, is thrown back to the earlier sadistic-anal level."[116] A "libidinal regression" of this type goes together with the development of an excessively strong super-ego, which is then responsible for the symptoms of compulsive cleanliness, exaggerated conscientiousness, and "ceremoniousness" in certain routine functions:

> The overstrict super-ego insists all the more strongly on the suppression of sexuality, since this has assumed such repellent forms. Thus, in obsessional neurosis, the conflict is aggravated in two directions: the defensive forces become more intolerant and the forces that are to be fended off become more intolerable.[117]

While the super-ego—grown harsh, tormenting and, in the wake of libidinal regression, "sadistic" as well—attempts to transform, along with the perverse impulses, almost all libidinal impulses "into [self]*reproach*,"[118] the warded-off impulses seek channels for substitute satisfaction. Although they are "opposed to one another," the two symptom-generating tendencies often meet: "symptom-formation scores a triumph if it succeeds in combining the prohibition with the satisfaction."[119] Such symptoms then oscillate in undecidable "ambivalence" between (sadistic-anal) fantasies of punishment and (perverse) fantasies of satisfaction. The obsessive neurotic becomes "quite conscious" of his "unpleasant obsessive ideas," whereas in the case of hysteria—where the process of repression is comparatively more successful—things are otherwise. Freud indeed adds the restriction that "usually only a distorted substitute" penetrates into consciousness, and that, in most cases, "the actual wording of the aggressive instinctual impulse is altogether unknown to the ego."[120] But whereas the hysteric has no suspicion that her cough conceals a fantasy of oral intercourse with her father, the obsessional neurotic attains to a recognition of the psycho-pathological character of his symptom-formation—although only at the cost of even aggravating an already torturously obsessional conscientiousness.[121] Furthermore: "A tendency to complete re-establishment of the repressed idea is, as a rule, unmistakably present."[122] In this finding, the accent lies on the word "complete." Negation, too, "is a way of taking cognizance of what has been repressed; properly speaking, it is already an overcoming of repression." It, too, makes conscious, in a largely undistorted form, "the pure content" of the repressed, while immediately rejecting it again through the symbol of negation. The symbol "no" (or "not") sharply separates the transitory admission of the repressed to consciousness from its affective appropriation.[123] By contrast, obsessional-neurotic symptoms succeed, even without the help of negation, in shielding the "intact" admission of repressed contents to consciousness against the strong affect of unpleasure which normally arises from the overcoming of repression. Even the undistorted (not negated) and hence "authentic re-establishment of the repressed idea"—the emergence of perverse impulses from the depths—does not undo the work of repression but rather remains, thanks to other "special techniques," integrated into its dynamic economy. The operation of wit and—as will soon become clear—the particular achievements of art constitute models of such manifest (obsessive-neurotic) engagement with repressed impulses, forms of open engagement which simultaneously suspend any release of unpleasure for the ego, or indeed simultaneous transform their potential unpleasure into an "incentive bonus"[124] of a peculiar sort:

> Special techniques have been evolved, with the purpose of bringing about such changes in the play of mental forces that what would otherwise give rise to unpleasure may on this occasion result in pleasure; and, whenever a technical device of this sort comes into operation, the repression of an instinctual representative which would otherwise be repudiated is removed. These techniques have till now only been studied in any detail in jokes.... We may suppose that the repressed exercises a continuous pressure in the direction of the conscious, so that this pressure must be balanced by an unceasing counter-pressure. Thus the maintenance of a repression involves an uninterrupted expenditure of force, while its removal results in a savings from an economic point of view.[125]

It follows that the obsessional neurotic behaves in a "witty" and economic way when he occasionally calls on certain "techniques" to make conscious (in an almost undistorted form) the "intolerable forces that are to be fended off." This implies that the "triumph" of obsessional-neurotic symptom formation can include explicit reflection on the "perverse" overcoming of barriers of disgust without in any way weakening the obsessional idea. In particular, Freud has observed two "symptom-forming activities of the ego" which, as "surrogates of repression," serve to neutralize the process of making the obsessional idea conscious: "*undoing what has been done* and *isolating*."[126] The techniques of undoing, understood as a "negative magic," operate through motoric symbolism designed deliberately to "blow away" events that have occurred.[127] By contrast, the techniques of isolation sever the event from its affect and, by suppressing all associations appertaining to it, make it fall into an "amnesia" of its own. Such "magical acts of isolation . . . [obey] one of the oldest and most fundamental commands of obsessional neurosis, the taboo on touching."[128] Where the traumatizing experience is "not forgotten," it can be given in "undistorted" form to consciousness in isolating representation, at the same time that it is actively withdrawn from consciousness: "The effect of this isolation is the same as the effect of repression with amnesia."[129] Hysteria does not need such witty and paradoxical techniques of non-repression as a continuation of repression. Without the help of the analyst, the hysteric's fantasies—whose "content . . . corresponds completely to the situations in which satisfaction is consciously obtained by perverts"—remain as a rule wholly "unconscious."[130]

In spite of all these distinctions, both forms of neurotic behavior are ways of processing *"repudiated repression."*[131] They both share the same point of departure and its subsequently refused "perverse" implications for choice of object and for sexual practices: "Obsessional neurosis originates . . . in the same situation as hysteria, namely, the necessity of fending off the libidinal demands of the Oedipus complex."[132] And they both develop their symptoms as a "negative of perversions," as deferred effects of the barriers of disgust instituted by culture and education in the face of "prehistoric" libidinal impulses. Perverted father, perverted maidservant or prostitute, desexualized mother, hysterical daughter, and obsessive-neurotic son—this, in Freud's view, is the "noxious" constellation that determines almost unavoidably the fate of sexuality ever since our "primitive" and "truly ineradicable," "animal impulses"—free of disgust and "perversion" as they originally are—entered into the field of upright posture and its "fateful" achievements (organic repression, foundation of the family, cultural repression). The "extinction of the human race" in the wake of systematic conversion of pleasure into disgust is evidently preventable (if at all), not through further progress of civilization but only through its deliberate withdrawal in favor of those forces which, in the form of "perversions" and "the negative of perversions," have tenaciously outlived the institution of disgust and shame. Freud's experience as analyst—his disclosure of "horribly perverse details" in the case of "all patients"[133]—thus not only confirms his cultural pessimism; it also forms the basis of the philosophico-historical, or better, evolutionary-theoretical hope implicit in his diagnosis of humanity's fate.

Excretion as Prototype of Social Acts, and the Copro-Erotics of Language

Freud's archaeological obsession not only has to do with the individual traces of abandoned "(virtual) sexuality" and its ineradicable presence even within the cultural barriers of disgust. What comes through so insistently in the life of "all patients" must also have survived and left traces in "the language, customs and superstitions of mankind today."[134] Linguistics, aesthetics, the study of folklore and religions all have something to contribute, therefore, to the story of how formerly disgust-free impulses from the age of prehistory, of paradise, of childhood, were repressed (with all the suffering this entails) on the one hand, while partly surviving in culture, on the other. For the scattered remains of a time when the genitals "were worshipped as gods,"[135] Freud refers to Richard Payne Knight's *Le Culte du Priape*.[136] His own speculations take their cue, above all, from excremental pleasure. If the affect of disgust is "originally . . . a reaction to the smell (and afterwards also to the sight) of excrement,"[137] then excretion represents a principal object of study where the conversion of pleasure into disgust and the persistent failure of this conversion is at stake. Freud was therefore the ideal author to write a foreword to the German translation (in an expensive collectors' edition from the Ethnologischer Verlag of Leipzig in 1913) of J. G. Bourke's monumental work of 1891, *Scatologic Rites of All Nations*. He made use of the occasion to recapitulate, in condensed form, his own findings about coprophilia. Once again, he begins with the moment "when *homo sapiens* first raised himself off Mother Earth," and he ends with the theme of neuroses and perversions:

> It may be said that the chief finding from psychoanalytic research has been the fact that the human infant is obliged to recapitulate, during the early part of its development, the changes in the attitude of the human race towards excremental matters, which probably had their start when *homo sapiens* first raised himself off Mother Earth. In the earliest years of infancy there is as yet no trace of shame about the excretory functions or of disgust at excreta. Small children show great interest in these, just as they do in other of their bodily secretions; they like occupying themselves with them and can derive many kinds of pleasure from doing so. Excreta, regarded as parts of a child's own body and as products of his organism, have a share in the esteem— the narcissistic esteem, as we should call it—with which he regards everything relating to his self. Children, indeed, are proud of their own excretions and make use of them to help in asserting themselves against adults. Under the influence of its upbringing, the child's coprophilic instincts and inclinations gradually succumb to repression; it learns to keep them secret, to be ashamed of them and to feel disgust at the objects of these interests. Strictly speaking, however, the disgust never goes so far as to apply to a child's own excretions, but is content with repudiating them when they are the products of other people. The interest which has hitherto been attached to excrement is carried over on to other objects—for instance, from feces to money, which is, of course, late in acquiring significance for children. Important constituents in the formation of character are developed, or strengthened, from the repression of coprophilic inclinations.
>
> Psychoanalysis further shows that excremental and sexual interests are not at first distinct from each other in children. The divorce between them occurs only later and it remains incomplete. Their

original affinity, which is established by the anatomy of the human body, still makes itself felt in many ways in normal adults. Finally, it should not be forgotten that these developments can no more be expected to yield a perfect result than any others. Some portion of the old preferences persist; some part of the coprophilic inclinations continue to operate in later life and are expressed in the neuroses, perversions, bad habits, and other practices of adults.

Folklore has adopted a quite different method of research, and yet it has reached the same results as psychoanalysis. It shows us how incompletely the repression of coprophilic inclinations has been carried out among various peoples at various times, and how closely at other cultural levels the treatment of excretory substances approximates to that practiced by children. It also demonstrates the persistent and indeed ineradicable nature of coprophilic interests, by displaying to our astonished gaze the multiplicity of applications—in magical ritual, in tribal customs, in observances of religious cults and in the art of healing—by which the old esteem for human excretions has found new expression.[138]

In "Character and Anal Eroticism" (1908), Freud detailed the transformation of coprophilic pleasure into qualities of character like "orderliness, parsimony, and obstinacy."[139] The amassing of money and gold allows an inverted, and therefore well concealed, continuation of the "interest in defecation."[140] In many cases, "superstition . . . connects the finding of treasure with defecation, and everyone is familiar with the figure of the 'shitter of ducats' *[Dukatenscheisser]*. Indeed, according to ancient Babylonian doctrine, gold is 'the feces of Hell.' . . . It is possible that the contrast between the most precious substance known to men and the most worthless, which they reject as waste matter (refuse), has led to this specific identification of gold with feces."[141] Elaborating on Freud's investigations, Sandor Ferenczi uncovered other middle terms in the transformation of the archaic-infantile interest in feces into "interest in money" (playing with mud, sand, pebbles, etc.).[142] Even the "fondness for substances with an agreeable odor, for perfumes," can then be recognized as a "consummate reaction-formation"—namely, "representation through the opposite"—of a merely superficially suppressed pleasure in excrement. For Ferenczi, "there can be no question that aesthetics in general has its principal root in repressed anal-eroticism." The "childish interest in flatus" and the "later fondness for music" are thus two related avenues of expression.[143] It is therefore precisely the primary matter for disgust—excrement—that defines, from two sides equally, the essence of civilized humanity: the process by which excrement becomes disgusting is the precondition and pathway for the sublimation of instinct and the identification with the super-ego, while the secret insistence of excrement as an object of pleasure leaves its impress on important attributes of character as well as on cultural capacities. Freud himself enriched his great myth of the fate of coprophilic interests above all through his theory of the gift-function of the disgusting matter of "feces." The handing over of this prized material serves to distinguish those presented with it, and this function can become not only the equivalent of paying money but also a model of giving birth and even of worshiping God:

> [The infant] feels no disgust at his feces, values them as a portion of his own body with which he will not readily part, and makes use of them as his first "gift," to distinguish people whom he values especially highly. Even after education has succeeded in its aim of making these inclinations alien to him, he carries on his high valuation of feces in his estimates of "gifts" and "money."[144]
>
> At a later stage of sexual development, feces take on the meaning of a *baby*. For babies, like feces, are born through the anus. The "gift" meaning of feces readily admits of this transformation. It is common usage to speak of a baby as a "gift." The more frequent expression is that the woman has "given" the man a baby; but, in the usage of the unconscious, equal attention is justly paid to the other aspect of the relation, namely, to the woman's having "received" the baby as a gift from the man.[145]

It is in keeping with the "disastrous" cultural destiny of our "most primitive" impulses that, in the case of feces, precisely "the first *gift* presented by the child, the first sacrifice on behalf of his affection,"[146] should fall prey to disgust. The "very first purpose to which feces are put—namely, the auto-erotic stimulation of the intestinal mucous membrane," paves the way for the libidinal cathexis of excrement *vis-à-vis* "particular privileged persons."[147] Before excrement is (almost) definitively converted into an object of disgust, Freud sees yet another and "new significance for the feces" in the development of the child: excretion becomes the prototype of castration, and anal eroticism thereby an integral element in the narcissistic "love of one's own penis." This investment of feces with the meaning of castration raises Freud's theory of excrement to new heights of structural abstraction:

> The handing over of feces for the sake of (out of love for) another person becomes a prototype of castration; it is the first occasion on which an individual gives up a piece of his own body in order to gain the favor of someone he loves. The love of one's own penis, which is in other respects narcissistic, is therefore not without an element of anal eroticism. "Feces," "baby," and "penis" thus form a unity, an unconscious concept—*sit venia verbo*—the concept, namely, of a "little one" that can be separated from one's body.[148]

Feces accordingly remain—even after their smell has become subject to "rejection" out of "disgust"—the secret "prototype" of our communicative acts ("gift") and our concepts ("concept of a 'little one' that can be separated from one's body"). Freud also wanted to trace back "our verbs" to coproerotic origins:

> A girl attending a sewing class that soon will come to an end is plagued by the obsessional idea: "No, you mustn't leave; you have not yet *finished;* you must still *make* more; you must still learn all sorts of things." Behind this lay the memory of childhood scenes in which she was put on the pot, did not want to remain there, and experienced the same compulsion: "You mustn't leave; you have not yet *finished;* you must still *make* more." The word "make" permits the later situation to be brought together with the infantile one. . . . An old fantasy of mine, which I would like to recommend to your linguistic sagacity, deals with the derivation of our verbs from such originally coproerotic terms.
> I can scarcely detail for you all the things that resolve themselves into—excrement for me (a new Midas!). It fits in completely with the theory of internal stinking. Above all, money itself. I believe this proceeds via the word "dirty" for "miserly." In the same way, everything related to birth, miscarriage, [menstrual] period goes back to the toilet via the word *Abort* [toilet] (*Abortus* [abortion]). This is really wild *[toll]*, but it is entirely analogous to the process by which words take on a transferred meaning as soon as new concepts requiring a designation appear.[149]

Once again, it is the letters to Fliess that disclose, in the most unguarded manner, Freud's deep-lying "fantasies." The substitutional relations of money and feces, the association of words like "money maker" and "shitter of ducats," the various tales from the treasury of "superstition" lead Freud, within a very short space, to a speculation in the study of religions by which the stinker par excellence—the devil—is characterized as a religious projection of our abandoned perversions:

> I read one day that the gold the devil gives his victims regularly turns into excrement; and next day Mr. E., who reports that his nurse had money deliria, suddenly told me (by the way of Cagliostro-alchemist-*Dukatenscheisser* [shitter of ducats]) that Louise's money always was excrement. So, in the witch stories, it is merely transformed back into the substance from which it arose. . . . I have ordered the *Malleus maleficarum,* and . . . shall study it diligently. The story of the devil, the vocabulary of popular swear words, the songs and customs of the nursery—all these are now gaining significance

for me ... I am beginning to grasp an idea: it is as though in the perversions, of which hysteria is the negative, we have before us a remnant of a primeval sexual cult, which once was—perhaps still is—a religion in the Semitic East (Moloch, Astarte). Imagine, I obtained a scene about the circumcision of a girl. The cutting off of a piece of the labium minor (which is even shorter today), sucking up the blood, after which the child was given a piece of the skin to eat. This child, at age 13, once claimed that she could swallow *one* piece of an earthworm and proceeded to do it ... I dream, therefore, of a primeval devil religion with rites that are carried on secretly, and understand the harsh therapy of the witches' judges. Connecting links abound.[150]

"DISGUSTING ABUSES," "PRIMEVAL DEVIL WORSHIP," AND THE EQUATION OF ANALYST AND TORTURER

To the extent that he understood sexual "perversions" as an antidote to the cultural barriers of disgust, Freud was almost obsessed with procuring for them an "ancient," indeed "primeval" pedigree within "culture," "rite" and "religion"; in the devil, this effort meets with its predestined emblem. The devil is the prime reprobate—stinking and abject—of official religion and, at the same time, he is the object of "secret" veneration; he is cast into hell, and yet remains mighty and ineradicable. The medieval theory of "possession" by the devil is, for Freud, "identical with our theory of a foreign body *[Fremdkörper]* and the splitting of consciousness."[151] For, in the case of neuroses as well, "the psychical trauma—or, more precisely, the memory of the trauma—acts like a foreign body which, long after its entry, must continue to be regarded as an agent that is still at work."[152] Sexual obsessions, demonized by the culture as perverted, are the prototype of all demonology and all possession by the "adversary."

The myth of the fate of disgust-free, animal sexuality in the domain of upright posture, together with the practice of psychoanalysis, thus provide an answer to the following two questions: "Why did the devil, who took possession of his miserable victims, invariably abuse them sexually and in a disgusting manner? And why are their confessions under torture so similar to the communications made by my patients in psychic treatment?"[153] To the extent that this letter characterizes the sexual abuses (which diabolically take possession of their "miserable victims") as disgusting, it is an exception to the rule; for, generally in Freud, perversions are conceived as transgressing the barriers of disgust, but are not themselves labeled "disgusting." Having taken up residence in our body, the devil represents the negative debasement of our own "primitive" impulses in the sphere of neuroticizing civilization. Like the child, like animal sexuality, he knows of no disgust; but unlike the child and the animal, he pays for this immunity with himself falling into abjectness and depravity. He is the insistence of what lacks all disgust, but as a being who is himself disgusting. As the medieval Inquisitors laid bare the *stigmata diaboli*, so the psychoanalyst uncovers the stigmata of perverse impulses and of their negative. Freud even has recourse to physical cruelties with needles and knives to deepen this parallel. Many hysterics insist on the presence of needles, felt as tormenting foreign bodies, in their body and, in this way, confirm the medieval conception of diabolic "pin pricks":

> Incidentally, the cruelties make it possible to understand some symptoms of hysteria that until now have been obscure. The pins which make their appearance in the oddest ways; the sewing needles on account of which the miserable victims let their breasts be mutilated and which are not visible by X-ray, though they can no doubt be found in their seduction stories! Eckstein has a scene [that is, remembers] where the diabolus sticks needles into her fingers and then places a candy on each drop of blood.[154]

Inquisitors uncovered the existence of the devil's stigmata by sticking needles repeatedly into the bodies of delinquents; as soon as they located "places that were anaesthetic and did not bleed *(stigmata diaboli)*," the victim was held to be convicted of witchcraft.[155] In this repeated probing of—and for—stigmata Freud recognizes the model of psychoanalysis. And he develops the secret identity between torturer/executioner and analyst even to the point of maintaining that the victims' needle-induced recollection of their childhood traumata simultaneously awakens an auto-analytic childhood memory on the part of the executioner:

> Once more, the Inquisitors prick with needles to discover the devil's stigmata, and in a similar situation the victims think of the same old cruel story . . . (helped perhaps by disguises of the seducers). Thus, not only the victims but also the executioners recalled in this their earliest youth.[156]

The "truth" revealed through torture, as through analysis, accordingly lies in the recollection of a repressed stigma, of a seduction that led to perversion or of a perverse impulse of one's own that was suppressed. At the same time, the drama uncovered in the life of a victim/patient awakens in the torturer/analyst—the cruel catalyst of this retrieval process—a memory of his own "childhood"; it recollects whatever hidden *stigmata diaboli*/traumata his or her childhood may have been marked by, and discloses the typical Freudian set of phenomena: that is, perversions brought on by a seducer and/or by one's own fantasies, incorporation of foreign bodies/obsessional ideas, deferred disgust.

From the perspective of the executioner/analyst, torture is thus always also a theodicy in the face of one's own "hell." Or, in biographical terms: the analyst Freud, in his obsessive investigation of perverse impulses and their negatives, is always also wrestling with his own neuroses.[157] The perverse fathers/seducers and the varied experiences with maidservants—core elements of so many case histories studied by Freud—shed light on his own experiences in these areas; they may also help to further the goal propagated by Nietzsche—the goal of overcoming disgust, of rumination without disgust, of recurring affirmation of one's own existence. The theory and practice of psychoanalysis are thus manifoldly oriented to the project of dis-charging disgust, of reclaiming the animal-like and childlike "freedom to enact perversions" and freedom from disgust.

"Why did the devil, who took possession of his miserable victims, invariably abuse them sexually, and in a disgusting manner? And why are their confessions under torture similar to the communications made by my patients in psychic treatment?" Freud's theory of "perverse" sexuality—understood as the proto-object of civilization's development of disgust and, at the same time, as the ineradicable power fueling all resistance to disgust—provides the answer to these questions. Freud took the motto for this theory from the closing line of the "Prelude in the Theater" from Goethe's *Faust:* "From heaven through the world to hell."[158] The devil, as the lord of hell, is the prosopopeia of Freud's theory of pleasure made disgusting—the limping, stinking (medieval) devil, that is, who enters into the compulsive ideas and actions of perverts and neurotics, and not the worldly, elegant and perfumed, provocatively self-indulgent devil of romantic satanism. In his abject immunity to the feeling of disgust, something he shares with the romantic Diabolo, he represents the (debased) counterpole to "aesthetic culture," as well as to the barriers of disgust which form the foundation of that culture and whose effect he nonetheless is. The "confessions under torture" and the drama of the unconscious under analysis attest to both: the cruel power of disgust's working in favor of civilization and its limits in face of the surviving "vestiges" of (supposedly) prehistoric pleasures.

Art as Suspension of Disgust and Guiltless "Enjoyment" of the Rejected

Given the conflict between the "barriers of disgust" and the childlike-archaic freedom from disgust and "freedom to enact perversions," the discontents of civilization are actually discontents with the severity of this conflict underlying civilization and with the suffering it brings to every single person in constantly new ways. Freud credits one form of human activity above all with processing this conflict differently—in a manner easier, more pain-free, more guiltless than neurosis, torture, and psychoanalysis are capable of. This form is art. It alone makes possible a playful intercourse with the dark continent of the abandoned and repressed—an intercourse which is both pleasurable and exempt from any severe sanctions. For Freud, the "innermost secret" of the creative writer, "the essential *Ars poetica*" resides "in the technique of overcoming the feeling of repulsion." This "poetics" rests upon the presupposition that an open "disclosure" of the writer's "fantasies" would normally trigger rejection both on his part and on that of his audience. For, according to the Freudian understanding of the archaic nature of human instinctive impulses, these fantasies would be at the least egoistical and frequently "perverse"; they would give the civilized ego all sorts of "reasons for being ashamed of them." The wondrous transformation of conscious repulsion into a "yield of pleasure" likewise serves to liberate readers from intellectual "barriers" shored up by morality and ego, "enabling us thenceforward to enjoy our own daydreams without self-reproach or shame."[159] Art is a technique of suspending disgust, of transforming repulsion into attraction; it makes enjoyable what otherwise gives rise to shame and disgust. In its very mode of overcoming disgust, the work of art releases a "formal—that is to say, aesthetic—yield of pleasure *[Lustgewinn]*," and this specific yield of pleasure is even said to entail a "liberation from tensions" within the entire psychic economy.[160] In this way, Freud carries over Kant's theory of a "freeplay" of mental faculties, producing an aesthetic "harmony" of otherwise irreconcilable conflicts, into an epistemological field in which the "thing in itself" has given place to the id, the "primary process," the unconscious, repressed and abandoned.

Freud concludes his discussion of the distinctive achievement of the writer, in his work "Creative Writers and Daydreaming" (1908), by positing an enjoyment without shame. In a lecture delivered shortly before this publication, he had already specified more fully the "preconditions for pleasure" appertaining not only to the artwork but also to its audience. The "precondition for this form of art" is there explained in terms of the classical aesthetic doctrine of "illusion":[161] artistic techniques of representation work to "spare" "a certain amount" of the "resistance" customarily mounted against uncivilized impulses, insofar as such techniques divert the intellectual "attention" of the spectator away from the (shocking) "incident."[162] Freud directly paralleled this technique (which combines a sparing in the expenditure of repression and a trickish discharge of repressed impulses) with his anatomy of wit published shortly before[163]—just as he later considered the obsessive-neurotic admission of the traumatizing idea, under certain conditions of irrealization, to be an analogue of "wit."[164] Techniques of dissimulation and distancing have for a long time been considered a "precondition" of artistic practice, especially for the dramatic conversion of represented suffering into spectators' pleasure. Freud lays emphasis on the fact that it is also and precisely the "identification" with the hero of tragedy and the "masochistic satisfaction in [his] defeat" that requires this "precondition of artistic form."[165] He sees, in addition, a special precondition for the reception of the modern "psychopathological" literature: "here, the precondition for enjoyment is that the spectator should himself be a neurotic." For only a neurotic—one who, by virtue of his own repressions, is "unstable" and "on the brink of failing"—is predisposed for the task of "deriving pleasure" from the represented conflict "between a conscious and a repressed source of suffering."[166] In neuroticizing "cultures," this special precondition for the "enjoyment" of repudiated impulses and sources of suffering is met not only by individuals but "possibly," Freud ventures to speculate, by "the whole of mankind."[167] The humanistic ideologem, according to which art advances the cause of "all human beings" and of "all humanity," is thus established on a new basis: that of neuroticizing disgust and its suspension and transformation into a pleasure free of guilt and shame.

RESEARCH ON DISGUST IN EMPIRICAL PSYCHOLOGY AFTER FREUD

Disgust is not among those concepts in Freud's work that are most often discussed by his readers. Even the general orientation of his thinking toward a vast realm of pleasure rendered disgusting has not made disgust a particular focus of interest in Freud-scholarship. By the same token, empirical psychology as a whole has produced only a few studies on the subject of disgust. The remaining pages of this chapter will be confined to certain elements of these studies that point in directions other than those laid down by Freud.

The first statistical-psychological analysis of disgust was undertaken in 1930 by Gustav Kafka, with thirty subjects participating in the investigation. A similar study by Andras Angyal followed in 1941. Neither of these studies, to be sure, fails to refer to Freud's better known theses on disgust, although both appear to be written in total ignorance of Aurel Kolnai's highly differentiated phenomenology of disgust of 1929—as is the case, since then, with all American research on this topic. Among the more interesting results of Kafka's and Angyal's investigations is the prominent part played by cognition in the disgust reaction: various sensible qualities—softness, sliminess, even many smells—were regularly felt to arouse disgust only when they were identified as belonging to particular objects.[168] The main focus of Kafka's study lies in the statistical confirmation of Freud's hypotheses concerning the disgust-overcoming power of sexuality. At the same time, Kafka attempts to extend Freud's functional thesis on the "restriction of the sexual aim" qua disgust to a thesis on the regulation (via restriction) of sexuality in general. Animals can lack the capacity for disgust, Kafka argues, "because here the sexual regulation depends on another factor, namely, the relatively brief duration of the estrual period and the correlative difficulty of finding a sexual partner."[169] In the absence of this particular regulation, two things may happen. Either "most remaining sexual inhibitions disappear along with the disappearance of the estrual period—and consequently the lower species of apes display an almost uninterrupted hetero-, homo- or autosexual activity." Or else an "inner inhibition"—which is precisely disgust—takes the place of the external inhibitions, "so as to prevent the sexual instinct, despite its temporally unrestricted operation, from attaining unrestrained dominance over human life. Such a regulation is accordingly nothing less than the precondition for the spiritual development of mankind."[170] This interpretation of disgust not only posits the spiritual development of mankind as a sort of natural end; it also insinuates something that Freud never actually maintained and that Hirsch himself[171] expressly denies: that *all* forms of human sexuality can be realized only in overcoming the inhibitions of disgust, and that the inversion of disgust is the unstable core of sexual experience in general. Angyal, on the other hand, offers an explanation of the disgust phenomenon that reinstates all the prejudices which Freud had called into question. "The waste products of the body," the chief causes of disgust, are for Angyal "something inferior and base"; from this he concludes, in the most simple-minded way imaginable, that "the *relevance of the disgusting object* consists in the threat of being debased through the mere contact with mean objects."[172]

Whereas Kafka's and Angyal's studies remained isolated excursions into a poorly explored terrain, Paul Rozin has devoted, in the 1980s and 1990s, a whole series of empirical studies to the phenomenon of disgust. Among the merits of these studies are: the statistical confirmation and measurement (to a very fine degree) of generally accepted disgust-sensitivities; the empirical differentiation of Freud's thesis on childhood freedom from disgust and on children's acquisition of disgust; the cataloguing of the customary forms of conditioning to disgust (like "toilet training") and of desensitizing against the disgust-reaction; the comparison between the danger of contamination that one encounters in disgust and archaic conceptions of negative magic.[173] The basic theoretical framework of Rozin's studies is very much in line with Angyal's thesis on the aversion to inferior, base substances. Rozin likewise sees in disgust, first of all, an effort of the human being to accentuate and preserve his difference from the "inferior" status of the animal:

> We start from the assumption that the category of disgust objects consists almost entirely of animals and their products.... In addition to the claim that all disgusts are of animal origin, we believe that *all* animals or animal products are potentially disgusting. That is, at some basic level (and perhaps at some point in human evolution), animalness was a necessary and sufficient condition of disgust.... Humans see themselves as quite distinct from (and superior to) other animals and wish to avoid any ambiguity about their status by accentuating

the human-animal-boundary. This view is consistent with the fact that there is a widespread aversion to consuming animals that are physically similar to humans or in close interactive relations with humans (e.g., pets).[174]

Hence, we repudiate our "waste products" and our sexuality as disgusting to the extent that they put us on a level with the animals: "Anything that reminds us that we are animals elicits disgust."[175] To be sure, this "very broad theory"[176] bears a remote resemblance to the Freudian story of the origin of digust in the evolution of upright posture and in the correlative turning away from animal four-footedness and animal olfactory and sexual behavior. But, in the specific form it assumes in Rozin, this theory contradicts certain data which Rozin himself in part deals with. The strongest feeling of disgust is in general directed toward *human* excrement, whereas animal excrement—from "horse manure" to "rabbit droppings"—is often enough perceived without disgust.[177] By the same token, we feel no disgust at all in the face of numerous other functions possessed in common with the animals: we breathe like them, sleep like them, and so forth. Most varieties of aesthetic and moral disgust have their basis, generally speaking, only in deformations of the specifically human skin or in specific relations between human beings. Rozin's examples for moral disgust in his questionnaire—the sight of photos made of the Nazi concentration camps by allied liberators, the reaction to the demand to put on Hitler's "sweater"—have nothing at all to do with securing the boundary between men and animals. Animals could never have committed the deeds of the Nazis.

It is, moreover, questionable whether Rozin's examples furnish adequate data for the statistical analysis of disgust. To make a fictive connection to Hitler's sweaty body into one of thirty-two "items" on a "Disgust Scale" says more about Hitler's negative star status in American mass media than about the phenomenon of disgust. In fact, the label "disgusting" seems hardly to fit the deeds of Hitler and the Nazi regime. Since organized genocide violates in a monstrous way explicit religious and cultural prohibitions of killing, the moral condemnation of the annihilation of the Jews implies a stronger intellectual dimension (one more detached from the bodily) than is found in disgust, even "moral" disgust. It would be more appropriate to describe the affective dimension of this judgment in terms of horror or abomination. The arousal of disgust, in the full sense of the term, pertains more readily to the Nazis' anti-Semitic propaganda—the portrayal of Jews as rats or as parasites in the "healthy" body of the Aryan *Volk*—or even to the hygienic regime of the concentration camps than to a moral reaction to these historical data. The absolutely reprehensible phenomenon of state-sponsored murder is hardly the predestined object for a disgust reaction, which is something grounded, in the last analysis, in the aesthetic sphere. Whoever assigns the crimes of the

National Socialists a maximal point on a scale of disgust testifies, certainly, to an especially high degree of disapproval, but not therefore to any specific reaction of disgust. Hitler's unwashed sweater—directly paralleled with bed linen used by strangers—may in fact arouse disgust; but it is nonetheless a piece of tastelessness, itself bordering on the disgusting, to make sacred or popular-fetishistic suspensions of disgust (the handkerchief of Saint Veronica, the T-shirts of sports stars) into the standard for an appropriate reaction to Hitler. Furthermore, it is not very convincing, from a psychological point of view, to test for what is morally disgusting by choosing examples so remote from one's own country, one's own body, and even one's own period—so remote that one's (self-righteous) pleasure in one's own integrity can count on not being seriously disturbed at any point. Empirical psychology since Freud has simply failed to provide a halfway convincing, let alone a fundamentally new, perspective on disgust. Wherever it has not limited itself to confirming, elaborating, or cautiously modifying the Freudian hypotheses, it has routinely lagged behind Freud himself.

7

The Angel of Disgust

Kafka's Poetics of "Innocent" Enjoyment of "Sulphurous" Pleasures

The figure of the female in Kafka's writings typically combines features of the disgusting *vetula* of classical aesthetics with features of the perverse maidservant, or perverse prostitute of the Freudian family romance. The hyperbolic representative of all these women is Brunelda: an evil-smelling, gigantic mass of flesh and a filthy prostitute, whose eating habits and other practices are thoroughly repellent. In *Amerika,* Brunelda assumes the role played by the court in *The Trial* and ascribed to the higher functionaries of the castle in *The Castle:* she simultaneously provokes desire and eludes the grasp; she is disgusting and, at the same time, the seat of all power. The *vetula*-prostitute Brunelda is the earliest figure of the 'absolute' to appear in Kafka's novels. The fusion of *vetula* and maidservant/prostitute—as attested in the writer's works, diaries, and letters—provides an especially conspicuous point of departure for an analysis of the ciphers, representational modes, and the poetics of the disgusting in Kafka.[1]

The following readings of Kafka's three novels and his short story "A Country Doctor" will show that the disgusting in Kafka is not simply a given subject matter or a thematic source of stimuli. Rather, Kafka's art consists precisely in making the presence and the strong affective value of a disgusting subject matter, openly presented as such, almost entirely invisible, imperceptible. The provocative exhibition of the disgusting in the literature of the "romantic" as well as the "fantastic" yields to a double strategy. On the one hand, Kafka develops more fully than perhaps any other writer nearly all traditional figurations of the disgusting. On the other hand, his narrative stance and his writing devices effect a simulation of a "childlike" absence of disgust, an "innocence" and "purity," which not only avoids being noticeably sullied by its subject matters but succeeds in completely "deceiving" the reader about their nature. According to the doctrine of classical aesthetics, what is disgusting destroys the formal conditions of aesthetic illusion. Hence, incorporations of the disgusting into works of art regularly break with the claim to aesthetic illusion—thus confirming the classical theory even while violating its precepts. Kafka's works, however, manage the considerable feat of both incorporating the disgusting and remaining true to a poetics of aesthetic "deception." Whereas the disgusting entails the scandal of undeniable real presence, and whereas most aesthetic doctrines of the disgusting wind up making this scandal their own, the effect of Kafka's mode of presentation is to transform the disgusting into phenomena that, even in their manifest presence at hand, appear strangely absent, impalpable—*not* present at all. Disgusting material, in Kafka, is precisely the unreadable, invisible, unsmellable dimension of an art that is nonetheless dedicated to "stench."[2] This deceptive nonpresence in literal manifestation of what is disgusting constitutes the "miracle" of a form of representation that, behind its power of making invisible, produces the positive semblance of "purity," "innocence" and sinless "enjoyment." Filth as purity, "grossness" and "loathsomeness" as "innocence," the devil as angel: this is the "deceptiveness" of a writing that, at the same time, "without deception" lays open its "hell."

7.1 Ugly Maidservants, Fat Old Whores, Sexual Disgust, and "Sulphurous" Obesssions

Felice and Other Women with Un-Greek Noses, Skin Defects, and Bad Teeth

On October 9, 1911, at the age of 28, Kafka takes the measure of his future life:

> If I reach my fortieth year, then I'll probably marry an old maid with protruding upper teeth left a little exposed by the upper lip. The upper front teeth of Miss K[aufmann], who was in Paris and London, slant toward each other a little like legs which are quickly crossed at the knees. I'll hardly reach my fortieth birthday, however; the frequent tension over the left half of my skull, for example, speaks against it—it feels like an inner leprosy which, when I only observe it and disregard its unpleasantness, makes the same impression on me as the skull cross-section in textbooks, or as an almost painless dissection of the living body, where the knife—a little coolingly, carefully, often stopping and going back, sometimes lying still—splits still thinner the paper-thin integument close to the functioning parts of the brain. (D, 70–71)

The two hypotheses miss the "truth" of Kafka's later life by only a little. The "old maid" with bad teeth—after the initial encounter with her, she is expressly named a "maidservant"—will be found soon afterward, but, despite two separate engagements, the marriage plans will founder in the end. And the fortieth year will reach its completion, but not the forty-first. The prophetic power of the diary entry, like all prophecy perhaps, derives from the recognition of obsessions which, in Kafka's case, announced themselves much earlier. What is most striking about the formulation and fulfillment of these prophecies are the details: from the ugly teeth of the old maid and his own "inner leprosy," to the vivisection of the brain integument. All these details have a strong affinity with traditional figures of disgust. Bad teeth—often in conjunction with repellently bad breath—belong to the typology of the disgusting *vetula*. "Leprosy" is the quintessence of disgusting disease and, at the same time, another name for the Philoctetean fate of being left exposed on account of triggering disgust. And the laying open of the quivering brain, the removal of its "integument," belongs with a series of many other variations which Kafka played on the flaying of Marsyas.

Although the paradigms of disgust informing Kafka's self-prognosis have widespread and outrightly uncanny repercussions throughout his writings, the category of disgust has not figured at all in the secondary literature on Kafka, which is certainly not lacking in special angles and perspectives. One reason for this may already be found in the diary entry just cited: despite the evocation of potentially disgusting phenomena, all feeling of disgust is effectively distanced, indeed avoided. Sources of disgust and feelings of disgust are desynchronized; the space of their disjunction is the field of a pleasure bordering in a variety of ways on the grotesque. The comparison of the middle teeth slanting toward each other with "legs which are quickly crossed at the knees" turns a permanent malformation into a "fleeting" gesture; it temporalizes it, insofar as it ascribes to the defective teeth a mobility, which is more likely to provoke amusement than disgust. Similarly, Kafka immediately brackets the affective value of ascribing to himself a sort of "leprosy" by adding: "when I only observe it and disregard its unpleasantness." To disregard its unpleasantness amounts to nothing less than disregarding precisely what constitutes the feeling of disgust as a feeling. Furthermore, through the medium of a sober clinical gaze and of modern medical technology (sustained by the words "painless," "coolingly," and "carefully"), the vivisection of the brain integument is thoroughly steeped in a stylistic (anti)pathos, which likewise spares the reader any spasms of disgust. Just as the fairy tale, according to Freud's observation, can present potentially uncanny phenomena without ever arousing a "feeling" of uncanniness,[3] so "Kafka's fairy tales for dialecticians"[4] have the capacity for making invisible and impalpable what they display almost exclusively: disgusting bodies, gestures, and actions.

The diary entry concerning Kafka's first meeting with the woman who was almost his wife, Felice Bauer, is framed by two sentences that could be borrowed from a classical choreography of spontaneous infatuation: "Miss F[elice] B[auer]. When I arrived at Brod's on August 13, she was sitting at the table. . . . As I was taking my seat, I looked at her closely for the first time; by the time I was seated, I already had an unshakeable opinion" (D, 207). The elided sentences, however, which anticipate and confirm this judgment of Kafka's, correspond so little to a logic of loving idealization that Kafka immediately adds in parenthesis: "I alienate myself from her a little by inspecting her body so closely." This "inspecting her body so closely" *[Auf-den-Leib-Gehen]* is more than "a little" removed from any infatuated ascription of virtues: "When I arrived at Brod's on August 13, she was sitting at the table. But she looked like a maidservant to me. I was not at all curious about who she was, but rather took her for granted at once. Bony, empty face that wore its emptiness openly. Bare throat. A blouse thrown on . . . Almost broken nose. Blond, somewhat straight, unattractive hair, strong chin." To Felice's friend Grete Bloch, Kafka writes about his "old maid" of twenty-six: "F.'s appearance varies; out of doors she generally looks very well, indoors sometimes tired and aged, with rough, blotchy skin. Her teeth, all of them, are in a worse condition than they used to be; each one has a filling. This Monday she started another round of visits to the dentist."[5] The sober and "precise" diagnosis—tired, aged, blotchy skin, bad teeth—is by no means offered in a heroic spirit, so as to allow the undeterred *constantia* of his own feeling to triumph. Rather, Grete Bloch becomes the witness to and medium of the unsettling attempt to transform "one of the most repulsive ailments" (LF, 327)—thus Kafka describes Felice's dental problems—into a source of pleasure:

> First of all, dear Fräulein Bloch, there are two errors in your letter. I didn't feign interest when you told me about F.'s toothache and the breaking off of her brother's engagement. Indeed, I was extremely interested, there was nothing I would rather have listened to; for my liking, you told me far too little about it; that's how I am, and surely that's not particularly remarkable; the abscess under the bridge, the piecemeal breaking-off of the bridge, I should like to have heard all about that with every detail and even asked F. about it in Berlin. Don't you get pleasure out of exaggerating painful things as much as possible? For people with weak instincts, it often seems to me the only way to drive out pain; like medicine, which is devoid of all good instincts, it cauterizes the sore spot. By so doing, of course, nothing definite is achieved, but the moment itself—and those with bad and weak instincts haven't time to worry about more than that—is spent almost pleasurable. It may be that other things played a part here, but at any rate I wasn't feigning; on the contrary, I was particularly truthful on this occasion. (LF, 330–31)

This cathartic-homeopathic theory of a working through, a salutary overcoming of disgust by means of a pleasurable intensification of its stimulus makes it seem that the lover's peculiar obsession obeys a well-grounded Aristotelian poetics. At the same time, the qualifying remark—"It may be that other things played a part here"—points enigmatically toward darker sources of pleasure.[6] A few months later, Kafka discloses another dimension of his passion for the disgusting set of teeth. In the foreground, now, is not so much the goal of cathartic discharge of disgust-feelings as the deliberate self-torment in the course of pursuing this goal:

> To tell the truth, this gleaming gold (a really hellish luster for this inappropriate spot) so scared me at first that I had to lower my eyes at the sight of F.'s teeth and the grayish yellow porcelain. After a time, whenever I could, I glanced at it on purpose so as not to forget it, to torment myself, and finally to convince myself that all this is really true. In a thoughtless moment, I even asked F. if it didn't embarrass her. Of course, it didn't—fortunately. But now I have become almost entirely reconciled, and not merely from habit (in fact, I hadn't the time to acquire a visual habit). I now no longer wish these gold teeth gone; but that's not quite the right expression, for I actually never did wish them gone. (LF, 406)

Kafka's prophecy of a bride with the "repulsive ailment" of tooth disease is as bewildering as the dento-taediological discourse he offers (once his strange wish is fulfilled) is eloquent and coherent. It was his go-between Grete Bloch who, as Felice's dental work was drawing to a close, provided an occasion—by means of her own toothache—for the continuance of Kafka's letters on tooth disgust:

> There is no doubt in my mind that a draft alone doesn't cause toothache in healthy teeth. Healthy teeth don't even begin to feel well until they are exposed to a draft. And if the deterioration of the teeth wasn't actually due to inadequate care, then it was due, as with me, to eating meat. One sits at the table laughing and talking (for me, at least, there is the justification that I neither laugh nor talk), and meanwhile tiny shreds of meat between the teeth produce germs of decay and fermentation, no less than a dead rat squashed between two stones./ Meat is the one thing that is so stringy that it can be removed only with great difficulty, and even then not at once and not completely, unless one's teeth are like those of a beast of prey—pointed, set wide apart, designed for the purpose of tearing meat to shreds. (LF, 407–8)

The tooth disease is "repulsive," therefore, not only because it adds to the aging skin the symptoms of decayed, yellowed, and (in Felice's case) also abscessed teeth. It is rather that the disease fits into a chain of associations with four other paradigms of disgust in Kafka's writing: eating, meat, corpse ("*dead* rat"), and repellent animal ("dead *rat*"). Kafka's prophetic diary entry—which mentions only two specific attributes of the future bride (she is "old" and has "bad teeth")—thus chose well. One of the caries-letters to Grete Bloch also builds a bridge between the paradigms of disgust and language (writing). The mouth, in which the dead rats of "germs of decay and fermentation" are rotting, is at the same time the place in which words are articulated. It may be due to this stigma of their origin that Kafka could find a novel hyperbolic image for "superlatives," for "these particular words—empty in their sheer immensity"; it is an image that turns the mouth and the teeth of the beloved and venerated girl into an object for disgust-lovers: "girls seem to disgorge them, while breathing labouringly, from their little mouths like huge rats."[7] In the chapter on perversion in his *Three Essays on the Theory of Sexuality*, Freud mentions in passing the relation one has to the teeth and oral cavity of a person one loves: "A man who will kiss a pretty girl's lips passionately, may perhaps be disgusted at the idea of using her teeth-brush, though there are no grounds for supposing that his own oral cavity, for which he feels no disgust, is cleaner than the girl's. Here, then, our attention is drawn to the factor of disgust, which interferes with the libidinal overvaluation of the sexual object but can in turn be overriden by libido."[8] Kafka's fixation on the "repulsive" tooth disease of his beloved in no way operates to diminish a heightened libido. Nor does it aim at the libidinal deactivation of the barriers of disgust, but instead at direct libidinal cathexis of certain "disgusting" qualities in the desired object, qualities that are explicitly recognized and not at all denied.

Felice is a maidservant with a bony, empty face, a broken nose, unattractive hair, a strong chin, and teeth that are rotting away; she lacks only the heavy down that Kafka likes to highlight in descriptions of other female faces. In his diaries, letters, and works, Kafka produces a whole series of such portraits, in which decidedly un-Greek noses are surrounded by ugly chins, folds of skin, and unattractive facial hair.[9] One further example may suffice here: "The woman wore a dress whose old, worn-out material and dirtiness gave it a light gray shimmer.... In her face, which I saw at first only in part, she had folds so deep that I thought of the uncomprehending amazement with which animals would have looked at such human faces. Especially striking was the small, upturned nose that stuck out of her face."[10] Only rarely is the unpleasant appearance an argument for rejection: "[The apartment] is inhabited by a woman and her daughter, of whom I recall nothing but a poisonously yellow blouse, hairy cheeks, and a waddling gait. One better gives up on this apartment" (LF, 450). Often enough, the meticulously described ugly features serve as a source of pleasure:

> Met Miss R. in the morning. Really an abysmal ugliness, a man could never change so. Clumsy body, limp as if still asleep; the old

jacket that I knew; what she was wearing under the jacket was as indeterminable as it was suspect. . . . Heavy down on her upper lip, but only in one spot; an exquisitely ugly impression. In spite of it all, I like her very much, even in all her undoubted ugliness . . . (D, 340)

The same ideal of beauty that implicitly, and by contrast, furnishes the paradigms for Kafka's descriptions[11] is regularly negated as a measure of male desire. Even in the case of the comparatively few women whom Kafka initially provides with traditional attributes of a pleasing appearance, he almost never ceases more or less subtly to undermine the beauty of the appearance.[12] To Leni's various attractions are added, as a provocative defect, a connecting web of skin between the fingers, which turns her hand into a "claw."[13] Frieda, who at first appears as a desirable and capable companion, changes within a few days into an ugly "old maid." K. soon notices the disappearance of everything that had made her "so wildly enticing": "K. sat down on a school bench and observed her weary movements. It had always been her freshness and resolve that had lent her paltry body a certain beauty, but now that beauty was gone."[14] Or, in Pepi's words: "Nobody realizes as keenly as Frieda herself how wretched she looks; the first time you see her letting down her hair, say, you clutch your hands with pity. . . . Had she really succeeded in pleasing him, that thin yellowish creature?" (C, 294, 297).

A pertinent example of the older conception of the disgusting woman is expressly cited: Swift's *Gulliver's Travels*. During his stay with the giants of Brobdingnab, Gulliver makes a discovery, without which the genre of the insect film would not exist—a discovery, moreover, whose technique corresponds closely with Kafka's own microscopic vision. Simple enlargements can make of beautiful appearances—flawless skin or a woman's breast—landscapes of ugly pores, secretions, and masses of flesh: "as Gulliver discovered," the "perishable . . . shapely contours" of the "slightly puffy, . . . soft flesh . . . are disfigured by sweat, fat, pores, and hairs" (L, 351). In the "slightly puffy" soft flesh, we may even hear echoes of Winckelmann's and Herder's conceptions of "smooth-drawn flesh" and "the softly blown corporeal," respectively. At the same time, these echoes are significantly distorted: for in the word *"aufgedunsen"* ("puffy"), the beautiful body that stands opposed to the disgusting body already in itself tends toward the latter. With regard to "leprosy" and conspicuous skin diseases, Kafka even more completely subscribes to classical verdicts on what is considered to elicit disgust; yet, it would not have occurred to the classical aestheticians to routinely imagine themselves—their own selves, their own bodies—as infected by a disgusting leprosy. The same day on which Kafka diagnoses in himself an "inner leprosy," while prophesying that his future bride will be "an old maid" with bad teeth, he notes down in his diary a memorable dream. In this dream, he is fingering a prostitute with great pleasure; he then discovers everywhere on her skin "large sealing-wax-red circles with paling edges, and red splashes scattered among them" (D, 72). What initially appears to him "the most beautiful entertainment" transforms itself, without being thereby condemned or abandoned, into the intercourse of one leprous being with another.

"Old Maids"

From classical antiquity to the aesthetics of the eighteenth century, the conception of an ugly and disgusting old age always presupposes an advanced biological decline—and, in the notorious case of Brockes' "old woman," old age on the doorstep of death. Kafka, by contrast, dynamizes the category of female old age in such a way that it includes all stages in the lives of grown "girls": once they are no longer simply children, they are almost always described as old or, at least, as basically aging. To be sure, Kafka revitalizes, on the one hand, a virulent paradigm informing the tradition from Aristophanes to Horace—the paradigm, namely, of the lascivious old woman who desires young men. The still very young Karl Rossmann, for example, is "disgustingly" abused by a thirty-five-year-old maidservant,[15] after which, in America, he enters into the dubious care of a fifty-year-old head cook, and then assumes the notable position of "servant" to an elderly prostitute. On the other hand, advanced biological age is by no means necessary for the topical *vetula*—predicates to be applied. In the case of "lovely young girls," Kafka simply adds the prospect that their "natural fancy dress" will soon be worn out, dusty, and puffy (S, 382–83), and, already at the age of twenty-six, his own bride Felice is described as an ugly "old maid" with yellowed, mottled skin and rotting teeth. In Kafka's view, old age is actually the essence of womanhood: "a man could never change so" (D, 340). He brings out in a radical way all the negative implications of Edmund Burke's memorable remark that beauty and a brief lifetime are correlative virtues.[16] The "perishability," the short-lived "shapely contours" of female "flesh" (L, 351) no longer require—as is still the case in Baudelaire—anticipations of a distant future for the artist to be able to address his beloved as a rotten cadaver. Baudelaire still knows the physical presence of the beautiful beloved and modes—however precarious—of an enduring existence of beauty in love and remembrance. With Kafka, on the other hand, the seeming stability of beautiful form becomes a "proof of the brevity of human life," and the illusion of presence is not only an imposture in the face of the future but a swindle—indeed, a shameless assault on the present itself:

> Four days in the city in summertime are to be sure a great deal: for instance, one could scarcely put up a longer resistance against the half-naked women. Not until summer does one really see their curious kind of flesh in quantities. It is soft flesh, retentive of a great deal

of water, slightly puffy, and keeps its freshness only a few days. Actually, of course, it stands up pretty well, but that is only proof of the brevity of human life. How short human life must be if flesh one hardly dares to touch because of its perishability, because its shapely contours last only a moment (which contours, as Gulliver discovered—but, most of the time, I cannot believe it—are disfigured by sweat, fat, pores, and hairs)—how short human life must be, if such flesh will last out a good portion of that life. (LF, 351)

In the conflict between "perishability," understood as the prime expressive value of female "flesh," and the doubtfully confirmed duration of such flesh for "a good portion of [the woman's] life," Kafka takes sides—by virtue of a disarmingly sophistical conclusion—with the only position conforming to the assumption that women are always already old: if such "flesh" lasts, then it can only be a matter of illusion and/or "proof" of the "brevity" of such duration. Brief duration is always already infiltrated by the imminence of its end; its substrate is from the beginning haunted by the curse of accelerated old age. This quasi-transcendental agedness of the female body almost from the very beginning appears all the more inexorable, insofar as Kafka uses the term "flesh" in a manner that allows no symbolizing ascension to the realms of "soul" or "personality." It is pure corporeality, pure materiality that he refers to; he ranges the female body within a series of phenomena that interweave "the flesh" with disgust. In doing so, Kafka once again takes care—by means of a style of pure observation—that virtually no association should arise between the "objective" theme of agedness and a subjective feeling of aversion. On the contrary: the catalogue of defects and deformities attaching to female old age can appear in description the more unrelenting, the more the author maintains his affective distance toward what is described, and the more he displays, in the gestures of his language, a "childlike" and "innocent" freedom from disgust:

> Yesterday met B[ailly]. Her calmness, contentedness, clarity, and lack of embarrassment, even though in the last two years she has become an old woman; her plumpness—even at that time a burden to her—that will soon have reached the extreme of sterile fatness; her walk that has become a sort of rolling or shuffle with the belly thrust—or rather carried—to the fore; and on her chin (at a quick glance, only on her chin), hairs now curling out of what used to be down. (D, 220)

Deleuze's and Guattari's thesis of a mediating function for young women in Kafka's novels[17] is doubly blind to Kafka's politics of age and sex. First, there are, strictly speaking, no young women in Kafka's works, but only more or less explicit figurations of the aged, or aging, *vetula*. And, second, these figurations—as will become clearer below—are not so much the means as the goal of a libidinal trajectory that conceals itself and its objects in innocent unreadabilty.

"I Want Only the Stout Older Ones"

Kafka's descriptions of facial deformations that are ugly to the point of disgusting—misshapen noses, sallow and mottled skin, rotting teeth—appear much more frequently in his diaries and letters than in his literary works proper. This may have to do with a symbolic difference between face and body: owing to the extreme variability of its changing expressions, the limited surface of the face is a highly developed linguistic organ that lends itself far more readily to the deciphering of meanings than does the functioning of trunk, limbs, and "fleshy" parts. Kafka's literary texts, however, favored and, indeed, originated a subtly bewildering, highly equivocal, and deconventionalized language of gestures, which better fits the semiotic material of the body below the head than the semiotic material of facial expressions. This fact helps to explain the marked preference of Kafka's writings for faceless and headless, not to say beheaded figures. Thus, Kafka's literary indifference toward the female face does not necessarily bespeak conformity with misogynistic ideology. The dominant trait in Kafka's presentation of the female body is corpulence—and, to be sure, a corpulence that, even in its more modest forms, already points discreetly to the disgust-values of its hyperbolic elaboration. The posthumously published fragment, "On What Is Your Power Based?" incorporates nearly all the elements of Kafka's imagination of "fat women." It involves a conversation between two men, one of whom admires the other for his power, "resolution," and "conviction," and asks about the origin of this power. The answer—"my power is based on my two wives"—meets with disbelief and entails some surprising revelations:

> "Do you mean the women I saw in your kitchen yesterday?"
> "Yes."
> "Those two fat women?"
> "Yes."
> "Those women. I hardly took any notice of them. Forgive my saying so, they looked like two cooks. But they weren't very clean, and they were sloppily dressed."
> "Yes, that they are."
> "Well, whatever you say I always instantly believe, only now you are being even more incomprehensible than previously, before I knew of those women."

"But there is no mystery, it is all quite plain, I shall try to tell you about it. Now, I live with these women, you have seen them in the kitchen, but it's seldom that they cook, most of the time meals are fetched from the restaurant opposite, Resi going one time, and one time Alba. Actually, no one is against the cooking being done at home, but it is too difficult, because the two of them don't get on together, that is to say, they get on excellently, but only when they live quietly alongside each other. For instance, they are capable of lying side by side on the narrow sofa for hours, quite peacefully, without sleeping, which is no small matter, if only because they are so fat. But at work they don't get on together, in less than no time they begin quarrelling, and from quarrelling they go to beating each other. For this reason, we have agreed—they are very ready to listen to reasoned argument—that as little work as possible should be done. This, incidentally, is in accord with their disposition. For example, they think they clean the apartment particularly well, and yet it is so dirty that it disgusts me to step over the threshold. But once I have taken that step, I get used to it quite easily.

Once work is out of the way, every occasion for quarrelling is removed, and jealousy, in particular, is utterly unknown to them. Whence should jealousy arise, anyway? After all, I can scarcely distinguish one from the other. Perhaps Alba's nose and lips are even somewhat more Negroid than Resi's, but sometimes, again, the opposite seems to be the case. Perhaps Resi has somewhat less hair than Alba—really, it is almost beyond what is permissible how little hair she has—but, after all, do I pay any attention to that? I stick to what I said, I can scarcely distinguish one from the other." (DF, 339–41)

Dirty, idle, lethargic, quarrelsome, almost hairless, and above all: fat—thus looms the source of all power; and thus appear the descendants of the "great mother." Freud's "authoress," the source of his "means for living and going on living,"[18] was likewise named Resi. Kafka's Resi is the grotesque return of Freud's serving girl. Both owe it precisely to their abject behavior—in which cleaning up and dirtying up are merged—that they are the secret generators of male power. This power is intimately linked with disgust—just as all positions of power in Kafka are tainted by the disgusting. Weaning from disgust is necessary to enter into power, and Kafka takes the overcoming of the distinction between clean and unclean to the point of no longer distinguishing at all between the two empowering women. When the nameless employee "come[s] home from work [in the] evening," the two women run "panting" to the door, and there ensues the following ritual:

> Then there is always the crossing of the hall, a journey of only a few steps, which takes from a quarter of an hour to a whole hour,

with them almost carrying me. I am indeed really tired after an anything but easy day, and one time I lay my head on Resi's soft shoulder, and one time on Alba's. Both are almost naked, only in their shifts, they go about like that most of the day; only when a visitor is expected do they put on a few dirty rags.

Then we arrive at my room, and usually they push me in, but they themselves remain outside and shut the door. It is a game, for now they begin fighting for the privilege of being the first to come in. It is not at all jealousy, not a real fight, only a game. I hear the light, loud slaps they give each other, the panting that is now really the result of being short of breath, and now and then a few words. Finally, I myself open the door and they tumble in, hot, with torn shifts and the acrid smell of their breath. Then we collapse on the carpet, and then everything gradually quiets down. (DF, 341–42)

A corpulence that leads, with any moving about, to "panting" and shortness of breath; "acrid" mouth odor; "deep, gurgling laughter"; and near nakedness habitually concealed by merely "a few dirty rags"—all these traits do by no means suffice to turn the sexual intercourse on the carpet—as indicated only by the words "collapse" and "quiets down"—into something repulsive and grotesque. As a final and additional 'kick,' Kafka even invents a scene of female wrestling, in order to be able to portray the "mere cohabitation" with two fat women as a unique source of power. (What any "healthy" Freudian father could ever wish for is, for the "I" of this narrative, the "hot" reality of his bachelor apartment: a field of happy "freedom to enact perversions" and freedom from disgust, without any impotence-threatening encroachment of bourgeois feelings of respectability or other disturbing inhibitions.)

Just as there are no young women in Kafka's writings but only aging women and "old maids," so also there are no slender women but only fat women or "stout girls." The figure of the slender woman which dominates the modern canon of beauty is entirely absent in Kafka's works; it yields to the transcendental corpulence of the female. The antithesis of the fat woman is not the slender woman but the thin, weak man.[19] "The door to the kitchen had been opened," Kafka writes in *The Castle*, "and filling the doorway was the mighty figure of the landlady; the landlord approached her on tiptoes in order to make his report" (C, 3–4). The typical Kafkan couple is reflected in the image of "voluminous women" and "smaller men . . . [walking] with short steps" (DF, 317). In his letters, Kafka occasionally portrays himself as a small "nervous dog," who runs around a large and serene female statue (Felice), "barking" (L, 140). Kafka's habitual rhetoric of self-belittlement and his professed unhappiness at his own leanness are not enough to adequately explain his obsession with the "fat woman." Two opposite tenets are equally relevant here: "Being fat, she is ugly to the point of being disgusting," and "Being fat, she is beautiful." The transitions between these points of view are brief and harsh:

> Last night I dreamed of her plump little legs. Such are the roundabout ways by which I recognize a girl's beauty and fall in love. (L, 26)
>
> There are also many summer visitors here, for example an unusually beautiful, unusually fat blonde woman, who, just as a man tugs at his vest, must stretch herself every few steps in order to straighten out her belly and breasts; she is dressed like a fine poisonous toadstool and smells—some people know no limits—like the best edible mushroom ... (L, 351)

After a visit with Alfred Kubin, Kafka notes with obvious fascination: "Loves fat women. Every woman he has had has been photographed. The bundle of photographs that he shows every visitor" (D, 289). A few months earlier, Kafka had already confessed:

> I intentionally walk through the streets where there are whores. Walking past them excites me, the remote but nevertheless existent possibility of going with one. Is that grossness? But I know no better, and doing this seems basically innocent to me and causes me almost no regret. I want only the stout, older ones, with outmoded clothes made voluminous, as it were, by various layers of adornments. One woman probably knows me by now. I met her this afternoon, she was not yet in her working clothes, her hair was still flat against her head, she was wearing no hat, a work blouse like a cook's, and was carrying a bundle of some sort, perhaps to the laundress. No one would have found anything exciting in her, only me. (D, 238)

While the notorious reference to the metonyms cooking and filth is introduced very discreetly here ("like a cook's," "to the laundress"), the attributes fat and old are linked much more conspicuously: fat older women in outmoded voluminous clothes. The deviant nature of this erotic taste ("only me") is openly, indeed almost proudly asserted. At the same time, the innocence of this intercourse with a prostitute-*vetula* is upheld against any suspicion of "grossness."

In Kafka's novels, this declared preference succumbs to a twofold distortion. Either it is displaced onto minor figures, and then soberly observed from K.'s perspective as something strange. Or else it is ascribed to K. himself, but only as something wholly unwilled which he suffers like an innocent victim. The mistress of the district attorney Hasterer exemplifies, in a relatively inconspicuous fashion, the first case: "She was a thickset older woman with a yellowish complexion.... At first, K. saw her only in bed; she usually lay there shamelessly" (T, 248). In the last analysis, all of K.'s own women friends too—even those called young and "beautiful"—participate in the paradigm of the fat and old, dirty and lascivious *vetula*. The canonic incarnation of this paradigm is Brunelda. On first meeting her, Karl Rossmann sees "only her double chin, which rolled in sympathy with the turning of her head.... [T]here was no room whatever on the couch beside Brunelda, in spite of its great breadth" (A, 225, 227). Brunelda is too heavy to negotiate the few steps to a ground-floor apartment without losing her breath (A, 234); she snorts loudly in her sleep, as she sometimes does while talking (A, 260). Most of the time, she merely lies upon an "evil-smelling" couch (A, 258), which, moreover, is so dusty that, when she bangs it with both hands, "you can't see her for dust" (A, 244). Her corpulence even prevents Brunelda from undressing herself:

> "How long you're taking!" cried Brunelda from the sofa; she had spread her legs wide where she sat so as to get more room for her disproportionately fat body; only with the greatest effort, gasping and frequently pausing to recover her breath, could she bend far enough forward to catch hold of her stockings at the top and pull them down a little; she could not possibly take off her own clothes; Delamarche would have to do that, and she was now impatiently waiting for him. (A, 229)

The men's job, accordingly, consists in dressing, undressing, washing, feeding, and transporting Brunelda. Kafka leaves it to K.'s antagonists to affirm the erotic appeal of this laborious business. Robinson describes his first encounter with Brunelda: "Maybe she was too tightly laced; anyhow, she couldn't get up to the top of these steps. But how lovely she looked, Rossmann! She was wearing a white dress with a red sunshade. You felt you could eat her. You felt you could drink her up. God, God, she was lovely. What a woman!" (A, 234). Although excluded from the washing sessions, Robinson knows still more to tell of:

> "She's a marvelous woman, of course. I say,"—and he gave Karl a sign to bend down so that he might whisper to him—"I once saw her naked. Oh"—and, in the memory of that pleasure, he began to pinch and slap Karl's leg until Karl shouted:
> "Robinson, you're mad!" and forcibly pushed his hands away.
> "You're still only a child, Rossmann," said Robinson ... (A, 231)

The disdain of the apartment house neighbors, the red sunshade, and the police license Karl has to display when he transports this giant beauty into

"Office No. 25"[20] (which is not hard to recognize as a bordello), associate Brunelda quite clearly with prostitution. On the other hand, precisely this association is systematically obscured: there is no talk of clients, and the three men "serve" Brunelda's "majesty" in a strictly hierarchical order. K. is initially repelled by the proposal to enter this service (A, 244), and he likewise abstains from the devotion paid to this foul-smelling mass of flesh, whose weight a policeman puts at "ten sacks of potatoes" (V, 380). Robinson's comment— "You're still only a child, Rossmann"—merely makes explicit what the narrative form as such continuously says, without saying. Because the childlike, innocent "hero," from whose perspective alone the reader views the action, has no feeling for Brunelda's "beauty," everything disgusting about her appearance and behavior is, by this means, diffracted in the prism of remote incomprehension. Hence, there is no direct engagement with the female-disgusting here—as there is in contemporary works by Kubin or Lovecraft, or in Kafka's own confession, reserved for his diaries, of attraction to fat old whores. Rather, it is as if Karl is surprised at having to narrate something that strikes him as coming from another planet. Other texts successfully create the impression that they are themselves even more nonplussed than their readers could be at having everywhere to deal with "people" who look "like fat old women," who stroke their bellies as if pregnant, and who remain, in the end, as incomprehensible as any other figuration of higher power in Kafka's world:

> I was not at all certain whether I had any advocates, I could not find out anything definite about it, every face was unfriendly, most people who came toward me and whom I kept meeting in the corridors looked like fat old women; they had huge blue-and-white striped aprons covering their entire bodies, kept stroking their stomachs and swaying awkwardly to and fro. . . . I am hanging about in these corridors where only these old women are to be seen, and not even many of them, and always the same ones, and even those few will not let themselves be cornered, despite their slowness; they slip away from me, float about like rain clouds, and are completely absorbed by unknown activities. (S, 449–50)

Disgust with Conjugal Sexuality Versus Pleasure in Disgusting Sex Outside of Marriage

It is a notorious fact that Kafka was unable to live in spatial and physical proximity to those of his female correspondents with whom he was passionately in love. Posterity has readily incorporated this fact into its image of the obsessive author; the popular concept of normative deviance associated with the literary genius and his poetic *mania* thus found a new canonical instauration. As a matter of fact, many of Kafka's diary entries read like a conscious and literarily sophisticated caricature of male anxiety in the presence of female sexuality. "The bursting sexuality of the women," begins a note from July 23, 1913, only to follow in quick succession with the elements of impurity, corpulence, bad teeth, pregnancy, and grotesque behind:

> The bursting sexuality of the women. Their natural impurity . . . the sight of a fat woman hunched up in a basket chair, one foot curiously pushed backwards, who was sewing something and talking to an old woman, probably an old spinster, whose teeth appeared unusually large on one side of her mouth. The full-bloodedness and wisdom of the pregnant woman. Her behind almost faceted by evenly divided planes. (D, 227)

The literary representation of sexuality in Kafka's works appears entirely consistent with the findings on hysterical sexual disgust. When, for example, Frieda and K. in *The Castle* roll around "among the small puddles of beer and other refuse scattered on the floor," the interpreters, faced with the metonymic contiguity of sex and "refuse" here, forget everything they have otherwise learned about the ambiguities and uncertainty relations in Kafka's work. Here, for once, things are simple and unequivocal:

> These horrible couplings obviously have very little to do with love or even with physical desire; they testify to an obsessively negative estimation of sexuality. Such . . . passages can hardly form an object of analysis for literary criticism; they speak for themselves in drastic fashion and require no extended commentary.[21]

Because the disgust with sexuality appears so evident, while the charm of Kafka's work lies in its endless complexity and subtle nuances, Kafka interpreters have usually been content to mention—or, more precisely, gesture toward—the findings on sexual disgust, in order then to turn their attention, with a smile of forebearance, to more important and more interesting questions. In this way, the regrettable inhibitions of the author, and the misogynist tendencies bound up with them, could be safely assumed to have no bearing on a reading of his work. Paradoxically, it is precisely the patency of sexual disgust that thus accounts for its latency as an object of analysis; the circularity of apparently clear understanding and marginalizing forebearance conceals the phenomenon under consistent good will. The following analysis amounts to three opposite claims:

1. Kafka's autobiographical and literary reflections obey models far more complex than the simple reference to sexual repression might suggest. To

these models belong, in particular, methods of neutralization and countercathexis of what is disgusting.
2. These modes of presentation, of countercathexis, and of visibly making invisible what is (sexually) disgusting are central to Kafka's entire literary project.
3. Kafka's intended "deception" of the reader proves itself—or founders—precisely in confronting that quality of the "real" in disgust which, according to eighteenth century aesthetics, shatters all "illusion."

The psychogram of sexual disgust delineated below is first of all Kafka's own—just as the extrapolation of an *écriture* of disgust avoids looking behind the back of the author. Kafka's pronounced tendency toward unflattering observations about himself is certainly no guarantee of their truth; in any case, they provide invaluable material for the establishment of a nuanced profile of sexual disgust. Forming the primary layer of this profile is the oft-mentioned "aversion" to "living together" with his family: "Yesterday I was choked with loathing *[Ekel]*," Kafka reports, on the occasion of an excursion to his family's summer home, where "disorder" increases in proportion to intimacy:

> Where cotton wool is to be found lying among the plates and a disgusting assortment of all kinds of objects on the beds; . . . where the little boy, because he can't help himself while being played with, does his business on the floor in the middle of the room, where the two maidservants jostle each other in the performance of various duties, where my mother insists on waiting on everyone, where bread is spread with goose-drippings which, if one's lucky, trickle only down one's fingers. (LF, 286)

"My aversion to it all," writes Kafka further, "is not, as you might think, an aversion to dirt." Nor is it an aversion to particular qualities of his relatives, but rather to their simple presence at hand as relatives: "I absolutely hate all my relatives, not because they are my relatives, not because they are wicked, . . . but simply because they are the people with whom I live in close proximity." If all disgust is an experience of (unpleasant) proximity, then for Kafka the people "with whom I live in close proximity" fulfill, in a virtually transcendental manner, the condition for the possibility of social disgust. Such disgust is occasioned not only by the actual presence of his relatives but also, and even more acutely, by the recollection that all family relation is grounded ultimately in acts of marriage and procreation. A relatively late letter to Felice contains a declaration of disgust for the site of his own conception—a declaration that, in its passion and trenchant formulation, is hardly to be surpassed:

> At home, the sight of the double bed, of sheets that have been slept in, of nightshirts carefully laid out, can bring me to the point of

retching, can turn my stomach inside out; it is as though my birth had not been final, as though from this fusty life I keep being born again and again in this fusty room; as though I had to return there for confirmation, being—if not quite, at least in part—indissolubly connected with these repulsive things; something still clings to the feet as they try to break free, held fast as they are in the primordial slime. (LF, 525)

The sight of the nuptial bed and of the bedsheets that have been slept in causes Kafka to sink back into the originary metaphor of all deformation disgust—into the "primordial slime" ("primal soup"). In a grotesque reversal of Nietzsche's affirmation of eternal return, he imagines his own imprisonment within the traumatic compulsion to "return," "again and again," to the birth canal and the place of conception for the sake of "confirming" his own existence, which is not yet "finally" uncoupled from these places of origin.[22] What the "retching" brings up is his own continual reconception and rebirth in his parents' double bed; what is vomited is the sticky slime that dooms the feet to a cycle of Sisyphean labors "as they try to break free." The stimulus for rejecting "these repulsive things" can be of two sorts. It can entail the paradigm of dirt and refuse (soiled sheets), but it can just as well derive its revolting quality from a painfully extreme orderliness and cleanliness, which appears displaced or pathological ("carefully laid out" nightshirts).

In Kafka's novels, such disgust with the proximity of relatives and the sexuality of parents can be retraced, if at all, only as the hidden power of successfully excluding all "these repulsive things." The novel *Amerika* begins at precisely the moment when the protagonist Karl Rossmann loses forever the sight of his parents' bedroom. Here, the fairy tale motif of the casting off of the innocent son *by* the parents may—as Maria Tatar suggests it actually does in the case of the "authentic" tales—realize in a distorted manner a repudiation *of* the parents by the son and thus fulfill a (forbidden) desire.[23] Whereas Karl Rossmann emerges from a rudimentary family prehistory, only to be increasingly severed from all family ties, Josef K. from the very beginning enters the scene as a confirmed bachelor without any family prehistory. The finished sections of *The Trial* recount nothing at all concerning the childhood and parents of the protagonist. An unfinished chapter mentions that K., despite various promises made to his mother, has not been to visit her in the past three years, while his half-blind mother, for her part, is no longer clamoring, with her "urgent invitations," to see him. It is precisely and solely on the basis of this complete loss of contact that K. plans a journey to his mother. The fragment, however, breaks off before depicting the reunion of mother and son (T, 263–66). The only sort of kinship which survives elimination in Kafka's first two novels is the relationship to an uncle. Indeed, Karl's and K.'s uncles both wear the guise of benevolent helpers, who seem to intervene unselfishly for the sake of their nephews. Yet this role of uncle as better father figure is subject, in both novels, to renewed structures of repudiation: Karl's uncle soon proves to be cruel and tyrannical, and merely reassumes the position of the boy's parents; K.'s uncle likewise—although remaining, for his part, good-natured—is implicitly brushed off after the dismissal of the lawyer he has chosen, and disappears from the novel without a trace.

In Kafka's last novel, *The Castle,* there is no longer an uncle and not the slightest recollection of the protagonist's parents. Having no parents and therefore bearing no trace of his conception or birth, exiled into an indeterminate foreign land, this hero has successfully left behind all remnants of that offensive contiguity which so grieved Kafka in regard to his own situation in the parental home. While Kafka's novels thus provide no occasion for disgust with the proximity of relatives and the sexuality of parents, two prominent early stories—and they alone—lead into the very center of the repudiated family romance. "The Judgment" shows the protagonist's sick father in dirty underwear and in a bed that is presumably the former nuptial bed; at the end it turns out that the father has usurped even the role of his son's friends, so that all independence in this sphere is impossible for the son. "The Metamorphosis" is unique among Kafka's stories in presenting a complete family scene, with father, mother, sister, and son; he promptly labeled it "exceptionally repulsive," "infinitely disgusting" (LF, 58). The mother, in this story, makes use of her sexual position to appease the aggressive father, while the son dreams of incest with his sister, presses his belly up against a (masochistic) fetish of a lady in furs, and, for the rest, is economically exploited. From the perspective of disgust with the proximity of family, Gregor Samsa's progressive exclusion could be read as a distorted wish-fulfillment, whose end result is that complete separation from the family which forms the point of departure for the action of the novels. "The Metamorphosis" banishes the son into an inner exteriority of the family, *Amerika* into an outer exteriority. These two sons are thus spared the sight of the parental bedroom and the experience of being stuck fast in the "primordial slime"; for both sons, the family takes over the arduous work of removal from disgusting proximity. Wish fulfillment merges with scenarios of punishment. In either case, the son comes out looking innocent.

As a consequence of this syndrome of disgust with familial dependence, proximity, and sexuality, Kafka's own myth of marriage quite logically involves sexual indifference, childlessness, and economic independence of the partners. "Coitus" is explicitly characterized as "punishment for the happiness of being together," and the greatest possible asceticism is proposed as "the only possible way for me to endure marriage." "But she?" adds Kafka, doubting whether Felice would ever accept marriage as a programmatic means for living ascetically—"more ascetically than a bachelor" (D, 228)—and, indeed, for living a strictly regulated "monastic life," in which "we shall have but *one* hour a day together" (LF, 309). In any event, the renunciation of marital sexuality—without Felice's agreement, to be sure—had already been in place as criterion for the selection of a bride:

> Later, . . . the body of every other girl tempted me, but the body of the girl in whom I placed my hopes (for that reason?) not at all. . . . Evidently, on account of my dignity, on account of my pride (no matter how humble he looks, the devious West European Jew!), I can love only what I place so high above me that I cannot reach it. (L, 273)

On this point, the diaries, letters, and works all paint the same picture: the tendency toward (hysterical) disgust *with* sexuality operates only in regard to the marital-parental bedroom. Outside the space of the family, there is no inhibition of sexual desire through the barriers of disgust, but instead a (perverse/obsessive-neurotic) discovery of libidinally charged disgust *within* sexuality. Numerous eroticized descriptions of girls in the diaries lend credence to Kafka's claim that "the body of every other girl tempted me." Kafka and his literary creations routinely have a sex life only outside of marriage. Its setting is most often anonymous hotel rooms, and there are generally two types of partners, neither of which is likely to yield a future spouse: travel acquaintances and prostitutes. The two emphatic sexual experiences of Kafka's life are connected to traveling abroad: "With F. I never experienced (except in letters) that sweetness one feels in a relationship with a woman one loves, such as I had in Zuckmantel and Riva" (D, 329). But the usual situation of Kafkan sexuality—the visit to a prostitute, or an encounter with a promiscuous maidservant—is less sweet. Whereas the dreams of visits to prostitutes or the reaction to prostitutes seen but not accosted detail with great vividness his "pleasure" in fat and, to some extent, disgustingly deformed older women, the few accounts of actual relations with prostitutes tend to be laconic and not very explicit:

> Otherwise I am so urgently driven to find someone who will merely touch me in a friendly manner that yesterday I went to the hotel with a prostitute. She is too old to be melancholy still, but feels sorry—though it doesn't surprise her—that people are not as kind to prostitutes as they are to a mistress. I didn't comfort her since she didn't comfort me either. (L, 45)

A letter to Milena provides the most thorough description of Kafka's "real" hotel room experiences with maidservants/prostitutes. The portrait of the very "first night" with a woman at all turns into the confession of a lasting and compulsive fixation on a sexual "happiness" that is bound up with "something slightly disgusting, embarrassing, obscene":

I remember the first night. We lived at that time in the Zeltnergasse, opposite a dress shop, in the door of which a shop girl used to stand, upstairs I, a little more than twenty years old, walked incessantly up and down the room, occupied with the nerve-wracking cramming of, to me, senseless facts required for my first State examination. It was summer, very hot, quite unbearable, I stopped each time by the window, the disgusting Roman Law between my teeth, finally we came to an understanding by sign language. I was to fetch her at 8 P.M., but when I came down in the evening someone else was already there—well, this didn't make any difference, I was afraid of the whole world, thus of this man too; even if he hadn't been there, I would *also* have been afraid of him. Although the girl took his arm, she nevertheless signed to me that I should follow them. Thus we arrived at the Schützen island where we drank beer, I at the next table, then we walked, I following slowly, to the girl's apartment, somewhere near the Fleischmarkt, there the man said good-bye, the girl ran into the house, I waited a while until she came out again, and then we went to a hotel on the Kleinseite. Even before we got to the hotel, all this was charming, exciting, and horrible, in the hotel it wasn't different. And when, toward morning (it was still hot and beautiful), we walked home over the Karlsbrücke, I was actually happy, but this happiness came from the fact that at last I had some peace from the ever-yearning body, and above all it came from the relief that the whole experience hadn't been *more* horrible, *more* obscene. I was with the girl once again (two nights later, I believe), everything went as well as the first time, but as I then left immediately for the summer holidays, where I played around a bit with another girl, I could no longer look at the shop girl in Prague, not another word did I exchange with her, she had become (from my point of view) my bitter enemy, and yet she was a good-natured, friendly girl, she followed me all the time with her uncomprehending eyes. I won't say that the sole reason for my enmity was the fact (I'm sure it wasn't) that at the hotel the girl in all innocence had made a tiny repulsive gesture (not worth mentioning), had uttered a trifling obscenity (not worth mentioning), but the memory remained—I knew at that instant that I would never forget it and simultaneously I knew, or thought I knew, that this repulsiveness and smut, though outwardly not necessary, was inwardly however very necessarily connected with the whole thing, and that just this repulsiveness and obscenity (whose little symptom had only been her tiny gesture, her trifling word) had drawn me with such terrible power into this hotel, which otherwise I would have avoided with all my remaining strength.

And as it was then, so it has always remained. My body, sometimes quiet for years, would then again be shaken to the point of not being able to bear it by this desire for a small, a very specific abomination, for something slightly disgusting, embarrassing, obscene, even in the best that existed for me there was something of it, some small nasty smell, some sulphur, some hell. This urge had in it something of the eternal Jew, being senselessly drawn, wandering senselessly through a senselessly obscene world.[24]

The choreography of this report to his beloved correspondent simultaneously magnifies and diminishes "a tiny repulsive gesture (not worth mentioning)," "a trifling obscenity (not worth mentioning)," a libinal fixation on something simultaneously acknowledged repulsive and obscene. In Freud's terminology: an overcoming of disgust in the interests of sexual desire—an overcoming felt to be excessive—is, on the one hand, stigmatized as a mundane diminutive of hell ("some sulphur, some hell"), while, on the other hand, it is defended against any moral censure and presented as a source of redeeming happiness ("I was actually happy," and, the second time, "everything went as well as the first time"). Not only is the admirer of the "shop girl"—in his combination of "fear," self-belittlement, and sexual inexperience—a prototypical innocent youth; the obscene word and the repulsive gesture of the girl—whose apartment, appropriately enough, lies "somewhere near the Fleischmarkt"—are likewise said to issue "in all innocence."

"Innocence" and "You Must Possess Every Girl!"

The *basso continuo* of Kafka's figuration of the sexual is the assumption (whether directly or obliquely) of a position of sexual "innocence"—innocence even in the enjoyment of abject sexual objects and sexual practices, indeed *precisely* in such enjoyment: "As a boy, I was as innocent of and uninterested in sexual matters (and would have long remained so, if they had not been forcibly thrust on me) as I am today in, say, the theory of relativity. Only trifling things (yet even these only after they were pointedly called to my attention) struck me, for example that it was just those women on the street who seemed to me most beautiful and best dressed who were supposed to be bad" (D, 418–19). Only seemingly is his own innocence evoked here as something in the meantime lost. For the sentence about the "most beautiful and best dressed" women on the street serves not so much to recall what he has learned through experience as to reactualize the gaze which sought out these women. It very effectively summons up the boy's former inexperience as a *present* stylistic gesture. What the narrative, by the use of "was," only seems to relegate to the past, the stylistic gesture, in the artfully naïve remembrance of "trifling things," reenacts and repeats as its own actual stance. This oblique bringing back to presence of vanished youthful innocence is an all the more astounding achievement, as it not only presents the appeal of prostitution in terms of an experience of sexual initiation, but also directly follows on "five guiding principles on the road to hell," of which the second and third run as follows:

2. "You must possess every girl!" not in Don Juan fashion, but according to the devil's expression "sexual etiquette."
3. "This girl you are not permitted to possess!" and for this very reason cannot. A heavenly *Fata Morgana* in hell. (D, 418)

Kafka has reserved the heavenly Fata Morgana of nonpossessability—which, according to the logic of the "principles," itself already belongs to the immanence of hell (as the opposite of the infernal etiquette, but *in* hell)—for potential wives like Felice Bauer and Milena Jesenska. Otherwise, the sexual etiquette of a comprehensive will to possess generally operates without Don-Juanism. This etiquette is the male correlate, if not the foundation, of the assumption of a universal female promiscuity. Without this etiquette, some form of Don-Juanism is needed to be able to captivate all the "girls," as Kafka's K. succeeds in doing without the slightest art of seduction. Whether it be Frieda, Amalia, Olga, Pepi, or the landlady: in *The Castle*, there is finally no woman who does not offer intimate relations to K. and whom he does not at least virtually possess. This "sexual etiquette of hell" likewise applies to the court and to the castle: the officials need only issue an order to have as many women as they want for their concubines.[25] They can thus dispense with a period of courtship, for "there's no such thing as an official's unhappy love affair" (C, 256). The woman's compliance, surprisingly enough, is only confirmed, in order to be absolved from every moral stricture: "And, strangely enough, it is not considered disgraceful for a woman to surrender to this temptation; on the contrary, in the opinion of many, this is something women have to go through, a debt which they pay to their sex. Moreover, it invariably takes the same course" (S, 440).

"Dirty Fellow," Dancing and Swinging Pigs, Stinking Bitches and Self-Knowledge

"Repulsive" and "obscene" sexual practices are something that Kafka—despite his declared obsession with "some sulphur" and "some hell" *in eroticis*—either left undescribed in his published works or else veiled in "innocence" by means of contexts and stylistic gestures. He is, quite rightly, not known as a pornographic author and could hardly compete with others in this line. The appeal of his figurations of disgust and sexuality is not a matter of any provocative display of the perverse; rather, it lies in the affective neutralization of a hell that is openly manifest and yet made invisible, unreadable. In the chapter "A Country House Near New York," Karl Rossmann is the object of what appears to be a barely concealed homosexual advance from his host Mr. Pollunder, who "put his arm round Karl and drew him between his knees" (A, 79). The following sentence, however, immediately neutralizes the ambiguity of this action by submerging it in the medium of Karl's inexperience, for which it can appear only as a fatherly gesture: "Karl submitted willingly, though for all intents and purposes he felt much too grown up to be treated this way." The stiffly mechanical qualifying phrase "though for all intents and purposes" *(trotzdem er sich im allgemeinen doch)* betrays, through its stylistic stumbling effect, something of the irritation it overcomes. Yet in confining this irritation to no more than a gentle smile over Karl's innocent blend of tolerance and faint inner protest, it immediately dissolves it again.[26] There are, however, two posthumously published prose texts that confront the reader with the "sulphur" of sexual "obscenities" in a manner unfiltered enough to come close to pornographic crassness in what they show and what they mean. In one of these texts, a bachelor returning home to his room from the office encounters a grotesque configuration of an unrecognizable face, large breasts, and a "long thick yellowish tail." The "spasmodic breathing" of the "creature" points to an advanced state of sexual arousal:

> Yellowish glittering eyes stared at me; large round woman's breasts rested on the shelf of the stove, on either side beneath the unrecognizable face; the creature seemed to consist entirely of a mass of soft white flesh; a long thick yellowish tail hung down beside the stove, its tip ceaselessly passing back and forth over the cracks of the tiles. (D, 288)

Shortly after this, the text breaks off. It is hard to imagine how the obscenity of the hybrid mass of flesh could ever have been integrated into a Kafkan gestus. Another bachelor fantasy—which short-circuits the function of landlady with the role of the old prostitute and unmasks her client as a coarsened "dirty fellow"—goes further in this direction:

> "Young man, said the woman, and her lower jaw jutted forward, you want to live here?"
> "Yes," the young man said, tossing his head upward.
> "You will like it here," the woman said, leading him to a chair on which she sat him down. In doing this, she noticed a stain on his trousers, kneeled down beside him and began to scrape at the stain with her fingernails.
> "You're a dirty fellow," she said.

"It's an old stain."
"Then you are an old dirty fellow."
"Take your hand away," he said suddenly, and actually pushed her away. "What horrible hands you have!" He caught her hand and turned it over. "All black on top, whitish below, but still black enough and"—he ran his fingers inside her wide sleeve—"there is even some hair on your arm."
"You're tickling me," she said.
"Because I like you. I don't understand how they can say that you are ugly. Because they did say it. But now I see that it isn't true at all."
And he stood up and walked up and down the room. She remained on her knees and looked at her hand.
For some reason this made him furious; he sprang to her side and caught her hand again.
"You're quite a woman," he then said, and clapped her long thin cheek. "It would really add to my comfort to live here. But it would have to be cheap. And you would not be allowed to take in other roomers. And you would have to be faithful to me. I am really much younger than you and can after all insist on faithfulness. And you would have to cook well. I am used to good food and never intend to disaccustom myself." (D, 271–72)

With her jutting jaw, black hands, hairy arms, thin cheeks, and her kneeling before the trousers of the young man, the landlady, who "whips up her skirts," fulfills all the conditions necessary to pass for a classic *vetula* of the Horatian type. It is this that makes her so repulsive and, at the same time, so pleasing to the young man. The arrangement he offers—manly youth in exchange for housing, good food, and sexual attentions—assumes the express form, in stipulating faithfulness as well, of a substitute for marriage. Daily meals, daily rubbing of trousers, proximity thereby to incest with the mother who provides for him—and all this at a cheap rate: a truly dirty deal. The text allows no inner distancing from its sordidness and produces no illusion—whether from the side of the landlady or from that of the young man—of inexperience and innocence. All the more pressing, therefore, is its need for a supplement that, at least on the surface, would make up for the missing effort to keep the disgusting at a distance and clearly demarcate the bachelor author from the bachelor represented in his text. This supplement, this kick against the text could hardly be more drastic: "Dance on, you pigs; what have I to do with it?" (D, 272).

Together with rats, mice, worms, and beetles, the pig has a place as well among the recurring figures of Kafka's bestiary of "repulsive animals" (LF, 115). "Hopelessly piggish" is the pig, according to Kafka, because with its "snout-face"—a "human face, in which the lower lip is folded down over the chin, while the upper lip, without affecting the eyes and nostrils, is folded up to the brow"—it "actually grubs up the ground. . . . You would really think that, just for testing purposes, it would be enough to poke at the thing in question with a foot, or to smell it, or if necessary to sniff at it from close quarters—but no, all this will not do, and the pig does not even try, but thrusts his snout right in, and if it has plunged into something horrid—all around me lie the droppings of my friends, the goats and the geese—then he snorts with delight" (L, 150). Converging, in this way, with the customary term of abuse, Kafka's anthropomorphized pig extends the semantics of the omni-eater—the pig making no distinctions and thus, like the child, knowing of no disgust—to a pleasure in grubbing in the disgusting. Both traits are disgusting: the indifference toward disgust and its (perverse) conversion to a preference for the disgusting. And what is true of the ugly, repulsive prostitutes, who offer themselves to everyone without distinction and without disgust, is once again true here: the pig, as a figure of the disgusting lack of disgust, in no way repels Kafka. On the contrary, he demonstrates a surprising sense for the "self-obliteration, sweetness," and "fastidiousness" of the pig; moreover, "[the pig] has elegant, delicately stepping feet, and the movements of his body seem to flow from a single impulse" (L, 150).

"Dance on, you pigs; what have I to do with it?" This sentence is so much a stranger to Kafka's linguistic cosmos that it was presumably felt to be even less suitable for publication than the little narrative that precedes it, and to whose protagonists it is addressed. The coupling of the "dirty fellow" story with a postscriptum sharply distancing the stance of the narrator from this story points *ex negativo* to a rule of superimposition which it violates: in its "ideal" form, Kafka's prose works to intertwine in a complex manner what here abstractly falls apart—an imagination of the disgusting and a censoring, a concealing of the pleasure taken in it. The seemingly rhetorical question—"what have I to do with it?"—a question to which, as a gesture of distantiation, the answer "Nothing!" appears certain, thus penetrates to the core of Kafka's writing. "What have I to do with it?" A great deal. This is the answer intimated by a longer diary entry, which compares the act of "self-scrutiny" with "the wallowing of a pig in muck":

> At a certain point in self-knowledge, when other circumstances favoring self-scrutiny are present, it will invariably follow that you find yourself execrable. Every moral standard—however opinions may differ on it—will seem too high. You will see that you are nothing but a rat's nest of miserable ulterior motives *[Hintergedanken]*. . . . These ulterior motives aren't all compounded merely of selfishness, selfishness seems in comparison an ideal of the good and beautiful. The filth . . . is the nethermost depth you will find; at the nethermost depth there will be not lava, no, but filth. It

is the nethermost and the uppermost, and even the doubts self-scrutiny begets will soon grow weak and self-complacent as the wallowing of a pig in muck. (D, 330)

Kafka is a master of the rhetoric of self-diminishment, indeed of self-sullying. His letters and notebooks never tire of putting on view his own self's "abomination"[27] and, after the outbreak of his lung disease, his physical "dissolution" (LF, 259) and the contagious "loathesomeness" of the infection (L, 264). The posthumously published text "A Life" replaces the comparison to the pig in the muck with the metonym of a stinking bitch, which, while still alive, already decomposes into "purulent and wormy flesh":

> A stinking bitch, mother of countless whelps, in places already rotting, but everything to me in my childhood, a faithful creature that follows me unfailingly, which I cannot bring myself to beat, from which, shunning her breath, I retreat step by step, and which nevertheless, if I do not decide otherwise, will push me into the corner between the walls, the corner that I already see, there to decompose completely, upon me and with me, right to the end—is it an honor for me?—the purulent and wormy flesh of her tongue upon my hand. (DF, 68–69)

To be sure, the "I" appears here as victim of an externalized principle of disgust which is unmistakably female, but since it recognizes in this principle its "all"—the desires and fixations of its own "childhood"—the "I" accepts the path of disgusting flesh as its own. Hence, the non-repudiation of the disgusting by no means ends in mere self-denigration. The parenthetical query—"is it an honor for me?"—points instead toward an affirmative dimension in Kafka's theme of the disgusting self. Its religious as well as literary model is the conversion of self-abasement into exaltation and redemption in (Christian) *sermo humilis*. Kafka seems to approximate this model when he distinguishes reflective self-disgust as the only sign of man's superiority to animals: "Only by one thing, by your disgust with yourself, are you richer than the wood louse that lies under that old stone, watching and waiting" (DF, 299). But he has expressly contradicted the hope that recognition or indeed confession of one's own secret baseness could result in one's "ridding oneself of oneself": instead of "reconquer[ing his] good and . . . free childhood" by means of his honesty, the "honest [sinner] . . . has only made the conquest of a brief folly and much subsequent bitterness" (DF, 205). That is, insofar as he lacks the "strength" to transform the negative self-recognition into a change of his attitudes and, finally, into creating a new self, he must, Kafka supposes, laboriously seek to "undo" the newfound self-knowledge. Otherwise, with no strength for a positive transformation of the self, his only alternative is to "destroy himself" in the face of his acquired knowledge. Thus, in the end, his self-recognition results in a gigantic camouflaging maneuver:

> But what has once happened cannot be undone, it can only be muddied. And to this end expedients *[Hilfskonstruktionen]* arise. The whole world is full of them: indeed, the whole visible world is perhaps nothing other than an expedient furthering man's wish to rest for a moment—a means for placing the fact of knowledge under suspicion, for making knowledge the goal. (DF, 44)

"World" here means the making invisible of a disgusting self that has recognized itself yet can derive no advantage to itself from the knowledge of its own "baseness," but only finds a momentary rest by muddying just this knowledge. The "goal" of self-knowledge proves to be an ideologem of its own negation: it is merely the mirage that hides "the fact of knowledge" and thereby serves as the most suitable form of its derailing. Thus, whether or not Kafka's *sermo humilis* can lay any claim to revealing genuine self-knowledge at all, it does in any event not imply a claim to dialectical heightening of the self. In fact, it cannot even be decided whether the systematic self-abasement is not itself already an "expedient" furthering the muddying of self-knowledge. The psychological as well as epistemological utility of Kafka's rhetoric of the disgusting self is thus fundamentally and irreducibly problematic. The positive achievements are to be looked for elsewhere: Kafka's *sermo humilis* remains, on the one hand, a thoroughly traditional method of gaining a practical advantage; on the other hand, from the perspective of writing, it opens up possibilities—as refined as they are deceptive—for transforming into sources of literary pleasure what, even through knowledge, cannot be altered.

Kafka the "Flabby Worm": The Method of Making "Abominable Peculiarities" Invisible through the Form of Their Disclosure

Kafka's correspondence with Kurt Wolff provided him with an occasion for expressly characterizing "self-denigration" as a success-oriented politics of understatement. Such a strategy compels the other party to counter with high praise—"not out of hypocrisy, which [Wolff] surely does not have to practice toward me, but because he is forced to by the method" of self-denigration itself.[28] As "truth," however, self-denigration produces "no successes; truth only shatters what is shattered." If Kafka's self-denigration as a writer were only the "truth," and not "also inevitably a strategy," then its success could reside only in the complete repudiation of the writings: "as such it would make me happy if I could take the repulsive little story out of Wolff's desk drawer and wipe it out of his memory" (LF, 326). The notorious self-abasement running through Kafka's letters to Felice and Milena shares in this duality of "truth" and "method." It is not a question here of any simple "fishing for compliments." What is uttered as "truth" may be perfectly and literally true. Only, it places Kafka as a potential companion in so unfavorable a light that it necessarily elicits reservations from his correspondents. A "truth," then, which, lacking plausibility, calls itself into question, shades seamlessly into a "method," by which the truth about oneself is muddied insofar as it is asserted. Kafka has explicitly called attention to this paradoxical effect of "self-denigration." In doing so, however, he has not charged himself with an especially perfidious form of deception, but rather reproached Felice for her deficient "belief" in what he writes. For Kafka, "the most important aspect of our relationship really seemed ... quite clear," given his utter frankness about his "abominable peculiarities" and their consequences for the (im)possibility of his living with someone else. Felice, however, would not take seriously what he said, preferring to dismiss it by assuming (in conformity with her wishes) that something quite different was being left "unsaid": "What was lacking was not discussion but belief. Because you were unable to believe the things you heard and saw, you thought there were things that had been left unsaid.... As a result, you were bound to misinterpret everything" (LF, 437).

Explicit self-denigration, accordingly, can bring about its own unreadability, insofar as it oversteps the bounds of the believable. In response to its unacceptable literal meaning, it then produces the illusion, the "expedient" of something left unsaid, which appears to contradict that explicit assertion whose effect it nonetheless is. Such a *sermo humilis* is "witty" in structure; indeed, it can be read as Kafka's variation on the "Jewish joke."[29] It exposes private weaknesses, allows forbidden desires to emerge from the censor's shadow, and thus saves itself the trouble of repression. At the same time, it takes care that a "real" self-denigration does not take place, but rather falls flat through the manner of its presentation or else is overlaid by secondary effects. The witty combination of a seemingly unconditional self-critique with a highly refined dissimulation of this very critique turns the (narcissistic) wound at the spectacle of the disgusting self back into a triumph of its own representational ability. It allows the writer to transfigure the "acting out" of his own "baseness" (LF, 545) into a subtle source of pleasure.

The "methodical" irony of a *sermo humilis* that, precisely through its frankness, muddies its own assertions has a clear practical value for Kafka's correspondence. The regularly repeated and merciless lashing of his own "abominable peculiarities" (LF, 437) by no means produces the horror one might expect in his female correspondents. Instead, it runs into the "melting" affect[30] of a compassion mixed with disbelief. And this seems to be exactly what Kafka intends. Whereas Lessing had seen in disgust the greatest enemy to the feeling of compassion, Kafka looks to the systematic representation of himself as abhorrent precisely for an effect of compassion. On further reflection, of course, the compassion induced through self-condemnation becomes for him something unpalatable:

> And what I fear is that even if I were to become abhorrent to you—after all, you are a girl, and want a man, not a flabby worm on the earth—even if I were to become abhorrent, your kindness would not fail you. You realize how completely I belong to you—but does one abruptly throw away a thing that belongs to one so completely, even if reasonable consideration for oneself demands it? And you of all people—would you do it? Could you overcome your compassion? You who are so deeply affected by the unhappiness of all those around you? On the other hand, there is me. I will not deny that I could very easily feed on someone else's compassion, but I certainly could not enjoy the fruits of any kind of compassion that would inevitably destroy you. (LF, 211)

The hypercomplex chess game, which Kafka plays against his female correspondents, periodically reaches the point at which the finespun net of absolute demands—based, as they are, on spatial distance as well as on disgusting self-representations—collapses. Yet the "method" survives these crises. Kafka does not cease attributing to himself things that, in their stench, arouse disgust: sulphur, hell, devil. This results, naturally, in a conflict with another predicate of Kafka's "self-condemnation": the miserable weakness whose hyperbolic depiction—for example, as a repulsive "flabby worm"—conjoins the quality of excessive softness, as adduced in Mendelssohn's theory of disgust, with a widespread stereotype of the physically degenerate Jewish body.[31] From this conflict between weakness and devlish strength, Kafka can even extract a discreet compliment to himself, within the framework of his methodical self-denigration: "If such types"—he is talking about himself first of all—"were 'powerful' into the bargain, they would be perfect devils; this is where Providence shows its kindness" (LF, 470).

7.2 The Transformation of the Abject into "Guiltless Enjoyment": Writing as Devlish-Angelic "Deceiving without Deception"

It is not just his sexual "baseness" and "abhorrent" obsessions that Kafka has described as sulphurous and devlish. Among the extended repertory of these figurations of a disgusting self belongs, in particular, the libidinal fixation on writing:

> Writing is a sweet and wonderful reward... for serving the devil. This descent to the dark powers, this unshackling of spirits bound by nature, these dubious embraces and whatever else may take place in the nether parts which the higher parts no longer know, when one writes one's stories in the sunshine. Perhaps there are other forms of writing, but I know only this kind.... And the devlish element in it seems very clear to me. It is vanity and the craving for pleasure *(Genußsucht)* which continually buzz about one's own or even another's *Gestalt*—and feast on it. The movement multiplies itself—it is a regular solar system of vanity.... The writer... has no ground, no substance, is less than dust. He is only barely possible in the broil of earthly life, is only a construct of the craving for pleasure. (L, 334–35)

The Romantic topos of unshackling the dark powers—including sexual aberrations ("dubious embraces")—is here entirely severed from any glamorizing of aesthetic genius. Whereas the language of genius—as a language of "nature" in the subject—grants to art a "ground"—however unavailable to itself—and the prospect of an enduring "substance," Kafka effectively cuts off the literary unshackling of "spirits" from any transcendental reference. Instead, he interprets it as a "construct," and this interpretation is analogous to his reading of the whole world as "an expedient furthering man's wish to rest for a moment," as the methodical falsification and muddying of a knowledge which cannot be lived. "The craving for pleasure" constructs a "figure" called the writer, who is wholly dedicated to the pleasure of observing himself. The "first prerequisite" of such a figure—for "self-forgetfulness is the writer's first prerequisite" (L, 334)—is to ensure the concealment of its structural narcissism. Because it is subject to the prerequisite of "self-forgetfulness," the writerly enjoyment of "one's own *Gestalt*"—a sin according to religious conceptions, a self-undermining abandonment according to the Ovidian prototype of Narcissus, and the maximum in what is morally disgusting according to Kant's harsh verdict[32]—escapes the censor on a lasting basis. A writer "constructed" in this way is an Anti-Christ. Like Jesus, he accepts our sins as given and, at the same time, delivers us from them. In sharp contrast to the action of Jesus, however, this redemption does not take the form of a vicarious atonement and purification of sin, but of a transformation of sin into an object and medium of artfully "innocent" enjoyment:

> The definition of a writer, of such a writer, and the explanation of his effectiveness, to the extent that he has any: He is the scapegoat of mankind. He makes it possible for men to enjoy sin without guilt, almost without guilt. (L, 335)

This definition reads almost like a quotation from Freud's article, "Creative Writers and Day-Dreaming" (1908), according to which the "innermost secret" of the creative writer and "the true *Ars poetica*" resides in "the technique of overcoming feelings of repulsion"; with this technique, the writer puts us "in the position of enjoying our own day-dreams without self-reproach or shame."[33] Kafka's anti-Christian "scapegoat," who, on the strength of his "construction," turns "sin" into an enjoyment without guilt, also recalls those leaps and gambols of the satyr in whom Nietzsche recognizes the emblem of an art and philosophy that has overcome disgust. All three—Nietzsche, Freud, and Kafka—hold fast to the traditional definition of art in terms of a specifically life-promoting pleasure. Precisely for this reason, the buttress of classical aesthetics—the experience of disgust as unpleasureable—remains central to their work. Even Kafka's distinctive technical motto for the artistic metamorphosis of sin into innocent pleasure relies, in its redoubled paradox, on the theories of aesthetic illusion. According to both the rationalistic and Kantian models, art deceives without deceiving: it pretends to be "nature," even while permitting the awareness (either subsequent or concurrent) that it is actually not nature but art. Kafka formulates the same goal: "I would like to deceive . . . without actual deception" (LF, 545). His explanation of his poetics of deception replaces the leading antithesis of classical aesthetics with a complex overlay of other oppositions: mean man versus kind man, loved versus "roasted," universally well-liked versus excluded, open versus concealed "baseness," sinner versus attribution of innocence:

> When I examine my ultimate aim, it shows that I do not actually strive to be good, to answer to a supreme tribunal. Quite the contrary, I strive to know the entire human and animal community, to recognize their fundamental preferences, desires, and moral ideas, to reduce them to simple rules, and as quickly as possible to adopt these rules so as to be pleasing to everyone, indeed (here comes the inconsistency) to become so pleasing that in the end I might openly act out my inherent baseness before the eyes of the world without forfeiting its love—the only sinner not to be roasted. In short, my only concern is the human tribunal, and moreover I would like to deceive this, however without deception. (LF, 545)

Kafka transcribed these sentences at least two other times. He copied them in his diary under the heading: "From a letter to F., perhaps the last" (D, 387). To Max Brod he passed on this "focal point of self-knowldege" with the comment: "What would you say to this dazzling piece of self-knowledge which I have just copied from a letter to F. It would make a good epitaph" (L, 152). As with any piece of self-knowledge, one might well be led astray by taking this epitaph seriously and literally—even more so since it acknowledges to be "*blendend*" (i.e., both brilliant and blinding, dazzling, deluding, and, as integral to Kafka's "self-condemnation," to be infected with methodical irony).

Nevertheless, in what follows, this "focal point of self-knowledge" will guide the reading of Kafka's poetics of disgust.[34]

How can the writer (this "construction" of a "craving for pleasure"), without any appeal to transcendental inspiration, "act out [his] inherent baseness before the eyes of the world" and, at the same time, suspend all negative judgment? Kafka's answer is bound up with that form of narration which, since Friedrich Beissner, has played a part—as "univocal narrative perspective"—in every discussion of Kafka.[35] In addition to various other effects, it makes it possible for Kafka's "narrative voice"[36]—even in the case of the greatest intellectual reflexivity—to confer on the protagonists a wholly unknowing innocence and to lead the reader's eye in a deceptive manner (deceptive insofar as it minimizes the complexity of the text) through the narrow opening of this pseudochildlike perspective of the protagonists. Josef K.'s response to Titorelli's question is at once the credo of all Kafka's protagonists and the self-delineation of a gestus founded in style:

> "Are you innocent?" he asked. "Yes," said K. The answering of this question gave him a feeling of real pleasure, particularly as he was addressing a private individual and therefore need fear no consequences. Nobody else had yet asked him such a frank question. To savor his elation to the full, he added: "I am completely innocent." "I see," said the painter, bending his head as if in thought. (T, 149)

All of Kafka's texts lay claim to such an innocence. Their protagonists, who simultaneously provide the primary narrative focus, simulate an attitude of innocence and even the role of an innocent victim: this is their structural childlikeness despite of all the author's enmity toward children. Translated into ages of mankind, the narrative voice refuses to acknowledge the biblical fall of man; it contributes to a poetics of undoing the fall and defiantly asserting a pre-lapsarian stance.[37] To be sure, this attitude of innocence is just as often called into question, as it is here in Titorelli's ambiguous "I see," but it is never wholly abandoned. What Kafka calls the "purity" of his writing refers to this consummate artistic overcoming of "obscenity" and "baseness" in an enjoyment of writing that, rather than celebrating itself in some romantic-diabolical vein as debased, simulates an innocence which frees the abject from every hint of repudiation. Even the antagonists must acknowledge this innocence in the very moment of its (presumed) unmasking. "An innocent child," cries Georg Bendemann's father, in his unexpected attack on his son, "yes, that you were, truly, but still more truly have you been a devlish human being!" (S, 87). Allowing for differences in context, these antithetical statements hold equally for many of Kafka's protagonists. Their interference belongs integrally to the poetics of deceiving without deception, which offers up to enjoyment a process of innocent sacrifice that it simultaneously presents as repellent "baseness." This innocence is, from the outset, as true and as false as the one Kafka claimed for his preference for fat old prostitutes (D, 238).

In light of this, one of the most famous of Kafka's "self-condemnations" appears to incline more to the side of "truth" than of "method," even while it provides renewed conceptual clarity precisely to the method of Kafka's writing, the overcoming of dirt in purity: "I'm dirty, Milena, infinitely dirty, which is why I make so much fuss about purity. No people sing with such pure voices as those who live in deepest hell; what we take for the song of angels is their song" (LM, 185–86). Accordingly, sulphur, hell, and dirt are predicates belonging also—and most properly—to the "angelic purity" of Kafka's prose. Everything repellent in the subject matter is merely the correlate of a "song" which, in its deceptive purity, mimics the opposite of all disgust. Just as in tragedy, according to Nietzsche, Dionysus speaks the language of Apollo and Apollo the language of Dionysus, so, according to Kafka, the "purity" of literature transfigures everything disgusting out of which it speaks; likewise, it is precisely hell which demands a presentation in angelic innocence: "The Diabolical sometimes assumes the aspect of the Good, or even embodies itself completely in its form.... *This* Good is more tempting than the genuine Good" (DF, 68). Kafka found a prototype for such angelic diabolicism in Gustav Roskoff's *History of the Devil*.[38]

> I have no literary interests, but am made of literature, I am nothing else, and cannot be anything else. The other day I read the following story in a *History of Devil Worship:* "There was a cleric with a voice so sweet and so beautiful that all who heard it were filled with joy. One day a priest heard the sweetness of these sounds and said: 'This is not the voice of a man, but of the devil.' In the presence of all the many admirers he exorcised the demon and drove him out, whereupon the corpse (for this body had been animated by the devil instead of a soul) disintegrated and stank." The relationship between me and my literature is similar, very similar to that, except that my literature is not as sweet as that monk's voice. (LF, 304)

Purity and beauty of voice—instead of bringing the soul to an immediate (self-)presence—call into question the position of the soul and, with it, the entire metaphysical model: "The existence of the writer is an argument against the soul" and a proof of demonic possession (L, 334). Now, the diabolical "I" of the cleric still has a separable existence behind the deceptive purity of the appearance; Kafka's "I," by contrast, is "nothing else, and cannot be anything else" than that deceptive "expedient" by means of which it conceals itself. The "demon" that animates the "construction" of "the writer" is therefore resistant to exorcism. In other respects as well, the "relationship between me and my literature" transcends the simple dualism of stinking "I" and sweet voice. Compared with the cleric, the writer is subject to more difficult conditions of angelic devlishness, since his voice is "not as sweet as that monk's voice." This deficiency corresponds to the more demanding character of his task: for the writer is called upon not simply to deceive but to deceive "without deception"—that is, without ceasing to manifest his sulphurous baseness. In this poetics, the ostentatious exhibition of the disgusting, distinctive of nineteenth-century satanism, gives way to a deceptive sublimation of the disgusting. The devil speaks in a twofold guise: as devil, in the manifest sulphur of disgusting subject matter, and as angel, in the form of a purification and dissimulation of this material. In this literary embodiment of an inverse satanism, Kafka's programmatic dictum, "Writers speak a stench" (D, 12) holds also and precisely for those passages that stink the least. Writers speak a stench—not because they subscribe to the production of unpalatable things, but because they are able, thanks to their "construction," to enjoy "with all their senses" everything, even the "most evil," and because their life is "sweeter than other people's" (L, 334). Such writers do not idealize, nor do they turn toward decay (whether romantically, naturalistically, or fantastically); rather, they make nonidealization invisible. In what follows, this figure of the dirty turned pure will be applied initially to the syndrome of disgust, sexuality, and innocence, then to the circulation of disgusting foods through Kafka's work, to the poetics of torture, execution, and stabbing, and finally to the danger of disgust incurred by words themselves.

7.3 Disgusting Sexuality in Kafka's Novels

Amerika, or the Trajectory of Male Innocence
in the Realm of "Repellent" Female Practices

The finished chapters of Kafka's first novel *Amerika* tell a story with a clear beginning and end: after being nearly raped, in a "disgusting" manner (A, 29), by a maidservant more than twice his age, the hero is "packed off . . . to America" (A, 27), only to end up there once again in the power of a fat old woman (Brunelda). In between, he meets with a similar fate at the hands of an athletic young woman (Clara Pollunder), who forces him onto a "sofa" with one of her martial-arts moves (A, 68). In the narrative unfolding of the novel, however, this strikingly clear sequence of events is effectively marginalized and concealed through various strategies. The initial episode of rape-near seduction is entirely overlaid by Karl's attempt to represent the grievances of the Stoker and by his first meeting with his uncle, the Clara episode by Green's unwelcome appearance and by the surprising discovery of the fiancé Mack, and the Brunelda episode by Karl's rivalry with the overpowering Delamarche and his unwanted intimacy with the latter's subaltern accomplice Robinson. In other ways as well, Kafka has insured that the following thesis must necessarily appear like a sacrilege in regard to his novel: the numerous scenes with repellent women are completely positive and libidinally charged in their working, and should be seen more as stages in the fulfillment of desire (Deleuze) than as the alienating negation of desire. Alongside this thesis stands a second, no less heretical: Kafka's novel (well in advance of Hollywood in this regard) is perhaps the first literary treatment of the assault on a man by several women.

In the opening scene of *Amerika*, on board the liner slowly entering the harbor of New York, Karl Rossmann suddenly notices "that he had forgotten his umbrella down below" (A, 3). The further significance of this object for the novel consists in the fact that it returns, in the first scene with Brunelda, as the "red umbrella" that identifies its bearer as a prostitute (A, 234). When he goes back below decks, Karl finds neither his cabin nor the umbrella. The course of his wandering is marked by a series of phenomena having to do, in every case, with things abject, dirty, and disgusting. The ship's stoker, on whose door he knocks, promptly orders him to crawl into his bed and proceeds to tell him the story of his impending dismissal from the ship's service as an instance of social expulsion, something governed by the opposition of Romanians versus Germans and of Chief Engineer versus Stoker. On their way to the office, the outcast Karl and the outcast stoker run first into "a rat which crossed [their] way" and then into "girls in dirty white aprons—which they splashed deliberately" (A, 10): a metonymic contiguity that, in the context of Kafka's distinction between clean and unclean, at the same time suggests a similarity between rats and girls' aprons. The apron is Kafka's most frequently used figure for articulating the difference between clean and unclean. The apron is supposed to keep clean what it covers, while itself absorbing the unclean. Accordingly, the protection from stains becomes the signal for defilement, and the sometimes deliberate dirtying of an apron (A, 10) becomes a sexual advance, drawing the man into the sphere of female impurity. Tying a dirty apron surreptitiously round the waist of a man thus belongs among the most obscene jokes which "the bursting sexuality of women" can permit itself: "This is really disgusting; they've tied a girl's apron on me" (A, 35).

The rat that crosses the Stoker's path leads to an unsuccessful attempt, on the part of this "outcast" man, to cast out another creature: "as he walked on, he kicked out sideways at the rat and tried to stamp on it, but merely drove it more quickly into its hole, which it reached just in time" (A, 10). This strange attempt at trampling underfoot by kicking out sideways, and the ironic manner in which an effort to kill the disgusting object serves to help it along its way, point—if only in passing ("as he walked on")—to a tenacity, an ineradicable presence of the disgusting. In the same year in which he composed this novel, Kafka—who, more than once, described himself as "a rat's nest" (D, 330)—occasionally asked Felice as well about her "secret drawer where old, neglected things gather like disgusting animals" (LF. 115). And just as Karl crosses paths with a rat on his arrival in New York, so K., during his first night in the Castle village, is "briefly disturbed once or twice by scurrying rats" (C, 5). A posthumously published note indicates that the rat crossing Karl Rossmann's way is, for Kafka, integral to the conception of the ocean liner: "The very lowest place of all in this ocean-going steamer, a chamber extending the entire length of the ship, is completely empty; to be sure, it is scarcely three feet high. The construction of the ship makes this empty chamber necessary. Actually, it is not quite empty, it belongs to the rats" (DF, 370). Empty, though not "completely empty," necessitated by the construction and at the same time home for a plague of the disgusting, the vilest, the "very lowest" of creatures: these offspring of the steamer's womb are a prelude to the first appearance of the dirty aprons and to the irresistible spread of female lasciviousness and promiscuity through the novel. Hardly has the stoker hailed "a girl called Lina," than she "coquettishly" resists his embrace and, "squirming under his arm," casts an eye toward the next object of desire: "'Where did you pick up that good-looking boy?' she cried after him, but without waiting for an answer. They could hear the laughter of the other girls, who had all stopped their work" (A, 11). Although the stoker had presumably offered Karl the favor of his bed only because there was no standing room in his cabin, Lina's remark raises the suspicion that he likes to "pick up" good-looking boys. The inopportune stay in the bed of a stoker repudiated by the rest of the ship's company, the rat that crosses their way, the girl's admonitory joke, and the coquettish familiarity of dirty-apron-wearer and outcast man—these things make no dent at all on Karl's ostensible innocence and inexperience. Without the slightest investigation of the matter, he makes the stoker's cause his own. Putting together improvised speeches to bolster open lies, he helps manufacture a story that portrays the stoker as a victim of ill treatment.

It is just here, where the role of innocence intersects with the state of deception in the face of a series of abject phenomena, that Karl's past history catches up with him. The fable Karl invents for the stoker passes over into the story of "disgustingly" seduced innocence which the uncle tells of Karl. As a doublet of Karl's plea for the stoker, which aims at helping out an accused rather than stating a truth, the story of Karl's expulsion merits at least as much doubt. Moreover, the first version of this story is told by someone who was in America while the reported event took place in Europe, and is based entirely on an account contained in a letter from the maidservant involved. According to this version, Karl was "simply thrown out" for allowing himself to be seduced. For Karl, the only positive aspect about this narrative is that at least "none of [those present] laughed." Karl's own recollection of the incident and the uncle's narration that precedes it have a common denominator in the affirmation of complete sexual innocence exposed to the "disgusting." "His transgression is of a kind that merely needs to be named to find indulgence," as the uncle had remarked (A, 26). Karl's version of the story transforms the explicit affirmation of innocence into an implicit function of the ignorant, misconstruing mode of presentation:

> But once she called him "Karl" and, while he was still dumbfounded at this unusual familiarity, led him into her room, sighing and grimacing, and locked the door. Then she flung her arms round his neck, almost choking him, and while urging him to take off her clothes, she really took off his and laid him on her bed, as if she would never give him up to anyone and would tend and cherish him to the end of time. "Oh Karl, my Karl!" she cried; it was as if her eyes were devouring him, while his eyes saw nothing at all and he felt uncomfortable in all the warm bedclothes which she seemed to have piled up for him alone. Then she lay down by him and wanted some secret from him, but he could tell her none, and she showed anger, either in jest or in earnest, shook him, listened to his heart, offered her breast that he might listen to hers in turn, but could not bring him to do it, pressed her naked belly against his body, felt with her hand between his legs, so disgustingly that his head and neck started up from the pillows, then thrust her body several times against him—it was as if she were a part of himself, and for that reason, perhaps, he was seized with a terrible feeling of yearning. With the tears running down his cheeks he reached his own bed at last, after many entreaties from her to come again. That was all that had happened, and yet his uncle had managed to make a big deal of it. (A, 29–30)

In order to let himself be drawn by the cook into her room, locked in there and laid in bed, and yet to be able to continue in the role of childlike innocence, Karl must insinuate a perspective of utter ignorance, which systematically misunderstands every single detail, while at the same time allowing the reader to come up with a different translation of the matter. Amorous expressions become grimaces, embraces become acts of choking and shaking, the offering of the female breast becomes an exercise in "listening" such as children practice in playing doctor, the stimulation of the male organ becomes a "disgusting" intrusion between his legs. Even the sexual union seems to have escaped Karl: it is registered only in the linguistic transformation into an exorbitant delusion ("it was as if she were part of himself") and in the inversion of traditional modes of description, which have the man becoming part of the woman. What this description brings out is not male disgust for the sexually active woman: rather, everything "disgusting" appears merely grotesque, indeed ridiculous, in light of the inner desynchronization of the two sexual partners that could hardly be greater. It is not the disgusting per se that makes for the great artistic mastery of this passage but rather the simulation of consummate male ignorance—an innocence that does not even understand what is happening to it. It is part of the paradox inherent in this mode of representation that the seduction is to some extent a violation, and yet the violated one shrugs off the whole experience with the phrase, "That was all that had happened," and cannot understand why anyone would "make a big deal of it."

The hero's assimilation to his American uncle's regimen is quickly followed by a first repetition of falling into sin and being expelled. A "stout gentleman" and "acquaintance" of his uncle invites Karl to his "country house in the neighborhood of New York," not without stressing that his daughter Clara in particular is expecting him there (A, 49–52). For Karl's renewed "transgression," this time with Clara, the term "seduction" is from the outset disqualified as the "suitable word" (A, 26). Karl has to overcome his uncle's manifest opposition in order (once again) to follow the wishes of a "girl." He cannot wait to fall into the arms of the unknown girl, and is "impatien[t] with the long journey" (A, 53). Clara seems to have "waited" just as impatiently, "at the gate" of the property, for her anagram Karl, and bluntly announces to him: "After dinner . . . we'll go straight to my room, if you would like that" (A, 57). For his part, Karl is twice sickened to the point of vomiting during the evening meal, before he finds that he is "heartily sick" of Clara too (A, 71):

> Mr. Green [put] a slice of pigeon into his mouth, where his tongue, as Karl chanced to notice, took it in charge with a flourish. Karl felt nearly sick and got up. Almost simultaneously, Mr. Pollunder and Clara caught him by the hands.
> "It's not time to get up yet," said Clara. And when he had sat down again, she whispered to him: "We'll escape together in a little while. Have patience."
> Meanwhile, Mr. Green had calmly gone on eating, as if it were Mr. Pollunder's and Clara's natural duty to comfort Karl after he had made him sick. (A, 60)

From disgust with eating, the text passes swiftly to (moral) disgust with sexual behavior. Although he is not very welcome that evening as a guest, Mr. Green treats his host's daughter like a ready and willing "poor little thing," despite the presence of her father: "Just look at the girl, how downcast she is," he went on, chucking Clara under the chin. She let him do it and closed her eyes. "Poor little thing!" he cried, leaning back, purple in the face, and laughing with the vigor of a well-fed man" (A, 61). Given his digust with Mr. Green, Karl fails to raise another question: why does Clara put up with this behavior? More amazingly still, it is only after witnessing Green's obscene gesture and Clara's consent to it that Karl notices the girl's beauty: "Ever since Mr. Green's gallantries began, he had been actually surprised by the beauty of which her face was capable, and especially by the brilliance of her lively eyes.

A dress which fitted so closely to its wearer's body he had never seen before; small wrinkles in the soft, closely-woven, yellowish material, betrayed the force of the tension" (A, 62). The "girl" must be degraded before Karl can see her beauty. Once he does see it, he comes to a significant conclusion: "And yet Karl cared nothing for her. . . . He did not like [the American girl], although she was very nearly as beautiful as he had pictured her" (A, 62).

The episode with Clara points up a noteworthy contrast: slender, good-looking girls with "sport-hardened bodies" (A, 68) are not Karl's type; incomparably greater, if also more ambivalent, is for him the attraction of the series of corpulent "old maids"—from the thirty-five-year-old Johanna, to the fifty-year-old Therese, to the almost immovable mass of flesh that is Brunelda. And yet, in the end, even Clara falls into the category of disgusting *vetula*. She shows herself, that is, to be not only a nymphomaniac, who makes open advances at Karl and tolerates Mr. Green's importunities, while her fiancé waits for her in the very same house. She also quite clearly becomes sexually excited in acting with relish the role of flagellating dominatrix. In this case, Karl must not, as with Johanna, play the innocent incapable of resisting, but rather must become refractory, disobedient, so as to bring upon himself the "punishment" of pleasurable abuse:

> [Clara] locked him in a well-applied wrestling hold, knocked his legs from under him by some foot-work in a technique strange to him and thrust him before her with amazing control, panting a little, to the wall. But there was a sofa by the wall on which she laid him down, keeping at a safe distance from him, and said: "Now move if you can."/"Cat, wild cat!" was all that Karl could shout in the confusion of rage and shame which he felt within him. "You must be crazy, you wild cat!"
>
> "Take care what you say," she said and slipped one hand to his throat, on which she began to press so strongly that Karl could only gasp for breath, while she swung the other fist against his cheek, touching it as if experimentally, and then again and again drew it back, farther and farther, ready to give him a buffet at any moment.
>
> "What would you say," she asked, "if I punished you for your rudeness to a lady by sending you home with your ears well boxed? . . . I feel enormously tempted to box your ears for you now that you're lying there. I'd probably regret it; but if I should do it, let me tell you that it'll be because I can't help it. And of course it won't be only one box on the ear I'll give you, but I'll let fly right and left till you're black and blue." (A, 68–69)

Having himself been "cast out" like a "cat" (A, 26), Karl meets here with a renewed configuration of cat and repellent sexual behavior. For the second time, he is overpowered by a woman and forced into a bed, where he is choked, struck, and abused. The stupor of helplessness returns as he submits to an immobility that, together with Clara's desire to inflict blows, directly recalls sadistic practices of chaining up. Again Karl appears to be placed exclusively in the position of victim. Nevertheless, this innocent abroad, outcast from his European homeland, has done everything in his power to follow the sexual lure of the waiting Clara. Has he merely gone astray, then, in sitting down to the disgusting dinner and in falling into the hands of the flagellating dominatrix? Or was he secretly expecting just these attractions in the vaguely forbidden country house? Faced with his uncle's letter of expulsion, Karl makes no attempt at all to defend his actions. Instead of justifying himself with arguments lying ready to hand, and setting into motion the well-oiled machine of Kafkan legal rhetoric, he merely asks Green who had conveyed the uncle's sentence after those personal belongings which remain as his only possessions in the wake of his renewed fall from grace: "Have you brought me my trunk and umbrella?"

The much-traveled umbrella, as mentioned earlier, has its provisional end in signaling Brunelda's connection to prostitution. Before this, however, Karl gives himself into the keeping of another powerful woman: the Manageress of the "Hotel Occidental." Delamarche and Robinson serve as connecting figures between Clara, the Manageress, and Brunelda. Initially, they appear as new comrades of the repeatedly outcast Karl; as their relationship to him unfolds, however, they increasingly function as adversaries and stumbling blocks in his way. After having quickly consumed Karl's provisions and traveling allowance, the two companions send Karl to the saloon of the Hotel Occidental. Karl at first gets hopelessly lost in the hectic bustle, and appears unable "to get a single thing anywhere in the place," until the Vienna-born Manageress suddenly appears like a fairy godmother. She not only solves the problem of victuals for Karl but also provides him with a place to stay and a new position. Her first words—"Then come with me, my boy" (A, 120)—point to the milieu of prostitution, as does her name Greta Mitzelbach, which alludes to the canonic Viennese prostitute's name Josephine Mutzenbacher.[39] This hybrid figure composed of fairy tale persona, mother, and prostitute, lodges Karl without further ado in a room of her own apartment and encourages him to feel "quite free and easy," the German *"ganz ungeniert"* even literally suggesting "altogether shameless," in a sexual sense (A, 136). At the same time, she establishes claims on him that are no less demanding than Johanna's: "you mustn't go away on any account. You mustn't offend me by doing that" (A, 134). The burden of her demands for loyalty is somewhat lightened for Karl by the fact that the fifty-year-old Manageress allows the sixteen-year-old Karl a relationship on the side with the unhappy kitchen maid Therese. As a liftboy, he also has the opportunity of occasionally being "kissed, . . . to say the least of it, in the lift" by fashionable ladies whose "external appearance gave not the slightest indication that such behavior was possible on [their] part" (A, 159). Karl's effusive comments about the hard "service" only incompletely conceal the ubiquitous sexualization of this workplace, the omnipresence of favorably disposed women. The notorious ladies' man Delamarche raises plausible suspicions of a hidden motive underlying Karl's decision to abandon the enervating "companions" in favor of the hotel: "Seeing that you're making such a parade of honesty, why not stretch your honesty a little farther, now that we're having a friendly heart-to-heart, and tell us why you really want to go to the hotel?" (A, 128).

Karl does not stretch his honesty that far. What he denies—above all, something disgusting about his own libidinal trajectory—haunts him, however, like a vengeance in his new place of work, oppressing him in the form of someone else who is utterly disgusting. It is a veritable orgy of vomiting that triggers Karl's third expulsion. The dismissed comrade Robinson shows up in the hotel foyer drunk and afflicted "with writhings which told their own story":

> And a stream poured out from Robinson's mouth into the deep. In the pauses of his sickness, he felt helplessly and blindly for Karl. "You're really a good lad," he would say then, or: "It's stopped now," which however was far short of being the case, or: "The swine, what sort of stuff is this they have poured into me!" In his agitation and disgust, Karl could not bear to stay beside him any longer and began to walk up and down. (A, 165)

The "scrupulously clean hotel" cannot tolerate this defilement by friends who spread disgust among both its employees and its clients. Once again, however, it is not Karl himself who is the "dirty fellow" and the agent of abominations; it is rather the ex-companion Robinson who performs this function. Nevertheless, Karl's reputation even with the Manageress is decisively impugned by the incident. The Head Waiter denounces her "angel boy" not only as the one responsible for the presence of disgusting pools of vomit in the wrong place but also as a notorious nightly visitor of bordellos:

> "My dear Manageress," he said, "to be quite frank, I wouldn't have believed that you were such a bad judge of character. I've just learned something about your angel boy which will radically alter your opinion of him, and I almost feel sorry that it has to come to your ears from me. This fine pet of yours, this pattern of all the virtues, rushes off to the town on every single free night he has and never comes back till morning. Yes, yes, I have evidence of it, unimpeachable evidence, yes. Now can you tell me, perhaps, where he gets hold of the money for these nocturnal adventures?" (A, 179)

Although more indulgent and loving than the rejecting parents and the rejecting uncle, the Manageress Mitzelbach/Mutzenbacher—intent, as she is, on loyalty—gives up her opposition to Karl's removal in the light of this suspicion. The seduced innocent is transformed into a libertine. But none of this troubles Karl or the reader in the least: Karl's innocence stands out the more brightly from all this dirt. And since the reader experiences things (almost) exclusively from Karl's perspective, he or she can only wonder anew at the miracle of a literature that sings the more purely, the more deeply it is enmired in sulphur and hell. Walter Benjamin has extolled "the entirely unmysterious, undefiled, and transparent figure of Karl Rossmann" for its display of "a very elemental purity of feeling," such as Franz Rosenzweig perceives in the Chinese "wise man."[40] But what if this undefiled innocence and purity were, in the final analysis, an artifice designed to make it possible, by means of a poetics of deceiving without deception, "openly to display" and "guiltlessly to enjoy" all the "horrors" that lie in Karl Rossmann's way?

Robinson's peristaltic performance in the hotel hall blends vomiting and ejaculation: the accusations of sexual defilement are implicitly corroborated by the rather unusual word used for vomiting here—"pouring out" *(Ergiessen)*— and by the spot utilized as a receptacle—a "shaft" leading into the deep. And as Karl, for his part, seeks to make good after his dismissal, he enters into an utterly abject servant relationship in the aftermath of Robinson's vomiting. Karl, for his part, gives the appearance of confirming the justice of his dismissal as, in the aftermath of Robinson's vomiting, he enters into an utterly abject servant relationship. He becomes the lowliest sort of valet de chambre for a monstrously fat, dirty, panting, lazy, inert, stinking, snoring, and moody old prostitute, who uses her money to keep a stable of young men and, at one point, defecates on an expensive present from her still loving husband, "so that the servant could hardly carry it away for disgust" (A, 237). This time, a police chase worthy of the silent film is staged, in order to be able to represent Karl's arrival in Brunelda's kingdom as involuntary and as the lesser evil in comparison with an unjustified incarceration. By himself expressing disgust for the "repellent position" he is being offered (A, 244), Karl does his part in making the display of disgusting femininity and perverse male obsession seem like a malevolent fate, a perfidious repetition compulsion, with which the "angel boy" himself has nothing to do. Nevertheless, Karl takes to the new "service" surprisingly quickly, overcomes all disgust, and earns praise for his eager and innovative performance as servant. As Milan Kundera has aptly remarked, Brunelda is "the erotic gem of *Amerika*."[41] Fellini's exuberant filming (in *Intervista*) of a group of actresses auditioning for the part of Brunelda is much truer to Kafka's writing than most of the delineations of this character set down by professors of German literature.

In the fragment "Brunelda's Journey," Karl is shown promoted to the rank of the only butler in the household, while Delamarche and Robinson, who initially figured as the ones holding all the strings and as the brutal guarantors of Karl's forced servitude, have evidently decamped. This fragmentary chapter likewise ends on a note of disgust with dirtiness, which Karl "had of course expected" in the "Firm 25": everything in the interior of this bordello, although it is "swept nearly clean," is somehow "covered with dust, . . . greasy and repellent." Karl, who in the meanwhile has become accustomed to cleaning work, sees "no possible way of cleaning all this up again," for the dirt is primarily a non-physical one: "looked at more closely, it was no physically graspable dirt" (V, 384). Yet despite the repellent mess everywhere, Karl looks on "with satisfaction" as Brunelda, whom he has just delivered to this place, makes a good impression on the superintendent. His initial attitude of disgust has altogether yielded to an attentive concern for Brunelda's "delicacy of feeling" (V, 384). This amounts to a complete inversion: in the eighteenth century, "delicacy of feeling" *(Zartgefühl)* occasionally bespoke a refined sensorium, "delicate" to the point of being all too sensitive, and therefore most acutely averse to everything potentially disgusting; in *Amerika,* on the other hand, delicacy of feeling becomes an attribute of the disgusting itself, and the erratic expression of such feelings on the part of what is itself disgusting goes so far as to constitute—along with the robust (that is, "indelicate") overcoming of disgust with the disgusting—a rule of conduct for the innocent and dutiful Karl.

In the finished Brunelda-chapters of *Amerika,* Karl's freedom of movement is once again negated by a kind of sexual fettering. What Clara managed with the aid of jiujitsu—to pin Karl to the sofa—Brunelda achieves through her mass alone. While Karl stands looking down on the street from the balcony, she squeezes him between herself and the railing: "And sighing deeply, she kept plucking . . . at Karl's shirt" (A, 250). Karl "suffered the weight of her arms on his shoulders," and, on top of that, is deprived of his sight—just as earlier, in bed with undressed Johanna, "his eyes saw nothing at all" (A, 29). Brunelda—this overpowering combination of Brunhild and Thusnelda, who is always loosening her "corset" and putting it on again (A, 231)—inadequately puts a pair of opera glasses before Karl's eyes and simultaneously immobilizes his head, "which was pressed against her breast"—the result being that "now . . . he could see nothing at all" (A, 252). His incapacitated vision is ironically replaced by an intensified olfactory stimulus: for "Karl's whole face was now exposed to her heavy breath." At this point, only the bite is lacking to bring to completion the canonical trope of today's horror-disgust films: namely, cannibalism. This last step is taken in one of Kafka's posthumously published stories:

> The wives of the emperors, pampered and overweening, seduced from noble custom by wily courtiers, swelling with ambition, vehement in their greed, uncontrollable in their lust, practice their abom-

inations ever anew. The more deeply they are buried in time, the more glaring are the colors in which their deeds are painted, and with a loud cry of woe our village eventually hears how an Empress drank her husband's blood in long draughts thousands of years ago. (S, 245)

Brunelda is far more than just the hyperbolic termination of a series of "repulsive" female figures and practices. For she is the only one to elevate her *vetula*-existence, by means of complicated prohibitions on any contact or proximity, into a transcendental dimension. Whereas all other women are unconditionally available to Karl, Brunelda's apartment is regulated by barely comprehensible rules of exclusion and inclusion. On the one hand, there is the rule of the shared bedroom and, with it, the fiction of intimacy: "This job has advantages that you wouldn't find in any other. You're always in close attendance on a lady like Brunelda; you sometimes sleep in the same room as she does, and, as you can imagine, there's lots of enjoyment to be got out of that" (A, 245). On the other hand, Karl remains excluded from the "actual waiting on Brunelda" (A, 245)—that is, from the washing, the dressing, the doing of her hair. And as for any sexual intimacy, there remains only the disturbance from her loud snoring. The unobstructed view of Brunelda is reserved for Karl's "archenemy" Delamarche alone; the two other servants are regularly banished from the room and often made to wait for long periods on the balcony. Sometimes, when she is taking a bath, Brunelda summons the two inferior servants by themselves, only to rage at them and berate them for their shamelessness and to apply strict sanctions. In short, even when she calls enticingly "Where are you, haven't you got a heart either?" she is taboo as far as seeing and touching goes, so much so that she responds to a transgression on Robinson's part with "nearly drowning" him. Robinson's glorified recollection, "I once saw her naked. Oh!" (A, 231), thus does not summon up any real and available referent, but only the phantasmagoria of an elusive one. The position of the disgusting—otherwise requiring, by definition, a spatial proximity—mutates into an ideal, an unavailable transcendental signifier with erratic rules for communication and provisions for maintaining distance. The inaccessible courtroom and the unapproachable castle, which seem to be without precedent in Kafka's first novel, have a deceptively concrete name there: Brunelda. The disgusting prostitute is Kafka's innocent-perverse variation on the absolute.

Her counterpart—for which, in the later novels, there is no longer any analogue—is "the great Theater of Oklahoma" (A, 272). The latter not only "calls" "everyone" but also—and this is precisely what makes it so "improbable"—engages "everyone without exception" (A, 272, 282). Within the compass of the words "Everyone is welcome," there are no longer any distinctions made between admission and exclusion: disgust is at an end. In psychogenetic terms, this is a childlike attitude; in terms of the theory of genres, it is the attitude of fairy tales; and in social terms, it is a utopian attitude. The fragment does not exclude the possibility that this theater without rules of exclusion, located in far-off America, triumphs, in a fairy-tale manner, over the diametrically opposed rules applying in the other parts of the novel. At the same time, there are numerous indications of a renewed restoration of distinctions, with the possible result that Karl will be excluded once again. The syndrome of disgust, pleasure, taboo, of authoritative exclusion and perverse inclusion—a syndrome activated ever more intensively from Brummer to Brunelda—would in that case have triumphed conclusively over the childlike and innocent phantasmagoria of non-perverse inclusion.

Loathsome Power and K.'s "Sexual Etiquette" in *The Trial* and *The Castle*

The seats of inaccessible power in Kafka's later novels—law/court and Klamm/castle—have been variously read as figures of negative theology and of the deconstruction of every transcendental signified. There is, however, at least *one* positive and relatively unambiguous fact regarding all these seats of power: like Brunelda, they are configurations of sexuality and the disgusting. The officials of the court and the castle everywhere have available to them women who are simply summoned to their sides. Disconcerted men are informed of the prostitution-duties of their wives, fiancées, or daughters with the remark: "Personal feelings cannot be taken into account, that goes without saying" (C, 273). The women themselves are summoned "in the vilest language, such as I had never heard before, and I could only half guess its meaning from the context" (C, 192). Associated with these (morally) disgusting practices of forced prostitution are the material insignia of the legal realm. The "lawbooks" which are "studied" by the judges are specimens of smut and sadopornography. When K. opens "the first of them," he finds "an indecent picture" showing a naked couple, and "the obscene intention of the draftsman was evident enough." Another lawbook, "a novel entitled: *How Grete Was Plagued by Her Husband Hans*," converts the misogynistic stereotypes of husbands plagued by their wives into the unambiguous promise of wives mistreated by their husbands. The servants of the gentlemen from the castle are a "wild, unruly horde, governed . . . by their insatiable impulses. Their shamelessness knows no bounds" (C, 222). For these servants, the women of the village who are made unconditionally available to them are, as one of the women observes, merely "a plaything, which in their fury they kept trying to break; throughout those two years I have never spoken an intimate word to any of them, nothing but hateful dissimulation, lies or craziness" (C, 226).

Even in the middle of court proceedings, there is a scene of open and noisy sexual intercourse, which arouses considerable interest among the spectators (T, 51). "Wholly depraved" thirteen-year-old child prostitutes form a lane on the stairs leading to the court painter's apartment and, in front of the visitor, lift their "little skirts, which [were] extremely short to begin with, with both hands" (T, 141). Kafka intimates Lolita sex for pedophiles also in describing the immediate environs of the Court of Inquiry: "Half-grown girls, apparently clad only in smocks, ran busily back and forth" (T, 40). The Flogger employed by the court serves to bring the not infrequent scenes of flagellation in Kafka's work—stick, whip, and birch rod are their stereotypical emblems—to a culmination in a display of leather homoerotics, and, in his pleasureable anticipation of the "first cuts" with the rod, he remarks, in a somewhat self-satisfied manner, of his "object": "Look how overweight he is—the first blows of the rod will be lost in fat" (T, 82). Apartments situated near the court have a look reminiscent of Brunelda's apartment: "in all the rooms the beds were still occupied, and one saw dirty petticoats and occupants wearing only their underclothes" (T, 40). Bad smells and generally stuffy, musty, oppressive air complete the metonymy of disgust in the courtroom. K.'s physical illness signals this disgusting character of the court. Kafka devotes seven full pages to the description of this revolt of K.'s senses. The description brings to light an affinity between disgust and seasickness, such as is strikingly attested by the English word "nausea": "He felt seasick. He felt he was on a ship rolling in heavy seas" (T, 78). However, this time there is no "pouring," as there is in Kafka's first great scene of vomiting in his first novel. Likewise, in *The Castle*, the disgust with the officials is kept down below the threshold of vomiting: "Truly, they are high-ranking gentlemen, but you have to make a great effort to overcome your disgust in order to be able to clean up after them" (C, 292).

What K. and the reader do not know of the court and the castle, or know only vaguely, is commented on with far greater exactitude than is the positive and by no means unclear information which the novels amply provide. In this, Kafka's poetics of "deceiving without deception" may have achieved one of its most brilliant strokes: the novels portray quite openly a rich spectrum of repellent practices, and yet all this "baseness" appears only as marginal, somewhat odd coloring in the involuntarily and absurdly heroic quest of innocently plagued heroes for the seat of authority, for the agents of this authority and the law directing these agents' actions. But what if *The Trial* and *The Castle* were also, first of all, novels which operate—in a form that simultaneously discloses itself and makes itself invisible—to process the vexed relations between disgust and sexuality, disgust and food, disgust and the injured, or tortured, body?

From Brunelda to the court, and on to the castle, the positions of the disgust-absolute become increasingly abstract. Yet, even this abstraction never fully conceals the imagination of a disgusting body and/or of bodily practices relating to disgust. Klamm, who, as castle secretary, metonymically represents the castle itself, confirms this fact by his name alone. Grimm's dictionary mentions, as the first meaning of the substantive *Klamm*, a pathological "spasm" and "compulsion." The connection with the peristaltic spasm and compulsion of vomiting in disgust is evinced primarily by the adjectival form of the word. Yet already the three definitions provided for the noun form *Klamm* make the connection sufficiently clear: "a disease in pigs, a growth on the roof of the mouth," "a dog infected with the *Klamm*," "a writing cramp in a writer's hands."[42] What connects the writer's cramp to the disfiguration of the disgusting pig (disgusting because it eats everything without disgust) is the field of disgust with the viscous, as indicated by the adjective *klamm*, "damp," "sticky," "clammy." As examples, the dictionary mentions "wash that is not completely dry" and "the limbs of someone who is lightly perspiring."[43] For Kafka, "Klamm" means—"klamm" is—the predominance of a disgusting (sexual) compulsion and a compulsive disgust, which knows itself as such and therefore stands before the alternative of self-repudiation or successful self-enthronement as law. In Klamm's being *klamm*, a *Klamm* in K. is furtively-clammily both insinuated and made invisible.

Power in this domain—though by no means only here—is first of all the power to define what is abject. This is made clear by the story of Amalia, which is only seemingly paradoxical. Unlike all the other girls of the village, she does not obey "the letter . . . couched in the vilest language" summoning her to the bed of a castle official. As a result, all the other villagers break off economic and social ties to Amalia and her family; even the family name is "no longer mentioned" (C, 211). This account of the development of a social and sexual abjection demonstrates the culturally bound character of all attributions of disgust. The power of power consists not least in the establishment of an informal code of disgust, which permeates even apparently private relations. K. recognizes this quite clearly: "How great, say, was the power Klamm wielded over K.'s service, which up to now had been no more than a formality, compared with the power Klamm possessed in actual fact in K.'s bedroom?" (C, 58). In order to enforce implausible rules of abjection and to license virtually unlimited "vileness," the Kafkan type of power requires no uniformed arm of the state but only a consistent form of self-disguise. This power is invisible not because it is always elsewhere, but because it is really invisible. And it is invisible because—despite its manifestly disgusting character—it presents itself as the refuge of all "delicacy of feeling" (C, 282), and hence also of all discrimination qua disgust. Klamm's chief attribute is his "great," indeed "extreme sensitivity" (C, 109)—already a main attribute of Brunelda. All regulations for preventing contact are ipso facto regulations preventing proximity and disgust. By their means, the power immunizes itself against any confrontation with competing rules of abjection. Where power is exercised, delicacy and vileness, shame and shamelessness become indistinguishable. Such mingling strikingly resembles Kafka's poetics of a simultaneously open and deceptive fusion of "vileness" and "innocence." In this respect, courtroom and castle represent a *mise-en-abîme* of Kafka's project of blending purity and disgust. This interpretation is strengthened by what is probably the decisive modification to the disgust-absolute, as it evolves from Brunelda to the court and to Klamm: the change in the indication of gender. To judge by their representatives, courtroom and castle are male institutions. Whereas in the figure of Brunelda, from Karl's male perspective, all disgusting desire appeared as a property of the female object, in *The Trial* and *The Castle* male power and male sexuality themselves occupy the position of the repellent *vetula*.

However, courtroom and castle occupy this position only through appearing as the absolute other of the protagonist K. And precisely this is one of the most amazing achievements to be found in Kafka's texts: the establishment and maintenance of a practically unbridgeable gulf between K. and Klamm. All the "vileness" of the officials comes to light as though from another shore, and is carried almost exclusively by rumor. In this way, the perspective of the hero is able to retain, if no longer Karl Rossmann's complete unknowingness, then nevertheless another type of "innocence." This latter is ideologically reinforced, insofar as the K.'s struggle more and more openly against the Klamms and readily see themselves in the role of "rescuer of maidens" (C, 290). They successfully generate the belief that they treat the "maidens" (whom they share with the officials) differently and better. In fact, the K.'s forgo the overt "vileness" of the castle officials and carry on long conversations with various women, something evidently taboo for the officials. On the other hand, the women make themselves no less willingly available to the K.'s than they do to the officials. The bank officer K. "paid a weekly visit to a young woman named Elsa, who worked at night and late into the morning as a waitress in a wine house, and by day received visitors only in bed" (T, 20). This regular provision of his sexual needs by a waitress-prostitute—Klamm's sweethearts are likewise servants at an inn—K. supplements through the no less willing Leni and through his play for his next-door neighbor Fräulein Bürstner. From an erotic point of view, the interrogation appears as an elaborately arranged ploy to enable him to look around virtually undisturbed in the room of the absent Fräulein Bürstner. Before this, K. "had exchanged no more than a few words of greeting," as he says to himself with barely concealed regret. Now, "the nightstand by her bed" is used as a desk for the Inspector, while her "white blouse" dangles decoratively "from the latch of the open window" (T, 12). The disorder resulting from the petty interrogation also provides a welcome opportunity for a visit later on. K. makes use of the occasion to quickly turn the due apology into an outrageous kiss—almost a piece of vampirism: "K. . . . seized her, kissed her on the mouth, then all over her face, like a thirsty animal lapping greedily at a spring it has found at last. Then he kissed her on the neck, right at her throat, and kept his lips there for a long time" (T, 33). The chain of associations—spring/lips/drinking—evokes, in all its "innocent" openness, the idea of a vampirish violation, and characterizes

K. with the same image of thirstquenching as applies to the jackal who drinks from the throat of a dead camel: "One was already at the camel's throat, sinking his teeth straight into an artery. Like a vehement small pump endeavoring with as much determination as hopefulness to extinguish some raging fire, every muscle in his body twitched and labored at the task" (S, 410). It is only the intervention of "a noise from the captain's room" that seems to keep K. from extending the parallel.

The employee Fräulein Bürstner allows K. to do as he pleases, "as if she were unaware of what he did," though by no means does she encourage any further advances. She appears to be the only woman in all of Kafka's novels who is almost capable of saying no. In response to his landlady's imputation of promiscuity—she claims to have met Fräulein Bürstner twice "this very month . . . already on outlying streets, and each time with a different gentleman"—K. angrily defends the Fräulein's "purity." But he does not really consider her an exception to the rule: "he knew that Fräulein Bürstner was an ordinary little typist who couldn't resist him for long" (T, 242). This assumption is given credence by her name itself: according to the Brockhaus' *Deutsches Wörterbuch*, "bürsten" is also a vulgar synonym for "to engage in coitus."[44] In *The Castle*, without exception, one woman is merely the ever more arbitrary metonym for the next, whom K., with utmost confidence, will manage to make his mistress. The second "guiding principle on the road to hell"— "'You must possess every girl!' not in Don Juan fashion, but according to the devil's expression, 'sexual etiquette'" (D, 418)—holds far truer for K. than for Klamm. In this regard, K.'s insight into "the power Klamm possessed in actual fact in K.'s bedroom" (C, 58) may function less as a recognition of an external influence than as a direct and literal acknowledgement of K.'s own innermost Klamm-being.

In Kafka's first novel, the spatial and social expulsion of the innocent hero is founded on a series of concrete "transgressions." In *The Trial*, K.'s exclusion remains to the end, to his very execution "like a dog," merely imminent; it diffusely pervades the otherwise intact everyday routine, and occasions endless puzzling over K.'s utterly unclear "guilt." In *The Castle*, finally, the question of guilt, as well as the fact of K.'s being originally in exile, is presupposed in quasi-transcendental fashion by the whole of the action. What has driven K. "into this desolate country," this bleak variation on the strange expanses of America? Why doesn't he think of returning, since he is not made use of as a "land surveyor?" The provenance, the prehistory of the hero remains closed, like a traumatic wound; for the first time, the hero's parents are not at all mentioned any more, even not as a dim memory. The decisive rejection has already taken place, and it conditions all doubts as to whether K. has actually "been accepted into the Count's service" (C, 22) or is not rather, according to the small print on this contract, "being thrown out" (C, 73). The complex unfolding of this difference between "being accepted" and "being thrown out"—or, in other words, between eating and vomiting, proximity/enjoyment and disgust—conceals a gap in the symbolic structure precisely through continually dancing around it. When Frieda proposes their emigration, K. is forced for the first and only time to acknowledge, enigmatically enough, a power of the past over the present which rules out a return "somewhere" into the other world, the world not of the castle:

"I cannot go abroad," said K., "I came here in order to stay here. I will stay here." And in a contradiction he didn't bother to explain, he added as if speaking to himself: "Now what could have enticed me to this desolate land other than the desire to stay?" (C, 136)

In this pathos and this unconcealed illogicality—both atypical of K.'s lucid analytical mode of thought—an abandoned continent is adumbrated, one which is no longer supposed to be touched upon. K. has no apparent arguments to raise against the fact of his emigration, nor does he blame any foreign powers for an unwarranted expulsion into the gloomy wasteland of the village. Rather, his own "desire" is never again to see the earlier world: "I came here in order to stay here." An unknown guilt, or injury appears otherwise unendurable. The act of casting out is thus completely displaced onto the hero. Precisely for this reason, the hero's putative guilt is rendered even more elusive than was the case where external authorities, such as parents, uncle, and court were involved. Nevertheless, the novel has not wrapped K.'s prehistory in total darkness. What K., upon his arrival, reveals casually, in the course of conversation, to the innkeeper points anew to the syndrome of disgust, sexuality, and family. Clearly, this standard theme of the biographically oriented Kafka criticism no longer needs to be disclosed as such. Yet the compulsive conclusiveness with which Kafka, by means of a poetics of deceiving without deception, inscribes this *theme* into the *performance* of his texts remains quite striking. The inscription of the family is rendered unreadable, and yet the abandonment of a family is openly conceded in all innocence: "'I still haven't met the Count,' said K., 'they say he pays good money for good work, is that so? Anybody traveling as far from his wife and child as I am wants to have something to take home with him'" (C, 5). K. introduces himself as a foreign worker looking for employment and thereby supplies the basis for a narration, which cuts off all further questions about the reasons for his arrival. He appears to have come in order to earn money and not, as he later asserts with desperate pathos, in order "to stay here." The guise of foreign worker and the fable of a return home are equally suspect; but what if the parenthetical admission of a far-off family tie were the one shred of truth in a web of lies? In the absence of any other visible explanation in the text, we might plausibly conclude that what drives K. irrevocably away is just a "wife and child." Karl Rossmann is removed from Johanna Brummer and his own child by the decision of his parents; K. leaves "wife and child" on his own. His "desire" to remain in the village conceals, within the positive commitment to the "desolate land," a negative truth about the break with his past.

In light of the abandoned children of Kafka's heroes in his novels, the poetics of deceiving without deception could actually be submitted to a statistical efficiency test: even good readers, when faced with the question of whether none, one, two, or all three of the bachelor heroes of Kafka's novels have children, might not as a rule fix on the number two. The fact of K.'s child might well fail to be credited, and even in the case of *Amerika* there is a good chance that the birth of the child will be forgotten as one encounters the sequence of repellent stories of seduction and violation. And yet the existence of the children is established no less literally and overtly than their removal from the action. Integral to this removal is the trick by which its "vileness" is written to be unreadable and is transformed into a condition of innocent victimization. The same repudiated children who literally exist and continue existing in the text are consistently erased from the imaginative register of this text, insofar as the self-conception and self-interpretation of the protagonists become—by means of the narrative perspective—the governing law of the narration. According to the classical model of aesthetic illusion, the level of the signifier makes itself as such "forgotten"[45] and, in this active self-obliteration, engenders the "illusion" of an immediate and living presence of the signified. In Kafka's "deception," by contrast, the presentation (level of the signifier) makes what is "immediately" present (the signified) disappear—without, however, concealing it or reducing it to a mere vehicle of its own procedure.

Two of the three Kafkan bachelor heroes, in the novels, have children; one of them is even married. None of them still torments himself about his parents. Far from being interchangeable with the life of the bachelor author Kafka, the life of his K.'s seems actually to have fulfilled Kafka's own unrealized intentions. Nevertheless, they are subject to the same logic of rejection that Kafka has applied so readily to himself, employing all his images of disgust. Kafka, it appears, outrightly 'refutes' his own projects of alternate forms of existence and consigns his heroes, far removed from "wife and child," to a succession of anti-familial sexual relations with maidservants and prostitutes, which terminates, either virtually or actually, in relations with "fat old whores." This course of events becomes more complex in the relationship with Frieda than it is elsewhere. Their first encounter, which is at the same time a scene of seduction, evokes "insane allurements" and breathes, even if not without ambiguity, a promise of happiness such as Kafka has conferred on no other "love scene." Frieda turns out the electric light and draws close to K., who is hiding beneath the counter of the bar in order to be able to observe Klamm in secret. It is not the notorious association of sexuality and dirt but rather the suspension of all disgust in the melodrama of "happy love" that causes K. pleasurably to "lose himself" further and further:

"My darling! My sweet darling!" she said in a whisper, but without touching K.; as though swooning with love she lay on her back and stretched out her arms, time must have seemed endless in her happy love, she sighed rather than sang some little song. Then she started, for K. was still silent, lost in thought, and like a child she began to tug at him: "Come, it's stifling down here," they embraced each other, her little body burned in K.'s hands; they rolled a little way in a state of unconsciousness from which K. repeatedly but vainly tried to rescue himself, bumped dully against Klamm's door, and then lay in the small puddles of beer and other refuse with which the floor was covered. There the hours passed, hours of shared breathing, of shared heartbeats, hours in which K. constantly had the feeling that he was losing his way or that he was wandering into a strange country farther than any human being had wandered before, a country so strange that not even the air had anything in common with the air in his homeland, and where one could only suffocate from strangeness, yet where the insane allurements were such that one could do nothing but go on and lose oneself further ... [K.] could say nothing, he was all too happy to hold Frieda in his arms, all too anxious and happy, for it seemed to him that if Frieda left him, he would lose all he had. (C, 41–42)

Here too, without a doubt, sex figures as the woman's natural habitat and as the equally natural land of strangeness for the insanely enchanted man. Yet in no other of his siren scenes has Kafka advanced so far from the deceptive promise to the happy possession of what is promised.[46] Of course, the grammatical reservation ("it seemed to him") will soon dissolve the illusion, and, to be sure, not least on account of K.'s intention to make Frieda his bride—and "very soon at that" (C, 46–47). Thus, it is not the abandoned wife, nor the suspicion of bigamy, but the principle of marriage itself that immediately plagues sexuality. Caught up in the prospect of married life, pleasure turns into a "duty," which is sought for desperately but in vain:

There they lay, but without abandoning themselves as fully as that time at night. She sought something and he sought something, in a fury, grimacing, they sought with their heads boring into each other's breasts; their embraces and arched bodies, far from making them forget, reminded them of their duty to keep searching, like dogs desperately pawing at the ground they pawed at each other's bodies, and, helpless and disappointed, in an effort to catch one last bit of happiness, they nuzzled and tongued each other's face. Only weariness stilled them at last and made them grateful to each other. Then the maids came up, "Look how they're lying there," said one, and out of pity she threw a sheet over them. (C, 45–46)

The grotesque depiction of the concept of "marital duty" in the dutifully searching action of dogs pawing the ground portrays living together as a married couple as a figure of the poetics of the pitiable. Kafka's heroes lick like dogs (T, 33), paw like dogs, and die "like a dog" (T, 231); they don't, however, like to be pitied with regard to their sexuality. The intended marriage with the former call girl Frieda thus represents only a transitory and hybrid attempt, after the abandonment of "wife and child," to link the road to the whores back to the principle of marriage. A childless bachelor living together permanently with a prostitute: this is also that obscene model of faithfulness within an alternative marriage which the text about the "dirty fellow" and the landlady openly dares to imagine, only to repudiate it in the end: "Dance on, you pigs; what have I to do with it?" K.'s relationship with Frieda—the only near-marriage ever represented in Kafka's work—verges on this dance of pigs.

K.'s tendency to use all women "not in a Don Juan fashion" naturally leads to the breakup of this near-marriage. In the last chapter of the novel, however, there are several indications that K. has now finally found the right sort of person for marriage with a "dirty fellow": namely, the old landlady. K.'s adversary during his relationship with Frieda, the old landlady nonetheless makes certain barely concealed offers to K. She casts a dreamy look in K.'s direction (C, 312), and she calls on him to advise her concerning her wardrobe, which consists of many "outmoded, overdone, frequently altered, worn out" dresses (C, 315). Her "weakness" for these clothes (C, 315) is as old as the constancy with which she clings to her role as call girl to the castle secretary Klamm, a role which at some point in the past she was forced to give up. To her husband, the slender landlord, the "door-filling figure of the landlady" maintains no relation at all. The wish recorded in Kafka's diaries—"I want only the stout, older ones, with outmoded clothes that have, however, a certain luxuriousness because of various adornments" (D, 238)—appears to be fulfilled in K.'s case: with a frankness that effaces itself and passes over into a peculiar sort of style-born "amnesia,"[47] with a literalness that produces precisely unreadability.

Perhaps this imminent, precarious 'happy-end' of K. 's final election by "a fat old whore" is one of the reasons for *The Castle*'s breaking off at precisely this point. Any further progress along the path toward this *vetula* would have destroyed the poetics of the novel. This poetics is successful only to the extent that it makes the interpretation given here impossible. On the other hand, such an interpretation works only insofar as it breaks the spell of Kafka's deceiving without deception, insofar as it manages, through rigorous philological investigation along the guiding lines of the disgusting, to play off the "without deception," the invisible frankness of Kafka's texts, against their absorption in visible aesthetic "deception." Of course, every claim to expose—by means of a reading against the grain of the novel's poetics—a hyperreal and hypervalid literalness beyond the difference between truth and deception remains, for its part, confined within the impossibility of proving the philological work of undeceiving to actually disclose an origin free of deception. The paradoxical model of a deceiving without deception serves rather, in several ways at once, to immunize the text and its reading against each other: in the event of successful deception, the question of deception does not even arise; on the other hand, once it does arise, the text is already left behind and done injustice since its stylistic features—working against the question to arise—have not been adequately appreciated. Even in being uncovered, the deception thus absorbs 'the real,' which it processes only in order to avoid being "roasted." In the period of classical aesthetics, the disgusting *vetula* represents the position of something 'real' which ought to be excluded—something real which altogether destroys aesthetic experience, because it is not amenable to illusion, because it remains indifferent to all "deception" of the senses. Kafka's writing answers the question how the disgusting old woman can obsessively occupy the place of desire, can appear in "innocent" openness, and yet can become invisible again in the type of second-order observation which is the working of literary representation. Kafka's work interweaves the romantic license to display the disgusting with the paradoxical return of the classical intention to neutralize it. The satanic provocation yields before an angelic one, whose infernal character consists precisely in its simulated innocence.

7.4 A Poetics of Eating and Vomiting

Broken Engagements and Disgust with Meat,
Spoiled Old Food, and Laxatives

Vegetarianism forms part of the image of Kafka. In multiple ways, the dietary convictions[48] of vegetarian discourse are informed by strong affective dimensions and by 'metaphysical' implications. In Kafka's case, the respect for the life and "soul" of other living beings seems to be irrelevant. Rather, vegetarianism appears here from the perspective of a self-pathologization, such as resembles Nietzsche's disgust with any vegetarianism subscribed to out of weakness, out of effeminate denial of one's own beast-of-prey nature: many a thing, Kafka writes, "nauseates me, not because it's nauseating, but because my stomach is too weak" (LM, 200). Kafka associates the eating of meat—indeed meat in general, in its sheer materiality—with heavily disgust-loaded ideas; at the same time, he disavows this disgust with meat as (in Hegel's words) a "lack of confidence," a means of fleeing conditioned by a constitutional inhibition on consumption. For the traditional image of Kafka, this has meant, by implication, a seamless connection between disgust with sex and disgust with meat. This connection is the more readily covered over in tactful regrets for the unfortunate author, and left unexplored, as Kafka's achievements as a "pure" writer in the positive sense manifestly cry out for quite different categories of interpretation—even though, negatively, the genesis of these achievements may bespeak an abyss of disgust. In what follows, this image receives a twofold correction. First, on the horizon of Kafka's disgust with meat, there emerges an obsession with excessive consumption of meat and a libidinal enjoyment of his own feelings of disgust, to the point of imagining cannibalism—all this, to be sure, not as Kafka's own practice but as object of his voyeuristic pleasure, or as wishes routinely even compulsively fantasized haunting him. Second, this libidinal countercathexis and reflective traversal of disgust with food and meat will be anchored anew within the innermost region of Kafka's poetics.[49]

"Yesterday I was . . . choked with disgust"—among the details of this prime attack of disgust is the fact that the "bread is spread with goose-drippings which, if one's lucky, trickle only down one's fingers" (LF, 286). Disgust at the sight of dripping animal fat is, however, exceeded by that aroused by the mechanics and chemistry of chewing on shreds of meat: "One sits at table laughing and talking, . . . and meanwhile tiny shreds of meat between the teeth produce germs of decay and fermentation no less than a dead rat squashed between two stones" (LF, 408). In Kafka's imagination, the prescribed eating of meat in the sanatorium becomes a grotesque violation carried out by a perverse senior physician-father: "I would like to go into the country, even more to stay in Prague and learn some craft, least of all do I want to go into a sanatorium. What shall I do there? Have the senior physician take me between his knees, choke on the lump of meat he stuffs into my mouth with his carbolic fingers and forces down my throat?" (LM, 210–11). The consumption of animal extremities turns this eating-choking into the worst sort of disgust: "Yesterday, today, worst days . . . nauseating meal: yesterday pig's trotters, today tail" (DF, 80–81). The habitual nausea in the face of animal nourishment is justified further by the danger of involuntarily eating unfit, forbidden meat:

> Four people ate a well-prepared roast cat, but only three knew what they were eating. After the meal the three began to meow, but the fourth refused to believe it, only when they showed him the bloody skin did he believe it, could not run out fast enough to vomit everything up again, and was very sick for two weeks. (D, 211)

Food and sex—the two canonical activities of the "grotesque body" (Bakhtin)—are also closely connected in Kafka, although (at first sight) in the form of a strict inversion of the Rabelaisian drinking bout. This inversion obeys a simple rule: whenever Kafka felt himself to be on the verge of sexual relations with a beloved woman who was neither a prostitute nor a traveling companion, but a potential wife; when, at the same time, precisely these relations were inhibited by Kafka's disgust with the contiguity of family life and sexuality, then a particularly strict and fastidious vegetarianism would figure as a sign system that classified *every* sort of "consumption of meat" as "indigestible" and inimical. In his first letter to Felice after the breaking of their engagement at the Askanischer Hof in Berlin, Kafka laconically disclosed the workings of this rule in the midst of his own "abominable peculiarities" and a sexual-political avoidance of meat:

> Moreover, these peculiarities (abominable peculiarities, I admit, abominable/above all to myself) manifested themselves more with you than with anyone else. That was inevitable, and happened not only out of obstinacy. You see, you were not only the greatest friend, but at the same time the greatest enemy, of my work, at least from the viewpoint of my work. Thus, though fundamentally it loved you beyond measure, equally it had to resist you with all its might for the sake of self-preservation. It had to do so in every single detail. I thought of it, for instance, when having a meal one evening with your sister consisting almost exclusively of meat. Had you been there, I would probably have ordered almonds. (LF, 437)

To Max Brod and Felix Weltsch, Kafka writes on the same occasion:

> But listen to what has happened to me. I am disengaged, have been in Berlin for three days, where everyone was my good friend and I was everyone's good friend. In addition, I clearly perceived that this was all for the best and so am not uneasy, as you might think, about the step, whose necessity had become so clear. But other things are not going so well.... I have put aside my apparent stubbornness, which has cost me my engagement, and eat almost nothing but meat. As a result, my stomach is upset and after terrible nights I wake early, with open mouth, and feeling my abused and punished body in the bed like an alien, disgusting filth *(wie eine fremde Schweinerei)*. (L, 110)

Where vegetarianism is overdetermined as a sign of "stubbornness"—a stubbornness that, according to Kafka's professions, requires of the bride a marriage without sex and without children—then it is only a small step to presenting it as the veritable cause of the break-up. In the shadows of this bold argument, the taboo on familial sexuality remains, on the one hand, intact, secretly grounding the clear "necessity" of the break. On the other hand, this taboo is weakened, as though by exorcism, in the deliberate attempt to adapt his own body to the consumption of meat so as, at least *post festum*, to cure the symptoms responsible for the dissolution of the engagement. To be sure, the cure does not make it past the stage of self-punishment, thus confirming that both the eating of meat *(Fleisch)* and the—social or sexual—intercourse with a beloved woman whom Kafka occasionally referred to as "fleshy" amount to " an alien, disgusting filth." But already the mere attempt at accustoming himself to such *"Schweinerei,"* to a heroic overcoming of disgust with meat, appears to give Kafka new courage for thinking about engagement and marriage. The letter to Brod and Weltsch, for example, moves from the metamorphosis into a pig with bad breath—and hence into a kind of meat that, according to Jewish dietary laws, is categorically tabooed—directly to a closing formula that appears nowhere else in his correspondence: "Regards to all your dear wives and brides."

The differentiation of disgust with nearness into two analogous and interwoven types of disgust with flesh still fits neatly into the traditional image of the ascetic artist who transforms bodily plights into solitary successes at the writing desk. But the (hysterical) disgust with eating meat attains poetological relevance only insofar as it is overlaid with a countervailing (compulsive-neurotic) fixation on what is repudiated. This fixation corresponds to the obsessive libidinal attraction to nonmarriageable, fat and disgusting old women, just as surely as the vegetarianism corresponds to sexual abstinence in regard to fiancées and wives. Side by side with the disgust in the face of actual and proper meat consumption, that is, exists a downright enthusiastic pleasure in either imagining or directly observing—to excess, and "without the slightest repugnance"—the tabooed consumption. The description of the greatest voyeuristic pleasure in others' consumption of meat brings the disgusting, the ratlike sausages, into the position of an intensely desired object:

> My attitude to the food and drink which I myself never, or only in dire need, eat or drink, is not as might be expected. There's nothing I'd rather see eaten than these things. If I am sitting at a table with ten friends all drinking black coffee, the sight of it gives me a feeling of happiness. Meat can be steaming around me, mugs of beer drained in huge drafts, those juicy Jewish sausages (at least here in Prague that's what they are like, plump as water rats) can be cut up by every relative all over the place (the sound of the taut sausage skin being cut has rung in my ears since childhood)—all this and worse gives me no sensation of distaste whatever; on the contrary, it does me a great deal of good. (LF, 163)

> Prof. G[rünwald] on the trip from Riva. His German-Bohemian nose reminding one of death, swollen, flushed, pimpled cheeks set on the bloodless leanness of his face, the blonde, full beard around it. Possessed by a voracious appetite and thirst. The gulping down of the hot soup, the biting into and at the same time the licking of the unskinned heel of salami, the solemn gulps of the beer grown warm, the sweat breaking out around his nose. A loathesomeness that cannot be savored to the full even by the greediest staring and sniffing. (D, 232)

Kafka's "greediest staring and sniffing" orchestrates the professorial gulping, biting, and licking around the unskinned heel of salami, with additional proven disgust-effects: warm beer, outbreak of sweat around the nose. Sexual references abound in these descriptions, which assert the voyeuristic pleasure to be virtually unbounded, and to know of no quantitative limit of turning into something disgusting: the "loathsomeness" of the 'objects' of this pleasure can never be "savored" to the full, can never sate. In regard to his own body, Kafka likes to imagine the gulping down of preferably old sausages and hard pieces of meat as a simultaneously oral and anal intercourse. He even presents this strange and, as he says, mechanical sex with the pork butcher's goods as his obstinate craving:

> This craving that I almost always have, when for once I feel my stomach is healthy, to heap up in me notions of terrible deeds of daring with food. I especially satisfy this craving in front of pork butchers. If I see a sausage that is labeled as an old, hard sausage, I bite into it in my imagination with all my teeth and swallow quickly, regularly, and thoughtlessly, like a machine. The despair that this act, even in the imagination, has as its immediate result, increases my haste. I shove the long slabs of rib meat unbitten into my mouth, and then pull them out again from behind, tearing through stomach and intestines. I eat dirty delicatessen stores completely empty. (D, 96)

This orgy[50] is the form which a Rabelaisian intoxication with entrails assumes in the context of Kafka's simultaneous disgust and perverse craving for "swinish" food. Here, what is important is not so much the affinity of excrement and food as the radical cancellation of the difference between the body's inside and outside. By means of its openings, the body is transformed, just as in Rabelais, from a solid figure into a medium for passing eaten and excreted matter. Kafka's credo, "The firm boundedness *(feste Abgegrenztheit)* of human bodies is horrible" (D, 396), has this much in common with the "grotesque body" (Bakhtin): they both explicitly repudiate the classical ideal of the beautiful figure as something "horrible." But whereas the grotesque body obeys the euphoric double rhythm of generating and dying matter, Kafka's unrestrained (fictive) eating of sausage transforms his own body into a place where "despair" and pleasurable self-dismemberment ("from behind, tearing through stomach and intestines") are the price paid for an overcoming of the fixed external boundaries of the body. The devouring of "all the bad, old, sharp foods" (D, 96) and the obsession with depraved, fat, old and foul-smelling "girls" are two analogous forms of a return of the grotesque body within the field of the libidinal countercathexis of a hypertrophically developed bodily disgust—a countercathexis which not only does not aspire to the classical avoidance and transfiguration of everything disgusting in beauty but actually shudders before such classicism as "horrible."[51] Kafka is a Rabelais under the conditions of modern neurasthenia: a Rabelais who has long since relegated all intoxication with entrails and with sluts to the register of obsessive wishful thinking, and who is constantly faced with the danger that the slightest fulfillment of his wishes will bode ill for him.[52]

The grotesque unity of intoxicated devouring and immediate anal evacuation by means of violent mechanical aids apes the bulimic cycle of eating and intentional vomiting. The fantasy of manually promoted and intestine-tearing immediate elimination of greedily devoured old food finds an echo in Kafka's surprising interest in a supposedly "mechanical" laxative. The latter forms a second dominant theme of the diary entries on the meetings with Kubin. Allied to his "love for stout women" is the detailed concern with the magic word "Regulin":

> The artist Kubin recommends Regulin as a laxative, a powdered seaweed that swells up in the bowels, shakes them up, is thus effective mechanically in contrast to the unhealthy chemical effect of other laxatives which just tear through the excrement and leave it hanging on the walls of the bowels. (D, 55)
>
> All evening he spoke often and—in my opinion—entirely seriously about my constipation and his.... When we had already said good-bye, he called to me again from the distance: "Regulin!" (D, 58)

Kafka's Regulin treatment does not seem to be further documented. But a postcard to Max Brod reveals how drastically Kafka was possessed by the idea of a simultaneously pleasurable ("I'm treating myself") and disgusting evacuation by means of mechanical aids—an idea which he considered self-evident. The postcard reads in full: "Dear Max, Lest I forget—if your sister is going to be in Prague Monday, you must write me today; if she is coming later, there is time, of course, for you to tell me on Monday. Tomorrow I am treating myself to having my stomach pumped; I have a feeling that disgusting things will come out./Yours, Franz" (L, 63). A year later, a similarly laconic postcard reports: "Kleist [a dentist, W.M.] ... shoots air into me as if I were an old pig's bladder" (L, 71).

On Hard Sausages and Filthy Breakfasts: Nutrition and Narration in Kafka's *Amerika*

Kafka's famous portrayals of two deaths by starvation—that of the bachelor/cockroach Gregor Samsa in "The Metamorphosis" and that of the hunger artist in the story of that name—are merely extreme instances of a comprehensive practice of self-dissimulation: the stories and novels routinely veil in unreadability the fact that they too are literally possessed by food and acts of eating. Karl Rossmann's sexual trajectory from Bummer to Brunelda is continually accompanied by these things. The "old, hard sausage" which it is Kafka's unrestrained "craving" to devour "like a machine"; the "unskinned heel of salami" which Kafka, with "the greediest staring and sniffing," watches a professor seated next to him "lick"—precisely these obscure objects of desire circulate through the novel, in a manner at once explicit and utterly discreet. The temporary "loss of the trunk," at the beginning of the novel, causes the hero to remember "that in the trunk there was a piece of Veronese salami which his mother had packed as an extra tidbit, only he had not been able to eat more than a scrap of it, for during the voyage he had been quite without any appetite, and the soup which was served in the steerage had been more than sufficient for him. But now he would have liked to have the salami at hand, so as to dedicate it to the stoker" (A, 9). Owing to the postponement of its consumption and its intended delegation to a third person, the hard sausage remains altogether inconspicuous at this initial entry into the novel. It may be that the somewhat ironic phrase, "dedicate it to the stoker *[sie dem Heizer verehren]*," betrays in a diffuse manner a symbolic-libidinal cathexis, such as is rarely accorded a piece of sausage. At the same time, the idea of passing on a partly consumed sausage anticipates the disgusting eating habits in Brunelda's apartment; there, it will be Karl's job to gather the remnants of other lodgers' meals as breakfast for Brunelda and her three "servants."

But before this happens, the salami believed lost surfaces a second and third time. After being expelled by his uncle, Karl unexpectedly gets back intact the trunk that has not been mentioned for almost one hundred pages of the novel: "Not the slightest thing was missing.... The only regrettable thing was that the Veronese salami, which was still there too, had bestowed its smell upon everything else. If he could not find some way of eliminating that smell, he had every prospect of walking about for months enveloped in it" (A, 101). And this seems to be what he does; at any rate, there is nothing to suggest that the smell is ever eliminated. It may indeed be that Karl is enabled to "savor" the smell of the old sausage to the full. Oral consumption, however, finally takes a detour through the mouth of another. On the road to Butterford— which not only through its name evokes the idea of a greasy paste for spreading on bread—Karl's new companion Delamarche undertakes to carry the trunk solely for the sake of the salami:

> But he kept grumbling about the weight of the trunk, until it turned out that all he wanted was to relieve it of the Veronese salami, to which it seemed he had taken a fancy before he left the inn. Karl had to unpack it, but the Frenchman grabbed it and with a knife somewhat like a dagger sliced it up and ate almost the whole of it himself. Robinson got only a piece now and then and Karl, who had

been forced to carry the chest again, seeing that he did not want to leave it standing on the road, got nothing at all, as if he had had his share beforehand. It seemed too silly to beg for a piece, but he began to feel bitter. (A, 110)

The business with the dagger-like knife recalls from afar Kafka's pleasure in the cutting up of the "taut sausage skin" of those juicy Jewish sausages "plump as water rats" (LF, 162). And the rising bitterness is by no means Karl's only share in the consumption of an object that has gained decisively in age and hardness through its months-long abode in the trunk. Rather, the virtually infinite deferment of the eating—accompanied by a permanent stimulation of the sense of smell—allows the hero a continuous anticipatory pleasure, a perpetual foretaste of the old European sausage. Nevertheless, the text endeavors quite successfully to attribute all disgusting and obsessive eating habits to Karl's antagonists and to leave the hero thereby in the "innocent" position of 'pure observer,' who for his part reacts only with disgust to the others' pleasure in their food. Karl's brief stay in the country house near New York consists, for the most part, in a dinner party that, as a consequence of Mr. Green's excessive eating habits, constantly brings Karl to the verge of vomiting:

> Mr. Green [put] a slice of pigeon into his mouth, where his tongue, as Karl chanced to notice, took it in charge with a flourish. Karl felt nearly sick.... The dinner was lingered out particularly by the exhaustiveness with which Mr. Green dissected each course, which did not keep him however from attacking each new course with fresh energy.... Mr. Green,... without looking up from his plate, frequently deplored Karl's extraordinary lack of appetite. Mr. Pollunder defended Karl's lack of appetite, although as the host he should have encouraged him to eat. And because of the constraint under which he had suffered during the whole dinner, Karl grew so touchy that, against his better judgment, he actually construed Mr. Pollunder's words as an unkindness. And it was another symptom of his condition that all at once he would eat far too much with indecorous speed, only to sit drooping for a long time afterward, letting his knife and fork rest on the plate, quite silent and motionless, so that the man who served the dishes often did not know what to do with him.
> "I'll have to tell your uncle the Senator tomorrow how you offended Miss Clara by not eating your dinner," said Mr. Green, and he betrayed the facetious intention of his words only by the way in which he plied his knife and fork. (A, 60–61)

The same scene in which Karl is reprimanded for a failure to eat—a failure allegedly offensive to women—shows him, then, suddenly engaged in eating "far too much with indecorous speed." The erotic subtext of this disgusting dinner party is only seemingly suited to help make its tormenting duration bearable. Not only is this subtext appropriated by Karl's antagonist and turned against him, but it also figures in Karl's second (near) rape, after the guests have risen from the dinner table, and in the new, now sexually conditioned disgust: "he was heartily sick of [Clara]" (A, 71). For Karl, having fallen from disgust with food to sexual disgust, the way back to the place of eating seems to be the lesser evil. And in fact, once arrived there, he receives not only the bad news about his uncle's casting him out but also the good news about the restitution of the lost trunk, together with the Veronese salami. Over and over, in the following episodes, the trajectory of Karl, chest, and salami is given its decisive turns by phenomena of seeking, taking in, and eliminating food. The first breakfast with the new companions Delamarche and Robinson is at the same time the first catastrophe. Disgust at the prospect of contact makes Karl simulate the hunger artist, for no "glasses" are provided with the "coffee-can": "So only one of them could drink at a time, while the other two stood by and waited. Karl could not bring himself to drink coffee in this way, but he did not want to offend the other two, and so, when his turn came, though he raised the can to his lips, he drank nothing" (A, 108). Robinson's table manners also play a part in repelling Karl:

> "I see," said Karl, staring at the quickly emptying basket and listening to the curious noise which Robinson made in drinking, for the beer seemed first to plunge right down into his throat and gurgle up again with a sort of whistle before finally pouring its flood into the deep. (A, 125–26)
> "Until we're rung for, we can't go in," said Robinson, opening his mouth to its full extent and devouring the oily bread, while in the hollow of one hand he caught the oil that dripped from it, making a kind of reservoir in which he dipped the rest of the bread from time to time. (A, 233)

Karl's attitude toward his temporary companions is determined in no small measure by these eating habits and by the expropriation of the Veronese salami. When he volunteers to procure food for them all in the "Hotel Occidental," he makes use of the first available opportunity to get free of his companions. Of course, the hotel guests themselves, as described in some detail, exhibit especially coarse and "uncouth" eating habits. The next station in Karl's American career is rung in when Robinson compromises him in his new post by an excessive effusion of vomit. This leads the innocent hero not only into the arms of Brunelda but also into a new terrain of disgusting table manners. Kafka exploits this in a revelatory ecphrastic passage, in which a discreet pleasure in 'pure' description amazingly neutralizes every affect of repugnance:

[In the landlady's eyes,] the remnants of the common breakfast seemed too good for these tenants; on the other hand, she had had enough of the importunity of the two servants, and so she grabbed a tray and shoved it up against Robinson's body. It took a moment before Robinson showed by his plaintive expression that he understood he was to hold the tray while the woman filled it with the food she consented to pick out. She then loaded the tray in a great hurry with an assortment of things, but the ensemble looked more like a pile of dirty dishes than a breakfast about to be served. Even as the woman was herding them out and as they—bent over, as though fearing insults or blows—hurried toward the door, Karl took the tray from Robinson's hands, for he felt it was not secure enough with Robinson.

Once they were far enough away from the landlady's door, Karl sat down with the tray on the floor of the hallway, in order first of all to tidy up the tray, to bring the various things on it into some kind of order, to pour the milk into one container, to scrape the various slabs of butter onto one plate, and then to remove all signs of previous use, to clean the knives and spoons, to cut straight the pieces of bread that had been bitten into, and thus to give a better appearance to the whole. Robinson declared these efforts to be unnecessary and maintained that often the breakfast would look much worse than this, but Karl was not to be deterred and was only happy that Robinson, with his dirty fingers, had no wish to help out. In order to keep him quiet, Karl had quickly slipped him—but only for this one time, as he made clear—some cakes and the thick deposit from a little jar that was earlier filled with chocolate. (V, 368–69)

It is just this repulsive composition out of "remnants" that procures for Karl the wondrous experience of appreciation and reward from the "fat little hands" of the lip-smacking and foul-smelling *vetula:*

Anyone who had seen the earlier stages of this breakfast would have been satisfied with the final result, although, as Karl had to admit to himself, there was still much about it that could be bettered. Fortunately, Brunelda was hungry. Well pleased, she nodded to Karl while he got everything ready, and frequently she would interfere with his work by reaching prematurely for some bit or other with her soft, plump hand, which quickly crumbled all it grasped. "He's done a good job," she said, smacking her lips, and she drew Delamarche, who had left the comb sticking in her hair for later application, down beside her on the easy chair. Even Delamarche grew friendly at the prospect of eating, both of them were very hungry, their hands quickly crossed to and fro over the little table. Karl realized that, in order to provide satisfaction here, it was merely necessary to bring in as much as possible and, recalling that he had left a number of usable food items lying on the floor of the kitchen, he said: "I wasn't sure how everything should be arranged the first time, but next time I'll do a better job." As he spoke these words, however, he remembered who it was he addressed, he had been too preoccupied with the business itself. Brunelda nodded in a satisfied way to Delamarche and held out a handful of biscuits as a reward to Karl. (V, 370–71)

The completed portion of the novel comes to a close with this breakfast scene. The tale of the outcast hero terminates, albeit in the mode of self-denial, in a perfect 'happy ending': the hero has met with approval in a social context, has gained access to sufficiently bad and old food, and has found a favorably inclined, fat old whore.[53] Regarded in this light, *Amerika* is a novel of wish-fulfillment, one, however, that presents itself as though it were the very opposite of a wish-fulfillment. Techniques of "isolation," together with the production of a second-order "amnesia" (Freud) and the radical desynchronization of the content of the action and the affective values arising from its presentation, make it possible for the novel to "display" sulphurous obsessions as estranged sufferings, devlish "stench" as angelic patience and purity, and to offer this all to an "innocent enjoyment."

Breakfast, Old Woman, and Arrest: The Opening Chapter of *The Trial*

Kafka's second novel, *The Trial*, begins where *Amerika* leaves off. It recombines the elements of landlady, breakfast, and Brunelda into a new configuration of "landlady," "breakfast," and "old woman":

> Someone must have slandered Josef K., for one morning, without having done anything evil, he was arrested. His landlady, Frau Grubach, had a cook, who brought him breakfast each day around eight, but this time she didn't appear. That had never happened before. K. waited a while longer, watching from his pillow the old woman who lived across the way, and who was peering at him with a curiosity quite unusual for her. (T, 3)

The fact of K.'s arrest (sentence 1) is primarily orchestrated through its connection with food (sentences 2 and 3) and sexual difference (sentence 4). Long before the warders accuse the thirty-year-old clerk of behaving like "a child," the latter has already, in the first sentence, immersed all that is to follow in a deceptive naïveté. For although, given his professional standing and his reference to the "state governed by law" (T, 6), he must be aware that an arrest is based solely on the difference between legal and illegal, he quickly shifts his reflections to the moral difference between good and evil. By means of this anachronistic misreading, the hero attributes to himself a type of unknowing innocence. On the other hand, this shift in his thinking may refer to the fact that K. rightly supposes the motive for the presumed "slander" to reside in the area in which he immediately chooses to defend himself: the field of offensive behavior, the gray area between breaking the law and transgressing a code of cultural ethics. Food and sexuality are the two 'arguments' which the chapter "The Arrest" promptly furnishes in support of his supposition. At the same time, abundant possibilities for overlooking just this supposition are offered the reader. Amazingly enough, the breakfast and the old woman become illegible not through any strategy of a merely casual mention but precisely through the insistence with which the opening chapter keeps returning to them. They attain in this manner an erratic significance which, in its grazing on the absurd, systematically annuls every rational recourse to a possible "guilt" in the accused. Approximately half of the first two pages is given over to the gesturally rich development of the following three theses: 1. "Anna is to bring me my breakfast." 2. "He says Anna is to bring him his breakfast." 3. "It can't be done." By no means does this exhaust the theme of breakfast. Rather, the guards later suggest the alternative of bringing "you a little breakfast from the coffeehouse across the way" (T, 10). The difference between the two breakfasts is twofold: the "little breakfast from the coffeehouse across the way" would not only cost more money, but it would above all be dirty ("the *filthy* all-night café"), and furthermore would represent contact with the sphere of prostitution ("filthy *all-night* café"). Even when K. refuses this offer, his persistent struggle for breakfast will draw him *ex negativo* into a sphere of filth and sin. The fact that he prefers to take "from the nightstand a nice apple" (T, 10), instead of ordering the filthy breakfast, connects on the one hand to the night-café-register of sin (Eve's apple). But the eating of the apple carries this allusion only insofar as it simultaneously conceals it through the countervailing feature of vegetarian purity. Hardly has he consumed "the first few bites," than K. feels "well and confident" (T, 10): he is back again in his element—the element of the sinful, as the Bible would have it—and he believes that everything will go on as before. He seals this confidence with a second supplement "to make up for his breakfast." In the world of Kafka's 'official' food politics, this second breakfast supplement is no less dubitable than the apple redolent of Eve. It consists in a drink of "good schnapps" of which K. proceeds to empty "a glass" and then "a second"—the latter "a mere precaution, in the unlikely event it might be needed" (T, 11).

From this trouble with breakfast, the beginning of the novel moves abruptly to the old woman. The mention of the filthy all-night café "across the way" as the source of a substitute breakfast later affords a direct bridge: the old lady "across the way" and the site of (sexual) filth are at least in close proximity, if not actually located in the same house. K.'s relation to this old, dirty woman seems to be highly charged with affective significance. Already her first mention betrays a customary relation: "from his pillow [K. watched] the old woman who lived across the way, and who was peering at him with a curiosity quite unusual for her" (T, 3). What is unusual is not the visual link between K. in bed and the old woman across the way, but rather the particular "curiosity" which the woman displays on the day of the arrest. Yet this unusual degree of curiosity is not itself the prime source of K.'s irritation, but rather the additional circumstance that the old woman draws other men into the intimate visual exchange with K. She first drags "an ancient man far older than herself to the window and [has] her arms wrapped about him" (T, 9). *Vis-à-vis* the latent (Horatian) norm of a sexual coupling between a young man and an old woman, the public exhibition of a *vetula*'s pairing with "an ancient man far older than herself" appears as a humiliation, indeed a castration of the young man. In this regard, K.'s reaction—he "had to bring this show to an end"—reflects not only his shame at the quasi-public visibility of his arrest but also a more-than-latent despair in the face of this exhibitionism (the "show") which the old woman in the embrace of an even older man provocatively engages in before K. A little later, another man appears behind the old woman, a man whose only distinguishing feature ("a shirt open at the chest") (T, 13) is coded in an unmistakably sexual fashion. A second man with the same attribute—the flogger in his dark "leather garment that left his neck and upper chest ... bare" (T, 81)—fully confirms the diffuse reference of the arrest scene to "repulsive" sexual practices.

K.'s desperate, futile attempts, in the presence of the Inspector and the two guards, to get rid of these witnesses (T, 15) indicate how closely bound to them he is. They are metonymically present throughout the scene of the arrest like some disgustingly sticky element. Like a curse, they are not to be shaken off, and in this respect as well the trio opposite not only recalls Kafka's description of his own "repulsive" craving for food and obsession with sex; they also provide a precise variation on the inescapable trio of the previous novel: flagelant Delamarche, disgusting old prostitute Brunelda, and weakling Robinson. The stubborn presence of sexual "sulphur" is completed through homosexual attacks: "The belly of the second guard—they surely must be guards—kept bumping against him in a positively friendly way" (T, 6). The abundance of references to oral and sexual "sulphur" conforms to the ambivalence of the first sentence: as an "infernal" phenomenon, the oral and sexual "sulphur" succumbs to the distinction between good and evil; at the same time, some of its violent and "perverse" dimensions are (were) subject to the code of legal and illegal. In the concept of "slander" Kafka has succeeded in establishing yet another point of indifference where moral and juridical reflection likewise apply, a concept that henceforth conditions every attempt to identify the grounds for the arrest. At the same time, in the phenomenology of the arrest—breakfast, old woman across the way, filthy all-night café, apple, Fräulein Bürstner—he has very discreetly disclosed obsessions on the part of his hero which provide clues to a possible defamation for reasons of "sexual dirt."

Orgies of Flesh-Eating and Intoxication with Blood in Kafka's (Hunger) Stories

Despite all the dangers of filth and sin, Joseph K.'s breakfast cannot come near those detailed descriptions of disgusting food and eating habits that punctuate every turn of the narrative in *Amerika*. On the other hand, *Amerika* is far and away surpassed by several short stories, as regards the representation of disgust with food and intoxicated consumption of meat. Licensing these representations throughout is the "illusion" of their being tied to foreign—even "exotic"—cultural contexts. Exportation into the Near and Far East distances and controls the threatening oral pleasure; at the same time, it renders its proximity illegible. In "Jackals and Arabs," the jackals raise that cry about purity *(Geschrei mit der Reinheit)* which Kafka has occasionally proclaimed as his own and rendered ironic (LM, 185–86). Purity—in the sense of cleansing from disgusting "filth"—is what the jackals argue for in demanding the genocide of the Arabs:

> "We want to be troubled no more by Arabs; room to breathe; a skyline cleansed of them; no more bleating of sheep knifed by an Arab; every beast to die a natural death; no interference till we have drained the carcass empty and picked its bones clean. Cleanliness, nothing but cleanliness is what we want"—and now they were all lamenting and sobbing—"how can you bear to live in such a world, O noble heart and kindly bowels? Filth is their white; filth is their black; their beards are a horror; the very sight of their eye sockets makes one want to spit; and when they lift an arm, the murk of hell yawns in the armpit. And so, sir, and so, dear sir, by means of your all-powerful hands slit their throats through with these scissors!" And in answer to a jerk of his head, a jackal came trotting up with a small pair of sewing scissors, covered with ancient rust, dangling from an eye-tooth. (S, 409–10)

The presumptive victims have merely a condescending smile for all this. With the help of a dead camel, they readily come to the service of the European narrator's ethnological view, providing graphic instruction in the unity of meat-eating, blood-drinking, and purification. In representing the irresistibly bewitching spell proceeding from the "stinking carrion," Kafka again brings about a complete neutralization of every barrier of disgust. The intoxicated consumption of the cadaver becomes utterly unironic proof of what "marvelous creatures" the jackals are:

> Four men came up with the heavy carcass and threw it down before us. It had barely touched the ground before the jackals lifted up their voices. As if irresistibly drawn by cords, each of them began to waver forward, crawling on his belly. They had forgotten the Arabs, forgotten their hatred, the all-obliterating immediate presence of the stinking carrion bewitched them. One was already at the camel's throat, sinking his teeth straight into an artery. Like a vehement small pump endeavoring with as much determination as hopefulness to extinguish some raging fire, every muscle in his body twitched and labored at the task. In a trice they were all on top of the carcass, laboring in common, piled mountain-high.
>
> And now the caravan leader lashed his cutting whip crisscross over their backs. They lifted their heads; half swooning in ecstasy; saw the Arabs standing before them; felt the sting of the whip on their muzzles; leaped and ran backwards a stretch. But the camel's blood was already lying in pools, reeking to heaven, the carcass was torn wide open in many places. They could not resist it; they were back again; once more the leader lifted his whip; I stayed his arm.
>
> "You are right, sir," said he, "we'll leave them to their business; besides, it's time to break camp. Well, you've seen them. Marvelous creatures, aren't they?" (S, 410–11)

A neighboring story, "An Old Manuscript," intensifies this orgy of flesh-eating to the point of consuming a live body. The price of this intensification is of course a restitution of the barriers of disgust on the part of an urban ("capital") culture, which finds itself helpless against an invasion of nomads who threaten civilization:

> As soon as [the butcher] brings in any meat, the nomads snatch it all from him and gobble it up. Even their horses devour flesh; often enough a horseman and his horse are lying side by side, both of them gnawing at the same joint, one at either end. The butcher is nervous and does not dare to stop his deliveries of meat. We understand that, however, and subscribe money to keep him going. If the nomads got no meat, who knows what they might think of doing; who knows anyhow what they may think of, even though they get meat every day.

> Not long ago the butcher thought he might at least spare himself the trouble of slaughtering, and so one morning he brought along a live ox. But that is something he will no longer care to repeat. I lay for a whole hour flat on the floor at the back of my workshop with my head muffled in all the clothes and rugs and pillows I had, simply to keep from hearing the bellowing of that ox, which the nomads were leaping on from all sides, tearing morsels out of its living flesh with their teeth. It had been quiet for a long time before I risked coming out; they were lying overcome around the remains of the carcass like drunkards around a wine flask. (S, 416–47)

From this point on, there is only one possible intensification left in the evocation of the repulsive consumption of flesh: that is, cannibalism. Kafka has taken this last step too.[54] A manuscript variant of "The Hunger Artist" introduces a "cannibal" as an old childhood friend of the hunger artist:

> "Yes," he said, "I am the one, the old cannibal who was so well-disposed to you and perhaps to you alone. I would like to make you a little visit so as to recover my strength in your sight and give my nerves a rest from those troublesome people." "You're a cannibal?" asked the hunger artist, pressing his hand to his forehead as though trying to recall something. "You have forgotten me?" said the cannibal, a little annoyed and even more surprised than annoyed. "Is it possible then? You don't remember how we used to play together?"[55]

Not only is the hunger artist an old friend of the cannibal. By the same token, the closing paragraph of the completed story "The Hunger Artist" brings a wild, flesh-eating animal to triumph over the just expired hunger artist. This animal, even more marveled at than the "marvelous" jackals, is a panther in whose jaws—otherwise the place of rat-like germs of decay—"freedom" seems to lurk, and whose "hot gamy breath" is celebrated as proof of "the joy of life" (S, 277).[56]

The substitution of the flesh-eating beast of prey for the deceased hunger artist may, moreover, throw light on an enigmatic feature of "The Metamorphosis," one entirely overlooked in the numerous readings of this story: that appearance of "a butcher's boy ... ascending proudly with a tray on his head" (S, 138) which seals the family's relief at Gregor's death by starvation. Just as the hunger artist at the end disavows his artistic achievement as unwilled necessity ("because I couldn't find the food I liked"), so also Gregor Samsa protests against a misunderstanding of his ostensibly voluntary pining away: "'I do have an appetite,' said Gregor sadly to himself, 'but not for that kind of food. How these lodgers are stuffing themselves, and here I am dying of starvation!'" (S, 129). "Appetite," as Kant had seen, is one of the most promising candidates for the difficult position of a direct conceptual opposite of disgust. Placed as it is, however, in contiguity with his observation of the lodgers at their food, Gregor's mention of his appetite at once becomes dubitable. For the eating habits of these gentlemen are distinctively repulsive and appetite-stifling: they ate "in almost complete silence," so that "among the various noises coming from the table [Gregor] could always distinguish the sound of their masticating teeth" (S, 129). Unlike the hunger artist, Gregor Samsa in his insect life is properly fed, at least initially. From a rich selection of fresh and half-decayed foods, he "greedily" chooses the most spoiled: a piece of cheese that, with his human senses, he "would have called uneatable two days ago," "old, half-decayed vegetables," and a "white sauce that had thickened" over "bones from last night's supper" (S, 107–8) These unpalatable foods serve as the medium of an intoxicated feed: "One after another, and with tears of satisfaction in his eyes, he quickly devoured [them]." But Gregor finds after some time that, instead of his choice and satisfying disgust-menu, "any food that was available" is being pushed into his room; "dirt" and "filth" (S, 125–26) do the rest to destroy his appetite.

The accumulation of all the "superfluous, not to say dirty, objects," which soon "found their way" into Gregor's room (S, 127–28), sets the scene for the "waste" disposal of his "completely flat and dry" hunger-corpse at the end (S, 137). For his family, the casting out of Gregor and all the other contents of his filth-filled room can only be complete if it includes the dismissal of those lodgers who were witnesses to the abject son finally removed from the apartment. Taken in so as to compensate for the loss of Gregor's income, the lodgers had not only maltreated Gregor with the mute concert of their masticating teeth occupied with "a piece of meat" (S, 128); they had also made use of his existence as a cause for reproaches against the apartment and the whole family. Their prompt expulsion after Gregor's death does not stop at the door of the apartment. The staircase outside becomes the scene of a farcical choreography of withdrawal and approach, of descent and ascent. This scene has its high point and conclusion in the redemptive, triumphant appearance of the butcher's boy "with a tray on his head":

> In the hall . . . all three [lodgers] took their hats from the rack, their canes from the umbrella stand, bowed in silence, and quitted the apartment. With a suspiciousness that proved quite unfounded, Mr. Samsa and the two women followed them out to the landing; leaning over the banister they watched the three figures slowly but surely going down the long flight of stairs, vanishing from sight at a certain turn of the staircase on every floor and coming into view again after a moment or so; the farther down they got, the more the Samsa family's interest in them dwindled, and when a butcher's boy met them on the stairs and then continued on his way high above

them, ascending proudly with a tray on his head, Mr. Samsa and the two women quickly left the landing and, as if a burden had been lifted from them, went back into their apartment. (S, 138)

In the slow progression from floor to floor, the staircase seems at first to lose itself in some enormous depth down below, before then gaining in the opposite direction an expansion ("high above them"), such as is hardly to be met with any central-European apartment house of Kafka's day. The shift in "the Samsa family's interest" from the descending, meat-eating lodgers to the ascending, meat-delivering young man bespeaks the triumph of young, fresh flesh—as which Gregor's sister then immediately offers herself on the marriage market (S, 139). In this triumph, it would seem, a world is once again restored to order, after being thrown into disorder by a disappointing son with a liking for rotten non-meat (cheese and vegetables) and sadomasochistic pin-ups. The fact that precisely this triumph of young, fresh flesh entails—no less here than in "The Hunger Artist"—a disgusting politics of traceless purification from what was repudiated, has no effect on the abysmal pleasure with which Kafka describes—as an analogue to the wild vitality of the young panther that takes the place of the deceased hunger artist—the pride of the butcher's boy ascending to and exceeding the place of the meat-refuser Gregor, who has just been disposed of. Hysterical abstinence from meat and perverse intoxication with it, vegetarian-bulimic hunger and cannibalism are the correlative extremes of a practice of (not) eating, which consistently suspends the distinction between scenes of punishment and scenes of wish-fulfillment. This politics is no more abstinent than Kafka's sexual politics. Rather, in more or less open fashion, it allows orgies of meat-eating to arise in the wake of disappearing bodies. Asceticism, like "self-condemnation," is another element of that "method" which, as a strategy of purification, promotes the repudiated pleasure, taken in its very opposite. "Certain ascetics," in Kafka's concise analysis, are "the most insatiable people" (DF, 300).

7.5 Incisions in Flesh and the Knife of Literature

To the eating of meat belongs the knife—belong acts of cutting and dividing. Kafka's memory of "those juicy Jewish sausages," which are "plump as water rats," is not least a memory of the way these sausages "can be cut up by every relative all over the place" and of "the sound of the taut sausage skin being cut." Whereas the continuity of smoothly drawn skin was the classical ideal of the beautiful, and at the same time the guiding value in all avoidance of disgust, Kafka effects a consistent caesura of the skin. The flaying of Marsyas returns as the obsessive desire to see all bodies cut, slit open, sliced up, tortured, indeed butchered. Kafka's texts are bizarre dances of bodies and knives.

And just as Lessing already saw, in the pathos of divine punishment by Apollo, Marsyas's opened body delivered from the "merely" disgusting to the monstrous, so Kafka's attacks on the skin bind all that is disgusting to the register of language, of truth, and of pleasure.[57]

The smoothly blown corporeal of the beautiful body possess a fullness but no corpulence; it consists of "uninterrupted portions" of a quasi-sacrosanct continuum of skin stretched over an invisibilized substratum. A Kafkan body, by contrast, is a divisible piece of matter, a block of wood, or a virtually raw piece of meat—one fit to be cut into, cut off, and consumed. The cut or thrust into this flesh makes it evident that the Kafkan body is not just a beautiful veil, or a properly blown hollow form. The story "A Fratricide" transforms the pleasure of cutting open the water-rat-sausage into "the bliss of murder." Just as the returned Odysseus, with premeditated murder in his heart, lovingly takes up the bow with which he is about to slaughter the suitors, feels along its length and plucks a resounding note on its taut string, so Kafka prepares for the "blissful" murder by having the murderer celebrate his weapon:

> His weapon, half bayonet and half kitchen knife, he kept firmly in his grasp, quite naked. He looked at the knife against the light of the moon; the blade glittered; not enough for Schmar; he struck it against the bricks of the pavement till the sparks flew; regretted that, perhaps; and to repair the damage drew it like a violin bow across his boot sole while he bent forward, standing on one leg, and listened both to the whetting of the knife on his boot and for any sound out on the fateful side street. (S, 402)

Before the victim appears on the scene, an onlooker is introduced: "Pallas, the private citizen." He not only tolerates the overt preparations for murder but bends far forward out of his window in order "not [to] miss anything." The allusion here to Pallas Athena may well recall the divinely sanctioned acts of murder and butchery in the Homeric epic. The victim of the murder, Wese, analogously looks up to the night sky for signs that might "interpret the near future for him." The absence of any such divine instruction provides further justification for the murder:

> The night sky invited him [Wese], with its dark blue and its gold. Unknowing, he gazed up at it, unknowing he lifted his hat and stroked his hair; nothing up there drew together in a pattern to interpret the immediate future for him; everything stayed in its senseless, inscrutable place. In itself it was a highly reasonable action that Wese should walk on, but he walked into Schmar's knife.
> "Wese!" shrieked Schmar, standing on tiptoe, his arm outstretched, the knife sharply lowered, "Wese! You will never see Julia

again!" And right into the throat and left into the throat and a third time deep into the belly stabbed Schmar's knife. Water rats, slit open, give out such a sound as came from Wese.

"Done," said Schmar, and pitched the knife, now superfluous blood-stained ballast, against the nearest house front. "The bliss of murder! The relief, the soaring ecstasy from the shedding of another's blood! Wese, old nightbird, friend, alehouse crony, you are oozing away into the dark earth below the street. Why aren't you simply a bladder of blood so that I could stamp on you and make you vanish into nothingness. Not all we want comes true, not all the dreams that blossomed have borne fruit, your solid remains lie here, already indifferent to every kick. What's the good of the dumb question you are asking?" (S, 403–4)

Provocatively enough, the stabbing of a human being is not only likened to the pleasurable slitting open of a water rat, but is actually presented as a source of bliss. Yet its taking the form of murder in this story effectively disguises the fact that here, in melodramatic disguise, Kafka's pervasive imagination of knife, body, and writing comes to the fore. In the diaries and letters, it is Kafka's own body that is stabbed, cut up, and pierced through. What Kafka, as an employee of an insurance company, had to prevent, if possible, or, in the case of injury, to regulate—accidents involving machines with rotating blades[58]—serves, as uninsured "fantasy," to govern the imagination of his own bodily self:

These are the fantasies or the wishes I indulge in when lying sleepless in bed: To be a large piece of wood, and to be pressed against her own body by the cook, who with both hands draws the knife toward her along the side of this stiff log (approximately in the region of my hip) and with all her might slices off shavings to light the fire. (LF, 201–2)

This morning, for the first time in a long time, the joy again of imagining a knife twisted in my heart. (D, 101)

Always the image of a pork butcher's broad knife that quickly and with mechanical regularity chops into me from the side and cuts off very thin slices which fly off almost like shavings because of the speed of the action. (D, 221)

Fantasies, for example that I lie stretched out on the floor, sliced up like a roast, and with my hand am slowly pushing a slice of the meat toward a dog in the corner—such fantasies are my mind's daily fare. (L, 95; see also LF, 230)

In these "daily" fantasies,[59] Kafka by no means allots to his body the role merely of stabbing victim, of object of the knife's action. Rather, the recognition of stabbing and vivisection as obsessional fantasies leads him to assume an active knife-role. To become the knife, in all coolness, is in fact the ideal of Kafka's self. The force of decision, *Entscheidung*, figures literally here as *Ent-Scheidung*, as the drawing of a knife from its sheath. Instead of substantially *being* its own "totality," the "I" can bring this totality into play only in an exteriorating act: namely an act of "butchering" in "the moment of decision" of decisive alienation. It must hold this totality, as though it were something utterly strange, "in [its] hand like a stone to be thrown, a knife for butchering *(ein Messer zum Schlachten)*":

> How are you even going to touch the greatest task, how are you even going to sense its nearness, even dream its existence, even plead for its dream, dare to learn the letters of the plea, if you cannot collect yourself in such a way that, when the decisive moment of decision comes, you hold the totality of yourself collected in your hand like a stone to be thrown, a knife for butchering? (DF, 65)

In the most favorable circumstances, the stabbing which the self suffers at the hands of its own knife-being, or through another knife, obeys a rule of idealization: "The main thing, when a sword cuts into one's soul, is to keep a calm gaze, lose no blood, accept the coldness of the sword with the coldness of a stone. By means of the stab, after the stab, become invulnerable" (DF, 73). Just as, in the children's game, the contiguity with the stone takes away the power of the knife and scissors to cut, so with Kafka the sword that cuts into the soul transforms the stone-like coolness of observation into paradoxical invulnerability. The obsessive imagination of self-mutilation thus serves a logic of immunization against the vulnerability to knife, stabbing, and cutting—a logic reminiscent of fairy tales. At the same time, the ideas of a bloodless cut into the flesh recalls from afar certain eminent achievements of bodily control through meditation. A narrative fragment composed in January 1915 imagines an involuntary mixture of yogi and sword-swallower:

> I had agreed to go picknicking on Sunday with two friends, but quite unexpectedly slept past the hour when we were to meet. My friends, who knew how punctual I ordinarily am, were surprised, came to the house where I lived, waited outside a while, then came upstairs and knocked on my door. I was very startled, jumped out of bed, and thought only of getting ready as soon as I could. When I emerged fully dressed from my room, my friends fell back in manifest alarm. "What's that behind your head?" they cried. Since my awakening I had felt something preventing me from bending back my head, and I now groped for it with my hand. My friends, who had grown somewhat calmer, had just shouted "Be careful, don't hurt

yourself!" when my hand closed behind my head on the hilt of a sword. My friends came closer, examined me, led me back to the mirror in my room, and stripped me to the waist. A large, ancient knight's sword with a cross-shaped handle was buried to the hilt in my back, but the blade had been driven with such incredible precision between my skin and flesh that it had caused no injury. Nor was there a wound at the spot on my neck where the sword had penetrated; my friends assured me that there was an opening large enough to admit the blade, but dry and showing no trace of blood. And when my friends now stood on chairs and slowly, inch by inch, drew out the sword, I did not bleed, and the opening on my neck closed until no mark was left save a scarcely discernible slit. "Here is your sword," laughed my friends, and gave it to me. I hefted it in my two hands; it was a splendid weapon, Crusaders might have used it. Who tolerates this gadding about of ancient knights in dreams, irresponsibly brandishing their swords, stabbing innocent sleepers who are saved from serious injury only because the weapons in all likelihood glance off of living bodies, and also because there are faithful friends knocking at the door, prepared to come to their assistance? (D, 327)

The politics of bodies and knives undergoes a repetition here which suffuses it in bewilderment and surprise. This distancing above all restores the innocence of the presentation in the face of all the stabbing and cutting, the swords and knives, in which Kafka's work abounds. A similar tendency is all the more pronounced in the case of texts geared, at least virtually, toward publication: letters and autobiographical notes affirm the lacerations of flesh as something self-willed, whereas works and fragments of works tend to delegate the knife and the act of killing, as a foreign power, to third parties and, correspondingly, tend to assume the role of "innocent victim." Not in regard to Kafka or to the K.'s, but rather to nomads from the North, it is then said: "They busy themselves sharpening swords, whittling arrows" (S, 416). It is only through such displacements onto foreign instances—which are often not only spatially removed but anachronistic as well (like the execution ceremony in "In the Penal Colony")—that a sadistic distance between the subject and the object of the knife emerges. In any case, Kafka disturbs all customary pragmatic orders of cutting and piercing. What in one case bespeaks "blissfulness" can, in another story of stabbing, make for the unexpected choreography of an execution:

> A singular judicial procedure. The condemned man is stabbed to death in his cell by the executioner without any other person being allowed to be present. He is seated at the table finishing a letter or his last meal. A knock is heard, it is the executioner.

"Are you ready?" he asks. The content and sequence of his questions and actions are fixed for him by regulation, he cannot depart from it. The condemned man, who at first jumped up, now sits down again and stares straight before him or buries his face in his hands. Having received no reply, the executioner opens his instrument case on the cot, chooses the daggers, and even now attempts to touch up their several edges here and there. It is very dark by now, he sets up a small lantern and lights it. The condemned man furtively turns his head toward the executioner, but shudders when he sees what he is doing, turns away again, and has no desire to see more.

"Ready," the executioner says after a little while.

"Ready?" screams the condemned man, jumps up and now, however, looks directly at the executioner. "You're not going to kill me, not going to put me down on the cot and stab me to death, you're a human being after all, you can execute someone on a scaffold, with assistants and in the presence of magistrates, but not here in this cell, one man killing another!" And when the executioner, bent over his case, says nothing, the condemned man goes on to say: "This singular judicial procedure was instituted just because it is impossible. The form is to be preserved, but the death penalty is no longer carried out. You will take me to another jail; I shall probably have to stay there a long time, but they will not execute me."

The executioner loosens a new dagger within its cotton sheath and says: "You are probably thinking of those fairy tales in which a servant is commanded to expose a child but does not do so and instead binds him over as apprentice to a shoemaker. Those are fairy tales; this, though, is not a fairy tale." (D, 368)

The *Ent-Scheidung*, or un-sheathing of the dagger—which is pointed at as the next step following upon loosening it in the sheath—presents anew the imminence of a decision but no longer acts on it. Can in fact the form of the execution be preserved without its being carried out? Is the stabbing without witnesses inverted into some fantastic deferment or even into a fantastic salvation? Or does the absence of official witnesses entail a mere collapse of the difference between murder and State-regulated execution? In the medium of such undecidable questions, Kafka makes it possible—in a manner at once open and hidden—for the incision into the beautiful continuous surface of skin to circulate through his works. What is manifest so dramatically in "In the Penal Colony" and *The Trial* lurks everywhere in Kafka's work: a knife ready to cut. Not only can a knife emerge at any moment, as though nothing were more natural, and be coldbloodedly stuck somewhere: "Then, without further ado, my acquaintance pulled a knife out of his pocket, opened it thoughtfully, and then, as though he were playing, he plunged it into his left upper arm, and didn't withdraw it" (S, 50). Even more radically: literature itself is to become this knife, even when it is not overtly concerned with knives. And the cuts and stabbings into flesh achieve not least a *mise en abîme* of the writing that cuts: "I'll jump into my story even though it should cut my face to pieces" (D, 28; see also L, 74).

In his concept of the "knife effect" *(Messerwirkung)* of literature (LF, 469), Kafka reformulates classical rhetorical assumptions concerning the weapon-like power of language. Longinus, for example, argues that the good orator can do the same with words as the man who strikes, beats, or cuts.[60] Of course, Kafka's ideal of a book that "wakes us up with a blow on the head" (L, 16) and Longinus's praise of Demosthenes for the "relentless blows" with which he attacks the minds of his listeners[61] are distinguished by virtue of the differing pragmatic functions assigned to the word-blows and word-cuts. The winning of a practical advantage through rhetorical surprise attacks on others gives way to a procedure of self-examination, in which self-torment, torture, and the quest for "truth" (LF, 469) are interwoven: "I think we ought to read only the kind of books that wound and stab us. . . . We need the books that affect us . . . like a suicide. A book must be the axe for the frozen sea inside us" (L, 16). Kafka's letters obey the same poetics: "'Poor dear Felice'—were the last words I wrote; is this to be the closing phrase to all my letters? It's not a knife that stabs only forward but one that wheels around and stabs back as well." (LF, 543–44) Once again, it is the reflective turning back, the boomerang effect of the word-knife, which transforms the traditional rhetorical model of verbal incision into a more complex figure. The relations between beautiful intact skin and disgusting dissection of the twitching innards are reversed in this field: in rereading his own most recent letters to Felice, Kafka testifies to extreme "repugnance, primarily because . . . I didn't feel stung by them, either deeply enough or often enough," and because "the desire . . . to make [these letters] even more decisive" had remained "impotent" (LF, 201). Love means "that you are for me the knife with which I dig into myself"; likewise, communication *(Mitteilung)* among two friends literally amounts to a shared dividing up *(Mit-Teilung)*, a "dissection" of two throats by the same knife:

> Dear Max, . . . Our correspondence can be very simple: I do my writing, you yours, and that is answer, verdict, consolation, inconsolability, whatever one likes. For it is the same knife against whose sharp blade our throats, our poor pigeons' throats, one here, one there, dissect themselves. But so slowly, so insidiously, with so little blood, so heartrendingly, so hearts-rendingly. (L, 139–40)

Kafka's last diary entry is at the same time the last variation on the poetics of cutting and stabbing. The provocative gesture there yields to a mixture of anxiety and consolation: anxiety at the uncontrollable turning of the word-spears against the writer himself; consolation, indeed "more than consolation," in the fact that he has "weapons" at all:

> More and more fearful as I write. It is understandable. Every word, twisted in the hands of the spirits—this twist of the hand is their characteristic gesture—becomes a spear turned against the speaker. Most especially a remark like this. And so *ad infinitum.* The only consolation would be: it happens whether you like or not. And what you like is of infinitesimally little help. More than consolation is: You too have weapons. (D, 423)

According to a much cited diary entry, Kafka's writing strives for the avoidance of metaphors in the desperate awareness of their unavoidability (D, 398). The cutting and stabbing with words, too, is no 'mere' metaphor. Nor is it simply a matter of the incisive effect which a speech is calculated to have on a listener. Rather, the cut with the knife comprises an objective moment in words themselves. From Homer to Saussure, the articulation of language has been repeatedly understood as a cutting and dividing. In his treatise *Von der Poesie im Recht* (1815), Jacob Grimm writes: "to speak is also to divide, for the speaker (or reader) cuts the word in his mouth (and in his senses); it is for this reason that Homer calls human beings in general *meropes*."[62] Saussure defined "the domain of articulations" as a field of dividing slices into a previously diffuse "nebula"; without the articulating achievement of the signs, the cloud of thoughts and sounds would forever remain a "shapeless . . . mass."[63] A particularly suggestive effect of articulation borrows its name directly from the idea of the cut *(Stich):* a *Stichwort* (keyword) has the capacity to cut through masses of data and thereby to serve up selective portions of the mass. But none of these indications really suffice for Kafka's poetics of the knife cut. Obviously, Kafka is interested neither in expounding a general doctrine of the articulation of signs nor in advancing the literature of cataloguing by means of keywords.

More specific clues into the function of literary cutting and piercing are provided by mythology and metrics. Among the animal prototypes for the writer, not the least significant is the bee: from Homer to Augustine, it appears over and over as representing a honey-sweet discourse which itself is grounded in acts of reading (in the sense of gathering and gleaning *(Auflesen).* The bee is an insect—from Latin *insecare,* "to cut into s.th."; itself articulated (cut) in segments and divisions, it is also quite capable of pointedly stinging. Thomas Schestag has shown that the paradigms of cutting, segmenting, and stinging are at least as relevant to the writer-bee mythology as the idea of persuasion through honeyed discourse.[64] What is perhaps the richest articulatory achievement of literary language—poetic verse—contains already in the terminology of metrics various references to cutting and piercing. In Greek, poetic verse as form of a linguistic cut is known as a *stíchos*, a finely articulated line of writing; phonetically, this line correlates with the battle line *(stíx, stichós)*,[65] in which it is literally a matter of swords and the "slaughtering" of living bodies. Moreover, in the line of verse there are particular points known as caesuras: dividing cuts which, precisely as empty places, as interruptions of the voice, indicate the position of the knife itself. Stichomythia is a speech and counterspeech that either cuts out all utterances according to the pattern of one single line of verse or even cuts the verse line itself, dividing it between two different speakers. The hectic exchange of such sharply cutout stichomythemes regularly indicates and produces situations of de-cision, where the course of dramatic action is poised on the (bare) edge of a knife blade.

As far as Kafka's work is concerned, another aspect of the cuts at work in lines of verse may be usefully adduced. A stichomythem is designed to strike home *(treffen)* in a twofold sense: formally, it should "meet" *(treffen)* the verse pattern, and, pragmatically, it is intended to "strike" *(treffen)* the addressee like a cut and thrust. It is, in an emphatic sense, a well-aimed *(treffendes)* word, fitting for its purpose like a stinging and cutting weapon. Kafka's poetics of the knife refers, through the medium of a radical literalization, to this category of the *treffendes Wort*, the well-aimed—because successfully stinging and cutting—word. At the same time, it interweaves this category of the "treffendes" word—a category which is scarcely viable as a rhetorical concept, while, in ordinary language, no longer felt as a powerful metaphor—with the conception of the sēma als sōma, of the word as body, and thus links it to the an-aesthetic of the disgusting, to the vivisection of the flesh. Well-aimed word, cutting of the flesh, and disgust are therefore the three moments a primal scene of inventing literary language consists of:

> While dictating a rather long report to the district Chief of Police, toward the end, where a climax was intended, I got stuck and could do nothing but look at K., the typist, who, in her usual way, became especially lively, moved her chair about, coughed, tapped on the table and so called the attention of the whole room to my misfortune. The sought-for idea now has the additional value that it will make her be quiet, and the more valuable it becomes the more difficult it becomes to find it. Finally I have the word "stigmatize" and the appropriate sentence, but still hold it all in my mouth with disgust and a sense of shame as though it were raw meat, cut out of me (such effort has it cost me). Finally I say it, but retain the great fear that everything within me is ready for a literary work. (D, 62)

In Kafka's account of the robbing of "a piece of flesh" (D, 62) from his body, all metaphysical dualism of the body-soul model—the body of the sign as the carrier of meaning, the incarnation of the spirit in the letter or of God's word in the body of Jesus—is doubly crossed out. In the first place, the flesh is posited as "raw meat," whereas the Christian and hermeneutic model always already implies a manifest symbolic moment of the sign-body itself. And secondly, this "raw meat" is not at all interpreted in terms of a signified, a spirit, a soul, but is itself already what is sought. Expected from it is not so much a meaning as a performative achievement: the resolution of a tormenting tension by dint of a power of striking, of hitting the mark. The correlate to this power of striking is precisely the cut into (one's own) flesh. Furthermore, the word disclosed through this cut into one's own flesh marks, for its part, a violent stamping of flesh: a "stigmatizing." The disgust at holding in his mouth the fittingly cut-out piece of raw meat by no means figures as an index of failure. Rather, it crowns the search, seals it as an analogue of "literary work," and produces a pleasurable foretaste of vomiting such words—a vomiting that, as Kafka immediately adds, brings with it, in the case of "literary work," a great "happiness," indeed a "heavenly dissolution (of tensions)." Just as Kant interprets vomiting in disgust as a lifesaving act in the face of a deadly danger, so Kafka witnesses to a power—apotropaic of death—in his vomited words, a power that for him signifies, first of all, "a real becoming-alive" (D, 62):

> The last letter, for example, wasn't written, it was (forgive the expression) vomited out; I was lying in bed and it occurred to me not as a sequence of sentences, but as one single terrible sentence which I felt would kill me if I did not write it down. (LF, 39)

Torture, Truth, and Disembowelled Pigs

If the pleasurable and disgusting vivisection of one's own body is the model of literary language, then Kafka's obsession with techniques of dismemberment, torture, murder, and execution concerns the project of his writing itself. This obsession—consistently favoring very detailed descriptions which, through their quasi-ethnologic gesture of objective, unempathic observation, border on the (morally) disgusting as well—may then be interpreted as the form in which Kafka's poetics of the knife and the disgusting cut presents itself most directly. As Milena Jesenska is translating a passage about torture from "In the Penal Colony," Kafka writes to her:

> It does indicate an affinity of taste that you have translated just this passage. Yes, torturing is extremely important to me, I'm preoccupied with nothing but being tortured and torturing. Why? For much the same reason as Perkins was and equally thoughtlessly, mechanically, and according to tradition—i.e., to learn the cursed word from the cursed mouth. (LM, 216)

In fully detached abstraction, Kafka reads torture, "according to tradition," as a method of finding hidden layers of language: as with his own poetics, the true or, at least, the desired word is forced from a body by means of knife cuts. To Freud's parallels between torture and psychoanalysis, between the stigmata diaboli and traumata (which, through repeated stabs of the executioner or the analytic process respectively are recalled and dissolved), Kafka gives a sadistic turn—while nevertheless remaining bound to the pseudonaïve quest for the legendary saving word. It is no mere *façon de parler* when Kafka keeps confessing to tormenting Felice with his letters, and even lays emphasis on this tendency in an offensive manner:

> These letters, as they are, are good for nothing but to torment, and if they don't torment, it's even worse. (LM, 223)
> What kind of person am I! I am tormenting her and myself to death. (L, 116)
> She is a real martyr and it is clear that I am undermining the entire basis on which she previously used to live, happy and in tune with the whole world. (L, 95)

To force "the cursed word from the cursed mouth"—that in fact seems to be the goal of Kafka's intentional tormenting by means of epistolary knives. His torturing reached its most ingenious heights where the language-cutting unity of "being tortured" and "torturing" is found: the cardinal trope of this self-reflective torture is the twisting of the knife in his own heart (D, 101).[66] The following sentences, written to torture Milena, exhibit the disgusting side of this torture- and execution-poetics in an especially drastic way:

> So that you can see something of my "occupations," I'm enclosing a drawing. These are four poles, through the two middle ones are driven rods to which the hands of the "delinquet" are fastened; through the two outer poles rods are driven for the feet. After the man has been bound in this way, the rods are drawn slowly outward until the man is torn apart in the middle. Against the post leans the inventor who, with crossed arms and legs, is giving himself great airs, as though the whole thing were his original invention, whereas he has only copied the butcher who stretches the disembowelled pig in his shop-front.

Even more disgusting than the comparison with impaling and pig-slaughtering is the pride with which the inventor regards the tearing apart of a human being by means of his torture machine.[67] Kafka told his beloved: these are my occupations, and I am the butcher represented here. He expressly warns her that "the person of whom you write doesn't exist" (LM,

(LM, 204–05)

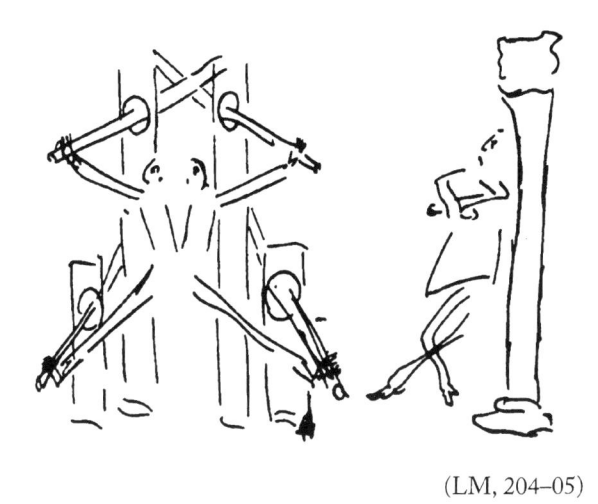

205), that Milena fails to get at the truth of her correspondent and therefore again and again portrays him "in all innocence, as though nothing had happened," instead of recognizing the devlish torturer for what he is. But it is precisely the unsparing candor with which Kafka confesses his obsession with torture that guarantees its unreadability and thus enables the deceiving without deception to continue: Milena will hardly believe that the drawing and its commentary are meant in all seriousness to reveal the truth about Kafka. And yet much argues for taking Kafka squarely at his word: the mode of detached observation applied on 'inappropriate' occasions—namely, where empathy might be expected—belongs integrally to the narrative gestus of Kafka's prose, and it is precisely through such pointedly 'misplaced' detachment that this prose speaks its cutting and lacerating knife-words. The cold-blooded acceptance of the knife-blade is the very ideal of Kafka's self (DF, 73). To this extent, the two figures represented on the drawing (the tortured victim and the detached observer) represent two aspects of Kafka's poetics, in which the cut into the flesh, the "opening out of the body" (D, 213), serves as the means for finding, for setting free the well-aimed *(treffend)* word, such as the poet-observer passionately seeks and cooly, acerbically notes down. With regard to Kafka's work and his self-scrutiny, the drawing articulates that cycle of "being tortured and torturing" of which Kafka writes to Milena a little later: "I'm preoccupied with nothing but [this]." At the same time, with respect to Kafka's correspondence with women, the drawing enables a different distribution of the roles of subject and object: it illustrates—in accordance with Kafka's repeated assertions—the premeditated torment, the systematic martyrdom, to which Kafka exposed his beloved correspondents with the help of his letter-knives. The crisis of disgust, which Kafka arouses in the reader with his unusual combination of picture and text, opens a deceptively clear prospect on Kafka's poetics of knife, flesh, disgust, and word. At the same time, it permits—and precisely here is its deceptiveness—a comforting diversion of attention away from this disturbing sight: for can the butchering and disembowelling of a pig really serve as a model for making literature, and especially in the case of a Jewish author?

It is not only in Kafka's memorable letter to Milena but also in other places that the self-reflection of the knife-poetics is associated with the killing of animals—this in addition to the phenomena of torture, execution, and murder. The kind and degree of affect invested in such killing is scarcely to be conceived without Kafka's "joy . . . [in] imagining a knife twisted in my heart" (D, 101). The "cattle bound for the slaughter-house," which cross Karl Rossmann's way after his departure from Clara's country house in New York, are said—in a pseudonaïve and cynical inversion of animal ignorance—to be "careless" (A, 109). And from his own country retreat in Zürau, Kafka reports with some relish on the latest happenings in the slaughterhouse: "Other news: One of the geese died of excessive stuffing, the sorrel has mange, the goats have been to the buck (who seems to be a particularly handsome young fellow; one of the goats, who had already been taken there, had a flash of remembrance and ran back to him again all the way from our house), and soon the pig is going to be butchered without more ado" (L, 172). It would seem that the association of horny and/or aged womanhood with the slaughtering of an (abject) animal was especially appealing to Kafka. A little earlier, he had already derived from this conjunction of two paradigms of disgust the following variation: "Today a slaughtered goose lay outside in the basin, looking like someone's dead aunt" (L, 171).

"Like a Dog": K.'s Execution as the Summa of Kafka's Knife-Poetics

The closing scene of *The Trial* brings the killing of an animal ("Like a dog!"), the vision of an ideal suicide, and the representation of a disgusting execution into one final accord, in which Kafka intermingles a number of the elements of his knife-cut poetics.[68] All "joy" in the turning of the knife in K.'s heart is well hidden, yet again Kafka offers here more than simply the nightmarish and punitive side of his poetics of stabbing and cutting. Whereas, earlier, the milieux of the court had brought K. literally to the verge of vomiting (because it appeared oppressive and evil-smelling, physically dirty and morally repulsive), the two executioners, who are reminiscent of "tenors," give rise to an opposite type of disgust: disgust with excessive cleanliness. In view of their age, their being "fat" (T, 225), and their "thick double chins" (T, 227), the two men still recall "voluminous women" like Brunelda; yet these "old supporting actors" are distinguished from the "fat old whores," and their ambivalent attractions, above all by the complete absence of dirt as well as of rude and aggressive behavior. And it is precisely for this reason that they appear to K. as a definite emetic: "He was nauseated *[ekelte sich]* by the cleanliness of their faces. You could practically still see the cleansing hand that had wiped the corners of their eyes, rubbed their upper lips, scrubbed the folds of their chins" (T, 227). The arrival at the execution site likewise becomes an immediate occasion for "the men" to tidy up: "they . . . wiped the perspiration from their foreheads with their handkerchiefs" (T, 229). No less "nauseating," for K., than their painfully clean appearance are the "courtesies" which these fat tenors continually exchange. At the end, they are seen "leaning cheek-to-cheek" to observe the decision *(Entscheidung)* being carried out on the body of the dying delinquent. As was already the case with the Flogger, this "nauseating" contact of two disgustingly clean male cheeks reveals a more-than-latent homosexuality in the pair of tenors, presented as they are as a unity. This seems to confirm Freud's diagnosis of the anal character of excessive cleanliness even down to its (potential) sexual consequences. The unsheathing *(Ent-Scheidung)* of the knife, which brings the decision *(Entscheidung)*—this cardinal trope of Kafka's poetics that vibrates with the mitigating foretaste of the cut, with the imminence of the caesura—is realized anew. And again, as in "A Fratricide" or the fragment about the execution without witnesses, it is realized through a "nauseating," indeed sadistically and perversely colored celebration of the naked knife edge. It is not just any knife, nor a regular weapon, that the executioners use, but a butcher knife. By this means, once again, the idea of butchering is evoked:

> Then one man opened his frock coat and, from a sheath on a belt that encircled his vest, drew forth a long, thin, double-edged butcher knife, held it up, and tested its sharpness in the light. Once more the nauseating courtesies began, one of them passed the knife across K. to the other, who passed it back over K. (T, 230)

Just as the distinction between clean and unclean is subject to an inverse evaluation (in that precisely the attributes "clean" and "courteous" evoke physical and moral disgust), so, too, the depiction of the fat tenors standing cheek to cheek entails a formal inversion: unlike situations elsewhere in Kafka, where the disgusting is stylistically neutralized and rendered invisible, here the disgusting is not so much obscured as obscuring. For its manifestation neutralizes another sort of knowledge that is no less disturbing: the knowledge, namely, that the cruel executioners are at the same time concealed helpers, who aid K. in recognizing the knife thrust as an ideal "duty." Whereas, earlier in the novel, the topography of the action had involved merely intracity distinctions between disgusting domains of the court and other places not connected with the court, the way from K.'s apartment to the site of the execution brings about K.'s definitive exclusion from the city. The way to the "open fields" and the "small stone quarry," which "almost without transition" leave the city behind (T, 229), at the same time makes it evident that the two repulsive tenors act as midwives to K.'s own will. Their "practiced and irresistible grip" (T, 226) provokes K.'s resistance only briefly; he soon discovers that the *Herren* are quite willing to follow his own lead: "now all three of them, in total accord, crossed a bridge in the moonlight, the men yielding willingly to K.'s slightest move" (T, 228). K. himself seeks to avoid patrolling policemen, instead of looking to them for help. The disgusting tenors thus function as helpers, who enable K. finally to overcome his habitual (inner) resistance. The reappearance of Fräulein Bürstner acts as an additional catalyst: "At that moment, coming up a small flight of stairs to the square from a narrow lane below, Fräulein Bürstner appeared before them" (T, 227). Her strange nocturnal appearance on the street seems to confirm the landlady's suspicions of disreputable conduct; it also recalls Kafka's own account of his covetous glances at "streetwalkers." While K. follows the direction taken by Fräulein Bürstner, the pursuit of the woman suddenly turns into a "reminder" or admonition *(Mahnung)* directed toward himself:

> Now they allowed him to choose the direction they should take, and he chose to follow in the steps of the young woman ahead of them, not because he wanted to catch up with her, and not because he wanted to keep her in sight for as long as possible, but simply not to forget the reminder she signified for him. (T, 227–28)

In a repetition of the beginning—a renewed pursuit of Fräulein Bürstner, of Fräulein "Sexual Intercourse"—K. breaks through resistances to self-knowledge and sees a "reminder" where before was only self-righteousness. This lends credence to the suspicion, as extrapolated from the opening scene, that the slander and guilt—if, in fact, they are more than mere rumor—have to do primarily with K.'s sexual practices and fixations. The impression of a "reminder" issuing from Fräulein Bürstner and the task of following in its path are two sides of the same coin. As in some psychoanalytical Hollywood story line, the breakthrough of knowledge appears immediately to leave its medium behind it and to lead to changed behavior: "In the meantime the young woman had turned into a side street, but K. could do without her now" (T, 228). Yet K.'s "grateful" recognition that "these half-mute, insensitive men [have been sent] to accompany me on this journey, and that it's been left to me to say to myself what is necessary" (T, 228) is not sufficient for the decisive act: the opening of his own breast, the cutting into his own flesh, so as to force "the cursed word from the cursed mouth." If literature is supposed to cut into us like an "axe," is supposed to "wound and stab us," effecting an (ideal) "suicide" (L, 16); if writing can be done only with "a complete opening out of the body" (D, 213), with a "hand that can reach to the body itself and that likes to do so" (D, 214); if the pleasure taken in twisting the knife in one's own heart is the correlate of a successful concentration of the self—the self that shall be "a whole, . . . a knife for butchering," then the possibility emerges that the executioners offer K. nothing less than the chance for an ideal opening and concentration of the self, as they hand the unsheathed knife back and forth across his uncovered body. K. grasps the import of this action, just as he understands Fräulein Bürstner's appearance as a "reminder": "K. knew clearly now that it was his duty to seize the knife as it floated from hand to hand above him and plunge it into himself" (T, 230).

There are other indications that K.'s repulsive "passing" (T, 228) realizes, in the mode of self-concealment and partial failure, Kafka's poetics of flesh, knife, cut, and word. The place where the knife is turned in his heart is a "small stone quarry" (T, 229). The word "stone" is repeated five times in this scene. The two men "[look] about the quarry *[Steinbruch]*," searching "for some suitable spot in the *Steinbruch*" (T, 229–30). The spot they finally discover "was near the quarry wall, where a loose block of stone *[Stein]* was lying. The men sat K. down on the ground, propped him against the stone, and laid his head down on it" (T, 230). In the preparations for the stabbing, then, K. becomes a metonym of the stone: in a stone quarry he lies near the quarry wall on a loose block of stone. He thus has every chance to share in the fabulous transformation of the stab by the stone: "The main thing, when a sword cuts into one's soul, is to keep a calm gaze, lose no blood, accept the coldness of the sword with the coldness of the stone. By means of the stab, after the stab, become invulnerable" (DF, 73). Although lying on a stone in the "cool night air," and surrounded by a stone quarry, K. fails in the task of accepting the coldness of the knife with the coldness of the stone. Or, since there is no mention of blood anywhere in this highly detailed scene, will he perhaps "by means of the stab, after the stab, become invulnerable?" Is he, in the end, a *Doppelgänger* of the dreamer who awakes unhurt with a sword lodged deep in his body? And what of the "light flicking on"—which comes from "the top story of the building adjoining the quarry?" (T, 230). Does this suggestion of a light at the periphery of the locale, a light as it were promising salvation, intimate a redemptive turn at the moment of "decision?"

The ending of *The Trial* seems to offer the language-disclosing configuration of knife and flesh, of stabbing and stone, only to the extent that it conceals this configuration behind fat, disgusting, clean and repulsively courteous "tenors," as well as behind the brutal act of slaughtering K. like an animal. The disgust, which Kafka's own poetics and ethics of butchering, execution, and suicide could arouse, is thus diverted onto the representation of its obstruction and failure. K. does not grab hold of the knife hovering above him, but "instead he twisted his still-free neck and looked about him." The turning of his neck may, in itself, recall Kafka's reflections on the best place to stab: "Between throat and chin would seem to be the most rewarding place to stab. Lift the chin and stick the knife into the tensed muscles. . . . You expect to see . . . a network of sinews and little bones like you find in the leg of a roast turkey" (D, 342). K.'s looking around completely distracts him from the acknowledged "duty" of plunging the knife into his own flesh. It enables a return to his favorite occupation: observing other observers. Just as, in the opening scene, he devotes more attention to the old woman in the window opposite than to his own arrest, so the appearance of a new observer in the window overlooking the quarry is a welcome occasion for an intense flow of questions and hypotheses. The result of these reflections on an unknown observer—"Who was it? A friend? A good person? Someone who cared? Someone who wanted to help? Was it just one person? Was it everyone?" and so forth—is concentrated into one gesture: K. "raised his hands and spread out all his fingers." Like so many other of Kafka's gestures, the spreading out of the fingers has no conventional communicative significance. Nevertheless, by indirect reference to its opposite, it carries a situational semantic charge. In the children's game, the balling of the fist stands for rock; this stone formed of fingers renders one invulnerable to the knife and scissors. In contrast to this gathering of forces into stone, the spreading of the fingers indicates a dispersal of forces. In this regard, it seals K.'s failure to become that stone upon which he lies and, as stone, to accept the stabbing which, as he recognizes, it is his "duty" to inflict on himself. Hence, the spreading of his fingers confirms K.'s skepticism regarding his possibilities: "He could not live up to the occasion; . . . the responsibility for this final failure lay with whoever had denied him the remnant of strength necessary to do so." By no means does K. lament the fact that he lacks the strength to take proper hold of the knife; it is rather "a remnant" of the necessary strength that he lacks. The two men supplement only this "remnant," as they open K.'s body with the unsheathed knife. As in the primal scene of the discovery of literary language, where Kafka holds the word "stigmatize" in his mouth "with disgust and a sense of shame, as though it were raw meat, cut out of me" (D, 62), so the cut into K.'s flesh wrests from him a *"treffendes Wort,"* a phrase that is right to the point—"Like a dog!"—along with the feeling of "shame." The "heavenly dissolution [of tensions]" and "the real becoming-alive" in the literary knife-work are, however, entirely concealed behind the mere slaughter of a putatively innocent victim:

> But the hands of one man were right at K.'s throat, while the other thrust the knife into his heart and turned it there twice. With failing sight K. saw how the men drew near his face, leaning cheek-to-cheek to observe the decision. "Like a dog!" he said; it seemed as though the shame was to outlive him. (T, 231)

What distinguishes the behavior of the executioners—the unempathic, indifferent observation, and the disturbing nearness ("near his face, leaning cheek-to-cheek")—is widely considered as characteristic of Kafka's narrative stance too: detached observation and a minutely detailed, close attention. Moreover, K.'s shame ultimately reflects the fact that he does not so much condemn the behavior of the fat tenors as deplore his own failure. Shame is experienced only in the face of an observer, whose authority is accepted and whose valuation is sought—regardless of whether this position of authority is one's own ideal- or super-ego or some third person. Shame is always shame in the face of a deficiency, a failure, which one discovers in oneself through the medium of another's observation. K.'s shame thus registers, as an affect and a bodily sign, his recognition of not standing the test of the knife hovering over him. Because the two men have to help him by supplementing "the remnant of strength necessary [for the deed]," they become witnesses to his weakness. Even his words spoken during the "decision" scarcely aim at any condemnation of the execution: as dogs are not ceremonially stabbed. K. is not killed or even slaughtered "like a dog"; if anything, he himself behaves "like a dog"—in the proverbial sense of someone who shrinks from making a demanding move, like "a wretched cur." In the concluding formula, K. above all criticizes himself, and in his feeling of shame he acknowledges the claim, the deed, and the observation of the two men. Thus at the end of *The Trial* too—in the form of a disturbing execution without hearing or sentencing, a ritual slaughter of a man performed by "old supporting actors"—there is inscribed an affirmative countercathexis with disgusting caesuras of the body—a body that is not *Gestalt* but first of all cuttable material, and that does not speak figuratively or symbolically but rather in words that are wrested from it through cuts.

In this context, a further reference for the words "Like a dog!" is not to be ruled out—a reference, namely, which furnishes a summary of the figurations of disgusting sexuality. In the famous footnote to *Civilization and its Discontents* in which Freud diagnoses upright posture as the "organic repression" of oral and anal sexuality, and as the means for making excrement and its olfactory stimuli disgusting, he asks at the very end why "man should use the name of his most faithful friend in the animal world—the dog—as a term of abuse."[69] The answer runs as follows: the dog is "an animal whose dominant sense is that of smell and one which has no horror of excrement"; like a child, it is unashamed of its sexual functions. Translated into the register of "normal" sexuality: the dog shamelessly enjoys those oral, anal, and nasal sexual practices which, in the evolution of mankind, have fallen before the barriers of disgust and which, as a result, bear the stigma of perversion. It would follow then that K. in fact behaves as reprehensibly, in his barely illuminated sexual relations, as the imagery at the beginning (including the excessive licking) suggests: he behaves precisely "like a dog." His reactive "shame," then, would be shame at his own shameless transgression of the cultural barriers of disgust.

This "shame" in fact outlives what it has defined as 'reprehensible;' indeed, only *as* the feelings of shame and disgust, only as articulated in the symptoms of shame and disgust, does it outlive what has driven K. and what—perhaps—caused him to be "slandered."

The ending of the story "A Crossbreed" transforms the close of *The Trial* into its opposite and yet continues with the same poetics of the butcher knife. The narrator of this text has inherited, as "a legacy from [his] father," "a curious animal, half kitten, half lamb" (S, 426). Among other characteristics, this animal crosses the line separating "the animal destined for the slaughterhouse" and "the housepet not destined for the slaughterhouse." Kafka's provocative extension of the application of butcher knives and slaughtering knives to the human body finds in the hybridization of this opposition an intra-animal analogue. Whereas the executioners in *The Trial* provide the offender with the remnant of strength necessary for the knife cut, "A Crossbreed" ends with the refusal of this "redemptive" deed: "Perhaps the knife of the butcher would be a release for this animal; but as it is a legacy I must deny it that" (S, 427). Once again, the irony of the talk of "redemption" seems above all designed to conceal a provocative literalness, which is laid bare before the eyes: deceiving without deception. The "heavenly dissolution" which Kafka promised himself from the (literarily) well-aimed cut into his own "raw flesh" is invoked only insofar as it is "denied."

The "Stupidity" of Torture

In many of Kafka's texts, a "knife for butchering" "hovers" over the scene, just as it does over K.'s exposed body in the stone quarry . On many occasions, this hovering of a knife occurs far less visibly, and shuttled back and forth not by fat tenors but by the "knifework" of the sentences themselves. The stabbing power of literature could be conceived in theory as entirely separate from every objectification as knife and cut. Obviously, Kafka does not seek such a separation of form from content, of stylistic-rhetorical methods from the embodiment of these methods. Such separation would have necessarily reduced the passage about the "axe" of literature to one of those "mere" metaphors which make Kafka "despair of writing" (D, 398). Characteristic of many of his works is rather a short-circuit from knife to knife: the categories of his poetics appear constantly and simultaneously as literal objects within the action. This doubling or, stated differently, this implosion of a difference oscillates between emphasizing the underlaying poetics, on the one hand, and concealing it through deceptive reification on the other. In this particular operation (which is always more than motivic), the knife that is brought forth and often actually celebrated can also be replaced by other forms of skin deformation and flaying of a body. Once again, Kafka has confided what is perhaps his most extreme fantasy of mutilation to his diary:

To be pulled in through the ground-floor window of a house by a rope tied around one's neck and to be yanked up, bloody and ragged, through all the ceilings, furniture, walls, and attics, without consideration, as if by a person who is paying no attention, until the empty noose, dropping the last fragments of me when it breaks through the roof tiles, is seen on the roof. (D, 224)

Compared with this, the scenes in which whipping and caning do the torture-work of the knife appear pretty mild.[70] Like the "joy" in the knifecut, the whip, cane, and rod are everywhere subject to a libidinal (counter)cathexis: as obscene objects (the male "cane"), requisites in sadistic torture scenes and occasionally also in the masochistic pleasure in being beaten ("The dream of the sick woman whom I serve in the ambulance and who canes me at my request" (N I, 406). A more specific reading would have to show how the repulsive scenes of whipping and caning likewise serve an enforcement of the *treffendes* word. The rhythm of whipping can even stand for the rhythm and pleasure of writing itself: "the ardor I write with! How the inkspots fly! . . . I delight in cracking the whip and am a man of importance" (LF, 142). This delight in whipping and the obsession with language-compelling torture, Kafka admits, naturally has its stupid and pathetic side:

The stupidity inherent in this (realization of stupidity doesn't help) I once expressed as follows: "The animal wrenches the whip from the master and whips itself so as to become master, and doesn't realize that it's only a fantasy caused by a new knot in the master's thong."/Of course torturing is pathetic, too. Alexander didn't torture the Gordian knot when it wouldn't come untied. (LM, 216; compare DF, 323)

No more than the recognition of stupidity helps against stupidity does the admission of negative attributes counteract the obsession admitted to. Rather, it may be assumed that Kafka considers stupidity and the pathetic to be supplemental and coextensive features of his literature of torture. Stupidity, in this context, may well appear as an element of the action, just as the knife does. Despite all their reflection on specific matters, Kafka's heroes often remain on the whole strikingly naïve and stupid. Precisely in this they attest to the pronounced affinities between Kafka's works and the form of fairy tales. For, as Maria Tatar has noted, stupidity is the basic characteristic of almost all the masculine heroes in the Brothers Grimm's fairy-tale collection. "'Innocent,' 'silly,' 'useless,' 'foolish,' 'simple' and 'guileless': these are the adjectives applied repeatedly to fairy-tale heroes in the Grimm's collection."[71] They would be the least likely to win prizes for "intelligence and good behavior,"[72] rather "the fathers of male heroes are eternally exasperated by the unrivaled obtuseness of their sons. To the question, Who is the stupidest of them all? most fairy-tale fathers would reply: my youngest son."[73] Precisely this dumbest son, then, is consistently chosen to make his way to fortune, for "in fairy tales all over the world, the one least likely to succeed paradoxically becomes the one most likely to succeed . . . fairy tales featuring male protagonists chart the success story of adolescents who lack even the good sense to heed the instructions of the many helpers and donors who rush to their aid."[74] Benjamin has interpreted this stupidity of the fairy tale heroes as a simulation of stupidity, as a "product of the dissolution of wisdom"[75]—a "dialectical" interpretation which is arguably more illuminating for Kafka's "fairy tales," with their complex poetics of deception, than for the traditional tales. Stupidity or "foolishness" is thus one of the themes of the planned, but unrealized revision of Benjamin's great essay on Kafka.[76] Kafka's heroes are intelligent *Dummköpfe* who meet with no success, precisely because, as it seems, they are more intelligent than the heroes of traditional tales and therefore fail to benefit from good advice, not out of any negligence on their part, but on account of the hypertrophied windings of the arguments. And since, in Kafka, the protagonist and the narrative voice, without detriment to all the complex differences and oscillations, for the most part coincide—or at least very effectively give the impression of coinciding—then this type of highly intelligent stupidity and naivete plays an integral part in the unfolding of Kafka's narratives of knives and whips. The same would hold for the pathetic side of torture. Many of Kafka's texts, in their own process of reflection, appear to do precisely what Alexander the Great cleverly avoided doing: unremittingly and desperately torturing the knot that will not "come untied"—as though, by these "stupid" means, a "heavenly dissolution," a "redemption" could be attained.

7.6 THE WOUND IN THE TEXT AND THE TEXT AS WOUND: THE STORY "A COUNTRY DOCTOR"

Cuts into flesh produce wounds, wounds can become infected, and such infection can lead to suppuration and infestation by worms: with this picture of illness, as drawn paradigmatically in the story "A Country Doctor,"[77] Kafka pens a new chapter in his processing of disgust, one powerfully rooted in tradition. The most salient prototype of this picture—the stinking and festering wound of Philoctetes—was the subject of wide-ranging discussion in the authoritative aesthetic-taediological treatises of the eighteenth century. Lessing and Herder agreed that, although Sophocles repeatedly describes the evil smell of Philoctetes' wound as unendurable, the wound is not simply disgusting but rather aesthetically admissable even where disgust is prohibited on principle. For it is no merely physical malady but semantically charged, and thereby weakened in its power to elicit genuin disgust: around the wound a complex social conflict is crystallized, and, in addition, the wound bears witness to divine intervention. In Kafka's "Country Doctor," the wound is rescued from the continent of disgust not first of all through its function but already through its description. The sober, detached gaze of the doctor, who is trained in displacing the barriers of disgust when faced with the sight of opened bodies, frees the reader as well from any exposure to the potential dangers of disgust. The finding of an open wound as big as the palm of a hand, with worms as thick as a finger, is communicated with perfect clinical coolness. At the same time, it is framed by narrative elements which are more likely to call up a faint smile than motions of disgust:

> I went toward [the boy who was lying in bed], he welcomed me smiling as if I were bringing him the most nourishing broth—ah, now both horses were whinnying together; the noise, I suppose, was ordained by heaven to assist my examination of the patient—and this time I discovered that the boy was indeed ill. In his right side, near the hip, was an open wound as big as the palm of my hand. Rose-red, in many variations of shade, dark in the hollows, lighter at the edges, softly granulated, with irregular clots of blood, open as a surface mine to the daylight. That was how it looked from a distance. But on a closer inspection there was another complication. Who could look at that without a low whistle? Worms, as thick and as long as my little finger, themselves rose-red and blood-spotted as well, were wriggling from their fastness in the interior of the wound toward the light, with small white heads and many little legs. Poor boy, you are past helping. I have discovered your great wound; this blossom in your side is destroying you. The family is pleased; it sees me busy; the sister tells it to the mother, the mother the father, the father several guests who are coming in, through the moonlight at the open door, walking on tiptoe, keeping their balance with outstretched arms. "Will you save me?" whispers the boy with a sob, quite blinded by the life within his wound. (S, 223–24)

The grotesque whinnying of the horses and the pleasure registered by the family serve to strengthen the distancing on disgust, a distancing which proceeds mainly from the doctor's reaction: "Who could look at that without a low whistle?" Mentioned before the object it refers to has been specified (other than through the empty deictic "that"), the hypothetical low whistle engages the reader in an effort to imagine possible objects suiting this reaction. The immediately succeeding explanation of "the sight" as "worms" generates a comic gap between the screen set up and the offered object: who gives a low whistle at the sight of an excessively alive wound, abounding with worms? Apart from a loud whistle as an expression of disapproval, whistling almost always has positive connotations. Self-induced whistling is conventionally taken to indicate the presence of a good mood, or light-heartedness; low reactive whistling has reference to phenomena demanding recognition mixed with amazement.[78] It is precisely the erotic variety of reactive whistling, the provocative whistle of admiration as a woman passes by, that belongs to the subtext of the country doctor's behavior. For the predicate first announced in the closer description of the wound ("Rose") is also the name of the "beautiful" servant girl whose assault at the hands of the groom is continually on the mind of the country doctor during his visit to his patient. Even the attribute "beautiful" *(schön)* belongs to the two roses equally: "quite blinded by the life" in the side of his own body, the boy reacts to the "rose-red" wound as though it were an aesthetic illusion, indeed an illumination, and shortly afterward calls it "a beautiful wound." It is beside this second beautiful "Rose" that the doctor is laid in the bed unclothed: The sexual significance of this close contact with a rose-red bodily opening hardly needs pointing out, and the swarm of white worms within it may well signify spermatozoa. As with Baudelaire's "carrion," a "flower" of disgust is cultivated—one charged at the same time with the rich erotic and religious semantics of the rose, in which love and death are interlaced. In contrast to Baudelaire's procedure, however, this counter-cathexis with the disgusting has nothing to do with any provocative satanic pose. Rather, it is presented as a "complicating" circumstance and an innocent misfortune in language transforming the shock, in the wake of such desensitizing, to a 'harmless' pleasure in observation.

In the criticism on "A Country Doctor," the boy's wound has been compared, most prominently, to Kafka's own lung infection, to Felice as the "sore" in his life, and to various wounds carrying a Christian-metaphysical significance (the wound in Jesus's side, Parsifal's wound, and the redeeming cohabitation with a leper in Flaubert's "La Légende de Saint-Julien l'Hospitalier"). The criticism on the story makes no mention of the eighteenth-century aesthetics of the (disgusting) wound, although this aesthetics offers a very useful language for analyzing the effects of Kafka's mode of representation. Not only has the genuinely aesthetic dimension of the wound been overlooked, but also a striking coincidence with a dream text reported in the diaries has seemingly escaped notice before now: in this text Kafka tells of the great "pleasure" he took in "fingering" and pressing "in regular rhythm" the thighs of a prostitute, whose back "was covered with large sealing-wax-red circles with paling edges, and red splashes scattered among them" (D, 72). Three features of this skin eruption converge exactly with the properties of the wound in "A Country Doctor": the basic color red/rose, the lightening toward the edges, and the scattered red splashes across the gradations of red and white. Finally, the ludicrous actions in which the country doctor becomes involved in the remote village—and particularly the half-public bedding down with the wound "Rose"—recall the presence of various other men in Kafka's bordello dream.

Of course, the sexual perverseness of the scene in "A Country Doctor"—an old man lies with a boy who has a female wound—is overlaid with the motivation provided by the story. The doctor does not voluntarily enter the bed of his patient; he is forcibly—although without resistance—undressed by the family members present, carried to the bed, and threatened with a ritual death if he fails to provide healing. The country doctor himself, however, does not dwell on this motivation for long, but instead abandons it without any problem as soon as he realizes he would far rather be back with the other Rose in his own house and his own bed.

The disgusting wound is thus a barely concealed screen memory of something else. Like much in this story, it lends itself, in a directness unusual for Kafka's writings, to an allegorical reading. The disgusting does not simply disappear in such a reading; rather, it is extended and transferred to the "first" Rose. Here, it appears explicitly both as a word and an acting figure: as "the disgusting groom" who brutally assaults the doctor's servant girl. It is this servant girl herself who comes up with the Freudian observation that the groom, apparently "a stranger" who emerges out of nowhere, is a repressed portion of the country doctor himself: "'You never know what you're going to find in your own house,' she said" (S, 220). This remark is framed by accumulating figurations of spatial penetration. Following an emergency ringing of the "night bell," by dint of which the outside invades the interior of the doctor's house, the doctor stands "in the courtyard all ready for the journey," while the servant girl searches through the village for a horse to borrow. The melodramatic effect of the scene depends on the premature appearance of the doctor in the courtyard: a solitary, forlorn hero, "muffled in furs," completely passive, and standing around without any protection in a fierce snowstorm until the busy girl should return. In retrospect, this disfunctional standing about in a snowstowm appears as an phantasmal image of erection, if not ejaculation—just as the appearance of furs in Kafka's writing (including the citation of Sacher-Masoch's *Venus in Furs* in "The Metamorphosis") is always sexually charged. Finally, the girl appears, alone, "in the gateway," without the sought-for horse, and "waved the lantern." The doctor promptly repeats the combination of passage through the gateway and rhythmical waving: in his confused distress he kicks "at the dilapidated door of the yearlong uninhabited pigsty," which flies open, flapping to and fro on its hinges, and gives a view of another swinging lantern. But not only the girl's instrument for signaling is found within the stall; it also harbors what she was vainly looking for—two horses, together with a groom. No sooner are they discovered than the horses pass through the door of the pigsty as through a birth canal:

> Two horses, enormous creatures with powerful flanks, one after the other, their legs tucked close to their bodies, each well-shaped head lowered like a camel's, by sheer strength of buttocking squeezed out through the door hole which they filled entirely. (S, 220)

The (second) birth of the unexpected horses immediately passes over into a vibrating sexual presence: "all at once they stood upright, their legs long and their bodies steaming thickly." These erect horses bring the doctor—who is "deafened and blinded by a storming rush that steadily buffeted all [his] senses"—from one open gateway to the next: "as if my patient's farmyard had opened out just before my courtyard gate, I was already there." Meanwhile, the groom, who has remained behind, breaks down another door in his pursuit of Rose: "I could just hear the door of my house splitting and bursting as the groom charged at it." After this forshadowing of a brutal rape, the text avoids any further direct representation of what happens in the doctor's house. Precisely through this device, the blindspot of the "actual" rape comes like a phantasm to dominate the entire story. The horses, by contrast, do not cease their acts of penetration in place of the doctor: before he can act on his impulse to push open a window, so as to clear the bad air in the sick chamber, the "ungovernable horses" do so—"these horses, now, they have somehow slipped the reins loose, push the windows open from outside, I do not know how; each of them sticking a head in at the window" (S, 222). The horsehead that appears in supernatural fashion in the interior of a room may well—especially since it is expressly compared to a camel's head ("each well-shaped head . . . like a camel's")—allude to another literary phantasm of penetration: to that camel's head in Jacques Cazotte's *Le diable amoureux*, which magically appears in a window and spews forth a white ejaculate.[79] Through a threefold repetition, the mention of the penetrating horses and the recollection of the supposed rape of Rose enter into a stable relation of contiguity. For the country doctor, it is as if the horses' pushing open of the window were summoning him to return to his house and servant girl. Yet soon after the wish to save Rose is sounded—"how could I pull her away from under that groom? . . ."—this altruistic motif is gradually replaced by the mere wish to land, without further ado, in his own bed. Nonetheless, the intention of returning remains stamped by the thought of Rose, so that the desire to jump into his own bed barely conceals a previously repressed claim to possess "the beautiful girl who had lived in my house for years almost without my noticing her."

The story thus appears as the discovery and acknowledgement of the desire to possess Rose, and the lying in bed naked next to a disgusting wound, which is likewise called Rose, appears as the final stage in the censuring of this desire. Suspended between a brutal rape and a perverse bedding down with a rose-colored patch of inflammation full of white worms, the wound lends itself to an allegorical interpretation, which—once again—displaces everything disgusting onto a sexual plane. In the doctor's resolve "to think of rescuing himself" and to "care" not for the present Rose but for the one at home, there briefly appears the possibility of a healing of the wound. Yet precisely this hope is abruptly extinguished: the quick return home which alone could close up the wound turns out to be a torturously slow wandering astray. The leap from anticipation to the reality of the journey toward home and rescue passes over delay and indefinite deferral to the recognition of the impossibility of return: "Never shall I reach home this way" (S, 225). Ruling out the possibility that the nocturnal journey from the site of a disgusting rape to the site of a disgusting wound closes reflectively upon itself through its reversal, the text establishes itself as the law of a festering wound, which knows of crisis and peripateia, to be sure, but not of healing.

From the beginning, the country doctor's awareness of himself exhibits a "vexed" mixture of intellectual superiority—"I am altogether composed and and superior to all [present on the scene]" (S, 224)—and the assumption of the role of victim in his practical existence. The claim of social superiority can take even the extreme form of a sense of one's distinction that verges on disgust: "in the narrow confines of the old man's thoughts"—that is, of the wounded boy's father offering him a glass of rum—the doctor almost physically "felt sick" (S, 222), whereas he is anaesthetized against disgust in the face of the worm-infested wound. The undisguised contempt for the "people ... in my district" (S, 224), for the "limber pack of patients" (S, 225), and the harsh tone taken with the groom—"'You brute,' I yelled in fury, 'do you want a whipping?'" (S, 221)—make appeal to a superiority which nevertheless provides no protection from defeat. Moreover, the doctor's ignorance of the inventory of his own stable reveals the limits of intellectual superiority where a proper recognition of one's own situation is concerned. It is not the doctor but his servant girl who comments, with psychoanalytic acumen, on the secret of the pigsty as the repressed element of the doctor's own psyche. The reaction of the two characters to Rose's Freudian remark—"we both laughed" (S, 220)—clearly brings to light, in the "we both" as subject of a shared laugh, a connection between the doctor and the servant girl which contradicts the doctor's claim to having barely noticed her. The next mention of the servant girl passes from the attribute "willing," ascribed to her from the doctor's perspective, to the wild sexual attacks which the groom initiates without fear of reprisal:

> "Give him a hand," I said, and the willing girl hurried to help the groom with the harnessing. Yet hardly is she beside him when the groom clips hold of her and shoves his face against hers. She screams and flees back to me; on her cheek stands out in red the marks of two rows of teeth. (S, 220–21)

The doctor's intention not to leave the aggressive groom behind with Rose is repulsed by the groom with a laconicism that betrays complete confidence in his own affairs: "I'm staying with Rose." Just before the doctor in his gig is "whirled off" like "a log in a freshet," the situation proceeds to a virtually certain rape scene that, in its imminence, is minutely observed:

"No," shrieked Rose, fleeing into the house with a correct presentiment that her fate was inescapable; I heard the door chain rattle as she put it up; I heard the key turn in the lock; I could see, moreover, how she put out the lights in the entrance hall and in further flight all through the rooms to keep herself from being discovered. (S, 221)

Kafka uses a very inconspicuous word here to nail down the inescapability, indeed to affirm it semantically: Rose's presentiment "that her fate was inescapable" is minimally heightened to a "correct *[richtigen]* presentiment." As a category of judgment, "correct" anticipates a having-already-happened, a sort of future II of what it is a presentiment of, and at the same time it implies an observational perspective which is in a position to make this judgment. Moreover, this perspective—which is that of the country doctor—must be sufficiently detached to react to panicked anxiety with the application of a theoretical judgment on what is "correct" or "faulty," instead of with spontaneous aid or a feeling of sympathy. The word *richtig* ("right" or "correct") itself feels slightly out of place here and, as a semantic irritation, continues the powerful rupture of grammatic tense, which conjoins the attack on Rose with the sudden shift to the present tense, indeed to the very presence of the story. "The willing girl *hurried* to help the groom with the harnessing. Yet hardly *was* she beside him when the groom *clips* hold of her and *shoves* his face against hers."[80] It is only with the word "clips" that the narrative reaches the present level of what actually happens, and from then on it stays with this temporality of the present. The combination of embrace and violence ("shoves") penetrates even the narrative past tense which leads to it. It posits a presence that is endowed with a peculiar duration: the question of whether the rape, which is imminent at the beginning of the story, is still threatening at its end, or else is already accomplished, is effectively left open at the story's close, the narrative present tense thus indefinitely maintaining the imminence of the event. It is this temporal structure which turns the rape into the persistent obsession of the story—the transcendental signified from which the disgusting wound works to distract attention. It is due solely to this indefinite imminence of the presentified violence that the country doctor is able, over and over, to return in his thoughts to the rape as possibly (still) occurring, as a sort of persistent present: "in my house the disgusting groom is raging; Rose is his victim; I do not want to think any further about it" (S, 225). With the irruption of the grammatical present, the raging and the victimization continue throughout the entire story, to outlast even its end. Kafka thus conceives a rape scene that simultaneously threatens to take place, has already occurred, and never ceases to take place. In other words, he conceives it as a structural violence rather than as a unique and temporally fixed act. He achieves this by inscribing the mode of action proceeding from the "disgusting groom" into the narrative structure as a whole. Perhaps there is no other work of fiction that is so thoroughly the story of a rape as Kafka's "Country Doctor" is—and precisely because it maintains the unnarratability of the traumatic "act itself."

The phrase "I do not want to think any further about it" corresponds to a tendency within the story to displace the rape to some place beyond the actually depicted scene. On the other hand, the clause is deceptive with regard to the effect of this fading out. For precisely this fading out of the rape, this putting it outside the scene first allows the doctor and the reader—indeed, compels them repeatedly during the visit to the patient—"to think about" (= *"ausdenken"* in the meaning of imagine) what is happening in the doctor's house, without ever being able to "think it to its final consequences" (= *"ausdenken"* in the meaning of to think to its end). The phrase "I do not want to think any further about it" thus straightforwardly obeys the Freudian law of denial: for the doctor thinks about hardly anything else. And his recurring thoughts disclose strange sorts of phantasms:

> The whole district made my life a torment with the night bell, but that I should have to give up Rose this time as well, the beautiful girl who had lived in my house for years almost without my noticing her—that sacrifice was too much to ask, and I had somehow to get it reasoned out in my head with the help of what sophistries I could muster, in order not to let fly at this family, which with the best will in the world could not restore Rose to me. (S, 223)

Despite the archaic rituals in the sick boy's village, nothing in the story suggests that the modern-minded doctor has ever possessed physical rights over his servant girl. How, therefore, can he imagine himself in the position of "giving up" the girl? And what is the country doctor himself sacrificing if Rose gets raped by someone else? What does it mean that the family gathered around "Rose's" wound "with the best will in the world could not restore Rose to [him]?" Rose's function as servant girl would not necessarily be compromised, or even suspended, by a rape. What cannot be restored to the country doctor must therefore be something else: either the archaic right of the master to dispose over Rose's virginity or else her life. The self-pitying lament for Rose's irretrievable "sacrifice" points to this second possibility, too: and with this, the rape looms as a potential sexual murder. Toward the end of the visit to the patient, however, another idea seems to have emerged. The raging of the groom appears to have first awoken the doctor's claims to sexual possession, and he wishes for a magical transfer out of the sick bed, where he lies naked with the wound named "Rose," into his own bed. In view of the manifest parallel action, the reader may readily supply the unmentioned fourth component of this transfer, the presence of the "first" Rose in his bed at home. But the horses—which, according to the psychological allegory of the beginning, represent repressed libidinal drives in the doctor himself—refuse to cooperate, thus dooming the doctor's "flourishing practice" to ruin and the servant girl to the precivilized raging of that "disgusting groom," who alone disposes over her and who moreover has sprung from the doctor's own long-forgotten "pigsty":

> My clothes, my fur coat, my bag were quickly collected; I didn't want to waste time dressing; if the horses raced home as they had raced on the way here, I should only be springing, as it were, out of this bed into my own. Obediently a horse backed away from the window; I threw my bundle into the gig; the fur coat missed its mark and was caught on a hook only by the sleeve. Good enough. I swung myself onto the horse. With the reins loosely trailing, one horse barely fastened to the other, the gig swaying behind, my fur coat last of all in the snow. "Gee up!" I said, but there was no galloping; slowly, like old men, we crawled through the snowy wastes; a long time echoed behind us the new but faulty song of the children: "O be joyful, all you patients,/The doctor's laid in bed beside you!"
> Never shall I reach home at this rate.... Naked, exposed to the frost of this most unhappy of ages, with an earthly vehicle, unearthly horses, old man that I am, I wander astray. My fur coat is hanging from the back of the gig, but I cannot reach it, and none of my limber pack of patients lifts a finger. (S, 225)

By means of their names—"Hey there, Brother, hey there, Sister!" (S, 220)—and by means of their function—which is to appear at just the right moment to fill a need on the part of the protagonist—the horses are initially introduced as the sort of helper animals one finds in fairy tales. But this role is increasingly overlaid by mythical features until it turns into the opposite. The "hero's" complete lack of control over the horses from the beginning on does not fit in with their status as magical helpers. Further, the fact that the groom demands the servant girl as "payment" corresponds to a mythical model of exchange more than to the model of happiness in the fairy tales. In these latter, heroes must usually display certain virtues, but they never pay for the help they get. As a matter of fact, there are quite concrete mythological reminiscences attaching to the groom who emerges from the pigsty and who lays claim to the doctor's "beautiful girl" as though he were fully justified in doing so. He is another Heracles who, after cleaning the gigantic pigsty of King Augeas, claims the king's (evidently promised) daughter and, as a punishment for not receiving her, wreaks havoc on Augeas's whole kingdom. Even more clearly, the "unearthly horses" show signs of mythical origins. In Plato's image of the chariot of the soul, which likewise consists of two horses and a driver, only one of the horses opposes the will of the driver with its violence and ungovernable sexual appetite; the other horse, by contrast, is cooperative and aids in the work of taming the instincts. In what is clearly a darkening of this model, the country doctor has to drive a chariot of the soul pulled by two "ungovernable horses."[81] This particular situation has its mythic prototype in another team of horses: those drawing the chariot of the sun which Zeus allows Phaethon to drive for one day. The "unearthly horses" of this carriage, as Phaethon's divine father Phoebus Apollo had urgently warned, prove altogether too much for the boy's powers. The uncontrolled chariot exposes the whole earth to a scorching, and Phaethon himself is fatally burned by a lightning bolt. In an exact reversal of these thermal aspects, the country doctor's team of horses is associated with an epochal frost ("the frost of this most unhappy of ages"), and they lead the country doctor, naked and unprotected, into "snowy wastes," from which there is no returning home for him. Beyond this negative correlation, there is a positive resemblance between Phaethon and the country doctor in the shared motif of "false" ambition: Phaethon is looking for an infallible proof of his divine origins and he dies in finding it; the country doctor everywhere asserts his intellectual superiority and yet falls victim to his patients, the groom, and the horses. Kafka heightens the loss of control in an image so full of disintegration that it affects even the syntax. As the country doctor, instead of climbing into the gig, swings himself onto one of the horses, it reads: "With the reins loosely trailing, one horse barely fastened to the other, the gig swaying behind, my fur coat last of all in the snow." This sentence no longer has a subject or predicate: it enumerates agrammatically the elements of a self-dissolving connection. The sorrowful rider, in this grotesque defiguration, mutates at the end into another "old man," who likewise "wander[s] astray" in a false age—into a Don Quixote, who is taken for a fool by his squire as by his horse, and whose erotic ambitions fall completely flat. The text can thus close on a note which emphasizes the doctor's role as victim, and in this way bringing together doctor and servant girl, if not yet in bed, then in shared victimhood: "Betrayed! Betrayed! A false alarm on the night bell once answered—it cannot be made good, not ever" (S, 225). This image of being confined to eternal and senseless wandering reactivates the same Ahasverus-topos by means of which Kafka had characterized his compelling "desire for . . . a very specific abomination" in terms of "some sulphur, some hell" within the sexual: "This urge had in it something of the eternal Jew, being senselessly drawn, wandering senselessly through a senselessly obscene world" (LM, 163–64).

The final turning in the narrative of the country doctor clearly does not bring the action to any resolution. It arbitrarily breaks off the description of the straying in the cold in favor of a reflective lament that is unconcerned about its own untenability. Despite the doctor's temporary fears, the ringing of the night bell was in this case certainly no "false alarm"; rather, a patient had sustained a "great wound." Nor was the doctor "betrayed" by the groom, who made his intentions *vis-à-vis* Rose quite clear. If anyone is "betrayed," it's the reader, who goes along with the doctor's oft-repeated claim to be a victim, even though the text, in keeping with the poetics of deceiving without deception, itself gives the lie to this deception. For that part of the doctor which emerges from its repression into the pigsty enjoys a lasting triumph in the end and lives out his "disgusting" sexual "raging," in a manner both unconstrained and fully unconcerned for the functioning of his practice. Even the socialized part of the doctor, the part that is dispatched on journeys, discovers unexpected forms by which to articulate its sexual desires.[82] The naked ride through the cold is in fact another of those elements which read almost like citations from Freudian psychoanalysis.[83]

"Dreams of being naked," Freud succinctly concludes, "are *dreams of exhibiting*."[84] They refer phylogenetically back to Paradise and ontogenetically back to childhood: "We can observe how undressing has an almost intoxicating effect on many children even in their later years, instead of making them feel ashamed. . . . When we look back at this unashamed period of childhood, it seems to us a Paradise; and Paradise itself is no more than a group fantasy of the childhood of the individual. That is why mankind were naked in Paradise and were without shame in one another's presence; till . . . expulsion followed, and sexual life and the tasks of cultural activity began. But we can regain this paradise every night in our dreams."[85] This regaining of paradise is made possible by the conservative tendency of the libido never quite to give up the sources of pleasure once enjoyed but instead to seek their repetition by assimilating them to new conditions. In the case of "perverse" exhibitionists, the "infantile impulse is raised to the status of symptom," insofar as this impulse is fixed in its childhood form. In the case of "normal" development, pleasurable exhibition of oneself without clothes is not only displaced into the dream but is also deprived of its happy shamelessness. Thus the dream of exhibiting oneself simultaneously brings to "language," in its repetition of childhood pleasure, the very "repression" which it partly overcomes; this is the price that must be paid in recompense for "the content of the scene of exhibiting having found expression in spite of the ban upon it."[86] Those to whom the exhibition is actually addressed are generally replaced by an anonymous crowd, who show no interest at all in the nakedness:

> I know of no instance in which the actual spectators of the infantile scenes of exhibiting have appeared in the dream. . . . What takes their place in dreams—"a lot of strangers" who take no notice of the spectacle that is offered—is nothing more nor less than the wishful contrary of the single familiar individual before whom the dreamer exposed himself. . . . For obvious reasons, the presence of "the whole family" in a dream has the same significance.[87]

The story "A Country Doctor" combines both models of displacement. Here too, a "whole family" is present at the disrobing of the doctor but, since this whole family is not that of the bachelor-doctor, the onlookers at the same time are "a lot of strangers" drawn from the "limber pack of patients." Among the members of the family gathered in its entirety, there is not the slightest sign of any erotic interest in the doctor's nakedness. Rather, the disrobing appears as a purely practical measure undertaken to keep the doctor in the bed of his patient until he should have healed him and, at the same time, to underline the seriousness of the threat: "If he doesn't heal, kill him dead!" (S, 224). The active exhibitionism is thus turned into a less shocking passive disrobing. However, the doctor's surprising refusal even to throw his clothes over himself for the homeward journey—something explained by the urgency of the situation and his expectation of a speedy journey through the snow—reveals the part played by the doctor himself in his exhibition. The doctor feels no shame in the presence of the onlookers. The censure is embodied in the unexpected retardation of the motion instead: the all-surpassing speed of the horses is reduced to a torturously slow crawl.

According to Freud, the "feeling of being inhibited . . . serves admirably in dreams to represent a *conflict in the will* or an act of saying 'no.'"[88] Freud reports on one of his own dreams in which he was very incompletely dressed and was going upstairs from an apartment on the ground floor to a higher story. The situation in the dream corresponds to that of his actual living arrangements, in which his living rooms and his consulting room were one floor apart in the same building. As a rule, he would take the public staircase separating the two floors in a few quick bounds: "I usually go upstairs two or three steps at a time; and this was recognized in the dream itself as a wish fulfillment."[89] In Kafka's "Country Doctor," this speed is fabulously heightened. Thanks to the two horses, "ten miles" is covered as quickly as the short staircase between two floors in Freud's dream. In Freud's case, an inhibition of his usual speediness—indeed, a sensation of being glued to the spot and unable to move—sets in at the very moment when a "maidservant" is coming down the stairs toward him. The same "feeling of being inhibited" that is stamped as "painful" by the claims of the censoring instance thus paradoxically serves to prolong the exhibition. It performs the trick of saying "no" and at the same time affirming what is being negated in its desire for continuation. Kafka fabulously heightens both sides of the conflict. The inhibition embodied in the prolongation of the motion over the snow already announces itself telepathically as the doctor is still ten miles away from the servant girl, hence long before Rose can ever see him riding naked on horseback. At the same time, his exhibition of himself is literally prolonged to infinity. It becomes absolute in a double sense: it has no temporal limit any more, but also no witnesses, no present object at which it is directed any longer. It neither ceases at any point nor begins at any point to be an exhibition. The indefinite deferral of the object, the "painful sensation" of never being able to reach his own bed (and Rose) back at home, is, however, countered not only by the paradisical prolongation of nakedness. For the old man's obscene riding about in Adamic attire may itself already symbolize a more than exhibitionistic reference to the (absent) object of desire: "rhythmic activities like *dancing, riding,* and *climbing*" are, according to Freud, predestined "representations of sexual intercourse."[90]

As the doctor slowly rides naked through the snow, he remains for a long time within hearing of the patient's village: "a long time echoed behind us the new but faulty song of the children: 'O be joyful, all you patients,/The doctor's laid in bed beside you!'" This strange song not only signals the lack of any forward progression by doctor and horses. It also forms a link back to the doctor's initial departure. For the adjective "faulty" *(irrtümlich)* negatively reflects the "correct *(richtig)*" used as the doctor rides off. It may be that these two adjectives—each in itself slightly out of place, although not logically incorrect—have their significance only in this opposition: Rose's presentiment of her unavoidable rape is "correct," whereas the assumption that the doctor's lying naked beside the wound "Rose" is the *skandalon* of the action is "faulty." This rectification appears necessary, for what "the disgusting groom" carries out is largely covered over by the archaic rites celebrated at the site of the disgusting wound. With this attribution of *richtig* and *irrtümlich,* the story expressly helps the reader in "correctly" identifying its prime disgusting matter. This is to be found, accordingly, not (so much) in the physical wound of the boy as in the repellent sexual practices, or wishes, of the doctor.

Considered as the protagonist of an allegorical psychomachy, the country doctor splits into a furious rapist—which he had kept repressed too long in his "pigsty"—and an inhibited exhibitionist. At the same time, however, the story succeeds in presenting the same country doctor as a plausible victim of hostile opponents and ungrateful patients, as a forlorn fairy-tale hero who, in solitude and without reliable helpers, is "exposed to the frost of this most unhappy of ages": "Betrayed! Betrayed! A false alarm on the night bell once answered—it cannot be made good, not ever." As narrated from the perspective of the country doctor, the story thus realizes Kafka's poetic "project" of deceiving without deception: the country doctor openly acts out his "inherent baseness" while yet retaining a claim "to be pleasing to everyone," and even to be "the only sinner not to be roasted." For eighteenth-century aesthetics, the disgusting was that which remained inaccessible to every aesthetic illusion and which without fail produced the impression of the real. For its part, this impression of the real could well be an illusion—no longer an aesthetic illusion, of course—since what produced the impression might just as well be entirely fictive as "real." Kafka derives a new variant of this complex configuration of disgust, aesthetic illusion, and non-aesthetic illusion. He discreetly credits, for the benefit of himself and his heroes, the presentation of disgusting practices and disgusting thoughts as proof of courageous self-analysis, and he makes use in this way of the transaesthetic affinity between the disgusting and the real as itself a stylistic effect. At the same time, he renders the roles of perpetrators and victims interchangeable and, to the end of redeeming openly committed "vices," he adopts what aesthetics had affirmed as disgust's indifference to the distinction between real and unreal. Thus, what is (potentially) disgusting can be used for literary strategies of deceiving, even though—or precisely because—on an aesthetic level the disgusting does not admit of deception.

As far as "A Country Doctor" is concerned, one of the models for the working of deception consists in the text's tendency to lend itself to psychoanalytic interpretation. Opportunities for such interpretation are openly and unequivocally presented—and precisely in this way enfeebled. The psychoanalytic perspectives on the country doctor's "baseness" may well be adequate and perfectly justifiable, yet their display as a kind of citation, their blatant application as ready-made frameworks of discourse, detracts from their plausibility. The doctor's self-righteousness, which, in its mixture of intellectual arrogance and lament for his own victimization, sets its seal on the narrative voice, is therefore not lastingly shattered by the psychological allegory. The allegorical interpretations offered by the text, on the one hand, and the protagonist's perspective, on the other, describe eccentric paths which never coincide. And only for this reason can the wound that does not close up serve as a model for Kafka's texts. The story of the country doctor unfolds between two sites whose intercommunication has been disturbed, and between two elements of action whose parallelism prevents any saving intervention from either side: the journey to the worm-inflicted "Rose" does no good for the latter, while simultaneously it provokes ample space and time for the imminent rape of the Rose on whom the "disgusting groom" has been inflicted. Other texts, too, could be read along these lines—that is, according to the model of an infliction of a wound against which any counteraction is thwarted. In Kafka's texts, there is always something that, from the beginning, "can never be made good"—whether this goes by the name of false alarm, defamation, seduction, metamorphosis, or something else. All petitions, accounts, and elaborated lines of reflection run aground on the massif of this wound and become, in turn, a traumatized tissue of text. "A Country Doctor" still knows of the Homeric motif of the return home to save the "girl" at home from her false suitors. But in the quixotic foundering of the *nostos*—the doctor at the end wanders hopelessly astray in a no-man's-land between Rose and Rose—the story refuses the reflective appropiation of the wound by means of 'dialectically' making its way through its externalization back to the doctor's home. The heroes of Kafka's novels learn to give up the project of return or "acquittal" in favor of more modest efforts, which aim at lowering the level of infection but no longer at healing the wound of the text. The lawyer's negotiations with the Chief Clerk of the Court cannot cause the charge to be dropped or the process of the case to take a positive turn; at the most, the successful outcome of these negotiations could be regarded, "to use a surgeon's expression, . . . as a clean wound and one could await further developments with an easy mind" (T, 122). By the same token, the idea of acquittal recedes, leaving behind merely the hope for an indefinite postponement of the judgment—a postponement which eternalizes the imminence of the execution, just as the endlessly deferred return of the country doctor eternalizes the rape of Rose. Kafka could thus look back on a developed poetics of the open wound, as he saw in the irreversible outbreak of his own "lung wound" a physical "emblem" of his existence and his writing.[91]

7.7 Beer Drinking Hearse Drivers and Cheerful Gravediggers

"I have discovered your great wound; this blossom in your side is destroying you" (S, 223). This sentence pronounced by the country doctor holds for many, if not all, of Kafka's protagonists: their appearance in his works stands under the sign of knives that are always already drawn somewhere, of irreversible wounds, metastases, and obsessions, of "unnatural" kinds of death (execution, murder, suicide) that are imminent from the start and often enough brought to pass. More than once, Kafka characterized his pleasure in the representation of death as a chief ingredient in his "construction" of the writer: "the best things I have written . . . always deal with the fact that someone is dying" (D, 321; L, 334). This "game" played with dying—"in the death enacted I rejoice in my own death" (D, 321)—has little in common with a romantic poetry of decay. Kafka's dying figures never pass over into the state of efflorescent carrion. As quasi-surgical material for cutting and caesuras, or else as dessicated, insubstantial hunger-bodies, they hardly evoke associations with disgusting decomposition. There is likewise no hint of any provocative diabolicism in the well-concealed pleasure taken in dying.[92] In view of all the many real and near-real corpses in his works, Kafka may be said to demonstrate precisely that capability which he denied to himself in periods of interrupted or suspended writing: "I ought to be able to invent words capable of blowing the odor of corpses in a direction other than straight into my own and the reader's face" (D, 29).

It is only in Kafka's posthumously published notebooks that one finds the beginnings of stories which literally and directly transmit the odor of corpses. Drivers of hearses and gravediggers are the heroes of these fragments. They expressly carry out the overcoming of taboos on contact which are based in the feeling of disgust—an overcoming, indeed, that is always already the implicit effect, the proper register of Kafka's mode of presentation:

> A hearse was driving around the countryside, it had a corpse aboard, but it did not deliver it to the cemetery, the driver was drunk

and believed he was driving a coach, but where he was supposed to be driving this coach was something he had forgotten too. So he drove through the villages, stopping at the taverns, and, when now and then his worry about his destination flashed upon him in his drunkenness, hoping that sometime good people would tell him all he needed to know. In this way he once stopped outside the Golden Cockerel and had roast pork ... [the text breaks off here, W. M.]. (DF, 298)

Twenty little gravediggers, none larger than an average pine cone, form an independent group. They have a wooden hut in a mountain glen, and there they rest from their heavy labors. There is much in the way of smoking, shouting, and singing to be found in this hut in the woods, as there is anywhere twenty workers get together. How cheerful these people are! No one pays them, no one equips them, no one has commissioned work for them. On their own initiative they have chosen their job, on their own initiative they perform it. (N 2, 363)

Hearse drivers who order roast pork, unpaid gravediggers who are cheerful: like the writer, these figures engage in a very peculiar relation to the corpse, one which precisely in bordering on the disgusting—as in the crossing of hearse and roast pork—exhibits a cheerful freedom from disgust. With the detail of "vultures' beaks instead of noses," the description of the gravediggers even alludes to the physical consumption of carrion.[93] Furthermore, the gravedigger's children provide Kafka with the opportunity to place contact with the abject under the deceptive sign of childlike "innocence" and lack of disgust. According to secular and religious ordinance, the corpse should be conveyed underground as soon as possible, since in it the body is both disfigured and desymbolized; not so in the case of the gravedigger's children:

Once, a coffin with a corpse in it lay beside us the whole night long—I no longer remember why. For us gravedigger's children, coffins were nothing unusual, we gave little thought, as we fell asleep, to the fact that a corpse lay in the same room with us.

When I awoke one night, an open coffin was standing in the middle of the room. From my bed I could see that an old man with a long white parted beard lay inside. (N 1, 420)

In the mode of 'pure,' indifferent observation, these scenes from the perspective of children—with their habitual cancellation of defense reactions—at the same time present an allegory of Kafka's writing. The catalogue of the classical emblems of disgust is thereby complete: disgusting old women, disgusting foods, open wounds and unburied corpses—everything offensive to aesthetics becomes, in Kafka, by means of the anaesthetizing of defense mechanisms, the innocent obsession of literature. Concealed in invisible visibility—the counterpart of the visible invisibility of the "soul" in the formal model of aesthetics—the repudiated not only circulates through the text in the form of abject matters, but it also determines the entire register of its mode of representation. "Writers speak a stench" (D, 12)—yet at the same time they transport us into a time before the invention of stench and into an order of things where nothing is sweeter than stench.

7.8 "Horrible Words" and Kafka's Physiology of Writing

In vague affinity with the semantics of disgust in Nietzsche and Freud, although in distinct contrast to Kafka's poetological engagement with the disgusting, the early twentieth-century's skepticism toward language denounced words as disgusting distortions of the authentic being of things and experiences: "O let the words go, they are harpies,/strewing disgust on life's blossoms!"[94] Just as civilized modern man's disgust effectively denies his beast-of-prey nature (Nietzsche), or censures his archaic libidinal impulses (Freud), so civilization's symbolic medium par excellence—language—is suspected of making all meanings and all reference disgusting. A few years after Nietzsche, Hofmannsthal also bore witness to a "great disgust," a disgust with language itself:

> People in fact are tired of listening to talk. They are profoundly disgusted with words. For words have usurped the place of things. Hearsay has swallowed up the world. The infinitely complex lies of time, the musty lies of tradition, the lies of offices, the lies of individuals, the lies of sciences—it all rests like myriad deadly flies upon our poor life. . . . Words do not lend themselves [to serving our purposes] but rather drain all our life away, just as, according to Goethe, women do to certain men. When we open our mouth to speak, always thousands of the dead speak with us.[95]

The famous crisis of language, announced by Lord Chandos, consists precisely in this: the consciousness that all words, and abstract words in particular, are merely "matters devoid of being" which crumble to dust "in the mouth like decaying mushrooms."[96] A disgust-based rule for the avoidance of contact is applied to the medium of language, and hence leads to a disruption of communication: "it . . . gradually became more difficult for me . . . to take into my mouth the words that everyone is in the habit of using without thinking."[97] Words are disgusting because they are *common*, in a double sense. First, they are common to virtually all people, and, second, insofar as they are imagined as concretely circulating things, they bring us into contact with numberless mouths—dead mouths included—which might elicit disgust. E. M. Cioran later gave expression to this type of disgust with words:

> There is something which rivals the basest whore in being dirty, worn, defeated . . . the *word*, any word. . . . They are tossed to us prechewed: yet we would not dream of swallowing food already masticated by others. The material aspect of speaking makes us vomit. A brief moment of speaking suffices to realize, under any word, an aftertaste of someone else's saliva.[98]

Language is disgustingly common, moreover, because it buries all that is individual under its worn-out generality and, instead of "truly" referring to something, puts into circulation only the "lies" of its own mediality. For this form of disgust as well, a female figure serves as emblem: not the whore touched and used by all, but the Harpies robbing or sullying all. Hofmannsthal evokes the monstrous, bird-like women—whose name means "those who rob, snatch up, and plunder"[99]—as a figure for the robbing of life by the generalizing act of signification. At the same time, he makes use of the association with excrement and defilement, an association found in the mythological account of the plaguing of Phineus: the Harpies leave behind their excrement on his banquet table. According to this logic, the words—*all* words—are disgusting *vetulae*: worn out prostitutes or contaminating harpies. No less an authority than Goethe is adduced to argue that the use of words brings about the same "draining away" of life that "certain men" experience in their relations to women. The close connection between the idea of disgust and the idea of woman is highlighted through the fact that even a quasi-transcendental critique of the generality of words has immediate recourse to the figure of abject women, the moment its argument touches on the affective value of disgust.

Fritz Mauthner has taken up Hofmannsthal's identification of the generality of words with their disgusting commonness, and shifted it out of the field of sexual politics to that of class politics. As a "common property," language is communism in action. To be sure, the inhabitants of cities also share the "poisoned light" coming from gas piping, the "contaminated water" coming from lead pipes, and the canals and fields irrigated with all sorts of "refuse." But the "charcoal fumes" and the "swamp water" at least need to be paid for according to the respective individual consumption. It is otherwise, and worse, in the case of language:

> In its rusty piping, light and poison, water and pestilence flow together, continually splashing aimlessly from the joints and inundating humanity; the whole of society is nothing more than a giant free-flowing fountain for this hodge-podge, every single person is a

gargoyle, and from mouth to mouth the turbid source spews forth, intermingling its pregnant and contagious, but unproductive and vile streams, and in the midst of it all there is no property and no law and no authority. Language is a common property. Everything belongs to everyone—everyone bathes in this common property, everyone drinks it, and everyone emits it.[100]

In Hofmannsthal's early work, the vileness of common sewer- and harpy-words is immediately opposed to the linguistic achievement of the great artist. This latter is capable of effacing the traces of disgusting common usage and restoring language to its function of "pure revelation": "He has finally trampled to death the myriad dead, and when he speaks, he speaks in his own right. Through his voice words regain their elementary power: they are armed tooth and nail, they entice like a smile or a gaze, and they become pure sensuous revelations of inner being. In his eloquence the soul comes to the fore like a bodily being."[101] By the time *The Lord Chandos Letter* is composed, this optimism has faded. Ranged against the tendency of language to make all "life" disgusting is only a speechless vision of the objects of daily life. The examples invoked are distanced as far as possible from the "commonness" of the city; they breathe the promise of pristine country life: "a watering can, a harrow left standing in the field, a dog in the sun, a rundown churchyard, a cripple, a small farmhouse—any of these can become the vessel for my revelation."[102] The letter attempts to describe more closely only one particular "vessel" filled with such "a prodigal surge of a more exalted life . . . that it beggars all words." As a verbalization of the transverbal purity and density of experience, this description is ensnared in a palpable contradiction: "But why resort to words again, the very words I have forsworn!" As if to do justice to this medial paradox, on the part of the subject matter serving as an example, too, Hofmannsthal chooses, as the cardinal paradigm of a "more exalted life" uncontaminated by words, the death throes of poisoned rats. Beyond the harpy-words that arouse disgust, even rats—the prototypical object of disgust—can become the "vessel" of a "pure sensuous revelation of inner being":

> Not long ago, for example, I ordered that a generous amount of poison be set out for the rats in the milk-cellars of one of my dairy farms. I then went out riding toward evening, thinking, as you can imagine, nothing further of the matter. Yet as I was cantering across the soft, newly turned soil of the fields, with nothing more ominous in sight than a startled brood of partridges and the large, setting sun in the distance above the rolling landscape, that cellar, crowded with the death throes of a swarm of rats, suddenly opened up inside me. All of it was there within: the cool, dank cellar air, pregnant with the sweetish, biting smell of the poison; the high-pitched death screams

echoing off mildewed walls; the contorted spasms of unconsciousness; all the confused and frenzied dashing about; the crazed search for exits; and the cold leers of rage when two of the beasts collided at a blocked crevice.[103]

This vision confirms Mendelssohn's theorem that the disgusting always produces an effect of the real, thus erasing the difference between its mere imagination, or artificial representation, and a genuine contact with its scandalous "nature." The rat-poisoning lord procures for himself, by merely *imagining* the creatures' death throes, a "vessel" that exalts him above all his doubts concerning the words' disgusting theft of reference and makes possible an uncontaminated "feeling": "It was both a good deal more and much less than pity: an overpowering empathy *[Anteilnehmen]*, a kind of flowing over into the hearts of those creatures."

Kafka found the "rat's nest" not in one of his dairy farms but in the "abominations" of his own self. In this regard, the rats which occasionally cross the paths of the heroes in his novels resemble the signature appearance of Alfred Hitchcock at inconspicuous spots in his films. From the observation of this rat's nest Kafka likewise expected a pleasure of a certain sort—that is, insofar as the self-regarding writer is "merely a construction of the craving for pleasure." But this pleasure has more in common with the "wallowing of a pig in muck" than with the "empathy" and "overpowering" feeling of communion experienced by a lord of the manor on the occasion of a mass death he has himself arranged. In particular, Kafka has nothing to do with the fundamentalist critique of the social constructedness of all communications media, understood as the "common" theft of all pure reference and all unfeigned "life." What is disgusting, in his mind, are not words per se, as they get chewed up and spat out by all and sundry, but always only specific, individual speech acts. And what is "repulsive" about them is to be found not in the defilement and dissimulation of a purity and aliveness ascribed to some preexistent signified, but rather in the performative disclosure of something disgusting which, without the words, would remain hidden. Kafka therefore considers observations on the "weakness of language" to be "quite fallacious." It sounds like a credo, maintained in opposition to the sort of *Sprachkritik* exemplified by Hofmannsthal or Mauthner, when he goes on to say:

> What is clear within is bound to become so in words as well. That is why one need never worry about language, but at the sight of words may often worry about oneself. After all, who knows within himself how things really are with him? This tempestuous or floundering or morasslike inner self is what we really are, but by the secret process by which words are forced out of us, our self-knowledge is brought to light, and though it may still be veiled, yet it is there

before us, wonderful or terrible to behold./So protect me, dearest, from these repulsive *[widerlichen]* words of which I have recently been delivering myself. (LF, 198)

Accordingly, all speaking, in the face of all resistance, is always also an "it speaks," a secret "being-forced-out" of words, an ungovernable medium of a "self-knowledge" accessible neither to pure intention nor to wordless perception. This psychoanalytic model of a structural unconscious of language subverts the theorem of a disgusting absence of reference on the part of the word-harpies and ennobles the "repulsive words" precisely as a symptom of the real. Of course, Kafka's poetics does not come to rest with this optimistic credo: rather, it looks for "expedients," by which immediately to reconvert the "fact" of self-knowledge into a "goal" once again, because it is only under this condition that writing can turn the "openly" acted-out "baseness" into a source of "guiltless enjoyment." Instead of a disgustingly common withdrawal of "life," the words thus demonstrate a double power: they unconsciously force out a "self-knowledge" which, in the interests of "life," they simultaneously obscure.

In this context, Kafka's phrase about the correlative clarity of words and what is within precisely serves to obscure something "repulsively" real, the scandal of which the latter states as follows: "The other day I wrote some offensive things about Lasker-Schüler and Schnitzler." The incriminated words run as follows:

> I cannot bear [Lasker-Schüler's] poems; their emptiness makes me feel nothing but boredom, and their contrived verbosity nothing but repulsion. Her prose I find just as tiresome and for the same reasons; it is the work of an indiscriminate brain twitching in the head of an overwrought city-dweller. But I may be quite wrong; many people love her, including Werfel, who talks of her with genuine enthusiasm. Yes, she is in a bad way; I believe her second husband has left her; they are collecting for her here, too; I had to give five kronen, without feeling the slightest sympathy for her. I don't quite know why, but I always imagine her simply as a drunk, dragging herself through the coffeehouses at night. . . . Away with you, Lasker-Schüler! (LF, 191)[104]
>
> [Schnitzler's] great plays and his great prose are full of a truly staggering mass of the most sickening drivel. It is impossible to be too hard on him. . . . Only when looking at his photograph—that bogus dreaminess, that sentimentality I wouldn't touch even with the tips of my fingers—can I see how he could have developed in this way from his partly excellent early work *(Anatol, La Ronde, Lieutenant Gustl)*. (LF, 193)

Felice must have responded with open perplexity to these violent attempts to inoculate her too with disgust at any contact with Lasker-Schüler and Schnitzler. Kafka reacts promptly with a mixture of childlike cry for help and methodical self-belittlement. To be sure, the negative judgments are obstinately adhered to ("How very right I was!"), but their expression is deplored as self-defiling. In a bold turnabout, Felice is summoned to make good once again the injuries he has done:

> Help me, dearest, I beg you, to put right the damage I have done in the last few days.... So protect me, dearest, from these repulsive words of which I have recently been delivering myself. Tell me that you understand it all, and yet go on loving me. The other day I wrote some offensive things about Lasker-Schüler and Schnitzler. How very right I was! And yet they both soar like angels over the abyss in which I lie prostrate. (LF, 198)

In this connection, the argument that inner clarity "is bound" to produce clarity in words as well serves simply to obscure all clarity about Kafka's "repulsive words." The affirmation of such clarity and the unequivocal avowal of his own degradation indeed simulate the gesture of penitent confession. But the rhetorical work of the letter aims to apply to himself only the exonerating negation of the anti-Hofmannsthal credo. If "what is clear within" makes possible clarity in language as well, then the reverse must hold: what is unclear in language refers to what is unclear within. And this, from the start, is Kafka's way out:

> I am driven by this feeling of anxiety in the midst of my lethargy, and I write, or fear I may at any moment write, irresponsible things. The wrong sentences lie in wait about my pen, twine themselves around its point, and are dragged along into the letters. (LF, 198)

If "wrong sentences" "lie in wait" about Kafka's pen and can be "dragged along into the letters," then, in the context of the optimistic theorem about clarity, this presupposes that there is in fact no inner clarity—and consequently no negative clarity either—that would merit unequivocal "disgust." Given the heroic credo—"I am not of the opinion that one can ever lack the power to express perfectly what one wants to write or say" (LF, 198)—a very specific, exonerating chain of reasoning then follows:

- Major premise: wrong sentences lie in wait about my pen and can be dragged into my letters.
- Minor premise: this cannot be due to any lack of expressive power.
- Conclusion: I am therefore lacking in clarity about what I want to write or say.

Instead of meriting Felice's criticisms of a manifest "baseness," Kafka manages, by such reasoning, to voice a claim for help in the difficult task of alleviating his own "chaos" *(Verwirrung)*: "When I look into myself I see so much that is obscure and still in flux that I cannot even properly explain or fully accept the dislike I feel for myself."

The stumbling block—"the damage I have done in the last few days"—is thus openly conceded, only to be immediately covered with a smokescreen. According to Hofmannsthal and Mauthner, *all* words defile true reference, since they are taken into the mouth and cast out in common and indistinct ways. This generalized disgust with language would make it unnecessary—and even impossible—for Kafka to claim, or indeed to produce, an excuse bearing specifically and exclusively on what is "repulsive" in his words only. It follows that Kafka also rejects the prostitute- and harpy-theory of language, the transcendental word-disgust propounded by Hofmannsthal and Mauthner, because it would preclude any possibility of polarizing the individual ways by which "words are [secretly] forced out of us," according to whether they are "splendid" or "repulsive,"—with the "chaos" looming at every point as a *tertium datur*. Insofar as his own words are concerned, the transition between the two poles is often a matter of only a small step. This corresponds to the (unresolvable) doubleness of self-abjection as "truth" and "method." At recurring intervals, Kafka pronounces physiologically buttressed condemnations of his writing: "My whole body warns me against every word" (L, 70); "The greatest part of it, I openly say, I find repulsive."[105] He sees "the pages being covered endlessly with things one hates, that fill one with loathing," and he explains this as the price to be paid for serving the devil, as the inevitable accompaniment of successful writing: "To have to atone for the joys of good writing in this terrible way!" (LF, 76). At such moments, the "construction" of the writer from out of the "pleasure" taken in language-based self-scrutiny becomes brittle—as does the confidence in a spontaneous correspondence of "feeling" and "word." The performative disclosure of inner states of mind through words appears to be disrupted: "When I was in the swing of writing and living, I once wrote to you that no true feeling need search for corresponding words, but [involuntarily] runs into them or is even forced out by them. Perhaps this is not quite true, after all" (LF, 225). The prudent "not quite" implies no fundamental revision but at most restrictions and modifications to the driving power of words. Kafka's faith in words is conjoined here to a complicating principle, one whose workings bear only a remote resemblance to the skepticism toward language exemplified by Hofmannsthal. Precisely the writerly encounter with words is burdened with doubt and is radically exposed to the nonoriginality of words:

> Every word, before it lets me write it down, first looks around in all directions. The sentences literally crumble before me; I see their insides and then have to stop quickly. (L, 70)

Almost every word I write jars against the next, I hear the consonants rub leadenly against each other and the vowels sing an accompaniment like Negroes in a minstrel show. My doubts stand in a circle around every word, I see them before I see the word . . . (D, 29)

Moreover, hardly a word comes to me from the origin, but is seized upon fortuitously and with great difficulty somewhere along the way. (LF, 225; compare D, 12)

On two separate counts, this type of doubt differs from the paradigms of a harpy-like flaying of reference or a prostitute-like attrition. Not only does it befall the word as much as the speaker/writer—indicating thereby that it is not some doubt originating from a position outside of language. It also has nothing to do with any naively referential adequacy of words, but rather concerns encounters, perceptions, and grasping maneuvers at issue in words as thing-like objects and in their always already self-referential mediality. At the same time, the characterization of one's own words as "repulsive" by no means entails the judgment that they have utterly miscarried and cannot be enjoyed. The pages that "fill one with loathing"—which, according to the classical logic, would constitute a threat to well-being and ultimately to life itself—are actually ennobled in accordance with the model of cathartic discharge, understood as a necessary means for the preservation of life: "Can you understand this, dearest: to write badly, yet feel compelled to write, if one is not to abandon oneself to total despair! . . . To see the pages being covered endlessly with things one hates, that fill one with loathing *[Ekel]*, or at any rate with dull indifference, that nevertheless have to be written down in order that one shall live" (LF, 76). In the physiology of Kafka's writing, even the "repulsive words" are to be preferred to the skeptical renunciation of language. Rather than leading into some uncontaminated purity of speechless vision, the stoppage of words results in the complementary evils of constipation and bodily expectoration: "Hardly ten days interrupted in my writing and already discarded sputum?" (D, 330). Just as the child, according to Freud, looks on his own excrement with pride, so Kafka, in the face of his own linguistic abject, develops a relation not of simple excretion but of pleasurable rumination: "In the afternoon I couldn't keep myself from reading what I had written yesterday, 'yesterday's filth'; didn't do any harm, though" (D, 343). Kafka is not only the jackdaw and the "rat's nest," not only the dung beetle and the mole, not only the pig who wallows in the muck, but also the cow, of whose disgust-overcoming rumination Nietzsche says: "To practice reading as an *art* . . . requires one thing above all, something which today more than ever has been thoroughly unlearned . . . [and] for which one has almost to be a cow, but certainly *not* a 'modern man': *rumination* . . ."[106]

8

Holy Disgust (Bataille) and the Sticky Jelly of Existence (Sartre)

"I believe that nothing is more important for us than to recognize that we are bound and sworn to what provokes our most intense disgust."[1] With changing nuances, Georges Bataille's thinking can be understood to gravitate around this credo: the anti-aesthetic thinking from the years of the journal *Documents* (1929–1930); the sociological from the late 1930s, especially the lectures in the Collège de Sociologie (1938–1939); and the important works *L'érotisme* und *Souveraineté* from the 1950s. The revolt against a "sickly" aesthetic culture's ideal of beauty is dedicated to the fascination of what is or renders debased, repellent, disgusting. Blending Nietzsche and Freud together with the "sociology of primitive peoples" (Durkheim, Mauss), Bataille's and Leiris' "sacred sociology" reveal the processing of what disgusts as constituting the very "heart of the existence animating us."[2]

ANTI-AESTHETIC OF THE "FORMLESS": MATERIALISM OF THE DEBASED, POLLUTION OF THE BEAUTIFUL, SELF-MUTILATION, AND THE "BLISS" OF ANAL-SADISTIC RAVAGES

Each of Bataille's short and very dense essays in *Documents* presents an element of an affirmative aesthetic of the repellent. As the polemic opponents of these texts, Bataille repeatedly cites "the idealistic conception of the Greeks,"[3] "ideal human aspirations,"[4] the ideas of form held by "academic men."[5] In its welcoming of the bestial, indeed the cannibalistic, the article "Mouth"—

accompanied by a photo of a gaping oral cavity—delivers a slap to the address of the famous Laocoön-rule;[6] "Academic Horse"[7] might be read as a gloss of Kant's equine examples in the *Critique of Judgment*. As the most human body part, since, Bataille observes, it owes its presence to upright gait, the big toe is subject to elaborate ascriptions of "baseness," of an appearance that is "hideously cadaverous and at the same time loud and proud."[8] To Bataille, the apes' "ignoble" anatomy and the spectacular malformations of human physique are of an interest as burning as is the scorn cast on them by the classical idealization of the beautiful figure. The eye, seat of attraction and ideal speech-organ of the soul, is not only treated, with Stevenson, as a "cannibal delicacy" and—with a reference here to the film *Un chien andalou* by Buñuel and Dali—as material for slicing.[9] As a "pineal eye" *(l'œil pinéal)*[10] it even becomes the anal counterpart to an equally anal sun:

> The pineal eye probably corresponds to the anal (in other words nocturnal) conception that I initially had of the sun and that I then expressed in a phrase such as "the intact anus . . . to which nothing sufficiently blinding can be compared except the sun (even though the anus is the night)." I imagined the eye at the summit of the scull like a horrible erupting volcano, precisely with the shady and comical character associated with the rear end and its excretions.[11]

Already in *The Solar Anus* (1927) Bataille had confronted the idealism of eye and sun with a process of fecal eruption. The text "Rotten Sun" leads the sun as the "most elevated conception" over into the most base of conceptions—the process of "combustion" emerging as a gigantic production of garbage and refuse, as an epileptic crisis and mental ejaculation.[12] This spitting, twitching sun is "situated at the bottom of the sky like a cadaver at the bottom of a pit." It is aligned with the "spectral attraction of decomposition . . . fecal like the eye painted at the bottom of a vase, this Sun, now borrowing its brilliance from death, has buried existence in the stench of the night."[13] The third, "idealistic" appendage on the line linking sun and eye is the beauty of flowers: this beauty, too, undergoes a radical transformation into "corruption." "Certain kinds of fat orchids" appear as "plants so shady that one is tempted to attribute to them the most troubling human perversions." Even the most beautiful blossom, Bataille argues, soon "rots indecently in the sun, thus becoming, for the plant, a garish withering."[14]

"Primitive art" and contemporary painters (Picasso, Dali, Miró) figure as exponents of such a violent "decomposition of forms," committing itself as it does to "base matter"[15] instead of aesthetic "elevation."[16] Images of apocalypse, slaughterhouse photographs, and contemporary painting are arranged around this common vanishing point: "Apparently, the very element of these paintings is horror—blood, a severed head, violent death, and all the overwhelming play of viscera severed alive."[17] To use an example from classical aesthetics, Marsyas's flaying advances to a model for all pictorial representation—and this with an abandoning of the punishment motif underlying the cruel act. Bataille here discovers a thoroughly positive fascination extending to an apogee of bliss *(beatitude)*.[18] At the same time, the images are meant to make us—"like drunkards"—"vomit . . . this servile nobility, this idiotic idealism that leaves us under the spell of a few comical prison bosses."[19] Such a vomiting is not bound to the literal presentation of vomitive stimuli—just as little as realizing an effect similar to a rotting corpse is bound to a corpse's material presence: "in a brusque enough fashion, the graphic arts [of our time] have brought into focus a process of disintegration and destruction whose view has been scarcely less painful for many people than the view of a cadaver's decomposition and destruction."[20] Beyond the literal presence of traditional disgust material in Bataille's writing, it is easy to overlook what is delegated in this sentence to the rhetorical structure of analogy ("scarcely less painful than"): in the articles from *Documents,* all mere signifieds of disgust are always simultaneously signifiers, or agents performing an active representational function. They are not (only) objects of artistic representation, but always—and above all—the formal element *(l'élément même)* of the operations comprising art itself.

The leading category of this anti-aesthetic is not form but "formless," *informe*.[21] Bataille stresses that what is here at play is not simply a turning from beautiful forms to their monstrous antithesis. He even declines any definition of what he means by informe. In order to introduce it as the performative agent of a task, informe, we read:

> is not only an adjective having a given meaning, but a term serving to degrade things in the world, generally requiring that each thing have its form. What it designates has no rights in any sense and gets itself squashed everywhere, like a spider or an earthworm.[22]

Neither word nor concept in the usual sense, but also not simply their antithesis, the "term" that serves for declassification and disorder is thus applied to itself. It is not only the operator of a decomposition of the very requirement of form that it itself presumes ("for academic man to be happy").[23] What it signifies can itself be squashed like a spider or earthworm rather than resting on a stable sense. It is no accident that the analogy comes from the realm of disgust at animals. Worms and spiders are not simply objects of human feet that threaten to squash their form. Fear of spiders, worms, and insects[24] also implies the opposite fear: that of the insects themselves taking on the role of a "degrading" term thus threatening—indeed mortally destroying—the integrity of the body.[25] To this extent, informe signifies a mode of generating pictures that only presumes the soothing forms of "philosophy" in order—

through an act of "degrading"—to confront them with an assertion itself claiming no legitimation through a "meaning": namely, the assertion that "the universe is something like a spider or spit."[26]

The articles and graphic contents of *Documents* leave no doubt that Bataille is not simply juxtaposing the crudities of excrement, blood, and flayed bodies to the world of beautiful forms; rather, what is at stake, are complex modes of pictorial production meant to be related to the imagination of "base material" in manifold ways. In this manner, informe practices can be read as the model for an (anti)aesthetic whose field extends through the entire twentieth century[27] (and, to be sure, was not first discovered by Bataille). In any event, already at the time of *Documents*, the self-implication of the informe in its own work of decomposition is at odds with explicit motivations ascribing a fairly unambiguous significance to the anti-aesthetic project. A threefold "return to reality"[28] hovers on the horizon of the informe: aesthetically, a desublimation of beautiful forms moving to the point of "base materialism"; psychologically, a "liberation" of violent sexuality; historically, a reactivation of archaic practices for generating and affirming societal life through feelings of repulsion and acts of sacrifice. Like Nietzsche, Bataille diagnoses most of his contemporaries as suffering from a self-disgust, emerging from weakness, at all predatory animal instincts.[29] Instead of "laughing lions" there are only castrated lions:[30] "So many animals in the world and everything we have lost: innocent cruelty.... There is thus an animal in every human being, locked up in prison like a convict, and there is a door, and when it is opened a crack the animal breaks out like a convict that has found an exit."[31] Nietzsche's laughing lion here blends with Freud's insight into the never fully tamed nature of human instincts, culminating in a particular ideology of liberation: that of and for "violence." On the one hand, this thinking's "black rage" *(colère noire)* is manifest as a forced, strategically motivated gesture of revolt against the desultory compromises of contemporary thought.[32] On the other hand, (Dionysian) violence is affirmed—without the controls offered in Freud's system, and without Nietzsche's moderation by the Apollonian—openly and absolutely as the core of eros, indeed of our entire existence. "The beneficent value of dirty, bloody deeds" that Bataille claims to discover in the facial expressions of "slaughterers in the slaughterhouse"[33] extends through the entire field of art, eros, and social life. Already for early Bataille, de Sade embodies "sacred" violence: "Art ... proceeds in this sense through successive destructions. To the extent it liberates libidinous instincts, these instincts are sadistic."[34]

In the field of these "instincts," the pivotal ideal of beautiful form receives new definition: its charm now lies solely in its capacity to intensify the pleasure at its own pollution and destruction. Henceforth, beauty is the substrate of a "filthy and glaring sacrilege" to be inflicted on it: "It seems, in fact, that desire has nothing to do with ideal beauty, or, more precisely, that it only arises in order to stain and wither beauty."³⁵ True, beauty does construct a ban on animality, a ban transformed into form—Bataille here confirming the classical rules for disgust avoidance and the diagnoses of both Nietzsche and Freud concerning the taboo inscribed within aesthetic culture.³⁶ But precisely through this process, it attracts the "transgression" of "desire." From this idea, the later text *L'érotisme (Death and Sensuality)* concludes, in complete seriousness, that ugly women are "depressing" for men because they offer nothing to "sacrifice," nothing to pollute:

> Beauty is desired so that it can be befouled. Not for its own sake, but for the joy tasted in the certainty of profaning it. In sacrifice, the victim was chosen in a manner allowing his perfection to render perceptible the brutality of death. Human beauty, in the union of bodies, introduces the opposition between purest humanity and the hideous animality of the organs. . . . For a man, there is nothing more depressing than the ugliness of a woman, from whom the ugliness of the organs or the sexual act does not emerge. Beauty's importance primarily resides in the assumption that ugliness cannot be befouled, and that befouling is the very essence of eroticism.³⁷

Self-mutilation is an additional channel for the transgressive violence of desire. Bataille aligns Vincent van Gogh's severing of his own ear with ritual self-inflicted injuries in sacrifices and initiations. He celebrates the "radical transformation" made possible through such acts:

> Such an action would be characterized by the fact that it would have the power to liberate heterogeneous elements and to break the habitual homogeneity of the individual, in the same way that vomiting would be opposed to its opposite, the communal eating of food. Sacrifice considered in its essential phase would only be the rejection of what had been appropriated by a person or by a group . . . the victim struck down in a pool of blood, the severed finger or ear, the torn-out eye—do not appreciably differ from vomited food. . . . The one who sacrifices is free—free to indulge in a similar disgorging, free, continuously identifying with the victim, to vomit his own being just as he has vomited a piece of himself or a bull.³⁸

Pollution of the beautiful, self-mutilation, and aesthetic practices of the *informe* all terminate in an affirmative relation to death in its material existence: corpse and decay. Against the cosmetic struggle against death's traces, Bataille's "heterology"—as a "science of what is completely other"³⁹—offers a "play of man and his own decomposition." Bizarre archaic festivals epitomize this play:

We are far away from the savages who hung the skulls of their ancestors on greasy poles during enormous festivals, who rammed the tibia of their fathers into pig-mouths the moment the slit-throat pigs vomited waves of blood. [. . . Today,] the play of man and his own decomposition continues in the most desultory conditions, without the former ever having the courage to confront the latter. It seems we shall never be able to stand in face of the grandiose image of a decomposition whose risk, intervening with each breath, is nevertheless the very sense of a life that we prefer, we do not know why, to that of another whose respiration might survive us. Of this image, we only know the negative form, the soaps, the toothbrushes, and all the pharmaceutical products whose accumulation allows us to painfully escape, each day, from filth and death.[40]

Bataille's assertion that the anti-aesthetic of the informe is not grounded in any "meaning" is here revised, and very openly: the "decomposition" to which it is consigned may *have* no sense, but it *is*, precisely, "the very sense of a life that we prefer." For Bataille, contemporary art, psychoanalysis, and sociology of "primitive peoples" marks a turn away from a castrating, cosmetic, utilitarian civilization, hostile to both waste and orgies: "The contrary attitude has only revealed itself openly in a recent epoch—an attitude involving the revelation that extreme fear of decay and bloody mutilation is tied to a violent seduction which all the world would very much like to hide."[41]

Disgust Prohibitions and Their Transgression as Societal "Core" and Stimulating Medium of Erotic Violence

With increasing emphasis, Bataille's sociological thinking of the 1930s defines the "seduction" or "fascination" through "that which disgusts and depresses—as I have mentioned, menstrual blood, bodily putrefaction"[42] as the "core" of the social itself. Using the example of a typical French village, he tries to show that positive "mutual attraction" alone cannot account for the making of social life. The church in the village's center does not only gather the inhabitants together for rites and festivals; at the same time, by articulating the difference between holy and profane, it establishes prohibitions on physical contact and surrounds itself in the graveyard with the corpses of ancestors.[43] In this manner, social communication transforms what we do not wish to touch (the corpse) or what we are not allowed to touch (sacred spaces) into both a medium of attraction and a bond. Strong prohibitions are required, along with an "intense repulsive force"[44] attached to the prohibited acts or objects, in order to release a "tonic sense,"[45] an "energetic charge"[46] comprising the appeal and the rhythm of life itself:

In effect, expending human life involves an exclusion of each ignoble, abject, filthy element, but an exclusion not aimed at consigning it to inexistence: rather, such exclusion creates the positive value thanks to which it becomes possible to make use of violent affective reactions. In sexual life, abject elements, even ones that have been denied, play the determining role of agents of erotic attraction, and this example makes clear that the value of such elements rests on the possibility—always latent—of transforming repulsion into attraction.[47]

Eighteenth-century aesthetics had focussed on the riddle of how tragedy's violent horror could serve as an object of intense pleasure for spectators. Bataille as well sees tragedy as a model for the transformation of repulsive into attractive phenomena. Still, the theory of tragedy he laid out in the *Collège de Sociologie* was very consciously not meant as an aesthetic, but as a theory of the social—one whose basic figures emerge from the sociology of Durkheim and Mauss. According to Durkheim, the "elementary forms of religious life" process nothing but the supra-individual energies of the society itself. The distinction between holy and profane is the elementary code in a crucial production of heterogeneity: one enabling the social community, through the interplay between negative and positive rules of behavior, to reaffirm its own powers. The ritual's negative side amounts to elementary prohibitions of proximity, contact, and consumption.[48] For Durkheim, its positive side is often an execution of precisely the tabooed behavior—with sacrifice being the key element within the rite's positive dimension. In sacrifice, forbidden food can be eaten; in many cultures even a human being can be slaughtered. Durkheim notes: "At bottom, there is no positive rite that does not actually constitute a sacrilege. For human beings cannot interact with sacred beings without crossing the barriers that ordinarily keep them separate. . . . Robertson Smith thought he could show that at the beginning the animal killed in the sacrifice must have been regarded as holy and as a close relative of those who killed it."[49] Hence by way of a detour through the "sociology of primitive peoples," Bataille renders Freud's presumption, based on contact-prohibition, that the pure and impure, holy and most strictly tabooed, share a core identity,[50] into a positive certainty. "It is only to the extend that a mind has been led to recognize the fundamental identity between the taboo marking impure things and the purest forms of the sacred that it is able to become conscious of the violent repulsions constituting the specificity of the general movements that create human community" (2, 329).[51]

In this way sacrilege belongs to the structure of the holy itself. The periodic transgression of elementary prohibitions does not destroy them but renews them; it releases strong affective energies through oscillating between repulsion and attraction, thus transforming the impure into the pure, the rejected into the holy. Bataille declares this transgression to be the core of the social, indeed of human existence: "The core of a settlement is the place where the left-hand holy is transformed into the right-hand holy, the object of repulsion into an object of attraction, and depression into stimulation."[52] As a result of the "tonic" alternation of disgust and lustful-joyous "release," Bataille no longer needs to define—as did Freud—the fundamental "violence" and perversity of human (meaning for him male) "desire" as civilization's archaic antidoton; rather, it now emerges as the first and positive constituent of social life. The moment, inscribed into sacrifice and ritual orgy, of (seemingly) unproductive expenditure of material resources is here read against the grain of the sociological precursors. For Marcel Mauss, it still serves to manifest and preserve positions of power, while for Bataille, to the contrary, it figures as an act of sovereign sadistic destruction, beyond all economy of usefulness. By way of the conceptual chain extending from the holy to sacrifice to expenditure, Bataille even applies the Freudian linkage of sadism to the phase of anal eroticism directly to the violence expressed in the holy. He maintains an "identical attitude towards shit, gods, and cadavers": "Religious organization represents the freest opening for excremental collective impulses (orgiastic impulses) established in opposition to political, judicial, and economic institutions" (II, 61–62).[53] "Agiology" and "scatology," knowledge of the holy and of excrement, are thus exchangeable doublets of the abstract concept of "heterology."[54]

For Bataille, such "heterology" exemplarily applies to tragedy. Transgressing the most deeply rooted prohibitions, confronting an assembled crowd with incest, the murder of one's spouse or mother, sending both perpetrators and victims down a path toward "mutilation" and becoming a "cadaver," tragedy produces a strong tonic sense, an intense affective cathexis of both social and individual existence.[55] It transforms acts that are in fact revolting and depressing into a positive "excitation" of what Bataille sees as most strongly driving us onward: passionate violence, "expenditure" until death, a "destruction sparing nothing."[56] In this sense, "tragic man is essentially one who becomes aware of human existence. He sees the violent and contradictory forces that stir him; he knows he is prey to human absurdity, prey to the absurdity of nature, but he affirms this reality which has left him no outlet other than crime."[57] By way of Freud, Durkheim, and Mauss, Bataille thus repeatedly ends up back with Nietzsche—with a tragic affirmation of existence that at the same time exposes itself to and overcomes disgust: "Nausea, then the overcoming of nausea, which follows the vertigo—these are the phases of the paradoxical dance regulating religious attitudes."[58] Nietzsche, however, sees Apollonian beauty of form as the vehicle for overcoming the disgust seizing us, in face of the profane world, upon returning from Dionysian intoxication. Bataille, on the other hand, understands the transformation of the repellent into our existence's *sens tonique* as taking place within the Dionysian festival itself. And Bataille's critique of Christianity is no longer aimed at its devaluation of worldly life in favor of the other-worldly, or the identification of Jesus with truth; it is rather aimed at a weakness—a "blindness" or "misperception"—of a different sort. The Christians, explains Bataille, do not possess the "tragic" pathos enabling them to recognize Jesus's murder as their own, desired deed—a deed constituting their very community.[59] Instead, they slough off the sacrilege, rendering it a sin they ascribe to the Jews; they can thus only identify with the victim, not with the perpetrators:

> Tragedy . . . is thus a more significant example and less obscure demonstration of society's central movement than the Christian church. Furthermore, it is the church's counterpart in the sense that it offers the perpetrator for the pathos-laden communion of those present, while the Christian ritual no longer has the power to do more than designate the victim.[60]

Despite this limitation, Bataille does not entirely give up on Christ's "murder" as a model of holy transgression. In the liturgy of *Felix culpa*, the joyous guilt of a crucifixion leading to salvation, he discovers at least distorted relics of a "proper" variant of the event—one not already completely dictated by the self-castration of violent human nature.[61] In this sense Bataille does see both "Dionysus and the crucified" as exemplary for "a tragic theory of bacchants and martyrs."[62]

Love between the sexes is read according to the same "tragic" schema. Lovers offer themselves to transgressive communication: "Love expresses a need for sacrifice. . . . By erotic frenzy . . . one is driven to tear oneself apart, to be lost at the same time as tearing apart and losing some other."[63] Once again, this act of a self-sacrificing "violent expenditure" is based on prohibitions and inhibitions whose affective value extends to disgust. Bataille needs and affirms these disgust limits because the power of transgression can only make itself known through them. This is the context for once more evoking the disgusting old woman: she no longer signifies the entirely other of aesthetic pleasure and the extremest border of male desire; rather, she is now inscribed within sexual love in general, since sexual love essentially consists in transgressing the barriers between attraction and repulsion—and can only prove its power through such transgression. As Bataille sees things, every woman, even the most desireable one, must partake, in sexual love, in the chimera of the disgusting old woman:

> Between two people whose movements are composed of exuberant life, the theme of reciprocal repulsion focused on sexual parts is present as a mediator, as a catalyst increasing the power of communication. Doubtless, the sexual parts are not truly repugnant unless they belong to a person devoid of charm—a fat old woman,

for example. But the most desirable woman's organs partake in the unspeakable nature of the organs of the woman who is old and obese. Thus they partake in the nature of the sacred nucleus; which is even less surprising because, as I have mentioned, this nucleus refers, among other tabooed horrors, to menstrual blood. (II, 318)[64]

Bataille's later books on eros and sovereignty endow an increasingly dogmatic substance to what the short *Documents* articles touch on as an aesthetic of the informe and what the *Collège de Sociologie* lectures theoretically schematize. These books integrate Nietzsche's critique of cultural self-disgust and his ideal of the laughing lion, Freud's theory of the endurance of perverse, especially excremental and sadistic drives, and Durkheim's description of holy sacrilege as a basic element of all social communication into Bataille's own doctrine: one oscillating between a fundamental anthropology and a philosophy of an essential because free "existence." A basic pillar of this doctrine remains the destructive violence characteristic of human beings. *Érotisme* interests Bataille precisely because it is "the domain of violence, the domain of violation."[65] That what is at stake is male violence, elevated to sacred existential rank, here becomes fully evident:

> The lover does not disaggregate the beloved any less than the bloody sacrificer does the immolated human being or animal. The woman in the hands of her assailant is dispossessed of her being. With her sense of shame, she loses the firm barrier that, separating her from others, rendered her impenetrable: she opens herself to the violence of the sexual play unfettered in the reproductive organs, she opens herself to the impersonal violence that overwhelms her from the outside.[66]

In a world of castrated lions, Bataille's thinking makes "safeguarding the grossest virility"[67] into a central goal. He views the very baseness at work here as standing for "human greatness":[68] an anti-idealist reversal and revaluation he liked to term "subversion."[69] The sacralizing of the forbidden and disgusting is a key element of this "subversion." Bataille understands the elementary civilizational prohibitions and the order of useful work as efforts at rejecting and severing oneself from one's own human (= male) violence.[70] However, just this rejection stimulates and intensifies the violence. For "in the domain of irrational behavior," Bataille holds, "the prohibition is there in order to be violated."[71] Even if violated, however, the taboo loses none of its basic quality of being "intangible." Rather, through its own transgressive energy, the "sovereign" violation intensifies and renews the energy of its counterpart. Transgression as the "unchaining of violence"[72] can only be as intense as the feeling of its being prohibited: "If the prohibition is no longer in play, if we no longer believe in the prohibition, transgression is impossible."[73] Accordingly, the elementary taboos are not required in order to tame, or civilize the human beings, but, contrarily, to provoke and set free repeated acts of human violence. To the extent that prohibitions ignite our violent transgressive energies and precisely such energies define our (culturally repressed) human essence, "the truth of prohibitions is the key to our human attitude. We must know, we can know precisely that prohibitions are not imposed from the outside."[74] Or, even more pathetically: it is "our aversions which constitute us and first make us human beings."[75] It is in this sense that for Bataille all social communication is "founded on disgust."[76] Freud had traced disgust barriers back to processes of organic and cultural repression always implying a loss of pleasure and the emergence of neurosis. Bataille, to the contrary, essentializes education for disgust—without any ambivalence, and with an exact reversal of the function of disgust maintained from Kant through Elias—into a sacred teaching animating and preserving all eroticism:

> Through mimic gestures and if necessary through violence, we have to teach our children the strange aberration that is disgust, touching us even to the point of fainting, and whose contagion has reached us from the earliest men through countless generations of scolded children.
> Our mistake is to take lightly sacred teachings transmitted to our children for millennia—teachings that nevertheless once had another form. In its ensemble, the domain of disgust and nausea is a result of these teachings.[77]

According to Bataille, our experience of the sacred and of sacrifice tends to be increasingly limited to feelings of disgust regarding the bloody "elements of the spectacle"; at the same time, the transfigurational "overcoming of nausea," and hence sacrifice's transgressive essence,[78] routinely goes unnoticed. Given this historical diagnosis, Bataille emphasizes the importance of clinging to the provocation experienced in disgust. For him, complete absence of the disgust-sensation would simultaneously amount to an annihilation of all transgressive intensity, and "violence," of all heterogeneity, of the sacred, even of the social altogether. Bataille sees all pleasure as fundamentally pleasure at disgust, or "disgust pleasure."[79] With the demise of prohibition and its affective representation in disgust, "the heart of the existence animating us"[80] would cease its beating—while Freud used to see a weakening of the libido, along with a danger of its complete extinction, in the way disgust barriers function.[81] For Bataille, a vanishing of (awareness of) the sexuality-based prohibitions would be the same as a vanishing of sexuality itself.[82] At the same time, it would devalue that "summit of transgression" Bataille furnishes with the name "Sade."[83] *"Sacred cannibalism"* is yet another example of "the prohibition creating desire: the prohibition does not create the savor of flesh, but it is the reason the 'pious' cannibal consumes it.

Within eroticism, we will also find this paradoxical creation of the value of attraction through prohibition."[84] Hence whoever affirms "violence" and its holy unchaining in transgression must also desire disgust and its overcoming. From this basic assumption Bataille derives a surprisingly simple genealogy of the disgust-linked prohibitions concerning incest and menstrual blood. He expressly rejects Lévi-Strauss's complex effort (especially in *The Elementary Structures of Kinship*) to define the incest taboo as a basic anthropological datum, reading it simply as a secondary effect of a primary postulate of "violence":

> Other prohibitions associated with sexuality seem no less reducible to the formless horror of violence than is incest: for instance the prohibition on menstrual blood or that of childbirth. These liquids are considered manifestations of internal violence. Blood is in itself a sign of violence. In addition, menstrual blood has the sense of sexual activity and the pollution emerging from it: pollution is one of the results of violence.[85]

Included in Bataille's "effects of violence" is the relation life establishes, in its most intense manifestations (sacrifice, love, orgy), with death. From this, an additional significance accrues to disgust and its transgressive overcoming. On the one hand, it confronts us with death's horror, most intensely in face of "putrefaction" and "decomposition." On the other hand, the same disgust grants us a sense of the shift of rotten matter into new, rampant life. Instead of damning putrefaction, with Rosenkranz, as the perverse life emerging from one's own death, Bataille celebrates it as a positive fermentation of life and hence as the appropriate object for "the triumph of nausea":

> This heaving, fetid, tepid matter, frightful to look at, site of fermenting life, this material teeming with eggs, germs, and worms, is at the origin of the decisive reactions we call nausea, vertigo, disgust. Beyond the annihilation to come, whose weight will fall, totally, on the being that I am . . . death will announce my return to the purulence of life. Hence I can anticipate—and live in expectation of—this multiplied purulence, celebrating in me, through anticipation, the triumph of nausea.[86]

In recollection of the fact that "death is also the youthfulness of the world,"[87] disgust-related acts of transgression—sacrifice, love, waste, in short: all forms of "holy" excretion—draw close to the medieval culture of festivals and laughter described by Bakhtin. Excretion and greedy gulping, birth, death, and new life mingle nearly seamlessly in the grotesque body of the carnival—to be sure, without disgust, the carnival's transgressions thus being categorically different in this respect from Bataille's "play of man and his own decomposition." Both

Bataille and Bakhtin describe the time of the festival not least of all in terms of lustful excesses involving otherwise disgust-imbued corporeal material and acts. Bakhtin's grotesque world of carnival has nearly the same structure as Bataille's "sacred world" and its artistic and erotic equivalents. "The sacred world," writes Bataille, "opens itself to limited transgressions. It is the world of the festival. . . . Par excellence, sacred time is the festival. The festival does not necessarily signify . . . the massive lifting of prohibitions, but in the time of a festival what is ordinarily forbidden may always be permitted, sometimes required. From ordinary time to the festival, there is an inversion of values."[88] Based on a study by Roger Caillois,[89] such sentences also document the points of contact between the texts of Bataille and Bakhtin, as distinct as they are in tone and philosophical horizon. It is consequently no coincidence that both authors place laughter at the center of their social theory. And once again, disgust, more specifically its relation to laughter, is what allows a marking of the difference between the theories. As a universal mode of degradation and exaltation, of foolish license for freedom and unofficial truth, Bakhtin's carnivalesque laughter does consistently recall the taboo to which it owes its existence. But only Bataille's laughter is in itself defined as excretion—as an analogon of anal-sadistic-excremental lust and thus as a performative traversing of a disgust taboo:

> Laughter as a spasmodic process of the oral orifice's sphincter muscles, analogous to that of the sphincter muscles of the anal orifice during defecation, is probably the only satisfying interpretation—in both cases taking account of the primary role in human existence of such spasmodic processes with excretory function. When it comes to outbursts of laughter, we must thus admit that the nervous discharge that could have normally been released by the anus (or by the adjacent sexual organs) is being released by the oral orifice.[90]

For his part, Bakhtin, declares that "shit is the joyful material."[91] From a similar insight, Bataille derives the quasi-identity of excretion and laughter, and with this perhaps his most surprising contribution to the theory of disgust and its overcoming: "The advantage of starting with a provisional characterization of shit in proportion to hilarity results precisely from the adaptation of laughter to this complexity of forms."[92]

"LA NAUSÉE: C'EST MOI"—
SARTRE'S ELEVATION OF DISGUST TO THE
SOLE AUTHENTIC EXPERIENCE OF EXISTENCE

Published in 1938, Jean-Paul Sartre's novel *La Nausée* appears stamped by a credo similar to Bataille's. Where Bataille discovers the holy-excremental core or "heart" of our existence in disgust, Sartre declares: "Nausea . . . is no longer an illness or a passing fit: it is I."[93] What dominates Bataille's early critical and literary texts, returns in 1952 as a description of Sartre's fictional œuvre in general: "The entire novelistic work of Sartre seems haunted by the obsession with a rotten, decomposed, moldy world, one full of sickening secretions."[94] Just as according to Nietzsche the feeling of disgust distinguishes the "elect man of cognition"[95] from the "horned animals," and just as Bataille views (sacred) disgust as only being adequately experienced by a few in the modern utilitarian epoch, the advent of disgust figures in *La Nausée* as an "event"—*événement*—of comprehensive revelatory quality. It distinguishes the protagonist in relation to his environment and his own former life hardly less than Musil's "other condition" does the subject of mystic experience. In Sartre's novel, moments of progress in the consciousness of one's own existence are simultaneously moments of progress in the experience of "Nausea" (the term is ordinarily capitalized by Sartre). Normal social life appears entirely caught-up in self-deception through false forms of legitimation and sense giving. Zarathustra "embarks" human beings on their "high seas" by shattering their "false shores and false securities," exposing them to "the great disgust, the great sea-sickness."[96] The crisis of nausea in Sartre's novel similarly opens a view of "things in themselves." As is the case with Nietzsche's image of seasickness, nausea signifies first of all a violent crisis of ordinary self- and world-perception, which suddenly experiences its very fundament as either absent or actively taken away: "Everything is groundless, this park, this city, and myself. When you become aware of that, it turns your heart upside down and everything begins to float: . . . that is Nausea."[97] Once the weave of "false shores and false securities," lies and deceptions is shattered, all phenomena appear in their unadorned arbitrariness and senselessness. Antoine Roquentin thus abandons his occupation—and his self-grounding. With the distance he owes to this "seasick" experience of absent grounding, he observes other bachelors, distinguished citizens, or young lovers, caught-up in the ideological patterns and social practices preventing them from becoming aware of the (absent) ground of their own existence. Like Descartes' *cogito, ergo sum*, like all philosophies of absolute self-consciousness, Sartre's "feeling of existence" first creates a tabula rasa.[98] It liberates the ego from any grounding, which is always an anchoring in the past, in favor of a pure actuality of the present; this, precisely, constitutes the "Nausea" of groundlessness.

Dizziness, seasickness, nausea, and disgust involve clearly distinct reactive models. Nevertheless, their affinity goes far beyond a potential convergence in the vomiting reflex—a convergence that in any event is of no significance for Sartre or Nietzsche or Bataille. In both Zarathustra's sayings and Sartre's novel, what connects the seasick groundlessness of vertigo and nausea to genuine disgust is the affected persons perceiving themselves as radically threatened—the emergency situation thus implying a particularly acute experience of their own "existence." In Sartre's work as in Nietzsche's, nausea or dizziness in bottomless space is only rarely—and never fully literally—described as a revolt of the stomach caused by seasickness; its phenomenology is rather always already displaced into the genuine imagistic field of disgust. To this extent, Sartre's novel depicts its nausea in the medium of disgust—and this may be the reason why it seems nearly arbitrary when its hero first speaks of his "Nausea," then of his "disgust in existing."[99] In contrast to Bataille's focus on "disgust"—*dégoût*—"Nausea" is Sartre's existential-philosophical category; yet the negative attributes of the existence grasped as "Nausea"—excessive thickness, fatness, softness, stickiness—themselves spark *dégoût*.

Sartre does indeed depict traditional objects of disgust, e.g. marked corporeal deformations and "perverse" sexual practices; but he seemingly does so only to exclude any possible confusion with the different referential horizon of his *nausée*. His hero, for instance, is not troubled by living in the "Street of Mutilated Persons" *(Rue des Mutilés)*,[100] where, equally untroubledly, he hears the streetcar pass by every hour on the way to the slaughterhouse;[101] he responds in strikingly "liberal," affectless fashion to the various material catalysts of disgust at play in his daily life: the postules and wrinkles in the ugly "ape face" of the historical figure he is researching;[102] the "rotten teeth" and "enormous nostrils" in the face of a random contemporary;[103] exhibitionism, pederasty, and his own, dispassionate sex with a restaurant proprietress. Roquentin's nausea is cast exclusively on what emerges behind the play of sexes, families, social hierarchies, even words. His *nausée* is the consciousness—in the form of a physical sensation, hence circumventing any theoretical objectification—of the utter contingency and senseless facticity of his own existence. In *L'être et le néant* (1943), Sartre correspondingly explains that for the individual experiencing it, nausea is the "non-positional apprehension of a contingency which he is, as a pure apprehension of self as a factual existence."[104]

Eighteenth-century aesthetics discovered the basis for pleasure in "unpleasant sensations" in their self-reflective dimension for the soul, the latter perceiving itself more strongly, thus as more alive, in proportion to the stimulus it experiences. In its violent defense against the approach of something unassimilable, the unpleasant disgust-sensation evokes a particularly intense awareness of self. For nothing less is at stake in disgust than the physical or moral integrity of those who feel it. Sartre's identification of *nausée* as an intense perception of one's own existence is grounded in this self-referential implication of all disgust.

In an early text written in 1935, Emmanuel *Lévinas* already read the moment of intensified self-perception within the violent affect of *nausée as* indicating an irremissible "one is there"—as an "experience of pure being:[105] " "Nausea as such only uncovers the nudity of being in its plenitude and irremissible presence."[106] To be sure, Sartre's *La Nausée* reserves the concept of *être* expressly for a disgust-free sphere of aesthetic justification transcending pure existence;[107] and Sartre does not describe the positive discovery made in nausea as a counter-reaction to "an impossibility of being what one is."[108] But for both Sartre and Lévinas, nausea no longer figures first and foremost as a psychic dam or negative stimulant. Its undeniable presence is now related entirely to itself "as something absolute," namely, as the experience of one's "very existence."[109] As a correlate of disgust, what remains of the aftereffect of Dionysian transport (Nietzsche), neurotic symptoms of repressed desires (Freud), and the indispensable intensifier of transgressive violence (Bataille), is the predicateless grasping of factual-haphazard existence. At the same time, as a rule Sartre's novel does not tie the pure grasp of existence in and as nausea to traditional disgust objects, but to the estrangement of apparently insignificant things. Suddenly, for instance, the hero can no longer hold a small stone[110] or lift a piece of white paper;[111] in the failure of such customary ways to grasp objects, he sees himself confronted with the phenomenon of a pure existence.

Since the late seventeenth century, literature has had another term than "disgust" available for the negative experience of "empty" contingency and melancholy lack of legitimation—*ennui*. "I stifled at the depths of this immense ennui"[112]—thus Roquentin himself occasionally translates the nausea he experiences in face of the groundlessness of existence into the older paradigm: "I am bored *(je m'ennui)*, that's all. From time to time I yawn so widely that tears roll down my cheeks. It is a profound ennui, profound, the profound heart of existence, the very matter that I am made of."[113] Boredom, senseless repetitions, lack of productivity, an absence of adventure, "privileged situations,"[114] and "perfect moments"[115]—the novel depicts all these features of the "disgust at one's own existence" (Kant) in ennui.[116] Even Sartre's own suggestion for the title—*Melancholia*—points in this direction: ennui and melancholia have traditionally been conceived of as fused together. Finally named *La Nausée* at the wish of publisher Gallimard, the novel both depicts and expels honorable old *ennui* in its images of physical *dégoût;* here as well, literature since Baudelaire has offered more than one model. And yet, traditional ennui constitutes only a first layer in Sartre's blending of nausea, disgust, and ennui. The blending's dynamic consists not least of all in a complete revaluation of the classical source of ennui. Contingency, senselessness, empty facticity cease to be grounds for melancholy despair. Instead, they emerge as thoroughly positive categories, doing justice to the "absurdity"[117] of existence precisely through their break with false legitimations and claims to meaning. This absurdity is no defect, but rather an irreducible *être de trop*:[118] a state of being superfluous and in excess, measured against any logic of meaningful grounding. In this manner, self-nausea mutates into a peculiar ecstasis, into the very epitome of the experience of existence. Ambivalent like all twentieth century disgust, Sartre's nausea is both itself and "just the opposite":[119] A "small happiness,"[120] if not "the goal of my happiness."[121] For nausea is the only way to authentically feel one's own existence:

> I am the thing. Existence, liberated, detached, floods over me. I exist.
> I exist. It's sweet, so sweet, so slow. And light: you'd think it floated all by itself. It stirs. It brushes by me, melts and vanishes. Gently, gently. There is bubbling water in my mouth. I swallow. It slides down my throat, it caresses me—and now it comes up again into my mouth. For ever I will have a little pool of whitish water in my mouth—a discrete pool grazing my tongue. And this pool is still me. And the tongue. And the throat is me.[122]
> I am the one who pulls myself from the nothingness to which I aspire: the hatred, the disgust of existing, these are as many ways *to make myself* exist, to thrust myself into existence.[123]

In its variation on Louis XIV's *L'état: c'est moi*, the phrase *"La Nausée ... c'est moi"*[124] brings nausea into a position of fullest power. As with Nietzsche's Zarathustra, "wings" actually grow from the disgust of Sartre's hero—wings allowing transferal of all repulsion into a yes-saying. The contingency and superfluousness is a "richness"[125] of its own sort. Its experience as a "great motionless beast,"[126] as color, secretion, and odor, leads to the following theoretical formulation:

> This moment was extraordinary. I was there, motionless and icy, plunged into a horrible ecstasy. But something fresh had just appeared in the very heart of this ecstasy; I understood the Nausea, I possessed it. To tell the truth, I did not formulate my discoveries to myself. But I think it would be easy for me to put them in words now. The essential thing is contingency. I mean that by definition, existence is not necessity. To exist is simply to be there; existing entities appear, let themselves be encountered, but you can never deduce them. I believe there are people who have understood this. Only they tried to overcome this contingency by inventing a necessary being, cause of himself. But no necessary being can explain existence: contingency is not a delusion, an appearance that can be dissipated; it is the absolute, consequently, perfect groundlessness. Everything is groundless, this park, this city and myself. When the moment comes where you become aware of that, it turns your heart upside down and everything starts to float: ... that is Nausea.[127]

The nonthetic experience of contingent-groundless existence is not only called "nausea" because, as its negative reverse side, it has taken up the ennui-qualities of empty existence and senselessly passing time. At the same time, the positive richesse in the revaluation of these qualities itself opens access to imagination of the disgusting. The *être de trop* of all existence is constantly in danger of shifting from a sweet feeling of happiness into quantitative disgust from excessive exuberance. This path follows the simple law that as soon as there is too much of it, anything pleasant can cause satietory disgust. In Sartre's novel, the philosophical recognition of contingency as *être de trop* thus moves into imagistic fields that vary paradigms of the excessively sweet, fat, damp, soft. The combination of excessively sweet and soft here furnishes that quality of stickiness whose disgusting contents—a diffuse blend of firm and fluid, non-consumable but also inescapable, taking revenge on every effort at appropriation and threatening our integrity with glue-like adherence—are defined so eloquently by Sartre in *Being and Nothingness* as a fundamental ontological factor in every psychoanalysis of objects.[128] In the intensification of *être de trop*, the experience of the pure contingency of existence, first greeted as a liberation and pleasing the palate like "bubbling water," turns into a confrontation with a monstrous, fat, sticky, and ubiquitously smearing jelly:

> Existence everywhere, infinitely, in excess, for ever and everywhere; existence—which is limited only by existence. I sank down on the bench, stupefied, stunned by this profusion of beings without origin: everywhere blossomings, hatchings out, my ears buzzed with existence, my very flesh throbbed and opened, abandoned itself to the universal burgeoning. It was repugnant.[129]
>
> Had I dreamed of this enormous presence? It was there, in the garden, toppled down into the trees, all soft, sticky, soiling everything, all thick, a jelly. And I was inside, I with the entire garden. I was frightened but above all furious, I thought it was so stupid, so out of place, I hated this ignoble jelly. It was there, it was there! Mounting up to the sky, spilling out everywhere, filling everything with its gelatinous slither, and I could see depths upon depths of it reaching far beyond the limits of the garden, the houses, and Bouville, I was no longer in Bouville, I was nowhere, floating. I was not surprised, I knew very well it was the World, the naked World suddenly revealing itself, and I choked with rage at this gross, absurd being. . . . I shouted "what filth, what filth!" and shook myself to get rid of this sticky filth, but it held fast and there was so much, tons and tons of existence, indefinitely.[130]

The excessively firm, soft, sweet, even the excessively tepid and sticky—all these disgust-qualities of existence's *être de trop* have feminine connotations and are occasionally directly defined as feminine: as "a soft, slimy, feminine activity," as "sweet, feminine revenge" of the in-itself (Ansich) on every effort of appropriation.[131] In all seriousness, Sartre compares the viscosity of honey to the "broadening and flattening of the somewhat mature breasts of a woman lying on her back."[132] The old woman can thus re-emerge with a new function.[133] Even the (equally feminine) *grande nature vague*[134]—as a vegetation growing over everything, as horror-sparking and disgusting luxuriance, as overanimated mixture of tepid fluids, secretions, sexual parts, putrefecatory materials, and insects—can allegorically depict pure existence in its *être de trop*. The excess is here intensified to a disgusting ecstasis, an apocalyptic paroxysm. The all too sweet, sticky, and fat experience of existence swallows up human civilization, driving it to a collapse into collective orgies of suicide.[135] Such imagery hyperbolically demonstrates that, in *Nausea*, the experience of pure existence constantly brings about a kind of death;[136] namely, the death of all false legitimations, those preventing us from genuinely experiencing existence.

The jelly of existence is the second negative limiting value of Sartre's *Nausée*. On the one hand, the experience of existence in itself executes an overcoming—indeed a direct countercathexis—of the disgust-qualities of ennui (as indicated, meaningless time-passage, empty factuality, boredom). On the other hand, the tendency toward suicide inscribed in ennui returns in the very feature of *être de trop* providing Sartre's Nausea with positive attributions of freedom and happiness. Or more succinctly: ennui's self-destructive potential persevers in the very mode of its overcoming. From the novel's opening onward, Sartre therefore supplies—in yet another variation on Nietzsche—an external counterpart to nausea's inner ennobling into a pure existential experience: the beauty of art. In complete agreement with classical aesthetics, Sartre defines as beautiful what from within itself appears to be "inevitable,"[137] what is so compellingly shaped that nothing part of it could be different. Put philosophically, beauty is the (seeming) transfiguration of art in nature, of contingency in necessity. In order to stress the contrast to the essential contingency of existence and its negative gradient of the (too) soft, damp, diffuse, tepid, Sartre ties the quality of art's "necessity" to the attributes of hardness, transparency, dryness, and clear coldness.[138] In *La Nausée*, an old jazz record serves as the only legitimate model for not simply having to affirm the contingency of existence in itself, but for being able to transfigure it into the necessity of emphatic meaning. Written by a sweaty hand, the jukebox tune is extracted from the unbearable heat of the New York summer, transforming bodies into "pools of melting fat";[139] the phrase *some of these days/you'll miss me, honey* even evokes a substance (honey) that plays a paradigmatic role in Sartre's specific sensitivity to disgust at sticky matter. In the middle of disgusting materials—warm beer, dirty mirror, body "with too much flesh"—the beloved record penetrates the "thick layers of existence," reaching something adamantine or "beautiful and hard as steel"[140]:

>[This little jeweled pain] does not exist because it has nothing superfluous *[elle n'a rien de trop]:* it is all the rest which in relation to it is superfluous. It is.
>And I, too, wanted *to be.* That's even all I wanted; this is the last word of the story. Within the apparent disorder of my life, I clearly see: at the bottom of all these attempts that seemed disconnected, I find the same desire: to drive existence out of me, to rid the passing moments of their fat, to twist them, dry them, purify myself, harden myself, to finally render the sharp, precise sound of a saxophone note.[141]

The brave affirmation of the pure facticity of existence experienced in nausea, in its contingent *être de trop,* is thus only the second best mode of overcoming ennui. Alongside the "small happiness of Nausea," there is "another happiness," belonging to an "outside" and "another time."[142] As was the case, already, in the older discussions of ennui, art here figures as the best antidote to disgust at one's own existence; as in Schopenhauer and Nietzsche, art is even attributed with the power of metaphysical salvation *(sauvés).*[143] In view of the jazz tune, Sartre's protagonist appears to recall Nietzsche's famous formula for overcoming disgust: "Only as an aesthetic phenomenon is existence eternally justified."[144] "The Negress sings. Can one justify one's existence then? A tiny little bit? I feel extraordinarily intimidated."[145] And Roquentin promptly searches, himself, for such a justification through art, as if it were "the actual metaphysical activity" (Schopenhauer). The novel ends with the uncertain project of a novel. In the writing of such a novel, Roquentin promises himself the next stage of his own *Bildungsroman.* The overthrow of all false existential groundings and the breakthrough to a pure experience of existence in nausea only seems to be the first step. Its result, the ecstatic *être de trop* of contingent existence, itself remains threatened with transformation into yet another source of disgust; it should thus ideally be subject to an activity providing access to an even higher order of self-perception:

>Naturally, at first it would only be a troublesome, tiring work, it wouldn't stop me from existing or feeling that I exist. But the moment would certainly come when the book would be written, when it would be behind me, and I think that a little of its clarity might fall over my past. Then, perhaps, because of it, I could remember my life without repugnance.[146]

To gain a disgust-free perspective on one's own life, wishing—as if with an art-work—to once more repeat (ruminate on) it: that was also the catalyst for the maximal overcoming of disgust Nietzsche propagated under the rubric of yes-saying to the eternal return.[147] Moderate echoes of Nietzsche's philosophy of disgust thus pervade Sartre's novel from start to finish: disgust as signature of the "elect men of cognition" who have gained distance from the systematic self-delusion of the "gregarious cow"; disgust as medium of cognition itself—and indeed of a "physiologically" grounded and immediate type of cognition; disgust as sign of an "insight" into the true "essence of things,"[148] of an authentic experience of existence; finally, art's beautiful illusion as the aesthetic legitimation and highest overcoming of the no-saying inherent in disgust. At the same time, Sartre could have drawn the material imagery coloring these elements in his novel almost completely from the disgust-phenomenology of Husserl-student Kolnai, which he very likely knew. Beyond this, Kolnai's comparative diagnosis of anxiety and disgust clarifies an inner-philosophical dimension of French thinking on disgust during the 1930s: at work there is a supplementary movement tied to—and distancing from—a philosophy centered on angst (Kierkegaard, Heidegger).[149] What literally remains in Sartre's thinking from the powerful disgust-continent of archaic violence (Nietzsche, Bataille), of excremental lust and the perversions (Freud, Bataille) are simply the regrettable obscenities of neurotic petty bourgeois citizens. The genuine Sartreian moment of *Nausée*—the affirmative nonthetic experience of "pure" existence in its contingent facticity—seems to have hardly made an enduring impact on twentieth-century art and culture.[150] It is all the more ironic that if only as a result of its title, Sartre's novel may well be the only work of art to be read, chiefly and consistently, from the perspective of disgust—although nearly always without taking account of the massive literature on and of disgust prior to Sartre.

9

Abject Mother (Kristeva), Abject Art, and the Convergence of Disgust, Truth, and the Real

In the 1980s, a new buzzword entered political and (in the wider sense) critical discourse—above all, critical discourse in the U.S. The word is "abjection," and it represents the newest mutation in the theory of disgust. Oscillating, in its usage, between serving as a theoretical concept and precisely defying the order of concentual language altogether, the term "abjection" also commonly appears as both adjective ("abject women," "abject art") and adjective turned into a substantive ("the abject"). Well-known women professors, who happened to be prominent public intellectuals and leading voices in feminist discourse, were affectionately caricatured as the "sonic mothers" of the "Party for Affirmative Abjection."[1] When the Whitney Museum of Modern Art chose to run one of its exhibitions under the title *Abject Art* (1993), it merely confirmed what had already come to seem unavoidable in discussing the work of Cindy Sherman and Robert Mapplethorpe, among others. Under the rubric "abject(ion)," the MLA Bibliography lists twenty-eight pages of titles of books and articles for the years 1982 to 1997, with a sharp increase in titles after 1988. Some representative examples: "Abject Bodies/Selves: Personal Narratives of Disabled Women," "Racialized National Abjection and the Asian-American Body on Stage," "Female Abjection in Inchbald's *A Simple Story*," "Homosexuality, Abjection, and the Production of a Late Twentieth-Century Black Masculinity," "The Abject: Kristeva and Antigone," "Women Speaking on the Ground of the Abject in the Plays of Maria Irene Fornes," "The Speaking Abject," "Anna Kavan's Narratives of Abjection," "Robert Frost and the Abject," "The Abject in Faulkner's *As I Lay Dying*," "Writing the Mother in the *Notebooks of Malte Laurids Brigge*. The Rhetoric of Abjection," "Charivari and the Comedy of

365

Abjection in *Othello*," "Eliot's Abjection," "Tattoos, Abjection and the Political Unconscious," "Coleridge, Wordsworth and the Textual Abject," "Reflections on Abjection, Anorexia, and Medieval Women Mystics," "Abjection and Organization: Men, Violence, and Management."[2]

The titles of all these books and essays bespeak a conscious recognition that the question of "abjection" was a particularly new and 'relevant' phenomenon. Other texts, by contrast, made use of this "concept" as though it were already a well-established given of all critical thinking. An author like Walter Benjamin has certainly before the 1990s been 'translated' into a variety of theoretical idioms, but he could be construed as a seismograph of abjection only after this evocative, if peculiarly elusive—"paradigm" had gained its ascendancy.[3] For speakers of German (at least until recently), words like *abjekt, das Abjekte*, or *die Abjektion* strike the ear as blatant neologisms; they have no tradition as naturalized loanwords, and hence their meaning can be deduced only through derivation from Latin *abicere* (to cast away) and *abiectum* (outcast). It is otherwise in the case of French and English: "abject" and "abjection" are customary (foreign) terms here, meaning, respectively, "lowly, mean, despicable," and "baseness, meanness, despicableness." Of course, these words have never belonged to a scholarly vocabulary. It was only by means of a double turnabout *vis-à-vis* its pejorative meaning that "the abject" could become the keynote of a discourse at once theoretically ambitious and politically loaded. All cultural rules and regulations had, first, to be read from the perspective of what they serve to rule out: that other—which they cannot or will not integrate—becomes in each case what is specifically abject—whether it be women, homosexuals, ethnic minorities, AIDS patients, or even offensive artworks. And, secondly, what was officially considered abject had to be embraced, more or less provocatively, as a positive alterity, thus challenging the legitimacy of the cultural discrimination at issue in each case.

REPRESSION, REPUDIATION, ABJECTION

It was the work of a psychoanalyst that provided the political-cultural arena with the new buzzword: Julia Kristeva's *Pouvoirs de l'Horreur. Essai sur l'abjection* (1980). Although an extraordinarily demanding book in itself—accessible only to readers familiar with psychoanalysis, philosophy, theology, and literary studies—this work has functioned (after the publication of an English translation in 1982) as the catalyst providing evocative and highly resonant means of addressing a variety of heterogeneous problems.

Among other things, Kristeva's theory is also, although not first and foremost, a theory of *dégoût*—of disgust in the face of the "unclean" body, and of nausea at the prospect of certain foods. The carefully elaborated theories of disgust, which philosophy and aesthetics have produced since Mendelssohn, have no resonance at all in Kristeva. She is evidently unfamiliar with them.[4] On the other hand, Kristeva also avoids any mention of a theory of disgust that, at least in some of its elements, was certainly known to her: the Freudian. This is all the more perplexing since the confrontation with Freud is precisely the medium in which Kristeva develops her "essay on abjection." Two terminological questions, therefore, ought to be raised at the outset of any discussion of Kristeva's book: Why does Kristeva feel it necessary to add yet another concept to the Freudian catalogue of defense mechanisms (repression, repudiation, denial, transference)—and, moreover, a concept which, at first sight, can be read as a newly proposed translation for "repudiation?" And why does Kristeva's *dégoût* keep apart from Freud's *Ekel?*

In his treatise entitled *Negation*, Freud derives the function of the pleasure-driven ego from an elementary code of ego-pleasure which governs the binary opposition between "introducing into myself" and "ejecting from myself":

> The attribute to be decided about [by intellectual judgment] may originally have been good or bad, useful or harmful. Expressed in the language of the oldest—the oral—instinctual impulses, the judgment is: "I would like to eat this," or "I would like to spit this out"; and, put more generally, "I would like to introduce this into myself and to keep that out." Which is to say: "It shall be inside me" or "it shall be outside of me." ... The original pleasure-driven ego wants to introject into itself everything that is good and to eject from itself everything that is bad.[5]

Analogously, Kant had based the exclusionary judgment of disgust on the difference between wholesome and unwholesome, life-promoting and life-threatening; Nietzsche had based it on the difference between yea-saying and nay-saying. In the passage cited, Freud does not speak directly about disgust; rather, his concern here would seem to be with pleasure and displeasure. What is not pleasing to the pleasure-driven ego—whatever is "bad" for it—is not in itself necessarily disgusting, although the highest degrees of displeasure border on the disgust reaction. Furthermore, there is another distinction to be drawn between the "ejecting from myself" of the pleasure-driven ego and the warding off in disgust: the latter is, structurally speaking, neurotic or neuroticizing, while the former is not. This distinction loses its significance, however, as soon as we focus not on the ejecting-from-itself of the archaic pleasure-driven ego but on its derivative, namely the intellectual judgment of denial. This judgment proceeds from the beginning within the field of cultural repression, and it is precisely as a linguistic act in the service of repression that such judgment interests Freud. Accordingly, he reads the statement of a patient—"You ask who this person ... can be. It's *not* my mother"—as symptomatic of the "correct" sentence "So it *is* his mother."[6] For this intellectual ejecting-from-oneself performed by means of the linguistic sign of negation, Freud also utilizes, in the passage cited, the concept of repudiation: "What he is repudiating ... is of course the correct meaning."

Lacan has made an influential attempt to interpret the Freudian concept of repudiation in a manner bearing specifically on the theory of psychosis.[7] According to Freud, "in a neurosis the ego, in its dependence on reality, suppresses a piece of the id (of libidinal life), whereas in a psychosis, this same ego, in the service of the id, withdraws from a piece of reality."[8] Freud's instructive example is a young woman's desire to marry her brother-in-law, as first expressed at the death-bed of her sister: "Now he is free and can marry me." The neurotic reaction to the forbidden desire would be its immediate repression, with the eventual consequence of later "hysterical pains." The neurosis "devalues the change that occurred in reality by repressing the libidinal demand associated with it—that is, the love for the brother-in-law. The *psychotic* reaction would have been a disavowal of the fact of the sister's death."[9] Psychosis, therefore, directly and entirely repudiates portions of reality. Neurosis, by contrast, distorts reality only, if at all, indirectly, namely to the extent that the repression of a libidinal demand implies distortions of reality, too. Primarily, however, neurosis brings about an adaptation to reality and precisely prevents the dissociation of the pleasure principle from the reality principle.

Freud's concept of repudiation is by no means limited to the mechanisms of paranoia and psychosis, from which Lacan has taken his cue in developing his concept of *forclusion*. The feeling of disgust, at any rate, has no place in the psychotic repudiation of reality. Whatever I spit out or deny as disgusting I must first have taken thorough "cognizance" of in its particular givenness.[10] To use Freud's examples: the judgment of denial "It is not [my] mother," or Dora's judgment "The (beloved) man's kiss is disgusting," are neurotic judgments of repression; their psychotic equivalents would take the form "I have no mother" and "There was no kiss." In terms of Freudian pathology, the judgment of disgust, like that of denial, belongs exclusively in the field of neurosis. And it is also exclusively in the context of neurotic repression—and of a cultural process which, even in its "normal" mode, tends to be neuroticizing—that Freud makes use of the concept "disgust." Hence, "repudiation" in no way signifies, as it does in psychosis, an achievement of the id, but always an achievement of the ego (or super-ego): as, for example, when it is said that "incestuous fantasies are overcome and repudiated,"[11] or when excremental pleasure is qualified with the series of predicates "disgusting, abhorrent, and abominable [*verwerflich*, literally: worth repudiation]."[12] The great letter to Fliess of November 14, 1897, defines "repudiation"—making reference to the quasi-geological redistribution, or more literally, the "throwing into a different order," of topical strata implied in the German "Verwerfung"—as actually a direct result of repression, while repression, for its part, is conceived as analogous to the warding off of a stinking object in disgust.[13] Hence, in the context of Freud's theory of neurosis—and in the terminology of this book on disgust—the occasional conjunction of the concepts of disgust and *"Verwerfung"* ("repudiation") is not intended to suggest a sharply demarcated defense mechanism in distinction to repression, denial, and so forth. Rather, this conjunction owes its semantic surplus (in excess of the more general concepts of defense and repression) exclusively to the physiological chain of associations "vomit—eject from oneself—*verwerfen*," and to the allusion to the dark powers of the earth, which occasionally eject older strata of the earth thus displacing the more recent ones *[Gesteinsverwerfungen]*. (Unfortunately, these layers of meaning underlying Freud's use of the German word *verwerfen*, are lost in the English translation.)

The repudiation at issue in Kristeva lays claim to a *tertium datur:* it is situated neither in the field of neuroses nor in that of psychoses. Even the fundamental meta-psychological presupposition for the mechanisms of repression and repudiation—the distinction between consciousness and unconsciousness—loses its validity where abjection and the abject are concerned.[14] The new word is meant to enlarge the map of psychoanalysis of new "existences" and new mechanisms of demarcation and exclusion: "there are existences not sustained by *desire*—desire being always for objects. Such existences are based on *exclusion*. They are clearly distinguishable from those understood as neurotic or psychotic, articulated by *negation* and its modalities, *transgression, denial,* and *repudiation*" (6). Neurotic and psychotic traumata— the material for psychic defense work, in Freud's conception—go back, in the rule, to culturally proscribed sexual practices: either the objects alone are forbidden (incest with the mother, daughter, etc.), or the libidinal impulses overstep normative barriers of disgust (homosexuality, coprophilia, oral intercourse), or it is a matter of combining perverse desires with forbidden objects. In principle, both objects and desires could be imagined or named as such. The case is different for the abject: "The abject is not an ob-ject facing me, which I name or imagine.... The abject has only one quality in common with the object—that of being opposed to the 'I'." (1) What sort of strange non-object and non-subject is this—one that precedes the distinction between conscious and unconscious, and always already must be "cast out" in order that some "speaking subject" can speak of itself as "I?" Kristeva's answer is: the maternal body—the maternal body not solely as nature and biological substance, but simultaneously in its relation to the symbolic order and to the pre-oedipal genesis of the speaking subject. This maternal body is further designated "semiotic," in order both to emphasize its function as "precondition of language," as the field of transition from nonsense to sense, and, at the same time, to mark its difference from the symbolic order of discrete linguistic signs (72). As such, Kristeva's "maternal body" has as little to do with empirical mothers as its counterpart (the father function in Lacan's sense) has to do with empirical fathers. Constituting the impersonal precondition, the boundary and "trustee" (72) of all future inscriptions, the maternal body is said to be equivalent to the Platonic *chora*.[15]

Kristeva's complex theory must be sharply distinguished from Georges Bataille's concept of "abjection," to which she occasionally refers. For Bataille, the "social abjection" befalling children from the poorest classes involves a fear of contact that is grounded in disgust: because their parents were not sufficiently able to keep them away from contact with "disgusting things," such children themselves become, in turn, a debased object of disgust.[16] To be sure, this simple structure of an *abjection humaine*, as predicated on an *abjection des choses*, may share with Kristeva's abjection of the maternal body the general feature of a constitution of (inter)subjectivity on the basis of a negative relation. Kristeva, too, understands the "inability" of destitute parents to provide adequate measures for the exclusion of filth as an index of the impossibility of ever fully mastering the "abject" and preventing its recrudescence (64). But nowhere in Bataille's schema of *abjection humaine* are to be found the libidinal-economic, psychohistorical, sexual, and decidedly non-objectival dimensions of Kristeva's originary *abjection* of the mother.

ABJECT MOTHER, SYMBOLIC ORDER, DESIRE

In the mother-child dyad, there are no clear distinctions of subject and object, inner and outer, "I" and others, but only fluid heterogeneities, rhythmic streamings of libidinal drives and matter.[17] For the child, the pregnant female body is an equivalent of Schelling's "absolute." In fact, Kristeva endows it with nearly all the qualities of the absolute in Idealist philosophy: it is preobjectival; it forms no circumscribed subject; it is undifferentiated; it is nameless—indeed, *the* nameless and unnameable; it is given in an athematic and pre-reflective mode of perception, and it transcends the antithesis of conscious and unconscious. In sum, it is *le lieu absolu*—"the absolute locus" (22). At the same time, this non-object is the inaccessible ground of all (future) distinctions and the source of a pleasure *(jouissance)* which exceeds all desire *(désir)* for an object and all satisfaction in objects. According to Kristeva, Freud's conception of the pre-oedipal relationship of mother and child was too idyllic and reassuring.[18] On the one hand, his picture of the infant being exempt, within the maternal womb, from all want and, hence, from all unpleasure, his description of an "economic situation" in which "[the mother] satisfies all [the infant's] needs without delay,"[19] does not attain to the Dionysian dimension of pleasure which Kristeva ascribes to the rhythmic pulsation of the symbiotic bodies of mother and infant and to the constant exchange of fluid matters between them. On the other hand, Freud does not see the "vital necessity" of a fundamental "matricide,"[20] a repudiation of the mother which precedes both her role as object of oedipal desire and the repudiation of this desire in the interests of the incest taboo. In order to be able to develop an idea of ego—whether in Freud's sense of a primary narcissism or in Lacan's sense of a mirror stage—the child has to abandon the *corps à corps* with the mother and seek to establish firm boundaries for its own bodily being and subjectivity. A (narcissistic) "subject" with a *corps propre*—with its own, pure and unalloyed body—can come into being only insofar as the maternal body, with its undifferentiated economy of fluidities and rhythmic impulses (14), is rejected as something unclean that threatens one's own proper boundaries. "The body must bear no trace of its debt to nature: it must be clean and proper in order to be fully symbolic" (102). This act of repulsion—so runs Kristeva's fundamental theorem—is the "primal repression"; it is only through and by means of such an act that a speaking subject, and with it the possibility of objects, first emerges (12).

The correlate of this repression—the non-object of the maternal body—receives the non-name of "abject" because, in phenomena of secondary repression that are keyed to (supposed) representatives of this body, it activates, on occasion, a perceptible "defensive position" (7), whose most intense bodily sign is the affect of disgust. Freud had interpreted the murder of the (perverse) father, amid the primal horde, as the primal scene of a necessary overcoming of paternal authority. The role of murderer here always fell to the son; to that extent, the struggle for authority was a purely masculine affair. Now, with the position of a "maternal authority" (72), which likewise disposes over life and death, Kristeva provides not only the son but also, and above all, the daughter with the motive and occasion for a virtually inevitable murder of the mother. Freud's work, from its beginnings all the way to *Moses and Monotheism*, is everywhere concerned with the authority of the father. Kristeva subscribes to this authority and, in her works published since 1980, uncovers some new aspects of it—now in accord with Lacan, now in opposition to him. But chiefly she sets up another, a maternal authority beside it—an authority that, although prey to "abjection" on a structural level, is, in terms of power, at least the equal of the father function.

The acquisition of language, the integration into the symbolic order, is for Kristeva coextensive with the development of the "speaking subject" and the simultaneous emergence of objects. By virtue of its own mechanism, all signification requires the repudiation of the undivided maternal being—assuming (with Saussure) that language is the field of discrete and differentiated articulation, the incision into presignificative "clouds" of sound and sense.[21] The linguistic sign is, seen from this perspective, an instance and trace of an originary repression of the maternal body:

> What is primal repression? Let us call it the ability of the speaking being, always already haunted by the Other, to divide, reject, repeat. Without *one* division, *one* separation, *one* subject/object having

been constituted . . . the abject confronts us . . . with our earliest attempts to release the hold of the *maternal* entity, even before ex-isting outside of her thanks to the autonomy of language. It is a violent, clumsy breaking away, constantly threatening to fall back under the sway of a power as securing as it is stifling. . . . The sign represses the *chora*. . . . (12–14)

The repression of the abject maternal body is thus constitutive for "each speaking being" (92)—precisely as, with Freud, "organic repression" and the "cultural repression" of particular libidinal impulses is constitutive for each civilized ego. Like everything repressed, the maternal body does not cease to return, thereby destabilizing the subject and the order founded on its own abjection. "Desire" and "affect" are two names for the insistence of repressed, undifferentiated *jouissance* under the conditions of the symbolic function and the constituted subject-object division:

Desire alone will henceforth be witness to that "primal" pulsation. (14)
This shell of ultra-protected signifier keeps breaking up—to the point of desemanticization, to the point of reverberating only as notes, music, "pure signifier" to be reparceled out and resemanticized anew. . . . And it is precisely at such a boundary [of language splitting] that *affect* leaves an imprint. Within the blanks that separate dislocated themes (like the limbs of a fragmented body), or through the shimmering of a signifier that, terrified, flees its signified, the analyst can perceive the imprint of that affect . . . (49)

Abjection, Disgust, and *Jouissance*

Like the cultural barriers of disgust, the neuroses and psychoses described by Freud are acquired only after the phase of primary narcissism, in which one first learns to speak. For Kristeva, therefore, these neuroses and psychoses are essentially tied to the field of the speaking subject, of its *désirs* and its possible objects. Abjection, however, first constitutes this very field. The disgust involved in the "feeling of abjection" is therefore rigorously distinguished from hysterical (sexual) disgust:

The disgust that is implied in [abjection] does not have the aspect of hysteric conversion; the latter is the symptom of an ego that, overtaxed by a "bad object," turns away from it, cleanses itself of it, and vomits it. In abjection, the revolt is completely . . . within the being of language. Contrary to hysteria, which provokes, or seduces the symbolic, but does not produce it, the subject of abjection is eminently productive of culture. Its symptom is the rejection and reconstruction of languages. (45)

This highly distinctive—pre- or, better, trans-neurotic—localization of the abjection-type disgust may lie behind Kristeva's decision, in her reflections on *dégoût*, to leave Freud's theory of disgust entirely untreated. The reference to hysterical disgust, in the passage cited above, appears to be the only instance in which (for purposes of comparison) she has brought Freud's wide-ranging and many-faceted theory of disgust within the compass of her own project. On the other hand, she clearly follows Freud in her attempt to make the concept of abjection the cornerstone of a comprehensive theory of culture, just as Freud had done with the concept of repression. To be sure, the feeling of abjection is only seldom identified, in any explicit way, with the feeling of disgust. Nevertheless, Kristeva's description of abjection, from the beginning, suggests an affinity with disgust: "There looms, within abjection, one of those violent, obscure revolts of being, directed against a threat that seems to emanate from an exorbitant outside or inside, hurled beyond the scope of the possible, the tolerable, the thinkable. It lies there, quite near, but it cannot be assimilated. It beseeches, worries, and fascinates desire, which, nevertheless, does not let itself be seduced. Apprehensive, desire turns aside; disgusted, it rejects" (1).

What is revolting to the senses is determined in every case, according to Kristeva, by the opposition between what is one's own and what is not one's own, what is pure and what is impure *(propre-impropre, pur-impur)*. This opposition, for its part, is nothing given in itself but rather a necessary function of becoming a subject: it is "*one* coding of the differentiation of the speaking subject as such, a coding of his repulsion *vis-à-vis* the other in order to autonomize himself" (82). Instead of being posited (as in Bataille) simply as the "effect" of a primordial "violence"—which, for the purpose of its "tonic" enhancement, has need of prohibitions and affective resistances—all representations and rituals of filth articulate, in some degree, "the boundary between semiotic authority and symbolic law" (73). The scandal of filth, of refuse, of the unclean consists in the infiltration of the (narcissistic) "clean and proper body"—an infiltration that reveals the body's laboriously achieved identity as brittle and deceptive (12–13).

The Kantian vital sense of disgust served to protect life and its well-being 'only'—but not any ego-identity of the subject, however it might be constituted; to be sure, Kant considered such an identity to be a necessary assumption, but not as something graspable through reflective thinking. For Freud, we process in the feeling of disgust the polymorphous-perverse inheritance of archaic libidinal impulses *together with* their repression; as symptom and, hence, as compromise formation, this feeling bespeaks the dividedness of our psychic system as much as the triumph of the cultural ego. Now, at issue for Kristeva, in the concept of abjection, is both preservation and shattering of the identity of the "subject"—a philosophic category, it may be added, whose absence in Freud's meta-psychology is probably not a mere coincidence. In this regard, Kristeva's example drawn from the sphere of disgust with foods is instructive: "that skin on the surface of milk" (2–3). This skin of milk does not smell bad (at no point in her book, not even when discussing the corpse, does Kristeva mention stinking as the cardinal experience of disgust); it also, perhaps, does not taste bad, but—like the clammy in Sartre—it shatters the boundaries of inner and outer, of firm and fluid, of *propre* and *impropre*.[22] It thus recalls the descent from the undividedness of the maternal body and the instability of the separations on which the integrity of one's own body is based.

Likewise, the corpse is not abject because it stinks, or because putrefaction begets overabundant life in a false place (Rosenkranz), but because it has "irremediably" "fallen" out of the symbolic order (3–4). As the "fundamental pollution" (109), the abject corpse is—within the realm of objects—the objective equivalent, indeed the sister, of the maternal body that can never be objectified: "Mother and death—both abominated, both abjected—slyly construct a victimizing and persecuting machine, at the cost of which I become subject of the Symbolic as well as Other of the Abject" (112). The prohibition of incest issuing from the position of the father, then, is merely the weak corroboration of a prehistoric incest phobia related to the abject mother whose body is the site where the boundaries of the subject are dissolved (61–64). Insofar as the disgusting old woman of classical aesthetics can be read as an emblem of the abject mother, Kristeva reformulates the primary figures of the abject in the construction of the aesthetic—the disgusting woman and the decomposing corpse—as elements of every subject-formation in the field of the paternal symbolic order.

For Kristeva, unlike Freud, "the spasms and vomitings that protect me" (2) are generated exclusively through phenomena that pertain to the paradigm of filth, refuse, secretions, and as such are directly associated with the disgust reaction. Disgust at something overly sweet or overly pretty has no place in Kristeva. Erratic disgust, in particular, such as hysterical disgust at the "wrong" time and with the "wrong" object, appears entirely irrelevant to the abjection that simultaneously constitutes and threatens the "speaking subject." Nevertheless, the feeling of abjection or of disgust, is, in Kristeva too, essentially a function of memory; it is in no way simply dependent for its power on something that "lies there, quite close" (1). All present and objective experiences of disgust, for Kristeva, can only have a phobic effect, because they recall that abject (because originally repressed) maternal body which lies behind all difference of subject and object—just as, in classical aesthetics, the feeling of disgust owes its unassimilable character to the "association" that recalls offenses to the sense of smell, and just as, in Freud, that feeling is linked to long past traumata of childhood or of phylogenesis. In Kristeva, the memory involved in the feeling of abjection includes, in the end, a "self-abjection." For the subject repudiates nothing other than its origin and its own (non)being in the maternal body.

> The abjection of self would be the culminating form of that experience of the subject to which it is revealed that all its objects are based merely on the inaugural *loss* that laid the foundations of its own being. There is nothing like the abjection of self to show that all abjection is, in fact, recognition of the *want [manque]* on which any being, meaning, language, or desire is founded. (5)

The originary loss, the experience of a lack—that which underlies the being of an object, as much as it underlies all signification of language—precisely this is what is meant by *l'abjection* (5). Already Freud had laconically observed that "the mother was not an object . . . and, at that time, there were no objects at all."[23] Objects first emerge, Freud goes on to say, only after the "loss of the object" par excellence—the separation from the mother. And it is precisely this originary object-loss—more precisely, this originary loss of *the* non-object—that first induces the infant to send "signals."[24] According to Kristeva, all corporeal-psychological states, all acts and affects that preserve the memory of an epoch prior to this constitutive lack (and thus prior to the emergence of objects, as well as of linguistic signs), call into question the identity and integrity of that self which owes its existence, from the first, to the "originary repression" of the maternal non-object. In terms of pathology, this fundamental threat to "all identity"—a threat posed by the undifferentiated "abject"—can come close to psychosis (44) even though the "originary" abjection always remains categorically distinct from psychotic repudiation.[25] What Kristeva brings, in a manifold way, into direct relation with (the language of) psychosis is not the pre-oedipal abjection that is constitutive for the subject but rather the post-oedipal modes in which the constituted subject strives to repudiate the repudiation that founds it and to seek out, once again, a connection to the abject *corps maternel*.[26] For, here, the *jouissance* of the primary process prevails against the reality principle of the symbolic order and thus entails the danger of a "psychotic" disintegration of ego and (paternal) world. To this extent, the literature of the "abject"—for Kristeva, the cardinal form of such second-order repudiation—is structurally psychotic. By contrast, the judgment of repudiation that speaks from Freud's concept of disgust belongs unequivocally in the field of "normal" or pathological neurosis.

Disgust, in Freud, always betokens past and/or repressed pleasure. The same holds for Kristeva's concept of abjection: it too is the joint connecting an apotropaic gesture with a prehistoric legacy of pleasure. Freud had occasionally judged precisely those "perverse" pleasures repudiated in disgust to be the supreme triumph of libido.[27] Kristeva similarly links all emphatic *jouissance*—which, in keeping with the Lacanian model, transcends "desire" and its objects (1), along with every symmetrical pleasure-unpleasure opposition—directly to abjection: "the advent of one's own identity demands a law that mutilates, whereas jouissance demands an *abjection* from which identity absents itself" (54). Furthermore, "*jouissance* alone causes the abject to exist as such. One does not know it, and one does not desire it; one joys in it *[on en jouit]*" (9). The *corps à corps* in the maternal body, the nearness of an "unnameable Otherness" within it, is the "solid rock of *jouissance*" (59) on which the "paternal function" shatters, just as, in Freud, the pleasure-repressing cultural process is shattered by indestructible archaic impulses. Corresponding to the double logic of the symptoms, the abject not only bespeaks the originary repression but also attests to the insistence of the repressed:

> The abject shatters the wall of repression and its judgments. It restores the ego to the abominable limits from which, in order to be, the ego has broken away—it restores it to the non-ego, drive, and death. Abjection is a resurrection that passes through death (the death of the ego). (15)

Accordingly, Kristeva derives the Freudian death drive, too, from the repudiation of the mother (112). For to *jouissance*—which can never be entirely repressed by this repudiation—belongs the pleasure in one's own non-being (as ego, as a speaking subject which can relate to and name objects only in the wake of an originary loss of *the* object). In its relation to the maternal body, this *jouissance* blends Freud's theory of the death drive and of the archaic triumph of the libido over all barriers of disgust and prohibitions of perversion with Bataille's *érotisme* of excess, of pleasurable self-abandonment, of death, of decomposition, and—not least—of perversions conceived as the royal road to a transgressive economy of expenditure. Still, the basic assumptions underlying the Dionysian transgression of the (official) self through a positive reappropriation of the repudiated differ in Bataille and Kristeva on various counts. Bataille's *érotisme* is grounded in an ontology of male desire: from the beginning, its primordial "violence" has need of feminine beauty as something to be befouled, and of feminine disgustingness as the energizing prerequisite to the most powerful and victorious discharge, overcoming all possible resistances. Kristeva, by contrast, presents the *économie biopulsionelle* of the preobjectival and "unnameable" maternal body as foundation of a theory of the subject's *emergence*, and the position of the female abject, in this theory, is by no means merely that of raw material for the "sacred" transgression performed by male violence. Despite the similarity in the respective rhetorics of revolt and subversion, the transformation from repulsion to attraction has entirely different functions. In Bataille, the acts of "subversive" self-expenditure—precisely in their difference from the order of the useful—found an archaic "core" in which, beyond the manifestations of (male-sadistic) power, the coherence of premodern communities was formed and confirmed. For Kristeva, on the other hand, the subl(im)ation of repudiation shatters every male order at its core, and exposes it to the repressed experience of *autorité maternelle*.

The double register of abjection—as necessary matricide and also *jouissance* in loss of self—makes for its fundamental ambiguity: "We may call it a border phenomenon; abjection is above all ambiguity. Because, while drawing a boundary *[démarquant]*, it does not radically cut off the subject from what threatens it—on the contrary, abjection acknowledges it to be in perpetual danger. But also because abjection itself is a composite of judgment and affect, of condemnation and yearning, of signs and drives" (9–10). Operating in the register of repudiation, and yet entailing the possibility of regaining the repudiated for a deterritorialized and deterritorializing pleasure, abjection remains—like the Freudian disgust and Bataille's *dégoût*—tied to the structure of perversion:

> The abject is related to perversion. The sense of abjection that I experience is anchored in the superego. The abject is perverse because it neither gives up nor assumes a prohibition, a rule, or a law; but rather turns them aside, leads them astray, corrupts them . . . (15)

The feeling of abjection could not affect us so strongly if a paternal gestus and the symbolic order had prevailed for all time over the authority of the maternal *chora*. The shattering of bodily boundaries in the "feeling of abjection" witnesses to the weakness of the father-function, and it is this weakness of the super-ego that "opens the door to perversion or psychosis" (63–64). To this extent, abjection is "at the crossroads of phobia, obsession, and perversion" (45). But Kristeva takes care not to confuse it with a "true perversion" (46). This borderline holds even for those "corpse fanciers" (109) and "devotees of the abject" (54) who break through the ambiguity of abjection in the interests of some affirmative eroticization of the abject. The libidinal cathexis of blood, excrement, and urine can be conceived of in terms of "perverse" impulses, as Freud understands them (54–55); but Kristeva provides another reading of this phenomenon. For Freud, excremental pleasure is in itself a given, an archaic inheritance, and a manifest form of behavior among children; it is only in the field of cultural repression, and of the barriers of disgust, that its untimely fixation takes on the cast of perversion. For Kristeva, on the other hand, the eroticization of bodily wastes is yet another function of the abjection of the mother—symptom of a particular manner of articulating the relation to the maternal body:

> Devotees of the abject . . . do not cease looking, within what flows from the other's "innermost being," for the desirable and terrifying,

nourishing and murderous, fascinating and abject inside the maternal body. For—in the miscarriage of identification with the mother, as well as with the father—how else can they maintain themselves in the Other? How, if not by incorporating a devouring mother, for want of having been able to introject her, and joy in what manifests her, for want of being able to signify her: urine, blood, sperm, excrement. (54)

The position of the analyst is stamped by such a quasi-perverse obsession with the abject. Thus, when addressing her own position, Kristeva surrenders all discriminatory caution and speaks bluntly of a "perverse *jouissance*" (210). Here, too, she works a variation on her psychoanalytic *Übervater* Freud, for whom the systematic disclosure of "perverse" instincts or experiences was the core of analysis, and who evidently derived both intellectual and affective pleasure from his discoveries. Through the agency of the abject mother, understood as the central reference point for perverse obsessions and psychotic losses of identity, Kristeva dethrones Freud's archaically perverse (seducer-) father—a figure who, in Lacan, becomes normalized in the "paternal function" of prohibitions, laws, and linguistic signs. She reformulates the project of psychoanalysis (namely, to trace the fate of drives, bodies, affects in the fissures of the symbolic order) in a pointedly philosophizing and politicizing terminology. And yet the confession of her own perverse pleasure is still best prepared through Freud:

> the analyst, since he interprets, is doubtless among the rare contemporary witnesses to our dancing on a volcano. If he draws perverse *jouissance* from it, fine. . . . Would he be capable . . . of displaying the abject without confusing himself with it? Probably not. (210)

LITERATURE AS (PERVERSE) RECLAMATION OF THE ABANDONED

Beyond the cure and the situation of transmission, the perverse pleasure of the analyst has an equivalent in art. According to Kristeva, literature repudiates the repudiation; to the "originary" abjection it responds with a second-order *rejet*.[28] To be sure, it does not entirely leave behind the symbolic order in favor of the "semiotic," but it "perversely" and "subversively" inscribes the movement of abject bodies and drives within the symbolic:

> The writer, fascinated by the abject, imagines its logic, projects himself into it, introjects it, and as a consequence perverts language—style and content. But, on the other hand, just as the sense of abjection is both judge and accomplice of the abject, so it is for

the literature that confronts it. One might thus say that with such a literature is realized a crossing over of the dichotomous categories of Pure and Impure, Prohibition and Sin, Morality and Immorality. For the subject firmly settled in its superego, a writing of this sort is necessarily implicated in the interspace that characterizes perversion. (16)

The aesthetic task—a descent into the foundations of the symbolic order—amounts to retracing the fragile limits of the speaking being, in closest proximity to its dawn, to that bottomless "origin" known as primal repression. In this experience, which is nevertheless undertaken by the Other, "subject" and "object" do not push each other away; they confront each other, collapse, and are redistributed anew—inseparable, contaminated, condemned, at the boundary of what is assimilable, thinkable: abject. Great modern literature unfolds over that terrain: Dostoyevsky, Lautréamont, Proust, Artaud, Kafka, Céline. (18)

Literature travels the "signifying path" *(trajet signifiant)*—murder of the mother and "murder of soma"[29]—in the opposite direction: not from the maternal body to the symbolic, but "from the symbolic" to the abject, to the "originally" repressed.[30] To be sure, what has been repressed finds no restitution here, for literature requires the symbolic and remains in its field. But literature "perverts" the symbolic, sets it vibrating, and breaks through resistances (134–35). Literature is the emergence of a "pure signifier" (23), which does not convey a homogeneous meaning, but rather disperses such meaning and discloses a "meaninglessness" *[non-sens]* (2). In Kristeva's psychoanalytic translation, this also means: the pure literary signifier is "abandoned by the paternal metaphor" (51), while allowing an opening (back) to the repudiated maternal body. "Might not modern art then be . . . the implementation of that maternal love, . . . a sublimated celebration of incest? . . ."[31] Kristeva can thus credit literature—in its unique blending of categories of (non)sense, the sexual, and the bodily—with a "sublimation of abjection" (16) and even a "reconciliation" with the repudiated (61). Or, in the philosophical terminology of subject and object, possible and impossible: literature is "the language—possible at last—of that impossibility which is a-subjectivity or nonobjectivity *[de cet impossible qu'est l'a-subjectivité ou la non-objectivité]*" (26). As a classical example of the (recurrent) intrusion of *jouissance* into the symbolic order, Kristeva, too, mentions the "unsublimated corporality of dance, song, and poetry" in those Dionysian festivals[32] which the young Nietzsche had already invoked in terms of the dissolution of the subject-object polarity and the voluptuous contact with a "primal ground" that, seen from without, provokes disgust. As the site of a radical dissociation of self, the author of modern literature is, at the same time, a reincarnation of the polymorphous-perverse figure of the child. Kristeva historicizes this role by means of a generalizing diagnosis of culture: in modernity, traditional superego positions (like religion or morality)—which had brought under semantic control the repressed, though insistent abject—forfeit their credibility in large part and thus also their power as a social bond. The semblance of their necessity shatters on the experience of their being arbitrary and power-based impositions indeed their impossibility and absurdity (16, 18). With this, the symbolic order is exposed as permeable and unstable; less encumbered by religious and moral prohibitions, the literary "revolution" of the symbolic order rapidly attains to the value of a psychotic disintegration of the subject in the interests of an abject *jouissance*. Modern authors may well avoid this clinical danger—one that, by the way, Kristeva holds to be far more serious for women authors than for men[33]—, yet their writing generally assumes the value of a perverse act. Despite this weakening of restrictive barriers, the modern author always preserves—for the sake of his "third degree repudiation,"[34] his symbolic revitalization of the abject—some measure of playful distance:

> The representation of the "character" who becomes the site of this process is something that normative consciousness finds intolerable. For this "character's" polymorphism is one that knows every perversion and adheres to none, one that moves through every vice without taking up any of them—un-identical, in-authentic, wisdom of artifice, without interiority, constant repudiation. As an unbearable monstrosity to the social body and its paranoid reality, which it does not so much ignore as toy with . . .[35]

Among the perversions reactivated through the structure of modern literature and the position of the modern author, Kristeva numbers not least the anal libido and its sadistic components. In Kristeva's view, the anal act of ejecting is the "precondition" for the symbolic, insofar as the latter depends on a casting out of the presymbolic as unclean, impure material; simultaneously, it is itself "what is repressed in the symbolic," insofar as the symbolic *corps propre* lacks precisely the capacity to excrete. It follows that the reactivation of anality—instead of being, as in Bataille, simply the archaic datum of a sacred-sadistic act of violence—can function to restore the drives of the body and the abject mother; indeed, in itself it can "make" the symbolic "a mobile *chora*."[36] The pleasure of texts—thanks to their negativity, their Dionysian disintegration of symbolic orders—is analogous to anal-sadistic pleasures:

> The texts of Lautréamont, Jarry, and Artaud—among others—explicitly point to the anal drive that agitates the subject's body in his subversion of the symbolic function. . . . Although psychoanalysis may speak of fantasies *[fantasme]* in literature, it never mentions the

economy of the subject that dissolves the symbolic and the language bound up with it. If the return of (excretionary) rejection *[rejet]*—by corrupting the symbolic and, with it, the sublimation in modern texts—attests to the presence of the death drive (that is, to the destruction of both the living being and the subject), then how can we neglect the jouissance harbored in this "aggressivity," this "sadistic component?" The jouissance of destruction (or, if you will, of the "death drive"), which the text manifests through language, traverses an unburying of repressed, sublimated anality.[37]

Rhythm, Laughing Apocalypse, Happy Guilt

For the literary dévotees of the abject, Kristeva sketches several elementary possibilities for traveling—in reverse direction, and via a specifically "poetic negativity"—down the paths of "symbolic negation and neurotic denial."[38] The term used most frequently for this reconquest of the maternal-material is "rhythm":

> This "material," repudiated by the sign and the judgment (operating beyond the range of *[hors des]* the first symbolizations), is now drawn away from the unconscious into language, but without being accepted there in the mode of "metalanguage" or of an intellection at all. The reiterated drive (of death: negativity, destruction) withdraws from the unconscious and *takes up a position, as already positivized and eroticized, in a language* that, by virtue of this emplacement, is organized into prosody or rhythmic timbres.[39]

The triad "rhythm, drive, the feminine" (180) reactivates, as far as rhythm is concerned, a set of conventional features, such as are familiar in rhetoric and poetics: as rhythmic phenomena, linguistic signs have an immediate relation to the dimension of affect, thanks to the features of temporal distribution and accentuation shaping the 'body' of the sign itself. This fluid corporeality of the rhythm has been traditionally associated with various functions: as an aid to goal-oriented persuasion, as accompanying or autonomous self-expression of speech, as the "pure music" of poetic language. Kristeva does nothing more nor less than to take up, in a rather vague form, the affirmation of "rhythm and music as . . . the ultimate sublimation of the unsignifiable" (23), and, without further ado, to ground it in the transcendental referent of her thought, the *économie biopulsionelle* of the maternal body. She provides no detailed argumentation for this parallellism of rhythmic linguistic body and primordial maternal body. Moreover, her concrete descriptions of rhythmic phenomena in literary works are rather disappointing and, from the perspective of literary criticism, break no new ground.

The thesis that "the abject resides, beyond the themes, . . . in the way one speaks" (23) is based not only on rhythm but on all the phenomena traditionally appertaining to the dimension of "style" (16). Kristeva's analysis of "Céline, the stylist" (188) is concerned above all with syntactic techniques.[40] The model for this analysis is that of a traditional stylistics focussing on features deviating from the 'normal': unconventional sentence types are interrogated for their "psychological value" (195). The idea that such stylistic innovations bring about a disturbance or even destruction of the symbolic order as well, and that, through their own bodily character, they open up pre-oedipal channels to the repressed body of the mother, cannot, of course, be deduced from a stylistic analysis in itself. Such a deduction requires a twofold external presupposition: first, one must accept Kristeva's basic theory and, second, one must consider it legitimate to short-circuit this basic theory with a rather conventional stylistic analysis. Kristeva herself may have experienced some dissatisfaction with the gulf that stretches between her empirical observations on style and the enormous theoretical freight with which they are loaded. Compared with the study entitled *Revolution in Poetic Language* (1974), the book on abjection (1980) betrays an effort to bring her own program more closely to bear on the material content of literature—at least insofar as this entails not simply some thematic material but also bears on the very (dis)position of speaking that is at work in a specific literary text. Pursuing this line, the protagonists and plot structures in the works regularly appear as (symbolic) prosopopeias of certain antitheses: semiotic versus symbolic, abject maternal body versus the law of the father. For Dostoyevsky, Proust, and Joyce, Kristeva has provided compressed formulations of such profiles of abjection within the highly charged field of repudiation and the repudiation of repudiation. These shorthand notes lay bare, with extreme simplification, the underlying pattern informing Kristeva's detailed analyses, too:

> Dostoyevsky has X-rayed sexual, moral, and religious abjection, displaying it as collapse of paternal laws. Is not the world of *The Possessed* a world of fathers who are either repudiated, bogus, or dead, a world where matriarchs lusting for power hold sway—ferocious fetishes but nonetheless phantom-like. And by symbolizing the abject, through a masterful delivery of the jouissance produced by uttering it, Dostoyevsky delivered himself of that ruthless maternal burden./But it is with Proust that we find the most immediately erotic, sexual, and desiring mainspring of abjection; and it is with Joyce that we shall discover that the feminine body, the maternal body, in its most unsignifiable aspect, shores up, in the individual, the fantasy of the loss in which he is engulfed or becomes inebriated, for want of the ability to name an object of desire. (20)

For Kristeva, such schematizations not only bear on matters of content, but on the project of literature itself in the work of the respective authors. They have direct consequences for the very position of speaking (137–38), and therefore pertain to the entire field of "style and content" (16), rather than simply to the content alone. To every author his specific abject—so runs the motto for these profiles in abjection, which have to do with the objective representatives of the nonobjective, unnameable "abject": "The abject, depending on the writer, turns out to be named differently when it is not merely suggested by linguistic deviations that are always somewhat elliptical" (26). At the same time, however, this "naming" misses the unnameable abject (unnameable because transcendent of the symbolic order): "It goes without saying that one can say nothing of such . . . heterogeneity without making it homologous with the linguistic signifier" (51). Therefore, what is "named" by literature must be read by Kristeva as a symptom—more precisely, a symptom of something "unnameable"—and hence be crossed out in its literality. Accordingly, the hysterical body—which speaks, within the symbolic order, the symptom-language of (oedipalized) neurosis—is explained, for its part, as an indirect representation of the pre-neurotic, pre-oedipal, and presymbolic body of the mother: "[Joyce] approaches the hysterical body so as to let it speak, so as to speak from its perspective of what eludes speech. This proves to be the body-to-body *[corps-à-corps]* of one woman with another, with her mother of course, the absolute (because primeval) seat of the impossible—of what is excluded, what is outside meaning, what is abject" (22). The relations posited here between a represented abject and an unnameable and primordial abject are, by their very nature, as little susceptible of empirical proof as the relations said to exist between rhythm and the maternal body.

Although the figures of the abject are different in the case of each author, and although, in a reading of the sort Kristeva proposes, their interpretation would presumably unfold in a manner not to be anticipated beforehand, her reading of Céline nonetheless provides a model that seems capable of some degree of generalized application. On the one hand, this reading focuses on certain "appropriate themes" (appropriate to the abject): themes of "horror, death, madness, orgy, outlaws, war, the feminine menace, the hideous delights of love, disgust, and fright." On the other hand, the focus on these themes is designed to produce a reading that is more than thematic. For what is at stake in such a reading is the articulation of an ambivalent position of speech suspended between apocalypse and carnival:

> My reading, however, will not be a thematic one—first, because of the very themes involved, but mainly because, with Céline, such themes always assume at least a double stance between disgust and laughter, apocalypse and carnival. (137–38)

"The laughing apocalypse" is accordingly a fundamental figure in the modern literary processing of *the* abject. The grotesque body, in Bakhtin's sense, returns—although remaining at every moment a repudiated one, too. The carnival expounded in Bakhtin's book on Rabelais thereby loses its ideological optimism stressing the procreation of living matter even in excretion and death and becomes a "bitter carnival."[41] The peculiar laughter of literature—Kafka's laughter may serve as an example here—resides in this tension "between disgust and laughter, apocalypse and carnival." Just as, according to Freud, prohibited tendencies find expression through wit, so does our attitude toward the unnameable abject through laughing: "For laughter is a way of placing or displacing abjection" (8).[42] With this, Kristeva—like Bataille before her—incorporates into her own theory what (since Nietzsche) is a key element in the philosophy of disgust: the element of laughter. As an act of expulsion, laughter in itself resembles the act of vomiting in disgust. On the other hand, the sudden discharge of tension in laughter, as in vomiting, makes for an overcoming of disgust, a successful (and, in this case, comical) contact with the abject, without psychotic disintegration on the part of the subject.

A second figure which Kristeva found recurrent among various ways of symbolizing the abject has its prototype in the interiorization of sin in the Christian confession of guilt. Confession does not cease to address the abject by means of subjecting it to the difference of pure and impure. But it no longer posits the impure as a threat coming from without:

> Abjection is no longer exterior. It is permanent and comes from within. Threatening, it does not entrench itself, but is reabsorbed into speech. Unacceptable, it endures through the subjection to God of a speaking being who is innerly divided and who, precisely through speech, does not cease purging himself of that speech. (113)

Whereas the originary repression, in establishing the (paternal) space of the sign, withdraws the antecedent "chaos" (61) of bodily and libidinal flux from all direct verbalization (49), the linguistic acknowledgment of sinfulness reabsorbs the "impure" into the symbolic order: "Sin as action—as action stemming from will and judgment—is what definitely integrates abjection into logic and language." (128–29) This absorption into language discloses the possibility of a "happy" abjection. The Roman Catholic Easter Night liturgy, in the *Exsultet*, knows of a felicitation reserved for Adam and sinful humanity: namely, the *felix culpa*, the sin that first made possible the redemption eventually brought about through Christ. Already Bataille had rediscovered, for his theory of sovereign transgression,[43] this theodicy (highly controversial within Christian dogma), which turns the transgression of a divine prohibition into the pathway to salvation. For Bataille, the sacred consists precisely in excess, in a violation of fundamental prohibitions. Kristeva's theory of abjection reinterprets Bataille's *interdit* as the prohibition that proceeds from the (Lacanian) father, from the ruler of the symbolic order; Bataille's position of the sacred, expenditure and self-loss, is replaced by the maternal body; and his idea of transgression is reinvented as the linguistic transgression that opens up within the symbolic order a way back to the forbidden maternal body. All these redistributions of Bataille's transgressive schema imply that it is not sin or ritual transgression itself that opens the way to the sacred (and 'salvation'), but rather the fact that the abject becomes language, that what is prohibited is incorporated into the very symbolic order which originally was constituted through the repudiation of the abject: "It is owing to speech, at any rate, that the lapse has a chance of becoming a happy one; *felix culpa* is exclusively a phenomenon of enunciation" (131). Art, for Kristeva, finds in *felix culpa* a model by which to adapt the representation of the abject to the conditions of aesthetic pleasure: "It is on this marginal potentiality of spoken sin, as happy sin, that art grounds itself" (131). The "happiness" that modern literature finds in the assertion of its own vileness is a functional equivalent of the laughter that accompanies the evocation of apocalypse. Both are figures of doubling and ambivalence by dint of which the *thèmes adéquats* of abjection come to play a more than thematic role in literature. (The reading of Kafka offered above corresponds, in various ways, to this more-than-thematic model of a *felix culpa* inherent in the processing of the abject.)

Abject Pleasure, Disgust, Truth, and the Real

"*Cette jouissance, cette vérité*" (this jouissance, this truth)[44]—with this identification, Kristeva finally projects her theory of the (potentially psychoticizing) pleasure in the "abject" on to the history of the philosophical concept of truth. Via the literature of the abject, the seemingly outmoded theorem about the truth of the beautiful is invested with new significance: "that language-practice in which the true is the beautiful."[45] This renewed identification of aesthetic language-practice with the true depends—and this is only apparently paradoxical—on nothing other than the intervention and structure of disgust (or abjection). Moses Mendelssohn had attributed to disgust the character of an unconditioned experience of reality and, thereby, a break with all media-based codifications. In his view, the feeling of disgust breaks through the binary opposition of nature and art, real and imagined, and hence unsettles the condition for the possibility of aesthetic symbolization. This feeling cannot be experienced as unreal; accordingly, it marks the irruptive impact of a hyperreality, beyond the simple antithesis of real and unreal. Kant had attributed to the life-promoting vital sensation of disgust a capacity that oversteps the bounds of our theoretical reason: an immediate intuitive—or, better, olfactory—knowledge of the things that concern us in their wholesomeness or harmfulness. Nietzsche saw in disgust both the indicator of a Dionysian insight into the "eternal being" of things and the privileged organ for an adequate judgment on temporal and contemporary issues, too. Freud traced out, in the defensive symptom of disgust, the "truth" of repressed pleasures and their neuroses, while Sartre detected, in the unavoidable feeling of presence entailed by disgust, the sole illusion-free access to existence in the *être de trop* of its contingent facticity. By the same token, Kristeva discovers at the site of the abject mother the call of an *autorité* and a potentially psychoticizing *jouissance*, which transcend the arbitrary and repressive laws of the symbolic order no less than the Lacanian "real" does.

The claim which disgust makes on the position of truth corresponds to a retreat by truth from its earlier positions. Since the time of Nietzsche, at the latest, we find metaphysical conceptions of truth—truth as God, as noumenal being, as idea, and so forth—appearing, if at all, only in starkly modified form. At the same time, there begins, with Nietzsche, a countermovement opposed to the tendency of academic philosophy to reduce the old doctrine of truth to the formal logic of correct propositions. Freud's discovery is probably the decisive one: in light of the operation of unconscious impulses and repressed desires, truth becomes a function not of our propositions and well-rounded sentences but of our slips of the tongue, our mistakes and defensive maneuvers. As Kristeva puts it, "Freud's work ... traces a movement in which *truth* is continually set up and knocked down—a process that ... destroys it as *identity* (Being, correspondence to Being, etc.) and leaves behind only a system of passages, folds, thresholds, catastrophes."[46] Truth is henceforth something that *posits itself* in the miscarriage of "normal" modes of symbolization, in the intermittent language of symptoms. Modifying Nietzsche and Freud, Benjamin has formulated a rehabilitation of metaphysical truth, which employs similar assumptions: according to Benjamin, the truth of art is, to be sure, a "being," yet one residing only in the interruption, in the breakdown of language, beauty, and semblance.[47] Now, disgust is in itself an operator of interruption: it interrupts every continuous approach and consumption. Likewise, it interrupts every unproblematic and continuous sense of self in favor of a sharp accentuation of the integrity of the self in the state of emergency, in the moment of decision between being and non-being. There is thus more than one point of convergence in the history of disgust and the history of truth.

In the twentieth century, disgust no longer pointed to only one truth among others, but rather made ready to occupy the position of *the* truth itself. Thus, a witness to the discourse on abjection captured very aptly a specific instance pointing to this larger context, when he wrote: "A special truth seems to reside in ... abject conditions, in diseased or disabled bodies."[48] This truth is not the truth of propositions. Nor does it consist in the representation of a particular sector of reality within the field defined by the tension of repulsion and attraction. Rather, it implies a more far-reaching claim: namely, in the dissolution of all constructions of reality, to let "the real" itself break through. Kristeva's term *le vréel* takes possession of this long prepared blending of disgust, truth, and the real with a striking neologism.

GRAND NARRATIVES OF THE HETEROGENEOUS

Kristeva's *Essay on Abjection* displays an impressive power of systematic integration. Freud had 'derived' the entire history of cultural development and the "destiny" of sexuality from the prehistoric transition to upright posture, from the devaluation of smell that accompanies this process, and from the archaic libidinal impulses that, once repressed with the rise of culture, enter the register of "perversions" while maintaining an indestructible insistence through human behavior, especially in the role of the "perverse father." Kristeva offers for a similarly comprehensive reflection—which likewise crosses the fields of human sexuality, language, art, and religion—a different transcendental reference point: the "absolute—because originary—site" of the maternal body. The originary repudiation of this body, its insistence as repudiated, its resemanticization, and its return, full of *jouissance,* in deformations of the symbolic order are the principal elements of a "grand narrative," by whose threads Kristeva attempts to weave together nearly all areas of sexual and cultural existence. The theory of abjection relates yet again—as Freud's narrative of disgust did before—the biological anatomy of the body directly to psychoanalysis and cultural theory. Kristeva's success stands in sharp contrast to all diagnoses of an end to grand narratives in "postmodern" times. Her book accomplishes a double achievement, one that resonates in various ways with major concerns of contemporary critical theory: it everywhere treats of the repressed dimensions—heterogeneous, unassimilable, untotalizable—of the maternal body, and thus of its own primary reference point; and yet it achieves in itself—insofar as it expounds the entire history of the subject and of cultural objectivizations in terms of the processing of this reference point—a truly exemplary totalization.

At first sight, the relation to the maternal body may appear to be a more convincing elementary anthropological datum than the preeminently traumatizing role which the young Freud assigns to the "perverse father," as the representative of our archaic libidinal dispositions. Moreover, Kristeva's incessant emphasis on the decisiveness of the very earliest phases of the infant's life for the entire shaping of the subject is borne out by a considerable body of more recent research indicating a highly developed psychic life already within the maternal womb. Nevertheless, Kristeva's central opposition between maternal body and paternal symbolic order leaves room for some qualifications. The question of biologism, and its incompatibility with the political ideas of feminism, can remain bracketed here. For the operation of the symbolic order,

Kristeva adopts an extremely reductive theory of language. The idea that the symbolic order, the acquisition of language, and the development of the subject are entirely governed by the *fonction paternel* is taken over, largely ready-made, as a valid insight from Lacan. Kristeva underlines the negative consequence implicit in this idea: as the law of the father, language for her is *ipso facto* the trace, medium and performative consummation of the repudiation of the maternal body (13). Language thus appears as noncorporeal, indeed anti-corporeal and anti-affective, sharply cut off from all "drive representations" (49). In a word, language is radically divested, at the first, from all mimetic, "poetic," and "maternal" dimensions, in order then to be invaded by these dimensions from without in the mode of a subversion and even destruction of "the symbolic." But what if *all* language has a "rhythm," and rhythm is not alone the privilege of poetic negativity and anal-sadistic dissolution of signifiers? What if "affect" is not the absolute other of the symbolic realm but rather—in keeping with the language theory of the eighteenth century—the "origin" of all linguistic behavior?

As far as the other side of the opposition is concerned (that of the *corps maternel*), a key feature, on which much of the theory relies, remains peculiarly vague. Kristeva does not restrict herself to the 'idyllic' evocation of the "body to body" relationship of mother and child, as enjoying a material-libidinal economy undisturbed by want and without clear divisions between inner and outer, solid and fluid, ego and other. Rather, she likewise maintains—and only this opposite feature accounts for the necessity of abjection as a kind of matricide—that the mother withholds and even takes life away as much as she gives life (161), that death threatens the "speaking subject" in the domain of the mother. The reason offered for this striking claim seems to lack sufficient explanatory power. Within the mother-child dyad, there is obviously no possibility for the child to be an autonomous ego. Any independent life demands, Kristeva therefore concludes, the abjection of the maternal body; conversely, any remembrance of the repressed *jouissance* enjoyed in the mother-child dyad is said to imply the pleasure in not yet being, or no longer being, an "autonomous" subject—and, hence, the pleasure in the death of the ego. Freud had also conceived the fantasy of a return to the womb as a regression back behind the achieved ego-differentiation—more precisely, as a "substitute for copulation" on the part of the "man who is impotent (that is, who is inhibited by the threat of castration)."[49] Yet it was by no means a pleasure in one's own death that he diagnosed in such a fantasy, but instead a neurotic defense against a threatened loss of the penis that Freud likened to a loss of the ego. Furthermore, there is simply no parallel in Freud to the striving of the child to become an "autonomous" subject,[50] and, for the sake of this presumed striving away from the maternal body, to have to repudiate it. Here, Kristeva appears engaged in building up the very fiction of autonomous subjectivity which elsewhere, and with great insistence, she works to undermine.

AIDS, DISGUST, AND AFFIRMATIVE ABJECTION: ON THE POLITICAL APPROPRIATION OF KRISTEVA

Kristeva does not command the often deceptive simplicity of style in which Freud was capable of presenting even his most speculative theorems. The great success which her extraordinarily difficult book has met with is therefore all the more amazing. This success—like that of other demanding theoretical texts—is first of all explained by the possibilities it offers for applications to a wide variety of fields. In the political field, various groups that felt themselves to be "abject"—in the sense of discriminated against or rejected—have used Kristeva's idiom in order to give a new articulation to their struggle for recognition, an articulation that allows both identification with and protest against their own "abjection." Homosexuals, in particular, whom Freud still occasionally called "the most repellent" perverts,[51] have thus been able, on the one hand, to condemn their own cultural abjection as a repressive function of patriarchal authority, while, on the other hand, provocatively affirming their abject existence as a socially unaccommodated way of life and source of pleasure. "An occupation or reterritorialization of a term that has been used to abject a population can become the site of resistance, the possibility of an enabling social and political resignification."[52] Such struggle for definition and counter-definition, for delimitation and liberation of the "abject," knows from the start that it is "entangled in the very thing one opposes." In the interests of "turning the prevailing authority against itself," however, this struggle forgoes all "'pure' opposition" and, instead, draws upon "resources that are unquestionably impure."[53] In undertakings of this kind, the radical alterity and unnameability of the abject, as Kristeva conceives it, is considerably moderated: "I do not claim that the abject gives us access to radical exteriority, merely that its invocation, under certain historical circumstances, can be used to renegotiate social relations in a contestary fashion."[54]

This sexual-political strategy bears a double analogy to Kristeva's conception of abjection and reconquest of the abject. Just as the speaking subject can be part of the symbolic order only by virtue of the originary repression of the *corps maternel*, which precisely in such repression becomes abject, so the formation of social identities requires the repression of all sexual impulses not in conformity with such socially prescribed identities. Here, too, what has been repressed in one's own history constitutes the "abject," and here, too, the "subversion" of abjection depends on a lack of power on the part of the dominant social order to enforce its rules without qualification. Just as the symbolic order can never entirely mute the insistence and the insurgence of the "abject," so the social normalizations of polymorphous-perverse childhood sexuality can never be absolutely effective; rather, they always leave some room for what escapes their effectiveness and thus open up entry points for modes of counter-cathexis: "The resignification of norms is accordingly a function of their ineffectiveness, and thus a question of utilizing weaknesses in the norm."[55]

The conditions for a homosexual politics of "affirmative abjection" have been altered, and rendered decidedly more difficult, by the phenomenon of AIDS. This phenomenon has strengthened both the older stereotype of the disgusting (male) homosexual and the homosexuals' own perception of their abject being. The classical aestheticians had, without exception, considered diseases of the skin and sexual organs to be "disgusting."[56] In doing so, they were thinking not so much of the occurrence of infection itself as of the visible disfigurement of the bodily surface. By contrast, whoever is diagnosed as HIV-positive becomes a potential object of disgust already at the "mere idea" of physical contact. Such disgust is founded not on seeing, touching, or smelling anything, but solely on the theoretical knowledge of the most common route of infection—homosexual anal intercourse—and of the fatal consequences of an invisible infection that might, in one way or another, invade our bodily integrity, too. With Kant—and, to some extent, even with Nietzsche—disgust could figure as *the* immune system that promptly, and in quasi-automatic fashion, defended body and mind against everything unwholesome. In this perspective, immune deficiency would be another name for the sickening of the health-protecting vital sensation of disgust—a sickening to which an intact defense-system can in turn respond with disgust, in the form of fear of contact.

In point of fact, association with persons diagnosed as HIV-positive does require strategies for overcoming disgust and for turning in a positive way to people whose immune system has been devastated. Blood, sperm, and anal pleasure—prime elements in the arousal of disgust, elements which Freud, Bataille, and Kristeva sought, at least in part, to extract and remove from the continent of disgust—appear, under the sign of AIDS, doubly liable to disgust, because infected in an especially perfidious manner: infected with that principle of infection itself which consists in the general disabling of the immune system. On the one hand, this immune system is heir to the old vital sense of disgust; on the other hand, it is far more uncanny than the latter. For it functions in complete detachment from consciousness; it fights against materials removed from sight, touch, or smell, and it generates no affective response in defense of the threatened self. The political strategy of "affirmative abjection" aims at affirming homosexual pleasure even in the face of AIDS-induced fear of contact and fear of death (a twin anxiety that is typical of the traditional feeling of disgust). Bataille's doctrine of an erotic transgression in which every lover abandons himself and the other, in ecstatic sacrifice, to death, finds in the clinical dimension of the potential course of infection a literal—and yet poisonously ironic—analogue. Having already encountered the barriers of organic-anatomical and cultural repression, the archaic pleasure in excrement, blood, and bodily secretions of all kinds now, in addition, runs up against medical prohibitions and taboos on contact. In light of this fact, the affirmation of "abject" types of pleasure requires an all the more intense energy of "negativity," and an all the more thorough break with culturally legitimated barriers of disgust. (The lesbian politics of the "abject" is subject, in this regard, to different conditions.)

Other groups discriminated against—ethnic minorities and marginal social groups of all kinds ("marginal" as measured by the fictive standard of the white American middle-class family)—struggle with rules of exclusion that often, at first sight, appear more pliant, since they are not always accompanied by bodily defense reactions. In fact, all social differentiation, as Pierre Bourdieu has shown,[57] makes use, in one degree or another, of "physiologically" grounded oppositions such as high versus low, or good versus bad taste, for the purpose of coding and giving emotional significance to distinctions which determine whether someone is part of a particular class (group, peergroup) or not. Here, by the way, is one of the reasons why the provocative politics of "affirmative abjection" no longer limits itself to the legalistic-rationalistic discourse of antidiscrimination: it also seeks to bring into play *feelings* of defense that border on disgust and tries to make them accessible to a revaluation, ideally to a direct countercathexis. The decidedly provocative element in the affirmation of abjection directly responds to the sense that anti-discrimination politics seemed to lose strength and even give way to a reverse trend. The official political scene in the United States has in fact witnessed a massive conservative "backlash" against everything that, under the rubrics of "affirmative action" and "antidiscrimination," had given juridical and political backing to the demands of the women's movement or to those of sexual and ethnic minorities. "Affirmative abjection" could thus be considered a combative answer to the crisis of "affirmative action": it turns the danger of a new calcification of traditional regulations of the abject into an aggressive intervention on behalf of the "lowly" and "rejected." The self-caricaturing program of the (fictive) "Party for Affirmative Abjection" got right to the heart of the matter: "It's time to imagine a state that could protect the inalienable right of its citizens to the pursuit of abjection. . . . *Affirmative abjection for all*, under many gods, multifarious and infinitely divisible. Only under such a regime could we be truly free and equal but different."[58]

Kristeva had linked the functioning of the paternal symbolic order and the formation of the speaking subject to the "originary" generation of an abject position; at the same time, she had looked for the insistence of this abject in "desire" and in literary methods of reconquering it. In similar fashion, the politics of "affirmative abjection" identified particular groups as abject (in relation to the prevailing order) in order to undertake the repudiation of repudiation and a countercathexis of the rejected. However, this parallel is tenable only from a misty bird's eye view which suppresses basic features of Kristeva's theory or even converts them into their direct opposites. The abject referent of the political discourse is always a specific historical and cultural phenomenon; this means that the rules concerning abjection are looked upon as changeable. "Abject identifications" are regarded as means for achieving an "appropriation and inversion of signs."[59] Through the countercathexis of the abject, the political struggle aims, in the end, to do away with the respective rules of abjection altogether. Kristeva's "abject," by contrast, is universally and biologically grounded (in the maternal body); likewise, the constitution of the speaking subject through the repudiation of the pre-objectival *corps maternel* and its pleasure belongs, for Kristeva, to the fundamental, unchangeable givens of subject-formation and of the symbolic order in general. Hence, the parallel drawn between Kristeva's abject mother and the figure of the abject homosexual would ultimately amount to turning the repudiation of homosexuality into an unavoidable law of culture. But this is clearly not the intent of the political appropriation of the term "abject." Rather, it replaces Kristeva's transcendental and non-objectival abject with one that is empirical and, indeed, an object (or, a subject, respectively). The position of the abject, in this way, not only assumes a different name but takes on an entirely different status.

This status is, in the final analysis, incompatible with Kristeva's theory. The only individually and historically relative variable in this theory is the degree and mode in which the "necessary matricide"—like all repression, in the end—meets with failure. In ever new and changing ways, religions, works of art, and individual biographies perform, on the one hand, the necessary abjection and conform to its objectival representatives (incest taboos, prohibitions on foodstuffs, and other barriers raised by disgust); on the other hand, they always bear traces of the insistence and recovery of the repudiated *jouissance*. Even as a substrate of "subversion," the *fonction paternelle* remains something necessary, positive, and indispensable—so much so, that Kristeva, alluding to the psychotic and suicidal tendencies of prominent women authors (Virginia Woolf, Sylvia Plath, Marina Zwetajewa), delivers a stern warning to women in particular to beware of abandoning the continent of paternal order in favor of too exclusive an attachment to the abject mother.[60] One would be hard pressed to find in the politics of those groups that called themselves abject anything that amounts to a similar affirmation of prohibitions and the order founded on them. Likewise, the overcoming of disgust with anal pleasure and with bodily secretions has a fundamentally different status. In Kristeva, these phenomena contribute to the destruction of the symbolic and function as symptoms of the maternal body, whereas in homosexual politics they function as something positive in themselves and thus undergo a far more direct counter-cathexis. In this way, Kristeva's unsettling theory is turned, in the last analysis, into a simple fable of repression and liberation. The evocative term "abjection" becomes the medium of an "identity politics":[61] the affirmation of the abject (which, in Kristeva, tends to be the psychotic counterpart of every subjective identity) promotes the self-confirmation of group identities. At issue here, it goes without saying, is not an objection to the widespread social and political appropriation of Kristeva's extremely adaptable term; these applications, interesting and legitimate in themselves, should not be confused, however, with Kristeva's own project.[62]

The Academic Career of the "Abject"

An adequate account of the academic career of the abjection paradigm could easily fill a whole book in itself. Viewed very abstractly, the academic concern with the "abject," as evidenced in various fields of the humanities, seems to be based on certain clearcut patterns. Positive references to and applications of Kristeva's work occur(red) preeminently among scholars who were clearly influenced by and susceptible to "deconstruction," but who never entirely adopted it. It is probably no accident that the statistical beginning of "Abject Studies" coincides not only with the turn against affirmative action but also with the institutional squeeze on "deconstruction" at U.S.-American universities. The Kristeva reception made it possible to adhere—at least in a theoretically lax fashion—to basic figures of deconstruction, while at the same time linking them to desiderata of a fundamentally different character. The interpretation of the subject, of language, and of the cultural order from the perspective of what these things repress in the interest of their identity, and what, simultaneously and inversely, keeps rendering this identity fragile—this psychoanalytic project of Kristeva's is similar to the project of deconstruction in more than a superficial manner. On the other hand, Kristeva disclosed positive elements of a genealogy of the subject, and of a theory of the sexes, of religions, and of literature, that would not have emerged through the practices of deconstructive reading alone. Furthermore, the abject mother in Kristeva plays a role that in many respects seems akin to that of a "transcendental signifier," and hence to a position in discourse deconstruction precisely tends to undo or reveal as ideological. To be sure, the "abject" cannot be subsumed under the category of "self-presence," which is central, according to deconstruction, to all "metaphysical" entities; for the abject maternal body appears only in a disjointed and refracted form, since it is always already and "originally" repudiated. And yet Kristeva imputes to the insistence of the maternal pleasure-body within the fissures of the symbolic order an emphatic role, one which will necessarily appear to hardnosed deconstructionists as ideological in tendency: the role of both the real and the true—*le vréel*. As a result, the reception of Kristeva's theory of abjection promotes a return to "the real"; precisely this tendency can be found, under various rubrics, in the scholarship on literature and the arts that made use pf Kristeva's term. Previous to this, the catchword *posthistoire* had signaled a putative end of history; the talk of medial "simulation" and technological "simulacra" had signaled the end of conventional reality; and the focus on the "(free) play of the signifier," with its capacity for infinite deferral, had signaled the impossibility of the traditional type of truth. With the upsurge of disgust and the reconquest of what is disgusting, all three of these things—history, reality, and truth—returned in an emphatic, strongly affect-charged manner. In light of this victorious return of truth and unconditional reality, the "Abject Studies" undertaken in the fields of literature, art history, and cultural history, simultaneously promised to resolve in some measure the pressing problem of legitimation in the humanities. They serve(d) to link up once again, in unexpectedly direct fashion, the philological reading practices of the ivory tower to the "truth" of the subject, of the sexes, and of culture. Thus, the striking proliferation of scholarly studies on the subject of abjection has the self-referential function of at least announcing, if not yet effectively bringing about, a marked political dimension within academic work. In many, if not most cases, these studies entail a reification of Kristeva's theory, similar to the one that typifies the political applications: the "abject mother" is almost always brought to light not, as with Kristeva herself, in the phenomena of rhythm, of laughing apocalypse, or of happy guilt, but rather in forms of direct or allegorical representation.

As operator of the truth, or of a trans-symbolic reality, the exorbitance of disgust/abjection converge(d) with the partly simultaneous interest in a different, older concept: that of trauma.[63] The self-reflective function of "abject studies," for the humanities, has an even more pronounced analogue in the parallel development of "trauma studies." Abjection and trauma were, or still are, the two faces of a "return of the real" in the humanities.[64] Scholars who embark on such studies tend to have a strong commitment to critical theory; they aim to avoid the diffuse positivism of "cultural studies," while, at the same time, they seek to open up poststructuralist theory to some "new-old" desiderata. In regard to trauma, too, it is a matter of processing an unassimilable alterity, an attack on one's own identity that often, quite literally, carries the threat of death—whether in the context of the sexual traumas of children, or the traumas consequent on accidents or war, or the persecution of the Jews by the National Socialists. In contrast to the disgust reaction, however, the defense mechanisms are, in the experience of trauma, not only mobilized to a particularly high degree; rather, they are effectively overpowered. This leads to the incorporation of what is harmful. Instead of being definitively and consciously vomited up once and for all, the traumatically harmful is repeatedly externalized—in a manner that both eludes consciousness and fails to provide permanent relief. One can master or take possession of disgust, as Sartre says *("je la possédais")*;[65] one can appropriate it as a form of knowledge. But there can be no such mastery for one who is subject to traumatic disintegration—at least not until psychoanalysis has done its work. Nevertheless, there is a striking similarity in the relation of abjection and trauma to the symbolic order: within this order, both appear only as disturbance or destruction. Having been driven out of the confines of communication, trauma is also a "truth" that can never, in consequence, find appropriate expression *as* trauma in the form of a regular linguistic proposition. In *Moses and Monotheism*, Freud outlined a correlation between trauma and character[66] that is just as strict as that later drawn by Kristeva, for very different reasons, between abjection and the formation of the subject, or that drawn by Sartre between *nausée* and the *moi*. Whereas, however, the insistence of accident trauma, war trauma, or persecution trauma in itself constitutes the paralyzing spell of an overwhelming experience of suffering, the insistence of abject pleasure marks a "*salutary*" attempt to elaborate the irruption of the real that leaves a hole in the symbolical weft."[67] To be sure, the reintegration into the abject entails the danger of a psychotic dissociation of the subject; nevertheless, Kristeva welcomes such a reintegration into or reappropiation of the abject above all as a chance for the "salvation [of] the speaking being."[68] As a *jouissance* that overcomes 'repressive' boundaries, on the one hand, and as overpowering experience of suffering, on the other, the abject and the traumatic represent two complementary forms of transcending the symbolic and thus, at the same time, two modes of "the truth" and "the real."

Both abjection and trauma provide a history to the subject. According to Nietzsche, tragedy, the freethinker, and Zarathustra all trace a path that exposes itself to disgust, that makes use of its potential for cognition, and yet in the end overcomes it. In an analogous way, for Kristeva, the history of the subject evolves along a path situated between prehistoric pleasure, the originary repression of the maternal body, and various forms which act out the conflict between the claims of the symbolic order and the insistence of abject pleasure. These forms oscillate between confinement in the abjection of the *corps maternel* and its reappropriation under the conditions of the symbolic order; the history of the traumatized runs a similar course between the poles of confinement in the trauma and its reintegration into the sphere of the symbolic. Neither of these two narratives follow linear curves. Their narrative logic obeys a discontinuous line of leaps, repetitions, and zigzags, of long latencies and manic as well as depressive episodes, of unclear goals and uncertain progress. The literary and art-historical scholarship since the late 1980s has seen repeated attempts, individual and institutionalized, to establish expertise in dealing with these erratic lines. These efforts more or less openly lay claim to the important role of a psychoanalyst of cultural objectivations—and this at a time when, particularly in the United States, the classical practice of psychoanalysis was, and still is, dramatically losing ground.

Abject Art

The academic and the political appropriations of Kristeva's evocative nonconcept intersect in the third field of its application: that of the art scene. At the same time, the distinctions between the abject and the traumatic have soon begun to blur: the abject occasionally appears to possess a traumatic dimension, and the traumatic an abject dimension. Cindy Sherman, Robert Mapplethorpe, Mike Kelley, Matthew Barney, John Miller, Gilbert & George, Kiki Smith, and Sue Williams are some of the artists who had a prominent role in promoting and discussing the label "abject art." Various other artists belonging to earlier generations—among them, Marcel Duchamp, Cy Twombly, and Claes Oldenburg—have also been singled out under the new designation. Leading the way in the display of abject art, it would seem, were works involving "degraded" bodily matter like "naked shit" (Mike Kelley, Gilbert & George) and works referring to anal pleasure (Robert Mapplethorpe's *Self Portrait*). Cindy Sherman, in one of her collections of photographs, presented still lifes depicting vomit, colored candies, earthworms, mold, mucus, bodily secretions, and infected pieces of skin.[69] Before this, in a long series of self-portraits exploring various forms of female "looked-at-ness," she had offered second-order materializations, as appealing as they were disconcerting, which turn the gaze of the spectator back upon himself, while breaking open from the inside various models of cultural fetishization. In her subsequent work (1985–1989), she completely eliminated all references to erotic and fashion photography and to the nostalgic quality of white American "Fiftyness." For Laura Mulvey, this radical break with all modes of fetishizing served to lay bare an abject interior of the female body; she therefore saw in Sherman's photos an imagistic correlative to Kristeva's theory:

> Finally, in the last phase, the figure disappears completely. Sometimes body bits are replaced by prosthetics, such as false breasts or buttocks, but, in the last resort, nothing is left but disgust—the disgust of sexual detritus, decaying food, vomit, slime, menstrual blood, hair. These traces represent the end of the road, the secret stuff of bodily fluids that the cosmetic is designed to conceal.[70]
>
> The late photographs are a reminder that the female psyche may well identify with misogynistic revulsion against the female body and attempt to erase signs that mark her physically as feminine. The images of decaying food and vomit raise the specter of the anorexic girl, who tragically acts out the fashion fetish of the female as an eviscerated, cosmetic and artificial construction designed to ward off the "otherness" hidden in the "interior."[71]

Cindy Sherman traces the abyss or morass that overwhelms the defetishized body, deprived of the fetish's semiotic, reduced to being "unspeakable" and devoid of significance. Her late work comes close to depicting the Kristevan concept of the abject: that is, the disgust aroused in the human psyche by lifeless, inanimate bodily matter, bodily wastes and the dead body itself.[72]

These sentences served as a point of departure for Rosalind Krauss in her general critique of "abject art" and of Kristeva herself. "Kristeva's project," Krauss writes, "is all about recuperating certain objects as abjects—waste products, filth, bodily fluids."[73] This tendency "to reify certain bodily products"[74] is said to correspond to a "thematizing approach,"[75] which reductively assigns to a variety of artworks an identical transcendental meaning: namely, to reveal in disgusting matter the truth about the female body as "traumatized" and "wounded."[76] In this way, for Krauss, all formal dynamics of the artwork are sacrificed to a univocal semanticization. The combination, in abject art, of both literally presenting crude, disgusting matter and ascribing a determinate thematic value to it amounts, in this perspective, to nothing more than a "childish move": "merely a way to characterize bodily substances so that the formerly disprivileged becomes the privileged."[77] Given these assumptions about the meaning of "abjection" and "abject," Rosalind Krauss can easily point out that the specific quality of Cindy Sherman's work cannot be adequately assessed within this framework. By contrast, Krauss emphasizes that "under the automobile hood" of Sherman's images all the signifieds of vomited matter operate simultaneously as signifiers of formal desublimation.[78] Before this, however, Laura Mulvey had interpreted Sherman's disgust still lifes not from the perspective of the objects alone but as a distinct stage in the evolution of techniques designed to unsettle the elementary laws of the visual order, along with its various fetishes. Beyond the somewhat misleading critique of Laura Mulvey's essay on Sherman, Krauss's polemic raises more general questions: Are not Gilbert & George's "Naked Shit Pictures" and other icons of "Abject Art" little more, in fact, than infantile provocations? And further: Can Kristeva's project be read as a reifying ennoblement of disgusting substances and as a transcendentalizing identification of the woman as wound?

The answer to the second question can only be no. The superimposition of the abject, the traumatic, and the wound goes back to Freud's description of the fetishization of particular traits of the woman as a phantasmatic compensation for her lack of a penis.[79] But Kristeva's *autorité maternelle* and *chora* are prior to the oedipal experience of the castrated mother and, in general, to every desire for the woman as object—with or without a fetish. Nowhere does she describe this pre-oedipal maternal body as a wound, as castrated, or as traumatized in any other sense. If anything constitutes the "truth" of this "abject being" and its objectival representations, then it is not its wound but its *jouissance*, in which there is neither an identity of the subject nor one of an object, nor of signifieds. In Kristeva's analysis, art's dedication to recuperating the (originary) abject results both in (anal-sadistic) forms of destruction—such as shatter the symbolic order and, with it, all established meaning—and in openings to the field of "non-meaning." It is simply not the case that, in the context of Kristeva's understanding of art, "rhythm puts in place the stability of form and the fullness of meaning."[80] The non-objectival, identity-shattering status of the *corps maternel* militates against any reading of Kristeva's texts in terms of simple thematic affirmations of the abject. In point of fact, Krauss pays no more attention to Kristeva's linguistic analyses of the operational modes of abject pleasure in the field of the symbolic than to her thoroughgoing efforts to integrate thematic concerns (laughing apocalypse, *felix culpa*, etc.) into a framework of questions bearing on form, too. Krauss's repeated invectives against Kristeva convincingly drive home an intellectual distaste with the "insistent spread of the 'abject' as an expressive mode," and with the diffuse promotion of the theme of the body; still as an interpretation of Kristeva's writings they do not hold up.[81]

"Abject Art" is not a category of art-historical scholarship but an evocative label belonging to the (self-)representation of the art scene and to strategies appropriate for its marketing. Rosalind Krauss's rather unflattering descriptions may well prove apt in the case of certain works under this label—or in connection with their interpretation in the catalogue to the exhibition *Abject Art*—more apt than they are in reference to Julia Kristeva's theory itself. The commonsensical question "Why do artists want to make objects that are abject?"[82] has the ring of déja vu: Why did Baudelaire sing of his beloved as carrion? Why did Romanticism embrace an affirmative poetics of disgusting decomposition, one which licences disgusting impotence, too? The explanations offered for "Abject Art" likewise ring a familiar note. For one thing, there is the pressure for innovation within the system of art itself, a pressure to which—in Friedrich Schlegel's words—the aesthetics of the "shocking," of the strongest possible stimuli, provides an especially viable response, one that has taken the most varied forms in the past two hundred years or so. The disgusting may well be the strongest possible stimulator of the human perceptual apparatus. It generates strong defensive affects which, at the same time, are powerful instants of self-perception on the part of the system forced to defend its own integrity. In this regard, artists of the "abject" could only welcome the outcry of conservatives such as Senator Jesse Helms. They actively provoked this beating by the "father": that is their "oedipal naughtiness." This naughtiness is the outward aspect of an attitude whose inner disposition has been saddled (by Hal Foster) with the suspicion of "infantile perversion."[83] In light of its routine recourse to mechanisms of shock and provocation, "abject art" soon appears to have lost much of its confidence in being an antidote to boredom (Baudelaire's *ennui*) or to other forms of cultural satiation. Correspondingly, the premeditated will to shock—which, for today's artists, entails testing the limits of one's own museability—is often checked by a self-irony signaled as though with a wink of the eye. The desired intensity of affect can blend as smoothly as one likes with the evocation of shoulder-shrugging indifference toward "lumpy things": "pure affect, no affect."[84]

No less well-established than the artist's wish to be as different and provocative as possible—a wish inherent to the very system of art—are the basic "civilizing" rules against which abject art appears to protest: "the shit movement in contemporary art may intend a symbolic reversal of the first step into civilization, of the repression of the anal and the olfactory."[85] This symbolic step back into a cultural stage already surmounted is, at the same time, imbued with the promise "that art refuses the age-old mandate to pacify the gaze, to unite the imaginary and the symbolic against the real. It is as if this art wanted the gaze to shine, the object to stand, the real to exist, in all the glory (or the horror) of its pulsatile desire."[86] Critical theory here interpolates—under the classical proviso of an "as if"—a new variant of a time-honoured claim enunciated in both rhetoric and aesthetics: namely, that art has the power of breaking through the wall of cultural formations (as well as the wall of its own mediality) in favor of a presence of the "thing itself" or "nature." But whereas aesthetics from Mendelssohn through Kant determined this "real presence" to be a "deception" or "illusion," abject art appears quite ready to affirm an "actual" real presence of the absolute in the form of "pulsatile desire." In the desublimation of that body whose total symbolization, cleaning from all disgusting matter, the system of aesthetics, the net of symbolization and its intertwining with the imaginary is allegedly torn open. This move is supposed to make possible the return of the real and, at the same time, to confer on the abject a peculiar truth status; it thus entails a truth inherent in the disgusting, or the affirmation of the disgusting as truth. Schooled in the vocabulary of Lacan and Kristeva (the symbolic, the real, *le vréel*), the conceptualizations of abject art thus repeat and blend the aesthetic, epistemological, and psychoanalytic configurations of disgust, reality, and truth: the disgusting as something unconditionally real in opposition to the imaginary and to the symbolic code of real versus imaginary (Mendelssohn); the disgusting as insight into the true "essence of things" and as signature of knowledge rooted in the body (Nietzsche); the disgusting as the repressed truth of archaic libido (Freud), as the pathway of transgressive desire (Bataille), and as the medium of an existential experience emancipated from all false justifications (Sartre). The abject even inherits the position of the absolute in Schelling's idealist philosophy of art. According to Schelling, art alone makes it possible—by dint of overcoming theoretical and practical objectifications—to experience the otherwise inaccessible (because constitutively displaced and dissimulated) "thing in itself." Piles of shit and parts of cadavers are more recent versions—in the field marked by the convergence of disgust, truth and the real—of a penetration to the "thing itself." It goes without saying that the increasing proliferation of disgust-stimuli in television, film, and everyday life gets well along without these ambitions attached to the evocative label "abject art" created, as it is, by critics at least remotely acquainted with Kristeva's demanding texts.

Those taboos which are based in disgust, and which concern elementary bodily matter and bodily acts, serve as ideal points of departure for renewed revolts against them, because even occasional acts of transgression do not overcome such taboos as though once and for all, but rather enhance their fundamental bearing, thus confirming Bataille's theory of the circle of prohibition and transgression. To be sure, the relative indestructibility of what Freud called civilizing barriers of disgust—a counterpart to the almost absolute indestructibility which Freud attributed to "perverse" impulses—may, in the twentieth century, have come to seem less assured. Yet without these barriers "abject art" would lose its point. And it is precisely these disgust taboos, so deeply established as to seem unconquerable, that prevent a purely "aesthetic" appreciation. Otherwise, abject art and its various precursors would run the danger of provoking merely yawns. For, compared with the orgies of defecation and copulation performed by the grotesque body in Rabelais, with the provocations of Vienna activists in the sixties, or with the widespread literary traditions of scatology and the obscene, the more recent turn to "shit" in works of art seems pretty harmless. Denis Hollier has made this point succinctly: "When I saw the 'Abject Art' show at the Whitney, I thought: What is so abject about it? Everything was very neat; the objects were clearly artworks. They live on the side of the victor."[87] Just as Cindy Sherman's disgust still lifes have a distinctive high-gloss beauty, so the "double defiance of visual sublimation and vertical form"[88] even in John Miller's work *Untitled* (1988), a work comprised of a "pile of shit," is once again resublimated by its pleasing geometric, indeed Pythagorean, form.

The same goes for works composed of parts from cadavers or still living, putrefying matter. Of course, the provision and preparation of such "materials" ran up against the combined powers of aesthetic, moral, and sometimes also—as in the case of Damien Hirst's denial of an entry visa into the United States—legal prohibition. Even so, the results of such artistic ventures often enough arouse anything but disgust. Damien Hirst's presentation, behind glass and steel, of a bull's skull in formaldehyde, or of various cadaver parts inhabited by living, dying, and proliferating insect populations, operates more to remove the fear of death than to augment it: "For all the weird stuff he uses, his work is meticulously well-made. It has an immaculate, trance-inducing presence about it. His compositions tend toward symmetry, and things are always placed just so."[89] Hence, the aesthetic and cultural taboo on the decomposing body is confirmed at the very moment when, for the first time, it is transgressed in a literal and material sense—as opposed to being merely represented through visual media or literary metaphors. This implies that the classical foundations of aesthetics—fixed as they are in the taboo on disgust, and in the ideal of a beautiful bodily surface free of anything disgusting—still survive, surprisingly secure, in the drastic forms of their transgression. These foundations are far more than just a historical episode of repressive demarcations or bizarre cosmetic retouching. In fact, they remain, in all their detail, part of the ongoing effort of artworks to be different from and to surpass all predecessors. Even the routinized orgies of perverse cruelty in "splatter videos" presuppose a remnant of prohibitionary consciousness—however diminished—in their customers. Without a rudimentary feeling for taboo (which is being battered by ever more intense sensations), all pleasure taken in the contemplation of such phenomena would pass into utter indifference, and the anti-aesthetic of disgust-horror-porno-videos would become anaesthetic—as it perhaps already is for *devotées* of this genre. The Classical aestheticians had discovered that the beautiful, for the sake of its own being, must not remain identical with itself, while writers of the Romantic period had found that, for the sake of art, the beautiful must be sacrificed again and again to other stimuli. It is much the same with what is disgusting: as maximal countervalue to what is beautiful, and as the strongest possible anti-aesthetic stimulus, it can never attain definitive victory over the idealization of form. Such victory would represent the end of the affective value of disgust, which requires a fierce nay-saying, and the end of art, since art thrives only on the continual generation of differences, and hence can never depend exclusively on the disgusting, considered as a prevailing and stable source of stimulation. We can therefore expect to see further—new and different—conjunctions of the beautiful and the disgusting, of the disgusting and the beautiful.

Notes

INTRODUCTION

1. Kant, *Anthropology from a Pragmatic Point of View*, 45.

2. Ibid., 40–41. Translation modified.

3. Cf. Kant, "Reflexionen zur Anthropologie," 804.

4. Cf. Kolnai, "Der Ekel," 524–26.

5. Compare the classification of disgust among the "feelings of basic universal emotions," which the neurosurgeon Antonio Damasio has offered on the basis of clinical observations (*Descartes' Error*, 149–50).

6. Freud, "Three Essays on the Theory of Sexuality," 177.

7. Benjamin, "Zur Moral und Anthropologie," 88.

8. Sophocles, *Philoctetes*. In *Greek Tragedies*, vol. 3, 48 (v. 38–39).

9. Ibid., 82 (v. 900).

10. Ibid., 47 (v. 7–9).

11. Ibid., 81 (v. 874–76).

12. Miller, *The Anatomy of Disgust*, 154.

13. Ibid.

14. Cf. ibid., 169.

15. Compare Kant, *Critique of Judgment*, 69, 160, and Bourdieu, *Distinction: A Social Critique of the Judgement of Taste*, 488–91.

16. Cf. 000, this volume.

17. Kolnai, "Der Ekel," 529.

18. Cf. 000, this volume.

19. Actually, Norbert Elias is treated only in passing. His thesis of the parallel progress of disgust and civilization is discussed in the context of similar theses by Nietzsche and Freud, as well as at the end of chapter 2. On the historical adequacy of Elias' thesis about disgust, see Miller, *The Anatomy of Disgust*, 170–78.

20. Mendelssohn, "82. Literaturbrief," 131.

21. Friedrich Schlegel, "Über das Studium der Griechischen Poesie," 254.

22. Bataille, *Œuvres complètes*, vol. 2, 321.

23. Kafka, *The Diaries*, 12.

24. Cf. the report, "Ungeziefer am Stiel als Leckerbissen" ("Insects on the Stick as Tidbit") in the *Frankfurter Allgemeine Zeitung* of June 21, 1996.

25. Cf. 000, this volume.

26. Issue number 129 (September 1997).

27. Cf. the catalogue of the exhibition, *Körperwelten: Einblicke in den menschlichen Körper*, mounted by the *Institut für Plastination* (Heidelberg) in the *Landesmuseum für Technik und Arbeit* in Mannheim (October 30, 1997 through March 1, 1998).

28. Christian Enzensberger, *Größerer Versuch über den Schmutz*, 100–1.

29. On disgust with the (anal-compulsive, neurotic) *absence* of dirt and disorder, see 000, this volume.

30. Michel, "Leib an Leib," 37.

31. Schaad, "Der öffentliche Stuhl," 54–55.

32. Cf. Streck, "Gefüllter Hund," 76, and Jeggle, "Runterschlucken," 15.

33. Streck, "Gefüllter Hund," 68.

34. Cf. Bourdieu, *Distinction*.

35. Michel, "Leib an Leib," 37. Michel, too, invokes, as epitome of the disgusting, a "corpulent" woman, smelling of perfumed sweat (27).

36. Cf. Marcuse, *One-Dimensional Man*, 71–94.

37. Michel, "Leib an Leib," 31. The present study likewise ventures no generalizing thesis to account for this snapshot portrait.

38. This obviously holds only for the "official" discourse, to which de Sade belongs so little as does the widely disseminated pornographic literature of the eighteenth century.

39. Hegel, *Philosophy of Right*, 11.

40. On which, see 000, this volume.

41. Subsequent citations from Kolnai's study are followed by their page numbers in parentheses in the text. The chapter "Der Ekel" in Hermann Schmitz's *System der Philosophie* (vol. 2, pt. 1, 240–45), merely repeats some of Kolnai's suggestive analyses.

42. Cf. 000, this volume.

43. Benjamin, "Zur Moral und Anthropologie," 88: "For every man, if he were but known with sufficient exactitude, it would be possible to deduce the animal that most keenly calls up his disgust."

44. Subsequent citations from Miller's *The Anatomy of Disgust* are followed by their page numbers in parentheses.

Chapter 1

1. J. A. Schlegel, "Anmerkungen über Ekel," 111. (Unless otherwise indicated, all excerpts from German sources are translated by J. G.)

2. Ibid., 112.

3. Mendelssohn, "82. Literaturbrief," 131.

4. Grimm, *Deutsches Wörterbuch*, vol. 3, col. 394.

5. Cf. Addison, *The Spectator*, vol. 3, 540: "There may, indeed, be something so terrible or offensive, that the horror or loathsomeness of an object may overbear the pleasure which results from its greatness, novelty or beauty; but still there will be such a mixture of delight in the very disgust it gives us, as any of these three qualifications are most conspicuous and prevailing." In contrast to Mendelssohn's paradigm, "horror" and "disgust" are here *not* distinguished in a strict and categorical manner. Addison appears to locate "disgust," without distinction, precisely within the field of mixed sensations from which Mendelssohn excludes it, as the "one exception" that cannot be reconciled with aesthetic pleasure.

6. Cf. 000, this volume.

7. Mendelssohn, "82. Literaturbrief," 132.

8. Mendelssohn, "Rhapsodie," 139–40.

9. Wezel, *Versuch über die Kenntniß des Menschen*, vol. 2, 153.

10. Ibid., 253–54. Cf. Goethe's remarks in the "Outline of a Theory of Color" (*Weimar Edition*, section 2, vol. 4, 198) concerning a form of disgust that "even the most beautiful color" can call forth, as soon as the eye is subject to it too long and without alteration.

11. Breitinger, *Critische Dichtkunst*, S. 225.

12. Kant, *Observations on the Feeling of the Beautiful and Sublime*, 102. Translation modified.

13. Satiation has served as a key paradigm for the psychology of disgust in the twentieth century as well. Cf. Kolnai, "Der Ekel," 545–47; Schultz, "Zur medizinischen Psychologie des Ekels Normaler," 197–201; Karsten, "Psychische Sättigung," 142–257; Miller, *The Anatomy of Disgust*, 87, 110–14.

14. Spinoza, *Ethics*, 140–41. Translation modified.

15. Barthes, *Fragments d'un discours amoureux*, 155.

16. Benjamin, "Denkbilder," 375.

17. Breitkopf, *Beschreibung des Reichs der Liebe mit beygefügter Landcharte*, fig. 3779.

18. Kant, *Observations on the Feeling of the Beautiful and Sublime*, 84. Translation modified.

19. On ancient variants, cf. 000, this volume.

20. Kerrigan, "The Personal Shakespeare," 186–87.

21. Kant, "Reflexionen zur Anthropologie," 473.

22. Kerrigan, "The Personal Shakespeare," 181.

23. Kant, *Anthropology from a Pragmatic Point of View*, 138. Translation modified.

24. Lessing, *Laocoön*, 19–20. Translation modified.

25. Kant, "Bemerkungen zu den Beobachtungen über das Gefühl des Schönen und Erhabenen," 61. In the cited passage, the additional stimulus is novelty—or at least its appearance ("if it does not appear to be new").

26. Ibid., p.19.

27. Kant, *Anthropology from a Pragmatic Point of View*, 184. Translation modified.

28. Kant, *Observations on the Feeling of the Beautiful and Sublime*, 83. Translation modified.

29. Kafka, *Tagebücher*, 372–73.

30. Adorno, *Aesthetic Theory*, 47–48.

31. Winckelmann, "Erläuterung der Gedanken von der Nachahmung der griechischen Werke in der Malerei und Bildhauerkunst," 95.

32. Ibid., 99.

33. Ibid., 97.

34. Kant, *Critique of Judgment*, 182.

35. Ibid., 183–84. Translation modified.

36. Ibid., 196.

37. Cf. ibid., 165–67, 195–96.

38. Ibid., 77.

39. Aristotle, *Poetics*, 1448b.

40. Cf. Lessing, *Laocoön*, 127.

41. Cf. Lucretius, *De natura rerum*, book 2, v. 1–22.

42. Mendelssohn, "82. Literaturbrief," p.132.

43. Charles Batteux, *Les beaux arts réduits à un même principe*, 100.

44. Mendelssohn, "82. Literaturbrief," 132. Cf. Mendelssohn, "Rhapsodie," 139.

45. The most reliable and detailed study is Carsten Zelle's *Angenehmes Grauen*. Cf. also Dieckmann, "Das Abscheuliche und Schreckliche in der Kunsttheorie des 18. Jahrhunderts" and Carroll, *The Philosophy of Horror or Paradoxes of the Heart*.

46. Approaches to the problem of disgust in eighteenth-century aesthetics are to be found in Dieckmann, "Das Abscheuliche und Schreckliche in der Kunsttheorie des 18. Jahrhunderts," 302–4 and 313–16; Derrida, "Economimesis," 19–25; Jacobs, "The Critical Performance of Lessing's 'Laokoon,'" 496–501; Zelle, *Angenehmes Grauen*, especially 247–51 and 381–95; Wellbery, "Das Gesetz der Schönheit. Lessings Ästhetik der Repräsentation"; Gustafson, *Absent Mothers and Orphaned Fathers*; and Kuhnle, "Der Ernst des Ekels," 269–76. Derrida, Jacobs, Wellbery, and Gustafson all

focus on individual aspects of the discourse on disgust starting with Kant or Lessing. However, a number of motives at work in this discourse—and moreover there entire configuration and concatenation—only become intelligible in a comparative look at all the related writings. While having a very good grasp of the sources, Carsten Zelle simply classifies the disgusting as one chapter in his own, particular theme, the horrible; at the same time, like Dieckmann before him, he considers the disgusting solely from the perspective of the greater or lesser liberality demonstrated by the authors under discussion in their licensing of disgust. The absence of any close interpretation put aside, this approach fails to identify the basic functions and points of intervention at work in the semantic locus termed "disgust." For his part, Kuhnle stakes a claim to presenting the conceptual history of disgust from Lessing to Freud in seven pages; he does not, however, appear cognizant of the most important texts before and after Lessing (J. A. Schlegel's notes to the Batteux-translation, Mendelssohn's "82. Literaturbrief," Herder's "Plastik," etc.). Mendelssohn's cardinal theorem that feelings of disgust are "always nature, never imitation" is thus ascribed to Lessing, who in fact simply cites it ("Der Ernst des Ekels," 272). Finally, note should be taken of Werner Hamacher's discussion of Nietzsche's outstanding reflections on disgust, as well as of several other interesting passages, mainly from Hegel's *Encyclopaedia (Pleroma. Reading in Hegel)*. Hamacher is not directly concerned with the elaborate pre-Hegelian discourse on disgust. His remarks do, however, bear at least obliquely on what is here under discussion for the eighteenth century.

47. According to Niklas Luhmann, the "self-description" of the modern system of art within aesthetics does not conform to the strict requirements of systems theory, since "as traditionally understood the idea of beauty impedes the distinction between codifying and programming." The highest programmatic value of the system (the beautiful) is thus burdened with the task of simultaneously reappearing as just one pole of its binary code—of the distinction between beautiful and ugly that generates all aesthetic "information." As Luhmann sees it, an adequate system-theoretical definition would need to identify such a confusion of code, program, and partly even function of art as the concealment of a paradox, then strive to disentangle this confusion (cf. idem, *Die Kunst der Gesellschaft*, 309–14). Regarding the development of art in the nineteenth and twentieth centuries, some of Luhmann's disciples have proposed other candidates as the aesthetic system's prime code value, such as the (romantic) distinction between "interesting" and "uninteresting" (cf. Werber, *Literatur als System*, 61–101). But already for the time when aesthetics emerged, as well as for the epoch of classical ideal beauty, it is doubtful that the distinction between beautiful and ugly is coextensive with aesthetic "information." If one views, in line with what is argued here, a *specific* distinction of pleasure and displeasure as the system's prime codificatory value, then Luhmann's problem concerning a presumed equivocation between code and programmatic ideal would simply disappear.

48. Mendelssohn, "82. Literaturbrief," 132–33. There is a similar passage in one of Kant's early reflections on anthropology: "Disgust is in itself and without recompense unpleasant. For this reason, the mind is not entertained by disgusting things, as it is indeed by sad ones. . . . In contrast, everything horrible is observed gladly, albeit with terror." ("Reflexionen zur Anthropologie," 218)

49. J. A. Schlegel, "Anmerkungen über Ekel," 111.

50. Condillac, *A Treatise on the Sensations*, 312.

51. Mendelssohn, "82. Literaturbrief," 131.

52. Kolnai, "Der Ekel," 524.

53. Kant, *Critique of Judgment*, 180. Translation modified.

54. Cf. Mülder-Bach, *Im Zeichen Pygmalions*, 50–66.

55. Herder, "Erstes Kritisches Wäldchen," 242.

56. Ibid.

57. Cf. Wellbery, *Lessing's Laocoön*.

58. Cf. Lessing, *Laocoön*, 78–120 and Mülder-Bach, *Im Zeichen Pygmalions*, 103–48.

59. Kant, *Critique of Judgment*, 174. Translation modified.

60. Mendelssohn, "82. Literaturbrief," 132.

61. Kant, *Critique of Judgment*, 180. Translation modified.

62. J. A. Schlegel, "Anmerkungen über Ekel," 112.

63. Cf. Freud, *The Complete Letters of Sigmund Freud to Wilhelm Fliess*, 264.

64. A good fifty years later, Goethe appeals to the same argument to explain his experience of violent "physical-aesthetic pain" upon reading Büsching's *Armer Heinrich*—a work in which the "most repulsive illness . . . serves as the motive for passionate deeds of love and chivalry": "It is hard to shrug off the disgust felt at a leprous man, for whom a most valiant young lady sacrifices herself. . . . The horrible disease here forming the basis of heroic action has at least such a violent effect on me, that from simply touching such a book, I have a sense of already being infected." Mere contact with the book is thus as violent and contagious as the "real evil"; indeed the disgust to which the reader is exposed will be more difficult to shrug off than disgust one feels outside the realm of art: a striking hyperbole of Mendelssohn's theorem. Cf. Goethe, "Tag- und Jahreshefte [1811]," *Weimar Edition*, section 1, vol. 36, 72–73.

65. Cf. Jacobs, "The Critical Performance of Lessing's 'Laokoon,'" 496–97.

66. Cf. von Mücke, "The Powers of Horror and the Magic of Euphemism," 163–80 and Wellbery, "The Pathos of Theory: Laokoon Revisited," 54–55, 58.

67. Cf. Kant's analogous observation: "Phantasy . . . often makes the object of imagination so strong that it seems real, e.g. dizziness from height. *Ekel* at the memory of disgusting things." ("Reflexionen zur Anthropologie," 807.)

68. I am in debt to a conversation with Robert Stockhammer for this latter point.

69. Mendelssohn, "Rhapsodie," 135.

70. Hegel, "Vorlesungen über die Ästhetik," vol. 13, 67. In the disgusting similitude arrived at in painted and "naturally" draped sculptures, Mendelssohn sees a border value of illusory imitation that must be avoided. Taking up this pre-Idealist critique of an imitative illusion intensified to the point of becoming disgusting, Hegel redirects it at the imitative foundation of art in general. Cf. Miller, *The Anatomy of Disgust*, 27: "Have you not seen dolls that disgust simply by being almost too good a likeness?"

Inversely, Tomkins writes of a "learned disgust . . . for the poor imitation." Cf. *Affect-Imagery-Consciousness*, 238.

71. J. E. Schlegel, "Abhandlung von der Nachahmung," 154.

72. Mendelssohn, "83. Literaturbrief," 133.

73. Lessing, *Laocoön*, 128.

74. Mendelssohn, "83. Literaturbrief," 133.

75. Lessing, *Laocoön*, 132–33. Translation modified. In his *System der Ästhetik* (1905), vol. 1, 451–52 and vol. 2, 17, 159–66, 420–22, and 469–75, Volkelt offers another account of how the disgusting can be made functional for the representation of the horrifying, sublime, and comic. However, his argument at no point goes beyond Lessing's. At the expense of some distinctions, Volkelt simply shifts the theme of the general irreconcilability of the disgusting with "aesthetic pleasure" from the pre-Kantian to a quasi-Schopenhauerian idiom (will vs. absence of will).

76. Sulzer, *Allgemeine Theorie der Schönen Künste*, pt. 2, 38.

77. Cf. Lessing, *Laocoön*, 133. Translation modified.

78. Ibid., 137.

79. Ibid. Goethe would later use a similar argument to criticize distorted performances of Schiller's *Robbers:* as soon as the "balance" of the characters is damaged, simple disgust emerges on the part of the spectator, as a dissociative product "of that great roughness filling us with astonishment in Schiller's play." As Goethe puts it, "the work of art is injured at the source of its deepest life; the gruesome accord vanishes, and what should excite dread in us excites only *Ekel*" (*Weimar Edition*, section 1, vol. 40, 172).

80. Lessing, *Laocoön*, p.137. Translation modified.

81. That this not only applies to painting but also to literature is evident in the example taken from Longinus of "Sadness with the running nose." Cf. 000, this volume.

82. Winckelmann, *History of Ancient Art*, vol. 2, 197–98.

83. Winckelmann, "Sendschreiben über die Gedanken über die Nachahmung der griechischen Werke in der Malerei und Bildhauerkunst," 48.

84. Herder, "Erstes Kritisches Wäldchen," 115–16.

85. Herder, "Plastik," p.34.

86. Herder, "Erstes Kritisches Wäldchen," 242.

87. Cf. Derrida, "Economimesis," 20–25 .

Chapter 2

1. Winckelmann, "Thoughts on the Imitation of Greek Works in Painting and Sculpture," 15–16. Translation modified.

2. Winckelmann, "Erinnerung über die Betrachtung der Werke der Kunst," 208–9.

3. Herder, "Plastik," 12. Cf. also "Studien und Entwürfe zur Plastik," 106.

4. Adelung, *Grammatisch-kritisches Wörterbuch der hochdeutschen Mundart*, col. 998.

5. Herder, "Studien und Entwürfe zur Plastik," 102.

6. Herder, "Plastik," 29.

7. Winckelmann, *History of Ancient Art*, vol. 2, 174.

8. Winckelmann, "Erläuterung," 96.

9. Herder, "Studien und Entwürfe zur Plastik," 106.

10. Winckelmann, *History of Ancient Art*, vol. 2, 108. Translation modified.

11. Cf. Winckelmann, "Thoughts on the Imitation of Greek Works in Painting and Sculpture," 9; "Sendschreiben," 52; *History of Ancient Art*, vol. 1, 233–34.

12. Winckelmann, "Sendschreiben," 61; cf. also *History of Ancient Art*, vol. 2, 188–89.

13. Herder, "Plastik," 27.

14. Herder, "Studien und Entwürfe zur Plastik," 90 and "Die Plastik von 1770," 140.

15. Herder, "Studien und Entwürfe zur Plastik," 105; Winckelmann, "Thoughts on the Imitation of Greek Works in Painting and Sculpture," 6–10.

16. Winckelmann, "Thoughts on the Imitation of Greek Works in Painting and Sculpture," 8. Translation modified.

17. Herder, "Studien und Entwürfe zur Plastik," 105.

18. Ibid., 94.

19. Cf. Hagedorn, *Betrachtungen über die Mahlerey*, pt. one, 119; Kant, "Versuch über die Krankheiten des Kopfes," 260; *Anthropology from a Pragmatic Point of View*, 212–13; "Reflexionen zur Anthropologie," 473; Goethe, *Weimar Edition*, section 2, vol. 27, 142 and vol. 36, 73; also *Weimar Edition*, section 2, vol. 13, 324.

20. Winckelmann, "Thoughts on the Imitation of Greek Works in Painting and Sculpture," 7 . Translation modified. Cf. Miller, *The Anatomy of Disgust*, 52–53.

21. Winckelmann, "Thoughts on the Imitation of Greek Works in Painting and Sculpture," 21.

22. Winckelmann, *History of Ancient Art*, vol. 2, 78. Translation modified.

23. Plato, *Phaidros*, 250 d.

24. Kant, *Critique of Judgment*, 189.

25. Winckelmann, "Erinnerung über die Betrachtung der Werke der Kunst," 207.

26. Diderot, "Pensées détachées sur la peinture," in *Œuvres Complètes*, vol. 12, 115.

27. Goethe, *Wilhelm Meisters Wanderjahre, Weimar Edition*, section 1, vol. 25, 88 and Goethe, "Zur Morphologie. Entwurf einer vergleichenden Anatomie," *Weimar Edition*, section 2, vol. 8, 64.

28. Winckelmann, "Vorläufige Abhandlung zu den Denkmalen der Kunst des Altertums," 110.

29. Cf. 000, this volume.

30. William Hogarth, *The Analysis of Beauty*, 7.

31. Ibid., 8.

32. Grimm, *Deutsches Wörterbuch*, vol. 25, col. 130.

33. Winckelmann, *History of Ancient Art*, vol. 2, 74. Translated modified.

34. Herder, "Plastik," 43.

35. Kant, "The End of All Things," 198–99.

36. Herder, "Studien und Entwürfe zur Plastik," 105.

37. Ibid.

38. Bakhtin, *Rabelais and His World*, 26–29.

39. Ibid., 321.

40. Winckelmann, *History of Ancient Art*, vol. 2, 60.

41. Winckelmann, "Erläuterung," 92.

42. Herder, "Studien und Entwürfe zur Plastik," 105.

43. Under the present-day circumstances of enhanced life expectancy, this calculation is of course only valid if the concept of "ripe youth" is substantially expanded.

44. Herder, "Studien und Entwürfe zur Plastik," 95.

45. Ibid.

46. Winckelmann, *History of Ancient Art*, vol. 2, 44.

47. Lessing, *Laocoön*, 19. Translation modified.

48. Goethe, "Paralipomena zu den Frankfurter Gelehrten Anzeigen," in *Weimar Edition*, section 1, vol. 38, 381. In his studies of sculpture, Herder had already drawn a similar conclusion: "As a result of their poetic essence, Ovid's metamorphoses cannot be visually represented; or the essence of visual art is ruined along with the essence of such metamorphoses." ("Studien und Entwürfe zur Plastik," 103.)

49. Bakhtin, *Rabelais and His World*, 317.

50. Ibid., 339.

51. Ibid., 348 . Translation modified.

52. Ibid., 321.

53. Winckelmann, *History of Ancient Art*, vol. 2, 172–74.

54. Winckelmann, "Thoughts on the Imitation of Greek Works in Painting and Sculpture," 26–27. Translation modified.

55. Lessing, *Laocoön*, 7–8. Translation modified.

56. Darwin, *The Expressions of the Emotions in Man and Animals*, 257.

57. Cf. Wellbery, "The Pathos of Theory: Laokoon Revisited."

58. Lessing, *Laocoön*, 19. Cf. Herder's critique in his "Erstes Kritisches Wäldchen," 94.

59. Ibid., 8–10.

60. Cf. Bakhtin, *Rabelais and His World*, 321.

61. Lessing, *Laocoön*, 23.

62. Bakhtin, *Rabelais and His World*, 315.

63. Ibid., 321.

64. *Der Kleine Pauly*, vol. 1, col. 50.

65. Hesiod, *The Homeric Hymns and Homerica*, 239. Translation modified.

66. Longinus, "On The Sublime" 9, 5, 145–46. Translation modified.

67. Lessing, *Laocoön*, 133.

68. Herder, "Erstes Kritisches Wäldchen," 242.

69. See Miller, *The Anatomy of Disgust*, 93.

70. Winckelmann, *History of Ancient Art*, vol. 2, 152. Translation modified.

71. Winckelmann, "Thoughts on the Imitation of Greek Works in Painting and Sculpture," 13.

72. Herder, "Plastik," 48.

73. Winckelmann, *History of Ancient Art*, vol. 1, 233.

74. Herder, "Studien und Entwürfe zur Plastik," 94.

75. Lessing, *Laocoön*, 133. Translation modified.

76. Winckelmann, *History of Ancient Art*, vol. 1, 233.

77. Lessing, *Laocoön*, 131. Translation modified.

78. If nevertheless "dilated nostrils" are once even attributed to beautiful Apollo, then only on grounds of a law of "expression" that is allowed to partially counteract the law of beauty. "Repose and equanimity in their highest degree" cannot be expected of Apollo, who has just dispatched the dragon Python with one of his arrows. What must be here displayed is his *"contempt"* for this victory, which is "minor for a god": "As the skillful artist wished to personify the most beautiful of the gods, he expressed only the anger in the nose—this organ, according to the old poets, being its appropriate seat—and the contempt on the lips." In this manner, a strong affect was transformed into a pair of relatively minor corporeal signs, so that the expression remained "as it were measured against the beauty" and could be "drowned out" by it. Cf. Winckelmann, *History of Ancient Art*, vol. 2, 113–14, 117–18. Translation modified.

79. Winckelmann, *History of Ancient Art*, vol. 2, 176–82.

80 Ibid., 276; ibid., 176–77. Translation modified.

81. Winckelmann, "Erläuterung," 88.

82. Winckelmann, *History of Ancient Art*, vol. 2, 191.

83. Herder, "Reisetagebuch," 576.

84. Ibid., 565.

85. Winckelmann, "Erläuterung," 89.

86. Herder, "Studien und Entwürfe zur Plastik," 112.

87. Lessing, *Laocoön*, 133. Translation modified.

88. Winckelmann, *History of Ancient Art*, vol. 2, 191. Translation modified.

89. Ibid., 192.

90. Cf. Bakhtin, *Rabelais and His World*, 322. Bakhtin, to be sure, does not recognize the extreme "ideality" of the suckling process here in question.

91. Herder, "Plastik," 52–53.

92. Cf. Mülder-Bach, *Im Zeichen Pygmalions*, 71–76.

93. Winckelmann, *History of Ancient Art*, vol. 2, 190. Translation modified.

94. Ibid., 60. Translation modified.

95. Ibid., 191. Translation modified.

96. Ibid., 61.

97. Ibid., 191. Translation modified.

98. Herder, "Studien und Entwürfe zur Plastik," 88.

99. Herder, "Plastik," 12–13.

100. Ibid., 19–20.

101. Herder, "Die Plastik von 1770," 134.

102. Winckelmann, "Thoughts on the Imitation of Greek Works in Painting and Sculpture," 21.

103. Herder, "Die Plastik von 1770," 137.

104. Bakhtin, *Rabelais and His World*, 26, 317.

105. Winckelmann, *History of Ancient Art*, vol. 2, 192. Translation modified.

106. Herder, "Plastik," 53.

107. The approach to the navel—a hollow and "elevation" at the center of the abdominal arch—is more moderate, but in the end analogous with that at play in the rules of diminishment for *ekle* bodily openings. On the one hand, Winckelmann observes that "the navel is markedly deep, especially in female figures"; on the other hand, he even rejects "this part" as unbeautiful on the Medici Venus, to the extent its rendition is "unusually deep and large." *History of Ancient Art*, 192. Translation modified.

108. Herder, "Plastik," 53.

109. Winckelmann, "Erläuterung," 82.

110. Winckelmann, "Sendschreiben," 52.

111. Winckelmann, "Erläuterung," 82.

112. Winckelmann, *History of Ancient Art*, vol. 2, 192–93. Translation modified.

113. Cf. Buchheit, *Studien zum Corpus Priapeorum*, 79–80.

114. Winckelmann, *History of Ancient Art*, vol. 2, 50. Translation modified.

115. Ibid., 51.

116. Winckelmann, "Vorläufige Abhandlung zu den Denkmalen der Kunst des Altertums," 106.

117. Winckelmann, *History of Ancient Art*, vol. 2, 53. Translation modified. On the hermaphrodite as an "idée fixe of German Classicism" and Classicism in general, cf. 000, this volume, and Pfotenhauer, "Gemeißelte Sinnlichkeit," 84–85, 100–02.

118. Herder, "Reisetagebuch," 603.

119. Winckelmann, *History of Ancient Art*, vol. 2, 53. Translation modified.

120. Winckelmann, "Vorläufige Abhandlung zu den Denkmalen der Kunst des Altertums," 112.

121. Winckelmann, *History of Ancient Art*, vol. 2, 50.

122. Herder, "Studien und Entwürfe zur Plastik," 90.

123. Diderot, *Ästhetische Schriften*, Bd. 1, S. 615. Diderot, "The Salon of 1765," 160. Translation modified. Cf. Pfotenhauer, "Gemeißelte Sinnlichkeit," 94–97.

124. Winckelmann, "Thoughts on the Imitation of Greek Works in Painting and Sculpture," 15–16.

125. Herder, "Studien und Entwürfe zur Plastik," 90.

126. Lessing, *Laocoön*, 204, note. Translation modified.

127. Herder, "Erstes Kritisches Wäldchen," 175–76.

128. Ibid., 221.

129. Ibid., 176.

130. Lessing, *Laocoön*, 133.

131. Herder, "Erstes Kritisches Wäldchen," 104.

132. Lessing, *Laocoön*, 10.

133. Ibid., 26. Translation modified.

134. Ibid., 133–34.

135. Ibid., 182; ibid., 137.

136. Ibid., 134. Translation modified.

137. Ovid, *Metamorphoses* VI 385–90, trans. Horace Gregory, quoted from: Lessing, *Laocoön*, 230.

138. Ibid., 134–35. Translation modified. Diderot openly defended flayed Marsyas as a *belle chose*—and this in the field of fine art: "But is not the dying gladiator indeed a *belle chose*? Are not the veins of Marsyas the satyr, torn out and quivering under Apollo's knife, indeed a *belle chose*?" (*Œuvres Complètes*, vol. 13, 91) Elsewhere,

Diderot himself draws a distinction between aesthetically productive *horreur* and antiaesthetic *dégout* in the contemplation of bloody, dismembered body-parts (vol. 10, 115–16); for that reason he rejects a painting that depicts Marsyas' flaying (vol. 13, 39). On the other hand, in the case of Chardin's *Rais dépouillée*, he finds even the *dégoutant* in itself to be aesthetically salvageable (vol. 10, 195). These few, heterogeneous passages appear to exhaust Diderot's "aesthetics" of disgust. Cf. Herbert Dieckmann, "Das Abscheuliche and Schreckliche in der Kunsttheorie des 18. Jahrhunderts," 302–4; Jean Seznec, "Un Laocoon français," 58–78, especially 63–66.

139. Chaouli has shown this convincingly in his essay "Devouring Metaphor: Disgust and Taste in Kleist's 'Penthesilea.'" In any case, I do not agree with Chaouli's argument that Kleist "launches an attack on one of the seminal works of aesthetics, Kant's *Critique of Judgment*, for nowhere is the opposition of taste and disgust enshrined as firmly and systematically" (125). As explained on page 000, this volume, Kant in fact would seem to be simply offering a late echo or indeed citation of a far more virulent debate unfolding in the 1750s and 1760s. And further, the figures that Chaouli explores, displaying a complex linkage of potentially disgusting objects to aesthetic representation, certainly do not need to be read as a "modern" deconstruction of Kant. Rather, they can be described more satisfactorily in the framework of—in fact—a pre-Kantian aesthetics: pleasure at mixed sensations, and semanticization and suspension of "true" disgust through double mixing-operations. To this extent, from both a historical and systematic-theoretical vantage, the deconstructive impulse of Chaouli's text loses its underpinning.

140. Bakhtin, *Rabelais and His World*, 207.

141. Ibid., 211.

142. Ibid., 207–08.

143. Nietzsche, "Aufzeichnungen aus der Zeit der Fröhlichen Wissenschaft," 193–94.

144. Lessing, "How the Ancients Represented Death," 215. Translation modified. Cf. von Mücke, "The Powers of Horror and the Magic of Euphemism," 172–80.

145. Lessing, "How the Ancients Represented Death," 182. Translation modified.

146. Ibid., 184.

147. Ibid., 213–14.

148. Ibid., 214.

149. Ibid., 215–16. Translation modified.

150. Herder, "Wie die Alten den Tod gebildet?," 449.

151. Ibid., 450–51.

152. Ibid., 450.

153. Nietzsche, *The Birth of Tragedy*, 38–40.

154. Lessing, *Laocoön*, 133. Translation modified.

155. Herder, "Die Plastik von 1770," 136.

156. Herder, "Plastik," 20. The two versions of Herder's work differ not least of all in the far more extensive and penetrating reflections on *Ekel* in the "Plastik" of 1770 than in the "Plastik" of 1778—which in any case was also mostly written between 1768 and 1770. (Compare 30–33 of the 1778 work with 145–49 of the 1770 work).

157. Kant, "Bemerkungen zu den Beobachtungen über das Gefühl des Schönen and Erhabenen," 155.

158. Kant, "Reflexionen zur Anthropologie," 804.

159. Ibid., 473.

160. Kant, *Anthropology from a Pragmatic Point of View*, 212–13.

161. Kolnai, "Der Ekel," 526.

162. Ibid.

163. Brockes, "Das durch die Betrachtung der Grösse Gottes verherrlichte Nichts der Menschen. In einem Gespräche auf das Neue Jahr, 1722," 441–42.

164. Horace, Epode 8; in The Complete Odes and Epodes, 11–12.

165. Cf. Oeri, *Der Typ der komischen Alten in der griechischen Komödie*.

166. Cf. Grassmann, *Die erotischen Epoden des Horaz*, 1–46.

167. Ibid., 31–32.

168. Cf. Freud's reference to the "unduly increased libido," that "the aging woman" develops during menopause—even to her own "horror" ("On the Grounds for Detaching a Particular Syndrome from Neurasthenia under the Description 'Anxiety Neurosis,'" 111).

169. In general, the edition hides Martial's frankness behind a wall of innuendo, paraphrase, and scholarly footnotes.

170. Goethe, "Nachträge zu den Gedichten," *Weimar Edition*, section 1, vol. 53, 12.

171. Rosenkranz, *Ästhetik des Häßlichen*, 368. In his notes, Rosenkranz cites Horace's eighth epode in full, simply adding a laconic comment: "I admit to not finding a spark of poetry in this repulsive depiction" (456–57).

172. Cf. Miller, *The Anatomy of Disgust*, 163.

173. On the following cf.: Zelle, *Angenehmes Grauen*, 247–51.

174. Brockes, "Das durch die Betrachtung der Grösse Gottes verherrlichte Nichts der Menschen," 445. Translation Eric Schwab.

175. Ibid., 439.

176. Ibid., 442.

177. Ibid., 441–42.

178. Bakhtin, *Rabelais and His World*, 25.

179. Breitinger, *Critische Dichtkunst*, vol. 1, 66–69. In a similar manner, Bodmer and Breitinger refer in their *Discourse der Mahlern* to an "enjoyment at seeing the loath-

some portrait of a wrinkled hag" (12). In his didactic poem "Gedanken von der Dichtkunst überhaupt," Heinrich Samuel von Brück likewise evokes an ugly old woman as the object of imitative pleasure (10). Despite a virtually complete parallelism of physical detail, the later paradigm of the disgusting is here still highly overlayered with an impression of the ridiculous and derisory.

180. J. E. Schlegel, "Abhandlung, daß die Nachahmung der Sache, der man nachahmet, zuweilen unähnlich werden müsse," 103.

181. Ibid., 98.

182. J. A. Schlegel, "Anmerkungen über Ekel," 111–12.

183. Hagedorn, *Betrachtungen über die Mahlerey*, 111.

184. J. E. Schlegel, "Abhandlung von der Nachahmung," 154.

185. Lessing, *Laocoön*, 121.

186. Ibid., 133–34.

187. For Baubo, see 000.

188. Bakhtin, *Rabelais and His World*, 366.

189. For a critique of the "ideological" identifications at work in Bakhtin's study of Rabelais, cf. Greenblatt, *Learning to Curse*, 67–69.

190. This a central thesis of Mülder-Bach, *Im Zeichen Pygmalions*. For the cited formulation, see 25, 155.

191. On the relation between disgust and pity cf. Wellbery, "The Pathos of Theory: Laokoon Revisited," 53–54.

192. Elias, *Über den Prozeß der Zivilisation*.

193. For a more discriminating approach cf. Pfotenhauer, *Gemeißelte Sinnlichkeit*, 81–94.

194. Herder, "Die Plastik von 1770," 140. Pfotenhauer, *Gemeißelte Sinnlichkeit*, 94–97 offers a more detailed discussion of the Classical rules for body hair.

195. Winckelmann, *History of Ancient Art*, 170.

196. Herder, "Die Plastik von 1770," 141–42.

197. J. E. Schlegel, "Abhandlung von der Nachahmung," 154.

198. J. A. Schlegel, "Anmerkungen über Ekel," 111.

199. Hagedorn, *Betrachtungen über die Mahlerey*, 112.

200. Douglas, *Purity and Danger*, 133.

201. Ibid., 132.

202. Ibid., 142.

203. Ibid., 4.

204. Ibid., 51–52.

205. Ibid., 157–58.

206. Ibid., 173.

207. Cf. Kant, *Critique of Judgment*, 80–81.

208. Herder, "Die Plastik von 1770," 149.

209. Ibid.

210. Winckelmann, "Thoughts on the Imitation of Greek Works in Painting and Sculpture," 8.

211. Winckelmann, *History of Ancient Art*, vol. 2, 75.

212. Winckelmann, "A Treatise on the Ability to Perceive the Beautiful in Art and Instruction in the Same," 100. Translation modified.

213. Winckelmann, *History of Ancient Art*, vol. 2, 91–92.

214. Winckelmann, "A Treatise on the Ability to Perceive the Beautiful in Art and Instruction in the Same," 100.

215. Herder, "Studien und Entwürfe zur Plastik," 88.

216. Cf. Edmund Burke, *A Philosophical Enquiry into the Origin of Our Ideas of the Sublime and the Beautiful*, 41–43. (In any event, other than Kant, Burke does recognize a reciprocal physical attraction of the woman to male beauty.)

217. Douglas, *Purity and Danger*, 158.

218. Kant, "Observations on the Feeling of the Beautiful and Sublime," 83.

219. Ibid., 84. Translation modified.

Chapter 3

1. At least to the extent of my familiarity with the literature on the third *Critique*.

2. Cf. Derrida, "Economimesis," 21–25. Placed against the backdrop of the elaborate *Ekel*-debate extending from J. A. Schlegel to Mendelssohn, Lessing, Herder, and Kant, many accents in Derrida's reading seem questionable. Derrida's consideration of the distinction in principle between the disgust-taboo and the forms of negative pleasure contained in the aesthetic itself thus involves an exertion of somewhat superfluous eloquence. For Kant is here simply following his predecessors. Derrida likewise overinterprets the absence of examples in the *Ekel*-paragraph of the third *Critique*: the absence, he explains, reflects ipso facto the "impossibility of finding examples in this case" demonstrating an essential "inability" on Kant's part (21). Accordingly, for Derrida disgust is "unrepresentable" and "unnamable in its singularity" (22), since it deconstructs the entire "logocentric system" (23, 25), every "hierarchizing authority" (25), and every "economy": "This impossibility cannot be said to be some thing" (25). But in his time, Kant could simply assume that every educated reader was familiar at least with the disgust-paragraphs in Lessing's *Laocoön;* he could thus spare himself a repetition of the examples treated there at great length. Crucially, in his anthropological texts Kant shows no hesitation in offering all sorts of examples of disgust connected

with nourishment, smell, sex, morality, and intellectual capacity. In doing so, he betrays no awareness of that basic inadequacy of all disgust-examples *actually* emerging from more careful scrutiny of the aesthetic debate over *Ekel*, cf. 000, this volume. But above all, Kant does his utmost to inscribe disgust as a most useful element in the economy of physical and intellectual life, hence into the same system of nature and logos whose aesthetic borders and transcendence he is demarcating. In the disgust-cipher's circulation through his writings, Kant always already accepts, indeed gladly so, what Derrida points to at the end of his essay: that every philosophy and every example—that the word *Ekel* itself—is already a remedy against the "absolutely heterogeneous" (22), the "scandal," to which it refers.

3. Among these texts, Derrida only considers the *Anthropology from a Pragmatic Point of View* of 1798.

4. Translator's note: the German word *Genuss (Geniessen)* ordinarily conveys a dual meaning of "enjoyment" ("to enjoy") and gustatory "consumption" ("to consume"); considering the context, I settle for the latter meaning here and below.

5. Kant, *Critique of Judgment*, 180. Translation modified.

6. Cf. Condillac, *A Treatise on the Sensations*, 312–13.

7. Kant, "Reflexionen zur Anthropologie," 107.

8. Kant, *Anthropology from a Pragmatic Point of View*, 45. Translation modified.

9. Cf. 000, this volume.

10. Bourdieu, *Distinction*, 488. Translation modified.

11. Ibid.

12. Miller takes up Bourdieu's reading of Kant's reflections on disgust (*The Anatomy of Disgust*, 169).

13. Kant, *Anthropology from a Pragmatic Point of View*, 45. Translation modified.

14. Ibid., 144. Translation modified.

15. Kant, "Reflexionen zur Anthropologie," 473.

16. Kant, *Anthropology from a Pragmatic Point of View*, 153. Translation modified.

17. Kant, "Reflexionen zur Anthropologie," 850.

18. Lessing, *Laocoön*, 135. Translation modified. Cf. Jacobs, "The Critical Performance of Lessing's 'Laokoon,'" 499–501.

19. Lessing, *Laocoön*, 135–37.

20. Lessing considers the correlation to be so distinctive a feature for the representation of hunger that he demarcates it as "*one* type of the terrible" (ibid., 135). Translation modified; italics added.

21. Kant, *Anthropology from a Pragmatic Point of View*, 45. Translation modified.

22. Ibid., 69, 178. Translation modified.

23. Kant, "Reflexionen zur Anthropologie," 804.

24. Kant, *Observations on the Feeling of the Beautiful and Sublime*, 93. Translation modified.

25. Ibid., 84.

26. Kant, "Bemerkungen zu den Beobachtungen über das Gefühl des Schönen und Erhabenen," 155.

27. Kolnai, "Der Ekel," 525.

28. Perhaps this more than latent inclination of all physical-aesthetic disgust toward ethical sexual disgust is responsible for the relative insignificance of "disgust" in the aesthetics and anthropology of 'hedonist' Goethe. Kant conceptualizes the ethical-anthropological implications of the classical-beautiful corporeal facade as an ambivalent rejection of enjoyment; Goethe pillories precisely that rejection as a disgust that is itself disgusting on the part of "ashamed criminals": "For me, finery and adornment remain disgusting, and in the end/doesn't a skirt of brocade lift the same as a wool one?" (*Römische Elegien, Weimar Edition,* section 1, vol. 53, 5–6). As Kant views it, beauty "contains in itself the concept of the invitation to the most intimate union with the object, that is, to immediate enjoyment" (*Anthropology from a Pragmatic Point of View,* 144); Goethe recommends following up on this invitation in any way possible, instead of aesthetically deferring "enjoyment" ad infinitum or ethically rejecting it as disgusting. To be sure, this call for "free pleasure" itself attests to the power of the disgust-cipher it defies; it thus negatively confirms that tendency of the aesthetic Kant both revealed as an ethical anthropologism and positively dogmatized.

29. Kant, *The Metaphysics of Morals,* 179.

30. Kant, "Physische Geographie," 379, 384.

31. Kant, "Reflexionen zur Anthropologie," 104. Kant draws here on Starke's *Menschenkunde.*

32. Kant, *Education,* 108–9. Translation modified. Kant draws here on Starke's *Menschenkunde.*

33. Cf. Kolnai, "Der Ekel," 525–26.

34. Condillac, *A Treatise on the Sensations,* 190.

35. Kolnai's formulation to the effect that disgust intends "to cleanse my proximity and weed out something from it" ("Der Ekel," 526) itself draws its action closer to an annihilatory intent than the declared dichotomy between disgust and hate would indicate. Particularly the Nazi genocidal project has shown that a deliberate use of an aesthetics of disgust—the Jews as a ubiquitous mass of ugly and subversive rats damaging to the "healthy" state and *Volk*—can render "cleansing" removal from proximity and direct murder into a cycle. For centuries, of course, disgusting odors, filth, and all sorts of contaminative traits have been stock elements of the antisemitic imagination (cf. Miller, *The Anatomy of Disgust,* 155–57). But only the Nazis set about degrading the Jews literally into stinking, excrement-soiled beings through the concentration-camp's hygienic regime. The purpose of this systematic debasement through making it impossible for the Jews to maintain basic disgust boundaries was not only to break the victims' self-respect, but also to lower the guards' inhibitions on murder. But even here, the feeling of disgust does not figure as a motive for murder in itself; it rather serves to neutralize the murder-taboo. Cf. Des Pres, *The Survivor,* 51–71.

36. Kant, *Anthropology from a Pragmatic Point of View,* 43.

37. Ibid., 44–45. Translation modified.

38. Kant, "Reflexionen zur Anthropologie," 106.

39. Ibid., 804.

40. Kant, *Anthropology from a Pragmatic Point of View*, 46. Translation modified.

41. Cf. Corbin, *The Foul and the Fragrant: Odor and French Social Imagination.*

42. Cf. Rozin et al., "Disgust," 58.

43. Cf. d'Holbach, *Système sociale ou principes naturels de la morale et de la politique*, 100: "Nous trouvons détestables des mêts qui sont trouvés délicieux dans d'autres pays par la seule raison que dès l'enfance notre palais ne s'y est pas accoutumé."

44. Kant, *Anthropology from a Pragmatic Point of View*, 144. Translation modified.

45. Ibid., 45. Translation modified.

46. Ibid. Translation modified.

47. Kant, "Reflexionen zur Anthropologie," 104–5. This conclusion converges with Derrida's theory of disgust's essential unnameability ("Economimesis," 20–25). On the specific unnameability of smells, cf. Engen, "Remembering Odors and Their Names" and Miller, *The Anatomy of Disgust*, 67–68.

48. Kant, *Anthropology from a Pragmatic Point of View*, 40–41. Translation modified. Despite extensive recourse to the *Anthropology from a Pragmatic Point of View* in "Economimesis," Derrida does not examine this central definition of disgust as an all-pervading "vital sensation," in distinction to the sensations of individual organs. Many of Derrida's expositions on mouth and nose as disgust's (or beauty's) sensory organs might be relativized from such a starting point.

49. Kant, *Critique of Judgment*, 98. Translation modified.

50. Ibid., 201. Translation modified.

51. Kant, "Reflexionen zur Anthropologie," 749.

52. Kant, *Anthropology from a Pragmatic Point of View*, 46.

53. Kant, *Critique of Judgment*, 203. Translation modified.

54. Kant, "Reflexionen zur Anthropologie," 744, 850.

55. Ibid., 850.

56. Kant, "Inquiry Concerning the Distinctness of the Principles of Natural Theology and Morals," 252–53. Translation modified.

57. Kant, *Critique of Pure Reason*, 273. Translation modified.

58. Kant, "Reflexionen zur Anthropologie," 665.

59. Kant, *Anthropology from a Pragmatic Point of View*, 45. Translation modified.

60. Kant, "Prolegomena to Any Future Metaphysics That Will Be Able to Come Forward as Science," 120.

61. Kant, *Groundwork of the Metaphysics of Morals*, 21–22. Translation modified.

62. Kant, *Anthropology from a Pragmatic Point of View*, 120. Translation modified.

63. Goethe, "Frankfurter gelehrte Anzeigen," *Weimar Edition*, section 1, vol. 36, 207, 211.

64. Goethe, "Letter to C. v. Knebel (November 1816)," *Weimar Edition*, section 4, vol. 27, 225.

65. Kant, *Critique of Judgment*, 23–25. Translation modified.

66. Kant, *Critique of Practical Reason*, 41.

67. Ibid., 29.

68. Kant, *Critique of Judgment*, 128. Translation modified.

69. Cf. Menninghaus, "Zwischen Überwältigung und Widerstand. Macht und Gewalt in Longins und Kants Theorien des Erhabenen," 14–19.

70. Kant, "Inquiry Concerning the Distinctness of the Principles of Natural Theology and Morals," 252.

71. Kant, "Reflexionen zur Moralphilosophie," 149.

72. Kant, *The Metaphysics of Morals*, 165.

73. Cf. Kant, "Reflexionen zur Anthropologie," 293. Here "love of honor" is defined as something approaching "the true and absolute good" in a "merely negative fashion," aiming only at the avoidance of contemptuous assessment by strangers "or even disgusting aversion."

74. Kant, *Critique of Judgment*, 180. Translation modified.

75. Darwin, *The Expression of the Emotions in Man and Animals*, 258.

76. Kant, *Anthropology from a Pragmatic Point of View*, 45. Translation modified.

77. Kant, *Observations on the Feeling of the Beautiful and Sublime*, 84. On the links between disgust and shame, cf. Miller, *The Anatomy of Disgust*, 34–35.

78. Kant, "Reflexionen zur Anthropologie," 741.

79. Kant, *Anthropology from a Pragmatic Point of View*, 45–46. Translation modified.

80. Goethe, "Italienische Reise," *Weimar Edition*, section 1, vol. 30, 221. Cf. Goethe's "Anmerkungen über Personen und Gegenstände, deren in dem Dialog Rameau's Neffe erwähnt wird," *Weimar Edition*, section 1, vol. 45, 199 and "Epigramme," *Weimar Edition*, section 1, vol. 53, 12.

81. Cf. Kant, *The Metaphysics of Morals*, 142–43.

82. Cf. Kant, "Religion within the Boundaries of Mere Reason," 191.

83. Kant, *Observations on the Feeling of the Beautiful and Sublime*, 77. Translation modified.

84. Ibid., 84–85. Translation modified.

85. Kant, *Anthropology from a Pragmatic Point of View*, 220. Translation modified.

86. Cf. ibid., 35, 45.

87. Ibid., 38. Translation modified. Cf. Schmitz, *System der Philosophie*, vol. 3, pt. 2, 220–41.

88. Goethe, *Dichtung und Wahrheit, Weimar Edition*, section 1, vol. 28, 209.

89. Ibid., 210.

90. Goethe, "Tagebücher (January 1779)," *Weimar Edition*, section 3, vol. 1, 77. Cf. "Italiänische Reise," *Weimar Edition*, section 1, vol. 32, 274; "Frankfurter gelehrte Anzeigen," section 1, vol. 36, 210; "Claudine von Villa Bella," section 1, vol. 38, 123; "Letter to C. v. Knebel (October 20, 1810)," section 4, vol. 21, 402.

91. Kant, "Reflexionen zur Anthropologie," 473.

Chapter 4

1. Mendelssohn, "82. Literaturbrief," 131.

2. Kolnai, "Der Ekel," 532–33. On the issue of disgust in acoustic phenomena cf. also H. M. Enzensberger, "Aus dem Leben eines musikalischen Opfers"; Eggebrecht, "Eeltöne"; and Miller, *Anatomy of Disgust*, 82–85.

3. Nietzsche, "Nachgelassene Fragmente," March 1875, 25.

4. All quotations refer to Hegel, *Enzyklopädie der philosophischen Wissenschaften II*, vol. 9, 492–93.

5. Rosenkranz, *Ästhetik des Häßlichen*, 39.

6. Schlegel, "Über das Studium der Griechischen Poesie," 254.

7. Rosenkranz, *Ästhetik des Häßlichen*, 321.

8. Schlegel, "Athenäums-Fragmente" 124, 185.

9. Cf. Praz, *The Romantic Agony*.

10. A parallel note clarifies the literary reference: "The depiction of absolute torment (Diderot's nun) itself basically belongs to modern poetry and to the novel's prolegomena." (Schlegel, *Literarische Notizen 1797–1801*, nr. 154.)

11. Cf. 000, this volume.

12. Rosenkranz, *Ästhetik des Häßlichen*, 381–83.

13. Like numerous formulations in the above passage, Rosenkranz took the formulation "beautiful disgust" directly from Julian Schmidt's *Geschichte der Romantik in dem Zeitalter der Reformation und der Revolution*, vol. 2, 385–87; this work abounds in a conservative critique of the "poison of Romanticism" and its decadent affirmation of a "broken being lacking any morale."

14. Schlegel, "Athenäums-Fragmente," nr. 116, 182.

15. For affinities between Baudelaire and Rosenkranz's *Aesthetics of the Ugly* cf. Fietkau, *Schwanengesang auf 1848*, 93–106.

16. Translated from: Baudelaire, *Œuvres complètes*, 5–6.

17. Tieck, *Das Alte Buch*, 829–30.

18. Ibid., 850–51.

19. Schopenhauer, *Die Welt als Wille und Vorstellung*, vol. 1, 246. Cf. Jean Paul's remark in the *Vorschule der Ästhetik* (427): "There are two feelings that cannot be admitted in any pure and free enjoyment of art, because they enter the viewer from the painting and transform the viewing into suffering: the feeling of *Ekel* and that of sensual love."

20. Rosenkranz, *Ästhetik des Häßlichen*, 312–13.

21. Kolnai, "Der Ekel," 547.

22. Rosenkranz, *Ästhetik des Häßlichen*, 313.

23. Herder, "Studien und Entwürfe zur Plastik," 88.

24. Mary Shelley, *Frankenstein or, The Modern Prometheus*, 99–105.

25. Rosenkranz, *Ästhetik des Häßlichen*, 314.

26. Tieck, *Das Alte Buch*, 850–51.

27. Ibid., 829.

28. Baudelaire, *Les Fleurs du Mal*, 31–32 (translated by Joel Golb). For a less literal and versified translation cf. the bilingual edition *The Flowers of Evil*, translated by James McGowan, 58–63.

29. Cf. Noyer-Weidner, "Stilempfinden und Stilentwicklung Baudelaires"; 186–94.

30. Cf. Kolnai, "Der Ekel," 540.

31. Winckelmann, "Erläuterung," 97. Cf. Benjamin, "Über einige Motive bei Baudelaire," 641, and Berger, "A vue de nez. Fragment d'une esthétique du dégoût," 111–19.

32. On Baudelaire's depiction of death, cf. Jackson, *La Mort Baudelaire;* on *"Une charogne,"* cf. especially 65–84.

33. I owe attention to this pun to an observation Joel Golb made in translating this chapter.

34. Baudelaire, *Les Fleurs du Mal*, 34.

35. Ibid., 89.

36. Weinberg, "Baudelaires 'Une Charogne,'" 110.

37. On Baudelaire's ironic Platonism cf., in relation to *"Une charogne,"* Hubert, *L'Esthétique des "Fleurs du Mal,"* 49–51 and Galland, *Baudelaire. Poétiques et Poésie*, 285–87. McLees, "Baudelaire's 'Une Charogne,'" has illuminated the general significance of caricature for the poem.

38. Cf. Ruff, *L'Esprit du mal et l'Esthétique baudelairienne*, S. 195–97, 298, 343.

39. Vgl. Grant-Tucker, "Pétrachisant sur l'horrible," 887–96 and Bersani, *Baudelaire and Freud*, 71.

40. Cf. Starobinski, *"Cadavres Interpellés,"* 71.

41. Cf. Ferran, *L'Esthétique de Baudelaire*, 47, 84, 94, 177 and Prévost, *Baudelaire. Essai sur l'inspiration et la création poétique*, 351–52.

42. Cf. Theile, "La toile oubliée," 309–17.
43. Weinberg, "Baudelaire's 'Une Charogne,'" 113–14.
44. Schlegel, "Athenäums-Fragmente," nr. 51, 172.
45. Cf. Menninghaus, *Unendliche Verdopplung*, 200–04.
46. Rosenkranz, *Ästhetik des Häßlichen*, 3.
47. Ibid. 6–7.
48. Ibid. 170–71.
49. Ibid., 32.
50. Ibid., 28–29.
51. Ibid., 166.
52. Ibid., 29–30.
53. Ibid., 325–26.
54. Tieck, *Das Alte Buch*, 829.
55. Ibid.
56. Rosenkranz, *Ästhetik des Häßlichen*, 317–18.
57. Ibid., 321.
58. Ibid., 315.
59. Lessing, *Laocoön*, 137. Translation modified.
60. Rosenkranz, *Ästhetik des Häßlichen*, 318.
61. Ibid., 320–21.
62. Ibid., 315.

Chapter 5

1. Kant, *Anthropology from a Pragmatic Point of View*, 39.
2. Nietzsche, *On the Genealogy of Morals*, 99. Translation modified.
3. Nietzsche, *Beyond Good and Evil*, 57.
4. Nietzsche, *Thus Spoke Zarathusztra*, 281.
5. Cf. Benjamin, "Zentralpark," 664, 683, 684.
6. Nietzsche, "Nachgelassene Fragmente," spring-autumn 1881, vol. 9, 461. After completion of the present discussion of Nietzsche, a short essay appeared with some overlappings of material and approach: Liessmann, "'Ekel! Ekel! Ekel!—Wehe mir!'"
7. Nietzsche, *The Birth of Tragedy*, 9. Translation modified.
8. Nietzsche, "Nachgelassene Fragmente," November 1887—March 1888, vol. 13, 70–71.

9. Nietzsche, *The Birth of Tragedy*, 9. Translation modified.
10. Nietzsche, "Nachgelassene Fragmente," spring 1888, vol. 13, 312.
11. Nietzsche, *The Birth of Tragedy*, 8–9. Translation modified.
12. Ibid., 8.
13. Nietzsche, "Nachgelassene Fragmente," autumn 1887, vol. 12, 565, 581.
14. Ibid., 381.
15. Nietzsche, "Nachgelassene Fragmente," autumn 1885—autumn 1886, vol. 12, 156.
16. Nietzsche, *On the Genealogy of Morals*, 101–2. Translation modified.
17. Ibid., 100. Translation modified.
18. Ibid., 132. Translation modified.
19. Ibid., 102–3. Translation modified.
20. Nietzsche, "Nachgelassene Fragmente," end of 1886—spring 1887, vol. 12, 321.
21. Nietzsche, *On the Genealogy of Morals*, 101.
22. Ibid., 115. Translation modified.
23. Nietzsche, *Daybreak*, 35.
24. Mendelssohn, "82. Literaturbrief," 131.
25. Nietzsche, *On the Genealogy of Morals*, 48. Translation modified.
26. Ibid., 133. Translation modified.
27. Ibid., 47–48. Translation modified.
28. Cf. Zelle, *"Angenehmes Grauen,"* 119, 147.
29. Nietzsche, *On the Genealogy of Morals*, 49.
30. Ibid., 48. Translation modified.
31. Nietzsche, *Ecce Homo*, 102. Translation modified.
32. Nietzsche, "Nachgelassene Fragmente," spring–autumn 1881, vol. 9, 471.
33. Ibid., 460.
34. Ibid., p 602.
35. Ibid., 460–61.
36. Nietzsche, *On the Genealogy of Morals*, 75. Translation modified.
37. Nietzsche, *The Gay Science*, 122. Translation modified.
38. Nietzsche, "Nachgelassene Fragmente," July–August 1879, vol. 8, 601.
39. Nietzsche, *Ecce Homo*, 21–22. Translation modified.
40. Ibid., 22. Translation modified.
41. Winckelmann, *History of Ancient Art*, vol. 2, 78.

42. Nietzsche, *Beyond Good and Evil*, 141. Translation modified.

43. Nietzsche, *The Birth of Tragedy*, 39–40.

44. Nietzsche, *On the Genealogy of Morals*, 103–4. Translation modified.

45. Ibid., 101. Translation modified.

46. Nietzsche, "Nachgelassene Fragmente," November 1887—March 1888, vol. 13, 75.

47. Cf. Nietzsche, *Ecce Homo*, 30 and Nietzsche, "Nachgelassene Fragmente," November 1887—March 1888, vol. 13, 75–92, 118, 404.

48. Nietzsche, *The Gay Science*, 289. Translation modified.

49. Nietzsche, *Twilight of the Idols*, 78.

50. Nietzsche, *Thus Spoke Zarathustra*, 121.

51. Ibid., 230, 307.

52. Ibid., 230.

53. Ibid., 121.

54. Nietzsche, *Beyond Good and Evil*, 35. Translation modified.

55. Nietzsche, *The Gay Science*, 85. Translation modified.

56. Nietzsche, *Beyond Good and Evil*, 57–58. Translation modified.

57. Nietzsche, "Nachgelassene Fragmente," summer 1886—spring 1887, vol. 12, 241.

58. Nietzsche, *Beyond Good and Evil*, 209. Translation modified.

59. Nietzsche, *Ecce Homo*, 50–51. Translation modified.

60. Cf. Bennholdt-Thommsen, *Nietzsches "Also sprach Zarathustra" als literarisches Phänomen*, 208–9.

61. Nietzsche, "Nachgelassene Fragmente," spring–summer 1888, vol. 13, 492.

62. Nietzsche, *Thus Spoke Zarathustra*, S. 216.

63. Nietzsche, *The Birth of Tragedy*, 40–41. Translation modified.

64. Nietzsche, "Nachgelassene Fragmente," spring–autumn 1881, vol. 9, 459.

65. Nietzsche, *Beyond Good and Evil*, 202–3. Translation modified.

66. Nietzsche, *Ecce Homo*, 92–94.

67. Nietzsche, "Nachgelassene Fragmente," spring–autumn 1881, vol. 9, 479.

68. Nietzsche, "On the Future of our Educational Institutions," 59–60.

69. Ibid., 59.

70. Occasionally, however, Nietzsche discovers more than isolated remains of a "reason" present as "instinctive" sediment. He then offers praise such as the following: "That resistance Wagner encountered among us Germans cannot be estimated and honored highly enough. The defense against him was like that against a disease,—*not with reasons*—one does not refute a disease—but with restraint, mistrust, bad temper,

disgust" ("Der Fall Wagner," 40). Once again, the explanation Nietzsche offers for possible collective remnants of an "instinct-scent for harmful stuff" points to the untimeliness of his disgust-knowledge model: the Germans are, precisely, "Europe's backward Culturvolk [sic]," "the *postponers* par excellence"—and this occasionally has "its advantages" (ibid. 41).

71. Nietzsche, *Ecce Homo* 50. Translation modified.

72. Nietzsche, *Beyond Good and Evil*, 152. Translation modified.

73. Cf. Nietzsche, "On the Uses and Disadvantages of History for Life," 109–10.

74. Nietzsche, *Beyond Good and Evil*, 152–54.

75. Nietzsche, *The Birth of Tragedy*, 40. Translation modified.

76. Ibid., 39.

77. Nietzsche, *The Gay Science*, 163–64. Translation modified.

78. Nietzsche, *The Birth of Tragedy*, 32. Translation modified.

79. Nietzsche, *The Gay Science*, 32–33. Translation modified.

80. Nietzsche, *Thus Spoke Zarathustra*, 281.

81. Ibid., 41. Translation modified.

82. Ibid., 40. Translation modified.

83. Ibid., 120–21. Translation modified.

84. Ibid., 180. Translation modified.

85. Ibid., 222. Translation modified.

86. Ibid., 230. Translation modified.

87. Ibid., 293–94. Translation modified.

88. Ibid., 320–21. Translation modified.

89. Ibid., 280.

90. Ibid., 280–81. Translation modified.

91. Nietzsche, *On the Genealogy of Morals*, 10. Translation modified.

92. Nietzsche, *Thus Spoke Zarathustra*, 326 . Translation modified.

93. Cf. Hamacher, *Pleroma. Reading in Hegel*, 276–80.

94. Cf. Nietzsche's praise of "that clever, bovine peace of mind, piety, and meekness of country pastors that lies in the meadow and *observes* life seriously while ruminating" (*The Gay Science*, 293. Translation modified).

95. Nietzsche, *Thus Spoke Zarathustra*, 67. Translation modified.

96. Cf. Hamacher, *Pleroma. Reading in Hegel*, 276: "But ruminating signifies—if it signifies at all—not merely the spitting-out of what is nauseous, but also its repeated eating. Reading signifies—if it signifies at all—not merely transsubstantiating the meaning of what is written into oneself, not merely spitting out again the externality and meaninglessness of the inscripted sign and its transformation in order to preserve

the purity of the self from the dangerously nauseous operation of another reading; it also signifies, before its repetition, before the nauseous, avoiding nausea at nausea itself." (In any event, spitting out is not a precondition for the cow's rumination—and probably also not for the readers.)

97. Cf. Kant, *Anthropology from a Pragmatic Point of View*, 45; and Goethe, *Dichtung und Wahrheit, Weimar Edition*, section 1, vol. 28, 210.

98. Nietzsche, "Nachgelassene Fragmente," spring–autumn 1881, vol. 9, 505.

99. Nietzsche, *The Gay Science*, 33. Translation modified.

100. Nietzsche, *Thus Spoke Zarathustra*, 321–22. Translation modified.

101. Ibid., 322. Translation modified.

102. Ibid., 324. Translation modified.

103. Ibid., 325.

104. Nietzsche, *Ecce Homo*, 50 . Translation modified.

105. Cf. Bennholdt-Thommsen, *Nietzsches "Also sprach Zarathustra" als literarisches Phänomen*, 209–12.

106. Nietzsche, *On the Genealogy of Morals*, 79. Translation modified.

107. Nietzsche, *Twilight of the Idols*, 33. Translation modified.

108. Nietzsche, *Thus Spoke Zarathustra*, 39.

109. Ibid., 335.

110. Ibid., 294.

111. Nietzsche, "Nachgelassene Fragmente," summer 1886–autumn 1887, vol. 12, 200–1.

112. Nietzsche, *Ecce Homo*, 42. Translation modified.

113. Nietzsche, *Beyond Good and Evil*, 38. Translation modified.

114. Nietzsche, *Ecce Homo*, 77. Translation modified.

115. Ibid., 82. Translation modified.

116. Ibid., 33. Translation modified.

117. Ibid., 17.

118. Nietzsche, "Nachgelassene Fragmente," spring–autumn 1881, vol. 9, 461.

119. Nietzsche, *Ecce Homo*, 69. Translation modified.

120. Herder, "Studien und Entwürfe zur Plastik," 112 and "Erstes Kritisches Wäldchen," 175–76.

121. Baudelaire, *The Flowers of Evil*, 38–41. Cf . Mathias, *La Beauté dans les "Fleurs du Mal."*

122. Cf. Derrida, *Éperons. Les styles de Nietzsche* and Hamacher, *Pleroma. Reading in Hegel*, 266–95.

123. Nietzsche, *The Gay Science*, 38. Translation modified.

124. Picard, "Die große Mutter von Kreta bis Eleusis," 104–6.
125. Devereux, *Baubo*.
126. Hahn, *Demeter und Baubo*, 58.
127. Cf. Picard, "Die große Mutter von Kreta bis Eleusis," 105–6.
128. Goethe, *Faust*, v. 3964–67.
129. Nietzsche, *The Gay Science*, 339. Translation modified.
130. Ibid., 125. Translation modified.
131. Nietzsche, *Thus Spoke Zarathustra*, 68. Translation modified.
132. Nietzsche, *Ecce Homo*, 8. Translation modified.
133. Ibid., 11. Translation modified.
134. Nietzsche, *The Gay Science*, 1127–28. Translation modified.

Chapter 6

1. Darwin, *The Expression of the Emotions in Man and Animals*, 256. Subsequent citations from Darwin are all from 256–58 of this book.
2. Cf., in particular, Richet, "Les causes du dégoût," 51–56, 83.
3. Ibid., 56–58.
4. Ibid., 53.
5. Ibid., 54.
6. Ibid., 69.
7. Ibid., 56.
8. Ibid., S. 83.
9. Ibid., 60–61, 68.
10. Ibid., 62.
11. Cf. Barnes, "Nutritional Implications of Coprophagy."
12. Freud, *The Complete Letters of Sigmund Freud to Wilhelm Fliess*, 249.
13. Ibid., 278–82.
14. Freud, "Fragments of an Analysis of a Case of Hysteria," 31.
15. Freud, *The Complete Letters of Sigmund Freud to Wilhelm Fliess*, 223.
16. Ibid, 279. Translation modified.
17. Freud, "On the Universal Tendency to Debasement in the Sphere of Love," 189. Translation modified.
18. Freud, *The Interpretation of Dreams*, 604.
19. Freud, "Three Essays on the Theory of Sexuality," 165.

20. Ibid., 177–78. Translation modified.

21. Ibid., 151.

22. Freud, "Preface to Bourke's Scatologic Rites of all Nations," 337. Translation modified.

23. Freud, *Civilization and Its Discontents*, 99.

24. Freud, "On the Universal Tendency to Debasement in the Sphere of Love," 189–90.

25. Freud, *Totem and Taboo*, 25.

26. Ibid.

27. Freud, *Civilization and Its Discontents*, 99–100.

28. Ibid.

29. Freud, "Inhibition, Symptoms and Anxiety," 89.

30. Freud, *"Hysterical Phantasies and Their Relationship to Bisexuality,"* 159; "Three Essays on the Theory of Sexuality," 166.

31. Freud, *The Complete Letters of Sigmund Freud to Wilhelm Fliess*, 281.

32. Freud, "On the Universal Tendency to Debasement in the Sphere of Love," 190.

33. Ibid., 189–90. Translation modified.

34. Cf. Kahane, "Freud's Sublimation: Disgust, Desire and the Female Body," 411–25.

35. Freud, *The Interpretation of Dreams*, 577.

36. Freud, "Thoughts for the Time on War and Death," 285–86. Translation modified.

37. Freud, "Leonardo da Vinci and a Memory of His Childhood," 96–97.

38. Freud, *The Interpretation of Dreams*, 604.

39. Freud, "Leonardo da Vinci and a Memory of His Childhood," 96–97.

40. Hirsch, "Ekel und Abscheu," 486.

41. Ibid., p.487.

42. Ibid., 493.

43. Freud, *Introductory Lectures on Psycho-Analysis*, pt. 1, 208–09. Translation modified.

44. Freud, "Fragments of an Analysis of a Case of Hysteria," 50.

45. Freud, "Three Essays on the Theory of Sexuality," 151–52.

46. Ibid., 150–51.

47. Ibid., 160–61. Cf. Krebs, "Ekellust."

48. Ibid., 157. On this point, cf. Rosenkranz, *Ästhetik des Häßlichen*, 456.

49. Freud, "Three Essays on the Theory of Sexuality," 159.

50. Ibid., 161–62. Translation modified. Citation at the end of Goethe's *Faust* ("Prelude in the Theater").

51. Freud, *The Complete Letters of Sigmund Freud to Wilhelm Fliess*, 252. Translation modified.

52. Ibid., 264.

53. Ibid., 230–31.

54. Cf. Krüll, *Freud and His Father*, 14–19, 91, 101, 110, 112–14, 121–22, 132–33, 137, 171, 179–80, 188.

55. Freud, *Briefe 1873–1939*, 206, 216.

56. I find equally questionable Krüll's thesis that Freud abandoned his early theory of seduction "precisely at a time when his self-analysis could have forced him to accuse his own father of being a seducer, of being perverse" (57–58). In the first place, Freud *has*—in two separate letters, and in an entirely unequivocal manner—characterized his own father as perverse; and no one, I suspect, will want to reproach him for not having publicized and substantiated with details this "accusation" (for Freud, a highly qualified one, to be sure). In the second place, especially in Freud's self-analysis qua dream-anamnesis, the seduction theory and the Oedipus theory merge seamlessly into one another, instead of the one replacing the other as an opposite tendency: for it is precisely his dream of being seduced by the nursemaid that contains the clearest Oedipal fantasy *vis-à-vis* his own mother.

57. Freud, *The Complete Letters of Sigmund Freud to Wilhelm Fliess*, 249.

58. Freud, "The Aetiology of Hysteria," 208.

59. Ibid., 214.

60. What he learned here also led Freud to wonder, later on, whether or not he had too successfully applied his own theory to his male and female patients.

61. Freud, *The Complete Letters of Sigmund Freud to Wilhelm Fliess*, 264. Translation modified.

62. Ibid., 220.

63. Ibid., 224–25. Translation modified.

64. Ibid., 288–89. Translation modified.

65. Ibid., 290. Written in Greek characters in the original; a play on the German *Dreck* (filth).

66. Ibid., 291. Translation modified.

67. Ibid., 288.

68. Ibid., 218. Translation modified.

69. Ibid., 223.

70. Ibid., 222.

71. Ibid., 213.

72. Freud, "On the Universal Tendency to Debasement in the Sphere of Love," 186. Translation modified.

73. Ibid., 185. Translation modified.

74. Freud, "Three Essays on the Theory of Sexuality," 191. Translation modified.

75. Freud, *The Complete Letters of Sigmund Freud to Wilhelm Fliess*, 217–18; cf. also 248.

76. bid., 218.

77. Ibid., 241. Translation modified.

78. Cf. Miller, *The Anatomy of Disgust*, 128–32.

79. Freud, "On the Universal Tendency to Debasement in the Sphere of Love," 186.

80. Ibid., 183. Translation modified.

81. Ibid., 186.

82. Freud, *The Complete Letters of Sigmund Freud to Wilhelm Fliess*, 43–44.

83. Freud, "On the Universal Tendency to Debasement in the Sphere of Love," 187.

84. Freud, *The Complete Letters of Sigmund Freud to Wilhelm Fliess*, 250.

85. Freud, *The Interpretation of Dreams*, 247–48.

86. Cf. Krüll, *Freud and His Father*, 119.

87. Freud, *The Complete Letters of Sigmund Freud to Wilhelm Fliess*, 268–69. Translation modified.

88. Krüll, *Freud and His Father*, 121. Cf. also ibid., 58–61 and 119–22, as well as Appignanesi and Forrester, *Freud's Women*, 16–18, 38–39.

89. Freud, *The Complete Letters of Sigmund Freud to Wilhelm Fliess*, 269–70.

90. Cf. Aristotle, *Poetics*, 1461b.

91. Freud, *Civilization and Its Discontents*, 100.

92. Freud, *The Complete Letters of Sigmund Freud to Wilhelm Fliess*, 223.

93. Ibid., 315.

94. Ibid., 212.

95. Ibid., 220.

96. Freud, "Three Essays on the Theory of Sexuality," 161.

97. Freud comes nearest to the stereotype of the disgusting pervert when, at one point, he characterizes "the sensual love of a man for a man" as "the perversion which is the most repellent for us";—the very same paragraph, however, emphasizes the "important social functions" of male homosexuality for a "people so far our superiors in cultivation as were the Greeks" ("Fragments of an Analysis of a Case of Hysteria," 50).

98. Freud, *Introductory Lectures on Psycho-Analysis*, pt. 1, 23.

99. Freud, "Three Essays on the Theory of Sexuality," 161.
100. Freud, *The Complete Letters of Sigmund Freud to Wilhelm Fliess*, 408.
101. Freud, *Introductory Lectures on Psycho-Analysis*, pt. 1, 144.
102. Freud, "On the Universal Tendency to Debasement in the Sphere of Love," 189.
103. Ibid., 190.
104. Freud, "Fragments of an Analysis of a Case of Hysteria," 50; "Three Essays on the Theory of Sexuality," 165; *The Complete Letters of Sigmund Freud to Wilhelm Fliess*, 227. (Italics added to accord with the German.)
105. Freud, "Three Essays on the Theory of Sexuality," 165.
106. Freud, "Fragments of an Analysis of a Case of Hysteria," 61–67, 81–88.
107. Freud, *The Interpretation of Dreams*, 570.
108. Freud, "Fragments of an Analysis of a Case of Hysteria," 52. Translation modified.
109. These studies have also established two other correlations, which invite reflection (not least concerning the methods of measurement): on the one hand, women are reported to be, on the average, distinctly more susceptible to disgust than men; on the other hand, there is supposedly a direct correlation between a higher level of education and a lower susceptibility to disgust. Cf. Rozin et. al., "Disgust," 590, and Templer et. al., "Assessment of Body Elimination Attitude," 758–59.
110. Freud, *The Complete Letters of Sigmund Freud to Wilhelm Fliess*, 281.
111. Cf. Freud, "Inhibitions, Symptoms and Anxiety," 114: "Moreover, the onset of [the obsessional] neurosis belongs to a later time than that of hysteria—to the second period of childhood, after the latency period has set in."
112. Freud, *The Complete Letters of Sigmund Freud to Wilhelm Fliess*, 144.
113. Ibid., 279–80.
114. Freud, "The Aetiology of Hysteria," 213.
115. Freud, *The Complete Letters of Sigmund Freud to Wilhelm Fliess*, 239. Translation modified.
116. Freud, "Inhibitions, Symptoms and Anxiety," 113.
117. Ibid., 116–17.
118. Freud, *The Complete Letters of Sigmund Freud to Wilhelm Fliess*, 144.
119. Freud, "Inhibitions, Symptoms and Anxiety," 112.
120. Ibid., 117.
121. Freud, "Fragments of an Analysis of a Case of Hysteria," 20.
122. Freud, "Repression," 157.
123. Freud, "Negation," 236.
124. Freud, "Creative Writers and Day-Dreaming," 153.

125. Freud, "Repression," 151.

126. Freud, "Inhibitions, Symptoms and Anxiety," 119.

127. Ibid.

128. Ibid., 121.

129. Ibid., 120.

130. Freud, "Hysterical Phantasies and Their Relation to Bisexuality," 162, 164–65.

131. Freud, *The Complete Letters of Sigmund Freud to Wilhelm Fliess*, 212.

132. Freud, "Inhibitions, Symptoms and Anxiety," 113.

133. Freud, *The Complete Letters of Sigmund Freud to Wilhelm Fliess*, p.270.

134. Freud, "Leonardo da Vinci and a Memory of His Childhood," 97.

135. Ibid., 97.

136. Freud cites the French translation (Brussels, 1883) of *A Discourse on the Worship of Priapus and Its Connection with the Mystic Theology of the Ancients*.

137. Freud, "Fragments of an Analysis of a Case of Hysteria," 31.

138. Freud, "Preface to Bourke's Scatologic Rites of all Nations," 336–37. Translation modified.

139. Freud, "Character and Anal Eroticism," 171.

140. Ibid., 173.

141. Ibid., 174 ("refuse" in English in the original).

142. Ferenczi, "The Ontogenesis of the Interest in Money."

143. Ibid., 324–25. Translation modified.

144. Freud, *Introductory Lectures in Psycho-Analysis*, pt. 2, 315.

145. Freud, "From the History of an Infantile Neurosis," 82.

146. Ibid., 81. Translation modified.

147. Ibid.

148. Ibid., 8. Translation modified.

149. Freud, *The Complete Letters of Sigmund Freud to Wilhelm Fliess*, 287–88.

150. Ibid., 227. Translation modified.

151. Ibid., 224.

152. Freud and Breuer, "Studies on Hysteria," 6.

153. Freud, *The Complete Letters of Sigmund Freud to Wilhelm Fliess*, 224. Translation modified.

154. Ibid., 224–25.

155. Cited in Freud, "Hysterie," 490 (it is not clear that Freud is himself the author of this text).

156. Freud, *The Complete Letters of Sigmund Freud to Wilhelm Fliess*, 225.

157. This is shown, altogether convincingly, in Marianne Krüll's *Freud und sein Vater*.

158. Freud, *The Complete Letters of Sigmund Freud to Wilhelm Fliess*, 220; "Three Essays on the Theory of Sexuality," 162.

159. Freud, "Creative Writers and Daydreaming," 152–53.

160. Ibid., 153.

161. Freud, "Psychopathic Characters on Stage," 302–09. On this matter, cf. Lacoue-Labarthe, *Le sujet de la philosophie*, 187–216.

162. Freud, "Psychopathic Characters on Stage," 309. Translation modified.

163. Cf. Freud's parallel passages in "Jokes and their Relation to the Unconscious," 136–37, "Psychopathic Characters on the Stage," 310, and "Creative Writers and Daydreaming," 152–53.

164. Cf. Freud, "Repression," 151, 000.

165. Freud, "Psychopathic Characters on the Stage," 305–06.

166. Ibid., 308–9. Translation modified. Cf. also 310.

167. Freud, *Civilization and Its Discontents*, 144.

168. Kafka, "Zur Psychologie des Ekels," 20–21.

169. Ibid., 43.

170. Hirsch, "Ekel und Abscheu," 491–92.

171. Ibid., 43.

172. Angyal, "Disgust and Related Aversions," 402.

173. Cf. the studies by Rozin listed in the bibliography.

174. Rozin and Fallon, "A Perspective on Disgust," 28–29, and Rozin, Lowry, and Ebert, "Varieties of Disgust Faces and the Structure of Disgust," 870.

175. Rozin et al., "Disgust," 584. Walter Benjamin appears to share this view of disgust: "In the case of disgust with animals, the predominant feeling is anxiety at being recognized by them through contact. The horror that stirs deep within man is an obscure awareness that something living in him is so akin to the disgust-arousing animal that it might be recognized by it." Human "disgust answers to the invocation" of this "bestial relationship with the creature." Cf. "One-Way-Street," 448.

176. Rozin and Fallon, "A Perspective on Disgust," 28.

177. Of course, disgust is greater in the case of carnivorous animals. Cf. Rozin and Fallon, "A Perspective on Disgust," 28.

Chapter 7

1. The following reading of Kafka deviates from methodological convictions to which I myself tend to subscribe (and still subscribe).

2. Kafka, *The Diaries—1910–1923*, 12: "Writers speak a stench." This volume is hereafter cited as D. Published translations of Kafka have been modified where necessary.

3. Freud, "The 'Uncanny,'" 246.

4. Benjamin, "Franz Kafka," 799.

5. Kafka, *Letters to Felice*, 355. Hereafter cited as LF.

6. If Freud's interpretation of "toothache" dreams were to be applied to Kafka's pleasure in imagining Felice's toothache and its treatment, it would follow that Kafka rejoices in something very close to dreams of masturbation: "I should like to draw attention to the frequency with which sexual repression makes use of transpositions from a lower to an upper part of the body. Thanks to them, it becomes possible in hysteria for all kinds of sensations and intentions to be put into effect, if not where they properly belong—in relation to the genitals—then at least in relation to other, unobjectionable parts of the body.... In our part of the world, the act of masturbation is vulgarly described as *sich einen ausreissen* or *sich einen herunterreissen* [literally, 'pulling one out' or 'pulling one down']. I know nothing of the source of this terminology, or of the imagery on which it is based; but 'a tooth' would fit very well into the first of the two phrases" (*The Interpretation of Dreams*, 387–88). On occasion, Freud interpreted the imagining of particular difficulties during this sort of tooth extraction in terms of a "transition from masturbation to sexual intercourse, which was apparently accomplished with great difficulty" (ibid., 391). On Kafka's relation to Felice's teeth, cf. also Lévy and Sabinus, *Kafka. Le Corps dans la Tête*, 214–17.

7. LF, 396. Kafka at times compared even his own stories to "a hollow or false tooth": "The disordered sentences of this story, with holes into which one could stick both hands. One sentence sounds high, one sentence sounds low, as the case may be; one sentence rubs against another like the tongue against a hollow or false tooth" (D, 104–5).

8. Freud, "Three Essays on the Theory of Sexuality," 151–52.

9. Cf. D, 10, 59, 73–74, 132–33, 336, 340. Cf. also Kafka's *Letters to Friends, Family, and Editors*, 157 (hereafter cited as L); and "Wedding Preparations in the Country," 9 (hereafter cited as DF). The latter text is reprinted in Kafka, *The Complete Stories*, 58 (hereafter cited as S).

10. This passage, dated October 31, 1911, is not found in the English language edition of the *Diaries*.

11. Compare Benjamin's observation: "The remarkable thing is that these whore-like women never seem to be beautiful." ("Franz Kafka," 797)

12. Kafka's first volume of prose *Meditation* (1913) makes the fixation on ugliness—and precisely in the case of "a beautiful girl"—the overt subject of two consecutive texts ("Clothes" and "Rejection"). Cf. S, 382–84.

13. Kafka, *The Trial*, 108. Hereafter cited as T.

14. Kafka, *The Castle*, 135. Hereafter cited as C.

15. Kafka, *Amerika*, 29. Hereafter cited as A. The translator has consulted the new English translation of *Der Verschollene: The Man Who Disappeared*, trans. Michael Hof-

mann (London: Penguin, 1996), which includes material missing from the version of the novel originally published by Max Brod in 1927 and translated as *Amerika*, in particular a section beginning "'Up! Up!,' cried Robinson" and the first of the fragments, "Brunelda's Departure" (184–201).

16. Burke, *A Philosophical Enquiry into the Origin of Our Ideas of the Sublime and Beautiful*, 116.

17. Deleuze and Guattari, *Kafka. Toward a Minor Literature*, 63–64.

18. Freud, *The Complete Letters of Sigmund Freud to Wilhelm Fliess*, 268–69. Cf. 000, this volume.

19. The other antithesis is the "little woman" (S, 317–24). Whereas the fat woman transmits power to the man from her own sources of power, the "little woman" undermines the man's self-esteem at its core with her continual reproaches, quarrelsomeness, and dissatisfaction.

20. Reference to a fragment, "Ausreise Bruneldas" (Brunelda's Journey), which is not translated in the English-language edition of *Amerika*. Cf. Kafka, *Der Verschollene*, 380–81 (hereafter cited as V).

21. Möbus, *Sündenfälle*, 8–9.

22. This is not disgust with the act of birth per se but rather with the idea of an incomplete birth—one condemned to repeating itself endlessly within the confines of this incompleteness—and hence with the idea of an eternally renewed parental cycle of conception and birth, from whose magic spell there is no escape for the child.

23. Tatar, *The Hard Facts of the Grimms' Fairy Tales*, 1987, 78.

24. Kafka, *Letters to Milena*, 163–64. Hereafter cited as LM.

25. Benjamin has interpreted the sexual availability of the women figures as material evidence of their "hetaeric" creatureliness and spoken, in moralizing fashion, of "swamp creatures" who, in "the dark womb of the deep, . . . perform that act of mating 'whose untrammeled voluptuousness,' to quote Bachofen, 'is hateful to the pure forces of heavenly light, and which justifies the term used by Arnobius, *luteae voluptates* [dirty kinds of lust]'" (Benjamin, "Franz Kafka," 809).

26. On homosexual elements in Kafka, cf. Gilman, *Franz Kafka: The Jewish Patient*, 156–68.

27. LM, 108. Cf. also DF, 323 ("Man is an immense swamp").

28. On this point, cf. Unseld, *Franz Kafka. Ein Schriftstellerleben*, 184–85.

29. Cf. Moszkowski, *Der jüdische Witz und seine Philosophie*, and Reik, "Psychology and Psychopathology of Jewish Wit."

30. Cf. Kant, *Critique of Judgment*, 133.

31. Cf. Gilman, *Franz Kafka: The Jewish Patient*, 41–100.

32. Kant, *The Metaphysics of Morals*, 179.

33. Freud, "Creative Writers and Day-Dreaming," 153.

34. Cf. Turk, "'betrügen . . . ohne Betrug.'"

35. Cf. Beissner, *Der Erzähler Franz Kafka*.

36. Cf. Vogl, "Vierte Person, Kafkas Erzählstimme." Vogl exposes the inadequacies of the Beissner-oriented approach to Kafka's narrative point of view, specifically in regard to the theory of the subject and the theory of the text. I leave open the question of whether, in fact, the concept of a "univocal narrative perspective" (Beissner) necessarily implies an uncritical unity of the subject and a reduction of language to the mere description of a prior perception. For Vogel's "narrative voice" likewise permits the supposition of at least a linguistic effect of focusing—if not as a simple given, then as the (imaginary) achievement of an 'actually' more complex structure.

37. On this point, cf. Neumann, "Hungerkünstler und Menschenfresser."

38. Roskoff, *Geschichte des Teufels*. Kafka's quotation is from 326 of vol. 1 of this work.

39. Cf. Stach, *Kafkas erotischer Mythos*, 108.

40. Benjamin, "Franz Kafka," 801.

41. Kundera, *Testaments Betrayed*, 47.

42. Grimm, *Deutsches Wörterbuch*, vol. 11, 934–35.

43. Ibid., 936.

44. *Deutsches Wörterbuch*, vol. 2, 552.

45. Mendelssohn, "Hauptgrundsätze der schönen Künste und Wissenschaften," 183.

46. Kundera makes a similar point in *Testaments Betrayed*, 49.

47. Compare Freud, "Inhibitions, Symptoms, and Anxiety," 120, and 000, this volume.

48. On Kafka's dietary and physical fitness regime, cf. Anderson, *Kafka's Clothes*, 74–97.

49. In his essay, "Hungerkünstler und Menschenfresser," Gerhard Neumann has already undertaken such a project from another perspective.

50. Guntermann sees in this orgy "nothing but self-laceration" (*Vom Fremdwerden der Dinge beim Schreiben*, 71).

51. Cf. Neumann's argument for Kafka's "revocation" of classical aesthetic "procedure" in "Hungerkünstler und Menschenfresser," 371–72. I doubt, however, whether Kafka's antitransfigurative "counterculture" (370) can stand in for "the truth of the body" and "the freedom from all compulsion" (367–68). Neumann appears to be offering an 'idealist' reading of an anti-idealist poetics.

52. On the phenomenon of disgust with foods and pleasure in disgusting foods, cf. Harris, *Wohlgeschmack und Widerwillen*; Raulff, "Chemie des Ekels und des Genusses"; Jeggle, "Runterschlucken."

53. Under the title "Pranzo Caprese," Benjamin has described a similar configuration of disgusting "old whore" and disgusting food, without implying, however, any recognizable libidinal (counter)cathexis: "She had been the Capri village cocotte, and

was now the sixty-year-old mother of little Gennaro, whom she beat when she was drunk.... She stood in the kitchen doorway dressed in a skirt and blouse, discolored items of clothing which you'd have searched in vain for any stains, so evenly, so uniformly was the dirt spread over them.... I now caught sight of her wretched husband inside the cottage, taking something out of a dish with a spoon. She went up to this dish. Immediately afterward, she reappeared in the doorway with a plate, which she held out to me without interrupting her flow of speech.... To taste it was of no importance. It was nothing but the decisive yet imperceptible transition between two moments: first between the moment of smelling it, and then of being overwhelmed, utterly bowled over and kneaded, by this food, gripped by it, as if by the hands of the old whore, squeezed, and having the juice rubbed into me—whether the juice of the food or of the woman, I am no longer able to say" (*Selected Writings*, vol. 2, 362–63.

54. Cf. also 000, this volume.

55. Kafka, *Nachgelassene Schriften und Fragmente II*, 648–49 (hereafter cited as N II).

56. For a more detailed interpretation of "The Hunger Artist," cf. Neumann, "Hungerkünstler und Menschenfresser."

57. Gilman has convincingly demonstrated affinities between Kafka's knife-stories and contemporary accounts of ritual murder and ritual slaughter supposedly, or actually, committed by Jews (*Franz Kafka: The Jewish Patient*, 112–56). The present study is concerned *solely* with the question of which system of *aesthetic* conventions Kafka brings into play and challenges, insofar as he incorporates such phenomena into literature and even defines them as the essence of writing.

58. Cf. Kafka, *"Hochlöblicher Verwaltungsausschluss!" Amtliche Schriften*, 134–41.

59. Compare also D, 71.

60. Longinus, *On the Sublime*, chapter 20, 2.

61. Ibid.

62. Jacob Grimm, *Kleinere Schriften*, vol. 6, 156.

63. de Saussure, *Course in General Linguistics*, 110–11.

64. Thomas Schestag, unpublished manuscript.

65. This association is not etymologically grounded, however.

66. Compare with this the similar formulation in Baudelaire's "Heauton Timoroumenos," in *Les Fleurs du Mal*, translated by Richard Howard, 80.

67. Cf. Gilman, *Franz Kafka: The Jewish Patient*, 87.

68. Cf. ibid., 154–56.

69. Freud, *Civilization and Its Discontents*, 99–100.

70. Cf. LM, 216; LF, 73, 142; DF, 298, 323; T, 84–90; S, 411. Cf. also Kafka, *Nachgelassene Schriften und Fragment I*, 406 (hereafter cited as N I).

71. Tatar, *The Hard Facts of the Grimm's Fairy Tales*, 86.

72. Ibid., 88.

73. Ibid., 87.

74. Ibid.

75. Cf. Benjamin, "Some Reflections on Kafka," and "The Storyteller," 144 and 87, respectively.

76. Cf. *Benjamin über Kafka*, 158.

77. The following reading is oriented exclusively toward the question of an (anti-)aesthetics of the disgusting. Particular details of this reading have already been considered in other contexts. Without any pretense to completeness, I refer here only to the works by Cohn, Goldstein, Hiebel, Kurz, Marson, Rösch, and Sokel, which are listed in the bibliography.

78. Theoretically, the whistling in reaction to the boy's wound might be read—to make use of a *terminus technicus* from psychoanalysis—as an *"Übersprungshandlung"* (i.e., as an affective response connected to an action of getting over or across something so as to resolve some tension)—for example, a narrow escape from a great danger. But a whistle of this sort can hardly be imagined in the case of the doctor's examining his patient's wound, for the doctor everywhere accentuates his professional distance and habitual superiority, and does not allow himself to feel threatened even in the face of danger to his own life.

79. Cazotte, *Le diable amoureux*, 59–60.

80. My emphasis (W. M.). Cf. Cohn, "Kafka's Eternal Present," 146–49.

81. Of the two horses attached to the Platonic chariot of the soul, Freud, too, has left only the one that tends to be ungovernable; the image of horse and rider thus serves to illustrate the relation between ego and id (*New Introductory Lectures on Psycho-Analysis*, 77; "The Ego and the Id," 25).

82. "In this case it [has] been possible," we may affirm with Freud, for an unpleasurable fantasy "to emerge into consciousness under the innocent disguise of making a complaint" (*The Interpretation of Dreams*, 618).

83. In the criticism on Kafka's "Country Doctor," so far as I have surveyed it, the relationship to Freudian psychoanalysis is, to be sure, touched on often enough—typical concerns are the stranger as the repressed self, the interference of physical and psychical manifestations of illness, the problems of curability, and so forth—but the striking parallels between the dreamlike nakedness of Freud and that of the country doctor have not been discussed.

84. Freud, *The Interpretation of Dreams*, 245.

85. Ibid., 244–45.

86. Ibid., 246.

87. Ibid., 245–46

88. Ibid., 246 (den *Willenskonflikt*, das *Nein*).

89. Ibid., 238.

90. Freud, *Introductory Lectures on Psycho-Analysis*, CW 15, 157.

91. Cf. L, 264. Like the wound in the boy's side, this wound is "always in motion," is a "constantly growing mass"; with all its disgusting qualities, it constitutes "nothing less than the very essence" of the miserable ego. As in Freud's *Moses and Monotheism* (75), trauma comes to form the character and essence of the traumatized person. In contrast to Freud, however, it is expressly embraced, indeed sought after, in the mode of self-analysis: "In any case my attitude toward the turberculosis today resembles that of a child clinging to the pleats of its mother's skirts. If the disease came from my mother, the image fits even better, and my mother in her infinite solicitude, which far surpasses her understanding of the matter, has done me this service also. I am constantly seeking an explanation for this disease, for I have not caught it by myself. Sometimes it seems to me that my brain and lungs came to an agreement without my knowledge. 'Things can't go on this way,' said the brain, and five years later the lungs said they were ready to help" (L, 138). In this context, cf. Gilman, *Franz Kafka: The Jewish Patient*, 169–228.

92. The short text "A Dream" is, in this respect, an exception. It ends with an openly rapturous phantasmagoria of self-burial, of a blissful and, at the same time, mole-like sinking into the unresisting earth. The text can be read as a secret signature of *The Trial*. In addition, it stages that "strange burial," that "illumination of my corpse," which the letter to Brod announces only years later: the artist or "writer, void of existence as he is *(etwas nicht Bestehendes)*, consigning the old corpse, the one being a corpse from the very beginning, to the grave" (L, 334).

93. Kafka occasionally characterized himself as a "vulture" too (L, 139), and, in one of his variations on the myth of Prometheus, he replaced the liver-devouring eagle with a foot-hacking vulture (DF, 84).

94. Hofmannsthal, *Der Abenteurer und die Sängerin*, 261.

95. Hofmannsthal, *Eine Monographie*, 265–67.

96. Ibid., 269.

97. Hofmannsthal, *The Lord Chandos Letter*, 19.

98. Cioran, *A Short History of Decay*, 161.

99. Cf. *Der kleine Pauly*, vol. 2, 944–45.

100. Mauthner, *Beiträge zu einer Kritik der Sprache*, vol. 1, 27.

101. Hofmannsthal, *Eine Monographie*, 267.

102. Hofmannsthal, *The Lord Chandos Letter*, 23.

103. Ibid., 23–24.

104. Compare Benjamin's very similar remark: "Then Else Lasker-Schüler saw me and invited me to join her at her table; I sat there between two young people for fifteen minutes without saying a word. There was a lot of crazy joking around, which Mrs. Lasker greatly enjoyed. . . . In company, she is shallow and sick—hysterical." (*The Correspondence of Walter Benjamin, 1910–1940*, 71.)

105. From a letter to Oskar Pollak, in which Kafka discusses early works of his that have not survived. Cited in Brod, *Franz Kafka: A Biography*, 58.

106. Nietzsche, *On the Genealogy of Morals*, 10. Translation modified.

Chapter 8

1. Bataille, "Attraction and Repulsion II," 114. Translation modified.
2. Ibid.
3. Bataille, *Œuvres complètes*, vol. 1, 161.
4. Bataille, "Base Materialism and Gnosticism." In *Visions of Excess*, 51.
5. Bataille, "Formless." In *Visions of Excess*, 31.
6. Bataille, "Mouth." In *Visions of Excess*, 59–60.
7. Bataille, "Academic Horse." In Bataille, *Œuvres complètes*, vol. 1, 159–63.
8. Bataille, "The Big Toe." In *Visions of Excess*, 22–23.
9. Bataille, "Eye." In *Visions of Excess*, 17–19.
10. Cf. Hollier, *La prise de la Concorde. Essais sur Georges Bataille*, 215–36.
11. Bataille, "The Jesuve." In *Visions of Excess*, 73–78; here: 74.
12. Bataille, "Rotten Sun." In *Visions of Excess*, 57–58.
13. Bataille, "The Pineal Eye." In *Visions of Excess*, 79–90; here: 84.
14. Bataille, "The Language of Flowers." In *Visions of Excess*, 12.
15. Bataille, "Base Materialism and Gnosticism." In *Visions of Excess*, 51.
16. Bataille, "Rotten Sun." In *Visions of Excess*, 57.
17. Bataille, *Œuvres complètes*, vol. 1, 166.
18. Ibid., 167.
19. Bataille, "The 'Lugubrious Game.'" In *Visions of Excess*, 28.
20. Bataille, *Œuvres complètes*, vol. 1, 253.
21. Cf. Didi-Hubermann, *La ressemblace informe ou le gai savoir visuel selon Georges Bataille*.
22. Bataille, "Formless." In *Visions of Excess*, 31. Translation modified.
23. Cf. Bois, "La valeur d'usage de l'informe" and the articles by Denis Hollier and Rosalind Krauss in Bois et al., *The Politics of the Signifier II: A Conversation on the Informe and the Abject*.
24. Bataille, "Eye." In *Visions of Excess*, 17.
25. Bataille, *Œuvres complètes*, vol. 1, 272.
26. Bataille, "Formless." In *Visions of Excess*, 31. Cf. Leiris, "Crachat: l'eau à la bouche."
27. This is the underlying assumption of the exhibition put together by Yve-Alain Bois and Rosalind Krauss, *l'informe. mode d'emploi*, in the Centre Pompidou, Paris 1996.
28. Bataille, "The Big Toe." In *Visions of Excess*, 23.

29. Ibid.
30. Bataille, *Œuvres complètes*, vol. 1, 218.
31. Ibid., 208–9.
32. Bataille, "The 'Lugubrious Game.'" In *Visions of Excess*, 24.
33. Bataille, *Œuvres complètes*, vol. 1, 167.
34. Ibid., 253.
35. Bataille, "The Language of Flowers." In *Visions of Excess*, 13.
36. Bataille, *Death and Sensuality*, 143.
37. Ibid., 144–45. Translation modified.
38. Bataille, "Sacrificial Mutilation." In *Visions of Excess*, 70.
39. Bataille, "The Use Value of D. A. F. de Sade." In *Visions of Excess*, 91–102; here: 97–98, 102.
40. Bataille, *Œuvres complètes*, vol. 1, 272–73.
41. Ibid., 114.
42. Bataille, "Attraction and Repulsion I," 111. Translation modified.
43. Ibid., 117–18.
44. Ibid., p.120.
45. Bataille, *Œuvres complètes*, vol. 2, 287.
46. Bataille, "Attraction and Repulsion II," 119.
47. Bataille, *Œuvres complètes*, vol. 2, 163.
48. Durkheim, *The Elementary Forms of Religious Life*, 303–04.
49. Ibid., 458–59. Translation modified.
50. Freud, *Totem and Taboo*, 24–25.
51. Bataille, "Attraction and Repulsion II," 121.
52. Ibid., 122. Translation modified.
53. Bataille, "The Use Value of D.A.F. De Sade," 94. Translation modified.
54. Ibid., 96, 97.
55. Bataille, "Attraction and Repulsion II," 122.
56. Ibid., 146. Translation modified. Bataille thus formulates the exact opposite of a moral sense- and sympathy-theory of tragedy, according to which pleasure at the horrific consists in the sparking of our pity, hence in a perception of our 'positive' humanity.
57. Ibid., p 147.
58. Bataille, *Death and Sensuality*, 69. Translation modified.
59. Ibid., 89–90.
60. Bataille, "Attraction and Repulsion II," 123. Translation modified.

61. Bataille, *Death and Sensuality*, 90.
62. Bataille, "Attraction and Repulsion II," 340. Translation modified.
63. Ibid., 337.
64. Bataille, "Attraction and Repulsion I," 112. Translation modified.
65. Bataille, *Death and Sensuality*, 16. Translation modified.
66. Ibid., 90. Translation modified.
67. Bataille, *Œuvres complètes*, vol. 1, 219.
68. Bataille, *Death and Sensuality*, 341.
69. Ibid., 217.
70. Ibid., 42–43.
71. Ibid., 64. Translation modified.
72. Ibid., 67. Translation modified.
73. Ibid., 140. Translation modified.
74. Ibid., 38. Translation modified.
75. Ibid., 58. Translation modified.
76. Bataille, *Œuvres complètes*, vol. 2, 285.
77. Bataille, *Death and Sensuality*, 58. Translation modified.
78. Ibid., 92. Translation modified.

79. On *Lustekel*, cf. Seelig, "Die Ambivalenz der Gefühle im Zuge des Sexualerlebens," 15.

80. Bataille, "Attraction and Repulsion II," 114. Translation modified.

81. Freuds famous assertion that "the sexual instinct in its strength enjoys overriding this disgust" ("Three Essays on the Theory of Sexuality," 152) does not mean—as Miller suggests in *The Anatomy of Disgust* (113–14)—that the disgust barrier first "heightens" or even "engenders" libidinal strength. Rather, Freud here defines this strength as an archaic drive *prior to* all disgust restraint; its transgressive power does not emerge from such restraint, as with Bataille. Seven years later, Freud does define the economy of prohibition as a necessary libidinal stimulus; but this type of stimulating prohibition is identified less as a disgust barrier than as purely conventional resistance to "sexual activity" in general: "It can be easily shown that the psychical value of erotic needs is reduced as soon as their satisfaction becomes easy. An obstacle is required to heighten libido; and where natural resistances to satisfaction have not been sufficient men have at all times erected conventional ones so as to be able to enjoy love" ("On the Universal Tendency to Debasement in the Sphere of Love," 187). By way of the libido's inner perversity, this structure is certainly related to Bataille's tonic overcoming of disgust inhibitions. But Freud diagnoses this overcoming as, precisely, an integral, indeed necessary part in the irresolvable conflict between the sex drives' archaic animalism and the cultural repressions imposed on them. He thus inscribes the working and overcoming of disgust in his narrative of culture's "universal tendency to debasement in the sphere of love" rather than using it, as does Bataille, to affirm a positive ontology which

identifies sexual desire with prohibition, pollution-fixated violence and "base material." Prehistorical and early-childhood sexuality transcend such an economy of prohibition, without being thought of by Freud as weak and lacking stimulus.

82. Bataille, *Death and Sensuality*, 38–39, 50, 115.

83. Ibid., 175. Translation modified.

84. Ibid., 72. Translation modified.

85. Ibid., 53–54. Translation modified.

86. Ibid., 56–57. Translation modified.

87. Ibid., 62. Translation modified.

88. Ibid., 68. Translation modified.

89. See Caillois, "Le sacré de transgression: théorie de la fête."

90. Bataille, *Œuvres complètes*, vol. 2, 71.

91. Bakthin, *Rabelais and His World*, 175. Translation modified.

92. Bataille, *Œuvres complètes*, vol. 2, 72.

93. Sartre, *Nausea*, 126. Translation modified.

94. Boisdeffre, "Sartre Romancier ou l'ange du morbide," 200.

95. Nietzsche, *Beyond Good and Evil*, 209. Translation modified.

96. Nietzsche, *Thus spoke Zarathustra*, 230.

97. Sartre, *Nausea*, 13. Translation modified.

98. Cf. Poulet, "La Nausée de Sartre," 217.

99. Sartre, *Nausea*, 99–100. Translation modified.

100. Sartre, *Nausea*, 10.

101. Ibid., 3.

102. Ibid., 1. Translation modified.

103. Ibid., 20. Translation modified.

104. Sartre, *Being and Nothingness*, 318.

105. Lévinas, "De l'évasion," 386. On disgust in Lévinas and Sartre cf. Kuhnle, "Der Ernst des Ekels," 286–303.

106. Lévinas, "De l'évasion," 387.

107. Sartre, *Nausea*, 175.

108. Lévinas, "De l'évasion," 386.

109. Ibid., 387.

110. Sartre, *Nausea*, 2.

111. Ibid., 9.

112. Ibid., 134. Translation modified.

113. Ibid., 157. Translation modified.
114. Ibid., 147.
115. Ibid., 148.
116. Cf. Kruse, "Philosophie und Dichtung in Sartres 'La Nausée,'" 218–25.
117. Sartre, *Nausea*, 129–30.
118. Ibid., 122, 128.
119. Ibid., 54.
120. Ibid., 21.
121. Ibid., 55.
122. Sartre, *Nausea*, 98. Translation modified.
123. Ibid., 100.
124. Ibid., 126.
125. Ibid., 131.
126. Ibid., 132.
127. Ibid., 131. Translation modified.
128. Sartre, *L'être et le néant*, 695–704. The English language version of Sartre's work does not contain the relevant section on existential psychoanalysis.
129. Sartre, *Nausea*, 133.
130. Ibid., 134. Translation modified.
131. Sartre, *L'être et le néant*, 700–01.
132. Ibid., 699.
133. Sartre, *Nausea*, 87, 154.
134. Ibid., 158.
135. Ibid., 155–60. The passage strongly evokes the disgust apocalypse in Alfred Kubin's novel *Die andere Seite*, 229–30.
136. Sartre, *Nausea*, 157.
137. Ibid., 22.
138. Ibid., 22–23, 173–78.
139. Ibid., 177.
140. Ibid., 175, 178.
141. Ibid., 175. Translation modified.
142. Ibid., 21.
143. Ibid., 177.
144. Nietzsche, *The Birth of Tragedy*, 32. Translation modified.
145. Sartre, *Nausea*, 177. Translation modified.

146. Sartre, *Nausea*, 178. Translation modified.

147. Cf. 000, this volume.

148. Nietzsche, *The Birth of Tragedy*, 39.

149. Cf. Kuhnle, "Der Ernst des Ekels," 296.

150. In its nonderivability and nongroundedness, the pure "there is" of existence has left more traces in the conceptual framework of the sublime than in that of disgust.

CHAPTER 9

1. Liu and Martim, "The Party for Affirmative Abjection," 216–17.

2. The titles are not all cited in full. Reference to the *Modern Language Association's Bibliography* (Arts and Humanities Citation Index).

3. Cf. Geyer-Ryan, "Abjection in the Texts of Walter Benjamin."

4. Hence, in American criticism as well, even where "disgust" is explicitly in question, the powerful intellectual potential of the German tradition of thought on this issue remains untapped, although Kristeva's *abjection* is certainly present. The exceptions to this rule are the few U.S. Germanists who have read Lessing's *Laocoön* and/or Derrida's reflections on the theme of disgust in Kant, and who have been able to forge a link to Kristeva's "abjection."

5. Freud, "Negation," 237. Translation modified.

6. Ibid., 235.

7. Cf. Laplanche and Pontalis, *The Language of Psychoanalysis*, 166–69 (entry on Verwerfung, "repudiation, foreclosure"); Lacan, "On a question preliminary to any possible treatment of psychosis"; Kaufmann, "Forclusion"; and Thom, "Verneinung, Verwerfung, Ausstossung."

8. Freud, "The Loss of Reality in Neurosis and Psychosis," 183.

9. Ibid., 184. Translation modified.

10. Freud, "Negation," 235.

11. Freud, "Three Essays on the Theory of Sexuality," 227.

12. Freud, *Civilization and its Discontents*, 100.

13. Freud, *The Complete Letters of Sigmund Freud to Wilhelm Fliess*, 279–80.

14. Julia Kristeva, *Powers of Horror: An Essay on Abjection*, 7. Page numbers for subsequent references to this work will appear in the text in parenthesis. Translations have been modified where necessary.

15. Cf. Oliver, *Reading Kristeva*, 103–06.

16. Bataille, *Œuvres complètes*, vol. 2, 217–21.

17. Cf. Kristeva, "Motherhood According to Giovanni Bellini," 237–38.

18. *Powers of Horror*, 59. Cf. also "Stabat Mater," 178–79.

19. Freud, "Inhibitions, Symptoms, and Anxiety," 137–38.

20. Kristeva, *Soleil Noir*, 38.

21. Cf. de Saussure, *Course in General Linguistics*, 110–12.

22. Miller speaks analogously—although more in the shadow of Mary Douglas than of Kristeva or Sartre—of the "taboos cultures place on whatever falls between essential categories" ("Disgust Reactions," 717).

23. Freud, "Inhibitions, Symptoms, and Anxiety," 138.

24. Ibid.

25. Elsewhere, Kristeva speaks of phobia as a "crossroad of neurosis and psychosis" (*Powers of Horror*, 64). She thereby converts Freud's negative conclusion—"that we need not rank [phobias with neuroses and psychoses] as an independent pathological process" ("Analysis of a Phobia in a Five-year-old Boy," 115)—into the positive assertion that it is a hybrid form sui generis.

26. Cf. Kristeva, "The True-Real"; *About Chinese Women*, 41; "Women's Time," 199; "Motherhood According to Giovanni Bellini," 239, 241.

27. Freud, "Three Essays on the Theory of Sexuality," 161–62.

28. This, at least, is the term by which *La Révolution du langage poétique* consistently evokes the aesthetic protest against the symbolic order (cf. especially 101–50: chapter A/II: "La Negativité: Le Rejet").

29. Kristeva, *Revolution in Poetic Language*, 75.

30. Ibid., 79.

31. Kristeva, "Stabat Mater," 177.

32. Kristeva, *Revolution in Poetic Language*, 79. Translation modified.

33. Cf. her discussion of the suicides of Virginia Woolf, Marina Zwetajewa, and Sylvia Plath, in *About Chinese Women*, 39–41; cf. also *Women's Time*, 199, and *Motherhood According to Giovanni Bellini*, 239–41.

34. Kristeva, *Revolution in Poetic Language*, 164. Translation modified.

35. Ibid., 156. Translation modified.

36. Ibid., 149.

37. Ibid., 149–50. Translation modified.

38. Ibid., 164.

39. Ibid., 163. Translation modified.

40. In her essay "The True-Real," Kristeva has highlighted the usage of deictic pronouns and proper names, in particular, as techniques for the inscription of the real in the symbolic ("The True-Real," 232–36).

41. Cf. Bernstein, *Bitter Carnival: Ressentiment and the Abject Hero*, 23–24.

42. Cf. also Kristeva, *About Chinese Women*, 29–30.

43. Bataille, *Death and Sensuality*, 89–90. Cf. 000, this volume.

44. Kristeva, "The True-Real," 236.

45. Ibid.

46. Ibid., 224.

47. Cf. Walter Benjamin, "Goethe's Elective Affinities," 340–41; and *The Origin of German Tragic Drama,* 29–38.

48. Foster, "Obscene, Abject, Traumatic," 123.

49. Freud, "Inhibitions, Symptoms, and Anxiety," 139.

50. As *sujet parlant,* this autonomous subject is of course from the beginning, in a different way, also heteronomous: namely, as conditioned by the paternal prohibition.

51. Freud, "Fragment of an Analysis of a Case of Hysteria," 50.

52. Butler, *Bodies That Matter,* 231.

53. Ibid., 241.

54. Taylor, "The Phobic Object: Abjection in Contemporary Art," 66.

55. Ibid., 313.

56. Cf. 000, this volume.

57. Cf. Bourdieu, *Distinction.*

58. Liu and Martim, "The Party for Affirmative Abjection," 217.

59. Houser, "I, Abject," 87.

60. Kristeva, *About Chinese Women,* 30–32.

61. Bois et al., "The Politics of the Signifier II," 6.

62. Many theoretically versed feminists have, in fact, called attention to the incompatibility between their own positions and the goals of Kristeva's theory.

63. On this, cf. Miller, "Disgust Reactions," 720–22.

64. Cf. Foster, *The Return of the Real.* Also Zizek, *Grimassen des Realen,* 139–86.

65. Sartre, *La Nausée,* 186.

66. Cf. Freud, *Moses and Monotheism,* 75.

67. Kristeva, "The True-Real," 230 (my emphasis, W. M.)

68. Ibid., 217.

69. Cf. *Cindy Sherman 1975–1993,* 126–65.

70. Mulvey, "A Phantasmagoria of the Female Body," 144.

71. Ibid., 146.

72. Ibid., 148.

73. Bois et al., "The Politics of the Signifier II," 3.

74. Ibid., 5.

75. Ibid., 7.

76. Krauss, "Informe without Conclusion," 97–98.

77. Bois et al., "The Politics of the Signifier II," 4.

78. Cf. the section "Disgust" in *Cindy Sherman 1975–1993*, 192–95.

79. Krauss, "Informe without Conclusion," 91–92.

80. Bois and Krauss, "A User's Guide to Entropy," 81.

81. In the struggle for the most appropriate catchword, Krauss's passionate distortion of Kristeva's "abject" goes together with an attempt to establish Bataille's *informe* as the better (and, in fact, antithetical) variant of a modernist aesthetics of "debasement" and deformation, one that unfolds in proximity to sensations of disgust. The results of this attempt are indeed impressive. At the same time, they evince a very uneven deployment of critical energies: whereas Kristeva's alleged ontology of the female body as wound meets with decisive rejection, Bataille's affirmation of rude masculine sadism (as something integral to the antiaesthetic of the *informe*) is not even mentioned.

82. Bois et al., "The Politics of the Signifier II" 21.

83. Foster, "Obscene, Abject, Traumatic," 117–18,

84. Ibid., 122.

85. Ibid., 118.

86. Ibid., 110.

87. Bois et al., "The Politics of the Signifier II," 20.

88. Foster, "Obscene, Abject, Traumatic," 118.

89. Saltz, "More Life: The Work of Damien Hirst," 83.

Bibliography

Adorno, Theodor W. *Aesthetic Theory*. Edited by Gretel Adorno and Rolf Tiedemann, newly translated and edited by Robert Hullot-Kentor. Vol. 88, *Theory and History of Literature*. Minneapolis: University of Minnesota Press, 1997.

Addison, Joseph. *The Spectator*. Vol. 3. Edited by D. F. Bond. London: Oxford University Press, 1965.

Adelung, Johann Christian. *Grammatisch-kritisches Wörterbuch der hochdeutschen Mundart*. Leipzig: Breitkopf und Härtel, ²1801.

Anderson, Mark. *Kafka's Clothes. Ornament and Aestheticism in Habsburg Fin de Siècle*. Oxford: Clarendon, 1992.

Angyal, Andras. "Disgust and Related Aversions." *Journal of Abnormal and Social Psychology* 36 (1941): 393–412.

Appignanesi, Lisa and John Forrester. *Freud's Women*. London: Weidenfeld and Nicholson, 1992.

Bakhtin, Michail. *Rabelais and His World*. Translated by Helene Iswolskya. Bloomington: Indiana University Press, 1984.

Barnes, Richard H. "Nutritional Implications of Coprophagy." *Nutrition Reviews* 20 (1962): 289–91.

Barthes, Roland. *Fragments d'un discours amoureux*. Paris: Seuil, 1977.

Bataille, Georges. "Attraction and Repulsion I," "Attraction and Repulsion II"; "The College of Sociology." All in Hollier, Dennis (ed.). *The College of Sociology 1937–39*. Minneapolis: University of Minnesota Press, 1988.

———. *Death and Sensuality. A Study of Eroticism and the Taboo*. New York: Walker and Co., 1962.

———. *Visions of Excess. Selected Writings 1927–1939*. Minneapolis: University of Minnesota Press, 1996.

———. *Œuvres complètes*. 12 vols. Paris: Gallimard, 1971–1988.

Batteux, Charles. *Les beaux arts réduits à un même principe*. Paris: Durand, 1747.

Baudelaire, Charles. *Œuvres complètes*. Edited by Claude Pichois. Paris: Gallimard, 1975.

———. *The Flowers of Evil*. Translated by James McGowan. Oxford and New York: Oxford University Press, 1993.

Beissner, Friedrich. *Der Erzähler Franz Kafka*. Frankfurt am Main: Suhrkamp, 1983.

Benjamin, Walter. *The Correspondence of Walter Benjamin, 1910–1940*. Translated by Manfred R. Jacobson and Evelyn M. Jacobson. Chicago: University of Chicago Press, 1994.

———. "Denkbilder." In *Gesammelte Schriften*, edited by Rolf Tiedemann and Hermann Schweppenhäuser. Vol. 4. Frankfurt am Main: Suhrkamp, 1972.

———. "Franz Kafka." Translated by Harry Zohn. In *Selected Writings*. Vol. 2. Cambridge, Mass.: Harvard University Press, 1999.

———. *Gesammelte Briefe*. Edited by Christoph Gödde and Henri Lonitz. Vol. 1. Frankfurt am Main: Suhrkamp, 1995.

———. "Goethe's *Elective Affinities*." Translated by Stanley Corngold. In *Selected Writings*. Vol. 1. Cambridge, Mass.: Harvard University Press, 1996.

———. "One-Way-Street." Translated by Edmund Jephcott. In *Selected Writings*. Vol. 1. Cambridge, Mass.: Harvard University Press, 1996.

———. *The Origin of German Tragic Drama*. Translated by John Osborne. London: Verso, 1977.

———. *Selected Writings*. Vols. 1 and 2. Cambridge, Mass.: Harvard University Press, 1996–1999.

———. "Some Reflections on Kafka." In *Illuminations*, translated be Harry Zohn. New York: Schocken, 1969.

———. "The Storyteller." In *Illuminations*, translated by Harry Zohn. New York: Schocken, 1969.

———. "Über einige Motive bei Baudelaire." In *Gesammelte Schriften*. Vol. 1, 605–53. Frankfurt am Main: Suhrkamp, 1974.

———. "Zentralpark." In *Gesammelte Schriften*. Vol. 1, 655–90.

———. "Zur Moral und Anthropologie." In *Gesammelte Schriften*. Vol. 6, 54–89. Frankfurt am Main: Suhrkamp, 1985.

Benjamin über Kafka. Texte, Briefzeugnisse, Aufzeichnungen, ed. Hermann Schweppenhäuser. Frankfurt am Main: Suhrkamp, 1981.

Bennholdt-Thomsen, Anke. *Nietzsches "Also sprach Zarathustra" als literarisches Phänomen. Eine Revision*. Frankfurt am Main: Athenäum, 1974.

Berger, Anne-Emmanuel. "À vue de nez. Fragment d'une esthétique du dégoût." *Europe* 69 (1991): 111–19.

Bernstein, Michael André. *Bitter Carnival. Ressentiment and the Abject Hero*. Princeton, N.J.: Princeton University Press, 1992.

Bersani, Leo. *Baudelaire and Freud*. Berkeley, Los Angeles and London: University of California Press, 1977.

Bodmer, Johann Jakob, and Johann Jacob Breitinger. *Die Discourse der Mahlern*. In *Schriften zur Literatur*, edited by Volker Meid, 3–19. Stuttgart: Reclam, 1980.

Bois, Yve-Alain, Benjamin Buchloh, Hal Foster, Denis Hollier, Rosalind Krauss, and Helen Molesworth. "The Politics of the Signifier II: A Conversation on the Informe and the Abject." October 67 (Winter 1994): 3–21.

Bois, Yve-Alain/Rosalind Krauss. "La valeur d'usage de l'informe." In *l'informe. mode d'emploi*, 8–37. Paris: Centre Pampidon, 1996.

———. *l'informe. mode d'emploi*. Paris: Centre Pompidou, 1996.

———. "A User's Guide to Entropy." In *October* 78 (Fall 1996): 21–88.

Boisdeffre, Pierre de. "Sartre Romancier ou l'ange du morbide." In *Métamorphose de la littérérature*. Vol. 2. *(De Proust à Sartre.)* Paris: Alsatia, 1951.

Bourdieu, Pierre. *Distinction: A Social Critique of Judgement of Taste*. Translated by Richard Nice. Cambridge, Mass.: Harvard University Press, 1984.

———. *Die feinen Unterschiede. Kritik der gesellschaftlichen Urteilskraft*. Frankfurt am Main: Suhrkamp, 1984.

Bourke, John G. *Scatologic Rites of All Nations*. Washington, D.C.: W. H. Lowdermilk & Co., 1891.

———. *Der Unrat in Sitte, Brauch, Glauben und Gewohnheitsrecht der Völker. Mit einem Geleitwort von Sigmund Freud*. Leipzig: Ethnologischer Verlag, 1913.

Breitinger, Johann Jacob. *Critische Dichtkunst*. 1740. Reprint, Stuttgart: Metzler, 1966.

Breitkopf, Johann Gottlieb Immanuel. *Beschreibung des Reichs der Liebe mit beygefügter Landcharte*. 1777. Reprint, *Oekonomisch-technologische Encyklopädie oder allgemeines System der Staats-, Stadt-, Haus- und Landwirthschaft*, ed. Johann Georg Krünitz, pt. 60. Berlin: Joachim Pauli, ²1802.

Brockes, Barthold Heinrich. "Das durch die Betrachtung der Grösse Gottes verherrlichte Nichts der Menschen. In einem Gespräche auf das Neue Jahr, 1722." In *Irdisches Vergnügen in Gott, bestehend in physicalisch- und moralischen Gedichten*, pt. 1, 423–57. Hamburg: Herold, 1734.

Brod, Max. *Franz Kafka: A Biography*. Translated by G. Humphreys Roberts. New York: Schocken, 1960.

Brück, Heinrich Samuel von. "Gedanken von der Dichtkunst überhaupt." In *Der Deutschen Gesellschaft in Leipzig Eigene Schriften und Übersetzungen*, edited by Johann Christoph Gottsched, 1–31. Leipzig: Breitkopf, 1730.

Buchheit, Vinzenz. *Studien zum Corpus Priapeorum*. München: Beck, 1962. (= Zetemata vol. 28)

Burke, Edmund. *A Philosophical Enquiry into the Origin of Our Ideas of the Sublime and Beautiful*. Edited by James T. Boulton. Notre Dame and London: University of Notre Dame Press, 1968.

Butler, Judith. *Bodies That Matter*. New York: Routledge, 1993.

Caillois, Roger. "Le sacré de transgression: théorie de la fête." In *L'homme et le sacré*, 125–68. Paris: Gallimard, 1950.

Carroll, Noel. *The Philosophy of Horror or Paradoxes of the Heart.* New York and London: Routledge, 1990.

Cazotte, Jacques. *Le diable amoureux.* Edited by Max Milner. Paris: Garnier-Flammarion, 1979.

Chaouli, Michel. "Devouring Metaphor: Disgust and Taste in Kleist's 'Penthesilea.'" *German Quarterly* 69 (1996): 125–43.

Cioran, Emile M. *A Short History of Decay.* Translated by Richard Howard. New York: Arcade Publishing, 1998.

Cohn, Dorrit. "Kafka's Eternal Present: Narrative Tense in 'Ein Landarzt' and Other First-Person Stories." *PMLA* 83 (1968): 144–50.

Condillac, Ètienne Bonnot, Abbé de. *A Treatise on the Sensations.* In Condillac, *Philosophical Writings*, translated by Franklin Philip with the collaboration of Harlan Lane, 153–339. Hillsdale, N.J. and London: Lawrence Erlbaum, 1982.

———. *Traité des sensations.* In *Œuvres philosophiques*, edited by Georges Le Roy. Vol. 1. Paris: Presses Universitaires de France, 1947.

Corbin, Alain. *The Foul and the Fragrant: Odor and French Social Imagination.* Cambridge, Mass.: Harvard University Press, 1986.

Damasio, Antonio. *Descartes' Error. Emotion, Reason and the Human Brain.* New York: Avon, 1995.

Darwin, Charles. *The Expression of the Emotions in Man and Animals.* Chicago: University of Chicago Press, 1965.

Deleuze, Gilles, and Félix Guattari. *Kafka: Toward a Minor Literature*, translated by Dana Polan. Minneapolis: University of Minnesota Press, 1986.

Derrida, Jacques. "Economimesis." Translated by R. Klein. *Diacritics* 2, no. 2 (Summer 1981): 3–25.

———. *Éperons. Les styles de Nietzsche.* Venedig: Corbo et Fiore, 1976.

Des Pres, Terence. *The Survivor. An Anatomy of Life in the Death Camps.* New York: Oxford University Press, 1976.

Deutsches Wörterbuch, ed. Jacob and Wilhelm Grimm. Leipzig: S. Hirzel, 1860, vol. II.

Devereux, Georges. *Baubo, la vulve mythique.* Paris: J.-C. Godefroy, 1983.

Diderot, Denis. *Œuvres complètes.* Edited by J. Assézat and M. Tourneux. 20 vols. Paris: Garnier, 1875–1877.

———. "The Salon of 1765." In *Diderot on Art*, edited and translated by John Goodmann. Vol. 1, 1–187. New Haven and London: Yale University Press, 1995.

Didi-Hubermann, Georges. *La ressemblace informe ou le gai savoir visuel selon Georges Bataille.* Paris: Macula, 1995.

Dieckmann, Herbert. "Das Abscheuliche und Schreckliche in der Kunsttheorie des 18. Jahrhunderts." In *Die nicht mehr schönen Künste. Grenzphänomene des Ästhetischen*, edited by H. R. Jauß, 271–317. München: Fink Verlag, 1968.

Douglas, Mary. *Purity and Danger*. London and Henley: Routledge and Kegan Paul, 1969.

Durkheim, Émile. *The Elementary Forms of Religious Life*. Translated by Karen E. Fields. New York: Free Press, 1995.

Eggebrecht, Harald. "Ekeltöne." *Kursbuch* 129 (September 1997): 145–51.

Elias, Norbert. *Über den Prozeß der Zivilisation. Soziogenetische und psychogenetische Untersuchungen*. 2 vols. Frankfurt am Main: Suhrkamp, 1976.

Engen, Trygg. "Remembering Odors and Their Names." *American Scientist* 75 (1987): 497–503.

Englisch, Paul. *Das skatologische Element in Literatur, Kunst und Volksleben*. Stuttgart: Julius Püttmann, 1928.

Enzensberger, Christian. *Größerer Versuch über den Schmutz*. München: Hanser, 1968.

Enzensberger, Hans Magnus. "Aus dem Leben eines musikalischen Opfers." *Kursbuch* 129 (September 1997): 1–4.

Ferenczi, Sandor. "The Ontogenesis of the Interest in Money." In *First Contributions to Psychoanalysis*, translated by Ernest Jones, 319–31. London: Hogarth Press, 1952.

Ferran, André. *L'esthétique de Baudelaire*. Paris: Hachette, 1933.

Fietkau, Wolfgang. *Schwanengesang auf 1848. Ein Rendezvous im Louvre: Baudelaire, Marx, Proudhon und Victor Hugo*. Reinbek: Rowohlt, 1978.

Foster, Hal. "Obscene, Abject, Traumatic." *October* 78 (Fall 1996): 107–24.

———. *The Return of the Real. The Avant-Garde at the End of the Century*. Cambridge: MIT Press, 1996.

Freud, Sigmund. "Analysis of a Phobia in a Five-year-old Boy." In *The Standard Edition of the Complete Works of Sigmund Freud*. 10 vols. Translated and edited by James Strachey. London: Hogarth Press, 1953–1974. (= *CW*)

———. "Character and Anal Erotism." In *CW* 9.

———. *Civilization and Its Discontents*. In *CW* 21.

———. "Creative Writers and Day-Dreaming." In *CW* 9.

———. "Fragments of an Analysis of a Case of Hysteria." In *CW* 7.

———. "From the History of an Infantile Neurosis." *CW* 10.

———. "Hysterical Phantasies and their Relation to Bisexuality." In *CW* 9.

———. "Hysterie." *Psyche* 7 (1953/54): 486–500. (It is not clear that Freud is himself the author of this text.)

———. "Inhibitions, Symptoms, and Anxiety." In *CW* 20.

———. *Introductory Lectures on Psycho-Analysis*. In *CW* 15/16.

---. "Jokes and Their Relation to the Unconscious." In *CW* 8.

---. "Leonardo da Vinci and a Memory of His Childhood." In *CW* 11.

---. *Moses and Monotheism*. In *CW* 23.

---. "Negation." In *CW* 19.

---. *New Introductory Lectures on Psycho-Analysis*. In *CW* 22.

---. "On the Grounds for Detaching a Particular Syndrome from Neurasthenia under the Description 'Anxiety Neurosis.'" In *CW* 3.

---. "On the Sexual Theories of Childen." In *CW* 9.

---. "On the Universal Tendency to Debasement in the Sphere of Love." In *CW* 11.

---. "Preface to Bourke's Scatologic Rites of all Nations." In *CW* 12.

---. "Project for a Scientific Psychology." In *CW* 1.

---. "Psychopathic Characters on Stage." In *CW* 7.

---. "Repression." In *CW* 14.

---. "The 'Uncanny.'" In *CW* 10.

---. "The Aetiology of Hysteria." In *CW* 3.

---. *The Complete Letters of Sigmund Freud to Wilhelm Fliess*, translated and edited by Jeffrey Moussaieff Masson, Cambridge, Mass. and London: Belknapp Press of Harvard University Press, 1985.

---. "The Ego and the Id." In *CW* 19.

---. *The Interpretation of Dreams*. In *CW* 4/5.

---. "The Loss of Reality in Neurosis and Psychosis." In *CW* 19.

---. "Thoughts for the Time on War and Death." In *CW* 14.

---. "Three Essays on the Theory of Sexuality." In *CW* 7.

---. *Totem and Taboo*. In *CW* 13.

Freud, Sigmund, and Josef Breuer. "Studies on Hysteria." In *CW* 2.

Fuhrmann, Manfred. "Die Funktion grausiger und ekelhafter Motive in der lateinischen Dichtung." In *Poetik und Hermeneutik III: Die nicht mehr schönen Künste. Grenzphänomene des Ästhetischen*, edited by H. R. Jauß, 23–66. München: Wilhelm Fink Verlag, 1968.

Galland, René. *Baudelaire. Poétiques et poésie*. Paris: Nizet, 1969.

Geyer-Ryan, Helga. "Abjection in the Texts of Walter Benjamin." In *Fables of Desire. Studies in the Ethics of Art and Gender*, 106–25. Cambridge: Polity Press, 1994.

Gilman, Sander. *Franz Kafka. The Jewish Patient*. New York: Routledge, 1995.

Goethe, Johann Wolfgang von. *Goethes Werke*, hg. im Auftrage der Großherzogin von Sachsen. Weimar: Böhlau, 1887–1919. Reprint München: Deutscher Taschenbuch Verlag, 1987. (= *Weimar Edition*)

―――. *Faust.* Translated by Walter Arndt and edited by Cyrus Hamlin. 2nd ed. New York and London: Norton, 2001.

―――. *Faust.* Edited by Albrecht Schöne. Frankfurt am Main: Deutscher Klassiker Verlag, 1994.

Goldstein, Bluma. "A Study of the Wound in Stories by Franz Kafka." *Germanic Review* 41 (1966): 202–17.

Grant-Tucker, Cynthia. "Pétrachisant sur l'horrible: A Renaissance Tradition and Baudelaire's Grotesque." *French Review* 48 (1975): 887–96.

Grassmann, Victor. *Die erotischen Epoden des Horaz. Literarischer Hintergrund und sprachliche Tradition.* München: C. H. Beck, 1966. (= Zetemata vol. 39)

Greenblatt, Stephen. *Learning to Curse. Essays in early modern culture.* New York and London: Routledge, 1992.

Grimm, Jacob. *Kleinere Schriften.* Vol. 6. Berlin: Dümmler, 1882.

Guntermann, Georg. *Vom Fremdwerden der Dinge beim Schreiben. Kafkas Tagebücher als literarische Physiognomie des Autors.* Tübingen: Niemeyer, 1991.

Gustafson, Susan E. *Absent Mothers and Orphaned Fathers. Narcissism and Abjection in Lessing's Aesthetic and Dramatic Production.* Detroit, Mich.: Wayne State University Press, 1995.

Hagedorn, Christian Ludwig. *Betrachtungen über die Mahlerey.* Pt. 1. Leipzig: Wendler, 1762.

Hahn, Eduard. *Demeter und Baubo. Versuch einer Theorie der Entstehung unsres Ackerbaus.* Lübeck: Selbstverlag, 1896.

Hamacher, Werner. *Pleroma. Reading in Hegel.* Translated by Nicholas Walker and Simon Jarvis. Stanford: Stanford University Press, 1998.

Harris, Marvin. *Good to Eat. Riddles of Food and Culture.* London and Boston: Allen and Unwin, 1986.

Hegel, Georg Wilhelm Friedrich. *Enzyklopädie der philosophischen Wissenschaften II.* In *Werke.* Vol. 9. Frankfurt am Main: Suhrkamp, 1970.

―――. *Philosophy of Right.* Translated by T. M. Knox. New York: Oxford University Press, 1967.

―――. *Vorlesungen über die Ästhetik.* In *Werke.* Vol. 13–15.

Herder, Johann Gottfried. "Die Plastik von 1770." In *Sämtliche Werke,* edited by Bernhard Suphan. Vol. 8, 116–63. Berlin: Weidmannsche Buchhandlung, 1892.

―――. "Erstes Kritisches Wäldchen." In *Schriften zur Ästhetik und Literatur 1767–1781,* edited by Gunter E. Grimm, 63–245. Frankfurt am Main: Deutscher Klassiker Verlag, 1993.

―――. *Plastik. Einige Wahrnehmungen über Form und Gestalt aus Pygmalions bildendem Traume.* In *Sämtliche Werke,* edited by Bernhard Suphan. Vol. 8, 1–87. Berlin: Weidmannsche Buchhandlung, 1892.

———. "Reisetagebuch." In *Italienische Reise. Briefe und Tagebuchaufzeichnungen 1788–1889,* edited by Albert Meier and Heide Hollmer, 560–613. München: Beck, 1989.

———. "Studien und Entwürfe zur Plastik." In *Sämtliche Werke,* edited by Bernhard Suphan. Vol. 8, 88–115. Berlin: Weidmannsche Buchhandlung, 1892.

———. "Wie die Alten den Tod gebildet? Ein Nachtrag zu Leßings Abhandlung desselben Titels und Inhalts." In *Sämtliche Werke.* Vol. 15. 1888. Reprint, Hildesheim: Olms, 1967.

Hesiod. *The Homeric Hymns and Homerica.* Edited by Hugh G. Evelyn-White. Cambridge and London: Harvard University Press, 1982, 220–53.

Hiebel, Hans H. *Franz Kafka: "Ein Landarzt."* München: Fink, 1984.

Hirsch, Julian. "Ekel und Abscheu." *Zeitschrift für angewandte Psychologie* 34 (1930): 472–84.

Hofmannsthal, Hugo von. *Der Abenteurer und die Sängerin.* In *Gesammelte Werke in Einzelausgaben.* Dramen I, 159–272. Frankfurt am Main: Fischer, 1953.

———. *The Lord Chandos Letter.* Translated by Russell Stockman. Marlboro, Vt.: Marlboro Press, 1986.

———. "Ein Brief." In *Sämtliche Werke,* edited by Rudolf Hirsch, Christoph Perels, and Heinz Rölleke. Vol. 31, *Erfundene Gespräche und Briefe,* 45–55. Frankfurt am Main: Fischer, 1991.

———. *Eine Monographie.* In *Gesammelte Werke in Einzelausgaben: Prosa I,* 265–70. Frankfurt am Main: Fischer, 1950.

Hogarth, William. *The Analysis of Beauty.* 1753. Reprint New York: Garland, 1973.

Holbach, Paul Henri, baron d'. *Système sociale ou principes naturels de la morale et de la politique avec un examen de l'influence du gouvernement sur les mœurs.* 1773. Reprint Hildesheim and New York: Olms, 1969.

Hollier, Denis. *La prise de la Concorde. Essais sur Georges Bataille.* Paris: Gallimard, 1974.

———, ed. *The College of Sociology 1937–39.* Minneapolis: University of Minnesota Press, 1988.

Horace. *The Complete Odes and Epodes.* Translated by David West. Oxford: Oxford University Press, 1997.

Houser, Craig. "I, Abject." In *Abject Art. Repulsion and Desire in American Art,* 59–84. New York: Whitney Museum of American Art, 1993.

Hubert, J.-D. *L'esthétique des "Fleurs du Mal." Essai sur l'ambiguité poétique.* Genf: Cailler, 1953.

Institut für Plastination, ed. *Körperwelten: Einblicke in den menschlichen Körper.* Heidelberg. Mannheim: Landesmuseum für Technik und Arbeit, 1998.

Jackson, John E. *La Mort Baudelaire. Essai sur les "Fleurs du Mal."* Neuchâtel: À la Baconnière, 1982.

Jacobs, Carol. "The Critical Performance of Lessing's 'Laokoon.'" *Modern Language Notes* 102 (1987): 483–521.

Jeggle, Utz. "Runterschlucken. Ekel und Kultur." *Kursbuch* 129 (September 1997): 12–26.

Kafka, Franz. *Amerika*. Translated by Willa Muir and Edwin Muir. New York: Schocken, 1962. (= A)

———. *Briefe an Felice, und andere Korrespondenz aus der Verlobungszeit*. Edited by Max Brod. Frankfurt am Main: Fischer, 1967.

———. *Briefe an Milena*. Edited by Jürgen Born and Michael Müller. Frankfurt am Main: Fischer, 1995.

———. *Briefe 1902–1924*. Edited by Max Brod. Frankfurt am Main: Fischer, 1958.

———. *The Castle*. Translated by Mark Harman. New York: Schocken, 1998. (= C)

———. "Clothes." Translated by Willa Muir and Edwin Muir. In *The Complete Stories*. New York: Schocken, 1971. (= S)

———. *Das Schloß*. Edited by Malcolm Pasley. Frankfurt am Main: Fischer, 1982.

———. *The Diaries—1910–1923*. Translated by Joseph Kresh and Martin Greenberg. New York: Schocken, 1976. (= D)

———. *Drucke zu Lebzeiten*. Edited by Wolf Kittler, Hans-Gerd Koch, and Gerhard Neumann. Frankfurt am Main: Fischer, 1994.

———. *"Hochlöblicher Verwaltungsausschuß!" Amtliche Schriften*. Edited by Klaus Hermsdorf. Frankfurt am Main: Luchterhand, 1991.

———. *Letters to Felice*. Translated by James Stern and Elisabeth Duckworth. New York: Schocken, 1973. (= LF)

———. *Letters to Friends, Family, and Editors*. Translated by Richard Winston and Clara Winston. New York: Schocken, 1977. (= L)

———. *Letters to Milena*. Translated by Tania Stern and James Stern. New York: Schocken, 1953. (= LM)

———. *Nachgelassene Schriften und Fragmente I*. Edited by Malcolm Pasley. Frankfurt am Main: Fischer, 1993. (= N I)

———. *Nachgelassene Schriften und Fragmente II*. Edited by Jost Schillemeit. Frankfurt am Main: Fischer, 1992. (= N II)

———. *Der Proceß*. Edited by Malcolm Pasley. Frankfurt am Main: Fischer, 1990.

———. "Rejection." Translated by Willa Muir and Edwin Muir. In *The Complete Stories*. New York: Schocken, 1977. (= S)

———. *Tagebücher*. Edited by Hans-Gerd Koch, Michael Müller, and Malcolm Pasley. Frankfurt am Main: Fischer, 1990.

———. *The Trial*. Translated by Breon Mitchell. New York: Schocken, 1998. (= T)

———. *Der Verschollene*. Edited by Jost Schillemeit. Frankfurt am Main: Fischer, 1983. (= V)

---. "Wedding Preparations in the Country." In *Dearest Father*, translated by Ernst Kaiser and Eithne Wilkins. New York: Schocken, 1954. (= DF) Reprinted in *The Complete Stories*. New York: Schocken, 1971.

Kafka, Gustav. "Zur Psychologie des Ekels." *Zeitschrift für angewandte Psychologie* 34 (1930): 1–46.

Kahane, Claire. "Freud's Sublimation: Disgust, Desire and the Female Body." *American Imago* 49 (1992): 411–25.

Kant, Immanuel. *Anthropology from a Pragmatic Point of View*. Translated by Victor Lyle Dowdell, edited by Hans H. Rudnick. Carbondale and Edwardsville, Ill.: Southern Illinois University Press, 1996.

---. *Anthropologie in pragmatischer Hinsicht*. In *Kant's gesammelte Schriften*, edited by Königlich Preußische Akademie der Wissenschaften. Vol. 7. Berlin: Georg Reimer, 1907.

---. "Bemerkungen zu den Beobachtungen über das Gefühl des Schönen und Erhabenen." In *Kant's gesammelte Schriften*. Vol. 20.

---. *Critique of Judgment*. Translated by Werner S. Pluhar. Indianapolis, Ind.: Hackett Publishing Co., 1987.

---. *Kritik der Urtheilskraft*. In *Kant's gesammelte Schriften*. Vol. 5.

---. *Critique of Practical Reason*. Translated and edited by Mary Gregor. Cambridge and New York: Cambridge University Press, 1997.

---. *Kritik der praktischen Vernunft*. In *Kant's gesammelte Schriften*. Vol. 5.

---. *Critique of Pure Reason*. Translated and edited by Paul Guyer and Allan W. Wood. Cambridge and New York: Cambridge University Press, 1998.

---. *Kritik der reinen Vernunft*. In *Kant's gesammelte Schriften*. Vol. 3.

---. *Education*. Translated by Annette Churden. Ann Arbor: University of Michigan Press, 1960.

---. "The End of All Things." In *Religion within the Boundaries of Mere Reason*, translated and edited by Allen Wood and George di Giovanni, 193–205. Cambridge and New York: Cambridge University Press, 1998.

---. *Groundwork of the Metaphysics of Morals*. Translated and edited by Mary Gregor. Cambridge and New York: Cambridge University Press, 1997.

---. "Inquiry Concerning the Distinctness of the Principles of Natural Theology and Morals." In *The Cambridge Edition of the Works of Immanuel Kant: Theoretical Philosophy 1755–1770*, translated and edited by David Walford, 243–86. Cambridge, New York, and Oakleigh: Cambridge University Press, 1992.

---. *The Metaphysics of Morals*. Translated by Mary Gregor. Cambridge, Mass.: Cambridge University Press, 1998.

---. *Observations on the Feeling of the Beautiful and Sublime*. Translated by John T. Golthwait. Berkeley and Los Angeles: University of California Press, 1960.

---. "Physische Geographie." In *Kant's gesammelte Schriften*. Vol. 9.

———. "Prolegomena to Any Future Metaphysics That Will Be Able to Come Forward as Science." In *Prolegomena to Any Future Metaphysics That Will Be Able to Come Forward as Science" with Selections from the "Critique of Pure Reason,"* translated by Gary Hatfield. Cambridge and New York: Cambridge University Press, 1997.

———. "Reflexionen zur Anthropologie." In *Kant's gesammelte Schriften.* Vol. 15.

———. "Reflexionen zur Moralphilosophie." In *Kant's gesammelte Schriften.* Vol. 19.

———. *Religion within the Boundaries of Mere Reason.* Translated and edited by Allen Wood and George di Giovanni. Cambridge and New York: Cambridge University Press, 1998.

———. "Versuch über die Krankheiten des Kopfes." In *Kant's gesammelte Schriften.* Vol. 2.

Karsten, Anitra. "Psychische Sättigung." *Psychologische Forschung. Zeitschrift für Psychologie und ihre Grenzwissenschaften* 10 (1928): 142–257.

Kaufmann, Pierre. "Forclusion." In *L'apport freudien. Éléments pour une encyclopédie de la psychoanalyse,* edited by Pierre Kaufmann, 139–40. Paris: Bordas, 1993.

Kerrigan, William. "The Personal Shakespeare: Three Clues." In *Shakespeare's Personality,* edited by Norman N. Holland et al., 175–90. Berkeley, Los Angeles, and London: University of California Press, 1989.

Kolnai, Aurel. "Der Ekel." In *Jahrbuch für Philosophie und phänomenologische Forschung,* edited by Edmund Husserl. Vol. 10. Halle and Saale: Max Niemeyer. 1929. Reprint 1974.

Krauss, Rosalind. "Informe without Conclusion." *October* 78 (Fall 1996): 87–106.

Krebs, Julius. "Ekellust." *Kursbuch* 129 (September 1997): 88–99.

Kristeva, Julia. *About Chinese Women.* Translated by Anita Barrows. London: Marion Boyars Publishers, 1977.

———. "Motherhood According to Giovanni Bellini." In *Desire in Language. A Semiotic Approach to Literature and Art,* edited by Leon S. Roudiez, translated by Thomas Gora, Alice Jardine, and Leon S. Roudiez, 237–70. New York: Columbia University Press, 1980.

———. *Powers of Horror. An Essay on Abjection.* Translated by Leon S. Roudiez. New York: Columbia University Press, 1982.

———. *Revolution in Poetic Language.* Translated by Margaret Waller. New York: Columbia University Press, 1984.

———. *Soleil Noir. Dépression et Mélancholie.* Paris: Gallimard, 1987.

———. "Stabat Mater." In *The Kristeva Reader,* edited by Toril Moi, 160–86. Oxford: Basil Blackwell, 1986.

———. "The True-Real." In *The Kristeva Reader,* 215–37.

———. "Women's Time." In *The Kristeva Reader,* 187–213.

Krüll, Marianne. *Freud and His Father.* Translated by Arnold J. Pomerans. New York: Norton, 1986.

Kruse, Margot. "Philosophie und Dichtung in Sartres 'La Nausée.'" *Romanistisches Jahrbuch* 9 (1958): 214–25.

Kubin, Alfred. *Die andere Seite*. Reinbek: Rowohlt, 1994.

Kuhnle, Till R. "Der Ernst des Ekels. Ein Grenzfall von Begriffsgeschichte und Metaphorologie." *Archiv für Begriffsgeschichte* 39 (1996): 268–325.

Kundera, Milan. *Testaments Betrayed*. Translated by Linda Asher. New York: Harper Collins, 1995.

Kurz, Gerhard. *Traum-Schrecken. Kafkas literarische Existenzanalyse*. Stuttgart: Metzler, 1980.

Lacan, Jacques. "On a question preliminary to any possible treatment of psychosis." In *Écrits. A Selection*, translated by Alan Sheridan. New York and London: Norton, 1977.

Lacoue-Labarthe, Philippe. *Le sujet de la philosophie (Typographies 1)*. Paris: Aubier-Flammarion, 1979.

Laplanche, Jean, and Jean-Bertrand Pontalis. *The Language of Psychoanalysis*. Translated by Donald Nicholson-Smith. New York and London: Norton, 1973.

Leiris, Michel. "Crachat: l' eau à la bouche." *Documents* 7 (Décembre 1929): 381–82.

Lessing, Gotthold Ephraim. *Laocoön. An Essay on the Limits of Painting and Poetry*. Edited by Edward Allen McCormick. Baltimore and London: Johns Hopkins University Press, 1984.

———. *Laokoon: Oder über die Grenzen der Malerei und Poesie*. In *Werke 1766–1769*, edited by Wilfried Barner. Vol. 5/2. Frankfurt am Main: Deutscher Klassiker Verlag, 1990.

———. "How the Ancients Represented Death." In *Laokoon and How the Ancients Represented Death*, translated by Helen Zimmern. London: G. Bell and Sons, 1914.

Lévinas, Emmanuel. "De l'évasion." *Recherches philosophiques* 5 (1935/36) 373–92.

Lévi-Strauss, Claude. *The Elementary Structures of Kinship*. Translated by James Harle Bell and John Richard von Sturmer. Edited by Rodney Needham. Boston: Beacon Press, 1969.

Lévy, Ghyslan, and Serge Sabinus. *Kafka. Le corps dans la tête*. Paris: Scarabée, 1983.

Longinus. "On The Sublime." In *Aristotele in Twenty Three Volumes*. Vol. 23. Cambridge, Mass.: Harvard University Press, 1982.

Liu, Catherine, and Avillez Martim. "The Party for Affirmative Abjection." In *Lusitania—A Journal of Reflection and Oceanography* 1, no. 4 *(The Abject, America)*, 216–25.

Liessmann, Konrad Paul. "'Ekel! Ekel! Ekel!—Wehe mir!' Eine kleine Philosophie des Abscheus." *Kursbuch* 129 (September 1997): 101–10.

Luhmann, Niklas. *Die Kunst der Gesellschaft*. Frankfurt am Main: Suhrkamp, 1995.

Marcuse, Herbert. *One-Dimensional Man*. Boston: Beacon Press, 1991.

Marson, Eric, and Keith Leopold. "Kafka, Freud, and 'Ein Landarzt.'" *German Quarterly* 37 (1964): 146–60.

Martial. *Epigrams* (lat.-engl.). Edited by Walter C. A. Ker. 2 vols. Cambridge and London: Harvard University Press, 1946 and 1950.

Mathias, Paul. *La Beauté dans les "Fleurs du Mal."* Grenoble: Presses Universitaires de Grenoble, 1977.

Mauthner, Fritz. *Beiträge zu einer Kritik der Sprache.* Vol. 1. Stuttgart and Berlin: Cotta, ³1921.

McLees, Ainslie Armstrong. "Baudelaire's 'Une Charogne.' Caricature and the birth of modern art." *Mosaic* 21 (1988): 111–22.

Mendelssohn, Moses. "Hauptgrundsätze der schönen Künste und Wissenschaften." In *Ästhetische Schriften in Auswahl,* edited by Otto F. Best. Darmstadt: Wissenschaftliche Buchgesellschaft, 130–37, 173–97, ²1986.

———. "82. bis 84. Literaturbrief." In *Gesammelte Schriften. Jubiläumsausgabe.* Vol. 5, 1, 130–37. (*Rezensionsartikel in Briefe, die neueste Literatur betreffend [1759–1765],* edited by Eva J. Engel.) Stuttgart: Frommann/Holzboog.

———. "Rhapsodie oder Zusätze zu den Briefen über die Empfindungen (1761)." In *Ästhetische Schriften in Auswahl,* 127–65.

Menninghaus, Winfried. *Unendliche Verdopplung. Die frühromantische Grundlegung der Kunsttheorie im Begriff absoluter Selbstreflexion.* Frankfurt am Main: Suhrkamp, 1987.

———. "Zwischen Überwältigung und Widerstand. Macht und Gewalt in Longins und Kants Theorien des Erhabenen." *POETICA* 23 (1991): 1–19.

Michel, Karl Markus. "Leib an Leib." *Kursbuch* 129 (September 1997): 27–37.

Miller, Susan B. "Disgust: Conceptualization, Development and Dynamics." *International Review of Psychoanalysis* 13 (1986): 295–307.

———. "Disgust Reactions: Their Determinants and Manifestations in Treatment." *Contemporary Psychoanalysis* 29 (1993): 711–35.

Miller, William Ian. *The Anatomy of Disgust.* Cambridge and London: Harvard University Press, 1997.

Möbus, Frank. *Sündenfälle. Die Geschlechtlichkeit in Erzählungen Franz Kafkas.* Göttingen: Wallstein, 1994.

Moszkowski, Alexander. *Der jüdische Witz und seine Philosophie.* Berlin: Eysler, 1923.

Mücke, Dorothea von. "The Powers of Horror and the Magic of Euphemism in Lessing's 'Laokoon' and 'How the Ancients Represented Death.'" In *Body and Text in the Eighteenth Century,* Veronica Kelly and Dorothea von Mücke, 163–80. Stanford, Calif.: Stanford University Press, 1994.

Mülder-Bach, Inka. *Im Zeichen Pygmalions. Das Modell der Statue und die Entdeckung der "Darstellung" im 18. Jahrhundert.* München: Fink, 1998.

Mulvey, Laura. "A Phantasmagoria of the Female Body: The Work of Cindy Sherman." *New Left Review* 188 (July/August 1991): 137–50.

Neumann, Gerhard. "Hungerkünstler und Menschenfresser. Zum Verhältnis von Kunst und kulturellem Ritual im Werk Franz Kafkas." *Archiv für Begriffsgeschichte* 66 (1984): 347–88.

Nietzsche, Friedrich. "Aufzeichnungen aus der Zeit der Fröhlichen Wissenschaft." In *Gesammelte Werke*. Vol. 11. München: Musarion, 1924.

———. *Beyond Good and Evil*. London: Penguin Books, 1990.

———. *The Birth of Tragedy*. London: Penguin Books, 1993.

———. *Daybreak. Thoughts on the Prejudices of Morality*. Edited by Maudemarie Clark. Translated by R. J. Hollingdale. Cambridge: Cambridge University Press, 1997.

———. "Der Fall Wagner." In *Sämtliche Werke. Kritische Studienausgabe*, edited by Giorgio Colli and Mazzino Montinari. München: Dutscher Taschenbuch Verlag/de Gruyter, 1980.

———. *Ecce Homo*. London: Penguin Books, 1992.

———. *The Gay Science, with a Prelude in Rhymes and an Appendix of Songs*. Translated by Walter Kaufmann. New York: Vintage, 1974.

———. "Nachgelassene Fragmente." In *Kritische Studienausgabe*. Vols. 7–13.

———. "On the Future of Our Educational Institutions." In *The Complete Works of Friedrich Nietzsche*, edited by Dr. Oscar Levy, translated by J. M. Kennedy. Vol. 6, 1–142. Edinburgh and London: T. N. Foulis, 1909.

———. *On the Genealogy of Morals*. Oxford and New York: Oxford University Press, 1996.

———. "On the Uses and Disadvantages of History for Life." In *Untimely Meditations*, edited by Daniel Breazeale, translated by R. J. Hollingdale, 57–123. Cambridge and New York: Cambridge University Press, 1997.

———. *Thus Spoke Zarathustra. A Book for Everyone and No One*. London: Penguin Books, 1969.

———. *Twilight of the Idols/The Anti-Christ*. London: Penguin Books, 1990.

Noyer-Weidner, Alfred. "Stilempfinden und Stilentwicklung Baudelaires im Spiegel seiner Varianten." In *Baudelaire*, edited by Alfred Noyer-Weidner, 180–212. Darmstadt: Wissenschaftliche Buchgesellschaft, 1976.

Oeri, Hans Georg. *Der Typ der komischen Alten in der griechischen Komödie, seine Nachwirkungen und seine Herkunft*. Diss. Basel: Schwabe, 1948.

Oliver, Kelly. *Reading Kristeva. Unraveling the Double-bind*. Bloomington: Indiana University Press, 1993.

Paul, Jean. *Vorschule der Ästhetik*. In *Werke*, edited by Norbert Miller. Vol. 5. München: Hanser, 1963.

Der Kleine Pauly, ed. Konrad Ziegler and Walther Sontheimer. München: Deutscher Taschenbuch Verlag, 1979.

Pfotenhauer, Helmut. "Gemeißelte Sinnlichkeit. Herders Anthropologie des Plastischen und die Spannungen darin." In *Um 1800. Konfigurationen der Literatur, Kunstliteratur und Ästhetik*, 79–102. Tübingen: Niemeyer, 1991.

Picard, Charles. "Die große Mutter von Kreta bis Eleusis." In *Eranos-Jahrbuch 1938 (Vorträge über Gestalt und Kult der "Grossen Mutter")*, edited by Olga Fröbe-Kapteyn, 91–119. Zürich: Rhein-Verlag, 1939.

Poulet, Georges. "La Nausée de Sartre." In *Études sur le temps humain III: Le point de départ*, 216–36. Paris: Plon, 1964.

Praz, Mario. *The Romantic Agony*. Translated by Angus Davidson. London and New York: Oxford University Press, 1970.

Prévost, Jean. *Baudelaire. Essai sur l'inspiration et la création poétique*. Paris: Mercure de France, 1953.

Raulff, Ulrich. "Chemie des Ekels und des Genusses." In *Die Wiederkehr des Körpers*, edited by Dietmar Kamper and Christoph Wulf, 241–58. Frankfurt am Main: Suhrkamp, 1982.

Reik, Theodor. "Psychology and Psychopathology of Jewish Wit." In *Jewish Wit*. New York: Gamut Press, 1962.

———. "Zur Psychoanalyse des jüdischen Witzes." In *Lust und Leid im Witz*, 33–58. Wien: Psychoanalytischer Verlag, 1929.

Richet, Charles. "Les causes du dégoût." In *L'homme et l'intelligence. Fragments de physiologie et de psychologie*, 41–84. Paris: Alcan, 1884.

Rösch, Ewald. "Getrübte Erkenntnis. Bemerkungen zu Franz Kafkas Erzählung 'Ein Landarzt.'" In *Dialog. Literatur und Literaturwissenschaft im Zeichen deutsch-französischer Begegnung*, edited by Rainer Schönhaar, 205–43. Berlin: Schmidt, 1973.

Roskoff, Gustav. *Geschichte des Teufels*. Leipzig: Brockhaus, 1869.

Rosenkranz, Karl. *Ästhetik des Häßlichen*. Darmstadt: Wissenschaftliche Buchgesellschaft, 1979.

Rozin, Paul, Jonathan Haidt, and Clark R. McCauley. "Disgust." In *Handbook of Emotions*, edited by Michael Lewis and Jeanette M. Haviland, 575–94. New York: Guilford, 1993.

Rozin, Paul, and April E. Fallon. "A Perspective on Disgust." *Psychological Review* 94 (1987): 23–41.

Rozin, Paul, Laura Lowery, and Rhonda Ebert. "Varieties of Disgust Faces and the Structure of Disgust." *Journal of Personality and Social Psychology* 66 (1994): 870–81.

Rozin, Paul, Linda Millman, and Carol Nemeroff. "Operations of the Laws of Sympathetic Magic in Disgust and other Domains." *Journal of Personality and Social Psychology* 50 (1986): 703–12.

Ruff, Marcel A. *L'Esprit du mal et l'Esthétique baudelairienne*. Paris: Colin, 1955.

Saltz, Jerry. "More Life: The Work of Damien Hirst." *Art in America* 83, no. 6 (June 1995): 83–87.

Sartre, Jean-Paul. *Being and Nothingness. An Essay in Phenomenological Ontology*. Special abridged edition. Translated by Hazel E. Barnes. New York: Citadel Press, 1965.

———. *L'être et le néant. Essai d'ontologie phénoménologique*. Paris: Gallimard, 1943.

———. *Nausea*. Translated by Lloyd Alexander. New York: New Directions Paperbook, 1964.

———. *La Nausée*. Paris: Gallimard, 1995.

Saussure, Ferdinand de. *Course in General Linguistics*. Edited by Charles Bally and Albert Sechehaye, translated by Roy Harris. London: Duckworth, 1983.

Schaad, Isolde. "Der öffentliche Stuhl." *Kursbuch* 129 (September 1997): 51–60.

Schlegel, Friedrich. "Athenäums-Fragmente." In *Kritische Friedrich-Schlegel-Ausgabe*, edited by Ernst Behler with the cooperation of Jean Jacques Anstett and Hans Eichner. Vol. 2. Paderborn, München, Wien, and Zürich: Schöningh, 1958.

———. *Literarische Notizen 1797–1801. Literary Notebooks*, edited by Hans Eichner. Frankfurt am Main, Berlin, and Wien: Ullstein, 1980.

———. "Über das Studium der Griechischen Poesie." In *Kritische Friedrich-Schlegel-Ausgabe*. Vol. 1.

Schlegel, Johann Adolf. "(Anmerkungen über Ekel)." In *Einschränkung der schönen Künste auf einen einzigen Grundsatz, aus dem Französischen übersetzt und mit verschiednen eignen damit verwandten Abhandlungen begleitet von Johann Adolf Schlegeln*, 106–20. Leipzig: Weidmanns Erben und Reich, 1770. 3rd augmented ed., pt. 2.

Schlegel, Johann Elias. "Abhandlung von der Nachahmung." In *Ästhetische und dramaturgische Schriften*, edited by Johann von Antoniewicz, 106–66. Darmstadt: Wissenschaftliche Buchgesellschaft, 1970.

———. "Abhandlung, daß die Nachahmung der Sache, der man nachahmet, zuweilen unähnlich werden müsse." In *Ästhetische und dramaturgische Schriften*, edited by Johann von Antoniewicz, 96–105. Darmstadt: Wissenschaftliche Buchgesellschaft, 1970.

Schmidt, Julian. *Geschichte der Romantik in dem Zeitalter der Reformation und der Revolution*. Leipzig: Herbig, 1850.

Schmitz, Hermann. *System der Philosphie*. 5 vols. Bonn: Bouvier, 1964–1980.

Schopenhauer, Arthur. *Die Welt als Wille und Vorstellung*. Erster Band, Wiesbaden: Brockhaus, 1949.

Schultz, J. H. "Zur medizinischen Psychologie des Ekels Normaler." *Psychologische Rundschau* 1 (1949/50). Reprint Amsterdam: Swets & Zeitlinger, 1966. 195–203.

———. "Zur medizinischen Psychologie des Ekels Abnormaler." In ibid., 276–84.

Seelig, Ernst. "Die Ambivalenz der Gefühle im Zuge des Sexualerlebens." *Zeitschrift für angewandte Psychologie* 36 (1930): 138–50.

Seznec, Jean. "Un Laocoon français." In Seznec, *Essais sur Diderot et l'Antiquité*, 58–78. Oxford: Clarendon, 1957.

Shelley, Mary. *Frankenstein or, The Modern Prometheus*. London: Penguin, 1985.

Sherman, Cindy. *Cindy Sherman 1975–1993*. Edited by Rosalind Krauss and Norman Bryson. Rizzoli: New York, 1993.

Smith, Adam. *The Theory of Moral Sentiments*. Edited by D. D. Raphael and A. L. Macfie. Oxford: Clarendon, 1976.

Sokel, Walter H. *Franz Kafka—Tragik und Ironie. Zur Struktur seiner Kunst*. München and Wien: Langen-Müller, 1964.

Sophocles. *Philoctetes*. Translated by David Grene. In *Greek Tragedies*. Vol. 3. Chicago: University of Chicago Press, 1960.

Spinoza, Baruch de. *Ethics*. In *The Ethics. Treatise on the Emendation of the Intellect. Selected Letters*, translated by Samuel Shirley, edited by Seymour Feldman, 31–223. Indianapolis and Cambridge: Hackett Publishing, 1992.

Stach, Reiner. *Kafkas erotischer Mythos. Eine ästhetische Konstruktion des Weiblichen*. Frankfurt am Main: Fischer, 1987.

Starobinski, Jean. "Cadavres interpellés. Fiction, mortalité, épreuve du temps chez Baudelaire." *Nouvelle Revue de Psychanalyse* 41 (1990).

Streck, Bernhard. "Gefüllter Hund oder die Grenzen des Geschmacks." *Kursbuch* 129 (September 1997): 67–78.

Sulzer, Johann Georg. *Allgemeine Theorie der Schönen Künste*. Hildesheim: Georg Olms, 1967.

Tatar, Maria. *The Hard Facts of the Grimms' Fairy Tales*. Princeton, N.J.: Princeton University Press, 1987.

Taylor, Simon. "The Phobic Object: Abjection in Contemporary Art." In *Abject Art. Repulsion and Desire in American Art*, 59–84. New York: Whitney Museum of American Art, 1993.

Templer, Donald I., Frank L. King, Robert K. Brooner, and Mark Corgiat. "Assessment of Body Elimination Attitude." *Journal of Clinical Psychology* 40 (1984): 754–59.

Theile, Wolfgang. "'La toile oubliée.' Ästhetische Reflexion und die Idee der Modernität bei Baudelaire (am Beispiel von 'Une charogne')." In *Romanische Literaturbeziehungen im 19. und 20. Jahrhundert. Festschrift für Franz Rauhut*, 309–17. Tübingen: Gunter Narr, 1985.

Thom, Martin. "Verneinung, Verwerfung, Ausstossung: A Problem in the Interpretation of Freud." In *The Talking Cure. Essays in Psychoanalysis and Language*, 162–87. London: Macmillan, 1981.

Tieck, Ludwig. *Das Alte Buch*. In *Schriften 1834–1836*. Edited by Uwe Schweikert, 733–854. Frankfurt am Main: Deutscher Klassiker Verlag, 1988.

Tomkins, Silvan S. *Affect-Imaginary-Consciousness*. New York: Springer, 1963.

Turk, Horst. "'betrügen . . . ohne Betrug.' Das Problem der literarischen Legitimation am Beispiel Kafkas." In *Urszenen. Literaturwissenschaft als Diskursanalyse und Diskurskritik*, edited by Friedrich A. Kittler and Horst Turk, 381–407. Frankfurt am Main: Suhrkamp, 1977.

Unseld, Joachim. *Franz Kafka. Ein Schriftstellerleben*. München: Hanser, 1982.

Vogl, Joseph. "Vierte Person. Kafkas Erzählstimme." Deutsche Viertel áhresschnift für Literaturwis-Senschaft und Geistesgeschichte 68 (1994): 745–56.

Volkelt, Johannes. *System der Ästhetik.* 2 vols. München: Beck, 1925 and 1927.

Voss, Johann Heinrich. *Hesiods Werke und Orpheus der Argonaut.* Heidelberg: Mohr und Zimmer, 1806.

Weinberg, Kurt. "Baudelaires 'Une Charogne': Paradigma einer Ästhetik des Unbehagens in der Natur." *POETICA* 12 (1980): 83–118.

Weissberg, Liliane. "Language's Wound: Herder, Philoctetes, and the Origin of Speech." *Modern Language Notes* 104 (1989): 548–79.

Wellbery, David E. "The Pathos of Theory: Laokoon Revisited." In *Intertextuality: German Literature and Visual Art from the Renaissance to the Twentieth Century,* edited by Ingeborg Hoesterey and Ulrich Weisstein, 47–63. Columbia, S.C.: Camden House, 1993.

———. *Lessing's Laocoon. Semiotics and Aesthetics in the Age of Reason.* Cambridge and New York: Cambridge University Press, 1984.

Werber, Niels. *Literatur als System. Zur Ausdifferenzierung literarischer Kommunikation.* Opladen: Westdeutscher Verlag, 1992.

Wezel, Johann Karl. *Versuch über die Kenntniß des Menschen.* 2 vols. Leipzig: Dykische Buchhandlung, 1784–1785. Reprint Frankfurt am Main: Athenäum, 1971.

Winckelmann, Johann Joachim. "A Treatise on the Ability to Perceive the Beautiful in Art and Instruction in the Same." In Denis M. Sweet, *An introduction to classical aesthetics in eighteenth-century Germany: Winckelmann's writings on art.* Ph.D. diss., Stanford University, 1978.

———. "Abhandlung von der Fähigkeit der Empfindung des Schönen in der Kunst." In *Kleine Schriften. Vorreden. Entwürfe,* edited by Walter Rehm, 211–33. Berlin: de Gruyter, 1968.

———. "Erinnerung über die Betrachtung der Werke der Kunst." In *Johann Winckelmanns sämtliche Werke,* edited by Joseph Eiselein. Vol. 1. Osnabrück: Otto Zeller, 1965.

———. "Erläuterung der Gedanken von der Nachahmung der griechischen Werke in der Malerei und Bildhauerkunst." In *Gedanken über die Nachahmung der griechischen Werke in der Malerei und Bildhauerkunst,* edited by Ludwig Uhlig. Stuttgart: Reclam, 1969.

———. "Sendschreiben über die Gedanken über die Nachahmung der griechischen Werke in der Malerei und Bildhauerkunst." In *Gedanken über die Nachahmung der griechischen Werke in der Malerei und Bildhauerkunst,* edited by Ludwig Uhlig. Stuttgart: Reclam, 1969.

———. "Thoughts on the Imitation of Greek Works in Painting and Sculpture." In *An introduction to classical aesthetics in eighteenth-century Germany: Winckelmann's writings on art,* edited by Denis M. Sweet. Ph.D. diss., Stanford University, 1978.

———. *The History of Ancient Art.* Translated by G. Henry Lodge. Vols. 1–2. Boston: James R. Osgood, 1873.

———. *Geschichte der Kunst des Altertums*. In *Johann Winckelmanns sämtliche Werke*. Vol. 3 and 4.

———. "Vorläufige Abhandlung zu den Denkmalen der Kunst des Altertums." in: *Johann Winckelmanns sämtliche Werke*. Vol. 7, 41–261.

Zedler, Johann Heinrich, ed. *Grosses Vollständiges Universal-Lexikon aller Wissenschaften und Künste*. Vol. 1–64, Suppl.-vol. 1–4, Halle 1732–1754.

Zelle, Carsten. *"Angenehmes Grauen." Literaturhistorische Beiträge zur Ästhetik des Schrecklichen im 18. Jahrhundert*. Hamburg: Felix Meiner, 1987.

Zizek, Slavoj. *Grimassen des Realen. Jacques Lacan und die Monstrosität des Aktes*. Köln: Kiepenheuer, 1993.